Child Development

Child Development

Perspectives in Developmental Psychology

M.D. Rutherford

OXFORD

UNIVERSITY PRESS

OXFORD
UNIVERSITY PRESS

8 Sampson Mews, Suite 204, Don Mills, Ontario M3C 0H5
www.oupcanada.com

Oxford University Press is a department of the University of Oxford.
It furthers the University's objective of excellence in research, scholarship,
and education by publishing worldwide in

Oxford   New York

Auckland Cape Town Dar es Salaam Hong Kong Karachi
Kuala Lumpur Madrid Melbourne Mexico City Nairobi
New Delhi Shanghai Taipei Toronto

With offices in

Argentina Austria Brazil Chile Czech Republic France Greece
Guatemala Hungary Italy Japan Poland Portugal Singapore
South Korea Switzerland Thailand Turkey Ukraine Vietnam

Oxford is a trade mark of Oxford University Press
in the UK and in certain other countries

Published in Canada by Oxford University Press

Library and Archives Canada Cataloguing in Publication

Rutherford, M. D.

Child development : perspectives in developmental psychology / M.D. Rutherford.

Includes bibliographical references and index.
ISBN 978–0–19–543298–5

1. Child psychology—Textbooks. 2. Developmental
psychology—Textbooks. 3. Evolutionary psychology—
Textbooks. I. Title.

BF721.R877 2011   155.4   C2010-906628-6

Cover image: Oleksiy Maksymenko/Acclaim Images

This book is printed on permanent (acid-free) paper ∞
which contains a minimum of 10% post-consumer waste.

Printed and bound in the United States of America

1 2 3 4 — 14 13 12 11

Dedicated to the memory of Margo Wilson (1942–2009)

Brief Contents

Contents

chapter 1 — What Is Developmental Psychology? 2

chapter 2 — Theories and Methods in Developmental Psychology 28

chapter 3 The Basics: Evolution, Genes, and Conception   62

chapter 4 Nature, Nurture, and Development   104

chapter 7 Core Knowledge Part I: Physics, Space, Biology, and Number 214

chapter 8 Core Knowledge Part II: Face Perception, Animacy Perception, and Theory of Mind 254

chapter 9 Language Development 296

chapter 10 Social Contexts for Development 336

From the Publisher

It is often difficult for us to appreciate the complexity of our psychological processes or indeed to appreciate that these processes are doing anything at all because they seem so automatic and inevitable. *Child Development* examines these mental processes during conception, prenatal and postnatal development, and even adolescence and explores important developmental concepts such as how we categorize, how we acquire knowledge, and how we make moral judgments.

The answers to these questions, and others, lie in M. D. Rutherford's fresh and balanced treatment of the key topics of developmental psychology—its history; important theories, theorists, and methods; and the various areas of development, including per-ceptual, cognitive, social, linguistic, and moral. This groundbreaking text takes an original approach to investigating the intersections between core areas in child development studies and evolutionary theories. Also new to the discussion of perspectives in developmental psychology is the innovative coverage of causality, facultative adaptations, learning mechanisms, and experience-expectant development that deconstruct the nature vs. nurture debate.

With a strong focus on research and practical applications of core concepts, this text urges students to become active participants in their learning and therefore includes a variety of tools to further enhance students' dynamic involvement in the study of developmental psychology.

FEATURES

With an awareness of the power of visual communication, we have included an array of vibrant and accessible features to bring developmental psychology to life. Students will appreciate the ways in which the visually engaging design helps them to quickly and easily identify essential information.

APPROACHABLE WRITING STYLE

The author's engaging tone draws introductory students into the fascinating discussions. Complex concepts are easy to understand with the apt use of analogies and comparisons.

COMPREHENSIVE COVERAGE

Discussions of the core areas of developmental psychology are combined with additional coverage of evolutionary theories in child development as well as the critical debate concerning the link between genetic and environmental factors in human development.

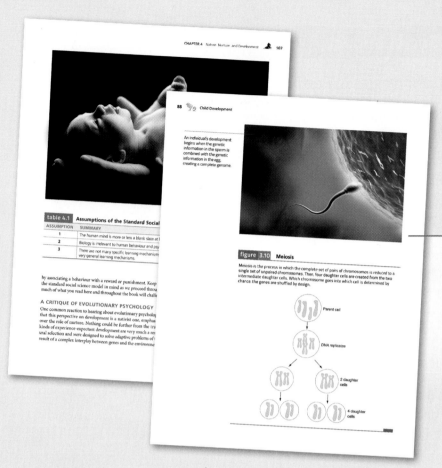

VISUAL REINFORCEMENT

With a multitude of figures, tables, and photos, students receive a visually engaging introduction to child development.

⸭ Culture and Community

Mosquito Tones

Researchers: D. W. Robinson and G. J. Sutton
Institution: Acoustics Unit, National Physical Laboratory, Teddington, Middlesex
Area of Research: Age-Related Changes in Auditory Perception
Page: 155

Cultural Differences in the Intuitive Understandings of Biology

Researchers: Kayoko Inagaki; Scott Atran, Norbert Ross, Douglas Medin, and John Coley
Institution: Chiba University, Japan; Northwestern University, Illinois
Area of Research: Cultural Influences on Children's Understandings of Biology
Page: 243

"CULTURE AND COMMUNITY" BOXES

compare and contrast the effects culture has on development, referencing international cultures and unique cultural experiences.

⁘ Assessing Social Impact

Alternative Technologies in Fertility

Researchers: Susan Golombok et al.
Institution: Centre for Family Research, University of Cambridge
Area of Research: The Social and Emotional Development of IVF Babies
Page: 90

The Carolina Abecedarian Project and Its Effects on IQ

Researchers: Isabelle Lewis and Joseph Sparling
Institution: FPG Child Development Institute, University of North Carolina at Chapel Hill
Area of Research: Socio-Economic Status and IQ
Page: 123

Bilingual Education

Researcher: Ellen Bialystok
Institution: York University, Toronto
Area of Research: Executive Control in Bilingual vs. Monolingual Children
Page: 320

Facebook: Good or Bad?

Researchers: John Cacioppo; Kaveri Subrahmanyam and Gloria Lin; Shima Sum; Laura
    Freberg; Charles Steinfield, Nicole Ellison, and Cliff Lampe
Institution: University of Chicago; California State University; University of Sydney;
    California Polytechnic State University; Michigan State University
Area of Research: Social Effects of Social Networking Sites
Page: 365

The Effect of Parenting Styles on Moral Development

Researcher: Diana Baumrind
Institution: University of California at Berkeley
Area of Research: Authoritarian, Permissive, and Authoritative Parenting Styles
Page: 450

"ASSESSING SOCIAL IMPACT" BOXES
discuss the impact socialization has on
development, ranging from authoritarian
parenting styles to the impact of Facebook.

Research in Action

Concordia Longitudinal Study

Researchers: Jane Ledingham and Alex Schwartzman
Institution: Concordia University, Montreal
Area of Research: Behaviour as a Predictor of Academic Success
Page: 48

Imaginary Friends

Researcher: Marjorie Taylor
Institution: University of Oregon
Area of Research: Children with Imaginary Companions
Page: 259

Infants' Understandings of Gender Stereotypes

Researchers: Diane Poulin-Dubois et al.
Institution: Concordia University, Montreal
Area of Research: Gender-Defined Expectations in Infants
Page: 397

"RESEARCH IN ACTION" BOXES highlight cutting-edge Canadian and international research in developmental psychology.

As children mature, their categories change to accommodate unusual category members; penguins and ostriches become acknowledged birds.

This study and others show that children do have concepts, that the concepts they develop are relatively consistent from one child to the next, and that these concepts are not just reliant on perceptual similarity (Gelman, 2000; Scholnick, Nelson, Gelman, & Miller, 1999; Wellman & Gelman, 1998). As an experimental control, when children were asked to judge the weight of each animal, they made judgments based on perceptual characteristics, not on category membership (Gelman, 1988). It is not that children avoid using perceptual similarity in general (in this respect Piaget was right); rather, they do not rely on perceptual similarity to assign category membership or to make inductions about biological properties. Inferences are tailored to the domain.

This is problematic for the Piagetian perspective that would predict perceptual fixedness. It is also problematic for a purely empiricist account, which would predict that children would only have knowledge about things they have had an opportunity to observe. These and similar studies make it evident that the child actually has an informationally rich category in his or her mind; the child has an understanding of those entities that are members of various categories and of what kinds of inferences are appropriate to make within specific categories. Like adult categories, children's categories are deeply functional, permitting inferences and generalizations from one category to the other.

6.11   Press Pause

Recent experiments show that children are not perceptually bound when forming categories as Piaget would have predicted.

Although children as young as 4 years old use category membership to draw a variety of appropriate inductions, not all category types lend themselves to rich inferences the way natural-kinds categories do. We know this, for example, from the Gelman and Markman experiments described above (Gelman & Markman, 1986, 1987). Children are selective, and

"PRESS PAUSE" FEATURES
ask students to stop and consider key points as they appear in the chapter.

---

boys who had not been anaesthetized during circumcision showed a more intense pain response than boys who were anaesthetized during circumcision (Taddio, Katz, Ilersich, & Koren, 1997).

TASTE

Newborns prefer a sweet tasting liquid over water, using longer sucks with fewer pauses to consume the sweeter drink (Crook & Lipsitt, 1976). Infants respond to sweet tastes by relaxing their facial muscles and show adult-like facial expressions in response to sour and to bitter tastes (Steiner, 1979). At birth, infants are neutral toward salty tastes but come to like them by 4 months of age (Beauchamp, Cowart, Mennella, & Marsh, 1994). For this reason, they will be ready to expand their repertoire beyond breast milk when solid foods are introduced around the age of 6 months.

⁂ Developmental Milestones

Perceptual Development Milestones

Age	Skills
At Birth	Interested in faces over other images
	Size constancy
	Slow and inaccurate eye movements
	Lightness perception well developed
	Can discriminate red and green but not more subtle colours
	Can detect motion
	Startle response to unexpected noise
	Prefers hearing mother's voice over that of a stranger's
	Prefers hearing a story they heard before birth over a different story
	Hears high-pitched sounds better than adults; low-pitched sounds worse than adults
	Likes sweet tastes
	Can discriminate smells; prefers human milk; likes the smell of bananas and chocolate
	Sense of touch well developed, especially around mouth, palms of hands, and bottoms of feet
1 Month	Looks mostly at the outline of faces
2 Months	Ocular dominance columns have developed
	Can see a variety of bright colours (blue, red, green, yellow)
	Shape constancy
	Brightness constancy (as long as the object is not too small)
3 Months	Looks mostly at the internal detail of faces
	Can see biological motion in a point-light walker
	Muscles needed to focus (by changing lens shape) are well developed
	Can track a moving object smoothly and accurately
4 Months	Adult-like colour vision
	Can discriminate more or less between saturated and unsaturated colours
	Colour constancy
6 Months	Visual acuity of 20/40 (can see at 20 feet what a normal adult can see at 40 feet)
	Consistently turns head toward direction of sound
9 Months	Depth perception develops along with self-locomotion
5 Years	Adult-like acuity

"DEVELOPMENTAL MILESTONES" TIMELINES
map out a child's development in the areas of perceptual, conceptual, cognitive, social, linguistic, sex and gender, and moral and prosocial development.

KOHLBERG

Lawrence Kohlberg (1927–1987) is the most well-known name in the field of moral development, and he is widely recognized to be the biggest contributor to the foundation of the field. Kohlberg worked on moral development later than Piaget and was influenced by his framework and his methods, especially the technique of presenting children with vignettes and asking them to evaluate them. Kohlberg gave children fictional stories that ended in a dilemma and asked them to tell him what the right thing to do would be and, very importantly for Kohlberg, why.

Like Piaget, Kohlberg was a stage theorist and was interested in describing and sequencing the stages that children went through on their way to mature moral reasoning. A famous story, and a good example of the method he used to approach moral development research, is the story about Heinz:

Lawrence Kohlberg is widely regarded as the biggest contributor to the foundation of the field of moral development. He was influenced by Piaget, adopting his stage perspective, cognitive perspective, and interview method. Kohlberg created scenarios, like the famous "Heinz" story, to probe moral development.

> A woman was near death from a special kind of cancer. There was one drug that the doctors thought might save her. It was a form of radium that a druggist in the same town had recently discovered. The drug was expensive to make, but the druggist was charging ten times what the drug cost him to make. He paid $200 for the radium and charged $2,000 for a small dose of the drug. The sick woman's husband, Heinz, went to everyone he knew to borrow the money, but he could only get together about $1,000 which is half of what it cost. He told the druggist that his wife was dying and asked him to sell it cheaper or let him pay later. But the druggist said: "No, I discovered the drug and I'm going to make money from it." So Heinz got desperate and broke into the man's store to steal the drug for his wife. Should the husband have done that? (Kohlberg, 1963, p. 19)

Kohlberg listened to the child's thoughts on whether this was right or wrong and encouraged the child to explain why he answered the way he did. Is the husband prevented from stealing because doing so is forbidden, or is the husband obliged to do so because of his responsibility for his wife's well-being? The child's stage of moral development was determined not by whether he (all of Kohlberg's subjects were boys) thought it was right or wrong to steal the drug but by the reasoning behind the choice. If the child appealed to authority, the law, and law enforcement, the child was at a lower level of moral development than a child who mentioned concern for the wife's health and well-being.

INNOVATIVE RESEARCH METHOD

Kohlberg described three levels of moral reasoning: pre-conventional, conventional, and post-conventional. Within each level, there are two stages. This means that there are theoretically six stages of moral reasoning, but according to Kohlberg it was exceptionally rare for anyone to reach the sixth stage. In fact, Kohlberg eventually stopped scoring that stage (Kohlberg, 1978).

There are, h[...] advantage is the amount of time it takes to collect the data. If you want to know the change in psychology over 5 years, you have to wait 5 years to get your answer. But there are deeper scientific problems: A longitudinal study is at risk of **selective attrition**. The researcher needs subjects to participate in the study more than one time, and some people who participated in an early session may leave the study before the later sessions have been conducted. Importantly, the participants who remain may differ from those who leave the study in a way that is significant to the research. For example, if a longitudinal experiment is about dyslexia and some families suspect that their child is developing dyslexia, those families are more likely to stay in the study than those who have less interest in the topic. Clearly, this can affect the results and jeopardize one's ability to draw valid conclusions. In addition, participants who continue in a longitudinal study may show **practice effects**. In this case, the participant may perform differently than naive participants in later testing sessions because they know how the tests works, they remember previous answers, or they feel more comfortable in the setting and with the researcher.

A well-known longitudinal study has been ongoing in Montreal for more than 30 years. The study was started in 1976 by Jane Ledingham (Ledingham, 1981). Initially, researchers screened over 4,000 kindergarten children in francophone public schools and selected a group of children who were normative in terms of aggression and withdrawal and a group of children who exhibited these characteristics to the extreme. The study has revealed that aggression and withdrawal are stable over time (Moskowitz, Schwartzman, & Ledingham, 1985), a conclusion that relies on the longitudinal design. The study also revealed that early measures of aggression and withdrawal predict future development in various areas, including school failure and a need for psychiatric care (Moskowitz & Schwartzman, 1989), and early measures of aggression in girls were associated with adolescent sexual activity and teen pregnancy (Serbin, Peters, McAffer, & Schwartzman, 1991). Early measures of withdrawal predict poor school achievement and negative self-perception in adolescence (Moskowitz & Schwartzman, 1989). These are all findings that were also made possible by the longitudinal design of the study.

selective attrition Attrition in which the subjects who quit a study or move away from a study location are different from the remaining subjects in some way that is relevant to the object of the study.

practice effects Participants in a longitudinal study performing differently over time as a result of prior exposure to the test or testing situation.

In order to test whether early measures of aggression and withdrawal predict future outcomes, one would need to use a longitudinal design.

AIDS TO FRAME CONTENT

Each chapter in *Child Development* begins and ends with recurring features that enhance the learning process by encouraging students to interact with the text as they progress.

OPENING VIGNETTES

engage the student with provocative stories of experiences that relate to the chapter topic. Each chapter opens with a vignette that is supported by a stunning visual image.

Opening Vignette: Core Knowledge

A young baby reaches out to grasp a toy rattle, picks it up by the handle, and watches the round rattle move toward her face. This simple and common action on the part of the developing infant actually relies on a great deal of knowledge about the physical world. She knows that the rattle is a physical object. The shape of her hand as she approaches the rattle reveals her knowledge of the size of the object. And she knows that the object is coherent, such that if she moves the handle toward her, the interesting part of the rattle will come too. In fact, recent research shows that even very young infants have a surprising understanding of some core domains of knowledge. Babies have an understanding of objects and an intuitive understanding of physics. They also have an understanding of numbers and simple addition. And children in early and middle childhood seem to have a precocious understanding of biology. These areas of early understanding have come to be known as *core knowledge*, and researchers in the field believe that these understandings had a functional, adaptive role in our EEA.

Chapter Outline

- The Acquisition of Knowledge
- Framing the Question of Knowledge Acquisition
- Core Knowledge
- Areas of Core Knowledge
- A Cross-Species Comparison

CHAPTER OUTLINES

allow students and instructors to see how the material within a chapter is cohesive.

Learning Objectives, Outcomes

- In this chapter you will learn about concepts, categories, and the cognitive strategy that children develop, called essentialism, that allows them to see members of special natural categories as having an unchanging "essence."

- You will learn to understand why our concepts and categories need an explanation: Category formation happens so naturally, and so universally, that people fail to think of it as something that needs explaining. But you will learn that many of the concepts that we have are universal to us but not to other species because they increased fitness in our ancestral past.

- You will obtain a clear view of what developmental psychologists have historically said about categories and concepts. You will read the classic view of categories, the prototype view, and Piaget's thoughts about children's concepts and categories. You will learn what kinds of concepts and categories young children do (and do not) have and what Piaget thought the developmental trajectory of concepts and categories was.

- Next you will read a functional account of concepts and concept formation that is consistent with evolutionary psychology. You will come to understand the function of concepts, including what functions concepts and categories served in the EEA as well as the functions at different ages throughout childhood. You will read evidence that adults' concepts are functional and that children most easily acquire concepts when they are functional.

- You will also read about the hierarchical organization of categories and the child's acquisition of basic-level categories. You will become familiar with the research on children's concept formation, including the induction and transformation experiments that reveal children's essentialist thinking. An understanding of *natural kinds* will help you to understand the child's thinking about essentialism.

- Finally, you will read an associationist account of concept formation and a reply to it.

Imagine you go for a walk and encounter a dog that you have never seen before. Without the concept of "dog" or an ability to include this new dog in your concept, you would have no information and no expectations regarding this new dog. But you are not, in fact, encountering a completely foreign and mysterious entity. Even though you have never met that particular dog, you know a lot about it because it belongs to your concept of dogs, and everything you know about dogs generally, you infer about that particular dog. Young children and even infants also have concepts and categories and the ability to include or exclude novel objects. They use these cognitive abilities to make sense of a world in which they frequently encounter novel entities.

Everyone categorizes: We group objects and events into classes of like kinds. That said, there are developmental changes in categorization. The groupings themselves change in age-related, predictable patterns (Bruner, Olver, & Greenfield, 1966; Inhelder & Piaget, 1964; Smith & Kemler, 1977; Vygotsky, 1962). The rules that younger children use to categorize are more likely than those of older children to refer to perceptual features, the features of an object that you can easily see (Flavell, 1963, 1985). And younger children are more likely to rely on global perceptual characteristics, the similarity of the broad shapes of objects, rather than a feature-by-feature comparison that older children prefer (Kemler, 1982, 1983; Smith, 1979, 1985).

LEARNING OBJECTIVES AND OUTCOMES

are listed at the beginning of each chapter to prep the student for upcoming concepts and ideas, providing a concise overview of the key areas to be covered.

CHAPTER SUMMARIES

are detailed, accessible, and supported with key visuals from the chapter and aid in reviewing for tests and exams.

SUMMARY

The first part of this chapter introduced you to the idea that concepts and categories are formed by our human psychology and that there are other possible and logical ways to classify the things we see, but the way humans classify them is largely universal. Hopefully this chapter allowed you to get beyond your instinct blindness and appreciate that the commonality of concepts across people and across cultures needs an explanation.

In this chapter you read some possible explanations for why our human psychology generates concepts and categories. Some people have suggested that we have to categorize because we are cognitively incapable of representing everything we encounter individually. This view is plausible but does not explain why the concepts and categories children create are so ubiquitous and logical. Perhaps a more fruitful view of categories and concepts is that they are functional because they allow for inference. If we know a lot about a fish, when we encounter one that we have never seen before, we already have a lot of information about it because we make inferences based on its category membership.

You also read about Piaget's view of categorization in children. First, Piaget approached the question with the classic definitions of categories, wherein every category had a list of necessary and sufficient features that qualified or disqualified items for inclusion. His research was focussed on discovering whether children had this kind of category, and he concluded that they did not: Children had complexes that were more fluid and less well defined than classic categories.

Finally, you read about a more contemporary, functionalist view of concepts and categories and their development in young children. There is good evidence that children develop natural-kinds categories, categorizing things into natural groupings that allow for maximal inference. Children often view members of these categories as having an essence, that special something that confers category membership no matter how many of the usual features are missing. You also read about important innovations in methods in this area, techniques such as the inductive method and the transformation experiment, that allow developmental psychologists to discover the nature of the categories and concepts that children have.

PRESS PAUSE SUMMARY

- Concepts and categories are very useful: They allow us to make predictions about what to expect from individual entities that we have never seen before.
- We do not notice the uniformity in the concepts people have, in part because we fail to imagine the myriad of other logically possible categories.
- Piaget saw categories as classic categories and tested whether infants and children have these classic categories. They did not, he concluded.
- Piaget, Vygotsky, and others have found that young children sort objects thematically, rather than taxonomically, and rely on perceptual features in their sorting.
- Categories and concepts allow for inference.
- Young children's developing categories are functional.
- As early as 3 months of age there is evidence that infants have some categories.

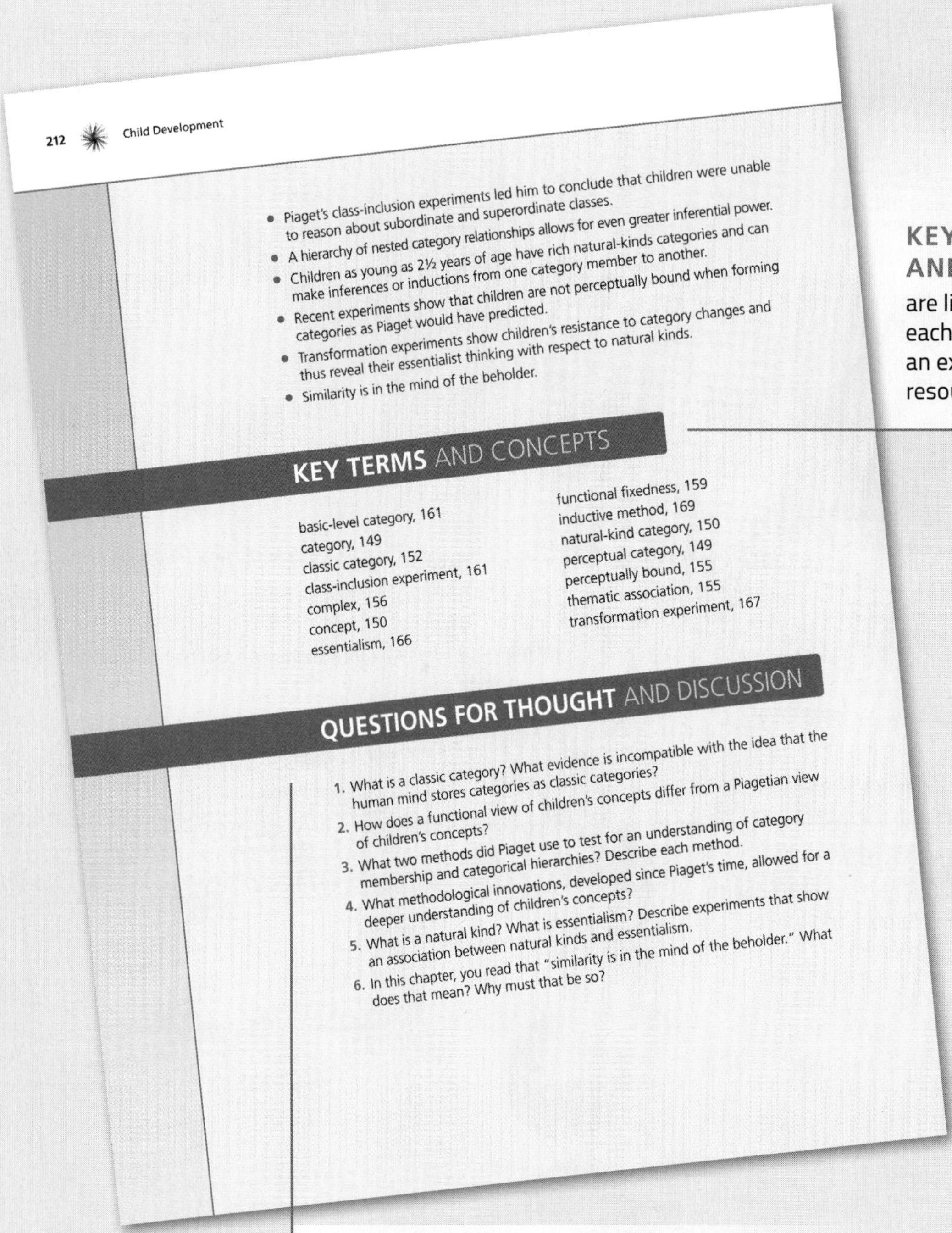

212   Child Development

- Piaget's class-inclusion experiments led him to conclude that children were unable to reason about subordinate and superordinate classes.
- A hierarchy of nested category relationships allows for even greater inferential power.
- Children as young as 2½ years of age have rich natural-kinds categories and can make inferences or inductions from one category member to another.
- Recent experiments show that children are not perceptually bound when forming categories as Piaget would have predicted.
- Transformation experiments show children's resistance to category changes and thus reveal their essentialist thinking with respect to natural kinds.
- Similarity is in the mind of the beholder.

KEY TERMS AND CONCEPTS

basic-level category, 161
category, 149
classic category, 152
class-inclusion experiment, 161
complex, 156
concept, 150
essentialism, 166

functional fixedness, 159
inductive method, 169
natural-kind category, 150
perceptual category, 149
perceptually bound, 155
thematic association, 155
transformation experiment, 167

QUESTIONS FOR THOUGHT AND DISCUSSION

1. What is a classic category? What evidence is incompatible with the idea that the human mind stores categories as classic categories?
2. How does a functional view of children's concepts differ from a Piagetian view of children's concepts?
3. What two methods did Piaget use to test for an understanding of category membership and categorical hierarchies? Describe each method.
4. What methodological innovations, developed since Piaget's time, allowed for a deeper understanding of children's concepts?
5. What is a natural kind? What is essentialism? Describe experiments that show an association between natural kinds and essentialism.
6. In this chapter, you read that "similarity is in the mind of the beholder." What does that mean? Why must that be so?

KEY TERMS AND CONCEPTS are listed at the end of each chapter and offer an excellent review resource.

QUESTIONS FOR THOUGHT AND DISCUSSION challenge students by testing their knowledge and asking them to think carefully about the material presented in the chapter.

be asked which of two children was naughtier: a child named Augustine who accidently knocked over a large glass of juice while helping set the table or a child named Julian who knocked over a small glass of juice while running in the house, a forbidden act. From these interviews, he was able to map developmental change in the seriousness of the "crime." Children younger than 6 considered only the amount of damage, whereas older children also considered the intentions of the actor.

Piaget's stages of moral development
Piaget described stages of moral development, including the morality of constraint stage, the transitional period, and the stage of autonomous morality.

Morality of constraint
The morality of constraint stage is the earliest stage and typically involves children younger than 7 or 8 years old who have not yet reached the stage of concrete operations. In the morality of constraint stage, children take rules as unchangeable and non-negotiable. A rule is a rule because an authority figure (parent, teacher, or other adult) says it is. Punishment, likewise, is justified because the authority figure says it is. Good and bad are clear and easy to define: Following the rules is good, and violating the rules is bad. According to Piaget, children in this stage overlook the intention of the actor; the consequence of the action, not the intention, determines whether the act was good or bad. The child in this stage evaluates morality in terms of objective consequences: A child who breaks several cups but does so unintentionally is naughtier than a child who breaks one cup but does so maliciously. (However, during this stage, children ages 2 to 4 do not have a concept of morality. They often play without rules and do not follow others' rules consistently. Although they may or may not follow a rule, it does not occur to them that they might question or negotiate a rule given by an authority figure.)

In Piaget's view, there were two reasons for the child's acceptance of rules as unalterable. First, because they were in an early stage of cognitive development, they could only understand rules as "things" like any other object whose existence could not be disputed. The second reason was more practical: Parents are bigger than kids and have power over kids, so small children are not in a position to enter into negotiations.

Is it worse to spill a small glass of juice while being naughty or a large glass of juice while trying to be helpful? To Piaget, a child's answer to this question would reveal his stage of moral development.

From the Classroom to the Lab
Imagine that you want to test the hypothesis that the changes described here that take place during the transitional period show a different course of time depending on whom the child interacts with. Perhaps rules become flexible with peers before they become flexible with adults. Design an experiment to test this hypothesis.

From the Classroom to the Lab: Follow Up
Consider the experiment you designed in response to the "From the Classroom to the Lab" challenge earlier in this chapter.

What age group(s) would you choose to participate? Why?

Describe your stimuli.

Describe your procedure.

What is your dependent variable?

What is your independent variable?

Imagine you have run your experiment. What results would indicate to you that the babies tested use colour as part of their object concept? What results would indicate that they do not?

"FROM THE CLASSROOM TO THE LAB" FEATURES

provide interactive exercises for students, helping them build practical research skills. Follow-ups, located at the end of the chapter, encourage students to further contemplate these exercises.

Glossary

5-alpha-reductase deficiency A developmental condition caused by the failure of the body to produce sufficient levels of 5-alpha-reductase. Babies with male genotypes, or an XY chromosome configuration, will be born with typical internal male reproductive organs but female-appearing external genitalia.

accommodation The process of changing one's current theory, understanding, or knowledge in order to cope with new information.

adaptation A trait that is designed and preserved by the process of natural selection because that trait confers a reproductive advantage in the environment in which it evolved.

adoption studies Heritability studies in which the correlation of a trait between adopted children and their adoptive parents is compared to the correlation of the trait between biologically related parents, children, and siblings living in different households.

allele One possible form of a gene that may occupy a particular locus (location) on the chromosome.

alloparents All of the people who contribute to the upbringing of a child other than the child's parents.

androgen insensitivity syndrome A condition in which a person has a mutation in the gene associated with the development of androgen receptors. Without functioning androgen receptors, a person with an XY karyotype can develop a female phenotype.

assimilation The process of interpreting new information in terms of previously understood theories and knowledge.

associationist perspective An approach that encompasses learning theories in general and social learning theory as well. This perspective suggests that people have only general-purpose learning mechanisms, allowing them to associate one stimulus with another. Other than these associationist learning mechanisms, the newborn mind is a blank slate.

attachment The emotional bond a young child feels with another specific person.

autism A developmental disorder that is defined and characterized by a deficit in social cognition, a delay in the development of communication, and an adherence to routine or repetitive behaviours.

autosome Any pair of chromosomes that are not sex chromosomes.

axon The long fibre that runs the length of a neuron, conducting the electric signal from the cell body to the terminals.

baby biography An intensive study first developed by Charles Darwin that describes the activities of an individual baby, typically the scientist's own child or a close relative.

basic-level category A category that is most easily processed at a basic level, first learned by children, and within which inferences are more generously drawn.

between-subjects design An experimental design in which each participant is included in only one group, and variables of interest are compared across groups.

bottleneck A situation in which the population is drastically reduced for at least one generation such that genetic diversity is lost.

Broca's aphasia A condition resulting from damage to Broca's area that involves single-word speech, or short word strings, lacking in grammatical organization.

by-product A trait that has come about as a result of natural selection, although it was not itself selected for.

categorical perception The perception of stimuli that differs continuously as being categorically or qualitatively different.

category A mentally represented collection of entities (objects, people, actions, or events).

chromosome A single molecule comprising a very large DNA helix. A single chromosome may include thousands of genes.

classic category A category that can be defined by a list of necessary and sufficient features.

classical conditioning A learning process in which a neutral stimulus comes to be associated with a naturally motivating stimulus so that each evokes the same response.

class-inclusion experiment An experiment used by Piaget and others in which children were tested to see if they would include a subset in a broader grouping.

clinical method A research method involving a semi-structured interview. The researcher approaches the interview with a planned set of questions but may have followed up on or probed areas of interest depending upon the child's responses.

complex A grouping that is more fluid and less well defined than a category and that did not rely on classic definitions. Piaget thought young children had complexes, not proper categories.

concept A psychological grouping together of entities, objects, events, or even characteristics on the basis of some more or less functional commonality, including some understanding of their interrelationship.

conditioned response In classical conditioning, the response to the conditioned stimulus once training has taken place.

conditioned stimulus In classical conditioning, the stimulus with which the unconditioned stimulus has been associated and which elicits a response after training has taken place.

congenital adrenal hyperplasia A condition in which the excessive production of androgens results in the masculinization of primary or secondary sex characteristics in developing girls.

constancy The perception of like objects as like (in terms of size, colour, lightness, and brightness) despite radically different projections on the retina.

A GLOSSARY
is available at the end of the book for easy reference to the important terms that have been boldfaced throughout the text.

SUPPLEMENTS

Child Development is supported by an extensive array of ancillaries that are designed to improve and enhance the teaching and learning experience—both for students and for instructors.

For the student

The **STUDENT STUDY GUIDE (9780195444827)** is full of test questions and other pedagogy to aid student comprehension. It includes a brief chapter summary, learning object-ives with page references, an extensive range of study questions (100 questions

STUDENT STUDY GUIDE

per chapter, with an answer key), suggested read-ings, and two practice tests per chapter with 25 questions per test. Also included are a practice mid-term and a practice final exam.

ONLINE RESOURCES

The Student Companion Website includes chapter summaries, learning objectives, key terms, a glos-sary, and review questions as well as the following:

- **Interactive Flash Card** exercises in question-and-answer style, with 15 to 20 questions per chapter;
- **A Practice Mid-Term Exam and a Practice Final Exam**, available in an interactive format.

For the instructor

The following resources are available online. Instruct-ors should contact their Oxford University Press sales representative for details on these supplements and for login and password information.

A Test Generator offers a comprehensive set of 60 multiple-choice questions per chapter for a total of 720 questions. Instructors can create and distribute their own tests using this software.

PowerPoint® Slides summarizing key points from each chapter and incorporating figures and tables from the book are also available. Approximately 15 to 20 slides are available for each chapter.

An Image Bank features every photo, figure, and table available in the text and also features bonus images of original photos from researchers conducting experiments in labs in Canada and the U.S.

 www.oupcanada.com/Rutherford

COMPANION WEBSITE

M. D. Rutherford

Child Development
ISBN 13: 9780195432985

Inspection copy request

Ordering information

Contact & Comments

About the Book

The first of its kind in Canada, *Child Development: Perspectives in Developmental Psychology* is a new topical introduction to child development, focusing on the psychological development of infants and children, with some treatment of adolescents. Written by Canadian professor M.D. Rutherford, the text covers all of the classic areas of developmental psychology, including a historical look at developmental psychology, important theories and methods (past and present), perceptual development, cognitive development, language development, moral development, and social development.

Instructor Resources

You need a password to access these resources. Please contact your local Sales and Editorial Representative for more information.

Student Resources

Preface

WHAT'S COMING UP IN THE BOOK?

This textbook embarks on a tour of developmental psychology. Chapter 1 begins with a description of the field and its history. In Chapter 2, you will learn some of the basics, including some of the methods used for scientific inquiry. In Chapter 3, you will learn about genes, genetic recombination and genetic inheritance, and conception. You will learn about natural selection and the processes that have been identified and described that lead to changes in gene frequencies across generations. In Chapter 4, you will learn about some possible solutions to the nature vs. nurture controversy. You will learn about the various resources that are available to the developing child, including genetic resources and various levels of environmental resources. You will learn that the effects that environmental inputs have on development are by design: facultative adaptations, learning mechanisms, and experience-expectant plasticity.

Chapters 5 to 8 are content chapters. Each will describe a research area within the field of developmental psychology. Chapter 5 is your introduction to perceptual development. You will learn about the functions of perception and the ways that instinct blindness make it difficult to appreciate what your perceptual systems are doing for you. In Chapter 6, you will learn about categories and concepts, how children develop and use them, and the functions that they serve. In chapters 7 and 8, you will learn about areas of core knowledge, that is, areas that children develop a rich and precocious understanding of. Chapter 7 introduces core knowledge in physics, space, biology, and numbers and reviews the evidence that children have a psychology specialized for understanding these areas. Chapter 8 focusses on social areas of core knowledge, including face and animacy perception and theory of mind. You will learn more about why people have a psychology specialized for understanding others and explore evidence that children develop this understanding early.

Chapter 9 reviews language development. You will read about the very specialized learning mechanisms that allow children all over the world to learn the spoken languages in their local environments. In Chapter 10, you will read about the social contexts for development, and you will learn about how people are designed to be sensitive to the environment in which they grow up, including family and peer situations, because different strategies will be best in different conditions. Chapter 11 is about sex and gender. You will read about the suite of adaptations that developed together to solve the adaptive problems faced by men and women in the EEA. You will learn about the early steps that lead to the development of one sex or the other, plus examples of conditions that result when the steps do not unfold in the typical way. Finally, in Chapter 12 you will learn about the development of prosocial behaviour. Contrary to what you might think about the competitive outcomes of the evolutionary process, you will learn how evolution by natural selection has designed human psychology to take others' interests into account and to form alliances, friendships, and morals.

M. D. Rutherford

Acknowledgements

A book like this is, naturally, the result of a tremendous amount of support, aid, and thoughtful feedback from a great number of people. It would be hard to adequately express my thanks. First, I deeply appreciate the support and tolerance given to me by my family, especially my wife Melanie. My work frequently took me away from family time as this book was being completed.

A number of people read an early draft of and offered comments on the book in its entirety: Elsa Ermer, University of New Mexico, Rachel G. Falcon, University of New Mexico, Janice W. Rutherford, University of Oregon, and Rhiannon West, University of New Mexico. I am grateful for their time and their suggestions. They helped create the vision and organization of this book.

Several people read one or two chapters and offered critical expertise. Robert Kurzban, University of Pennsylvania, Sandeep Mishra, University of Lethbridge, and Selena Connealy, Museum Education Group, Albuquerque, read Chapter 1. Donald Symons, University of California at Santa Barbara, read Chapter 3. Robert Kurzban, University of Pennsylvania, read Chapter 4. Jack M. Loomis, University of California at Santa Barbara, and Cathy Mondloch, Brock University, read Chapter 5. Larry Fiddick, James Cook University, and Max Krasnow, University of California at Santa Barbara, read Chapter 6. Clark Barrett, University of California at Los Angeles, and Valerie Kuhlmeier, Queens University, read Chapter 7. Francys Subiaul, George Washington University, and Cathy Mondloch, Brock University, read Chapter 8. Jenna Cheal, McMaster University, read Chapter 10. David Feinberg, McMaster University, Pat Barclay, University of Guelph, and Melanie Parish, read Chapter 11. And Debra Lieberman, University of Miami, and Marla V. Anderson, McMaster University, read Chapter 12. Others who attended a discussion group and provided feedback on developing chapters were Ilanit Tal, Annie Caldwell, Joshua M. Tyber, Elizabeth Eadie, Leslie Merriman, and Melissa Franklin, all of the University of New Mexico. Jen Dawson and Gail Rappolt also read sections and offered comments.

I appreciate the input of the following and anonymous reviewers who read the whole book and offered detailed comments: FangFang Li, University of Lethbridge; Ori Friedman, University of Waterloo; Trudy Kwong, Grant MacEwan University; Clark Barrett, UCLA; and Melanie Soderstrom, University of Manitoba. Their comments helped me organize the book's content and flesh out areas outside of my own expertise.

I would like to thank my collaborators at Oxford University Press. Thanks to my acquisitions editor, Jacqueline Mason, who made it as easy as she said it would be. And thanks to Amanda Maurice, a careful copy editor and a pleasure to work with.

I am indebted to Steve Gangestad, University of New Mexico, who hosted me while I wrote this book; he even cleaned out his office so I would have a place to write. I am grateful to the Department of Psychology at the University of New Mexico, especially the front office staff, for supporting and indulging me for an academic year.

And I thank Margo Wilson for her encouraging enthusiasm as I told her about this book. I'm sorry that she never got to read it.

About the Author

Dr. M. D. Rutherford is Canada Research Chair in Social Perceptual Development and Associate Professor in the Department of Psychology, Neuroscience & Behaviour at McMaster University in Hamilton, Ontario.

Born in Portland, Oregon, Dr. Rutherford grew up in Oregon's Willamette Valley. After graduating from McMinnville High School, Rutherford attended Yale College in New Haven, Connecticut. He graduated from Yale with a B.A. in Psychology and Biology and with a new-found fascination with evolution by natural selection and its applications to human psychology.

A Fulbright Fellowship allowed Dr. Rutherford to study and collaborate with Simon Baron-Cohen at Cambridge University, England, where Rutherford began studying social cognitive development, especially the workings of theory of mind processing. In collaboration with Professor Baron-Cohen, Rutherford developed the Reading the Mind in the Voice test while at Cambridge.

Dr. Rutherford earned a Ph.D. in Psychology with an emphasis in Human Development from the University of California at Santa Barbara where he studied with both Leda Cosmides and David H. Brainard. Rutherford spent time at UCSB's Center for Evolutionary Psychology, studying evolutionary psychology with some of the founders of the field. At UCSB, he learned about evolutionary psychology, which is the foundation of his current thinking about psychology, and the psychophysical methods that are essential laboratory techniques in his current research.

While working with Bruce Pennington and Sally Rogers at the University of Denver as a postdoctoral fellow, Dr. Rutherford continued studying early social cognitive development, began studying the development of people with autism, and participated in a longitudinal study that examined the role of theory of mind in the development of autism. Still using psychophysical techniques, he asked questions about how those with and without autism perceive fundamental social stimuli.

Currently working at McMaster University, another of North America's hubs for evolutionary psychology, Dr. Rutherford's current research centres on early social perceptual development and encompasses work in face perception, theory of mind, and the early detection of autism. His research has been supported by the Natural Sciences and Engineering Research Council of Canada (NSERC), the Social Sciences and Humanities Research Council (SSHRC), the Canadian Institutes of Health Research (CIHR), the Canada Foundation for Innovation (CFI), the Canada Research Chairs (CRC), and the Canadian National Autism Foundation (CNAF). Rutherford is a member of the Society for Research on Child Development (SRCD), the Vision Science Society (VSS), and the Human Behavior and Evolution Society (HBES). In addition to dozens of peer-reviewed empirical reports, Rutherford's research has been described in *The Globe and Mail, The London Times, The Chicago Times*, CBC Radio's *Quirks and Quarks*, and *The Discovery Channel* as well as many AP newspapers around the world.

Dr. M. D. Rutherford lives in Dundas, Ontario, with his wife and twin sons.

Child Development

chapter 1

What Is Developmental Psychology?

Opening Vignette: *7 Up!* to *49 Up*

In the fall of 1962, Canadian journalist Paul Almond went to Britain to make films. He noticed that although England's Labour Government had claimed to have created a classless society, social class in England actually determined a child's opportunities and eventual outcome. In a unique use of film, Almond and collaborator Michael Apted created a longitudinal series, following the same set of children at regular intervals over a long period of time, to test the hypothesis that class influences were so strong, at least in England, that a child's outcome could be determined at birth.

The film *7 Up!* introduces fourteen 7-year-olds, selected to represent a range of classes. Three boys came from the wealthy suburb of Kensington, another attended a prestigious boarding school, and one girl came from a wealthy background and was filmed at her boarding school. Some children came from a working-class neighbourhood in London, and one child came from London's East End, known for overcrowded, underprivileged living conditions and high crime rates. Two boys came from a charity-based boarding school, another from a small farm in Yorkshire, and two more were from middle-class suburban schools near Liverpool.

A new film was produced every 7 years, *49 Up* having been released in 2005. The films show the development of these children, including their career paths, marital status, and parenting styles. In some cases, the children's paths seemed very predictable: Two of three boys from a wealthy pre-preparatory school ended up in a prestigious preparatory school and attended Cambridge or Oxford. Others were less predictable: A middle-class child who appeared happy and hopeful at age 7 was homeless and unemployed by age 21 but had found some stability in housing and employment by the time *49 Up* was filmed. As the series' creators suspected, the films show quite a lot of class stability, but there were some surprising exceptions.

By reading about the numerous influences on a child's development and the way these influences work together to create a developing person, you, like the creators of the *Up* series, will discover that examining data from real developing children can answer your questions but may also yield some surprises.

Chapter Outline

- The purposes of this chapter are to introduce you to developmental psychology and to prepare you to read about evolutionary psychology and learn about research in the field of developmental psychology, starting with a description of the discipline and its history.

- You will read about the classic nature vs. nurture question, dating back to the earliest writings about human development, and how our contemporary understanding of human psychology as a product of evolution by natural selection gives us a solid starting point for thinking about nature and nurture working together rather than independently.

- You will understand how natural selection works and how our psychological processes have resulted from evolution by natural selection. When thinking about what natural selection has designed modern humans to do (from seeing to digesting to parenting), one needs to think of the environment in which the relevant selection pressures acted, the environment of evolutionary adaptedness (EEA).

What Is Developmental Psychology?

developmental psychology
The scientific study of recurrent psychological changes across the human lifespan, focussing on development from the prenatal period to early, but sometimes middle and late, adulthood.

Developmental psychology is the scientific study of changes across the human lifespan, often from the prenatal period to early, but sometimes middle and late, adulthood. Developmental psychologists use the *scientific method* to answer questions about the development of people and sometimes animals. This method involves a consensus about how data is collected, how it is analyzed, and what conclusions are warranted based on the results. Because developmental psychology is a science, the ideas and beliefs within this field change over time as a result of the scientific method. Scientific research advances our understanding of infants' and children's psychological development.

In the field of developmental psychology, the scientific method can be used for *description*, that is, reporting at what age children typically show particular skills and understandings. This method can also be used for *explanation*, that is, testing current beliefs (called *hypotheses*) that predict that changes in a given variable will affect another variable. Hypotheses are educated guesses that can and should be tested. Following the tradition of the scientific method, hypotheses can be wrong, regardless of how widely believed, dearly held, or politically convenient they might be. If the experiments that are designed to test a hypothesis reject that hypothesis, the hypothesis needs to be modified or abandoned.

1.1 Press Pause

Hypotheses are educated guesses that can and should be tested.

figure 1.1   Developmental psychology is a science

The scientific method involves a consensus about how data is collected, how it is analyzed, and what conclusions are warranted based on the results.

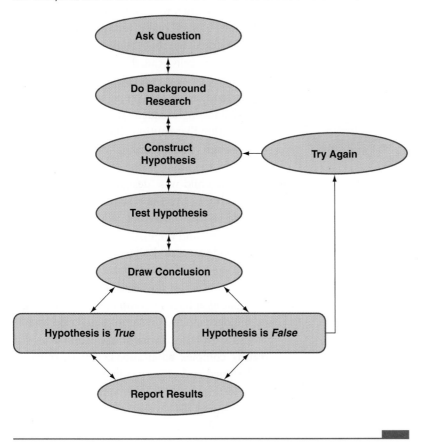

Furthermore, because developmental psychology is a science, what we believe to be true about it needs to be consistent with what we know from other branches of science. For example, a hypothesis that is inconsistent with what we know about cell development cannot be true unless what we know about cell development is incorrect. Our developmental hypothesis needs to be consistent with what we know about genetics, developmental biology, and biochemistry. Even though astrophysics does not provide too many productive constraints on our thinking about developmental psychology, we know that we cannot reasonably make proposals that are incompatible with it.

But developmental psychology encompasses more than just genetic development. It includes a wide range of psychological processes, including motor development, perceptual development, conceptual development, cognitive development, social and emotional development, language development, gender and sexual development, and moral development, to name a few other areas of interest.

What Is Development?

Development is a fundamental scientific field of inquiry, not just in psychology, not just in humans, but throughout the field of biology. Development is inevitable: The death of an individual creates an available niche, and mechanisms for bringing new individuals into the world evolve. For some species, including humans, this means the creation of sex cells and sexual reproduction; in others, a spore contains the genetic information

figure 1.2 — Scientific knowledge is consistent throughout disciplines

Developmental psychology is a science, and what we believe to be true about developmental psychology needs to be consistent with what we know from other branches of science.

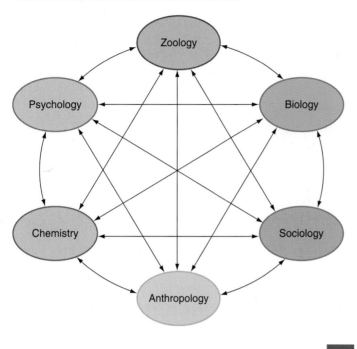

gamete One of two sex cells, egg or sperm, that fuse together during fertilization.

adaptation A trait that is designed and preserved by the process of natural selection because that trait confers a reproductive advantage in the environment in which it evolved.

species-typical environment The environment that provides the features that the genome needs or "expects" in order to develop typically.

that is necessary for the next generation. In any case, the life cycle of any species that involves death also involves life as a new generation develops into adulthood. Intuitively, and scientifically, development begins when the *genome* of a new individual is complete. In sexually reproducing organisms, this is marked by conception: the union of two **gametes** (sex cells) called the *egg* and the *sperm*. From there, cellular specialization, systems development, and increasing complexity and functionality unfold through sequential periods of functional specialization that continue into adulthood.

Although the beginning of development is marked by the union of the complete genome, the developing child was "designed" by natural selection making use of the resources that were likely available to our ancestors (e.g., physical, nutritional, social, and linguistic resources). The developing child was also designed by natural selection to solve age-specific problems.

Note the use of the word *designed* in the previous paragraph. It is common for psychologists and biologists to use this term to describe what the process of evolution by natural selection does when creating complex **adaptations**, that is, traits that are designed and preserved by the process of natural selection because they confer a reproductive advantage in an organism's current environment. Do not be misled. Saying that an organism is designed for a certain kind of problem-solving, or that an organ or mechanism is designed for a certain function, does not imply that there was a designer, design, or intention that led to its original formation. In this chapter and the next, you will read more about how natural selection works, how it creates devices that solve adaptive problems, and moreover, how such devices appear to be *designed* to solve those problems.

1.2 Press Pause

Development happens in all species because all individuals die, creating a niche for new individuals.

Why Study the Developmental Psychology of Children?

One reason for studying psychological development in children is that it gives us insight into our universal human nature. We can learn what kinds of human universals are robust across **species-typical environments**, how information in these environments interacts with the developing child to bring about lasting changes, and how deviations from the environments, whether experimental or accidental, will affect development.

A second reason for studying the developmental psychology of children is that doing so may provide information into adult psychological processes, which may be complex

Every species has a life cycle: Individuals die, creating an opportunity for new individuals to be born. Therefore, every species develops although, the timelines, sequences, and processes differ.

and thus difficult to study. Observing the development of these processes may yield clues as to developmental components and precursors. Studies of language development, for example, may shed light on the rules underlying adult language production.

A third motivation for studying child development is the possibility that, whether as parents or as educators, people want to know how their interactions with children affect their development. Does it matter whether a parent speaks to a pre-verbal child? What rewards and punishments should an adult offer to help a child internalize morality? What visual experiences are important in development? Real-world, practical applications result from reading and research in the area of developmental psychology.

A Historical Look at Developmental Psychology and the Nature vs. Nurture Debate

Discussions and debates on child development long predate any experimental research in the area. Some of the earliest known writings on child development were those of Aristotle and Plato in the 4th century B.C.E. Aristotle's writings showed an early recognition of individual differences: Why did one child grow up with a particular set of interests and skills and another child with a different set? He suggested that the ideal education can only be developed if tailored to each individual child. Plato and Aristotle believed that children, especially boys, were naturally unruly and aggressive, so discipline and self-control were important parts of childhood education, and both philosophers were interested in asking whether a child's development could be attributed to inborn factors (nature) or environmental factors (nurture).

Plato, thought to be the classic **nativist**, believed that children were born with innate knowledge. Indeed, according to Plato, young children did not need to learn but only had to recollect information that was available. For example, in the first year of its life a baby would recognize an animal as an animal, having that concept innately and not needing any specific teaching or experience in order to understand it.

nativist One who views development as being driven primarily or exclusively by internal forces. The information needed for development is assumed to exist within the developing child. Often this information is thought to be preserved in the genes.

Plato (left) believed that children were born with innate knowledge and that they did not need to learn. That is, children had only to "recollect" information that was already available from within, whereas Aristotle (right) believed the mind of a newborn baby was a blank slate on which knowledge would be written by experience. These two juxtaposing views are the historical roots of the nature vs. nurture debate.

empiricist One who believes that all knowledge depends upon direct experience or empirical observation. The newborn's mind is a blank slate and requires exposure to information in order to gain knowledge.

Even though he was a student of Plato, Aristotle became the classic **empiricist**, asserting that the mind of a newborn was a blank slate on which knowledge would be written by experience. Everything that a developing child needed to know was available to him in the real world and could be understood simply via empirical observation, according to this perspective. These two juxtaposing views are the historical roots of the nature vs. nurture debate.

1.3 Press Pause

> The seeds of the nature vs. nurture debate can be seen in the writings of Plato and Aristotle, from the 4th century B.C.E. Plato is the classic nativist, and Aristotle is the classic empiricist.

THE ENLIGHTENMENT AND CHILD DEVELOPMENT

Early European philosophers were still wrestling with the question of human knowledge acquisition in the 17th and 18th centuries. To a large extent, the empiricist tradition was lauded on the British Isles, and the nativist view, also called *rationalism*, was supported on the European continent. English philosopher John Locke (1632–1704) was an empiricist like Aristotle and viewed the newborn's mind as a blank slate or, in Latin, a *tabula rasa*. Locke rejected the suggestion that infants had any innate knowledge or concepts. He held the extreme view that all knowledge was a result of experience and that the mind simply accepted the knowledge that was imparted by virtue of sensory inputs. Nurture was all-important, parental and societal influences shaped the development of the child, and all knowledge as well as all reason came from experience, according to Locke. Experience was the only avenue to knowledge. Even one's character was open for shaping: Locke believed that because the child's mind was a blank slate, the parent could potentially mould and form the child to be whatever type of person the parent desired through means such as reward and punishment, example, and explicit instruction. A child, conversely, could do little to

Is the child's mind a blank slate? Early empiricists thought so.

influence his or her own development. Locke discouraged corporal punishment in school, since it might, consequently, have led to a child's aversion to formal learning. Locke's empiricist beliefs served as the foundation for 20th-century behaviourists, described below.

According to empiricism, if a person was a talented artist or inventor, their childhood environment was to be credited. Similarly, if one grew up to be a criminal, it was due entirely to a poor upbringing. Also important to Locke's legacy was his belief that all children were created equal. This is a logical implication of the idea that each child's mind is a blank slate, and the perspective became an important philosophy to American colonists as they developed their new government. That all people are seen as equal in the eyes of the law can be traced to John Locke.

John Locke was an empiricist and viewed the newborn's mind as a blank slate. All knowledge was a result of experience, and the mind simply accepted the knowledge that was imparted by virtue of sensory inputs, according to Locke.

French philosopher Jean-Jacques Rousseau (1712–1778) is credited with having carried on the nativist tradition. Rousseau opposed the idea that children's minds were blank slates; instead he thought children had conceptual understandings and knowledge (including concepts of justice and fairness) that unfolded through maturation. Children would, by their own activities and explorations, be largely responsible for their own development. Adult tutoring would only interfere with the child's natural development, Rousseau believed, although he did acknowledge the role of the environment and the child's interaction with the environment in the process of maturation.

Rousseau thought that children, or *noble savages* as he referred to them, should therefore be given as much freedom as possible in service of their education. Until the age of 12, when the child reached "the age of reason" and could choose and discriminate among information sources, they should be left to explore on their own. He illuminated his views on childhood in a novel called *Émile* (1762), which tells the story of the development of a child from infancy to adolescence. Ultimately, he used the novel as a mechanism for conveying his own child-rearing advice, emphasizing the effects of free exploration over formal instruction.

Jean-Jacques Rousseau opposed the idea that children's minds were blank slates. He thought children were endowed with both an inherent plan for development and a sense of right and wrong early in life.

Because developmental psychology is a science, there came a point when conjecture was no longer productive, and early disagreements about the development of children and the acquisition of knowledge and expertise created a controversy that could only be resolved via empirical research.

1.4   Press Pause

The empirical study of child development started in earnest in the late 19th and early 20th centuries.

EARLY MODERN DEVELOPMENTAL PSYCHOLOGY

Charles Darwin

It may surprise you to know that early modern work in child development was spurred on by none other than Charles Darwin and his theory of evolution by natural selection.

In response to his work, contemporary scientists recognized the importance of understanding child development as a window into the nature of the human species. In 1877, Darwin published an article entitled "A Biographical Sketch of the Infant," which was a description of his infant son's development. The method Darwin developed for this intensive study came to be known as the **baby biography**. One of his observations was the similarity of early prenatal development across the species that he was able to explore. The prediction that followed, that human children would develop in the same way that other young animals develop, turned out to be an inaccurate simplification but prompted some of the first careful observations of human development and children's behavioural development nonetheless.

The empirical field of child development research started to thrive in the late 19th and early 20th centuries. Around this time, universities began supporting research programs in developmental psychology, and academic journals about the discipline were emerging. Developmental psychology was becoming a genuine and respectable field of scientific inquiry.

G. Stanley Hall

G. Stanley Hall (1844–1924) is considered the founder of developmental psychology, having begun the first psychology laboratory in the United States at Johns Hopkins

University in the 1880s and being among the first to use a scientific approach to child development. Hall was an early developmental psychologist who was also interested in evolutionary theory. He read and was influenced by the work of Charles Darwin and was inspired by Darwin's theory of natural selection.

Hall was primarily interested in studying child development and educational psychology. He thought that children should be educated according to their emerging needs and abilities and that these could be illuminated by considering human evolutionary history. He advocated the scientific reconstruction of the evolutionary history of the human mind, human behaviour, and human culture and espoused the theory of recapitulation: the idea that developmental changes parallel the species' changes through evolutionary time.

Hall emphasized the *maturational process* that characterized child development. He believed that children developed following an inherent plan that would unfold more or less automatically given the proper circumstances (Hall, 1904). Hall conducted the

In 1877, Charles Darwin published "A Biographical Sketch of the Infant," the first baby biography. One of Darwin's observations was the similarity of early prenatal development across the species that he was able to explore.

baby biography An intensive study first developed by Charles Darwin that describes the activities of an individual baby, typically the scientist's own child or a close relative.

G. Stanley Hall is considered the founder of developmental psychology. He began the first psychology laboratory in the United States in the 1880s and is credited with starting scientific research in the field.

first large systematic study of development in North America and is perhaps most well known for having started the **normative approach** in which he worked to define the norms of development. He measured the development of large numbers of children, computed averages that represented typical development, and then identified children whose development fell outside of this normal range.

The theoretical ideas that drove Hall's work, and his belief that development recapitulates evolution, are no longer held in high regard, but his impact on the field is unmistakeable. He trained the first generation of developmental psychologists in the methods of research, established scientific journals that served to report research findings in the field, and founded the American Psychological Association, which is still in operation today.

normative approach The study of development in which norms or averages are computed over a large population and individual development is compared to these norms.

Arnold Gesell

Arnold Gesell (1880–1961) was a student of G. Stanley Hall. Gesell started the Yale Clinic of Child Development in 1911 and spent the next 50 years there doing research on the normative development of typical children. Like Hall, Gesell's view of development was that it followed a maturational process, an unfolding of normal biological processes. Gesell believed that for typical healthy children, development would follow a predictable pattern that was the same for each child. Thus, he was very interested in the normative approach and spent much of his career documenting and describing the norms of development.

Arnold Gesell measured and described the norms of typical development and made this information available to parents and physicians so they could know what milestones to expect at a given age.

Using the normative approach, Gesell found a great deal of uniformity in the development of the hundreds of children that he studied. Following his methods, one was able to tell whether or not an individual child was developing normally in areas such as motor, social, and personality development. Gesell was the first person to see value in making this information available to parents so that they could know what milestones to expect with their baby's age.

1.3 Press Pause

G. Stanley Hall and his student Arnold Gesell started the normative approach. Gesell watched the development of many, many children and documented the age at which skills normally develop.

John B. Watson

John B. Watson (1878–1958) is often called the Father of Behaviourism after the sub-field of psychology that he described, named, and popularized. Of the developmental psychologists who made the field a science, he was the first to follow Locke's assertion that what drives behaviour and shapes development is a person's learning based on experience. Watson was an empiricist in the extreme, as he believed that variation between individuals was not at all due to any endogenous differences between people but was entirely due to differences in how they were reared. Indeed, he is popularly known for having said

John B. Watson, the Father of Behaviourism, followed Locke's tradition. Watson was an empiricist and believed that variation between individuals was not due to any inherent differences between people but was entirely due to how they were reared.

Give me a dozen healthy infants, well-formed, and my own specified world to bring them up in and I'll guarantee to take any one at random and train him to become any type of specialist I might select—doctor, lawyer, artist, merchant-chief and, yes, even beggar-man and thief, regardless of his talents, penchants, tendencies, abilities, vocations, and race of his ancestors. (Watson, 1930, p. 82)

In essence, Watson and other behaviourists believed that a person's (or animal's) behaviour could be entirely controlled via reward and punishment training. The central belief of behaviourism was that behaviour is a result of conditioning processes: A person or animal had been conditioned to associate two events (classical conditioning) or a behaviour and an outcome (operant conditioning). Watson's perspective was rooted in Ivan Pavlov's discovery of classical conditioning, which showed that dogs could be trained to salivate in response to a trained stimulus (e.g., a bell), whereas untrained dogs only salivate in response to actual food. Watson assumed that humans and other animals were endowed with a small number of general-purpose learning mechanisms that could associate any stimulus with any other stimulus, or with any response. All human behaviour, and that of other animals, could be attributed to a series of simple associations made over time. He dismissed the idea that studying cognition or thought was possible or even that it might be scientifically interesting, thinking instead that psychologists should focus only on measurable behaviour.

Watson is also famous for his "Little Albert" experiments, conducted in 1920 at Johns Hopkins University (Watson & Raynor, 1920). In order to demonstrate the classical conditioning of fear, Watson trained an 11-month-old boy Albert (who prior to the experiments showed a typical range of emotions) to fear white rats. It followed, according to Watson, that parents should be able to control children's behaviour by controlling the stimulus and response pairings that the child encounters.

Although behaviourism has lost all of its former popularity, and the extreme views of empiricism are rejected by contemporary developmental psychologists, Watson did make some lasting and valuable contributions to developmental research. He insisted on objective methods, which made the study of development more rigorous and more interpretable. The rigidity of his experimental design is still important to developmental psychologists today.

Jean Piaget

Jean Piaget (1896–1980) was enormously influential to developmental psychology. It would be impossible to overstate his influence on the field of cognitive development, and therefore his views and research are presented throughout this book, including a broad review in Chapter 2.

Jean Piaget is the developmental psychologist who has made the greatest impact on the field. His theoretical and methodological contributions are still important today.

Piaget was a Swiss psychologist who worked in and essentially created the field of cognitive development. He was interested in science even as a child, and his early work on animal behaviour may have had an influence on his thinking about child development. After earning a Ph.D. in Switzerland, he moved to Paris and was hired to administer intelligence tests to school-aged children. This was his entré into developmental psychology. He noticed not just quantitative differences in responses due to age (older children responded correctly to more questions), but he also noticed qualitative differences (children at different ages saw and understood things differently).

After two years of work in France, Piaget returned to Switzerland and began his own cognitive development studies. He was more interested in examining how children think and how knowledge changes during development than in what children did and did not know. He called this study of knowledge development **genetic epistemology**.

Piaget's theory of cognitive development was a stage theory: When children attained a certain stage of cognitive development, they were limited to the skills characterized by that stage until they reached the next stage, at which point a whole new set of cognitive skills were available to them. At the earliest stages, experience was very important, especially perceptual experiences. Piaget believed young children were perceptually bound and that they brought very few pre-existing cognitive structures to the process of knowledge acquisition.

In a field that was still new and in need of scientific methods, Piaget was methodologically innovative. Unlike previous developmental psychologists who observed children while trying not to interfere with their behaviour, Piaget actually presented children with challenging tasks (e.g., having them sort items into groups) and asked them questions and then had them explain their answers. Thus, Piaget created the clinical method. The **clinical method** was a research method involving a pre-planned, semi-structured interview in which the researcher may have followed up on or probed areas of interest depending upon the child's responses. Again, Piaget was more interested in how children think than whether their answers were right or wrong. The clinical method is still in use today.

Piaget's work did not become influential in North America until the 1960s, both because behaviourism had such a strong hold on the thinking of North American psychologists and because Piaget's concepts and terms were unfamiliar to them.

> **1.6 Press Pause**
>
> Piaget was the most influential figure in the emerging field of cognitive development.

genetic epistemology
Genetic epistemology, according to Piaget, describes the process of cognitive development from birth through late adolescence.

Piaget's theory of cognitive development
Piaget described children's development through stages, which predicted that children attained a certain set of cognitive skills at a certain stage. Children were thought to be limited to the skills characterized by that stage until they reached the next stage, at which point a whole new set of cognitive skills were available to them.

clinical method A research method involving a semi-structured interview. The researcher approaches the interview with a planned set of questions but may have followed up on or probed areas of interest depending upon the child's responses.

Lev Vygotsky

Lev Vygotsky (1896–1934) was an early Russian developmental psychologist and a contemporary of Piaget. Unlike Piaget, who had a background in science, Vygotsky's background was linguistics, literature, and law. Because of his emphasis on social development and the importance of the social context on development, he is described as a "social constructivist."

Vygotsky worked in the new Soviet Union, just after Marxism had replaced the czarist system of government. During that historical period, there was a tremendous emphasis on culture, collectivism, and socialism. In this context, Vygotsky developed his theory of social development, which emphasized the influence of culture as well as the influence of other people on a child's development, knowledge, and thinking.

Lev Vygotsky was an influential Russian developmental psychologist. Working in the collectivist Soviet Union, Vygotsky emphasized the influence of culture on a child's development.

Vygotsky described and studied the relationship between language development and thought. In contrast to Piaget, Vygotsky stressed the cultural context of a child's development and the effect that culture could have as the child moved through the stages of cognitive development. Vygotsky was interested in the transmission of cultural values, beliefs, attitudes, and skills to the next generation. He focussed on co-operative dialogues between children and their elders as a means of cultural transmission. He thought cultural influence was so strong that it could disrupt the order of the stages, whereas Piaget did not believe that a child could go through the stages in anything but the canonical order.

Vygotsky thought that much of the child's cognitive development resulted from the **dialectical process**, a process of shared problem-solving. In this process, an adult and a child repeatedly work through a problem or task together. At first, the adult takes the lead, performing, modelling, and instructing. Over time the child takes more and more responsibility for executing the task. Eventually, the child internalizes the knowledge and the way of thinking modelled by the adult. The concept of the **zone of proximal development**, one of Vygotsky's lasting contributions, was thought to be the child's growing edge, or next step in development, and describes the tasks a child can complete with and without adult support.

Vygotsky died before ever knowing what an impact he would have on the English-speaking world. His work was not translated into English until the 1960s, after which point it became part of the scientific exploration of child development and subjected to scientific study. Not only did he not live to see his work considered by Western psychologists, but he was also unread in his home country, where his work was banned.

dialectical process A process of shared problem-solving.

zone of proximal development The tasks a child can complete with and without adult support.

Nature and Nurture, Working Together to Make a Person

In the last section, you read about early discussions of the nature vs. nurture debate and its roots in ancient Greece and later in Europe. You have heard the nature vs. nurture question before, no doubt. You probably have some sense of what it means and of what people mean by *nature* and *nurture* when the terms are used either in casual conversation or in the media. Maybe you think it means that you can measure how much of an individual is a result of their genes and how much of that individual is a result of their environment. Maybe you think it means that you can measure how much of a trait (e.g., shyness, thrill-seeking, sexual orientation) is built by genes and how much of that trait is built by the environment. But the nature vs. nurture question is an untenable one: Without genes, nothing develops, and without the necessary environmental input, nothing develops. Every person and every trait of every person is a result of genetic and environmental interaction.

Despite debates about the relative contribution of nature and nurture to the development of an individual, you have likely been told, maybe in an introduction to psychology course or in a biology course, that the nature vs. nurture question is not a meaningful one. To ask "What determines how a person develops: heredity or the environment?" makes no sense. Does it make sense to you to ask whether a trait is social or biological, innate or learned, genetic or environmental? Thinking this way is not fruitful when considering human development. It is like asking which contributes more to the area of a rectangle: the width or the height. Thinking in terms of nature vs. nurture is so intuitively appealing that it is difficult for some people to think beyond it until they learn a sensible alternative way to approach development.

Nature and nurture work together to make a person.

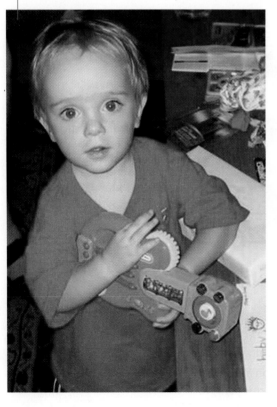

1.7   Press Pause

Because the nature vs. nurture dichotomy is so intuitively appealing, it is very difficult for some people to think beyond it until they learn a sensible alternative way to approach development.

An Evolutionary Perspective on Development

Evolutionary psychology clarifies developmental psychology, and likewise, developmental psychology informs evolutionary psychology. Children develop as a result of an intricate interaction between the environment and the developing child, and they do so as a result of developmental demands that recurred in the environment in which our ancestors evolved. Here we will consider what the field of evolutionary psychology has to offer the traditional field of developmental psychology and then how the understanding of developmental psychologists can contribute to the work of evolutionary psychologists.

EVOLUTIONARY PSYCHOLOGY'S CONTRIBUTION TO DEVELOPMENTAL PSYCHOLOGY

Evolutionary psychology is a productive perspective to consider and understand when working in the field of developmental psychology for a couple of reasons:

1. It promotes research that is consistent with what is known about evolution by natural selection.
2. It provides guidance in terms of hypothesis testing.

It behoves developmental psychologists to have an understanding of evolutionary psychology because proposals in the field of development need to be consistent with what is known about evolution. One example of a potential inconsistency is the idea that the infant's mind is flexibly teachable without constraint and without biological imperatives, the blank slate idea. If simple learning mechanisms such as classical and operant conditioning were all a child had, anyone could teach the child to do anything, even if it violated the child's biological interests. This contradicts evolutionary theory, and the idea that psychological processes promote survival and reproduction.

1.8   Press Pause

Theories about developmental psychology need to be consistent with other scientific knowledge, including natural selection.

Another way in which evolutionary theory contributes to developmental psychology is by providing guidance in terms of hypothesis testing. The complexity of a system (here, the developing child) determines the potential number of hypotheses that could possibly be tested. Human behaviour, human development, and the human brain are very complex, so the number and scope of hypotheses that could be tested is unimaginable. There are clearly practical limits to testing as well, limits such as money, available participants, laboratory space, research assistants, writing time, and the scientist's life span. Evolution-

evolutionary psychology
An approach to the study of psychology that holds that being well informed about the process of evolution as well as the circumstances in which our ancestors lived during our evolutionary history will aid us in understanding the function and design of the human mind.

ary theory, thankfully, narrows the hypothesis space significantly; one does not need to test hypotheses that are known to be inconsistent with evolutionary theory.

In general, an evolutionary perspective is important to the field of psychology, especially developmental psychology, because it frames our inquiry. It allows us to ask why the human mind is designed the way it is, what functions various psychological processes serve (e.g., face recognition, attachment, or depth perception), and how our unique human psychology was adaptive in the environment in which our ancestors evolved. The functional perspective that the evolutionary framework provides allows us to make sense of the interaction between a developing organism and its environment.

1.9 Press Pause

> An evolutionary perspective allows us to make sense of the interaction between a developing organism and its environment.

In order to understand how a psychological process works, we need to know what it was designed to do. What adaptive problem in our ancestors' hunter–gatherer environment was it solving? Vision? Language? Social cognition? Moral development? How is the mind designed so that a child can come to understand his or her physical, linguistic, and social world? With what learning mechanisms must the child be endowed? What parts of the environment inform these learning mechanisms? Only evolutionary psychology lends a coherent framework for answering these questions.

DEVELOPMENTAL PSYCHOLOGY'S CONTRIBUTION TO EVOLUTIONARY PSYCHOLOGY

A consideration of developmental psychology is advantageous for evolutionary psychologists for the following reasons:

1. It provides insight into how an adult comes into being.
2. It allows an opportunity to examine how changes in the environment during development lead to changes in the adult.

Studies in the field of developmental psychology allow us to examine the interaction between genes and the environment.

figure 1.3   Evolutionary Psychology

Evolutionary psychology can inform developmental psychology, and vice versa.

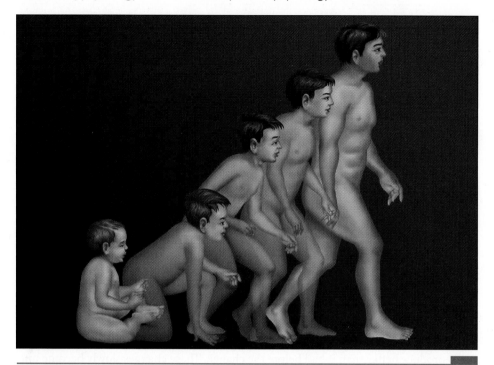

3. It buffers evolutionary psychologists from accusations of "genetic determinism."
4. It allows them to study non-adult adaptations.

Like most sub-fields of psychology, contemporary evolutionary psychology focuses on adults, whereas developmental psychology asks how a developing infant comes to realize the adult form. As early as the 19th century, scientists knew that reliable information about child development would lead to a greater awareness of the human species, and so evolutionary psychologists study developmental psychology because it lies at the heart of understanding how an adult organism comes to have the features of that species that were designed by natural selection.

Some studies in the field of developmental psychology allow scientists to examine the interaction between genes and the environment by observing the effects of variance in the developmental surroundings. In some cases, this involves naturally occurring variance, such as differing access to nutrition or a change in paternal care. In other cases, unusual circumstances create environments that are not species-typical, such as when children grow up in an orphanage without a consistent caregiver or, even more unusual, when children grow up "feral."

If you have heard of evolutionary psychology, you may have heard evolutionary psychologists described as genetic determinists. Evolutionary psychologists are sometimes perceived erroneously as supporting genetic determinism, the idea that a gene or genetic ensemble, in every case, leads to a particular phenotypic outcome (whether morphological, psychological, or behavioural). This is not how development works. It is clear that genes do not inevitably lead to predetermined outcomes. Evolutionary psychologists consider genetic inheritance as well as all of the other developmental resources available to the growing child (broadly, the environment), without relying on genes as a complete explanation for development. Paying serious heed to developmental psychology rescues them from the genetic determinism attack.

> **1.10 Press Pause**
>
> Genes do not inevitably lead to predetermined outcomes.

There is another way in which developmental psychology contributes to evolutionary psychology. Evolutionary psychologists ask questions about adaptations to understand what complex psychological adaptations have evolved as a result of evolution by natural selection. By focusing exclusively on adults (who are, of course, interesting because they reproduce and parent, among other things), a psychologist will miss a host of interesting non-adult adaptations. Infants have adaptations designed to help them be infants. Three-year-olds have adaptations designed to solve the problems of a three-year-old. Pubescent adolescents have a suite of physiological, psychological, and morphological adaptations designed to solve problems at that stage in the life cycle. And post-pubescent adolescents have psychological, social cognitive, and other adaptations that solve the problems that are unique to adolescence. By taking developmental psychology into account, evolutionary psychologists can study both adult and non-adult adaptations.

Adaptationism and Functionality

Above we touched on the idea of adaptations. Through the adaptation process, described by Darwin, small changes that confer a fitness advantage allow an individual to survive and reproduce better than it had before the change. These changes slowly become universal in a population, resulting in complex adaptations. Indeed, evolution by natural selection is the only scientific theory capable of explaining complex adaptations.

Evolutionary psychologists use the concept of adaptations and functional design to organize and direct their empirical research. An evolutionary perspective holds that the interesting traits or units of scientific analysis are those functional sub-components, sometimes called *organs*, that were sculpted by natural selection. With respect to mental processes (processes such as learning language, learning to walk, and bonding with one's mother), it is almost a trademark for evolutionary psychologists to look for many specialized adaptations, each designed to solve a particular adaptive problem and each mediated by psychological machinery specialized to that particular task (Barkow, Cosmides, & Tooby, 1992; Pinker, 1997).

How did this moth come to have eye patches on its wings? Evolution by natural selection is the only scientific theory capable of explaining complex adaptations.

THE EVOLUTION OF AN ADAPTATION

Darwin offered the first and only viable scientific explanation of the origin of adaptations. Before he spelled out and then published his theory of evolution by natural selection, the common and popular explanation for the complexities in the natural world was divine design, or creationism. How, for example, did the vertebrate eye, so exquisitely complex and functional, come to be? It very clearly did not come about by chance. The same was true of the human heart and circulatory system, the decoy eyes on the back of a polyphemus moth, and the decoy lure that a fish uses to capture another fish. How do you explain their existence?

1.11 **Press Pause**

Only evolution by natural selection can explain otherwise improbably complex traits.

Let us review Darwin's original arguments for the evolution of complex adaptive traits:

1. Natural species have enough "potential fertility" to increase exponentially, blanketing the planet with individuals, if unfettered.
2. Populations tend to remain more or less stable.
3. Natural resources, such as food, water, and suitable shelter are limited.
4. There is a struggle to acquire resources and survive. The winners of this competition are those best suited to solve the challenges of their current environment.
5. There is variability in the population with respect to many traits, some relevant and some irrelevant to survival and reproduction.
6. These variables are heritable.
7. Success in this struggle to survive is not random: There is an advantage to those whose genetic inheritance is well suited to their current environment. The unequal success with respect to survival and reproduction due to genetic inheritance is natural selection.
8. Over many generations of natural selection, individuals become better and better suited to their environment, with adaptations that are more complex, efficient, effective, reliably developing, etc. (Mayr, 1985).

The Environment of Evolutionary Adaptedness

Selection pressures are environment-specific, and adaptations are designed by natural selection to solve adaptive problems in a particular environment. Therefore, in order to understand adaptations in general, and human adaptations in particular, we need to know something about the environment to which the adaptations are suited. What was the environment that prevailed during the time when these traits were being shaped by natural selection? Imagine a population of moths, some of which are black and some of which are white. If the variance in colour is statistically related to the presence of a specific gene, a moth is more likely to develop black wings if that gene is inherited from a black-wing parent and to develop white wings if inherited from a white-wing parent. In an environment where the surfaces on which the moth rests are black, predators will overlook the black moth and so it will out-compete the white moth. The black moth will live longer, reproduce more, and its genes will spread throughout the population in that environment.

When considering human adaptations, we need to consider the hunter–gatherer environment our ancestors lived

Some environments will be favourable to white moths, whereas others will be favourable to black moths. In any case, adaptations increase an organism's fitness with respect to a particular environment.

EEA The "environment of evolutionary adaptedness" is the condition under which our ancestors lived, and to which our morphological and psychological features are adapted.

and evolved in, the "environment of evolutionary adaptedness," or the **EEA**, a term coined by John Bowlby. Different aspects of the EEA are important for examining different characteristics, traits, or psychological mechanisms. For example, if you were primarily concerned with the study of vision, the features of the EEA that would be of interest to you would be terrestrial light sources and the illumination of surfaces with biological relevance, such as food. The vertebrate eye and visual system have been evolving for millions of years with essentially the same source of light and essentially the same range of illuminations. The fact that light is reflected differently between sunrise and sunset is relevant to the evolution of the visual system because it creates selection pressure. For our species and our immediate ancestors, who picked ripe fruit from green foliage, having a visual system that discriminates between the "reds" of fruit and the "greens" of foliage, for example, may have been important. Indeed our colour-sensitive photoreceptors, cones, are maximally sensitive to greens and reds.

On the other hand, if you were primarily concerned with the study of language, the EEA that would be relevant would be the linguistic environment. Compared to

figure 1.4 | An adaptation is adaptive with respect to a particular environment

Here, the bunnies are selected to have white fur because their environment is white. Had the environment been different, the adaptation would have been different.

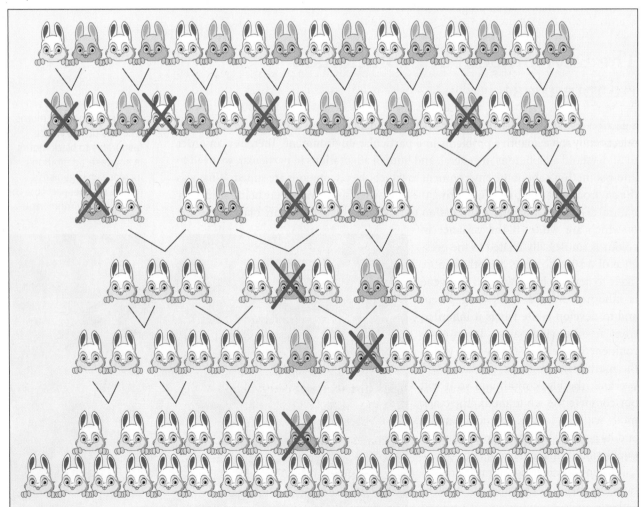

the visual system, the psychological mechanisms underpinning human language have only been evolving for perhaps the last 50,000 years, which is a very short period of time geologically. It is fairly impossible to pinpoint the start of human language, both because it evolved so gradually and because it left no fossil trace, so even prehistoric cultures that are otherwise fairly well understood are opaque with regard to language.

1.12   Press Pause

The aspect of the EEA that is relevant depends on the psychological process you wish to study (e.g., vision or language).

VARIANCE ACROSS CONDITIONS IN THE EEA

When we think about the EEA of our hunter–gatherer ancestors, we must take into account the variance among the possible environments into which they might have been born. For example, what language did they speak? What type of climate existed, and what resources were available as a result? Was it a time of war or peace? What were the levels of paternity certainty and paternal support? A baby just coming into the world has no way of knowing which of many possible environments she is being born into. That information cannot be encoded in her genes. We have evolved to detect and solve the adaptive problems of not just the most likely environment but various environmental conditions. Indeed, there is evidence that children are equipped to detect which kind of environment they are born into and adjust their strategies accordingly.

The word *strategies* in the last paragraph is not meant to imply conscious decisions. When an organism is shaped by natural selection such that reproductive success is competitively maximized, evolutionary thinkers may use the term to refer to a strategy that seems to be pursued as a result of a psychological or morphological adaptation (e.g., a pitcher plant follows a carnivorous strategy, although the plant itself cannot intentionally strategize).

Maladaptive Behaviour in the Modern World

In many ways, our behaviour is adaptive in the current environment: We instinctively select fresh fruit, we quickly avoid falling objects, and we love our children utterly. But there are certain behaviours that are not adaptive, not fitness-enhancing.

FAST FOOD AND FAST CARS

Obesity is a result of the mismatch between our EEA-shaped psychological adaptations and our modern environment. In the EEA, food was relatively scarce and very much a limiting factor in survival and reproduction. There was a strong evolutionary pressure for psychological adaptations that motivated people to hunger for particularly important but scarce nutrients, like sugars (the source of energy for all of the body's operations, including brain function), fats (essential for healthy hair and skin, some cell functions, and maintaining body temperature), and salts (necessary for nerve and cell function and regulating water content). (Incidentally, in the current environment, we lack the adaptive pressure to hunger for fibre because in the EEA, the foods we ate were extremely fibrous, and we never had to crave fibre in order to consume a sufficient amount of it.) Because of the psychological adaptation motivating us to seek, acquire, and ingest sugars, fats, and salts, we have created a modern world replete with them. We created fast food. And in some way, we have created obesity.

Our psychological mechanisms are adapted to solve the problems of the environment in which we evolved. Elements of our modern environment, like fast food and fast cars, can be dangerous because we do not have adaptations to deal with them.

1.13 Press Pause

In some ways the modern world is like the EEA, and in others it is not, depending on the psychological processes of interest.

Another example of how our modern world is different from the EEA is technology. Our psychological mechanisms for fear motivate us to avoid natural phenomena that would have been dangerous in the EEA (e.g., high cliffs, spiders, snakes, fire). However, because there are certain dangers in the current environment that did not exist in the EEA, such as fast cars, there was no selection pressure to create adaptations to them. For example, we do not necessarily fear cars, guns, and electricity even though some of the leading causes of accidental death are motor vehicle accidents, gunshot wounds, and electrocution. Some behaviours are maladaptive because our psychological adaptations sculpted by the selection pressures of the EEA do not lead to adaptive behaviours in the modern world.

WHY BEHAVIOUR IN THE MODERN WORLD MIGHT BE MALADAPTIVE

Our psychology is not designed to optimize fitness in the current environment. There are several reasons for mismatch: In short, (a) natural selection works on adaptations, not on behaviours; (b) evolution is slow; (c) the evolution of complex adaptations is particularly slow; (d) increasing complexity makes beneficial mutations less likely.

Natural selection leads to adaptations, not adaptive behaviours per se. You may be familiar with the idea that natural selection has shaped our physical characteristics, our body plan (internal organs, limbs, etc.), but you may also be starting to think about the role of natural selection in shaping our psychological adaptations as well. Be careful: Natural selection does not shape behaviour directly; it can only shape our psychological processes, the processes that underlie behaviour. You might think that natural selection has selected for adaptive behaviours, such as eating high-calorie foods or finding warmth when it is cold, or you might expect that natural selection should cause people to behave adaptively no matter how the environment changes, but natural selection can only affect and build psychological adaptations (following Darwin's arguments above) via neural architecture, the strength of excitatory and inhibitory neural connections, and carefully orchestrated hormonal changes.

1.14 Press Pause

Natural selection builds psychological adaptations; it cannot build behaviour directly.

This leaves us vulnerable to changing environments. We have psychological adaptations that worked really well (i.e., that produced adaptive behaviour) in the EEA, such as our hunger for sugars, fats, and salts. Because these nutrients were scarce, those who were motivated to seek them out had a better chance of surviving and thus producing more offspring than those who were indifferent to the consumption of these nutrients. But this psychological adaptation is maladaptive in the current environment where fats, sugars, and salts are not scarce. Because natural selection created a mechanism that made us crave nutrients that were scarce in the EEA, people in the EEA ate more adaptively, but the behaviour itself was not selected for directly.

The flip side of the idea that natural selection only builds adaptations, not behaviours is that psychological adaptations that have no behavioural manifestation are "invisible" to natural selection. If, hypothetically, you had a psychological adaptation that resulted in no change in behaviour, the adaptation would neither be selected for nor selected against. If you had an emotion that made you feel a certain way, but did not motivate you or change your behaviour in any way, it would not and could not be selected for or against, since it would have no effect on the frequency of genes for that emotion.

Second, we are still adapted to the EEA because, in general, evolution by natural selection is slow. How quickly a beneficial allele (alternate forms of a gene) spreads depends upon the strength of the selection pressure. Generally speaking, with a new generation beginning every 20 or so years, there has not been enough time for beneficial mutations to make significant inroads, let alone become universal, in the 10,000 years that humans have lived in post-hunter–gatherer circumstances.

Another reason that we have not evolved psychological mechanisms that are well adapted to a modern, industrial world (e.g., with defences against fast food and the effects of sitting in front of a computer all day) is the vast length of time that it takes to evolve complex psychological adaptations. Complex adaptations (e.g., the vertebrate eye or the immune system) rely on not one but many alleles in their development. Building any adaptation takes time, but for multi-gene adaptations to evolve, each new mutation has to arise separately and spread universally throughout the population. A complex adaptation is built when one mutation (one among thousands that happens to be beneficial rather than deleterious) spreads throughout an entire species until it becomes part of that species' typical genome (which would take hundreds or thousands of generations, depending upon population size, mating habits, the strength of the selection pressure, and many other factors). This one mutation must then be followed by another, and another, until the many (perhaps dozens, or hundreds of) genes involved in the development of this complex adaptation have, one by one, become universal in the population.

Lastly, there is reason to believe that the progress brought about by evolution by natural selection is slower today than it might have been in the past, or than it might be in less complex organisms, because the more complex an organism is, the less likely a random mutation will benefit or improve the final product. Imagine a car with many interrelated mechanisms. If you randomly change one of those mechanisms, the car is not likely to work better. This is true of any functioning machine, but more so of more complex machines. Beneficial mutations occur less frequently because changes in the system are less likely to be beneficial. Because complexity increases slowly, evolutionary change decreases slowly.

As a result, we encounter **generative entrenchment** (Wimsatt & Schank, 1988), the idea that development itself becomes entrenched, unable to evolve in radically different ways. This is especially true of the earlier developmental processes because small perturbations early in development lay the foundation for later development. On this view, random changes introduced by random mutations are likely to be disastrous, and the earlier in development those changes are expressed, the more developmentally disastrous they are likely to be, especially in the most complex organisms, which therefore slows the evolution of developmental processes.

In sum, in thinking about the adaptations of the human mind, we consider the evolutionary pressures of our EEA because modern or recent evolutionary pressures are negligible when considering the origin of a complex adaptation. But are natural selection, genetic variability, and competition for resources leading to differences in reproductive success factors in our current environment?

generative entrenchment
A phenomenon that slows the evolution of developmental processes. Because early perturbations in development can have catastrophic effects later in development, random mutations that affect early development are unlikely to be beneficial.

1.15   **Press Pause**

Modern or recent evolutionary pressures are negligible when considering the origin of a complex adaptation.

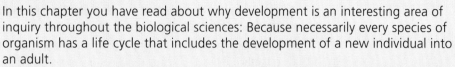

SUMMARY

In this chapter you have read about why development is an interesting area of inquiry throughout the biological sciences: Because necessarily every species of organism has a life cycle that includes the development of a new individual into an adult.

You have been introduced to the history of developmental psychology, including ancient Greek philosophers who created a focus on the nature vs. nurture question in the field of child development. Early modern developmental researchers were still thinking about the relative contribution of nature and nurture and using empirical research to explore their theories and test their predictions.

Next you read an introduction to some of the ideas of evolutionary psychology, which will serve as a guiding and organizing perspective for the rest of this book. You read about how an evolutionary perspective gives developmental psychologists a starting point to look for potentially fruitful avenues of research in a potentially infinite field of untested hypotheses. Thinking in terms of evolution by natural selection allows us to examine the functions of traits and features of the developing child but requires us to think about this functionality in terms of the environment in which our ancestors would have developed, the environment of evolutionary adaptedness.

PRESS PAUSE SUMMARY

- Hypotheses are educated guesses that can and should be tested.
- Development happens in all species because all individuals die, creating a niche for new individuals.
- The seeds of the nature vs. nurture debate can be seen in the writings of Plato and Aristotle, from the 4th century B.C.E. Plato is the classic nativist, and Aristotle is the classic empiricist.
- The empirical study of child development started in earnest in the late 19th and early 20th centuries.
- G. Stanley Hall and his student Arnold Gesell started the normative approach. Gesell watched the development of many, many children, and documented the age at which skills normally develop.
- Piaget was the most influential figure in the emerging field of cognitive development.
- Because the nature vs. nurture dichotomy is so intuitively appealing, it is very difficult for some people to think beyond it until they learn a sensible alternative way to approach development.
- Theories about developmental psychology need to be consistent with other scientific knowledge, including natural selection.
- An evolutionary perspective allows us to make sense of the interaction between a developing organism and its environment.
- Genes do not inevitably lead to predetermined outcomes.
- Only evolution by natural selection can explain otherwise improbably complex traits.
- The aspect of the EEA that is relevant depends on the psychological process you wish to study (e.g., vision or language).

- In some ways the modern world is like the EEA, and in others it is not, depending on the psychological processes of interest.
- Natural selection builds psychological adaptations; it cannot build behaviour directly.
- Modern or recent evolutionary pressures are negligible when considering the origin of a complex adaptation.

KEY TERMS AND CONCEPTS

adaptation, 6
baby biography, 10
clinical method, 13
developmental psychology, 4
dialectical process, 14
EEA, 20
empiricist, 8
evolutionary psychology, 15
gamete, 6

generative entrenchment, 24
genetic epistemology, 13
nativist, 7
normative approach, 11
Piaget's theory of cognitive development, 13
species-typical environment, 6
zone of proximal development, 14

QUESTIONS FOR THOUGHT AND DISCUSSION

1. Who were some of the earliest people to frame the nature vs. nurture debate in ancient Greece? What were their beliefs about the topic? Who added to the nature vs. nurture discussion in Europe during the Enlightenment? What were their positions on the debate?

2. What is evolutionary psychology? What are the implications of evolutionary psychology for the field of developmental psychology? List as many as you can.

3. What is an adaptation? How does Darwin's theory of evolution by natural selection explain the existence of adaptations? Are there other possible explanations for improbably complex adaptations?

4. What is the environment of evolutionary adaptedness (EEA)? Why is it important to think about when considering evolutionary psychology? Why is the relevant aspect of the EEA different for different topics of psychological research?

chapter 2

Theories and Methods in Developmental Psychology

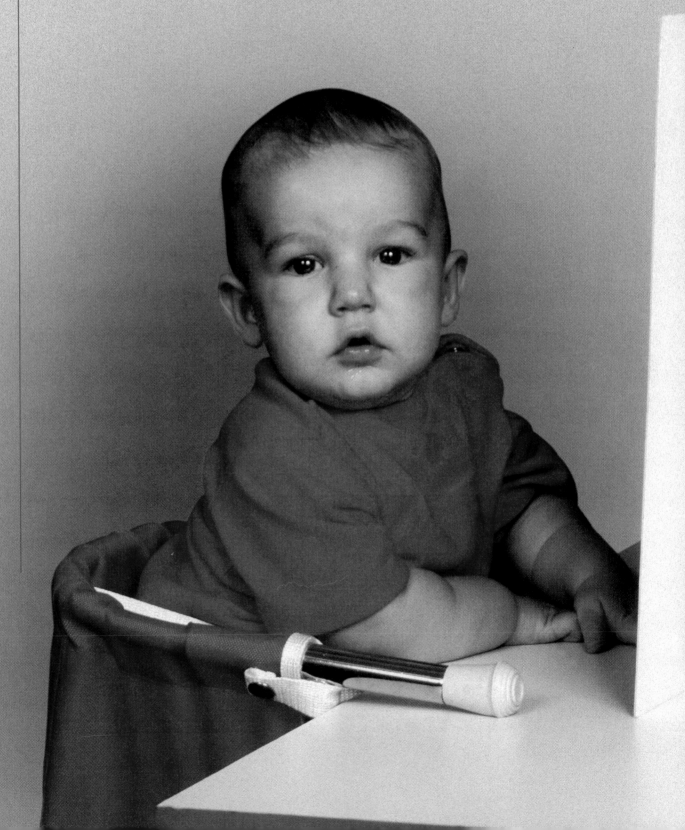

Opening Vignette: New Theories Test Old Methods

An 8-month-old infant sits and plays quietly with his favourite toy. He is completely absorbed by the toy and enjoys manipulating it with his hands and putting it in his mouth. As he sets it down, a washcloth is lowered onto it and covers it completely. The toy is no longer visible to the baby. What do you suppose he will do? Surprisingly, he does not search for the beloved toy. He does not even look in its direction. Judging by his actions and facial expression, he appears to have forgotten that it ever existed.

This was what Jean Piaget's interpretation was. In the 1950s (Piaget, 1954) Piaget repeatedly performed this experiment with young infants and concluded that infants younger than 8 months lacked object permanence, or a child's understanding that an object continues to exist even when it can no longer be observed directly. He believed that these infants did not actually have any representation of objects that were not directly and currently perceivable. The development of object permanence was an important milestone in Piaget's stage model.

Fast forward several decades. In 1985, Baillargeon, Spelke, and Wasserman published an article describing a new method for testing whether infants have object permanence. If an infant watches a rotating solid plank pass through a spot where they think a solid object is sitting, an impossible event, they look at this event for a long time, longer than if the plank is instead blocked by the object, a possible event. This new method allowed researchers to find evidence that 5-month-old infants do have a representation of objects, even when those objects are out of sight.

In this chapter, you will read about theory and methods in developmental psychology. Sometimes innovations in methods allow old theories to be tested with new approaches. And sometimes, as in the case above, the theory has to be radically re-evaluated in light of the new information.

Chapter Outline

- Piaget's Theory of Cognitive Development
- Associationism and Social Learning Theory
- Developmental Systems Theory
- Evolutionary Psychology
- Methods of Developmental Psychology
- Within- and Between-Subjects Design
- Techniques for Developmental Research

- In this chapter you will be introduced to four of the major theoretical approaches to the study of developmental psychology, and you will read about the methods that are available for its scientific study. First, you will read about Piaget's theory of development, the only approach of the four that can be attributed to a single individual. You will then read about his methods, observations, and conclusions.

- Next you will read about the associationist, or learning, perspective. You will read about John B. Watson's work, influenced by classical conditioning, and B. F. Skinner's work, influenced by operant conditioning. Then you will read about how Albert Bandura championed observational learning and how that changed the field.

- You will learn how developmental systems theory (DST) reminds us to view development as a result of interactions throughout a great system. Genes, behaviour, brains, parents, and culture continually interact and can have surprising effects throughout the system.

- You will read about evolutionary psychology and how our understanding of the environment in which our ancestors evolved applies to modern developmental research.

- You will also read about the methods that developmental psychologists use to study developing children. Have you ever wondered what a pre-verbal infant knows? How might you study whether the development of one cognitive skill is a prerequisite for another? You will learn about the different experimental designs and laboratory techniques that researchers use to answer these questions.

Piaget's Theory of Cognitive Development

In the last chapter, you were introduced to Jean Piaget, the most influential researcher in developmental psychology to date and a pioneer in the field. Here we will go through his theory of cognitive development. It is important to understand Piaget's theory because much of contemporary cognitive development involves experiments designed to reply to his claims.

Piaget's long-reaching influence is due to many factors: He worked and published in the field for nearly 60 years; he covered tremendous breadth in terms of ages, examining development from the neonatal period to late adolescence; and he touched on a range of topics of development, from the understanding of physical properties, time, and language to numbers, other people's perspectives, and many other topics.

First, one needs to understand Piaget's view of development as a stage theory. Rather than viewing the development of the child as continuous, Piaget believed that children spent some period of time in a given stage with an unchanging set of skills, and that they rather suddenly moved into a new stage, exhibiting a whole array of new skills in a number of areas more or less at once. In other words, Piaget saw development as discontinuous. He saw radical qualitative changes, as between a caterpillar and a butterfly, rather than continuous quantitative changes, as a tree gaining only in height and circumference. According to Piaget, children everywhere moved through the stages in the same order. There would never be any backtracking or skipping of stages.

Piaget's model of psychological development was a stage theory. Children were thought to complete each stage in turn, always in the same order.

table 2.1	Piaget's Four Stages of Development	
STAGE	**AGES**	**DESCRIPTION**
Sensorimotor	Birth to 2 years	Initially endowed with only reflexes, the infant interacts with the physical and social world on a physical basis. The infant is perceptually bound. She makes progress by associating sensory experiences and her own actions.
Preoperational	2 to 7 years	In this stage, the child learns to use symbols such as words and numbers.
Concrete Operational	Approximately 7 to 11 years	The child can now perform mental operations, which allows the logical problem-solving that preoperational children cannot do. Still, the child can only apply these operations to concrete objects.
Formal Operational	12 years to adulthood	The child can now perform mental operations on abstract or hypothetical entities.

THE FOUR STAGES

Here, let us examine each of Piaget's four general stages in detail, unpacking the sub-stages as we go along. Table 2.1 summarizes the stages described below.

The first stage is called the *sensorimotor stage.* This stage covers birth to approximately 2 years of age. In this stage, Piaget emphasized the use of motor activity and physical interaction for knowledge acquisition. The infant is constantly engaged in experimenting by trial and error, does not predict reactions, and does not use symbols, including pretend play. The development of physical interactions with objects is virtually synonymous with cognitive development at this stage. Early language development starts during this stage, and according to Piaget, **object permanence** develops at around 8 months of age.

Piaget described six sub-stages that make up the sensorimotor period. This is the only period that was divided into sub-stages. These six sub-stages are summarized in Table 2.2.

Piaget's second stage is called the *preoperational stage* and covers the period from about 2 years of age through early childhood, around 7 years of age. Cognitive development is rapid in this stage and includes language, memory, and the development of pretend or symbolic play. Children in this stage understand past and future, but knowledge is still very egocentric and very concrete.

The third stage is called the *concrete operational stage* and covers the period from 7 to 11 years of age. Children in this stage begin to understand and use symbols, according to Piaget. Thinking is less egocentric, and children understand concrete operations such as conservation of number, mass, and liquids but not yet abstract or formal operations.

object permanence
A child's understanding that an object still exists even when it can no longer be observed directly. A major development in the sensorimotor period, according to Piaget.

Jean Piaget, the most influential researcher in developmental psychology to date, worked and published in the field for nearly 60 years.

figure 2.1 Conservation of liquids

In a test of concrete operations such as conservation of liquid, Piaget would start with equal amounts of liquid in two containers, and then pour one into a taller container. A child in the preoperational stage would be sure that there was more liquid in the taller container. A child in the concrete operational stage would understand that the amounts are still equal.

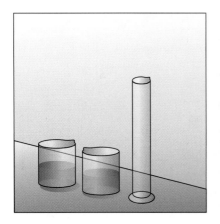 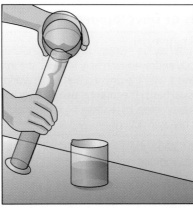 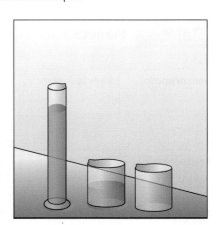

The fourth and final stage is called the formal operational stage. It starts in early adolescence, around the age of 12, and persists through adulthood. People in this stage are adept at using symbols and can relate them to abstract concepts. In this stage, people can think about multiple variables to predict outcomes and can formulate hypotheses about either concrete or abstract relationships. Although people continue to learn new information, once this stage is reached no new structures develop.

table 2.2 The Six Sub-Stages of the Sensorimotor Stage

SUB-STAGE	SUMMARY	AGES	DESCRIPTION
1	Exercising Reflexes	Birth to 1 month	Piaget grants the infant only reflexes in this stage. They respond automatically to specific stimuli.
2	Developing Schemes	1 to 4 months	Schemes are action patterns the infant uses to interact with the world, like sucking or grasping.
3	Discovering Procedures	4 to 8 months	More interest in the world. Uses procedures to reproduce events.
4	Intentional Behaviour	8 to 12 months	The child can separate means from ends, and make a plan to achieve a goal or overcome obstacles.
5	Novelty and Exploration	12 to 18 months	The infant can generate new schemes and novel solutions. Tool use starts.
6	Mental Representation	18 to 24 months	The infant can represent the world mentally, so experiments don't need to be overt anymore. Solutions can be imagined.

| figure | 2.2 | **Piaget's stages of development** |

Piaget's four stages describe cognitive development from birth through adolescence.

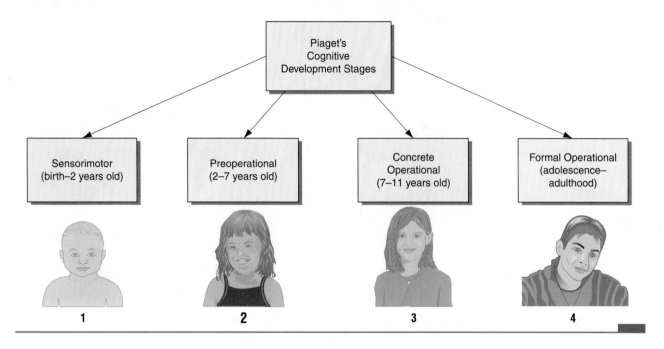

2.2 Press Pause

According to Piaget, as children moved from one stage to the next, corresponding changes took place across domains all at once.

SOURCES OF DEVELOPMENTAL CHANGE

Piaget described three sources of developmental change: assimilation, accommodation, and equilibration. **Assimilation** is the process of interpreting new information in terms of previously understood theories and knowledge. When an adult or a child hears something new, they can translate it into information that makes sense. Perhaps a child knows about cows, and upon seeing a gazelle for the first time, the child views it as a cow. Or, an infant might have a sucking scheme that is useful at nursing time but then grabs a cellphone and begins sucking on the antenna. The new object, the phone, is assimilated into the familiar scheme.

Accommodation is the process of changing one's current theory, understanding, or knowledge in order to cope with new information. This is a learning process, and the process by which a child may develop new categories. The child will learn new categories of animals and continue to refine his or her understanding of animals, plants, and all types of artifacts. Do you remember the first time you heard that plants could be male or female? To understand this, you may have had to employ accommodation, in Piaget's terms.

Finally, **equilibration** is Piaget's process of balancing assimilation and accommodation in order to maintain a stable understanding of the world while still allowing for development. If one were to accommodate every time one saw a novel object, the world would be very hard to make sense of. If one were to never accommodate, learning and development would never take place. If children come to a state of disequilibrium, then

assimilation
The process of interpreting new information in terms of previously understood theories and knowledge.

accommodation
The process of changing one's current theory, understanding, or knowledge in order to cope with new information.

equilibration
The process of balancing assimilation and accommodation in order to maintain a stable understanding of the world while still allowing for development.

Piaget may have underestimated the importance of the social and emotional contributions to development.

they are not satisfied that they can make sense of a new experience with their current understanding. As a result, their understanding changes, and they return to equilibrium.

SHORTCOMINGS OF PIAGET'S COGNITIVE DEVELOPMENT THEORY

The most striking shortcoming of Piaget's theory is that Piaget greatly underestimated the cognitive competence of infants and children. In several of the following chapters, you will read about new research findings that would have surprised Piaget because they challenge his understanding. In large part, this is due to radical advances in methods. Piaget relied largely on children's ability to explicitly report their own understandings. He also used difficult tasks that were conservative with respect to how they could be interpreted: One could be sure that a child that passed such a task had the cognitive ability in question, but one could not be sure that children who failed the task lacked the ability.

2.3 Press Pause

Although Piaget contributed tremendously to developmental psychology, more contemporary evidence suggests that he underestimated the cognitive sophistication of children.

A second major shortcoming that modern developmentalists have found in Piaget's theory is that the stage model is overstated. That is to say, Piaget thought that a child's stage determined modes of thinking in a wide number of domains and that thinking was consistent until the child moved into a new stage. There does not seem to be any evidence, however, of concurrent changes across a large number of domains at the moment of stage change, as Piaget's theory required. More recent research shows more variability across domains: Whether a child is thinking about biology, numbers, or other people determines her way of thinking. To his credit, Piaget noticed toward the end of his research the variability in cognitive strategies within a stage, but he had no way to deal with it in his theory.

A third shortcoming of Piaget's theory is Piaget's underestimation of the importance of social and emotional contributions to development. His focus was on cognitive development and on the child's own interaction with the physical world as the impetus for cognitive change. Modern developmental psychologists have a better understanding of the tremendous role other people play in development. From birth, children are completely dependent upon the adults in their lives, and throughout childhood and adolescence, parents and peers play a crucial role in development, in many domains.

Associationism and Social Learning Theory

A second theoretical perspective that recurs throughout this book is the **associationist perspective**, which encompasses learning theories in general and social learning theory as well. Here, we will trace the historical beginnings of this view starting with John Locke and then consider the more recent modifications: classical conditioning and the era of John B. Watson, operant conditioning and the contributions of B. F. Skinner, and social learning theory as conceived by Albert Bandura.

You read in the previous chapter that John Locke extended Aristotle's empiricist thinking. Locke's perspective is summed up in his quote "I imagine the mind of children as easily turned, this or that way as water itself." Locke's empiricist perspective, as you will recall, emphasized the role of experience in development and knowledge acquisition. Human behaviour, in this view, is best understood and explained as a result of experiences a person has had in his or her lifetime. Likewise, more contemporary adherents to this viewpoint expect that development and learning are a result of a very few, very general-purpose learning mechanisms, such as classical conditioning and operant conditioning. This may be the default assumption in developmental psychology, and this perspective is consistent with the standard social science model described in detail in Chapter 4.

associationist perspective An approach that encompasses learning theories in general and social learning theory as well. This perspective suggests that people have only general-purpose learning mechanisms, allowing them to associate one stimulus with another. Other than these associationist learning mechanisms, the newborn mind is a blank slate.

CLASSICAL CONDITIONING

Classical conditioning is a form of learning associated with the work of Ivan Pavlov. In classical conditioning, a neutral stimulus becomes associated with a psychologically meaningful stimulus. Pavlov's dogs learned, through repeated pairing, to associate a neutral stimulus (the sound of a bell) with a meaningful stimulus (food).

classical conditioning A learning process in which a neutral stimulus comes to be associated with a naturally motivating stimulus so that each evokes the same response.

Pavlov's experiments with dogs in 1890 led to the discovery of classical conditioning, which is still an important concept to learning theorists.

unconditioned stimulus
In classical conditioning, the stimulus that elicits a response before any training has taken place.

unconditioned response
In classical conditioning, the response that follows the presentation of the unconditioned stimulus.

conditioned stimulus
In classical conditioning, the stimulus with which the unconditioned stimulus has been associated and which elicits a response after training has taken place.

conditioned response
In classical conditioning, the response to the conditioned stimulus once training has taken place.

As summarized in Figure 2.3, the **unconditioned stimulus** is the stimulus that served to elicit the response before the training, in this case the food. The **unconditioned response** is the response to this stimulus that followed the presentation of the food, in this case salivation. By repeatedly pairing the bell and the food, the learner makes an association between the two: the neutral stimulus and the unconditioned stimulus. Once that association has been made, the neutral stimulus, which has become the **conditioned stimulus**, is effective in eliciting a response, in this case salivation. This learned response is known as the **conditioned response**.

BEHAVIOURISM

John B. Watson was very much an empiricist and believed that a child's behaviour and development was best explained by his or her experiences in life. Watson was a fan of Ivan Pavlov's work and emphasized learning through conditioning. Famously, Watson endeavoured to demonstrate the power of conditioning in young children with his "Little Albert" experiments (Watson & Raynor, 1920). Watson showed little Albert, a typically developing 11-month-old, a white rat. Albert was interested in and initially quite comfortable with the rat, the neutral stimulus. In training sessions, Watson paired the presentation of the rat with a loud startling noise that frightened little Albert and served as the unconditioned stimulus. After repeated pairings, Albert began to associate the loud noise with the rat. The rat became the conditioned stimulus, and Albert developed a lasting phobia of rats.

| figure | 2.3 | **Classical conditioning** |

Through the process of classical conditioning, the unconditioned stimulus comes to be associated with the conditioned stimulus, thus eliciting the conditioned response when presented alone.

BEFORE CONDITIONING

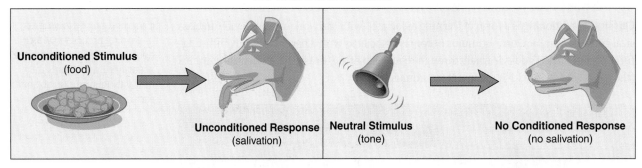

DURING CONDITIONING   AFTER CONDITIONING

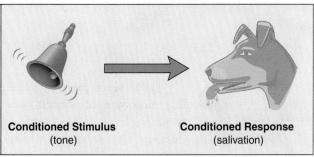

Watson's demonstration sparked years of research as well as practical applications of classical conditioning. This conditioning approach can be used for systematic desensitization, a treatment in which people who have unwanted fears and phobias are exposed to the object of fear. But instead of pairing the object with a fear response, the object is paired with a reward. After repeated exposure, the object is no longer feared (Jones, 1924).

Watson had a huge influence on child rearing in North America (Watson, 1928). He advocated strict discipline. To this day, his idea of a regimented feeding schedule is widely employed. He believed that if conditioned to eat at regular intervals, a child would not be hungry or cry in between feedings. Watson discouraged parents from kissing and hugging their children, or even letting them sit on their lap. He told parents to shake hands with their child in the morning and "Give them a pat on the head if they have made an extraordinarily good job on a difficult task" (p. 81). This perspective was pervasive in North America until Dr. Spock introduced his childcare book, which gave parents permission to show affection to their children.

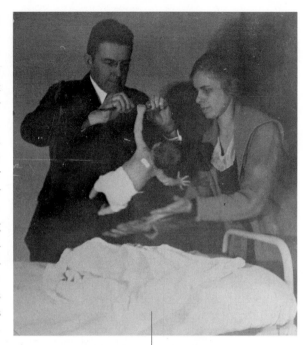

John B. Watson believed that a child's behaviour and development was best explained by his or her experiences in life. He advocated strict discipline. To this day, his idea of a regimented feeding schedule is widely employed.

2.4 Press Pause

Watson emphasized the importance and effectiveness of Pavlov's classical conditioning.

OPERANT CONDITIONING

Another type of learning that is recognized by associationists is operant conditioning. Unlike classical conditioning, **operant conditioning** is a type of learning in which a specific behaviour becomes more or less likely as a result of rewards or punishments. Learning theorists see operant conditioning as playing a major role in child development and potentially child rearing. If a child occasionally produces a particular behaviour, say cleaning up after a spill or putting his shoes away, and that behaviour is followed by positive consequences, the behaviour may become more likely in the future. Any consequence that makes a behaviour more likely to occur is called a **reinforcer**. Reinforcers may work for negative as well as positive behaviours: Just as a smile from a friend reinforces a child's sharing behaviour, placating a child with a treat in a store reinforces a temper tantrum. There need not be an intentional agent providing the reinforcement: If the door to the house opens reliably when you kick it, then the kicking behaviour may become more likely to occur. If behaviour leads to a consequence that makes the behaviour less likely, that unpleasant consequence is called a **punisher**.

operant conditioning
A type of learning in which a specific behaviour becomes more or less likely as a result of rewards or punishments.

reinforcer In operant conditioning, any consequence that makes a behaviour more likely to occur.

punisher In operant conditioning, any consequence that makes a behaviour less likely to occur.

BEHAVIOURISM AND OPERANT CONDITIONING

Operant conditioning was championed by B. F. Skinner. Like Watson, Skinner was a strong empiricist, believing that a child is passively shaped by his or her environment. Skinner's beliefs regarding the power of operant conditioning were extreme: He believed that every behaviour is a result of the operant conditioning that came before it. Given this, and the unfettered malleability of children, Skinner believed that with careful and precise child rearing, a utopian civilization was possible in which everyone behaved in ways that were good for society, and no evil behaviours ever happened.

B. F. Skinner believed that a child is shaped by his or her environment. Skinner's beliefs regarding the power of operant conditioning were extreme: He believed that every behaviour is a result of the operant conditioning that came before it.

Some of Skinner's ideas have a broad influence, even today. For example, Skinner recognized that the attention an adult paid to a child could serve as a reinforcer. A child might act disruptively "just to get attention" (Skinner, 1953, p. 78). This observation has parenting implications: If a child has a temper tantrum or acts out, just turning your attention to him may make that unwanted behaviour more likely. To this day, parents take this idea to heart when they place an unruly child in "time out," thus temporarily withdrawing the reinforcer.

SOCIAL LEARNING THEORY

The name most associated with social learning theory is Albert Bandura (Bandura, 1977; Bandura & Walters, 1963) who studied and described it in the 1960s though it had already been growing for a few decades at that point. Like other empiricists, Bandura sought to explain a child's behaviour and development in terms of experience, and social learning theorists explained all behaviour in terms of stimulus and response learning. Unlike his predecessors, Bandura focussed on personality and social development; the focus of social learning theory was the process by which adults taught children to behave as proper adults. In addition to classical and operant conditioning, Bandura described the importance of imitation. Social learning theorists had argued that imitation was one of the most powerful forces when it came to socialization (Miller & Dollard, 1941).

observational learning
The learning process by which an actor's behaviour changes as a result of observing a model.

Bandura, still mindful of classical and operant conditioning, emphasized the role of **observational learning**, a learning process by which an actor's behaviour changes as a result of observing a model. Bandura recognized that children could learn new behaviours just by watching others. Furthermore, the rewards and punishments that children witnessed (but did not receive) affected the likelihood that they would perform the behaviour, and operant conditioning alone did not explain that.

Although most contemporary developmental psychologists would resist being called associationists, the impact of all of these learning theories reverberates throughout the field. As you read more about contemporary research, particularly in evolutionary developmental psychology, you may notice that experiments are often designed to show that a phenomenon cannot be explained by simple associationism. Experiments are frequently designed to falsify simple associationist pairings in order to reveal more powerful, better-designed psychological mechanisms.

Albert Bandura emphasized observational learning. If a child witnessed a behaviour, that child was likely to imitate the behaviour unless they also witnessed the actor being punished for the behaviour.

SHORTCOMINGS OF THE ASSOCIATIONIST AND SOCIAL LEARNING VIEWS

Associationist accounts deeply underestimate the power and specificity of learning mechanisms. We will return to this topic throughout this book, but briefly, it is now recognized that any two variables are not equally easily associated. A rat can learn to avoid a specific food if the punisher is nausea but not if the punisher is an electric shock (Garcia, Kimeldorf, & Koelling, 1955). A monkey can learn, from observation, to fear a snake but not to fear a flower (Cook & Mineka, 1989).

Throughout this book, look for evidence of powerful learning mechanisms as you read about attachment, the development of language, and the effects of social context on development, for example.

> **2.5   Press Pause**
>
> Associationist learning models underestimate the specificity as well as the number of learning mechanisms that account for child development.

An even bigger problem for associationists is describing how the child knows when two objects or events are similar. For classical conditioning to work, one has to recognize different instances of the neutral stimulus as the same and different instances of the meaningful stimulus as the same. This seems trivially easy (as though anyone should be able to do this without requiring a specific cognitive explanation) in the controlled laboratory situation, but in the real world, recognizing two objects (e.g., two bears) as the same is real psychological work. We need to suspend our humanness in order to appreciate how difficult it is. This is one place in the associationism model where what counts as similar has an evolutionary history; it involves perception and categorization, concepts, and a whole host of assumptions.

Finally, even if their theories are correct, associationists cannot ignore evolution since no matter how simple the learning rules are, their rewards have an evolutionary history: If a rat is motivated to work for food or a child is motivated to be near his mother, it is because these rewards increased fitness in our EEA. As well, the processes of operant and classical conditioning must have an evolutionary history. To claim that these are the processes that comprise human learning is to claim that these learning mechanisms have been able to outcompete other possible developmental strategies.

Developmental Systems Theory

One group of theorists, those who work in an area called **developmental systems theory** (DST), have articulated the interaction between factors in development particularly well (Lickliter & Honeycutt, 2003; Oyama, 2000, 2001; Oyama, Griffiths, & Gray, 2001). Borrowing from the dynamic systems theory that was developed for complex systems in physics and mathematics, DST researchers emphasize that when it comes to complex systems, the whole is more than the sum of its parts (Thelen & Smith, 2006).

This view translates easily to development. This approach is primarily characterized by the view that all of the developmental resources act together as a system to create the developing organism. Developmental psychologists in this area speak of "the multiple, mutual, and continuous interaction of all the levels of the developing system, from the molecular to the cultural" (Thelen & Smith, 2006, p. 258).

These resources include DNA; the cell in which DNA is housed; the prenatal environment (the inter-uterine environment for those organisms that develop in utero); the social environment; the pathogenic, microbial environment; terrestrial regularities like the sun, seasonal cycles, and moderate cycling temperatures; the chemical environment; and any other factors that might play a part in development. Developmental systems theorists caution us to regard all of these resources as equally important to development. There is no one part that has causal primacy; without all of the resources the organism would not develop as it does, and altering any of the resources would change the outcome. Thus, the developmental systems view rejects the person vs. the environment dichotomy since the person in the environment is to be regarded as a system, and all parts of the environment, including the macroenvironment, are to be

developmental systems theory A perspective that emphasizes that when it comes to complex systems, the whole is more than the sum of its parts. This perspective reminds us to consider all of the resources contributing to development, genetic and environmental, rather than emphasizing the contribution of one over the other.

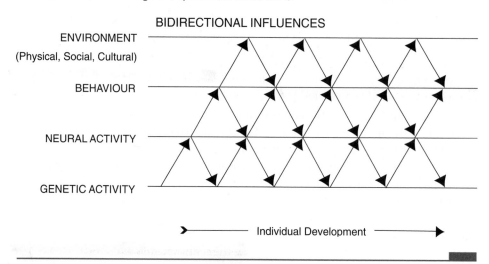

figure 2.4 Bidirectional influences

Developmental systems theorists remind people to think of genes as having a bidirectional influence on behaviour such that genes, the brain, behaviour, and the environment continually influence each other during development (Gottlieb, 1991).

regarded as integral to development and capable of influencing and being influenced. This view is summed up by Oyama (2000):

> What is transmitted between generations is not traits, or blueprints, or symbolic representations of traits, but developmental means (or resources, or interactants). These means include genes, the cellular machinery necessary for their functioning, and the larger developmental context, which may include the maternal reproductive system, parental care, or other interaction with conspecifics, as well as relations with other aspects of the animate and inanimate worlds. This context . . . changes with time, partly as a result of the developmental processes themselves. (p. 29)

In addition, developmental systems theorists think of the resources as being hierarchical, from the gene to the gene's environment to the cell's environment to the organ's environment to the organism's environment. Influences throughout the levels of the hierarchy are bidirectional. Genes not only influence other levels of the hierarchy, but they are also influenced by them. This bidirectionality is a cornerstone of DST theorists' thinking.

These theorists encourage people to think about a developing organism's inheritance not just as the genome but also as everything in the environment that the organism inherits from the previous generation. This includes aspects of the environment that the organism might have manipulated or affected itself. For example, when termites build a termite mound, and the mound outlasts the generation, the subsequent generation inherits the mound and must adapt to a world with the mound in it. Similarly, developmental systems theorists encourage us to remember that human environments include many aspects that are inherited from one generation to the next and that are as much a part of a newborn's developmental inheritance as the genome (e.g., cars, antibiotics). Indeed, even in species that do not obviously manipulate their environments, the species-typical environments that are necessary for normal development are part of what an individual inherits (Lickliter & Berry, 1990; Oyama, 2000).

One implication of developmental systems theory is that small initial changes in the system early in development can have a far-reaching and massive effect for years to come. For example, the fact that the presence or absence of a girl's father in early life has an effect on the age of first menstruation (as we will discuss in Chapter 10) (Ellis, McFadyen-Ketchum, Dodge, Pettit, & Bates, 1999) is both interesting and believable to a developmental systems theorist since all of these processes are part of one system, and any one part of the system could affect any other part. The brain itself is complex, and developmental systems theorists acknowledge (indeed emphasize) the continual interaction among genes, the brain, behaviour, and the environment during development (Karmiloff-Smith, 2009).

Developmental systems theorists see an organism's inheritance not just as the genome but also as everything in the environment that it inherits from the previous generation. A termite mound is part of what a termite inherits from its parents.

2.6 **Press Pause**

Developmental systems theorists emphasize the continuous, bidirectional interaction between developmental resources: genes, the brain, behaviour, and the environment.

SHORTCOMINGS OF THE DST PERSPECTIVE

Developmental systems theory has certainly made a contribution to developmental psychology. Thinking of development as a multi-factor interaction is an improvement over arguing which contributes more to development, genes or the environment. (It is similarly nonsensical to claim that genes and the environment make an equal contribution.) But making this interactionist claim is just a trail marker. It does not answer the complex question of development. We can say that genes and the environment contribute to every trait or characteristic, but as curious developmental psychologists, we want to know how they interact.

More critically, developmental systems theorists insist that no component of the system be credited with a special role in either development or evolution. Consequently developmental systems theorists reject the definition of evolution as "a change in gene frequencies across generations" since such a definition accords a special role to genes. For developmental systems theorists, evolution happens whenever a change in the system is preserved across generations, even if gene or relative allele frequency has not changed. It is only because selection acts on the genome to preserve successful characteristics and carve out new solutions that complex functionality in biological systems can emerge and be maintained. Nothing else can explain the exquisite complex functionality seen in, say, the vertebrate eye, the human heart, or the human mind. Indeed, without selection acting on alternative alleles, entropic tendencies would lead to complete disorder; complex organs would not be preserved generation after generation (Tooby, Cosmides, & Barrett, 2003). In other words, all complex systems tend toward less order, less complexity, and less functionality. Imagine an iPad sitting in a field for 500 years. Over time it would lose complexity and functionality and tend toward entropy or disorder. So too would our genome if some force was not countering the entropy, and that force is natural selection.

2.7 **Press Pause**

DST acknowledges that numerous developmental resources interact, but it does not acknowledge a special role for genes in evolution.

Evolutionary Psychology

Evolutionary psychology is an approach to psychological research that is mindful of our evolutionary history and the processes by which complex organisms are created and that scientists believe will be a benefit to those trying to understand the human mind. Here, let us consider how the field of evolutionary psychology has been shaped over the last many decades as well as the contributions it has made to the field of development.

DARWIN ON PSYCHOLOGY

Charles Darwin, in his original writings on evolution by natural selection, anticipated that this perspective on the origins of living systems would illuminate our understanding of psychology as well as the physical traits of organisms. In the final pages of *The Origin of Species*, the book in which he laid out his theory of natural selection, Darwin wrote "in the distant future I see open fields for far more important researches. Psychology will be based on a new foundation, that of the necessary acquirement of each mental power and capacity by gradation. Light will be thrown on the origin of man and his history" (1859).

So Darwin understood that the theory of natural selection would be important to psychology. And he contributed to the field of developmental psychology with his detailed observations and the innovation of the baby biography. But among this impressive body of work, he did not draw out the connections that could be made between evolution and developmental psychology, leaving that to future generations.

2.8 **Press Pause**

Charles Darwin anticipated that the theory of evolution by natural selection would be important to psychology.

ETHOLOGY

ethology The study of fitness-enhancing behaviours that were shaped by natural selection.

The next important steps in the understanding of evolution as it relates to developmental psychology happened in the field of ethology, mostly in middle of the last century. **Ethology** is the study of fitness-enhancing behaviours that were shaped by natural selection.

Some of the best known names in ethology at that time were Konrad Lorenz (1903–1989), Niko Tinbergen (1907–1988), John Bowlby (1907–1990), and Irenäus Eibl-Eibesfeldt (1928–). Lorenz was interested in issues that are very relevant to development, including his studies of **imprinting** in birds, the psychological process by which newborns first identify their mother and then strongly attach to her psychologically. Lorenz famously caused several batches of young birds to imprint on him as a means of exploring the factors that were relevant to the process (Lorenz, 1935, 1952). Imprinting serves to ensure that the infant is always near the mother, which ethologists recognized as having tremendous adaptive value.

imprinting The psychological process by which newborns first identify their mother and then strongly attach to her psychologically.

There are several lasting legacies from classical ethology in the field of developmental psychology. First is the idea of a sensitive period or critical period. Ethologists discovered that some things were more easily learned in a discrete period during development. Each species of bird studied had a specific window of time immediately after birth during which imprinting could happen. Evidence for these species-typical constraints on learning was problematic for a pure associationist account of learning. The concept of critical periods or sensitive periods for learning is still an important concept in developmental psychology as you will learn when as you read about language development, visual development, and social development, for example.

Eibl-Eibesfeldt (1975, 1989) was another classical ethologist who explicitly made connections with human development. He is credited with being the founder of human ethology, that is, the first to apply the idea of evolved adaptive behaviour to humans, although some researchers in the field of developmental psychology took notice of the possibilities beforehand.

One significant advance in developmental psychology that can be attributed to ethology is the idea of attachment. Like newborn birds and other mammalian species, human infants form a strong attachment to their mothers. Cues such as sight, sound, and smell orient the baby to its mother, and once attached, an unknown but competent caregiver is not an adequate substitute. Bowlby (1969), who described the process of attachment in human infants, was explicitly borrowing from the ethological point of view, and like ethologists, he saw attachment as an evolved behaviour with adaptive value. You will read much more about attachment in Chapter 10.

Charles Darwin anticipated that evolutionary psychology's perspective on the origins of living systems would illuminate our understanding of psychology as well as the physical traits of organisms. While studying the Galapagos finch, Darwin realized that the size and shape of these birds' beaks had evolved in order to maximize their nutritional success in different climates.

SOCIOBIOLOGY

The next step in the history of evolutionary psychology is the era of **sociobiology**, the study of the biological basis of social behaviour. The field is most closely associated with E. O. Wilson (Wilson, 1975). Wilson focussed on social behaviour such as altruism, co-operation, mating, and aggression, working to explain these behaviours in adaptive terms and test predictions that came out of these explanations. Much of his work revolved around human social behaviour, but he was interested in other social species as well. Sociobiologists' thinking on parenting, mating, and social hierarchies still has an influence on psychological research today.

When Wilson was working to explain and popularize his ideas regarding the evolutionary basis of human social behaviour, especially in the late 1970s, he was met with

sociobiology The study of the biological basis of social behaviour, popularized by E. O. Wilson in the 1970s.

E. O. Wilson is known as the champion of sociobiology, the study of the biological basis and adaptive value of social behaviours such as altruism, co-operation, mating, and aggression.

tremendous politically motivated resistance. Watson's and Skinner's belief that human behaviour was endlessly malleable was still ubiquitous. Many were offended at the suggestion that biology informed people's behaviour, and they did not wish to think of their actions as influenced by processes that were shaped by natural selection. Protestors called for Wilson to be fired, and a bucket of water was dumped on his head as he tried to give a talk to the American Association for the Advancement of Science. His claims about the evolutionary history of social behaviour in other species were less controversial.

MODERN EVOLUTIONARY PSYCHOLOGY

The ideas of ethologists and sociobiologists have been expanded and built upon by modern evolutionary psychologists (Barkow, Cosmides, & Tooby, 1992; Buss, 1995; Daly & Wilson, 1983; Symons, 1979). Evolutionary psychology does not apply to any one sub-field, and you will see in this book that the approach has been applied to the study of vision, language, and conceptual, cognitive and social development, among other areas of psychology.

One way in which modern evolutionary psychology differs from its predecessors, sociobiology and ethology, is its emphasis on the environment of evolutionary adaptedness, the EEA, or the conditions under which our ancestors lived and to which our morphological and psychological features are adapted. You can imagine the EEA as a hunter–gatherer society hundreds of thousands of years ago in the African savannah.

Evolutionary psychologists recognize that the selection pressures of the environment in which our ancestors evolved, such as the African savannah, are the pressures that shaped our human psychology as well as our physiology and our bodies.

Evolutionary psychologists recognize that the selection pressures of that environment (i.e., the struggles toward survival and reproduction) are the pressures that shaped our human psychology as well as our physiology and our bodies. To the extent that our modern environment is the same as the EEA (e.g., the colour spectrum of terrestrial sunlight), our psychological adaptations work well; to the extent that there is a mismatch between our current environment and the EEA (e.g., technology), our behaviours may not be adaptive.

2.9 Press Pause

To the extent that our modern environment is the same as the environment of our ancestors, our psychological adaptations work well. However, if there is a mismatch, our behaviours may not be adaptive.

A second way that evolutionary psychologists have added to the thinking of the sociobiologists is an explicit consideration of psychology. That is to say, ethologists and sociobiologists focus on behaviour and the adaptive value of the behaviour. While there is clearly a relationship between behaviour and psychology, evolutionary psychologists made it clear that it is the psychological processes, not the behaviours themselves, that are a product of evolution by natural selection. Although behaviour is still expected to be adaptive to the extent that current conditions are similar to species-typical conditions in the EEA, the adaptive value of the behaviour can change either as circumstances change over historical time or as inputs are carefully manipulated in the laboratory.

Methods of Developmental Psychology

So far in this chapter we have read about theories in developmental psychology. Theories are very important to research because they suggest fruitful hypotheses to test; the methods of developmental research are just as important. Here, we will consider some of the methods and some of the practical issues involved in research that is designed to answer questions about the psychological development of children.

CROSS-SECTIONAL AND LONGITUDINAL DESIGNS IN DEVELOPMENTAL RESEARCH

In developmental psychology research, a researcher often wants to answer questions about how children change with age. A convenient way to compare children at different ages is by using a cross-sectional design. In a **cross-sectional design**, one compares different ages of children as a group in a *between-subjects design* comparing measures that are taken at the same time. One might compare 2-year-olds, 4-year-olds, and 6-year-olds on some aspect of grammatical mastery in language development.

The cross-sectional approach has some clear advantages: All measures are collected at once, so one's research question can be answered relatively quickly. Each subject needs to be measured only once, so there is no risk of attrition or practice effects. One clear disadvantage is that this between-subjects design does not actually measure the development of an individual, which is likely to be the researcher's primary interest. The researcher is left to infer development based on differences between individuals at different ages. In addition, a vulnerability of this approach is that one could be inadvertently measuring cohort effects. If some new teaching method, for example, has been introduced in the local school system, then differences between a group of Grade 1 students and a group of Grade 6 students might be exaggerated or mitigated.

cross-sectional design
A type of developmental study in which children of different ages are measured at the same time and compared in order to infer age-related change.

In a cross-sectional design, one compares different ages of children as a group (e.g., this group of Grade 6 students and this group of Grade 12 students) in order to see what difference the passage of time makes in their development.

An example of an experiment with a cross-sectional design is one focussing on how children's friendships differ with age. Researchers compared the responses of Grade 6 and Grade 12 students who were asked to name their best friends. Researchers found that older children named fewer friends, but the people they named were more likely (compared to younger children's purported friends) to name them as friends in turn. Some things did not change with age: Children who were part of the ethnic majority in their school were more likely to be identified as friends compared to children who were members of an ethnic minority group (Urberg, Degirmencioglu, Tolson, & Halliday-Scher, 1995).

A stronger (but more time-consuming) approach to comparing children at different ages is the longitudinal design. In a **longitudinal design**, one takes multiple measurements of the same child or group of children as time passes. This is a *within-subjects design*. The longitudinal study could span months or years. The advantage to this somewhat stronger design is that it directly measures the effect of the passage of time, eliminating possible cohort effects and allowing the researcher to measure both general trends (changes that happen to all the participants) and individual differences in development.

longitudinal design A type of developmental study in which a group of children are studied first at one age and later at another age, or many ages, in order to observe age-related changes.

The *7 Up!* series that documented the development of a group of people, discussed in Chapter 1, gave viewers an opportunity to ask the following questions: What life stages do people go through? How do early circumstances influence later development? How are people the same, and how are they different?

There are, however, disadvantages of the longitudinal approach. One practical disadvantage is the amount of time it takes to collect the data. If you want to know the change in psychology over 5 years, you have to wait 5 years to get your answer. But there are deeper scientific problems: A longitudinal study is at risk of **selective attrition**. The researcher needs subjects to participate in the study more than one time, and some people who participated in an early session may leave the study before the later sessions have been conducted. Importantly, the participants who remain may differ from those who leave the study in a way that is significant to the research. For example, if a longitudinal experiment is about dyslexia and some families suspect that their child is developing dyslexia, those families are more likely to stay in the study than those who have less interest in the topic. Clearly, this can affect the results and jeopardize one's ability to draw valid conclusions. In addition, participants who continue in a longitudinal study may show **practice effects**. In this case, the participant may perform differently than naive participants in later testing sessions because they know how the tests works, they remember previous answers, or they feel more comfortable in the setting and with the researcher.

A well-known longitudinal study has been ongoing in Montreal for more than 30 years. The study was started in 1976 by Jane Ledingham (Ledingham, 1981). Initially, researchers screened over 4,000 kindergarten children in francophone public schools and selected a group of children who were normative in terms of aggression and withdrawal and a group of children who exhibited these characteristics to the extreme. The study has revealed that aggression and withdrawal are stable over time (Moskowitz, Schwartzman, & Ledingham, 1985), a conclusion that relies on the longitudinal design. The study also revealed that early measures of aggression and withdrawal predict future development in various areas, including school failure and a need for psychiatric care (Moskowitz & Schwartzman, 1989), and early measures of aggression in girls were associated with adolescent sexual activity and teen pregnancy (Serbin, Peters, McAffer, & Schwartzman, 1991). Early measures of withdrawal predict poor school achievement and negative self-perception in adolescence (Moskowitz & Schwartzman, 1989). These are all findings that were also made possible by the longitudinal design of the study.

selective attrition Attrition in which the subjects who quit a study or move away from a study location are different from the remaining subjects in some way that is relevant to the object of the study.

practice effects Participants in a longitudinal study performing differently over time as a result of prior exposure to the test or testing situation.

In order to test whether early measures of aggression and withdrawal predict future outcomes, one would need to use a longitudinal design.

THE BEST OF BOTH

cross-sequential design
A type of developmental study in which different-aged groups of children are studied at the same time, once initially and then later after a set period of time, in order to observe age-related changes.

It is possible to combine a cross-sectional and a longitudinal design in what is called a **cross-sequential design**. In this type of study, researchers follow two or more age-defined groups and collect data on them when they reach a certain age. Researchers will first take measures from each group, as in a standard cross-sectional design. Then, after some interval of time has passed, they will measure each group again, providing the advantages of a longitudinal design.

So, for example, imagine that a researcher studied a group of 4-year-olds (Cohort 1) and a group of 8-year-olds (Cohort 2) in the year 2006, yielding interpretable results of a cross-sectional comparison of 4- and 8-year-olds. Then, imagine the researcher administered the measures 4 years later in 2010. She can compare the performance of Cohort 1 as both 4-year-olds and 8-year-olds to make inferences about development during that time period. Practice effects might be estimated by differences in performance between Cohort 1 at Time 2 and Cohort 2 at Time 1.

The cross-sequential design is replete with scientific advantages: It allows researchers to study the passage of time and individual differences, and it buffers against the effects of selective attrition. It even allows one to determine whether differences are

⁘ Research in Action

Concordia Longitudinal Study

A longitudinal design offers unparalleled benefits to developmental research. Only a longitudinal study can allow one to make inferences about the effects of early experience on later development or the persistence of individual traits and characteristics. Still, in addition to the financial cost and the tremendous wait before results can be interpreted, one of the biggest disadvantages to longitudinal studies is attrition. After the first few experimental sessions, important participants in the study might stop being involved, in some cases because they have moved away. How might you guard your study against this problem?

One group of researchers at Concordia University in Montreal was able to curtail this problem by focussing their study on the demographic group that is the most geographically stable in urban Canada. Who might that be? The francophone community of Montreal. Jane Ledingham and Alex Schwartzman started the Concordia Risk Study in 1976, and it is still active today. The study's participants were originally recruited when they were in Grade 1, 4, or 7, and those participants were followed through childhood, adolescence, young adulthood, and into parenthood. Imagine the possibilities: One can ask whether early measures of childhood characteristics predict adult relationships and parental success.

Based on some early measures in the study, Ledingham and Schwartzman discovered that aggression in early childhood predicts academic trouble in adolescence, for both boys and girls (Moskowitz & Schwartzman, 1989). Considering just the girls as a group, early aggression also predicts precocious sexual behaviour and teen pregnancy (Serbin, Peters, McAffer, & Schwartzman, 1991).

Measureable withdrawal in young children also predicted later problems. Withdrawal in early childhood predicted academic trouble and low self-esteem during adolescence for both boys and girls. And if a child is both aggressive and withdrawn, the combination is additive. These children would later have greater social and behavioural problems than children who had just been withdrawn or just been aggressive (Moskowitz & Schwartzman, 1989).

The original participants are still involved in the study, and now their children are participating too. Current research in the study is focussing on intergenerational transfer of traits and behaviours that have been observed and measured for decades now. If your mother was withdrawn or aggressive in her early childhood, does this predict how you will act with peers or with authority figures? Early analyses suggest that the answer is yes (Serbin et al., 1998). This ongoing, exciting longitudinal study reveals more about continuity in personality traits over generations, as only a longitudinal study could.

driven by cohort effects. At the same time, the cross-sequential design is a very time-consuming and expensive undertaking.

MAKING INFERENCES

Studies in developmental psychology can have one of several different experimental approaches, each specialized for asking certain kinds of questions. A study employing **naturalistic observations** is a study in which data are collected in everyday settings, usually without manipulating the subject's experience. One might use this method to study peer interactions in a daycare or language development in 3-year-olds, situations in which the researcher is interested in natural behaviour in everyday environments. A natural observation study has high external validity, and thus generalizability, but it allows for little experimenter control (you get what you get) and does not allow for strong conclusions regarding causation since it lacks **random assignment.** For example, if you were studying peer interactions of language development, some children might be approached more often than others, thus enjoying more opportunities to display their social or language development skills.

In a **correlational design** the researcher will observe the relationship between two variables in a group of subjects without manipulating either variable. Perhaps a researcher wants to know the relationship between watching television and aggressive behaviour. In a correlation study, the researcher would measure the time spent watching television and would also measure aggressive behaviour but would not manipu-

naturalistic observations
A study in which data are collected in everyday settings.

random assignment
A procedure that ensures that each participant in a study has an equal chance of being assigned to any group in the experiment.

correlational design
A research design in which the researcher will observe the relationship between two variables in a group of subjects without manipulating either variable.

---

figure 2.5   Correlational design

This figure depicts correlations of various magnitudes. If two variables are correlated, it could be that one causes the other, but we cannot know which variable, if any, is the cause. Furthermore, a third, unknown factor may be affecting both variables, which could also lead to a correlation. One should be cautious about making inferences from correlational data.

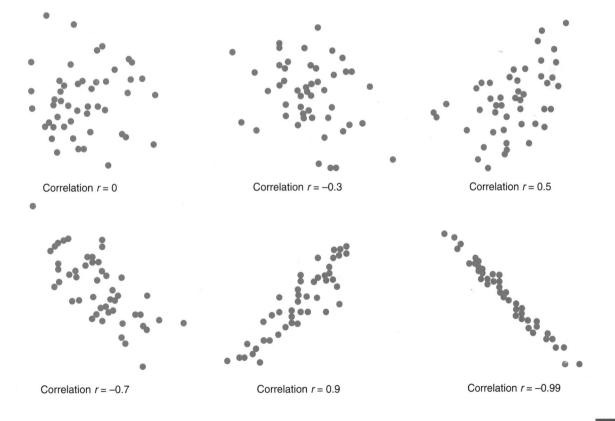

Correlation $r = 0$ Correlation $r = -0.3$ Correlation $r = 0.5$

Correlation $r = -0.7$ Correlation $r = 0.9$ Correlation $r = -0.99$

correlation coefficient
A number between -1 and +1 that describes the correlation between two variables in terms of direction and strength.

correlation The relationship between two variables. Reports of correlation include direction and strength.

experimental design
A research design in which the researcher carefully controls one or more variables and observes the effect on another variable. Subjects are randomly assigned to conditions.

independent variable In an experiment, the variable that is systematically manipulated to test its relationship to the dependent variable.

dependent variable In an experiment, the variable that is expected to be affected by, or dependent on, the experimental manipulation.

within-subjects design An experimental design in which participants are exposed to multiple experimental treatments, and measures taken from the same individuals are compared.

between-subjects design
An experimental design in which each participant is included in only one group, and variables of interest are compared across groups.

late either. Given these measures in a group of children, the researcher can calculate the **correlation coefficient**, which reveals both whether the relationship between the two variables is positive or negative and how strong the relationship is. A correlational design might offer some advantages in terms of expense or ethical considerations, but it has some scientific limitations. If one has only measured a **correlation**, then one cannot infer any causal relationship. Perhaps television viewing has caused aggressive behaviour, or perhaps an aggressive disposition has attracted a child to television viewing. A third, unknown factor may also be causing kids both to (a) want to watch television and (b) display an aggressive behaviour after the experiment. Viewing violent television may not have caused group differences.

Experimental design is the strongest design with respect to drawing conclusions about causality. The experimenter chooses and administers the manipulation to the subjects. Importantly, subjects are randomly assigned to the conditions. For example, one group might watch violent television while the control group watches nonviolent television. If the experimenter randomly assigns each subject to one group or the other, then any group differences seen after the manipulation can be attributed to the manipulation. This random assignment is critical in an experimental design. If the experiment lets any factor determine which subject gets assigned to which group (e.g., who shows up to the experiment first, who wants to be in which group), then one's conclusions about causation are not warranted. Variables that are measured in an experimental design are called either **independent variables**, those that the researcher manipulated and expects to cause an effect, or **dependent variables**, those whose values the researcher expects to depend upon the independent variable.

2.11 Press Pause

Stronger inferences can be made based on experimental findings compared to correlations.

Within- and Between-Subjects Design

Another consideration when designing a research project is whether to use a within-subjects design or a between-subjects design. In a **within-subjects design**, multiple measurements are taken with the same subject, and measurements taken at Time 1 are compared with measurements taken at Time 2. Sometimes, a manipulation is conducted between measurements, such as training the subject in a given skill. Other times, especially in developmental research, the independent variable of interest is age, so no manipulation, save for the passage of time, distinguishes Time 1 from Time 2. A longitudinal study is necessarily a within-subjects design, and the design is ideal for measuring the effect of a given manipulation. Because you are comparing a group of subjects to themselves, you have already controlled for a number of variables such as ethnicity, IQ, sex, and socio-economic status.

In a **between-subjects design**, two different groups of subjects are compared. Perhaps you want to know which of two teaching methods for reading is more effective. Clearly you could not use the same group for both methods without cross-contaminating the treatments. Instead, you would use one naive group and teach them with one method and a different naive group and teach them with the other method. Then you would compare the reading ability across groups. For this to be an experiment, you would need to ensure that each participant was randomly assigned to the group. As suggested above, in this method, you might want to ensure that the groups are matched on demographic factors such as ethnicity, IQ, sex, and socio-economic status.

Techniques for Developmental Research

PSYCHOPHYSICAL METHODS

The methods that are used in the laboratory in child development research are necessarily different from those used with adults. One might be able to get reasonably reliable data using a multi-page questionnaire with adults, but this technique will obviously not work with children. Even with children who are old enough to be verbal, methods have to be adapted so as to capture and hold their interest. The task needs to be clear enough for children to perform it. Studies with pre-verbal infants pose a particular problem. How do you ask babies what they think and what they know? We will see examples of experiments throughout this chapter and this book that solve exactly this problem. One thing to remember is that when a researcher finds evidence that children have developed a particular cognitive skill at a particular age, this does not give anyone the licence to infer that the skill is absent before that age. The last several decades in developmental psychology research have been characterized by novel and innovative methods revealing cognitive skills that were previously thought to be absent in children of a certain age.

Preferential-looking paradigm

Much can be inferred based on very simple behaviours such as eye direction. Using the preferential-looking method, there is evidence that pre-verbal babies can tell the difference between two things (i.e., they can categorize) and that opens the doors for research on many topics, from perception to social cognition.

The **preferential-looking paradigm** was developed and refined in the 1970s by Davida Teller, who was the first to use it experimentally, as a binary choice. In this type of experiment, an infant is presented with two side-by-side visual displays. In between these two displays is a viewing aperture, intended to be unnoticed by the infant, through which an experimenter observes the infant's gaze direction. The experimenter is naive to which stimulus is displayed on which side, so that there is no particular expectation about where the baby is likely to look. If the baby cannot discriminate between the two displays, then neither can the experimenter. If the baby shows a clear preference for one display over the other, this is taken as evidence that the baby can distinguish the two. Teller was working in the field of visual development, but her paradigm has been used in many areas since. Look for examples throughout the book.

The logic behind the preferential-looking technique is still employed, but technology allows for greater precision and accuracy. Researchers using this paradigm today will almost certainly present the stimuli using a computer. Computer presentation ensures that each subject sees the same stimuli, under the same lighting conditions, for the same duration. Computer software designed for psychology experiments also makes it easy to counterbalance the order of the stimuli presented: You can show one baby the stimulus of interest on the left side first, and show the next baby the stimulus of interest on the right side first, so that you know that a preference for one side over the other does not drive your effect.

Another modern addition to the preferential-looking paradigm is the use of eye-tracking technology. Eye trackers are like cameras that detect and record the light that is reflected off of the observer's eye. By first measuring the light that is reflected when we know where an observer is looking, we can then infer where on the computer screen the observer is looking based on those measurements. By coordinating the stimulus presentation with the eye tracking, we can easily tell if the baby is looking at one stimulus longer than another. The results are both more efficient and more accurate than the 1970s' methods allowed.

preferential-looking paradigm An experimental design in which an infant is presented with two visual stimuli at the same time. If the looking time differs reliably between the two, the experimenter infers that the infant can discriminate between the two stimuli.

---

figure 2.6 A modern preferential looking task

In modern research, the preferential-looking paradigm makes use of computer displays and eye-tracking technology.

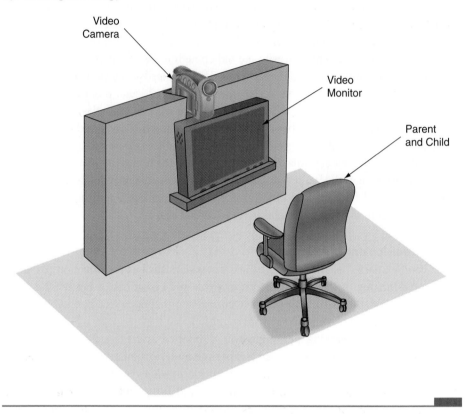

Video Camera

Video Monitor

Parent and Child

2.12 **Press Pause**

If infants reliably look at one stimulus more than another, researchers infer that the infant can tell the difference between them. This is the logic of the preferential-looking paradigm.

The habituation paradigm

habituation paradigm
An experimental design that takes advantage of an infant's declining response to (habituation to) a repeatedly presented stimulus. If a new stimulus elicits a recovery in response, the experimenter infers that the infant can discriminate between the old and the new stimulus.

Another method for determining whether pre-verbal babies can discriminate between two stimuli is the **habituation paradigm**. First, the baby is presented with pictures of the same thing over and over until she is bored. For example, the baby might be shown the colour green, and then a slightly different green, and then another example of green, etc. The baby first finds this interesting (we know by measuring looking time) but then habituates to the stimulus. Green is no longer novel and exciting, and habituation is evinced by a sharp decrease in looking time. Now, we can present the baby with a new stimulus, say the colour blue, and in essence ask the baby if the new display is the same or different as the previous display. If the baby looks at the blue display significantly longer than she did the green, this dishabituation is evidence that she has seen a difference. If looking time does not increase, perhaps the two displays fall into the same category for the baby. Notice that neither of these techniques can be used to falsify the hypothesis that the baby can discrimi-

nate between two things, but it can only be used to falsify the
hypothesis that the baby cannot discriminate between them.

The violation of expectation paradigm

Another method used to find out what a non-verbal baby is
thinking is the **violation of expectation paradigm**. The idea is
that infants will look longer at events that are impossible. Any
impossible display will surprise the infant, and looking time will
increase. This technique was introduced in the 1960s and 1970s (Bower, 1974; Charlesworth, 1966) and was employed by Baillargeon et al. (1985) in the experiment described
at the start of this chapter. Infants first watched a solid panel (imagine a piece of card-
board) rotate on one edge: First it was flat, and then it rotated around while one edge
stayed on the ground until it was flat again as in figure 2.7. Once the infant had habituated to this motion, a solid object was placed behind the panel so that it should have
appeared to prevent the panel from going all the way down. If the panel stopped on the
object, the baby's looking time did not increase; that was the expected outcome. If the
panel appeared to pass through the object, continuing all the way to the floor, looking
time increased; the authors inferred object permanence.

Notice the logic here is different from a typical habituation paradigm, in which the
infant is attracted to and looks longer at a novel event. In the violation of expectation
paradigm, the infant looks longer at an event that is impossible. This provides a window
into the infant's expectations about the world.

Non-visual psychophysical techniques

Some effective ways to ask pre-verbal infants questions do not involve eye direction.
For infants as well as for adults, changes in the autonomic nervous system, which are
both involuntary and often unnoticed, can respond to psychological states and are
thus measurable proxies for those states. Researchers can measure changes in heart
rate, pupil dilation, and the conductance of the skin. In the case of infants, sucking
time also has a measurable response to changes in psychological states: Infants will
suck faster if they are interested in what they are seeing (DeCasper & Fifer, 1980).

In some cases, measuring physiological responses may be a more sensitive measure
than looking time: If an infant is staring at a stimulus but not attending to or process-

INNOVATIVE
RESEARCH METHOD

**violation of expectation
paradigm** An experimental
procedure in which an infant
is expected to look longer at
an event that violates a belief
or expectation that the infant
holds.

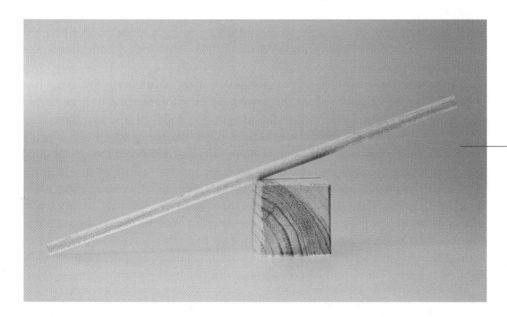

If a solid plank appeared to
pass through a solid block,
that would be surprising,
and an infant would look at
the event longer. By using
a violation of expectation
paradigm, researchers can
discover what expectations
infants have about how the
world works.

figure 2.7 A habituation task

This figure shows the violation of expectation paradigm. Having seen that a solid object is behind a screen, a baby will be surprised (i.e., look longer) if the screen falls flat. If no object is behind the screen, the flat screen is no surprise. This is evidence that infants as young as 3 ½ months have object permanence (Adapted from Baillargeon et al., 1985).

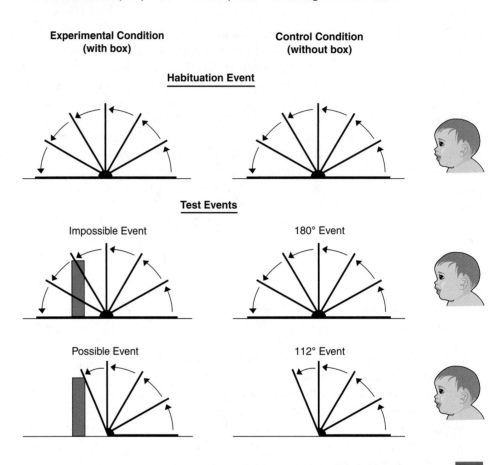

ing it, her heart rate will be stable, whereas if she is staring at it attentively with great interest, her heart rate will decrease (Fox & Card, 1998). The baby's eye direction would not distinguish the two.

Throughout this book, you will read about creative and innovative research that is designed to ask questions about the developing mind of the child. Whenever you see "Innovative Research Method" in the margin, you will read about an interesting methodological approach. You will see that researchers have come up with some pretty clever and interesting ways to find out what is on a child's mind even though the child is not able to describe their own psychological development.

INNOVATIVE
RESEARCH METHOD

Some methods that are available to researchers allow them to assess brain activity more directly. The electroencephalograph (EEG) measures electrical activity that is generated in the brain, via electrodes that are placed non-invasively on the scalp. For example, EEG recordings have been used to show that when infants listen to speech sounds, there is more activity on the left side of the brain than on the right side (Molfese & Molfese, 1979). The same is true for adults.

Here is Renee Baillargeon. employing a radically different research method, Baillargeon, Spelke, and Wasserman (1985) found that infants much younger than 8 months show object permanence. New methods provide new ways to test theories, and theories change as a result.

RELIABILITY AND VALIDITY

Research is not intended to be kept a secret but is meant to be shared and to influence others' thinking and scientific conclusions. Because of this, researchers strive to make sure that their results are trustworthy and meet the standards of the scientific community. Researchers want to ensure the reliability and validity of their results.

Reliability is the extent to which research results are repeatable. If you were to take the same measurements, with the same participants, under the same circumstances, would you get the same results? You would if your results are reliable. Results should not depend upon who the experimenter or observer is: Results should be repeatable by other observers, even those who are naive to the results you are hoping for. Indeed, in observational research, one standard measure of reliability is called *inter-rater reliability*. Reliability can also be measured across separate administrations of a test, a measure called *test–retest reliability*. Reliability can be estimated within a given testing session if, for example, different items on a questionnaire are thought to be measuring the same underlying psychological phenomenon. In that case, the agreement between these items is an index of reliability.

reliability The consistency in repeated measures of the same variable using the same measurement method.

The **validity** of a research test is the extent to which the test actually measures what the experimenter wants to measure, as opposed to memory, reading ability, or test anxiety, for example. If you do not have reliability you do not have validity Without reliability, you are not measuring anything in particular. But the problem of validity is even harder than just having reliability. Do your results predict the kind of performance that you would expect on independent tests? If you think you are measuring mathematics ability, do your measurements predict performance on math in school? There are two different kinds of validity to consider. *Internal validity* is the extent to which internal conditions of the study allow for a measure of the intended phenomenon. One can fail to have internal validity by having inadequate recruiting and screening standards, devising the test improperly, or creating biasing distractions in the test setting. *External validity* refers to the extent to which the research measures generalize the intended factor outside of a research situation. If the researcher intends to measure attention to

validity The extent to which a measuring technique measures the attribute that it is designed to measure.

If a researcher asks a child to work on a task that has no solution, the child might feel frustrated and stressed. What other psychological risks might research involve?

eye direction, will her findings generalize the way people pay attention to eye direction in the real world or only on stimuli that resemble those used in the experiment?

ETHICAL CONSIDERATIONS FOR RESEARCH WITH CHILDREN

Research participants must be treated ethically. Children participating in research might be exposed to physical risks, perhaps in the case of medical research where a specific treatment is being studied, but it is possible that they might be exposed to psychological risks as well. A researcher might want to observe children when they are asked to answer a problem they cannot solve, or when they are asked to deny themselves a tempting treat, or when they are exposed to violent behaviour. The treatment that the child is exposed to during the experiment might cause negative feelings, stress, or discomfort.

Research in any field of psychology balances risks and benefits with regard to those who participate in the research: In order to be considered ethical, the benefits of the research must exceed the risks to the participant. Clearly psychological research has benefits, both in terms of illuminating the workings of the mind, and answering theoretical questions, and also in terms of discovery with practical, even therapeutic, applications. But to what extent should a subject be exposed to the risk of possible harm in order to answer the important and valid scientific questions that researchers have? Who makes that decision?

Today, all research that is conducted with human subjects, whether in the field of psychology, anthropology, sociology, or even history, is reviewed by an institutional review board (IRB), a panel of objective and knowledgeable individuals who determine whether the benefits of a particular research project exceed the risks. They may make suggestions to the researcher about how to reduce the risks. They can deny permission to conduct the research if risks are too high or if benefits are too low: If they think the design of the experiment would not yield interpretable answers, they may deem it unworthy of human participation. All universities have an IRB, as do research hospitals, research institutes, and other organizations that conduct research. In the current climate, research would not be possible without such a review: Funding agencies require the review in order for a researcher to use their funds, and scientific journals require the review before findings can be published.

2.13 Press Pause

Institutional review boards (IRBS) make sure that research projects reach the ethical standards set out by the research community.

Researchers, whether they are psychologists, medical doctors, or historians, follow strict ethical guidelines when dealing with human subjects. Researchers who deal with children follow an even stricter, more specific set of guidelines established by organizations such as the Canadian Psychological Association (2000), the American Psychological Association (2002), and the Society for Research in Child Development (1993).

table 2.3 Society for Research in Child Development's Ethical Standards for Research With Children

PRINCIPLE	TITLE	DESCRIPTION
1	Non-Harmful Procedures	The investigator should use the least stressful research procedure possible.
2	Informed Consent	The procedure should be described to the child and consent obtained in a language that is comprehensible to the child.
3	Parental Consent	Consent of a parent of legal guardian should be obtained in writing.
4	Additional Consent	If the object of study is the child's interaction with a third party, such as a teacher, the consent of the third party should be obtained.
5	Incentives	Incentives should be reasonable, so as not to be coercive.
6	Deception	Deception is permissible only if employing it is the only way to answer the experimental question. If deception is employed, the participant should be debriefed, and the reason for the deception should be explained.
7	Anonymity	Information obtained about research participants should be kept anonymous and obtained with permission.
8	Mutual Responsibilities	The researcher, parent and any other authority such, as a participating teacher, are mutually responsible, and should be clear with each other about each one's role.
9	Jeopardy	If the researcher becomes aware of information suggesting that the child's welfare might be in jeopardy, this information needs to be shared with a parent or guardian.
10	Unforeseen Consequences	Should unforeseen consequences arise, the researcher should immediately make necessary corrections to the procedure.
11	Confidentiality	Any information obtained about the participant should be kept confidential.
12	Informing Participants	General findings should be reported in a language the participant can understand.
13	Reporting Results	Caution should be exercised in reporting results or giving advice to parents and children.
14	Implications of Findings	When presenting research findings, be clear about the limitations of the research with respect to what conclusions can be drawn.
15	Scientific Misconduct	Misconduct is the fabrication or falsification of data, plagiarism, or serious deviation from research practices commonly accepted within the scientific community.
16	Personal Misconduct	Personal misconduct that results in a criminal conviction of a felony may be sufficient grounds for a member's expulsion from the Society.

Source: Ethical Standards for Research With Children, SRCD

The ethical standards of the Society for Research in Child Development

Let us consider the standards set by the Society for Research in Child Development (SRCD), which are detailed in Table 2.3. Compared to adults who participate in research, children are less able to comprehend the risks and benefits associated with it. They may be more vulnerable to stressors than adults: We do not always know how seemingly mild stressors affect a developing child. Therefore, the SRCD's standards describe 16 specific principles. The first is the principle of "non-harmful procedures," meaning the investigator should use the least stressful research procedure possible.

The next three principles have to do with consent. The right to informed consent means that the research must explain, in child-appropriate language, what they will experience during the research session, including anything that might affect their decision to participate. A parent or guardian must also provide informed consent on a child's behalf. In the case of infants and pre-verbal children, a parent or guardian's consent is normally regarded as sufficient.

Another principle has to do with the use of deception. In some cases, a researcher would not be able to test her hypothesis if she explained the whole procedure to the participants. If the researcher deems that deception is necessary in order to conduct the research, and the institutional review board agrees, than deception can be used. Still, the participant should be debriefed at the end of the study, and the researcher should ensure that the participant feels all right about their experience before they leave.

The child's right to privacy means the researcher must protect the child's identity when discussing or reporting results from the research. One principle speaks to the question of anonymity, another to confidentiality. The research should preserve anonymity when possible. The researcher should also keep any information obtained confidential. This obligation on the part of the researcher extends even to informal conversations about the research.

Participants also have the right to knowledge of results, which means that if the child wants, the researcher will provide results of the study in language that is meaningful to the child. And if the research project involves a therapy that may be beneficial to children, but the child has been assigned to the control group who will not get the treatment as part of the research project, the child has the right to alternative beneficial treatments if available.

SUMMARY

In this chapter, you read about four theoretical perspectives that frame most of the research you will read about in this book. First you read about Jean Piaget, whose contributions to cognitive development underlie nearly all current research in the field. Piaget's theory was a stage theory of development, and he thought that when children matured into a new stage, thinking across all domains shifted simultaneously.

Next you read about the associationist tradition that started with Aristotle and was supported by Watson and Skinner in the last century. Associationist learning models propose a very small number of very general learning mechanisms that are common across species and that should be able to explain all learning.

You also read next about the developmental systems theory, a relatively new way of thinking about development. One strength of this theory is that it reminds us of the intricate and bidirectional interaction between genes and all levels of the environment; one of its weaknesses is its failure to acknowledge a special role of genes in evolution and in maintaining the complexity of living beings.

The final theoretical perspective you read about was evolutionary psychology as it pertains to development. The child was designed by natural selection to develop in interaction with the species-typical environment. To the extent that our modern environment is the same as the environment of our ancestors, children will develop as designed. If there is a mismatch, it is hard to predict what effect this will have on development.

Lastly, the methods you read about in this chapter are those used by scientists trying to understand the development of children. Longitudinal, cross-sectional, and cross-sequential designs all have strengths and weaknesses. Experimental studies allow for the strongest inferences, but sometimes practical considerations mean correlational or observational studies are preferred. Laboratory techniques have advanced over the last few decades, and strong inferences can be made based on where an infant is looking by using a preferential-looking, habituation, or violation of expectation paradigm. Advances in these techniques have given new insights into what infants know, as you will discover throughout this book.

PRESS PAUSE SUMMARY

- Piaget's model of psychological development was a stage theory. Children were thought to complete each stage in turn, always in the same order.
- According to Piaget, as children moved from one stage to the next, corresponding changes took place across domains all at once.
- Although Piaget contributed tremendously to developmental psychology, more contemporary evidence suggests that he underestimated the cognitive sophistication of children.
- Watson emphasized the importance and effectiveness of Pavlov's classical conditioning.
- Associationist learning models underestimate the specificity as well as the number of learning mechanisms that account for child development.
- Developmental systems theorists emphasize the continuous, bidirectional interaction between developmental resources: genes, the brain, behaviour, and the environment.

- DST acknowledges that numerous developmental resources interact, but it does not acknowledge a special role for genes in evolution.
- Charles Darwin anticipated that the theory of evolution by natural selection would be important to psychology.
- To the extent that our modern environment is the same as the environment of our ancestors, our psychological adaptations work well. However, if there is a mismatch, our behaviours may not be adaptive.
- Cross-sectional and longitudinal designs are both used in developmental research. Each has advantages and disadvantages.
- Stronger inferences can be made based on experimental findings compared to correlations.
- If infants reliably look more at one stimulus than another, researchers infer that the infant can tell the difference between them. This is the logic of the preferential-looking paradigm.
- Institutional review boards (IRBs) make sure that research projects reach the ethical standards set out by the research community.

KEY TERMS AND CONCEPTS

accommodation, 33
assimilation, 33
associationist perspective, 35
between-subjects design, 50
classical conditioning, 35
conditioned response, 36
conditioned stimulus, 36
correlation, 50
correlation coefficient, 50
correlational design, 49
cross-sectional design, 48
cross-sequential design, 41
dependent variable, 50
developmental systems theory, 39
equilibration, 33
ethology, 42
experimental design, 50
habituation paradigm, 52
imprinting, 42

independent variable, 50
longitudinal design, 46
naturalistic observations, 49
object permanence, 31
observational learning, 38
operant conditioning, 37
practice effects, 47
preferential-looking paradigm, 51
punisher, 37
random assignment, 49
reinforcer, 37
reliability, 55
selective attrition, 47
sociobiology, 43
unconditioned response, 36
unconditioned stimulus, 36
validity, 55
violation of expectation paradigm, 53
within-subjects design, 50

QUESTIONS FOR THOUGHT AND DISCUSSION

1. What are the key hallmarks of Piaget's theory of child development?

2. What methods were used most by Piaget?

3. What is a stage, according to Piaget? How is a stage theory different from other theories of child development?

4. Compare and contrast classical conditioning and operant conditioning. Which developmental psychologist is associated with each?

5. What are some shortcomings of the associationist learning views? Can you think of a rebuttal to these shortcomings?

6. Summarize the developmental systems theory. What are its strengths and weaknesses?

7. What advances were made by the study of ethology? What connections were made between ethology and developmental psychology?

8. How does modern evolutionary psychology differ from the sociobiology that it was built upon?

9. Compare and contrast a longitudinal design and a cross-sectional design.

10. Compare and contrast the preferential-looking paradigm, the habituation paradigm, and the violation of expectation paradigm.

11. What inferences do correlational and experimental research allow? Why?

12. What ethical considerations are unique to child research? What ethical considerations are common to child and adult research?

From the Classroom to the Lab: Follow Up

Consider the experiment you designed in response to the "From the Classroom to the Lab" challenge earlier in this chapter.

Would your experimental method meet the ethical standards expected by the field? What risks does your experiment involve? What benefits are likely?

What is your dependent variable?

What is your independent variable?

What kind of design does your experiment have (e.g., experimental, correlational)?

Imagine you have run your experiment. What results would indicate to you that the babies tested can discriminate between two sounds? What results would indicate to you that the baby cannot discriminate between two sounds?

chapter 3

The Basics
Evolution, Genes, and Conception

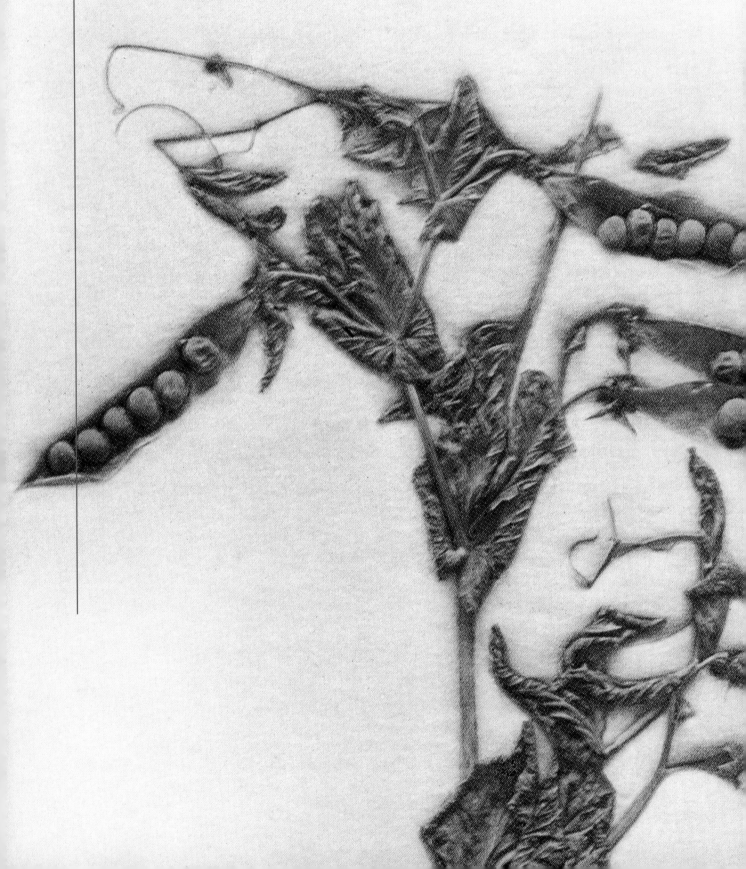

Opening Vignette: Charles Darwin and Gregor Mendel

On 27 December 1831, the *Beagle* set sail from Plymouth, England, with Charles Darwin aboard. Darwin spent 5 years circumnavigating the globe. He spent the 5 years collecting, examining, and classifying geological and animal specimens. Partly as a result of the data he collected during this voyage, Darwin conceived the theory of evolution by natural selection, the idea that some heritable traits would lead to greater reproductive success, greater representation in future generations, resulting in changes in a population over time. Darwin's revolutionary theory was published in 1859, in *On the Origin of Species by Means of Natural Selection, or the Preservation of Favoured Races in the Struggle for Life*. The first edition sold out immediately, and the book attracted international attention.

On 20 July 1822, Gregor Mendel was born to a German family in Austria. He grew up on a farm where his childhood tasks included gardening and beekeeping. In 1843, Mendel joined an abbey and became a monk. He attended the University of Vienna starting in 1851 but upon completion returned to the abbey. His experimental work resulting in the discovery of the particulate method of inheritance largely took place between 1856 and 1863. Mendel presented his findings at a conference in 1865 and in a published paper in 1866. Upon publication, his work was largely unnoticed and only cited three times over the following 50 years. The scientific community was extraordinarily slow in recognizing the implications of Mendel's work. In 1868 Mendel was promoted to the position of abbot and no longer had time for scientific pursuits.

Darwin and Mendel were contemporaries, and together their two transformative discoveries are known as the *modern synthesis*: the modern understanding that the gene, Mendel's particulate mechanism of inheritance, was the heritable matter that Darwin's theory of evolution relied upon. During their lifetimes, however, Mendel and Darwin were unaware of each other's existence and of the importance of each other's work to their own.

Chapter Outline

- A Modern Understanding of Evolution
- Darwin's Problem: Blending Inheritance
- Mendelian Inheritance
- Chromosomes, Genes, and Alleles
- Evolutionary Processes
- Adaptations, By-Products, and Noise
- What Does DNA Do Anyway?
- Interactionism: The Bidirectional Influences of Developmental Resources
- Meiosis, Conception, and Pregnancy
- Brain Development

- In this chapter, you will read about some of the basic concepts and processes that are important in the study of evolution. You will read about genes, what they are and what they do, and you will read about conception and pregnancy.

- You will learn about the modern understanding of evolution involving Darwin's idea regarding the change of heritable traits in a population over time and Mendel's discovery that the heritable material that gives rise to these traits is particulate, or made out of separable particles.

- You will also learn about some of the evolutionary processes such as bottlenecks and the founder effects, and you will learn more about adaptations, by-products of adaptations, and exaptations, those adaptations that are currently used for a new purpose.

- You will develop a clearer understanding of what chromosomes are, what DNA is, and what a useful understanding of a gene might be. You will read about what DNA does and how it leads to the production of functional proteins. You will also learn why the function of the protein is not solely determined by the DNA sequence.

- You will also read about meiosis, the process in which genetic material is shuffled to create new sex cells to pass along to the next generation. You will read about conception and about how twinning can occur in the first few days after conception. You will read about development during pregnancy and about some of the adaptations that mother and fetus are equipped with that keep the fetus safe during pregnancy.

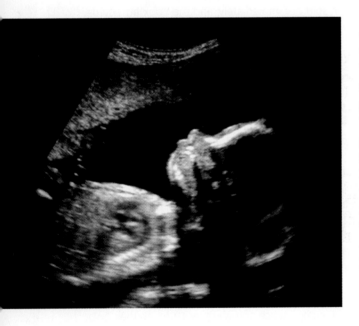

A Modern Understanding of Evolution

Contemporary scientists now understand that evolution involves genes and that genes are particulate and inherited as a whole, a "bit" of information. As it is understood by contemporary biologists and psychologists, evolution is the change in the relative frequency of alleles over the course of successive generations. For example, if an allele that tends to lead to the development of white wings in normal developmental circumstances decreases in frequency in a population of moths, while an alternative allele that tends to lead to the development of black wings in normal developmental circumstances increases in frequency in the population of moths, evolution is happening.

The idea that evolution involves particles (that we now call genes) is a big leap forward from Darwin's day, when people thought that what was passed from parents to their offspring was somehow fluid, rather than discrete particles. In this chapter we will talk about genes, their expression, and the processes that lead to changes in gene frequency over time: the processes of evolution. Darwin worked without the knowledge of genes or genetics, without the knowledge of dominant and recessive genes, and without any knowledge of how traits were passed from parent to offspring. The **modern synthesis**, sometimes called Neo-Darwinism, is the pairing of Charles Darwin's theory of evolution by natural selection and Gregor Mendel's discovery of the particulate nature of genes. In a later section (What Does DNA Do Anyway?), we will describe genes and the process by which they are transcribed, thereby taking part in the developmental process.

As developmental psychologists, we are interested in natural selection because it is the only process in evolution that can give rise to adaptations and thus the only process that can explain the complex design that we see in living beings. If we want

modern synthesis The modern understanding that the gene, Mendel's particulate mechanism of inheritance, was the heritable matter that Darwin's theory of evolution relied upon.

Evolution is the change in the relative frequency of alleles over the course of successive generations. If an allele that tends to lead to the development of black wings increases in frequency in a population, evolution is happening.

to understand the development of visual perception, the development of attachment to caregivers, or the developmental influences of peers, it is helpful to understand the psychological processes that were shaped by natural selection in the environment in which we evolved. Natural selection is not, however, the only process that leads to changes in gene frequency, as we will see later in this chapter. Before we get into the details of how evolutionary processes change a population over time, first let us look at what a gene is and what a gene does.

There are two main goals of this section. One is to describe how Mendel's discovery of the particulate character of inheritance solved Darwin's problem of describing how traits are preserved and selected from generation to generation. The second goal is to steer you away from thinking about genes as destiny. Genes are really just sections of very large molecules that code for proteins. We will look at what they do and the role they play in development as well as in the operation of various adult systems.

3.1 Press Pause

There is nothing magical about chromosomes; they are just very large molecules that can be transcribed into proteins.

Darwin's Problem: Blending Inheritance

Darwin had a problem. He did not know about genes and, in fact, had no idea how heritable traits were inherited. He held the view, widespread at the time, that whatever was inherited from parent to offspring was fluid. This inherited "stuff" would come from the mother and from the father and then blend together in the way that two fluids would. The implication was that traits would average. If a plant with red flowers and a plant with white flowers were crossed, all of their offspring would be the same, and in this case, all of their offspring would be pink. If a tall person mated and reproduced with a short person, all of their children would be of intermediate height.

Darwin believed that offspring would carry characteristics of each parent, so a flower with a red parent and a white parent might be pink. This blended inheritance was a problem for the theory of natural selection since advantageous new trait would be diluted.

mutation A spontaneous error to create a true replica in the process of DNA replication, resulting in a novel sequence.

This was a big problem for Darwin because this model of inheritance did not lend itself to his theory of evolution by natural selection. A novel mutation that had beneficial effects could never take hold and could never spread throughout the population. (A **mutation** is a spontaneous error to create a true replica in the process of DNA replication.) Worse, blending inheritance would mean the new mutation would essentially disappear. Imagine that for a given population of rabbits there is an advantage to having dark fur (because rabbits with lighter fur are more visible to predators). Imagine then that a mutation comes along that will, given normal developmental conditions,

---

figure **3.1** **Darwin's problem: Blended inheritance**

Suppose a new mutation came along that led to an advantage. When the lucky individual with this advantageous gene passes it on, the gene is blended with that of the other parent, leading to offspring who are intermediate. The advantage is diluted more with each generation and will never have the chance to spread.

New Mutation!

The Next Generation

The Next Generation

lead to darker fur. When this lucky, darker-furred individual passes this advantageous new gene onto her offspring, the gene is blended with that of her lighter-furred mate, leading to offspring who are intermediate in colour. The advantage has been diluted by 50 per cent. In the next generation, the advantage is diluted by 25 per cent, 12.5 per cent in the next, and so on. The new mutation will never have the chance to spread and become universal throughout the population. This was a problem for Darwin. He knew it and his critics knew it.

3.2 Press Pause

Darwin's evolutionary explanation for complex functionality would not work if inheritance was blended.

Mendelian Inheritance

A great irony in the history of science is that Mendel, who discovered the answer to Darwin's trouble with inheritance, was a contemporary of Darwin, yet Darwin did not learn of Mendel's work during his lifetime. Mendel discovered particulate inheritance.

figure 3.2   Mendel's solution: Particulate inheritance

A tall and a short pea plant, of the sort Mendel might have used.

He made this discovery by conducting a series of experiments in a species of peas that had distinct and heritable traits such as pod colour, height, and pea texture. Indeed he is sometimes called the Father of Modern Genetics.

Mendel conducted an enormous number of experiments, growing and testing almost 30,000 pea plants during his career, but he is most well known for two critical experiments. Mendel first started with two purebred strains of peas, a purebred short plant and a purebred tall plant. For this purpose *purebred* means descended from many generations of just short plants on the one hand or just tall plants on the other hand, resulting in homogenous populations that had only the gene associated with short plants or only the gene associated with tall plants.

Next Mendel created a hybrid plant by cross-pollinating the two purebred parents. What do you think these hybrid offspring looked like? Remember that if Darwin's blending model was correct, all the hybrid offspring should be an intermediate of the two parents; in this case, plants of medium height. But this is not what Mendel found at all. All the offspring in this first hybrid generation were the same, but they were all tall. Did the short parents contribute anything to their offspring? Yes, they did, and this showed up in the next generation, when Mendel bred the first-generation hybrids among themselves.

---

figure 3.3   **Mendel's Experiment**

Mendel found that when a purebred short plant and a purebred tall plant were crossed, although the first hybrid generation was uniformly tall, the second hybrid generation had short plants. There was no irreversible blending of traits, and a trait not seen in one generation could reappear in the next.

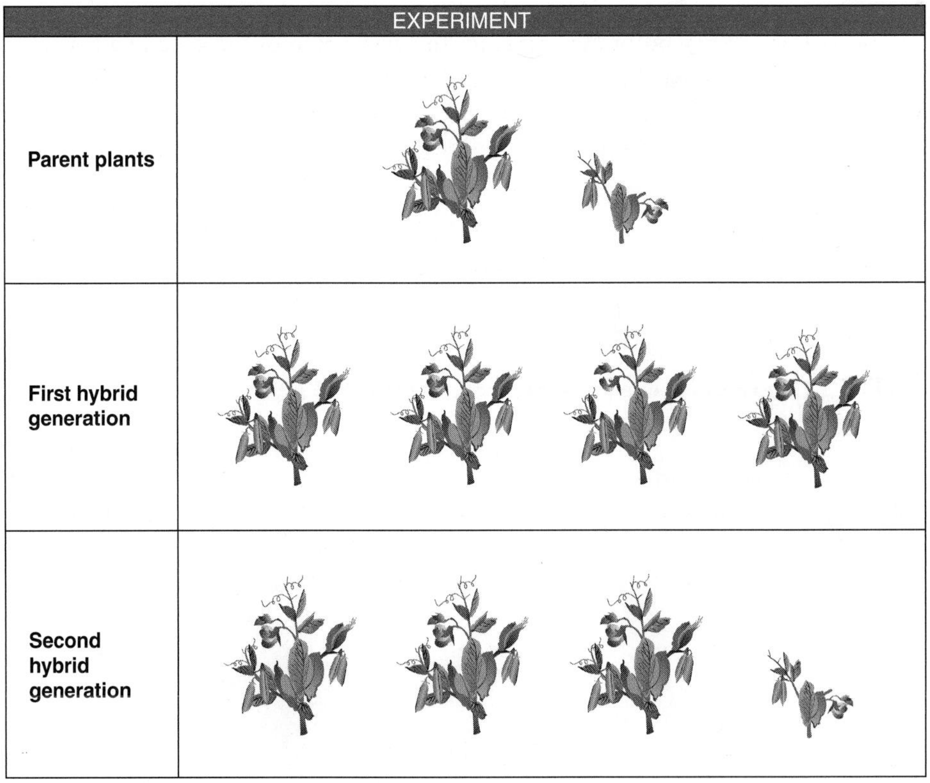

In the production of this second hybrid generation, if the blending model were correct, again, all these tall parents would have to produce tall offspring. Instead about three quarters of the plants in this second generation were tall and about one quarter of the plants were short. Mendel replicated these results with various other traits (e.g., colour and texture) and always found that the first hybrid generation was uniform, showing one form or the other of the trait in question, and the second hybrid generation was made up of three-quarters individuals who showed the same form as the first hybrid generation, and one quarter who showed the alternative form. How would you explain that?

Mendel concluded that the inherited factor was not fluid and did not blend or average across generations. It was clear to him that inheritance from parent to offspring was particulate: The information was contained in coherent bits that retained their character, even in generations in which they were not expressed in the physical features of the plant. In the model of heredity that he derived from these two experiments, Mendel drew four conclusions:

1. Whatever was inherited was particulate, not fluid.
2. Each individual carried two copies of each of these particulate units of inheritance. (Today we could call them *genes* or *alleles*, but these terms were not available to Mendel.)
3. Each parent gives one copy of the heritable particle to its offspring.
4. The heritable particle (what we now call a *gene*) given by one parent does not change the nature of the gene inherited by the other parent (each gene can be passed on intact), but it can influence the expression of the gene in a particular individual. This was Mendel's idea of dominant and recessive genes. Genes that came from the tall purebred parent were dominant to the genes that came from the short purebred parent, so the first hybrid generation appeared tall, even though each plant had one tall gene and one short gene.

For a quick review, see "The Gregor Mendel Rap" by Parish Monk Education, available at http://www.youtube.com/watch?v=KxiuTtozG2M.

> ## From the Classroom to the Lab
> Mendel's work focussed on traits for which there were two variants: colour was either green or yellow; surface was either smooth or wrinkled. Scottish terriers have three coat colours: black, brindle, and wheaten. Design a breeding experiment to find out which of those colours is associated with a dominant gene and which are associated with recessive genes. Imagine that, like Mendel, you get to start with "pure" breeding stock.

Chromosomes, Genes, and Alleles

Let us define some terms. Although a gene is a component of a chromosome, it turns out that it is much easier to define a chromosome than it is to define a gene. A **chromosome** is a single molecule, so big that it can be seen under a microscope. It is a large DNA double helix, so it looks like a twisted ladder. A single chromosome includes thousands of genes. (It also includes silent sections that are not "transcribed" into proteins the way genes are. There is more about transcription later in this chapter.) In a sense, chromosomes keep your genes tidy. The chromosomes spend most of their time neatly gathered up in the nucleus of each cell in your body, uncurling just when they are involved in replication or transcription.

Defining exactly what a gene is has turned out to be more interesting and more controversial. It would be convenient to say a gene is a certain length, say 10 letters of the chromosome, but this is not going to be useful. In many cases, this chunk

chromosome A single molecule comprising a very large DNA helix. A single chromosome may include thousands of genes.

of chromosome will not code for anything: There is a lot of DNA that is never transcribed. You could define a gene in terms of transcription, a sequence on the chromosome that is transcribed, but this is problematic because a given stretch of DNA might be involved in the transcription of one protein along with its neighbours on one side and in the transcription of a different protein along with its neighbours on the other side.

3.3 Press Pause

Defining a gene is not as easy as you might think! It is not as easy as defining a chromosome.

Keeping evolution by natural selection in mind will help us find a working definition of a gene. In order to reasonably discuss a gene as being passed from generation to generation, it needs to have some integrity during reproduction. Here is how Dawkins defines a gene:

> A gene is any portion of chromosomal material that potentially lasts for enough generations to serve as a unit of natural selection. . . . No matter how long or short it is . . . this is what we are calling a genetic unit. It is just a length of chromosome, not physically differentiated from the rest of the chromosome in any way. (Dawkins, 1976)

gene A functional sequence of DNA that remains across a large number of generations, potentially for long enough for it to function as a significant unit of natural selection.

Dawkins rejects the idea that the length of the sequence defines the gene: The gene may be long or short, as long as it fits the above definition. He also allows for overlap: Two genes might occupy overlapping sections of a chromosome. Furthermore, Dawkins allows that one gene could be entirely contained within the area that defines another gene. Since it is not physically differentiated from the rest of the chromosome, you could not identify it by looking at it under a microscope. It is defined by what it does.

Again, since we are interested in evolution by natural selection, this definition works for us, as Dawkins clarifies: "The **gene** is defined as a piece of chromosome which is sufficiently short for it to last, potentially, for long enough for it to function as a significant unit of natural selection" (Dawkins, 1976). This is the definition we will use throughout this book because it fits our purposes and will facilitate our discussion, but keep in mind that there could be alternative ways to define a gene, depending on your purposes (e.g., in biochemistry, chemistry, or fetal development).

You may have heard people suggest that a gene is like a blueprint, code, plan, or recipe. Do not worry too much whether the "claim" that a gene is a blueprint is true or false because it is a metaphor. Like the metaphor of the brain as a computer and other metaphors that you may have heard in psychology, gene metaphors are sometimes very helpful in allowing you to understand what genes do, but sometimes they are misleading. Note that this is different from, say, the claim that the heart is a pump. The heart actually *is* a pump; that is not a metaphor. Whatever is true of pumps is generally also true of the heart. But the gene is only a metaphorical blueprint, so something that is true of a blueprint may or may not be true of a gene. A

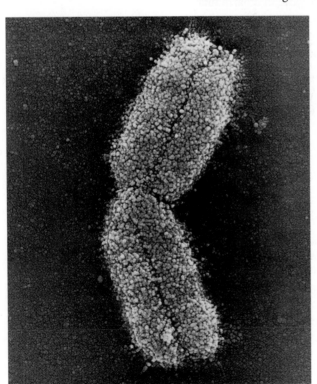

A chromosome is a large DNA double-helix single molecule. A single chromosome includes thousands of genes. It is so big that it can be seen under a microscope.

deeper understanding of what genes do will help you avoid the pitfalls of this metaphor, but before learning about what genes do, first we have to define an allele.

An **allele** is one possible form or variant of a gene that may occupy a particular locus (location) on the chromosome. For example, in the human species, there are alleles that are associated with the development of blue eyes and, alternatively, alleles that are associated with the development of brown eyes. Mendel studied the effects of alleles that were associated with the development of green or, alternatively, yellow pea pods and other allele pairs that were associated with the development of smooth or, alternatively, wrinkled surfaces. You can think of the process of natural selection as selecting for one allele or the other: If one allele provides any advantage in terms of reproduction, even a small advantage, then selection pressure in favour of that allele will cause it to increase in frequency over time. All else being equal, the allele will spread and eventually become universal. But keep in mind that a catastrophe or other random event could keep even a favoured allele from spreading, especially early in its existence when it has only a small presence. Also important to remember is that we use the term *allele* only when there is a common functional alternative in that species. The word comes from the Greek *alleles*, which means "each other." Once it is selected to the point that it is universal, we call it a *gene* by convention.

In the human genome, about two thirds of loci have only one form of a gene, that gene being essentially universal. That is to say everyone all over the world has the same allele, the same gene, at the same location on the chromosome. For about one third of loci in the human genome, there are currently two or more viable alleles in the human

allele One possible form of a gene that may occupy a particular locus (location) on the chromosome.

In the human genome, about two thirds of loci have only one form of a gene, that gene being essentially universal, and in the other third, there are currently two or more viable alleles, a source of variance in a human population.

population. The amount of variance can change over time, and any particular locus that is now universally occupied by a common allele once was not.

If a particular allele has not become universal after some time, then there has not been a strong enough selection pressure throughout the species with respect to the alternative alleles. If a population of peas has some alleles that create wrinkled pea surfaces, and some alleles that create smooth pea surfaces, then these alternatives are not different from each other in terms of the advantage that they provide to the pea. In most cases where an allele provides an advantage, an adaptation will become species-typical (Tooby & Cosmides, 1990), so if there was a difference, the existence of alternative alleles would not persist: One of the alternative alleles would be selected to the point that it became universal. (We will set aside, for now, cases where two different versions of a gene find an equilibrium.)

3.4 **Press Pause**

An allele is only an allele as long as there are alternatives in the population at a particular locus on the chromosome.

Evolutionary Processes

Mutation is one process that leads to changes in gene frequency. Mutations are not as rare as you might think. In humans, estimates have ranged from approximately 30 mutations in an individual's lifetime (Wells, 2002) to 175 mutations per lifetime (Nachman & Crowell, 2000). A mutation occurs in a given individual, and if it occurs in a somatic cell (a cell that is not passed to the next generation) nothing remarkable will come of it. If the mutation occurs in a sex cell (the egg or sperm that may be passed to the next generation) then it has the potential for "exposing" itself to natural selection. Although mutations are believed to be random, both with respect to location and with respect to outcome, the process of mutation is the "creative" process in evolution. The process is not intentionally creative or innovative, with a goal or drive toward some outcome, but rather it generates the possibility of change. It is only because mutations can and do occur that novel options are available for natural selection to operate on.

In order for natural selection to act on alternative alleles, the mutation need not necessarily be recent. There is enough genetic variability in natural populations that phenotypic changes can occur without the occurrence of new mutations, as demonstrated by artificial selection. When an early farmer wanted to create a cow that produced a lot of milk, there was enough variance in milk production in the available population that generations of selecting the highest milk producers for breeding led to an increase in milk production in the population. In that case, the selection pressure was novel, but the mutation was not.

Because the outcome of a mutation is random, not planned or directed, adaptations should not be thought of as optimal. The adaptation that results from the process of selection is not necessarily the best possible design or the best engineered option. It is simply the option that was selected for. Better options may be conceivable but may not have been available because the necessary mutation did not, by chance, arise. An example that may illustrate this point is the idea of the centaur, the mythical creature who is part human and part horse. This would be a great design: all the strength, speed, and agility of a quadruped organism and all the dexterity of a bipedal organ-

figure 3.4 Mutations

In this figure, a mutation results when a single **nucleotide** is erroneously replaced, creating a nonsense sequence. In humans, estimates have ranged from 30 to 175 mutations in an individual's lifetime (Adapted from US National Library of Medicine).

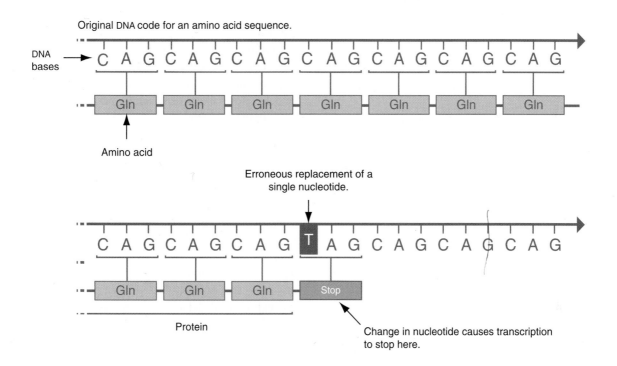

ism. But no such animal exists. No creature has four legs *and* two hands (Raff, 1996). Why? Because natural selection can only select among the possible designs that arise; it cannot drive evolution in any direction, despite the fact that such a direction might ultimately be well adapted. Nonetheless, incredibly complex and precise adaptations do evolve.

GENETIC DRIFT, FOUNDER EFFECTS, AND BOTTLENECKS

Natural selection, although the only viable explanation for complexity and adaptive traits, is not the only cause of evolutionary change. There are other causes of change in gene frequency. **Genetic drift** is the change in gene frequency that results from the fact that genes passed from parent to offspring are selected randomly. For example, if a parent has one allele associated with the development of blue eyes, and one allele associated with the development of brown eyes, one will be selected at random to pass to the first child. Because the selection is random, the second child could get the very same allele as the first child (there is no mechanism ensuring a fair distribution). Even the third and fourth offspring could get the same allele since there is no counterbalancing. Changes due to genetic drift can be beneficial, deleterious, or neutral. Genetic drift is relatively unlikely to have big effects in large populations but has the potential to have major effects in small populations.

A special case of genetic drift, which is likely to occur only in very small populations, is called the **founder effect**. The founder effect is the outcome of a situation in

nucleotide One of the compounds constituting the basic building blocks of DNA and RNA. In the structure of DNA, the four nucleotides are guanine, adenine, cytosine, and thymine.

genetic drift The change in gene frequency that results from the fact that genes passed from parent to offspring are selected randomly.

founder effect A special case of genetic drift in a small "founder" population.

figure 3.5   Centaur

Although it would be handy to have four legs and two arms like the mythical centaur, natural selection can only select among the possible designs that arise; it cannot drive evolution in any direction.

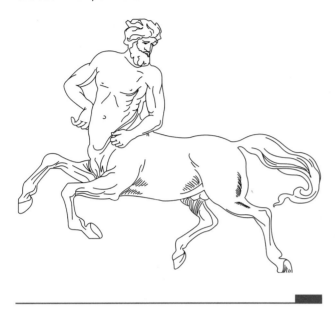

which a small number of individuals colonize a region and allow no other inflow into the population's gene pool. Because the population is small, genetic drift can have a dramatic effect, and neutral or even deleterious alleles can get a foothold. Think of a geographic barrier, such as an island, that isolates a group of people; political and social factors can lead to the isolation of a gene pool as well. Founder situations can allow otherwise rare alleles to spread throughout the population, even though they are not selected for. This strong over-representation of deleterious alleles can then be preserved over time as the population grows, creating ethnic groups that are susceptible to specific genetic disorders.

Here is how the founder effect works: Imagine a large population in which a recessive gene is associated with people developing deafness. This recessive gene has no phenotypic effect if it is paired with the dominant allele, but if a person inherits two such recessive genes, one from each parent, that person is likely to develop deafness. In a large population, that recessive gene can exist quietly for a long time: The more infrequent the gene becomes, the less likely that two people with the gene will mate, so the less exposed the deleterious gene is to natural selection. No force is reducing its frequency.

Then imagine that a small group of people from this population get on a boat and colonize an island. Imagine that deleterious allele comes with them. Now in that small population, there is less opportunity for outbreeding, and more inbreeding is likely to occur. Someone with the recessive gene is more prone, in such a small population, to mate with someone else who has that allele. The deleterious effect, deafness, which may not have been expressed in dozens of generations, can now become a problem for the population.

A real-life example is the Cajun population in Louisiana. This population descends from the people of Acadia (on the East Coast of Canada) who were exiled by the monarch of England. They were forced out to sea, and some of them ended up, unintentionally, in southern Louisiana, forming the Cajun culture. A small number of these people carried a gene for Usher syndrome, which can lead to deafness and blindness. In other circumstances, where this relatively infrequent gene is passed in a large gene pool, the gene would rarely be expressed, since it is unlikely that two people with the gene would marry. In this founder situation in southern Louisiana, however, the gene was able to become relatively frequent in the population. This example describes a deleterious gene, but founder effects can allow an opportunity for beneficial genes to spread as well.

The founder effect might allow the gene to spread to a small colony of, say, several hundred people and then ultimately have a higher probability of becoming universal when the colony encounters others. Remember that a new mutation occurs at first in only one individual. What if that person is eaten by a lion or dies of infection before passing the new mutation on to his offspring? Even if the mutation is passed to a small number of immediate family members, they may share a common fate if food or water or shelter is scarce, even if only for a season.

When the people of Acadia were exiled and forced out to sea, they sailed to southern Louisiana and founded the Cajun culture. A small number of these people carried a gene for Usher syndrome. Until then, the deleterious effects of the gene were rarely seen. In this founder situation the gene was able to become relatively frequent in the population.

Indeed, one idea of how human adaptations, including cognitive adaptations, were able to take hold and spread is that in the EEA, climate cycles would alternatively lead to isolated fertile patches separated by vast, impassable deserts (a founder situation) alternating with lush vast expanses, over which formerly isolated populations could cross and meet each other (Fagan, 2004).

A similar phenomenon with related consequences is a population **bottleneck**, a situation in which the population is drastically reduced for at least one generation such that genetic diversity is lost. One recent example of this is the world population of northern elephant seals. These seals were hunted to near extinction, with as few as 20 individuals remaining at the end of the 19th century. Because of the reduction in the population, some alleles were lost: Certain variants of some genes did not make it through the bottleneck. Now the population has blossomed again, and there are over 30,000 individuals, but the alleles that were lost are gone forever, and the population has less genetic diversity than it did before the bottleneck.

bottleneck A situation in which the population is drastically reduced for at least one generation such that genetic diversity is lost.

3.5   Press Pause

Natural selection is not the only evolutionary process that causes a change in gene frequency.

Northern elephant seals were hunted to near extinction to the point where as few as 20 individuals remained at the end of the 19th century. The population lost some alleles. Now there are over 30,000 individuals, but the alleles were permanently lost, and the population has less genetic diversity because of the bottleneck.

Adaptations, By-Products, and Noise

You have read about adaptations and will continue to read about them throughout this book. As you read in Chapter 1, an adaptation is a trait that is designed and preserved by the process of natural selection as a result of its having conferred a reproductive advantage in the environment in which it evolved. It is a trait that was selected for and maintained by natural selection because it solved (or was part of the solution to) an adaptive problem during a species' evolutionary history (Tooby & Cosmides, 1992). Adaptations are one product of the process of evolution by natural selection, and indeed, natural selection is needed to explain the existence of complex adaptations. Since there is a tendency toward randomness or inertia (known as the *second law of thermodynamics*), natural selection is needed to explain the persistence of adaptations as well: Without some force driving a form toward a functional organization, things would instead gradually tend toward disorder.

by-product A trait that has come about as a result of natural selection, although it was not itself selected for.

But there are at least two other products of the process of evolution by natural selection: by-products and noise. A **by-product** is a trait that has come about as a result of natural selection, although it was not itself selected for and has not historically performed adaptive functions. The cutest example of a by-product is the belly button: It does not do anything functional for the child, but it did come along for the ride when the umbilical system was selected for as a solution to the problem of delivering nutrients and gases to the developing fetus. Another example is the colour of blood: Hemoglobin was not selected for because it is red but because it binds to the oxygen molecule with just the right level of stability. Similarly, the colour of bones was not selected to be white, but calcium, which is white, was selected for its strength in bones. Notice that in order to identify a trait as a by-product, there must be an adaptation of which it is a by-product. It is not helpful to claim that some trait is a by-product if there is no identifiable adaptation that might have inadvertently led to its selection (Tooby & Cosmides, 1992).

The third product of evolution by natural selection is noise. Noise comprises of the random effects that were not selected for. These might result from mutations (which, remember, are non-directed so might be beneficial, deleterious, or inert) or from new circumstances in the environment, for example. If new changes in the genome or in the environment lead to a poorly functioning individual, then we would expect natural selection to play a role in decreasing the frequency of that gene–environment pairing over time. But if the effect is neutral with respect to selection, a new and inconsequential characteristic could exist for a long time and could even become more prevalent due to genetic drift. It is extremely unlikely that without selection pressures this noise will become a characteristic of the entire species, but it might become prevalent in a local population.

In principle, it should be possible to distinguish adaptations from by-products and from noise. Even though it may take a very long time to persuade researchers in the field to the point of practical consensus, scientists look for evidence that a trait is an adaptation by looking for these hallmarks: efficiency, economy, precision, and reliability (Williams, 1966). To put it more simply, Pinker suggests that if it takes you longer to describe the parts of the thing than it takes you to describe the purported function of the thing, it is probably the product of design (Pinker, 1997).

> **3.6 | Press Pause**
>
> A trait that is observed in a human (or any other species) could be an adaptation, it could be a by-product of an adaptation, or it could be a result of noise.

EXAPTATIONS

But wait! What if something was selected for, crafted to complex and exquisite function by natural selection, and then began to be used for something else? Moreover, what if its new use was functional and contributed to (or replaced) the original evolutionary pressure such that the new function was actually maintaining the trait? The idea of an exaptation to describe this situation was introduced not too long ago (Gould & Lewontin, 1979; Gould & Vrba, 1982). An exaptation is "a feature, now useful to an organism, that did not arise as an adaptation for its present role, but was subsequently co-opted for that function" (Gould, 1991, p. 43). For example, it is widely believed that bird feathers evolved in order to keep birds warm. They were selected to solve the adaptive problem of thermoregulation. Subsequently they came to be used in flight, and their role in flight is both crucial and clearly adaptive.

The concept of exaptations is appealing because it reminds us that natural selection does not have an end product in mind. Natural selection would not be expected to take the shortest path to a solution, as an engineer or software designer might. Natural selection modifies the existing organism, working with and sculpting all the available parts.

> **3.7 | Press Pause**
>
> An exaptation is a feature, now useful to an organism, that did not arise as an adaptation for its present role but was subsequently co-opted for that function.

Many scientists believe that bird feathers were originally adapted to solve the problem of thermoregulation and that they later became adaptive because of their role in flight. If so, then they are exaptations.

Like by-products of adaptations, exaptations have an adaptive history. If one wants to make the claim that some observed human trait or cognitive ability is an exaptation, the onus is on that scientist to identify the adaptation and the adaptive pressures that led to its evolution (Rutherford, 2002). The exaptation is still an adaptation.

The distinction between exaptations and adaptations is a bit difficult to define. If something was originally selected for one function but is now maintained by natural selection for another, is it still an exaptation? What if it has served its current function for longer than it served its original function? What if it has since been extensively modified? The boundary is not always clear, even to scientists working in the field.

What Does DNA Do Anyway?

Now, let us talk, step by step, about what DNA does and what kinds of resources a gene must interact with in order to do the interesting things that genes do. DNA has two special functions: (a) it can replicate itself, and (b) it can be transcribed in a process that results in a protein. By the end of this section, it should be clear to you what the process of transcription entails and what results. But first, some background.

Your body is made out of trillions of small cells. Despite the fact that cells are very specialized, and can look very different from one another depending upon their function, they have some commonalities. Each cell has a cell membrane that protects the cell and selects what kinds of molecules can move into or out of it. The cell membrane is full of cytoplasm, a fluid in which all the organelle (the tiny organ-like structures within the cell) float about. In the cytoplasm, in almost every cell in your body, is the nucleus, which is itself surrounded by its own membrane, the nuclear membrane. Within that cell nucleus are the large molecules we call *chromosomes*, the **DNA** (or deoxyribonucleic acid). DNA can store information because it is made

DNA Deoxyribonucleic acid, which can store information because it is made of sequences of four types of nucleotides. Two strands of DNA zip together to form a double helix.

---

figure 3.6   A cell

Each cell has a cell membrane that is full of cytoplasm, a fluid in which all the organelle float about. In the cytoplasm is the nucleus, which is enclosed in the nuclear membrane. Within that cell nucleus are chromosomes, which comprise DNA.

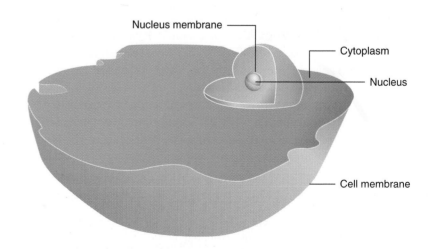

figure 3.7 **What does DNA do anyway?**

The DNA molecule can replicate itself. The two strands, which are weakly bound to each other, unzip and then form bonds with complementary bases that are available. The result is two new, identical DNA strands.

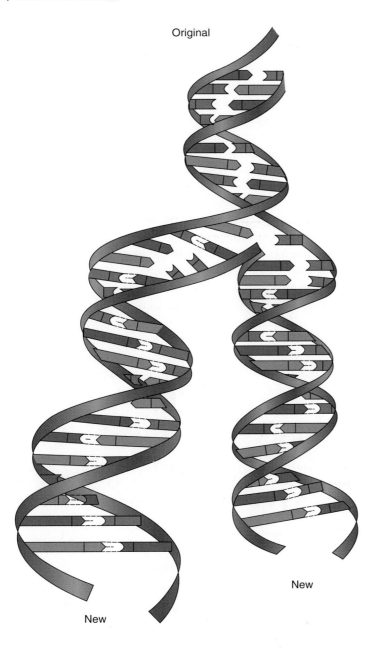

Original

New

New

of sequences of four types of nucleotides. Two strands of DNA zip together to form a double helix. All of this applies not just to you but to cats, dogs, trees, and many other plants and animals.

In each of your somatic cells, that is, the non-sex cells that are found throughout your body, there are 23 pairs of chromosomes. Of each pair, one chromosome comes from your mother and one comes from your father. Similarly, although the number of chromosome pairs differs, in many sexually reproducing species, an individual receives one of the chromosome pairs from each parent. All of an individual's DNA together is called a *genome*, that is, your complete genetic endowment. All of the somatic cells have the same full set of chromosomes. It is not the case, for example, that the hand cells just have genes for making a hand and that the liver cells just have genes for making a liver.

You read earlier that a chromosome is a double helix. What this means is that the molecule that is the chromosome is made up of complementary strands of chemicals, and those two strands are weakly bonded to each other, while the molecules within each strand, called *bases*, are strongly bonded to one another. It is as if a ladder was split down the middle, each side (strand) strongly attached to half a rung (base), but when the two rung halves (base pairs) meet in the middle, they snap loosely together via a magnetic attraction. There are only four types of bases, and they can be thought of as letters in an alphabet, arranged in a particular sequence in order to facilitate the transcription of particular proteins. Let us call the four types *A* (adenine), *C* (cytosine),

figure 3.8 Transcription

Proteins are created via two steps: The DNA is transcribed into messenger RNA, and then the messenger RNA is translated into a protein.

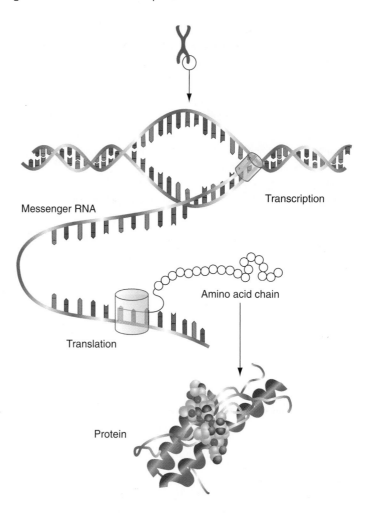

G (guanine), and *T* (thymine). Each of these types can only form a weak bond to one other type: *A* can weakly bond to *T*, and *C* can weakly bond to *G*, but *A* cannot weakly bond to *C* or *G*, and *C* cannot weakly bond to *A* or *T*, and so on. Remember that the weak bond is the bond that forms the rung of the ladder, in our analogy.

A DNA molecule does something really unusual that makes it a special kind of molecule: It can replicate itself. To do so, the molecule "unzips" and creates copies of itself that are made up of the same bases in the same sequence. All it needs for raw materials is a supply of free bases of various sorts (like a typesetter needs a variety of loose letters to create a word).

In terms of development, here is where the action is: DNA is transcribed into proteins. This transcription is what really gets things done. Remember that genes are just inanimate particles that are a part of a very large molecule. Basically, although genes do not "do" anything intentional, they code for proteins and that is all they contribute to development.

Proteins are sequences of amino acids. Proteins have a huge variety of different functions throughout our (and others') bodies. Our bodies use 22 different types of amino acids to make proteins. Amino acids combine and fold in specific shapes in order to create unique, functional proteins. Structurally, proteins are similar to DNA insofar as they are made up of a strand of components in a particular sequence (though in the case of proteins, the components are called *amino acids,* not bases). This similarity is important in understanding how proteins are made using the information stored in DNA.

Proteins are created via two major steps: The DNA (the section of it that we are calling the *gene*) is transcribed into **messenger RNA**, and then the messenger RNA is translated into a protein. Transcription produces a single strand of messenger RNA, which yields a single strand protein.

The information in the DNA is encoded such that three adjacent bases along the strand of DNA will "represent" a specific one of the 22 amino acids. For example, G-A-C specifies (and leads to the production of) leucine. This formula yields a 64-letter alphabet since four bases can make 64 different three-base combinations.

Here is how the process works: First the DNA molecule has to unzip so that the template strand is exposed. An mRNA molecule is then created when nucleotides pair up with the template strand and create the single mRNA strand. This process is very much like the replication of DNA that we just discussed except that mRNA is always single-stranded and thus does not form a double helix. Each of the bases in the DNA (A, C, T, and G) will form a bond with an available complementary mRNA nucleotide.

This new mRNA molecule is then "read" like a ribbon. The alphabet of the RNA is read three nucleotides at a time, and that triplet, called a *codon*, is matched up with the corresponding amino acid. The codon specifies which amino acid is to be attached to the growing protein next. One by one, the amino acids are attached until the protein is complete.

protein A sequence of amino acid that combines and folds in specific shapes in order to accomplish specific functions.

messenger RNA A molecule that serves as an intermediate step when DNA is transcribed to make a protein. The sequence of the messenger RNA is read from the DNA molecule, and the messenger RNA is then translated into a protein.

3.8 **Press Pause**

The gene is transcribed into messenger RNA, and then the messenger RNA is translated into a protein. Proteins are the only mechanism by which DNA has an effect on development or on adult functioning.

This simplified description is enough to prepare you for the following discussion of development and its relationship to DNA. But there is one more wrinkle in the relationship between DNA and its effects that should nudge you away from thinking about DNA as "determining" outcomes. So far, what you have just learned about DNA could be summarized as follows: DNA stores information in the form of bases sequences, which are read by RNA, and are used to create proteins. Proteins serve a huge variety of functions in our bodies, and the function of a particular protein is determined by its shape, which is determined by which amino acids attach to the protein in which order, which is determined by RNA, which is determined by DNA. Right? Hold on! The shape of the resulting protein, and hence its function, can be affected by environmental factors within the cell when it is produced, including the local pH (a measure of acidity) and temperature (Johnston, 1987). This means the function of the resulting protein derived from a given sequence of DNA can differ as pH and temperature differ. So even at this early stage, the relationship between DNA and outcomes is not deterministic, although it is, indeed, complex and interesting.

And here is one more example that should get you to stop thinking of DNA in terms of genetic determinism: A particular segment of DNA can (and does) make different proteins, with entirely different functions, depending upon which cell type the DNA segment is in. Here is how that works: Overall, most of the DNA in your genome is not transcribed at all (Maynard Smith, 1993; Neumann-Held, 1998). The proportion of DNA that is transcribed is not all contiguous (bases will be read for a stretch, then several bases will be ignored, then some more bases will be read, etc.), so a structure inside the nucleus splices the useful bits together (using special start and stop codes it finds on the DNA) so they can go on to make a protein. But when the cell's splicing structure finds the start and stop codes to put the RNA together, some cells find some start and stop signals, while other cells find other start and stop signals (Smith, Patton, & Nadal-Ginard, 1989). For example, the same DNA code can be spliced to make a neurohormone if the cell is in the nervous system but can be spliced to make a protein that regulates calcium if it is any other cell type (Amara, Jonas, Rosenfeld, Ong, & Evans, 1982). Again, even at this early stage there is no determinism with respect to what DNA produces: It depends on where in the body it gets transcribed.

3.9   Press Pause

> The relationship between DNA and the outcome protein is not deterministic, but it is designed to be influenced by the environment right from the start.

Essentially, that is the simple version of what DNA does. The four-letter "alphabet" (the four types of bases that make up DNA) line up to create "recipes" for particular proteins. There are a lot more details known about these processes, which you may be interested in researching, but the point here is to give you a sense of what DNA does in order to remove the mystery about it. Ultimately, it engages in a chemical process that results in protein production. There is nothing magical and nothing predetermined about it. Genes do not do anything but store the information that codes for proteins, and even the process of transcription is a passive process that is done without any intention or volition. A gene is not actually trying to do anything.

PLEIOTROPY

pleiotropy The phenomenon of a single gene having effects on more than one phenotypic trait.

Pleiotropy refers to the phenomenon of a single gene having effects on more than one phenotypic trait. One gene might affect multiple developmental outcomes, and the outcomes could be disparate in terms of which body systems are affected. For example, a single gene mutation might cause different outcomes in cognitive function and in skin pigmentation.

Pleiotropy has been used to explain diseases, cancers, and senescence (the deterioration that takes place with aging): If a gene has a pleiotropic effect that leads to greater reproductive success early in adulthood, but to disease later in life, the early success "hides" the later cost from natural selection. One of the interesting implications of this adaptationist perspective is that senescence, in its evolutionary biological meaning, is not confined to old age, but begins at reproductive maturity. As soon as a gene might have an opportunity to increase reproductive success (which is true at the moment of sexual maturity) then any pleiotropic effect, whether beneficial, neutral, or even deleterious, may get a "free ride" and increase in frequency in spite of its not contributing to reproductive success. Even if the gene is costly at some point later in life, it can be selected for and spread throughout the population.

Such a phenomenon seems to be true of testosterone: Higher testosterone leads to higher fertility in young men but also leads to prostate cancer in middle-age men. In some situations, selection pressure will be additive: The effect the gene has on each trait is beneficial, so it will be selected for as a result of both of its effects. In some cases, it may be subtractive: The effect the gene has on one trait could be beneficial, while the effect it has on another trait is deleterious. Selection will compete against itself, and the winner will depend on the strength of the selection pressures as well as the timing in terms of when the effect is revealed in the individual's life history.

3.10 Press Pause

Pleiotropy is the phenomenon of a single gene having effects on more that one trait. If one effect is beneficial, the gene may get selected for in spite of other effects.

Interactionism: The Bidirectional Influences of Developmental Resources

In the first chapter, you read about the historic roots of the nature vs. nurture debate. You also read that instead of thinking of development as being a result of nature and nurture, you should be mindful of how the interaction of nature and nurture work together as development unfolds. Actually, no scientist working in contemporary developmental psychology is either a nativist or an empiricist in the extreme sense. No one thinks that infants come with all their mental processes fully formed or that they come with no specialized mechanisms designed to enable development in a species-typical environment. Everyone agrees that development is the result of an interaction between genes and the environment, a view known as **interactionism**.

To illustrate, we will walk through three specific examples of interactions between genes and environment. The examples are important for two reasons. First, it is never sufficient to replace the nature vs. nurture idea with a quick claim of interactionism and then to move on since it does not actually answer the developmental question. We want to know *how* genes and the environment interact to produce a trait, and the answer to that question will be different for different traits. Second, understanding a couple of examples in more detail will illustrate the point that the nature vs. nurture question is meaningless. As we walk through these examples, keep in mind that it would not make any sense to talk about the contribution of the genes independent of the environ-

interactionism The perspective in developmental science that development unfolds as a result of the interaction between genes and all other "developmental resources."

ment or vice versa. In each case, the developing infant is designed to interact with the environment in a specific way so as to facilitate development.

The examples of interactions in this chapter are offered to help illustrate the idea, to get you thinking about what an interaction between genes and environment might mean. But remember that all of development is interaction. The development of every individual, of every trait, and of every psychological process described in this book is the result of an interaction.

GENETIC SUSCEPTIBILITY TO DEPRESSION? IT DEPENDS ON THE ENVIRONMENT

A recently reported longitudinal study has revealed strong evidence for an interaction between a genetic susceptibility to depression and environmental factors. A group of researchers located in England, the United States, and New Zealand followed a large group of children in New Zealand from birth through early adulthood. They measured, among other things, depression and suicidality, environmental stressors, and which type of allele the child had for a serotonin transporter gene.

One thing that is interesting about the serotonin transporter gene (called 5-HTT by those who study it) is that it is polymorphic: A person will get one of either of two possible alleles of this gene. The serotonin transporter gene is an example of a gene that has two viable alleles, each fairly common in a given human population. Remember that some genes have more than one form currently available in the population, in which case we call the alternate forms *alleles*. In the case of the 5-HTT gene, one can inherit the short allele or the long allele. Serotonin is a neurotransmitter, and as you may know, neurotransmitters are part of what allows *neurons* to communicate with one another and to excite or inhibit one another. The serotonin transporter gene codes for a protein that helps regulate how much serotonin gets into neurons and thus how serotonin affects the neurons. So it is not surprising that the serotonin transporter gene has an effect on brain function, and in this case on depression and suicidality. But what is interesting is that the effect is not straightforward: Knowing that a person has

| figure 3.9 | Serotonin transporter |

There are two types of the serotonin transporter gene, one short and one long. The shorter allele is associated with depression, but only in some environments. This is an example of a known gene–environment interaction.

Long Allele

Promoter region   Translated region

Short Allele

Promoter region   Translated region

one allele or the other does not allow you to predict whether that person will be depressive, at least not without knowing about some specific environmental factors. Researchers discovered that it was not that one of the alleles (in this case the shorter) led to people being depressed. It was not even that, overall, the shorter allele led to a greater proportion of people being depressive, at least not in all environments. The environmental factors a person was exposed to mattered. People who were exposed to a major stressor or trauma in childhood *and* who had the short version of the serotonin transporter gene were at increased risk of depression and suicidality compared to others in the study. There was an interaction between the two factors: genes and the environment (Caspi et al., 2003).

In this fish species, an individual's rank in the social hierarchy affects the expression of the gene that codes for androgen and estrogen receptors. The environment can affect the genes if that is how the system is designed.

SOCIAL STATUS AFFECTS GENE EXPRESSION

The widespread view of genes and their relationships to adult behaviour is that genes are "upstream," on the causal end of the relationship, and when you think of the relationship between genes and, say, social status, you probably think about it in terms of how genes affect social status. Maybe you wonder whether having a particular allele would predict higher social status in some social environments, for example. But here is a twist on that way of thinking: Social status affects gene expression.

In one species of fish that has been studied (*Astatotilapia burtoni)*, an individual's rank in the social hierarchy affects the expression of the gene that codes for androgen and estrogen receptors (Burmeister, Kailasanath, & Fernald, 2007). This means that

Even in humans, the environment can affect gene expression. One study identified 209 genes that were expressed differently in lonely and non-lonely people.

if the fish is higher in rank, his DNA makes more receptors for these sex hormones; if lower in rank, his DNA produces fewer of these hormones. This leads to differences in behaviour: Those with more hormone receptors behave more dominantly; those with fewer receptors lay low and stay out of trouble so that the dominant fish will leave them alone. More hormone receptors also mean more sexual behaviour, so the dominant fish can reap the benefits of his higher rank, and the less dominant can avoid offending the higher-ranking males. Social rank is also known to affect the expression of some genes in rats as well (Pohorecky et al., 2004). There are even examples in humans wherein events in the social world and other stressors affect gene expression. Loneliness has an effect on the expression of some genes: One study identifies 209 genes that were expressed differently in lonely and non-lonely people (Cole et al., 2007).

3.11 Press Pause

Events during the lifetime of an adult can affect the expression of some genes.

SANDRA SCARR'S NICHE-PICKING THEORY

Finally, our last example of research revealing the interaction between genes and the environment is the research of Sandra Scarr. Prior to Scarr's work, the traditional view of the role of family (and the environment more generally) in development was that the family environment made a causal contribution to the development of the child. If the family has a lot of books and reads to the child, the child will become an avid reader. If the family is musical, the child will develop a taste for music. If the parents are harsh disciplinarians, the child will display aggressive tendencies, according to the traditional view.

Early in life, a child can produce an "evocative gene–environment" relationship by showing her parents what she is interested in. In later childhood, a child produces an "active gene–environment" relationship by choosing his own environment. Scarr's niche-picking model does not ignore or discount the role of either genes or the environment: Genes influence the child's tastes and temperament and the environments the child picks. These environments then contribute to the development of the child.

Scarr sees a much more active role for the child: The child to some extent determines her environment, or picks her niche. Early in life, a child can produce an "evocative gene–environment" relationship: A child who shows a great deal of interest in books and reading may evoke a book-reading response in her parents. A child who shows a great deal of interest in music may evoke a music-playing response in his parents.

In later childhood, the child produces an "active gene–environment" relationship. The child at this point has the autonomy to more actively control his environment and to more actively pick his niche, in Scarr's terminology. The child can choose extracurricular activities, from music to athletics, and can even select among academic pursuits.

Scarr's niche-picking model does not ignore or discount the role of either genes or the environment. In her view, genes may influence the child's tastes and temperament, which in turn influences the environments the child picks. These chosen environments then contribute to the development of the child (Scarr, 1992, 1993).

The above examples of interactions between genes and the environment are not offered because they are the *only* instances of gene–environment interactions during development. Every trait develops as a result of interactions between genes and environments. The above examples were chosen because substantial research into these areas has revealed *how* genes and the environment are interacting to cause these traits. In most cases, the developmental story is not yet known, leaving lots of room for future researchers like you! Again, these examples are meant to carve another chip out of the idea that genes serve as a blueprint for the fully formed adult. Not only are there complex interactions between genes and the developing organism, but as a result of their evolutionary history, events during the lifetime of an adult can affect the expression of some genes.

Let us wrap up our discussion about interactions. Traditionally, and very naively, people have thought of an evolutionary perspective on development as being deterministic, as predicting that genes would be on only one side of the causal chain. Here we have seen that genes are part of a developmental system. They interact with the environment, and they do so in predictable ways in order to develop specific traits. Remember that these interactions themselves are a result of evolution by natural selection, just as development is a product of evolution by natural selection.

Notice also that there are two possible ways to talk about a gene–environment interaction. You can boil it down to statistically identifiable contributions to the variance in the population. In this case we are talking about heritability, which we will discuss in detail in Chapter 4. Or you could ask about how genes and the environment are employed in the development of a given trait, which is really at the heart of developmental research. Just be clear which question you are asking and which question is being answered.

Meiosis, Conception, and Pregnancy

The fertilized egg is called a **zygote** and has a full complement of human genetic material: half from the mother, and half from the father. In humans, the zygote lasts for about 4 days and then divides, grows, and develops from there. In this section, you will read about how that zygote is formed and how it develops.

zygote The fertilized egg, which is still in the single-cell stage.

MEIOSIS AND THE CREATION OF SEX CELLS: DNA COPIES ITSELF

Remember that a person's complete genome has 23 *pairs* of chromosomes: 23 chromosomes that came from the mother and 23 chromosomes that came from the father. So if half of a person's genetic information comes from mom and half comes from dad, how come all children of a pair of parents are not identical? What creates the difference between offspring in reproduction? The answer is meiosis.

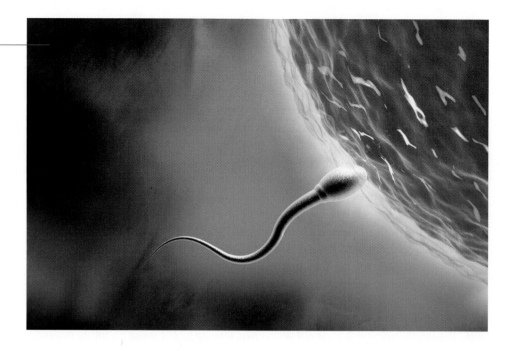

An individual's development begins when the genetic information in the sperm is combined with the genetic information in the egg, creating a complete genome.

| figure | 3.10 | **Meiosis** |

Meiosis is the process in which the complete set of pairs of chromosomes is reduced to a single set of unpaired chromosomes. Then, four daughter cells are created from the two intermediate daughter cells. Which chromosome goes into which cell is determined by chance: the genes are shuffled by design.

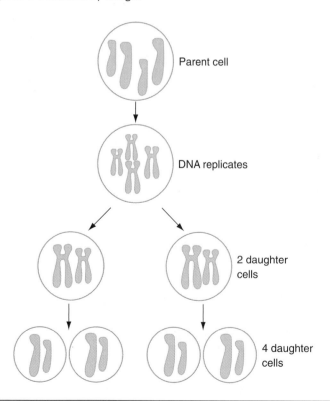

Parent cell

DNA replicates

2 daughter cells

4 daughter cells

figure 3.11 Crossover

Before the chromosomes migrate into new cells, crossover may occur. Part of the chromosome that came from mom's mom and part of the chromosome that came from mom's dad are swapped. This crossover will result in a brand new, never-before-seen chromosome and is a significant source of genetic diversity.

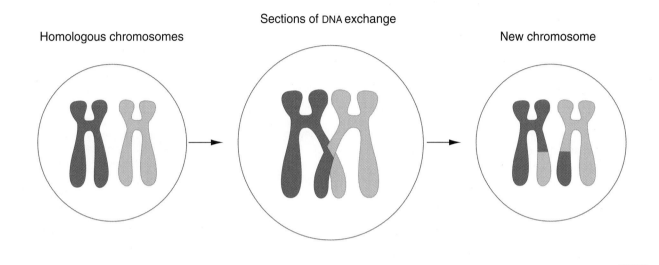

Homologous chromosomes   Sections of DNA exchange   New chromosome

Meiosis is the process by which sex cells—eggs and sperm—are produced. It occurs in the mother, who produces one egg, and the father, who produces four sperm during a meiosis event, and occurs in all sexually reproducing animals and plants. Meiosis consists of two cell divisions, one after the other, called Meiosis I and Meiosis II.

Humans (as well as most sexually reproducing animals and plants) are diploid, which means that each cell has two copies of each chromosome, one that the individual got from his or her mother and one that came from his or her father. The result of meiosis is four haploid cells: cells that contain half of the genetic material of the original cell. It makes sense that there should be a reduction division in the process of creating sex cells. The number of chromosomes should be cut in half to make a gamete because it is about to be combined with another person's gamete to create a full genome. Without such a division, each generation would have twice the genetic material of the previous generation.

Meiosis I is the first division, and it is often called the *reduction division* because in this phase the 23 pairs of chromosomes that are found in every human cell (except the sex cells) are reduced to a single set of chromosomes. In this phase, the two homologous pairs of chromosomes separate and migrate to two different cells. The cells are created when the original cell closes in the middle and the cell membrane forms completely around the two separating cells. So, the result of Meiosis I is two haploid daughter cells.

Here is the interesting step, a significant source of genetic diversity: Before the chromosomes migrate into what will become two different cells, an event called *crossover* may occur, in which a pair of homologous chromosomes (one from the maternal grandmother and one from the maternal grandfather) pair up and exchange sections of DNA. A section of the chromosome will break off, and the homologous section on the matched-up

meiosis The process by which sex cells–eggs and sperm–are produced.

⠿ Assessing Social Impact

Alternative Technologies in Fertility

You know how babies are made, right? The textbook story, one you have probably heard since elementary school, involves the introduction of sperm into the female reproductive tract where it meets and fertilizes the egg. However, modern technological advances in fertility allow for alternative methods of creating a family. Prospective parents might use alternative technologies if they are gay or lesbian, if a single woman wishes to become a mother, if the male member of a straight couple does not produce viable sperm in a sufficient quantity to result in conception, or if a woman is having trouble conceiving or maintaining a pregnancy, for example.

One method of conception that a couple might choose is donor insemination. In this case, the semen, which carries millions of sperm cells, is introduced into the female reproductive system in a medical procedure. This procedure may be "intrauterine insemination," which means that the sperm is injected directly into the uterus. Remember that during sexual intercourse, semen is ejaculated into the vagina and has to travel through the mucus plug in the cervix that protects the uterus, whereas intrauterine insemination delivers sperm through that natural barrier, thus increasing the chances of conception. In addition, the doctor who places the sperm will likely use ultrasound imaging in order to place the sperm in the best location, again increasing the odds of fertilization. The "donor" in the donor insemination procedure could be the male member of a couple who has been unsuccessful in their attempts to conceive, or it could be a known or anonymous sperm donor.

Another effective method of creating a pregnancy is in vitro fertilization (IVF). In this method both the sperm and the eggs are removed from the donors' bodies and are introduced to each other in the laboratory. Conception happens in the lab, and after a period of a few days, the conceptus is placed in the uterus in the hopes that a pregnancy will result. The conceptus can be placed in the uterus of the woman who donated the eggs or in a different woman. If there are two women, they will have to have synchronized their menstrual cycles so that the recipient is ready to become pregnant just when the conceptus is ready to implant in the uterine wall. This method can be used by a variety of different families, including gay or straight couples who need to employ a surrogate to carry the pregnancy, straight couples who have been unable to conceive using more conventional methods, and lesbian couples who each wish to participate actively in the pregnancy.

The first successful IVF procedure resulted in a live birth in 1978, and now it is estimated that as many as a half a million babies have been born resulting from IVF. How are they doing? Susan Golombok and colleagues at Cambridge University's Centre for Family Research set out to test the prediction that the social and emotional development of these babies might be poor compared to typically conceived children, reasoning that the complication of their birth or lack of genetic connection with a parent or parents might be problematic. They measured development using interviews, observations, and tests, first when the child was about 6 years old and then when the child was about 12 years old. They compared three groups: children conceived via alternative fertility methods, children conceived naturally living with their biological parents, and children conceived naturally living with their adopted parents.

The results may surprise you: At the 6-year assessment, parents of children conceived via alternative fertility methods were warmer, more responsive to their children, and more emotionally involved with their children compared to the control children conceived naturally. Both mothers and fathers in the alternative fertility condition spent more time interacting with their children. The families with adopted children were comparable to the families who had used alternative fertility methods (Golombok, Cook, Bish, & Murray, 1995).

By the time of the 12-year assessment, these differences had disappeared and no measureable differences were found. Furthermore, at neither assessment was the behaviour, development, or psychological adjustment of the children distinguishable (Golombok, MacCallum, & Goodman, 2001). Incidentally, that first IVF baby who was born in 1978 has given birth to a baby of her own . . . conceived the old-fashioned way.

---

chromosome will break off, and then each section will attach to the other chromosome. Notice that this crossover will result in a brand new, never-before-seen chromosome. Notice also that those genes that happen to be close together on the chromosome (a smaller "genetic distance") have a greater chance of sticking together generation after generation than genes that happen to be farther apart on the chromosome.

In Meiosis II, four daughter cells are created from the two intermediate daughter cells. In essence, each chromosome from the intermediate cell splits in half, resulting in a chromotid (one half of the symmetric chromosome); each of the four daughter cells has one chromotid, which is ready to pair up with the homologous chromotid that is introduced as a result of mating. Which chromotid goes into which cell is determined by chance: the genes are shuffled by design. The end product here is the sex cell, either the egg or the sperm, and each sex cell contains 23 chromosomes, each one brand new and unique!

WHERE DO TWINS COME FROM?

In the next chapter, we will look at how twins contribute to our understanding of heredity by examining twin studies that are designed to estimate the heritability of various traits. Here, let us look at how different types of twins are formed. Remember that the fertilized egg is called a *zygote*. The two common types of twins are monozygotic twins and dizygotic twins. **Monozygotic twins** form from one zygote, as the name implies, and thus have identical genomes. They are what people commonly call *identical* twins, although we will see that this is a misnomer. **Dizygotic twins** develop from two completely different zygotes and thus have different genomes. They are commonly called *fraternal* twins because they are as genetically related to each other as two brothers would be.

Dizygotic or fraternal twins result when the mother releases more than one egg into her fallopian tubes during ovulation. Each egg is fertilized by a different sperm, forming two zygotes, each with its own complete genome. Dizygotic twinning is somewhat heritable but must be in the mother's family since nothing about the father influences the probability that the mother's ovaries will release multiple ova. However, if fraternal twinning is common in the father's family, he may pass genes that increase the probability of multiple ovulating to his daughter and thus is more likely than average to have fraternal twin grandchildren. Other factors are also associated with fraternal twinning: As the mother ages, the probability of fraternal twins increases. The more children the mother has already had, the more likely that each subsequent pregnancy will involve fraternal twins. Women who are tall, who are not underweight, and who have a sufficiently nutritional diet are more likely to have fraternal twins. Fraternal twin births account for 1 in every 85 births in Canada and 1 in 38 births in the United States.

Monozygotic twins result when a single zygote divides within the first few days of conception. In humans, no variables are known to be associated with monozygotic twinning, although some experimental research with animals has found factors in embryonic development that make such twinning more likely (e.g., temperature, oxygen levels, and the age of the ovum when fertilized). Monozygotic twinning accounts for about 1 in 285 births.

Monozygotic twins may develop in the same amniotic sac or in two different amniotic sacs, and that depends upon how early in development the two developing fetuses divide from one another. Monozygotic twins result when the inner cell mass divides. This division typically takes place just a few days after conception, before the amniotic sac has developed. In this case, each twin develops his or her own amniotic sac. If the division happens just a few days later, after the formation of the amniotic sac, then the twins will share the existing amniotic sac, live and develop in exactly the same fluids throughout gestation, and possibly become entwined with each other. If delivered in a modern North American health facility, nearly every twin pair sharing an amniotic sac will be born at around 34 weeks (6 weeks earlier than is typical) because medical professionals consider the pregnancy too dangerous to the babies after that point.

But wait, there's more. Monozygotic twins may or may not share a placenta, again depending upon the exact day when they divide. About two thirds of monozygotic twins form when the zygote splits on the fifth through the ninth day post-conception. If the membrane that forms the placenta (it is called the *chorion*) has already developed at this point, these twins will share a placenta. About one third of monozygotic twins form when the zygote splits before the fifth day post-conception. The chorion

monozygotic twins Twins that form from one zygote and thus have identical genomes.

dizygotic twins Twins that develop from two completely different zygotes and thus have different genomes.

has not yet formed, so each new zygote will form its own. These twins will not share a placenta. Apparently this relationship can affect development: Monozygotic twins who shared a placenta are more similar than those who did not share a placenta on measures such as IQ (Melnick, Myrianthopoulos, & Christian, 1978), on 20 different personality measures (Sokol et al., 1995), on birth weight, and congenital anomalies (Beekmans et al., 1993).

Monozygotic twins: Not so identical after all

As you just read above, monozygotic twins have an identical genome and are often called *identical* twins in common parlance. Not only do they have the same genes, but they tend to look very much alike, sometimes indistinguishable to those who do not know them well. But monozygotic twins are not actually identical.

First of all, some monozygotic twins have non-identical prenatal environments, perhaps having different placentas (and thus different avenues of access to maternal resources) and perhaps having their own amniotic fluid. The evidence reviewed above suggests that these prenatal differences can lead to differences in cognitive and personality development.

Even in cases when twins do share the prenatal environment, and apparently share everything else, the two individuals are still not identical. Consider Chang and Eng, to

Monozygotic twins develop from the same zygote and have the same genome. They are commonly called *identical* twins but are not, in fact, identical people.

this day the most well-known set of conjoined twins. Conjoined twins are monozygotic twins who split after 9 days post-conception such that the separation is not complete, and the two babies are physically attached, or conjoined, when they are born. Chang and Eng were born and reared in what is now Thailand, then called Siam (hence the term *Siamese twins*). They were born joined at the sternum by a muscular band of tissue and, because surgical solutions were not available at the time, spent their entire lives connected to each other's sides. Chang and Eng, who had identical genomes, were forced to have identical environments; nonetheless they developed into different people. They could easily carry on independent conversations with different people. Chang was said to be moody and melancholy, whereas Eng was quiet, cheerful, and contemplative (Gould, 1985). People who know other monozygotic twins know very well that they are distinguishable by their personalities.

Why and how do monozygotic twins become different? First, there is some stochasticity in the process of development that developmental biologist Conrad Waddington called *developmental noise* (Waddington, 1957). This term describes developmental differences that cannot be accounted for by differences in genes or by differences in the environment (Lewontin, 1983). Have you ever seen a dog (or a person) with two different coloured eyes? This is not because different genes contributed differently to the development of each eye or, presumably, because of differences in prenatal circumstances. This may be an example of developmental noise.

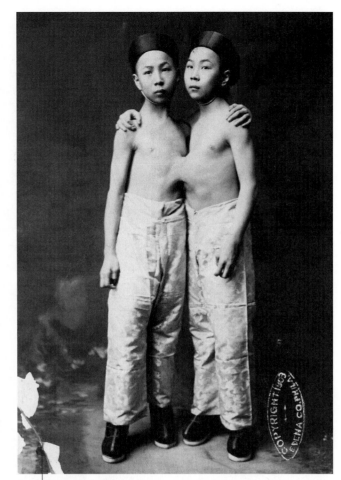

Chang and Eng were famous conjoined twins. In spite of having the same genome, the same prenatal environment, and being around each other constantly, they developed into distinct people with their own personalities.

But there are likely more interesting and more adaptive sources of differences between monozygotic twins. It may actually be strategically disadvantageous to be identical. In a community, there is some tactical social advantage to being unique, individual, and what some evolutionary psychologists call *irreplaceable* (Tooby & Cosmides, 1996). Siblings, including twins, may have psychological adaptations designed to steer them toward different specializations, or niches, in order to reduce direct competition between them in their local environment. We will read more about the idea of adaptive differentiation in Chapter 10.

3.12 Press Pause

There are adaptive reasons why identical twins are not identical: people specialize.

AFTER CONCEPTION

In prenatal development, the first two weeks after conception are called *germinal*, the third to eighth week after conception are called *embryonic*, and the remaining weeks of pregnancy are referred to as the *fetal* period. The embryo is supplied nutrients and

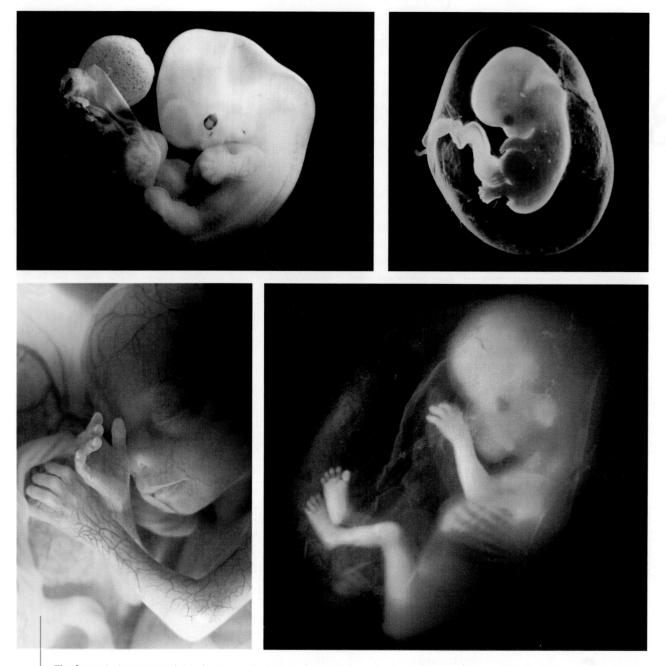

The fetus during prenatal development. Clockwise, shown at 6 weeks, 8 weeks, 12 weeks and 20 weeks.

oxygen by the placenta and the umbilical cord. These same structures remove waste and carbon dioxide. The amniotic sac fills with amniotic fluid that protects the fetus. From the fourth week on, prenatal development is cephalocaudal, meaning that the features near the head develop sooner than the rest of the body. By 12 weeks after gestation, the fetus engages in a wide range of behaviours, including moving the chest walls, or practice breathing, and swallowing amniotic fluid.

PREGNANCY TIMELINE

The development of an individual starts when a sperm passes through the outer covering of an egg, the process known as *conception*. The result of conception is a zygote.

From that moment through approximately the first two weeks of development, the individual undergoes rapid cell division. The germinal period ends with the conceptus implanting in the uterine wall.

At four weeks after conception, the tiny embryo has a basic body plan: The face has four folds of tissue that will become facial features, and a primitive heart has formed, beats, and circulates blood. The embryo has arm and leg buds, and the body is curved tightly, like a shrimp. The central nervous system develops early, from about the end of the second week after conception through early in the sixth week.

By eight weeks after conception, the embryo has a recognizable (though not adult-like) face with eyes, nose, and a mouth. By nine weeks, all internal organs are present but still developing. Sexual differentiation has started: Different external and internal sexual characteristics are developing. External genitalia develop from about the seventh week through about the twelfth week. The embryo has fingers and toes and even nails at this age. The embryo also moves, but movement increases dramatically in the second half of pregnancy.

At 28 weeks, the fetus may be well-developed enough to survive on its own since the brain and lungs are sufficiently developed. At this point, the eyes open and the auditory system functions. Brain development (as measured by brainwave activity) is similar to that of a newborn. The biggest job left for the fetus at this point is to grow!

Human infants are born early, indeed, compared to other primates, even prematurely (Krogman, 1972; Gould, 1980), meaning that if the timing of birth were predicted based on the relative maturity at birth in other primates, humans would be expected to be born at around 18 months of gestation (Corballis, 1991). But human infants are born at the end of nine months of gestation. The limiting factor in the duration of the gestational period is the conflict between the mother's pelvis size and the infant's brain growth. If the infant gestated for a longer period and grew a larger head, the mother's pelvis would have to be even wider than it is, but any increase in an adult woman's already wide pelvis would compromise her mobility, not a trivial consideration in the EEA.

THE PLACENTA: CO-OPERATIVE VENTURE OR BATTLEGROUND?

In humans and other mammals, the fetus is connected to the mother via the placenta, a highly vascularized spongy organ through which oxygen and nutrients arrive into the fetus and carbon dioxide and waste are removed. A classic view of the placenta was that it was a structure that mother and fetus built together, the original cite of maternal nurturance. Recent research and more recent views tell a different story of its development and use.

The placenta develops from the blastocyst, the multicellular conceptus, as it implants into the uterine lining. That is to say, its development relies upon the genome of the fetus, not of the mother. Moreover, it seems to be a structure designed to be exquisitely parasitic. The placenta invades the uterine wall, bores into the mother's blood vessels, and reconfigures them such that they literally cannot constrict: The mother cannot resist sharing nutrients with the fetus without reducing the nutrients circulating within her blood. Given this set-up, the fetus now has unrestricted access to the mother's blood supply and can (and does) release hormones into her in order to influence the amount of nutrition available. The fetus raises the mother's blood pressure and blood sugar.

Mother would, of course, like to invest in the developing fetus (her opportunity for genetic representation in the next generation) but only to an extent. She would also like to be able to recover from the pregnancy with enough stores to some day support another pregnancy. The fetus has some evolutionary interest in mother's other offspring but only half as much interest as the fetus has in itself. But what of the father? If the father is a long-term mate of the mother, his interests are quite aligned with hers, but if the pregnancy is a result of a short-term liaison, then he has no evolutionary interest in the mother's future offspring. From his point of view, the mother should overinvest in his developing fetus. And there is evidence that when it comes to the development of the nutrient-guzzling placenta, "the paternal genome appears to play a greater role than the maternal genome in placental growth" (Haig, 1993, p. 499). We know this from the development of aberrant conceptuses in which there is an over-representation of paternal genes. In these cases there is a "massive proliferation of placental tissue" (Haig, 1993; p. 499).

ADAPTATIONS IN PREGNANCY

In human development, there are adaptations that are species-typical and universal but that are only expressed during a particular finite period in the individual's lifetime (e.g., language learning and other types of learning that involve critical periods or sensitive periods). Similarly, there are clearly physiological changes in humans that take place only during pregnancy. Recently, there has been accumulating evidence that certain psychological and cognitive adaptations are expressed during pregnancy as well.

One adaptation that has now been explored fairly extensively is pregnancy (or morning) sickness. At one point, not that long ago, pregnancy sickness was considered maladaptive. It was seen as a sickness that could be treated. Thanks to the work of Margie Profet and others (Hook, 1978, 1976; Profet, 1988), it is now understood that pregnancy sickness is actually an adaptation that protects the developing fetus from toxins in the diet, just at the time when the fetus's developing systems are most vulnerable to the exposure of such toxins. Organ development and the development of the central nervous system occur during the first trimester, and it is during this time that a pregnant woman may have a strong aversion to foods bearing plant toxins. A woman in her first trimester of pregnancy may be immediately repulsed by the smell of coffee, for example. We know now that women who experience morning sickness are less likely to have a miscarriage than women who do not have morning sickness, and among women who have morning sickness, those who vomit are even less likely to miscarry (Flaxman & Sherman, 2000). Women who have severe nausea and vomiting in pregnancy experience fewer preterm births as well (Cziezel & Puho, 2004). What was once thought of as a malady is now understood to be a mechanism that protects the developing fetus. There is also evidence that pregnant women form common aversions to animal products, which may be contaminated by pathogens and toxins (Flaxman & Sherman, 2000; Fessler, 2002).

3.13   Press Pause ─────────────────────────────

Pregnancy sickness, once thought to be an illness, is an adaptation that protects the fetus.

There is also growing evidence that other cognitive adaptations are expressed in pregnant women. For example, in spite of the commonly held belief (supported by some psychological research) that women who are pregnant lose cognitive function, especially short-term memory (Brett & Baxendale, 2001), women who are pregnant have a better memory for male faces than non-pregnant women. This finding was predicted because women who are pregnant have pressing adaptive needs, such as avoiding dangers and protecting their developing fetuses, including the social threat that unknown males might pose (Anderson & Rutherford, 2008). Pregnant women have also been shown to express increased negativity toward unknown people compared to non-pregnant women. Again, this difference is attributed to a drive to protect the fetus, as unfamiliar people may carry novel pathogens (Navarrete, Fessler, & Eng, 2007). Everyone prefers to look at healthy rather than unhealthy faces, but this is even more true of pregnant women, and this may serve the protective function of staving off people who may bear pathogens and thus threaten the mother and her fetus (Jones et al., 2005).

Brain Development

All psychological processes emanate from the brain. Whether you are studying emotions, behaviour, cognition, attitudes, beliefs, attachment, or language, you are studying the processing of the brain. As we continue to lay the groundwork for our study of developmental psychology, let us consider brain development.

The basic units of the brain's information processing are cells called **neurons**, of which the mature human brain has over 100 billion. Information is transmitted through a neuron when an electrical pulse enters via the **dendrite** and travels down the **axon**. Information is conveyed between cells chemically, in a process involving neurotransmitters. The junction between neurons is called the **synapse**.

The fetus's brain is the fastest growing organ, by weight, and this aggressive growth rate continues through infancy. By the age of 3, a child's brain is 80 per cent of its adult weight, whereas the rest of the body has reached only 20 per cent of the adult weight. By the age of 6, the brain is 90 per cent of its adult weight.

NEUROGENESIS, NEURON MIGRATION, AND DEVELOPMENT

An individual will produce nearly all of her neurons between the third and eighteenth week post-conception. During this peak in production, the fetus is creating 250,000

neuron A nerve cell. A cell specialized for conducting information between the brain and other body parts or within the brain.

dendrite One of the fibres extending from the cell body of a neuron, designed to receive a signal from a nearby neuron.

axon The long fibre that runs the length of a neuron, conducting the electric signal from the cell body to the terminals.

synapse The gap between two neurons, across which a chemical signal is transmitted.

figure 3.12   Neuron

The structure of a generic neuron, although individual neurons may be specialized and look somewhat different from this example.

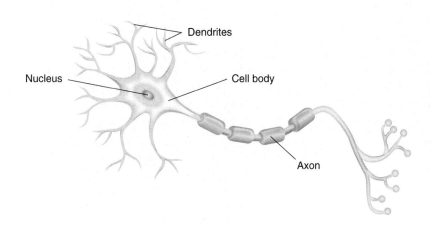

new neurons per minute (Cowan, 1979). Neuronal production is almost complete by 18 weeks after conception (Rakic, 1995), although some areas of the brain are capable of neuron production in adulthood (Tanapat, Hastings, & Gould, 2001).

Neurons, which are produced near the centre of the brain, then move toward their destination. Some are passively pushed out of the centre of the brain by cells that are created after them, but others actively seek their destination, which could be anywhere in the body, using a chemical attraction between the migrating neuron and the target. Cell migration is complete by 7 months of gestation (Huttenlocher, 1990).

Each cell also develops by becoming more elaborate. The neuron first grows an axon, which in some cases can be quite long, and then grows a dendrite, which forms an elaborate bush-like structure. The dendrite can become extremely complex as it grows new branches and forms spines on those branches. This *arborization*, as it is called, clearly increases the neuron's capacity to form connections with other cells. The peak of this type of growth and development in the cortex is after birth but continues for years afterward. Finally, the process of **myelination** encases the long axon of neurons in a myelin sheath, which serves as insulation and allows the transmission of an electrical impulse with great efficiency. Myelination is known to continue into adolescence.

SYNAPTOGENESIS

As axons and, even more so, dendrites, grow, the neurons are able to create synapses, a process called **synaptogenesis**. Most neurons have connections with thousands of other neurons, resulting in trillions of connections in the brain. Synapse formation starts prenatally and proceeds rapidly before birth and after birth. Synaptic density peaks at about 1 year of age, and the average number of connections for each neuron is about 16,000 at the peak. That said, the developmental timeline differs in different parts of the brain. For example, although synaptic density peaks in the visual cortex at around 1 year of age, it does not peak in the prefrontal cortex until an individual is just less than 4 years of age.

SYNAPTIC PRUNING

Synaptogenesis results in a huge surplus of neural connections (Rakic, 1995). Indeed, there are major connections between brain areas that do not appear to need connections, such as between the visual cortex and the auditory cortex or between these areas and taste and smell centres. **Synaptic pruning**, a process during which synaptic density decreases as synaptic connections are lost, appears to be an important part of the developmental process. Synapses that are used are preserved, and synapses that are not used disappear; this describes one mechanism of learning at the neural level. This is a normal part of development.

Like synapse formation, synaptic pruning peaks at different times in different parts of the brain. In the visual cortex, synaptic pruning takes place between 1 and 10 years of age. It occurs later in the prefrontal cortex, continuing into young adulthood. At its peak, as many as 100,000 synapses disappear per second (Kolb, 1995).

This developmental process, by which a huge excess of neurons are created and then pruned and sculpted based on experience, is thought to provide a great deal of plasticity. The human brain is surprisingly good at recovering from injury, provided the injury happens early in life when there is a surplus of synaptic connections.

myelination The development of a fatty sheath around the axon. This sheath serves as insulation, allowing for signals to travel faster.

synaptogenesis The growth of synapses between neurons.

synaptic pruning The developmental process by which synapses are eliminated.

HEMISPHERIC SPECIALIZATION

The two hemispheres of the human brain are somewhat specialized. For one thing, the left side of the brain is involved in processing sensory information and sending motor commands to the right side of the body, while the right side of the brain processes sensory information and sends motor commands to the left side of the body. Furthermore, the left side of the brain processes language information, whereas the right side of the brain is thought to underlie spatial thinking and visual imagery.

Some hemispheric specialization appears quite early. There are differences between the size and shape of the two hemispheres that are already evident at birth. There is evidence that even infants use the left hemisphere to process speech-related information (Molfese & Molfese, 1979). Still, hemispheric specialization is not complete in infancy, and specialization continues to develop through childhood (Werker & Vouloumanos, 2001).

SUMMARY

In this chapter you were introduced to the basics of evolution, and the process by which genes contribute to development, as well as conception and pregnancy. With this, you should now be ready to learn about development in the following chapters without being vulnerable to the pitfalls of thinking about nature vs. nurture or thinking in terms of genetic determinism. (You should understand that nature and nurture, and all available developmental resources, always work together to create any trait and that gene transcription is a chemical process and that its product depends on circumstances early in the process of transcription.)

This chapter started with a historical look at the two discoveries that formed the modern synthesis and thus a contemporary understanding of evolution. You read about Darwin's proposal that in an environment characterized by competition for resources, heritable factors that give an organism a competitive reproductive advantage will increase in frequency in a population from generation to generation. You also read about Mendel's experiments that lead to his inference that the heritable factor was particulate and does not blend during sexual reproduction. You then learned about the modern definition of evolution (a change in gene frequency across generations) and about some different ways that gene frequency can change across generations including, importantly, natural selection.

In this chapter you learned quite a bit about DNA and what it does. DNA is a big molecule that is neither animate nor intentional. You read about how DNA is transcribed and how an RNA molecule is created, then moved outside of the cell nucleus, and then used to make a protein. And you also learned about some factors that affect which protein is produced, even at that earliest stage of DNA expression, critically challenging the idea of genetic determinism.

Finally you read about conception and pregnancy. You learned about the creation of sex cells, eggs and sperm, a process that is designed to create a novel genome. And you read about some of the adaptations in pregnancy that are designed to ensure the safety of the fetus such as changes in a pregnant woman's food preferences and the experience of nausea in the first trimester, which are adaptations designed to protect the fetus from toxins that mothers can otherwise process in their diets. Cognitive changes during pregnancy also protect the fetus by making a pregnant mother more cautious and more attentive to dangers in the environment.

PRESS PAUSE SUMMARY

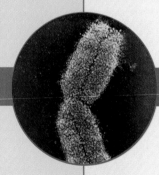

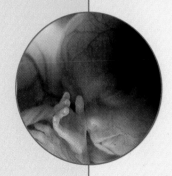

- There is nothing magic about chromosomes; they are just very large molecules that can be transcribed into proteins.
- Darwin's evolutionary explanation for complex functionality would not work if inheritance was blended.
- Defining a gene is not as easy as you might think! It is not as easy as defining a chromosome.
- An allele is only an allele as long as there are alternatives in the population at a particular locus on the chromosome.

- Natural selection is not the only evolutionary process that causes a change in gene frequency.
- A trait that is observed in a human (or any other species) could be an adaptation, it could be a by-product of an adaptation, or it could be a result of noise.
- An exaptation is a feature, now useful to an organism, that did not arise as an adaptation for its present role but was subsequently co-opted for that function.
- The gene is transcribed into messenger RNA, and then the messenger RNA is translated into a protein. Proteins are the only mechanism by which DNA has an effect on development or on adult functioning.
- The relationship between DNA and the outcome protein is not deterministic, but it is designed to be influenced by the environment right from the start.
- Pleiotropy is the phenomenon of a single gene having effects on more than one trait. If one effect is beneficial, the gene may get selected for in spite of other effects.
- Events during the lifetime of an adult can affect the expression of some genes.
- There are adaptive reasons why identical twins are not identical: people specialize.
- Pregnancy sickness, once thought to be an illness, is an adaptation that protects the fetus.

KEY TERMS AND CONCEPTS

allele, 71

axon, 97

bottleneck, 75

by-product, 76

chromosome, 69

dendrite, 97

dizygotic twins, 91

DNA, 78

founder effect, 73

gene, 70

genetic drift, 73

interactionism, 83

meiosis, 89

messenger RNA, 81

modern synthesis, 64

monozygotic twins, 91

mutation, 66

myelination, 98

neuron, 97

nucleotide, 73

pleiotropy, 82

protein, 81

synapse, 97

synaptic pruning, 98

synaptogenesis, 98

zygote, 87

QUESTIONS FOR THOUGHT AND DISCUSSION

1. What did Darwin believe about the nature of inherited material? Why was this belief a problem for his theory?

2. Why was the second-generation pea plant so critical in Mendel's experiments? How did the outcome in the second generation allow him to infer that inheritance was particulate?

3. Describe how information stored in a chromosome becomes a protein. What influences the shape of the protein besides the DNA sequence?

4. What does *interactionism* mean? Describe an example of an interaction.

5. What function does meiosis serve? What function does crossover serve? How does crossover work?

6. Describe a protective process during pregnancy that is believed to be an adaptation. Why do some people think it is an adaptation?

From the Classroom to the Lab: Follow Up

Consider the experiment you designed in response to the "From the Classroom to the Lab" challenge earlier in this chapter. Imagine you have run your experiment.

How many generations would you have to breed in order to answer the question?

What results would you expect in the first (F1) generation? How do you interpret those results?

What possible outcomes would there be in the next (F2) generation? How would you interpret those results?

Create a Punnett-like square to chart at least one possible outcome. How do you infer dominant and recessive traits given your chart?

chapter 4

Nature, Nurture, and Development

Opening Vignette: Who, If Anyone, Shot Henry Ziegland?

The following story about Henry Ziegland's demise may or may not be true, but in any case, it illustrates the difficulty of identifying a single cause in a chain of events.

As legend has it, Henry Ziegland was a young man who lived in Honey Grove, Texas. In 1893, he walked out on his girlfriend, leaving her so upset that she killed herself. Her brother was distraught by the tragedy and decided to avenge her death by shooting Ziegland. The brother's attempt was unsuccessful, and the bullet only grazed Ziegland's face, barely hurting him at all. The bullet actually lodged itself in the trunk of a tree that was on Ziegland's property. The brother, thinking he had hit Ziegland, and satisfied that his sister was avenged, turned the gun on himself.

Twenty years later, in 1913, Ziegland decided to get rid of the tree that served as a reminder of that unpleasant day. He found that he was unable to chop it down, so he decided to blow it up with dynamite instead. The tree was successfully destroyed, but in the process, the bullet was blown out of the tree trunk and struck Ziegland in the head. He died.

So the question is, "Was Henry Ziegland killed, and if so, who killed him?" The bullet that the brother had fired intending to kill Ziegland did, in fact, kill him by striking his head, as the shooter intended. But the bullet did not travel a direct path and was actually at rest for 20 years.

Naturally, you won't find the answer to this question here; the story is offered in order to point out that a single unique cause of an event is not always identifiable. In fact, a "cause" of an event is something our minds are designed to perceive, not something the world is obliged to supply. This more complicated way of thinking about causality is preparation for considering nature and nurture as causes of development. Throughout this chapter, you will be discouraged to think about nature as opposing nurture or of one or the other as the sole cause of development. Nature and nurture, of course, contribute to the development of people, but neither, by itself, can be seen as any more or less causal than the other, just as the bullet without the dynamite would not have killed Henry Ziegland, and the dynamite without the bullet would not have killed Henry Ziegland.

Chapter Outline

- Understanding Nature and Nurture
- Causality
- Heritability
- The Heritability Statistic
- IQ Heritability as an Example
- Wrapping up Heritability: What It Is Not
- Facultative Adaptation
- There Are Many Types of Learning
- Prepared Learning

- This chapter is meant to help you think about nature and nurture working together to produce an individual and to produce every trait in the individual. First you will be introduced to the Standard Social Science Model: the assumptions about human nature that pervade lay conversations.

- In the first half of the chapter, you will discover the logic behind the idea that nature and nurture must work together. For this purpose, a discussion of causality is necessary: It is impossible to identify a single unique cause of any event, although our minds are designed to seek explanatory causes.

- You will then learn about the heritability statistic, how it is calculated, what it means, and what it does not mean. The heritability statistic cannot tell you how much genes cause a trait and how much the environment causes a trait, but it can tell you, for a given population, how much of the variance in the population can be attributed to variance in the genes. We use the heritability of intelligence as a case to explore what the heritability statistic might mean. You

will next read about the heritability of IQ as an example of how the heritability statistic might be used. You will read about the measurement of IQ, and the history of IQ tests. You will see that the heritability of IQ depends on the study population, can change across groups, and can be experimentally manipulated.

- In the second half of the chapter you will explore how nature and nurture work together by design. You will learn about facultative adaptations: adaptations that are designed to respond to stimuli in the environment in order to better calibrate the individual to his or her circumstances. Learning mechanisms are examples of facultative adaptations, and you will learn about some examples, thinking of learning not as an alternative to natural selection but as a product of natural selection.

- As the chapter concludes, you will read about experience-expectant and experience-dependant learning, and their respective functions. You will read about prepared learning, the discovery that not all stimulus pairs are equally easily learned but that people and other organisms seem prepared to learn pairings that were relevant in our evolutionary history.

SSSM The standard social science model is a summary of current thoughts about human nature, including the assumptions that underlie most undergraduate curriculum and popular press reports on human issues.

Understanding Nature and Nurture

THE STANDARD SOCIAL SCIENCE MODEL

The common view of human nature in recent decades was labelled the standard social science model (or **SSSM**) by Cosmides and Tooby (Barkow, Cosmides, & Tooby, 1992). This model is a summary of current thought, including the assumptions that underlie most undergraduate curriculum as well as the assumptions usually made in the popular press when reporting human issues.

First, central to its proponents, the standard social science model assumes that the human mind is more or less a blank slate at birth: the mind has no initial content, and everything that the adult "knows" has been "learned." (We will discuss more about what these terms might mean later in the chapter.) Second, the standard social science model assumes that biology is irrelevant to human nature, and that the influences of biology on culture are, at best, minor. A third assumption of the model is that there are not many specific learning mechanisms but rather one or very few general learning mechanisms that account for all of the learning a human can do. The standard social science model acknowledges classical conditioning and operant conditioning—the ability to learn associations between things, but typically no more than that. Those few very general tools must do all of the work of learning, according to this model. We also call this *associationism*: Learning happens by associating one stimulus with another, or

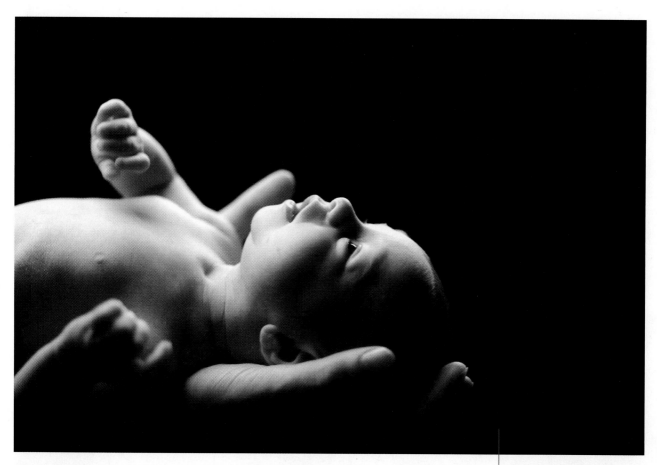

Implications of the blank slate view of the mind at birth, an assumption of the standard social science model, are that biology is irrelevant to human culture and history and that the human mind has only a few general learning mechanisms.

table 4.1	Assumptions of the Standard Social Science Model

ASSUMPTION	SUMMARY
1	The human mind is more or less a blank slate at birth.
2	Biology is irrelevant to human behaviour and psychology.
3	There are not many specific learning mechanisms but rather very few, very general learning mechanisms.

by associating a behaviour with a reward or punishment. Keep this characterization of the standard social science model in mind as we proceed through this chapter because much of what you read here and throughout the book will challenge these assumptions.

A CRITIQUE OF EVOLUTIONARY PSYCHOLOGY

One common reaction to hearing about evolutionary psychology is the misconception that this perspective on development is a nativist one, emphasizing the role of nature over the role of nurture. Nothing could be further from the truth. Learning and other kinds of experience-expectant development are very much a result of evolution by natural selection and were designed to solve adaptive problems of the EEA. Every trait is a result of a complex interplay between genes and the environment.

EEA Environment of Evolutionary Adaptedness.

Asking whether any trait (e.g., eye colour, shyness, or height) is more a result of nature or nurture is like asking whether a cake is more a result of the recipe or the ingredients.

4.1 Press Pause

Every trait is a result of a complex interplay between all available resources: genes and the relevant environmental factors.

Asking the nature vs. nurture question may be intuitively appealing, and it certainly has widespread popular appeal. If you ask a group of your friends what the relative contribution of genes vs. the environment is for any given trait (e.g., intelligence, height, or extroversion), they will likely find the question sensible. They are even likely to offer an answer. It seems that you are asking a reasonable question: What part of a given trait is a result of things that have happened during our lifetime, and what part of the trait is a part of our essence, immutable and determined before "experience"? But it is not sensible to ask which is more important for part of a given trait, nature or nurture. Our modern understanding of what genes do does not support the idea that some traits are a result of nature and some are a result of nurture. As discussed in Chapter 3, genes simply code for proteins and even that is something they do only metaphorically since there is no way of encrypting the code.

Asking whether a trait was shaped by genes or the environment is like considering a freshly baked cake and asking which is more important in determining the outcome: the recipe or the ingredients. We could change the ingredients, and doing so would affect the outcome of the cake. Likewise, we could change the recipe, which would also affect the final outcome, but knowing that still does not mean that the final outcome could be attributed to one or the other. So it is with the nature vs. nurture question. A change in genes may very well change the development of the person, and a change in relevant environmental inputs might change the development of the person, but knowing this does imply that one is more important than the other.

Reading here about the idea of the standard social science model gives you an opportunity to ask whether you recognize these assumptions and, if you have them, to identify them as you read about development and the complex interaction of nature and nurture.

Causality

When people ask the nature vs. nurture question, they are asking about causality: Which is the cause of the trait, nature or nurture? We often find ourselves seeking a single cause of some outcome, but there is never a single cause. There are always multiple causes. Recall our discussion of Henry Ziegland's death and the fact that many preceding events had to happen in order for the eventual outcome to unfold.

This point is amusingly illustrated in the movie *The Curious Case of Benjamin Button*, when Benjamin, here acting as a narrator, describes the causal factors leading to the accident in which his lover, Daisy, shatters her leg when she collides with a taxicab. In order for the accident to have occurred, each of a series of factors that affected the taxi's timing had to have happened, including a woman answering a phone (thus causing her to catch a later taxi), the cab driver stopping for coffee, a man crossing the street (delaying the taxi and its passenger because the man's alarm clock had not gone

When we think of causes, we overlook factors that are usually present. We do not think of oxygen as being the cause of a fire, although if oxygen were not there, there would be no fire. Keep this in mind when thinking about the causes of development.

off and he was running late), the taxi being delayed waiting for a female passenger at a shop because the clerk had not prepared her package due to the break up of a romantic relationship the previous night, and a delivery truck blocking the street. Similarly, other events affected the timing of Daisy's accident, including her waiting for a friend with a broken shoelace and being the last to get dressed after rehearsal. Benjamin laments that if any of those things had happened differently, the taxi would not have hit Daisy. In some sense, each of those events was causally related but none on their own was the singular cause of the accident.

Furthermore, there are factors which make an event possible but which we do not consider to be the cause because we take them for granted. For example, in order for your house to burn down, there needs to be plenty of oxygen available. But if your house were to burn down, you probably would not think of oxygen as the cause of the fire: You take the presence of oxygen for granted and do not think about it as causal.

We can isolate the contribution of a single cause statistically, and this is what we do experimentally. For example, in an experiment that demonstrates that people are faster at locating a target when an actor's eyes are looking at the target instead of away from the target, one might conclude that the eye gaze is the cause of the response time. Let us say that the two trial types have the following things in common: The subjects are well-fed, middle-class young adults; it is daytime; we are in a time of peace; and the experiment room is a comfortable temperature. In a different experiment, the researcher could manipulate any one of these factors and may conclude that *that factor* is the cause of the response time.

4.2 Press Pause

It is harder than you think to assign a single cause to an. Likewise, it is not possible to assign a single cause to development.

The discussion of causality applies more broadly as well. We have a very strong intuition that we should be able to identify a single cause for any event. This is sometimes called the *fallacy of exclusive determinism*. The intuition that an event has a single, identifiable cause is also part of your human psychology. This intuition is functional. For example, it facilitates our thinking about justice: If something bad happens, we want to blame it on someone and seek revenge. Notice that our legal system assumes that death has an identifiable, single cause and that traffic accidents have an identifiable, single cause.

In any case, the point is that the cause that you identify will depend upon your goals and upon the alternative outcomes that you are considering. Again, the perceived cause of an event is in part a product of your mind. Certainly, there is something "real" about causes: They are antecedents to the events that we are trying to explain, and if the cause is manipulated, the outcome is manipulated. But if you take an antecedent event for granted (because you have not been exposed to or considered alternative possibilities), then you may not identify that antecedent as a cause. And that is the result of a functional mind: If alternatives are rare and unlikely, it may not be computationally efficient to consider that antecedent as a cause. But scientists can move away from this intuitive limitation and acknowledge that events have multiple causes, as do artifacts and organisms. Keep this in mind when reading about the description and definition of the *heritability statistic*.

4.3   Press Pause

The fallacy of exclusive determinism describes our desire to identify a single cause of an event. It is an adaptive part of human psychology.

Heritability

You may have read about heritability in the news, perhaps when a breaking story announced that risk-taking or business acumen is heritable. It may be that you have heard heritability being discussed in relation to the heritability of IQ or autism. Do you have a clear belief about what heritability means? If you were to read, for example, that the heritability of attitudes toward abortion is 0.54 (Olson, Vernon, Harris, & Lang, 2001), what does that mean? Do you think that it means that for a given individual, his attitude toward abortion is 54 per cent determined by genes and 46 per cent shaped by experiences that unfolded during his lifetime? If that is your interpretation of a heritability statistic, you are not alone. The idea that the heritability statistic tells us what proportion of a trait was built by genes and what proportion was built by the environment is a common understanding when people encounter a heritability statistic in the media. Let us be very clear: That perspective is wrong. A heritability statistic does not tell you how much of an individual's attitude toward abortion (or whatever trait you are reading about) was caused by genes and how much was caused by the environment.

4.4   Press Pause

The heritability statistic does not tell you how much of a trait in a given individual was caused by genes and how much was caused by the environment.

Let us try again. If you read a study that claims that the heritability of autism is 0.90 (Freitag, 2007), what does that mean? It that bad news? Does it mean that if a child is born into a family with known cases of autism, that child has a 90 per cent chance of developing autism? If, instead, you read a study reporting that autism has a heritability of 0.57 (Hoekstra, Bartels, Verweij, & Boomsma, 2007), would that be much better news? Would the lower heritability suggest a relatively greater contribution of the environment and therefore suggest that the trait is that much more malleable? Does this lower heritability now suggest that, at least, treatment has a shot of being effective? Again, if this is your interpretation of the heritability statistic, you are not alone, but again, you would be wrong. Many people interpret higher heritability as suggesting immutability, or a "deterministic" developmental outcome, and a lower heritability as suggesting a more malleable, plastic developmental trajectory.

4.5   Press Pause

The heritability statistic does not tell you how malleable a trait is or whether that trait is unchangeably "determined."

There is persistent confusion in people's conversations as well as in media reports about what the heritability statistic means and, especially, what it does not mean. You cannot be blamed for your erroneous beliefs about what heritability is since the popular media often reports new information about heritability as if it tells you something about the relative contribution of genes and the environment to the development of a given trait, or as if it tells you how open to influence a trait might be. Furthermore, those scientists who write in the field, although they probably understand the limitations of the heritability statistic, sometimes write in such a way that they almost invite the common, but erroneous, interpretations. Reporting on the impressive 0.90 heritability of height, renowned behavioural geneticist Robert Plomin writes

> . . . results indicate significant genetic effects. . . . This estimate . . . indicates that, of the differences among individuals in height in the population sampled, most of the differences are due to genetic rather than environmental differences among individuals. (Plomin, 1994, p. 44)

This description is not incorrect, but it will lead you to draw erroneous conclusions unless you notice that Plomin does not say that height is due more to a genetic contribution than to an environmental contribution; rather, he says that *differences* among individuals are due more to *differences* in genes among individuals than *differences* in environmental input among people. This distinction is crucial and one which you must come to understand.

In order to illustrate this distinction, psychologist David Moore invites us to consider the formation of snowflakes. If you wanted to fully describe the formation of snowflakes, you would have to know about the features of a water molecule and the factors, such as temperature, that can lead to a change (freezing) in a water molecule, keeping in mind that ambient pressure affects whether or not a water molecule will

What causes a snowflake? Imagine that instead of understanding the development of a child, you were trying to understand the development of a snowflake. You could easily measure differences in snow production across areas that differ in humidity or temperature and that would be analogous to generating a heritability statistic. It does not, however, tell you how snowflakes are formed.

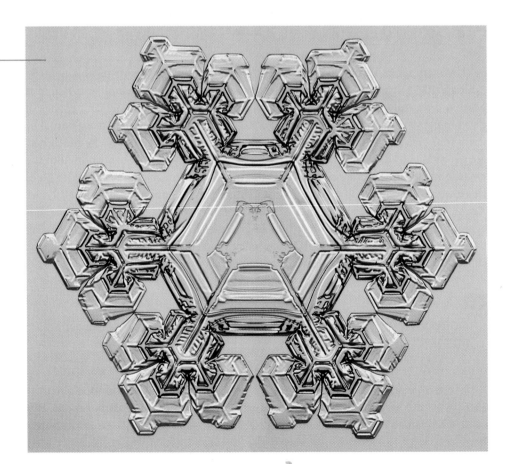

freeze. And you would have to know how and under what circumstances frozen or freezing water molecules bind together. I suppose you might also want to look into what a cloud is and why we have clouds in the first place. Remember from our discussion about causality that no one factor is ever the cause of an outcome (or the development of a trait) and so it is with snowflakes: No one factor caused the snowflake.

A much easier question, and, as we will see, the question that the heritability statistic can address with respect to trait formation, is what factors account for the *difference* in snowflake formation between two defined areas? As an example, here borrowing from Moore, consider the formation of snowflakes on a given, hypothetical day in the North Pole and in the South Pole. On this hypothetical day, it is well below freezing (0°C) at both poles, and it snows in the North Pole but not in the South Pole. What accounts for this difference? In this case, humidity. All of the variance in snowflake formation is statistically accounted for by the variance in humidity. Now consider snowfall on a given hypothetical day in two locations in Costa Rica. Humidity is high in both locations, a rainforest and a mountaintop, but it only snows on the mountaintop. There is no snow in the rainforest. What accounts for the difference in snowfall? In this case, only temperature. All of the variance in snowflake formation is statistically accounted for by the variance in temperature (Moore, 2001, pp. 41 and 44).

4.6 Press Pause

Asking if a trait is a result of genes or the environment is like asking if a snowflake is a result of temperature or humidity.

These examples are analogous to what the heritability statistic can and cannot tell you. In either of our snowflake comparisons, by asking and answering the simple question about what statistically accounts for differences in snowfall, you do not have a

---

figure 4.1   North and South poles

What accounts for the difference in snowflake formation in two different areas? In the case of the poles, where temperatures are below freezing in both places, the difference is accounted for by humidity. Does humidity cause snowflakes?

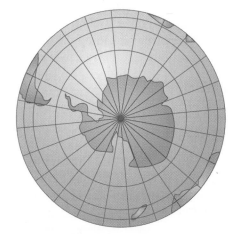

North Pole   South Pole

What accounts for differences in snowflake formation? Across these two locations, both humid, the difference is accounted for entirely by temperature. But temperature alone does not cause snow just as genes alone do not cause a highly heritable trait.

very complete understanding of how snowflakes are formed. You do not know how much "humidity" and how much "temperature" went into making an individual snowflake. Similarly, by asking and answering how much variation in a human population can be statistically accounted for by differences in genes (or the environment), one does not have a very complete understanding of human development. Indeed, it would be easy to argue that addressing this question tells us nothing about human development. In the following examples of heritability, you will see that it can change across time and location as well as age as you define the population of study differently. These differences in the heritability statistic do not necessarily reflect any change in how the trait in question develops.

The Heritability Statistic

The heritability statistic is a modification of the correlational statistic that was discovered by Sir Francis Galton in his pursuit of a way to measure the extent to which traits "breed true," meaning the extent to which traits that are seen in parents will develop in subsequent generations.

Galton was Charles Darwin's cousin, and he was aware of Darwin's thinking about evolution by natural selection years before Darwin's work on the subject was published. As a result of this exposure, Galton was interested in how traits were inherited. Galton was the first person to use the terms *nature* and *nurture* to describe what he saw as the alternative contributors to development. His first inquiry into human heritability focussed on "eminence" and was based on information on the most distinguished, accomplished people of England in the 18th and 19th centuries. Because people who had reached eminence were

---

figure | **4.2** | **The heritability statistic**

This is the heritability statistic. It tells you how much of the variance (V) in the entire population is accounted for by the variance in genes. It does not tell you how a trait develops.

$$\text{Heritability} = \frac{V(\text{genes})}{V(\text{genes}) + V(\text{environment}) + V(g*e)}$$

likely to be related to each other, Galton concluded that nature was a greater contributor to eminence than nurture. By contemporary standards, this conclusion is suspect since Galton made no attempt to control for environmental factors: All of the people he was talking about were reared in privileged, upper-class, well-educated circumstances. But he did introduce the idea that psychological traits and characteristics, not just physical features, might be heritable.

In 1875, Galton proposed the use of twins to estimate the heritability of a trait. Although he did not know anything about genes, chromosomes, or the differences between monozygotic twins and dizygotic twins, he observed that twins who were similar as children (presumably monozygotic twins) remained similar into adulthood, and those who were less similar remained relatively dissimilar into adulthood, even if their environmental circumstances were the same. Again, he concluded that nature trumped nurture.

Some of Galton's lasting contributions were his statistical innovations. Based on comparisons between people

Sir Francis Galton created the statistical analysis from which the modern heritability statistic derives. He was interested in the extent to which various traits, such as eminence, "breed true." He was the first to use the terms *nature* and *nurture* in this sense.

and their parents on myriad measures (height, weight, breathing power, etc.), he created the regression analysis: a statistical analysis that allowed him to estimate the relationship between various measures. He later realized that the regression analysis was a special case of the more general analysis that he called the *co-relation*, what we call a *correlation*. The correlation statistic is a measure of the relationship between any two sets of numbers. After Mendel's work on the particulate nature of heritable factors became known, others were able to modify the correlation statistic to create the heritability statistic.

Heritability is a statistical estimate of the proportion of the measured variance on a trait among individuals in a given population that is attributable to genetic differences among those individuals. The **heritability statistic** tells you how much of the variance in the entire population is (statistically) accounted for by the variance in genes. Stated more mathematically, it is the variance in the genes divided by all the variance, where all the variance is variance due to genes, plus variance due to the environment, plus variance due to the interaction between genes and the environment.

heritability statistic
The estimate of the proportion of the measured variance in a trait among individuals in a given population that is attributable to genetic differences among those individuals.

4.7 Press Pause

The heritability statistic quantifies how much of the differences among people are statistically accounted for by differences in genes. The focus on differences is crucial.

IQ Heritability as an Example

To illustrate heritability, its implications, and measurement, let us consider IQ. The heritability of IQ has been a focus of intense study, so much is known about the heritability of IQ under different circumstances, at different ages, and across historical periods. You will see, as you read this chapter, that heritability can tell you something about the sources of statistical variance but cannot tell you much about the development of intelligence. At best, knowing the heritability of IQ can provide clues about what hypotheses might be promising with respect to development.

From the beginning, the aim of measuring intelligence was different from the purpose of some other types of developmental testing. The original intention in measuring intelligence was to measure differences between individuals. In contrast, Piaget, Vygotsky, and others who were interested in child development have looked at ways in which children, as a group, move through developmental stages together at roughly the same age, showing emerging mental skills at predictable ages. Whereas other approaches to child development are normative, that is, they focus on observing and describing normal development, the study of IQ has always been ideographic, describing individual differences, measuring development only in comparison to the development of others.

THE ORIGINAL DEVELOPMENT OF IQ TESTING

The modern enterprise of measuring intelligence started early in the last century in France. Alfred Binet and Théophile Simon set out to create a way to measure intelligence as a way to identify schoolchildren who needed special or remedial education. Binet believed (contrary to the wisdom of the time) that intelligence, and thus success in school, would be associated with higher-level cognition demonstrated by complex problem-solving, memory, language comprehension, reasoning, and spatial reasoning. The two psychologists created the Binet–Simon Intelligence Test with this theory in mind, and they were indeed successful in predicting children's success in school. The test was correlated with grades in school both at the time of testing and for years to come. Intelligence testing was embraced in the United States by the US Army for the purposes of testing recruits during World War I. During this time, the US Army administered IQ tests to 1.75 million recruits.

IQ testing continued to improve and to be refined and standardized throughout the 20th century, especially in North America and in Europe, and researchers in the fields of psychology and behavioural genetics became very interested in the heritability of IQ, especially for social and political reasons.

CURRENT IQ TESTS

One IQ test that is currently in use is the Stanford–Binet Intelligence Scale. This test is derived directly from the Binet–Simon test and preserves several key features. Like the original, it assesses quantitative reasoning, fluid reasoning, visual–spatial processing, general knowledge, and working memory. And, also like the original, it is intended for use with school-aged children, although it can be used to measure adult intelligence.

More common today are the Wechsler tests, designed by David Wechsler. Children aged 4 to 6.5 years old can be assessed using the WPPSI-III (The Wechsler Preschool and Primary Scale of Intelligence), and children aged 6 to 16 years old can be assessed using the WISC-IV (the Wechsler Intelligence Scale for Children). Like the Stanford–Binet test, these tests focus on skills that are relevant to school performance.

In addition, the scores on the Wechsler tests are subdivided into four scales: verbal comprehension (including vocabulary and general knowledge), perceptual reasoning (e.g., using coloured blocks to reproduce a pattern), working memory, and processing speed (scanning an array for target symbols or copying symbols that have been paired with numbers).

TEST VALIDITY

One obvious question regarding the measurement of intelligence is whether these tests are valid. In other words, do they measure what they claim to measure? There is some evidence that standardized intelligence tests can, indeed, predict the kinds of success they purport to be associated with. The Stanford–Binet is correlated with academic performance, and the measured correlations usually range from 0.5 to 0.6 (Sternberg, Grigorenko, & Bundy, 2001). They also correlate with adult occupational status (Hunter & Hunter, 1984). In other words, they are associated with the kinds of intelligence they are meant to measure but are clearly not perfect predictors of achievement.

> **4.8   Press Pause**
>
> IQ scores are associated with academic and professional achievement, just as they were designed to be.

STABILITY OF IQ

Another question is whether IQ is stable over time. The answer, again, is "somewhat." Table 4.2 shows the correlation between pairs of ages. As you can see, there is a strong relationship between IQ measured at one point in childhood and IQ measured at another point. You can also see that the relationship is not perfect. IQ can change somewhat as a group of children ages. The correlation diminishes as the age interval increases.

table 4.2	**Correlations between IQ and Age**			
AGE 3	**6**	**9**	**12**	**18**
3	0.57	0.53	0.36	0.35
6		0.80	0.74	0.61
9			0.90	0.76
12				0.78

This table shows the correlation of IQ when a given pair of ages are compared. Adapted from "The Stability of Mental Test Performance between Two and Eighteen Years," by M. P. Honzik, J. W. MacFarlan, and L. Allen, 1948, *Journal of Experimental Education, 17*, p. 323. Published by Heldref Publications, 1319 Eighteenth St. N.W., Washington, D.C.

METHODS FOR ESTIMATING HERITABILITY

A standard method for estimating heritability is to compare the concordance among people who are closely related, genetically, to the concordance among people who are less closely related. For example, in **family studies** of intelligence, IQ is compared across known genetic relatedness. The relationship in IQ can be compared to genetic relatedness. As you can see by looking at Table 4.3, correlations in IQ are associated with genetic relatedness. This relationship is strong but not perfect; genetic relatedness does not account for all of the variance in intelligence.

family studies Studies designed to estimate the heritability of a trait in which the concordance of a trait between people is compared to their genetic relatedness. Researchers then estimate how much of the variance of the trait in the population is accounted for by genetic relatedness.

table 4.3	Familial Studies	
RELATION	**RELATEDNESS**	**CORRELATION**
Full sibling	0.50	0.55
Parent–child	0.50	0.50
Grandparent–grandchild	0.25	0.27
First cousin	12.5	0.26
Second cousin	0.3	0.16

Correlations in IQ are associated with genetic relatedness. This relationship is strong but not perfect. The correlation can and does change across populations. Any estimate of heritability only pertains to the population for which the estimate was made. Adapted from "Genetics and the Development of Intelligence," by S. Scarr-Salapatek, 1975, in *Review of Child Development Research, Vol. 4*, p. 33, Ed. F. D. Horowitz, Chicago, IL: University of Chicago Press.

adoption studies

Heritability studies in which the correlation of a trait between adopted children and their adoptive parents is compared to the correlation of the trait between biologically related parents, children, and siblings living in different households.

Clearly, familial studies alone can be hard to interpret since families do not just share genes, but they also share many aspects of their environment, education, and economic circumstance. In addition to familial studies, a second important method for estimating IQ is **adoption studies**. In adoption studies, the correlation between the IQ of adopted children and that of their adoptive parents can be computed, and the correlation between the IQ of biologically related parents, children, and siblings living in different households can also be computed. Findings from these studies tend to show a greater concordance of IQ between biologically related relatives living in different households than between adoptive family members, indicating that IQ is somewhat heritable.

Unfortunately, adoption studies are not as unambiguously interpretable as they sound. Adoption agencies will often match an adoptive child and parent on a number of factors, building in an environmental association you thought was controlled for. Adoptive families as a whole are a non-random group, having a motivation and socio-economic status that allowed the adoption in the first place. And the IQs of

Comparing monozygotic twins to dizygotic twins can help disentangle shared genes and shared environments.

adopted children in these studies are often higher than average, a result of the families' differences.

A third design that allows an estimate of heritability is **twin studies**. Comparing monozygotic twins (who share the same genome) to dizygotic twins (who are only as genetically related to each other as any two full siblings would be) can help disentangle shared genes and shared environments. The observation that siblings are similar on measures of IQ would be hard to interpret since siblings share some genes and also share many environmental factors. What would you infer if monozygotic twins who were reared in different households were more concordant on IQ measures than dizygotic twins who were reared in the same household? It should be apparent that by comparing differences across households between people who have the same genome and those with different genomes, one can estimate the contribution of variance in genes and the environment to the variance across the population as a whole. In fact, the heritability of a trait can be estimated using the following formula:

$$\text{Heritability} = (\text{correlation between monozygotic twins} - \text{correlation between dizygotic twins}) \times 2$$

One estimate reports that among siblings reared together, monozygotic twins had a concordance of 0.86, dizygotic twins had a concordance of 0.60, full siblings had a concordance of 0.50, and non-genetic siblings of approximately the same age (perhaps step- or adopted siblings) had a concordance of 0.26 (Segal, 2000). You can probably see that creating this statistical estimate does not tell you very much about how intelligence develops in a child.

twin studies A special type of family study in heritability. Concordance of a trait among monozygotic twins is compared to the concordance of the trait among dizygotic twins, allowing for the estimate of genetic relatedness contributing to the variance of the trait in the population.

4.9 Press Pause

Family studies, adoption studies, and twin studies are used to estimate the heritability of various traits, including IQ.

figure 4.3 Heritability: How can it be estimated?

This figure shows the correlations of IQ across various relationships. By comparing these correlations, heritability can be estimated for a particular population. (Adapted from "Familial Studies of Intelligence: A Review," by T. J. Bouchard, Jr. and M. McGue, 1981, *Science, 212*, pp. 1055–1059. Reprinted with permission from AAAS.)

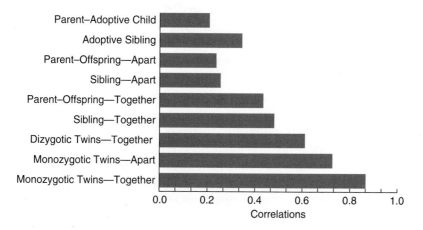

The heritability statistic must be calculated over a large population, like a country or at least a significant region. You would never try to calculate heritability in, say, your school or your hometown. The results would be skewed and would deviate from the statistics derived from larger populations, especially for rare traits such as autism or schizophrenia. In a very large population, it is the amount of variance in a trait (e.g., risk aversion or height) that is statistically accounted for by variance in genes divided by all other variance (which will amount to the variance that is attributed to variance in the environment plus the variance that is attributed to an interaction between genes and the environment). Notice also that there has to be appreciable variance in the trait you are asking about or the heritability statistic is meaningless. For example, you could not calculate the heritability of the number of stomachs: Everyone has one. There is no variance to attribute to either genes or other sources.

In practice, the only part of the heritability statistic that can actually be directly measured is the variance in the expressed trait (often called the *variance in the phenotype*). You can measure everybody's height, and there are ways to measure people's IQ and extroversion, but there is no direct way to measure the variance in genes for height, IQ, or extroversion, and there is no way to measure the variance in the environmental factors that influence the development of height, IQ, or extroversion in a person's lifetime. (Note that these are practical not theoretical barriers. We simply do not have enough information about the development of these traits to know what we should be measuring. In theory, if we did, there would be no reason we could not measure those factors.)

THE ELUSIVE HERITABILITY OF IQ

Now, you may have the impression that heritability is a "fact" about a trait. Perhaps you think that heritability does not change, that the heritability of IQ is something about IQ; it is what it is and that is that. In fact, heritability statistics are specific to the population for which they were calculated, and depending on the factors that are causally related to development, the heritability of a given trait can change from one population to the next and can change in a given location over historical time periods. Different studies of the heritability of IQ yield different heritability estimates and not just because of methodological differences: The heritability of IQ is, in fact, different in different populations (Bouchard, 1981; Bouchard, Lykken, McGue, Segal, & Tellegen, 1990; Pedersen, Plomin, Nesselroade, & McClearn, 1992; Plomin & DeFries, 1980). For instance, a recent study reported that in a large North American sample, the heritability of verbal IQ was 0.57 for the overall sample, only 0.26 for those people whose parents had a high-school education or less, and 0.74 for those people whose parents had a post-secondary education (Rowe, Jacobson, & van der Oord, 1999). Below are more examples to get you thinking less in terms of heritability as a fixed attribute of a trait and more of heritability as a statistic that describes a trait in a temporally and geographically defined population.

The heritability of IQ increases with age (Jensen, 1998, pp. 179–181) and is estimated to be as low as 20 per cent in infant populations and 40 per cent in middle childhood. By late adolescence, the heritability of IQ increases to around 75 per cent (Neisser et al., 1996, p. 85). In other words, in late adolescence, the heritability of IQ is higher than the heritability of IQ in infancy. To put it more concretely: As they grow through childhood into late adolescence, the measured IQ of adopted children is increasingly correlated with their birth parents, not their adoptive parents (Bouchard, 2004). The IQ of adopted children decreases in correlation with their adoptive parents (Plomin, Fulker,

figure 4.4   Heritability by age

The heritability of IQ is not a fixed characteristic of a trait, but it increases with age.

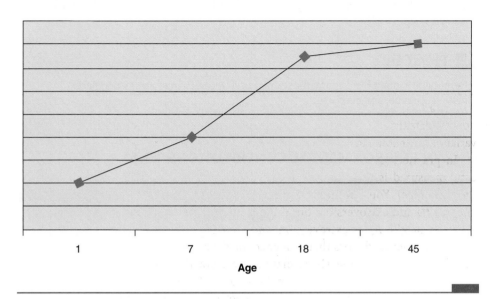

Corley, & DeFries, 1997; Scarr & Weinberg, 1983; Scarr, Weinberg, & Waldman, 1993). Furthermore, there is an extremely low correlation between teenagers and their adopted siblings (Scarr & Weinberg, 1976). Then, the heritability of IQ continues to increase through late adulthood (Cyphers, Fulker, Plomin, & DeFries, 1989; Pedersen et al., 1992), so the heritability of IQ at around 45 years of age is even greater than that at 18 years of age (Pedersen et al., 1992).

This example of the elusive heritability of IQ first makes it clear that heritability is not an immutable feature of a trait. The heritability of IQ changes as you define the population differently and measure it in that population. Second, it probably surprises you that heritability could increase with age. You may have been less surprised if the heritability of IQ decreased with age since the older you get more the more experience you have (the more environment you are exposed to) and the greater one would expect the relative contribution of the environment (as opposed to genetics) to be. The IQ of an individual is not some proportion genetics and some proportion environment. The development of IQ is a result of a complex but intricately designed interaction between all available resources, including genes and the environment. Also, the heritability statistic does not tell you that, say, 52 per cent of an individual's IQ comes from her parents while 48 per cent of her intelligence comes from her environment. If this were true, how could heritability increase with age or even change with age?

Another point to consider is that over time, as environments become more uniform, heritability rises. You can easily see this logical necessity by considering the heritability statistic: If there is less variance in environments, there will be less variance in IQ, but of the remaining variance in IQ, more of it will be attributable to variance in genes. If the variance in environments approaches zero (which it cannot, but if it could), then the heritability of IQ would approach 100 per cent. Clearly, environments are not standardized across childhood, but public schooling and programs, as well as standardized provincial curricula, that are designed to ensure that all children have access to educational resources lead to somewhat less variance in the environment and thus a higher heritability of IQ. Finally, we know that the more general the IQ test is, the more heritable IQ is. Conversely, the more the tasks on the test are restricted to a particular domain or cognitive skill set, the less heritable IQ is (Cyphers et al., 1989; Pedersen et al., 1992).

4.10 Press Pause

Heritability is not a fixed characteristic of a trait. It can change across population, historical period, and even age.

KNOWN ENVIRONMENTAL CONTRIBUTIONS TO IQ

From the Classroom to the Lab

You have read that heritability is sometimes estimated by comparing the similarity of a trait in monozygotic twins to the similarity of that same trait in dizygotic twins. How would you measure the heritability of twinning?

Measuring the heritability of IQ does not reveal how intelligence develops, but two longitudinal studies have revealed some factors in the home environment that are associated with IQ. One longitudinal study followed children from the age of 4 until they were 14. This study measured and identified a number of risk factors: an unemployed head of household, a mother with no high-school diploma, four or more children in the family, an absent father, authoritarian parenting, unusually high maternal anxiety, poor mental health on the part of the mother, and a lack of affection from the mother. Any combination of these factors was associated with a decline in IQ, and the more risk factors there were, the greater the decline in IQ (Sameroff, Seifer, Baldwin, & Baldwin, 1993).

The other longitudinal study also followed changes in IQ across childhood, this time focussing on parenting, and identified a number of factors. Researchers found that in families where parents emphasized intellectual acceleration, the children's IQ increased, and in families where parents made little effort to contribute to the child's intellectual development, IQ decreased. In addition, families with consistent discipline saw an increase in the child's IQ, but families with either extremely severe or extremely lax discipline saw a decrease in the child's IQ (McCall, Applebaum, & Hogarty, 1973).

What environmental factors affect changes in IQ? Children whose parents take an active interest in their academic achievement have higher IQ scores.

ETHNICITY AND IQ

There is replicable evidence that there are ethnic group differences in performance on IQ tests. Compared to Caucasian children, IQ scores are lower for children who are Black (Loehlin, 2000), Hispanic (Sattler, 1988), and First Nations (Dolan, 1999). Although there is a great deal of overlap in IQ scores, and there is more variability within groups than between groups, there is still a consistent difference to explain. Many factors may be contributing to group differences in these scores. First, there is a persistent tendency for economic differences between ethnic groups; minority children are more likely to live in poverty (Duncan & Magnuson, 2005). It is clear that access to nutrition, medical care, and educational resources, all of which can be reduced in poor economic situations, can affect performance on IQ tests. Ethnic differences in parents' beliefs and attitudes about education can also affect performance on academic tests. Mothers' beliefs that school performance can be affected by effort regardless of ability is associated with better school

⁙ Assessing Social Impact

The Carolina Abecedarian Project and Its Effects on IQ

One known correlate of IQ is socio-economic status (SES): Children who come from poor families have lower IQ scores compared to children who come from affluent families. The old conventional wisdom was that IQ scores were unalterable: Children who were not doing well academically would not likely benefit from educational help (Jensen, 1973).

Some researchers were not convinced, and Isabelle Lewis and Joseph Sparling started the Carolina Abecedarian Project with two objectives in mind: (a) delivering educational resources to low SES groups of children with the hope of raising their IQ scores and (b) carefully measuring and comparing the results of different educational approaches so as to determine what kind of assistance was most effective. What was radically different about this project, compared to earlier efforts, was that Lewis and Sparling started their intervention before their subjects were 6 months of age.

Starting in 1972, infants were recruited and randomly assigned to different groups, either receiving the early educational intervention plans or participating in the control group. The infants were from father-absent families with low incomes and low maternal education. From infancy until the age of 5, the children received an intensive educational intervention that was tailored to their needs. They spent their days in specially designed daycare centres that were essentially open all day, from 7:45 a.m. to 5:30 p.m.

The educational activities were designed to be delivered as games that the child played on a daily basis. For the youngest children, the focus was on motor development as well as social and cognitive development. For the older children, language development was emphasized, and they were also introduced to math, science, and music. Children in the control group got health and nutritional intervention but no educational benefit. Follow-up studies were conducted when the children were 12, 15, and 21. The results were remarkable.

At the age of 21, there was a measureable IQ difference (5 points) between the intervention group and the control group (Campbell et al., 2001). Although the intervention was initiated early and ended when the children were 5 years old, their academic achievement, particularly in math and reading, was higher through young adulthood. The children who participated in the intervention were more likely to attend college and stayed in school longer than the control children.

It appears that the success of this project depended on starting early, delivering intensive intervention, and continuing that intervention for a significant period of time. A later study that provided educational programming until the age of 3 did not show the same robust advantages, neither with respect to gains in IQ nor improved academic achievement (Burchinal, Campbell, Bryant, Wasik, & Ramey, 1997; Ramey et al., 2000).

What about the question of heritability? The success of this project shows that IQ is malleable. We can also use it to illustrate some of the concepts around heritability that you have just been reading about: (a) heritability can change, and (b) the heritability of a trait depends on the population being studied. First, this project would have greatly increased the heritability of IQ within the test group. If you were able to measure the heritability of IQ in the group studied, you would find that since the educational environment had been standardized, the contribution of variance in the environment to variance in IQ would be reduced, and relatively more of the variance among people would be accounted for by variance in genes, yielding an increased heritability of IQ. Second, the population studied matters: If you calculated IQ across the entire community, you would find IQ to be less heritable. Having introduced an environmental manipulation to only some of the children, variance in the environment would contribute relatively more to variance in IQ.

performance (Chen & Stevenson, 1995). Furthermore, some have argued that the IQ instruments have an inherent cultural bias, such that Caucasian children find them easier to navigate and that the general-knowledge questions may probe information that is general only in the majority culture. Also, the communication style may be more familiar to Caucasian children than to minority children. And achievement on a standardized test may be valued in some families more than others, accounting for some of these group differences.

Wrapping up Heritability: What It Is Not

Let us be clear about what heritability is *not*. It is not the proportion of a given trait that is attributed to genes. It does not tell you whether something is malleable or open to developmental change based on experience. It does not (and this may be surprising) tell you whether something is inherited.

Heritability is not the number that tells you how much of a trait comes from genes and how much of it comes from the environment. If we say, for example, that IQ is 52 per cent heritable, this does not mean that 52 per cent of an individual's intelligence comes from her genes and 48 per cent comes from her upbringing. Resist thinking this way. To start with, heritability cannot be computed for an individual, and it tells us nothing about an individual. The heritability statistic is an index of the relative

If you estimate the heritability of plant height within either of these environments, it will be very high: Genetic variance accounts for all the differences in height. If you estimate heritability across the two groups, it will be low: Environmental differences account for all the differences in height.

contribution of *differences* in genes or *differences* in an environment to *differences* in a given trait between people. Just as knowing what accounts for differences in snowfall tells you nothing at all about how a snowflake is made, accounting for differences in a given trait tells you nothing about the development of that trait.

One study reports that IQ is 0.70 heritable (Bouchard et al., 1990). Does this mean that genes cause 70 per cent of a person's intelligence and that the environment causes 30 per cent of it? No. Genes could do nothing without their interaction with the environment, and the environment could not create an intelligent person without a genome to play off of. A person's intelligence is a result of both genes and the environment, influencing each other throughout development in intricate and poorly understood ways.

In a now classic illustration, consider the height of some experimentally cultivated plants. Imagine we plant a handful of seeds in a tightly controlled environment, Environment A, in which every plant gets the same resources: plenty of food, water, and sunshine for healthy, vigorous growth. In a different environment, Environment B, every plant is again given identical, carefully controlled resources but in this case just barely enough for the plants to survive. After the plants have grown, we can calculate the heritability of height within each population. First consider Environment A. In this population, the plants are all tall, but there is some variance in height (not a lot, but some). Since we know that we have very carefully controlled the environment, none of the variance in height is attributable to differences in the environment. All of the variance must be due to differences in the genes between the plants. In this population, the heritability of height is 100 per cent (Lewontin, 1970). Likewise, if you consider Environment B, in which the plants are relatively short but also display some variance in height, again there is no difference between the plants and their environment. All of the variance in height is due to variance in the genes. In this population, the heritability of height is also 100 per cent. From this example, can we conclude that genes determine height? That genes alone cause height? That height is due to genes but not the environment? Clearly not. If you estimate heritability across the two groups, it will be low: Environmental differences account for all the differences in height. Likewise, if humans had a trait with extremely high heritability environmental circumstances could still exist that would affect the development of that trait.

Furthermore, heritability does *not* tell you whether a trait is immutable. If genetic variance accounts for 52 per cent of the variance in extroversion, this does not tell you that it is 48 per cent changeable and 52 per cent an immutable part of the person's nature. Learning that a particular kind of intellectual disability, phenylketonuria, is highly heritable might lead you to think that it is therefore genetically determined, immutable, and untreatable. Not so. Phenylketonuria is a kind of intellectual disability that affects individuals who cannot process the amino acid phenylalanine. All you need to do is remove phenylalanine from the individual's diet entirely, and no intellectual disability will develop. If you want to understand the development of a trait (whether for therapeutic or other reasons) heritability tells you very little.

In the variance of height example above, all of the plants in Environment B are short, and the heritability statistic of height calculated in that environment is 100 per cent. Does this mean that height is not malleable? No. Add more water, food, and sun, and the plants will grow to be tall. Similarly, if you measure IQ in a particular population and find it to be very heritable, does this mean that programs designed to promote intellectual development have no chance of success? Not at all. The high heritability of IQ says nothing, absolutely nothing, about its malleability. Environmental influences could still have dramatic effects on IQ.

The heritability estimate does not tell you whether something is inherited. Although we think of having fingers and toes as an inherited trait, the heritability of the number of fingers and toes is essentially zero.

The third point is that heritability does not tell us anything about whether or not a trait or characteristic is inherited. This may strike you as particularly odd since the question of whether or not something is inherited was, originally, the enterprise for which the heritability statistic was conceived. But a trait with a very low heritability may, nonetheless, be inherited.

Philosopher Ned Block invites us to consider, for example, a trait that intuition tells us is inherited: the number of fingers and toes a person has. We certainly think of this trait as having been inherited from one's parents, who in turn inherited it from their parents. But what would happen if you went about calculating the heritability of the number of fingers and toes? Remember, the heritability statistic is the amount of variance due to genes divided by all variance. Well, all of the variance in the number of fingers and toes is pretty small: Most folks have 10 fingers and 10 toes. But among those who have a different number, what do you suppose accounts for the variance? Block suggests that variance will largely be due to accidents and to drugs that a mother ingested during pregnancy, especially thalidomide (Block, 1995). Most of the variance in the number of fingers and toes is due to non-genetic factors, making the heritability statistic very small. The number of fingers and toes has low heritability, and yet we are certain that it is inherited. So it is with most of the features that we think of as standard parts of the human package.

Similarly, if you are used to thinking about things that are highly heritable as biological, and things that are much less heritable as environmental, social, or cultural, then here is something else that might surprise you: Adaptations have a very low heritability, approaching zero. Here is why: natural selection uses up variance. Imagine a group of rabbits living in a snowy field. Imagine that hawks eat the rabbits. Imagine that at the beginning of our experiment, there are a variety of different-coloured rabbits: white, black, grey, brown. A hawk can more easily see the darker-coloured rabbits against the snowy background and will target them first. Therefore, the white rabbits will out-survive, and out-reproduce, the other rabbits. There is selection pressure for being white. If this condition exists over a long enough time period, the white rabbits will become universal. That seems straightforward, right? But notice that at the beginning of our experiment, colour may have been highly heritable, but at the end of our experiment, it is not. At the beginning, there was a lot of variance in the population in terms of fur colour and that variance could be statistically accounted for by differences in genes (i.e., the presence of particular genes predicted specific fur colour). At the end of the experiment, the variance in hair colour simply did not exist, and as the variance in hair colour diminished to zero, the heritability became indefinable. Contrary to common expectation, the adaptation (white fur) does not have a high heritability.

---

figure 4.5 Natural selection uses up variance

Traits that have been strongly selected for are likely to be low in variance throughout the population and thus low in heritability. This applies equally to psychological traits such as face preference, attachment, and language acquisition, which you will read about in coming chapters.

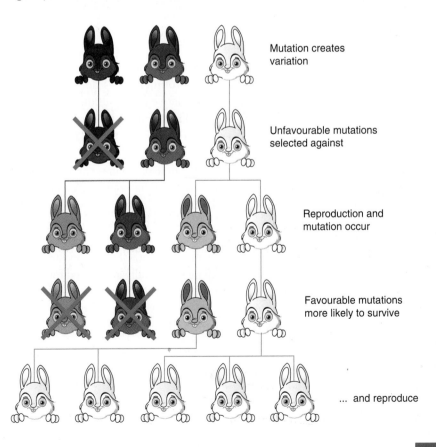

Mutation creates variation

Unfavourable mutations selected against

Reproduction and mutation occur

Favourable mutations more likely to survive

... and reproduce

This is, of course, true for humans too and for human psychological adaptations. We do not expect high heritability for adaptations, and the traits that are human universals do not have high heritability. Until some time ago, there was considerable debate around whether or not there were any human universals. The issue has been more or less settled, and anthropologist Don Brown, who was originally sceptical of the idea of human universals, has now done considerable research and has written a book on the subject (Brown, 1991). In this book, Brown chronicles hundreds of human universals, that is, traits and characteristics that you would find in any human group on earth. Many of the universals that Brown describes are behavioural: Humans are social, they live in groups, and they have status and hierarchy within groups. They have and observe rules regarding politeness and etiquette. They live in families, exchange gifts, keep track of favours and insults, retaliate, celebrate, make music, dance, etc. But what underlies these behavioural universals is, in each case, an evolved cognitive adaptation that is universal throughout the human world. These traits, therefore, would not be highly heritable, although they are inherited as part of our biological endowment.

4.11 Press Pause

Contrary to common expectation, adaptations are not associated with high heritability.

Finally, here is one last thought experiment that might help you abandon the idea that heritability is an unchangeable part of a trait: Heritability can be artificially manipulated. If you standardize the environment such that everyone is exposed to a very small range of environment types, there will be a relatively small contribution of variance due to the environment: Heritability will be low. Let us take, for example, skin colour. On the one hand you could take a large number of people from all over the world, from Scandinavia, Africa, the South Pacific, and take them to a place (any place) where their environment is standardized (e.g., where their exposure to sunlight is equal). Because their experience or environment does not differ in terms of the relevant factors (in this case sunlight), the relative contribution of variance in the environment will be small. The heritability of skin colour in this group of people will be very high. (Go ahead and look at the heritability statistic formula above and check it out.) Now, on the other hand, consider a new group of people who have similar ethnic backgrounds, say a large group of Asian people of Japanese descent. Let us send some of them to the African savannah, some to Australia, some to Scandinavia, some to Ecuador, and let us send some to Alaska in the middle of winter. Now, when we measure heritability in this group of people, there will be considerable variance in the environment, specifically the relevant aspect of the environment: sun exposure. Some of the people will become quite tanned and some will not. Of all of the variance in skin colour in this group, relatively little of it will be statistically accounted for by variance in the genes, and much more of it will be accounted for by variance in the environment. Heritability of skin colour in this group will be very small. So, what is the heritability of skin colour? It can only be calculated with respect to a defined population.

Facultative Adaptation

This next section introduces the idea of a facultative adaptation and uses learning as an illustration of a facultative adaptation. Although you have likely heard "learning" offered as an alternative to evolution as an explanation for psychological traits, knowledge, or processes (as in "evolved vs. learned" or "biological vs. learned"), nothing

Heritability can be artificially manipulated. If you standardize the environment in a genetically diverse group, differences in skin colour will be associated with differences in genes. If you manipulate the environment in a genetically homogenous group, skin colour will have a very low heritability since genes are not sources of variance.

could be further from the truth. In fact, learning mechanisms are designed by natural selection. You might think that if research results show that some trait or skill is learned, that the skill in question must not be an adaptation. In fact, when anything is learned, it is learned as a result of an adaption: Natural selection has designed psychological mechanisms that are meant to be shaped by experience. It is easy to see why this is true: In many cases, responding to and adapting to environmental input will result in greater fitness compared to the result of a rigidly unfolding developmental program.

facultative adaptation
An adaptation that is designed to respond to specific cues in the environment, thus preparing organisms for the varying conditions that were possible in the EEA.

> ### 4.12 Press Pause
>
> Organisms respond to the environment by design. Nurture is not in opposition to nature in development; nature and nurture act together by design.

Facultative adaptations are adaptations that are designed to respond developmentally to specific stimuli in the environment in order to optimize the fit between the individual and the environment. These adaptations evolve over time because developmental plasticity increased fitness in the EEA. Can you think of any features of your mind or body that change for the better in response to exposure to some environmental factor? Some commonly mentioned examples of facultative adaptations such as these include the calluses that one develops on their feet or hands as a result of friction on the skin in these areas and the suntan that one gets in response to the skin's exposure to ultraviolet radiation. These are changes that take place in response to given conditions, and, importantly, they are changes that take place by design, as a result of an adaptation that is designed to respond to the environment.

Facultative adaptations prepared organisms for the varying conditions that were possible in the EEA and remind us that just because something is a product of evolution it does not mean that it is immutable or determined: Some adaptations are designed to develop differently based on the context in which the person grows up. Across the possible environments that one could have been born into in the EEA, there was variance in ecology, economy, food availability, paternal commitment, exposure to sunlight, and the amount of activity required to meet one's caloric needs, etc.

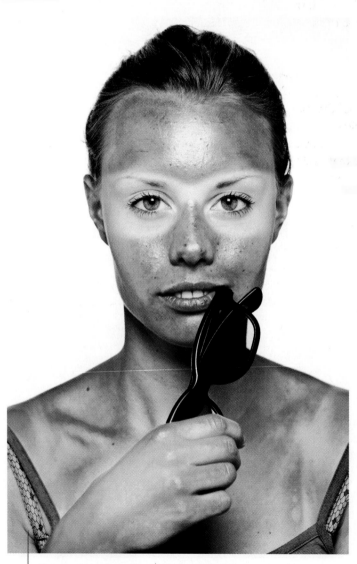

Facultative adaptations allow an individual to adjust to a particular environment in order to increase fitness. Our ability to suntan balances our need for sunlight with our need for protection from the sun.

In addition to simple examples like calluses and suntans, more complex examples are psychological facultative adaptations such as language learning, developmental differences resulting from parenting styles, and the development of attachment styles, which you will read about in detail in Chapter 10. In brief, parental investment is affected by ecological situations and varies across cultures. In some cases fathers contribute to their offspring because their contribution will make a difference in their children's survival and success. In other cases, fathers' contributions would not make a substantial difference. The level of parental investment one experiences in early childhood signals to the developing child which life-cycle strategy (early development and reproduction or abstinence until marriage) will be the most fruitful strategy, and evidence suggests that physiological and psychological adaptations develop in order to employ the most fruitful strategy in the local environment.

THE BENEFITS OF FLEXIBILITY

Are you surprised to learn that evolutionary psychologists are interested in learning and plasticity? Some people think that *learning* is the opposite of *evolved*, and that if evidence of learning is found, then this will be problematic for an evolutionary perspective. There are, broadly, two tremendous evolutionary advantages to being born cognitively immature and yet equipped with learning mechanisms. First, storing information in the environment, not just the genome, may be an efficient way to pass regularity on to the next generation in cases where reliable information is available in a species-typical environment. Second, to the extent that circumstances are not identical across lifespans, learning mechanisms allow an individual to optimize his or her compatibility with the current environment.

A baby's reliance on external stimuli for development may be a necessary design. Human brains have over 100 billion neurons, and billions and billions of synapses, yet there are only about 30,000 genes in the human genome. There are simply too many connections for each to be determined by the genome. Since the human genome does not have enough information to genetically specify the development, location, pathway, and connections of all the neurons in the brain, it follows that a developing nervous system as complex as the human nervous system relies on exogenous information to develop.

One solution to the problem of insufficient genetic information is for the genome to "store information" in the environment, figuratively speaking. In any case where a certain aspect of the environment is reliable across many, many generations, it will be more efficient for a germ line (i.e., the genetic information passed from generation to generation) to rely on this information in the environment rather than to create and store it in DNA. There are environmental cues specific to each organism that are reliable enough to be depended on for development. These cues are species-typical. For example, if the sun rises reliably and predictably every day over many generations, it will be efficient to calibrate internal schedules to this pattern rather than building self-contained timing devices into the neural system. Day and night are reliable, observable phenomena as are the changing seasons and fluctuating hours of daylight.

Furthermore, remember that an evolutionary perspective leads us to expect that the developing child's mind will be well designed to interact with the EEA. Remember, too, that there was some environmental variance in the EEA. Sometimes a child has to learn what his or her circumstances are and then adjust accordingly. The child might even have to make changes in life strategies as a result of information encountered in early childhood.

4.13 Press Pause

Learning based on reliable environmental cues may be an efficient developmental trick. It may also solve the problem of unpredictable variance in possible environments.

Evolutionary psychologists broadly distinguish between adaptations that are facultative (those that develop when they become functional in the current environment, as evidenced by a specific cue the organism can detect) and those that are obligate (those that develop reliably as long as the individual is developing in a species-typical environment). Developmental psychologists can make a further distinction between experience-expectant learning and experience-dependent learning.

EXPERIENCE-EXPECTANT LEARNING

There is a subset of facultative adaptations that are psychological. Learning, for example, is a kind of facultative adaptation. Knowing this, it is important to understand that learning is not just one kind of psychological adaptation (learning to walk

Here is an example of experience-expectant learning: A 2-day-old chick will find, pick up, and eat mealworms in normal circumstances. If the chick is fitted with shoes immediately after hatching and therefore cannot see its own feet, the chick will be oblivious to mealworms.

is not accomplished by the same learning mechanisms as learning to talk), but rather it involves many adaptations, each designed to solve a specific learning problem. There are a variety of different types of learning mechanisms, each designed to acquire a specific type of content. In broad terms, we can categorize two large classes of learning mechanisms: experience-expectant learning mechanisms and experience-dependent learning mechanisms.

Both experience-expectant and experience-dependent learning are changes in the brain, by design, in response to stimuli that are external to the developing individual. The difference is that **experience-expectant learning** relies on some stimuli that all members of the species experience in a species-typical environment. So in normative development, experience-expectant plasticity unfolds as a result of the interplay between reliably present elements of the organism (including the genome) and reliably present elements of the environment. As was made clear in the discussion of developmental systems theory in Chapter 2, part of what a developing young individual inherits is the relevant environmental resources. Ideally, the individual will inherit the species-typical environment, which is to say, the environment that provides the features that the genome needs or "expects" in order to develop typically. Greenough and others have described experience-expectant processes in detail (Greenough, Black, & Wallace, 1987; Johnson, 1998). Early in development, the organism can take advantage of environmental regularities, such as the presence of vertical and horizontal lines in terrestrial light. Neural development prepares an organism to react to a specific stimulus in the environment that is reliably present in species-typical environments (Greenough & Black, 1992).

Normal brain development relies on exposure to the appropriate stimuli during the relevant critical period, and changes in either the developing organism or the environment could lead to unexpected abnormalities in development. Developmental psychologists have long recognized that some forms of learning can only take place during a **critical period**, the time period in development during which a specific kind of learning can take place, or during a **sensitive period**, the time period in development during which a specific kind of learning takes place most easily.

Here is an example of experience-expectant learning taking place in a species-typical environment. A 2-day-old chick will find, pick up, and eat mealworms given normal developmental circumstances in a species-typical environment. However, if the chicks are fitted with shoes immediately after hatching, such that they cannot see their own feet, they will be oblivious to mealworms. Why? Researchers speculate that in order to develop the ability to perceive and pursue mealworms, a chick must be able to see his own toes because a chick's toes resemble mealworms in size, colour, and segmentation (Moore, 2001; Wallman, 1979). Notice too that the visual stimuli of the chick's own toes is part of the species-typical environment; the young chick has always had that stimuli available, and the stimuli is available during the critical period, the first few days of life. The fact that the toes have nothing to do with the mealworms is no reason why the chick's developing visual system cannot rely on the toes to develop competence with respect to finding mealworms.

Other examples are involved in the development of the visual system: A developing cat needs to see vertical and horizontal lines in order for its visual system to develop normally. The natural world provides plenty of vertical and horizontal lines, so in the species-typical environment, a cat's visual system will develop typically. If the developing cat is experimentally deprived of horizontal or vertical lines, the perception of such lines does not develop (Hubel & Wiesel, 1962). In the case that the developing animal was not exposed to the necessary visual stimulus during the critical period, vision will never be normal. Animals that were completely deprived of stimuli to one eye were

experience-expectant learning mechanism A learning mechanism that is designed to respond to species-typical environmental input, usually during a critical period, in order for normal brain development to result.

critical period
The time period in development during which a specific kind of learning can take place if the necessary stimuli are present.

sensitive period
The time period in development during which a specific kind of learning takes place most easily.

blind in that eye. Animals that were selectively deprived of, say, vertical lines could never see that particular stimulus. Research on humans who were born with cataracts reveals that failure to view patterned light during a critical period results in a permanent deviation from developmental norms (Maurer, Lewis, Brent, & Levin, 1999).

For humans, a language community is reliably present during development, so language does not need to be fully specified in the genome in order to be a species-typical characteristic of humans. Very young children orient selectively to faces in their visual environment (Goren, Sarty, & Wu, 1975; Maurer, 1985; Wilcox, 1969) and then build a face template based on the faces that they are exposed to (Meltzoff, 1995; Morton & Johnson, 1991). The genome and the environment are selected by natural selection to mesh so that their interaction produces a stable, reliably developing species-typical design. What has evolved by natural selection is a coordination, a system if you will, between genes and the environment. The genome by no means bears the whole burden.

4.14　Press Pause

Experience-expectant learning mechanisms may take advantage of regularities in the species-typical environment in the course of development.

EXPERIENCE-DEPENDENT LEARNING

experience-dependent learning mechanism A learning mechanism that responds to individual, specific information.

Experience-dependent learning is what we call the kind of learning mechanism that responds to individual-specific information. This kind of learning includes the learning mechanisms designed to optimize the relationship between one's brain and one's own idiosyncratic environment (Black & Greenough, 1986; Greenough & Black, 1992). For example, one needs to learn not just attachment in general but who, specifically, one's mother is. One needs to learn not just language in general but, specifically, the vocabulary of one's local community. This information is important to an individual and could not, even in theory, be specified in the genome. One has to have exposure to this information in the environment in order to develop an understanding of it.

In contrast to experience-expectant learning, experience-dependent learning happens throughout the lifespan, not just during a restricted critical or sensitive period. One revealing set of experiments involving rats showed differences in brain development as a result of being reared in a complex, interesting environment compared to rat pups who were reared in a simple, deprived environment. Those who were reared in an environment with physical challenges and objects to explore made more dendritic extensions on their neurons, more synapses on each neuron, more synapses overall, and developed a thicker cortex. Not only that, but they were better at learning new things later in life (Juraska, Henderson, & Muller, 1984).

There are some studies that have shown evidence of experience-dependent learning in humans as well. Compared to other musicians, violinists and cellists (who use their left hand to manipulate strings) have more cortical cells in the brain area controlling the left hand and receive sensory information from the left hand (Elbert, Pantev, Wienbruch, Rockstroh, & Taub, 1995). Similarly, compared to matched control subjects, those who can read Braille have more cortical cells dedicated to the hand they use to read it with (Pascual-Leone et al., 1993).

4.15　Press Pause

The genome is designed to interact with the species-typical environment in order to produce the adult phenotype.

NORM OF REACTION

In the fields of ecology and genetics, the term **norm of reaction** represents the relationship between a specific environmental factor and a measurable phenotypic expression, keeping genetics unchanged across environmental changes. For example, a plant of a given genotype might grow tall in lower altitudes but not in higher altitudes. Graphing height vs. altitude for this plant would illustrate its norm of reaction.

There is no one-to-one relationship between an environmental factor and its phenotypic effect: Different genomes respond differently across various levels of a given environmental factor (altitude, rainfall, nutrition, etc.). Indeed, norms of reaction are oft en plotted in order to compare across genomes. If you have ever gone to a gardening store to buy grass seed, you may have noticed that one type does well in wet conditions, one in dry conditions; one does well in sunny spots, another in shady spots. Each type has a different norm of reaction with respect to these specific environmental factors: water and sunlight.

norm of reaction The relationship between a specific environmental factor and a measurable phenotypic expression.

---

figure 4.6   Norm of reaction

The norm of reaction describes the relationship with an environmental factor, here altitude, and the expression of some trait, here height, without changing the genotype.

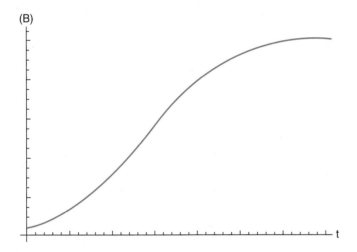

The point here is that in many species, including humans, different environments lead to different but predictable phenotypic outcomes, and this happens by design. The developing organism is designed to develop a phenotype that is adapted to the environment. The EEA offered a range of normal developmental plans because a range of different environments were possible. Finding evidence that the outcome of development is influenced by environmental factors is not a challenge to evolutionary theory but rather a sign of a well-designed organism.

As you can imagine, research capable of mapping out the norms of reaction in humans would be impossible for practical and ethical reasons. Indeed such research on any species is costly and time-consuming. Still, there is some evidence that people react developmentally to specific environmental factors in predictable ways, as you saw above when you read about research on the development of intelligence and as you will see later when reading about parenting, attachment, and the life history theory in Chapter 10.

| figure | 4.7 | **Norm of reaction of two different genotypes** |

Norms of reaction can vary dramatically from one genotype to another. This is why when you buy grass seed, one type does well in wet conditions, one in dry conditions; one does well in sunny spots, another in shady spots.

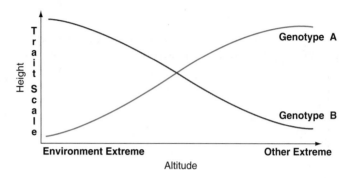

| 4.16 | **Press Pause** |

In many species, including humans, different environments lead to different phenotypic outcomes, and this happens by design.

There Are Many Types of Learning

Not only is the nature vs. nurture question a false dichotomy but so are the biology vs. culture and learned vs. innate dichotomies. If a child learns something, this is because there is a learning mechanism that allowed the child to learn. Where does this learning mechanism come from? It was designed by natural selection. There really is no serious debate within the scientific community regarding whether the human brain is a product of natural selection (what else could explain its existence?). What is contentious is what the implications of our evolutionary history are. The standard social science model, as mentioned earlier, disregards our evolutionary history, with the assumption that knowledge of that history will not be useful in informing our inquiry in psychology and psychological development.

And how does that learning mechanism learn? It depends very much on what kind of learning we are talking about. Learning language relies on very different cognitive processes (described in Chapter 9) than learning to walk or learning maternal attachment. The interesting question is not how much is innate and how much is learned but rather what is the design of the child's mind that allows it to learn? How does that particular learning mechanism learn? What content is needed? What input is needed? What are the effects of manipulating the inputs within the range of naturally occurring circumstances? What are the effects of manipulating the input outside of that range?

The effect that the environment has on learning depends on how the learning mechanism was designed. Indeed what counts as "the environment" depends on how the learning mechanism was designed. The child's mind has to have a structure that allows learning, or he cannot learn anything at all. The blank slate remains blank.

4.17 **Press Pause**

Different kinds of learning require different psychological adaptations, not one general-purpose learning mechanism.

Prepared Learning

Blank-slate or associationist views dominated psychology and especially developmental psychology at least until the end of the last century. To John Watson and B. F. Skinner, the idea of a completely malleable infant mind, and a newborn who could be taught to do anything, value anything, and believe anything, was appealing. Skinner wrote books for a popular, non-scientific audience (books that included *Walden Two* and *Beyond Freedom and Dignity*), encouraging people to think that modern advances in the understanding of psychology could be used to create a utopia, free of war and free of hunger resulting from competition, by controlling the behaviour of the population.

As appealing as his promised utopia might be, John Garcia's and Susan Mineka's research offered evidence that the human mind might not be a blank slate, equally able to learn whatever association or pairing a teacher might want to teach. John Garcia was studying the effects of radiation during the 1950s, using rats as subjects, when he noticed that a rat seemed to develop an aversion to a food if two things were true: (a) the rat ate the food just prior to being exposed to radiation, and (b) the food was previ-

An example of prepared learning is Garcia's discovery that rats avoid foods that they have eaten just prior to becoming nauseous but not foods that they have eaten just prior to being shocked. Arbitrarily paired stimuli are not equally easily associated.

ously unknown to the rat prior to radiation. Garcia probed this finding experimentally by first letting rats taste sweetened water and then exposing them to mild radiation, strong radiation, or no radiation. He then allowed them to freely consume sweetened water. Relative to those rats who had not been exposed to radiation, those who were radiated drank less water, and the more radiation the rats were exposed to, the less water they drank. The effect, Garcia reasoned, was mediated by the nausea the rats experienced after exposure to radiation. In more natural circumstances like the EEA, experiencing nausea after eating usually meant that something was poisonous and that it would be best to avoid eating it in the future.

This discovery was surprising at the time because learning after a single exposure had not yet been documented. Learned associations that took place in the laboratory usually took hundreds of trials. Secondarily, it was surprising because there was an unusuali long delay between the stimuli. Traditionally the two stimuli that were to be associated with one another were presented within milliseconds. Here, for the first time, Garcia observed long-lasting learning following a single exposure. This was regarded as evidence of **prepared learning**: learning that is easier to induce than a random paired association would be because of its importance in our evolutionary history.

prepared learning
Learning that is easier to induce than a random paired association would be because of its importance in our evolutionary history.

But perhaps the most important lesson from Garcia's series of experiments on taste aversion was the violation of the assumption of equal associations. It had been assumed, indeed it was part of the classical conditioning model, that any two stimuli could be paired. (Associationists at the time paid no heed to perception or attention, so they would not have worried that some things would not have been perceived, and if they were perceived, that they may or may not be attended to. All stimuli would count as a candidate for an association.) A learned food aversion, Garcia discovered, is selective. When Garcia exposed the rats to radiation, which led to nausea, and paired that unpleasant stimulus with a red light, the rats never learned to avoid the red light, but they did learn to avoid a food when it was paired with nausea, a learning mechanism that clearly served a valuable function in the EEA. In another condition in the experiment, Garcia paired sweetened water with an electric shock, but the rats did not learn to avoid the sweet water. Instead, they tried to avoid the location in which they got shocked. Rats could learn to associate the shock with the red light, however. The fact that some associations were learnable and some were not was very much counter to the prevailing beliefs at the time. Any association should have been learnable (Garcia, Kimeldorf, & Koelling, 1955).

A similar lesson was learned from experiments about learned fears, conducted by Susan Mineka. Again, a blank-slate associationist account would predict that any stimulus could be learned to be feared and that all stimuli are equally easily feared. Mineka's experiments disproved this. Her experiments involved the acquisition of fear, using rhesus monkeys as subjects. Preliminary to the actual experiment, she videotaped a monkey's fearful reaction to a snake. Mineka then manipulated the image such that in one video, the monkey appeared to be displaying fear at the sight of a boa constrictor, and in another video, the monkey appeared to be displaying fear at the sight of a flower. To round out the conditions, Mineka also created two more videos, again splicing footage such that in one video, the monkey appeared to be calm and showed no fear at the sight of a flower, and in the other, the monkey again appeared to be calm and showed no fear at the sight of a boa constrictor.

In a between-subjects design, these four videos were shown to different laboratory-reared monkeys that did not fear the displayed objects. Each monkey was exposed to one of the four conditions for just a few minutes. Finally, the dependent measure was recorded: How much time would it take for each monkey to retrieve a food item if they had to reach past the object (a flower or a snake) that they had seen in the video? Prior to seeing the video, there was not a significant difference in the monkey's willingness to reach past a flower or a snake; laboratory-reared rhesus monkeys with no prior exposure to snakes did not show a fear of them. However after exposure to the video showing the monkey displaying fear at the sight of a snake, the subjects took significantly longer to collect food near a snake than a flower. Monkeys that had seen the video showing the display of fear toward a flower did not change from pre-experimental levels of fear. The video made them no less willing to collect food near a flower (Mineka, 1986).

Similar to these findings in other primates, there is evidence that humans may be prepared to learn, quite easily, to fear objects that would have been a danger in the EEA compared to objects that would not have existed in the EEA. Emotional fear responses of snakes and spiders are more easily conditioned than fears of other stimuli (Seligman, 1971). Clinical phobias are much more likely to be the fear of an evolutionarily relevant stimuli (spiders, snakes, heights, enclosed spaces) than objects that may be more dangerous to us today but that were not present in the EEA (guns, cars, knives) (Nesse, 1990). And fears of these evolutionarily relevant stimuli are much less easily treated or extinguished compared to fears of modern objects (Cook, Hodes, & Lang, 1986; Öhman, 1986).

These results may not seem surprising to you, but they were pretty devastating to the prevailing view at the time. The blank slate view of development assumed that prior to exposure and training, all stimuli were equal; it could not tolerate evidence that stimuli were different with respect to how easily one could learn to fear them. Mineka's results showed that monkeys have special learning mechanisms that allow them to learn to fear snakes based on another monkey's display of fear in the presence of a snake. The same learning mechanism could not be used to learn to fear flowers.

4.18 Press Pause

People and other animals learn by design. Learning does not oppose nature; rather, learning is designed by nature.

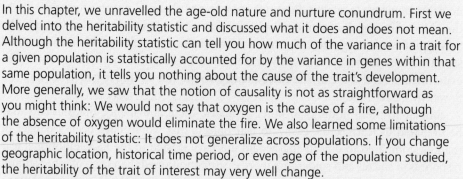

SUMMARY

In this chapter, we unravelled the age-old nature and nurture conundrum. First we delved into the heritability statistic and discussed what it does and does not mean. Although the heritability statistic can tell you how much of the variance in a trait for a given population is statistically accounted for by the variance in genes within that same population, it tells you nothing about the cause of the trait's development. More generally, we saw that the notion of causality is not as straightforward as you might think: We would not say that oxygen is the cause of a fire, although the absence of oxygen would eliminate the fire. We also learned some limitations of the heritability statistic: It does not generalize across populations. If you change geographic location, historical time period, or even age of the population studied, the heritability of the trait of interest may very well change.

You read that the fact that the environment affects development is by design, not by accident. Indeed, there is no reason to think of genes and the environment as being in opposition to each other since the developing organism is designed by natural selection to make use of information available in the environment. You also read about facultative adaptations: adaptations that are designed to respond developmentally to cues in the environment. A subset of facultative adaptations are learning mechanisms, and experiments by Garcia and Mineka show that learning mechanisms are not even-handed with respect to stimuli as the blank slate view of development would predict. Learning mechanisms are designed to accomplish specific types of learning. The discussion on norms of reaction described how the developing organism can "choose" one developmental strategy or another based on which of several environment types it is developing in. The developing organism is designed to interact with the species-typical environment in order to produce the adult phenotype.

Finally, you learned that developmental psychologists rejected the blank slate view of the developing child long ago and have recently begun to form a viable alternative: there are specific learning mechanisms designed to learn specific things. Experience-expectand and experience-dependant learning operate differently. Experimental evidence from Garcia and Mineka demonstrates the biases and constraints to guide learning.

PRESS PAUSE SUMMARY

- Every trait is a result of a complex interplay between all available resources: genes and the relevant environmental factors.
- It is harder than you think to assign a single cause to an event. Likewise, it is not possible to assign a single cause to development.
- The fallacy of exclusive determinism describes our desire to identify a single cause of an event. It is an adaptive part of human psychology.
- The heritability statistic does not tell you how much of a trait in a given individual was caused by genes and how much was caused by the environment.

- The heritability statistic does not tell you how malleable a trait is or whether that trait is unchangeably "determined".
- Asking if a trait is a result of genes or the environment is like asking if a snowflake is a result of temperature or humidity.
- The heritability statistic quantifies how much of the differences among people are statistically accounted for by differences in genes. The focus on differences is crucial.
- IQ scores are associated with academic and professional achievement, just as they were designed to be.
- Family studies, adoption studies, and twin studies are used to estimate the heritability of various traits, including IQ.
- Heritability is not a fixed characteristic of a trait. It can change across population, historical period, and even age.
- Contrary to common expectation, adaptations are not associated with high heritability.
- Organisms respond to the environment by design. Nurture is not in opposition to nature in development; nature and nurture act together by design.
- Learning based on reliable environmental cues may be an efficient developmental trick. It may also solve the problem of unpredictable variance in possible environments.
- Experience-expectant learning mechanisms may take advantage of regularities in the species-typical environment in the course of development.
- The genome is designed to interact with the species-typical environment in order to produce the adult phenotype.
- In many species, including humans, different environments lead to different phenotypic outcomes, and this happens by design.
- Different kinds of learning require different psychological adaptations, not one general-purpose learning mechanism.
- People and other animals learn by design. Learning does not oppose nature; rather, learning is designed by nature.

KEY TERMS AND CONCEPTS

adoption studies, 118

critical period, 133

experience-dependent learning mechanism, 134

experience-expectant learning mechanism, 133

facultative adaptation, 107

family studies, 117

heritability statistic, 115

norm of reaction, 135

prepared learning, 138

sensitive period, 133

SSSM, 106

twin studies, 119

QUESTIONS FOR THOUGHT AND DISCUSSION

1. Describe the beliefs held by the standard social science model (sssm). How are these beliefs inconsistent with other ideas that you learned in this chapter?

2. Why is it hard to identify a single cause for a given event? Can you think of a counter-example (an event that does have a single cause)? How does thinking about identifying a single cause affect the way you think about developmental psychology?

3. What does the heritability statistic of a trait tell you? Does this surprise you? How is this similar to or different from what you expected? How is it similar to or different from the way you have heard heritability talked about in the media or among your friends?

4. What are facultative adaptations? What is experience-dependent learning? How has what you read in this chapter challenged the biological vs. learned dichotomy with respect to developmental psychology?

5. What is associationism? What is prepared learning? Why is it that experiments that reveal prepared learning are a challenge to the associationist perspective?

From the Classroom to the Lab: Follow Up

Consider the experiment you designed in response to the "From the Classroom to the Lab" challenge earlier in this chapter.

Describe the design of your experiment.

What is your dependent variable?

What is your independent variable?

What are the possible outcomes of your experiment? How will you know what you are entitled to infer, based on these results?

Would you estimate the heritability of monozygotic and dizygotic twinning in the same experiment or in different experiments? If in different experiments, how would they differ?

chapter 5

Perceptual Development

Opening Vignette: Michael May

Michael May was born in 1954, a typical child with a typical visual system. At the age of 3½ he was completely blinded by a chemical explosion and lived the next 43 years without sight. Although May holds the record in downhill skiing by a totally blind person, if that record should be beaten, he could not challenge it because he is no longer blind. In 2000, at the age of 46, May underwent an innovative procedure for sight restoration in which a new cornea was transplanted and connected with the rest of his visual system. The procedure was successful. Sounds perfect, doesn't it?

As with other cases of sight that have been restored in adulthood, May's vision is not that of a normal adult (Fine et al., 2003). He cannot recognize his sons or his wife by looking at their faces. He cannot tell the difference between a man and a woman by looking at their faces. He cannot see three-dimensional objects as three-dimensional unless they are rotating. May once describing a cube as "a square with lines" (Fine et al., 2003, p. 915), adding "It was really weird to have a three-dimensional sense of something on a flat surface, because it was such a foreign experience to someone dominated by a tactile ability," (Associated Press, 2003).

Cases in which people's vision was restored in adulthood sheds light on the development of the visual system. Their non-normative adult sight makes it clear that a species-typical visual experience early in life is necessary for the development of the visual system. In May's case, where he had sight before the age of 3½, we can learn something valuable about the critical periods of different components of the visual system, which will be discussed later in this chapter.

Chapter Outline

- The Function of Perception: Adaptive Behaviour
- Early Competencies and Interests
- Prenatal Perceptual Development
- Postnatal Perceptual Development
- Intermodal Perception
- Constancies
- The Nobel Prize-Winning Work of Hubel and Wiesel: Experience-Expectant Development
- Visual Deprivation and Development in Humans
- Associationist Accounts of Visual Development

- In this chapter you will read about instinct blindness. This is a relevant concept throughout the book. Instinct blindness is one's inability to appreciate the complexity of one's own psychological processes or indeed to appreciate that one's own psychological processes are doing anything at all. Of course, this "blindness" is by design.

- You will learn about the constancies in the visual system, especially size, shape, brightness, and colour: tricks that the visual system uses to make similar objects appear dissimilar, even under different viewing conditions. You will learn about procedures used to test constancies in infants and about evidence that infants employ such constancies in their visual systems.

- You will explore what is known about perception during development: prenatally, postnatally, and through childhood. You will read about perception via each of the senses as well as the development of intermodal perception. You will also read about innovative research

that reveals developing perceptual skills, including prenatal perception and learning.

- Next you will read about sight restoration in adults. You will read about individual case studies and the limits to the success that sight restoration has had. You will be encouraged to think about what these experiences reveal about perceptual development and to think about the importance of visual input during critical periods.

- You will review experimental work regarding critical periods in visual development. You will learn about the Nobel Prize-winning work of David Hubel and Torsten Wiesel as they discovered specific relationships between visual inputs and visual development in cats. You will read about "natural experiments" in people who have been deprived of visual input early in development. And you will read about the discovery of "sleeper effects," which are changes to development that can only be measured some time after the critical period for exposure.

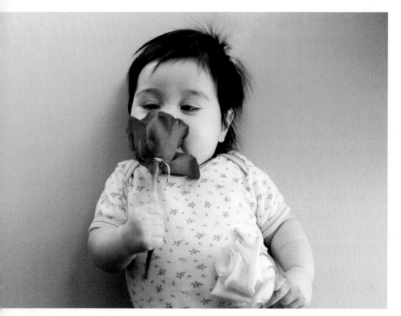

The Function of Perception: Adaptive Behaviour

In this chapter we will explore the development of the senses. We will look at the prenatal and postnatal development of the senses and the relationship between development and the stimuli available in species-typical environments. But first, our exploration of the topic will be more focussed if we are clear about what the function of perception is.

To start, let us consider what the function of perception is not. A traditional view of the function of perception might be that it enables us to see the world as it really is. In this view, we use our senses to passively absorb the truth about our surroundings. Indeed, this view is at the core of the empiricist view of the acquisition of knowledge wherein we know things because we have seen or experienced them. Even some modern thinkers in cognitive science hold to this intuitively appealing view: Jerry Fodor states, "What the perceptual system must do is to so represent the world as to make it accessible to thought" (Fodor, 1983, p. 40).

Another proposed function of perception, sometimes advocated by poets and theologians, is that it allows us to appreciate all that is spectacular in the world. But the function of perception is not simply to let us see and hear beautiful and spectacular things. It is not for our pleasure that we have sensation and perception. Indeed, pain, burning, and bitter tastes are very functional and adaptive and not at all fun to experience. These unpleasant sensations allow us to avoid dangerous and poisonous hazards; without them we would be in great peril.

figure 5.1 Hearing range of various animals

Different animals hear different pitch ranges. Each animal has a hearing range that includes that species's voice range. There is no reason to perceive everything, just the things that help each animal make functional decisions.

The function of perception is to allow us to behave sensibly in the world with respect to our survival and our reproductive interests. Notice that we do not have to know everything about the world; we do not have to know the "truth"; we do not have to have knowledge for the sake of knowledge. We derive a benefit from perceiving those cues in the world that inform our decisions, information that changes our behaviour in one way or another. For this reason, different species are sensitive to different kinds of information in the environment; they need and can make use of this information depending upon the adaptive problems that they have to solve. Sense organs have a cost: There is a cost to build them as well as a metabolic cost to operate them and process the information they generate. The benefit of having access to that type of information must outweigh the costs in order for any particular kind of perceptual sensitivity to evolve. For example, generally speaking, larger animals are able to hear sounds that are lower in frequency, and smaller animals are able to hear sounds that are higher in frequency because those are the sounds, respectively, that are likely to be relevant and that inform decisions about what behaviours to engage in.

Different animals have different perceptual ranges. Bats can hear things we cannot, and this serves an adaptive function. Some cave-dwelling fish develop without eyes because the cost of developing eyes outweighs the benefits.

5.1 **Press Pause**

The function of perception is to allow us to behave sensibly in the world with respect to survival and reproductive interests.

Here are a couple of examples that illustrate that the function of perception is adaptive behaviour rather than knowledge. First, there is a disconnect between people's ability to judge distance correctly when you ask them to report a distance and when you ask them to walk it blindfolded. Ask people how far away a landmark is, and their guess is typically inaccurate. Jack Loomis and his colleagues realized that this was not the only way to measure whether or not the brain was representing distance accurately and that guessing distance visually was probably not what our perceptual system was designed to do. They blindfolded participants and asked them to walk to a landmark. The accuracy of the subjects' guesses, as measured by their walking accuracy rather than explicit reporting, was much improved (Loomis, Da Silva, Fujita, & Fukusima, 1992).

Second, there is evidence that physical fatigue affects people's perception of the slope of a hill, an estimative task that one might think of as a simple perceptual skill. In multiple trials using differently sloped hills, experimenters asked participants to estimate the steepness of a slope before and after performing physical activities that led to fatigue. When fatigued, participants judged the hills to be steeper than they were. Researchers also showed that people judge hills as steeper if they are in poorer physical condition or are older than other participants (Bhalla & Proffitt, 1999; Proffitt, Bhalla, Gossweiler, & Midgett, 1995). Our perceptual systems are not designed to see the truth about the world but are instead designed to help us produce adaptive behaviours.

INSTINCT BLINDNESS

It is hard, if not impossible, for people to recognize the complexity of their own psychological processes. Nowhere is this phenomenon more evident than when we use our perceptions. It is difficult to appreciate how our perceptions are formed by our species-typical perceptual systems and that they are not just "given" to us. Like a fish oblivious to water, we have no access to what our perceptual systems are doing when

figure 5.2   The function of perception

Although people find it very difficult to verbally report the distance to an object in a darkened room, they can accurately point to or walk to that object in the dark. The function of perception is to allow us to behave adaptively, not to know or to be able to report the truth about the world. (Based on Loomis et al., 1992. Figure courtesy of Dave Munger, http://scienceblogs.com/cognitivedaily.)

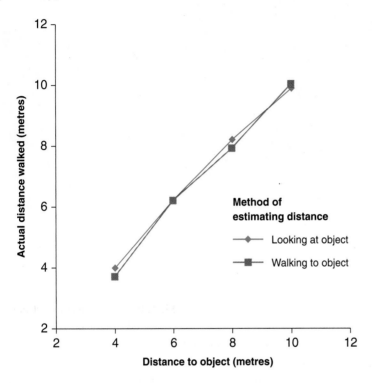

we see an object, feel a surface, or hear a noise. We simply have a strong sense that we are perceiving something that is really there, whether we perceive a solid object, a face, an emotion, an animate movement, or the colour blue. **Instinct blindness** is our inability to appreciate the complexity of our mental processes because they seem automatic and inevitable to us.

Let us take vision as an example. It seems as though we open our eyes and see the world as it really is. In one sense, this is true, but in another sense, this masks a dramatically complex set of processes that are well designed to allow us to perceive what is most useful for us to perceive. Legend has it that in the 1960s, renowned cognitive scientist Marv Minsky assigned a student a summer project that involved making a machine see colours (Hulbert & Poggio, 1988). In fact, colour vision is such a difficult and intricate problem that, five decades later, a computer that can see colours has still not been created. This story, whether true or not, illustrates that because colour vision happens so easily and automatically when we open our eyes, we are blind to the complexities of the problem of colour vision.

instinct blindness Our inability to appreciate the complexity of our mental processes because they seem automatic and inevitable to us.

5.2   Press Pause

Instinct blindness makes it hard to appreciate perception and hence the complexity of the adaptations underlying vision.

Some research suggests that people will judge hills to be steeper if they are fatigued, in poor physical condition, or elderly. Our perceptual systems are not designed to see the truth about how steep a hill is but rather to help us make decisions that promote survival.

AESTHETICS AND INTEREST

The information that our brain is exposed to by virtue of our visual system is constructed by specialized psychological mechanisms, stored and processed by other psychological mechanisms, and used by yet other specialized psychological mechanisms to produce behaviour that increases survival and ultimately reproductive success.

That which is interesting or that which is beautiful is not determined by the world, but by our minds. That is to say, things that are inherently beautiful or inherently interesting do not exist. To a dung beetle, the most beautiful thing in the world is dung. Beauty is truly in the eyes of the beholder. Things are beautiful because our visual system is designed to perceive them as beautiful and that, in turn, is because our attraction to them increases our reproductive success. For example, flowers are beautiful to us, and flowers in a natural environment (excluding flowers that have resulted from artificial selection) indicate the presence of a fertile, literally fruitful environment and portend the coming of a rich food source: fruit. A human face is more interesting to us than other objects in a room because that face conveys information that may be important to our social standing. The function of vision is not just to see for the sake of seeing, or to see things because they are interesting or beautiful, but vision, like the other senses, is ultimately a means of increasing reproductive success.

It is difficult to overstate how much our brain and our visual system construct the things that we see. We open our eyes and see objects easily and automatically. But figuring out what an object is is not the product of a blank slate. The ability to meaningfully process visual information does not come for free, but requires computation. Our visual system is designed to parse the visual scene into objects and has a number of built-in strategies that allow for this possibility.

One example that may help you to understand that our mind constructs the things that we see is motion pictures. There is a scene in the movie *An Education* that shows the main character running down a street in London. When you watch the movie, you clearly perceive motion: The character is running fast. But there is actually no motion happening in front of you. When a motion picture is shown, a still image is displayed onscreen for a fraction of a second and is quickly replaced by another still image in

Did you see Carey Mulligan racing down the street in *An Education*? When you watch a movie, your brain perceives motion even though there are only a series of still photographs displayed on the screen.

which objects appear at a slightly different location. Then that image is also replaced, and so on and so on. There is never anything in front of you but a still image, and yet your perceptual system perceives motion because that is what your visual system constructs.

5.3   Press Pause

Our brain and visual system construct the things we see.

Early Competencies and Interests

A significant challenge to the developing organism is that the vast amount of potential information available in the environment would all be useless without some type of information-selection process. Earlier we mentioned that different species are capable of perceiving a different subset of cues in the world, dependent on whether the benefit of that perception outweighs the cost. Likewise, a developing child will have specific visual and auditory interests and will be interested in perceiving high-value stimuli. Whether one considers visual stimuli, auditory stimuli, or tactile stimuli, for example, there is a constant torrent of information and sensations that each developing organism is exposed to, what William James famously referred to as a "blooming, buzzing confusion" (James, 1891).

How is the developing infant to make sense of this overwhelming barrage of stimuli? He or she must have specialized mechanisms to orient to, interface with, and exploit the regularities and potential observations in the environment. It is not just that there are more possible objects and events than one can process but indeed that what counts as an object or an event is not determined in the environment but is in large part a product of the mind (Baldwin, Baird, Saylor, & Clark, 2001). Because of this information overload, and because of the complexity of the biological system, the interactionist story demands

Infants look at face-like images longer than they look at scrambled facial features or other images. An infant's interests are adaptive: Very young infants will orient to social information, allowing them to observe just what they need to learn about the world.

that the developing organism have a mechanism that orients to developmentally relevant (and not superfluous) regularities in the environment. Orienting devices are necessary to allow the system to attend to, select, and use developmentally relevant information. Infants prefer to look at social information, including faces.

We know that children are interested in faces as early as 2 months of age because they look at face-like images longer than they look at scrambled facial features or blank images (Goren, Sarty, & Wu, 1975; Morton & Johnson, 1991). When looking at a face, infants are particularly interested in eyes (Maurer, 1985). Another sign that infants prefer social stimuli is the preference for direct gaze over averted gaze, which is evident even in newborns (Farroni, Johnson, Brockbank, & Simion, 2000; Hains & Muir, 1996; Vecera & Johnson, 1995).

Very young children pay attention to the direction of others' eyes. Hood, Willen, and Driver (1998) showed that infants as young as 3 months old shift their gaze in the direction of an adult's eye gaze. Other researchers have shown that at 6 months old, infants begin to look in the direction of an adult's eye gaze if they can see both the adult's eyes and head turning and if the object of interest is already within their visual field (Moore & Corkum, 1998; Phillips, Baron-Cohen, & Rutter, 1992).

The scan path that infants follow when looking at a face develops over the first few months of life. In an early study of infant scan paths, researchers projected the image of a face onto a one-way mirror in order to observe infants while they looked at the face. Results showed that a 1-month-old spent more time looking at the outline of the face while a 2-month-old looked more at the internal details of the face (Maurer & Salapatek, 1976). These days, researchers have eye-tracking equipment that allows them to record what an infant is looking at based on the reflectance of the cornea. Other research confirms that when looking at a complex object such as a human face, infants develop from an immature pattern of focussing only on the outer contour to looking at both the outer contour and the inner details (Haith, Bergman, & Moore, 1977; Salapatek & Kessen, 1966).

This precocious interest in social stimuli is thought to be adaptive. Not only will it allow infants to attend to the social inputs needed for social development, but following others' eye gazes and attending to objects that are of interest to others will lead to learning about non-social objects that are of interest to people. This may sound insignificant, but remember the huge number of possibilities that could attract the infant's interest instead.

| figure | 5.3 | **Scanning and tracking** |

An early scan-path experiment showed that the part of the face that infants look at develops between one and two months of age. A 1-month-old (a) looked more at the outline while a 2-month-old (b) inspected the internal features more. (Adapted from Maurer and Salapatek, 1976.)

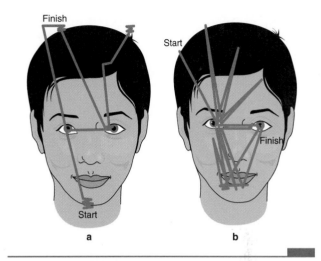

a   b

5.4   Press Pause

An infant's interests are adaptive: Very young infants will orient to social information allowing them to observe just what they need to learn about the world.

Prenatal Perceptual Development

Learning does not start at the moment of birth: Plenty of learning takes place prenatally. Life in the womb is not simply existence in a silent, dark chamber with no impinging sensations. There are sounds and tastes in the uterus, including the sound of mother's voice and the tastes of the foods she eats. Infants experience and learn tastes and sounds prenatally.

VISION

Vision is the most altricial (least developed) of the senses at birth. There is probably not a lot of visual sensation in utero since the interior of the uterus is largely dark and the infant's visual system is quite undeveloped, as described below. Likely, the only visual perception is of undefined lightness during the day, contrasted with increased or complete darkness at night.

HEARING

Can a fetus hear prenatally? In order for prenatal infants to be able to hear, two things would have to be true. First, the auditory system would have to be sufficiently well developed, and second, there would have to be sounds that could travel through the mother's tissues and arrive at the fetus's auditory system. In fact, researchers have been able to record sounds within the uteruses of pregnant women, and we now know that

figure 5.4 How do you ask an infant what he likes to hear?

By placing an electrode in an artificial nipple and rewarding newborn babies' sucking behaviours with a recording of their mothers' voices, researchers determined that newborn babies like to hear the voices of their mothers over the voices of strangers.

with the extreme distension of an abdomen at full-term pregnancy, ambient sounds, including the mother's voice, pass into the uterus pretty clearly (Querleu & Renard, 1981). We also now know that infants can hear other people's voices prenatally (e.g., mom talking to others and others talking to mom) as well as sounds that are internal to the mother, such as her heartbeat and sounds from her digestive system.

How would you ask a baby whether he heard his mother's voice in utero? DeCasper and Fifer devised a clever experiment based on newborn babies' sucking behaviours to find out if they preferred their own mothers' voices over those of strangers, thus showing evidence that they had been able to hear their mothers' voices before they were born. DeCasper and Fifer put a recording device inside an artificial nipple so that they could record the baby's sucking and present stimuli based on the infant's behaviour. When infants suck on a nipple, the sucking is not constant but occurs in bursts that last several seconds followed by a rest period. Newborns were rewarded by getting to hear their mothers' voices (or a stranger's voice) through headphones if they increased their rest period between sucking (in another condition, newborns were rewarded if they decreased their rest period between sucking). Newborns in the first condition came to rest longer between sucking bursts, and those in the second condition came to take shorter rest periods. They were motivated to hear their mothers' voices but not the voice of an unknown woman (DeCasper & Fifer, 1980).

In a later experiment, DeCasper and Spence tested more directly whether auditory experiences before birth could affect preferences after birth. They gave mothers who were seven months pregnant a story to read out loud twice per day until the baby was born. Using the same sucking paradigm, whereby they could train a newborn to rest for longer or shorter periods between sucking bursts, DeCasper and Spence showed that newborns preferred to hear the story that was read to them in utero than hear an unfamiliar story that was similar in length and complexity. In fact, newborns preferred to hear the familiar story even if it was read by a stranger than to hear the unfamiliar story read by their own mothers (DeCasper & Spence, 1986). This was pretty convincing evidence that postnatal preferences could be affected by prenatal experiences. The authors noted that "the most reasonable conclusion is that the target stories were . . . preferred, because the infants had heard them before birth" (p. 143).

INNOVATIVE
RESEARCH METHOD

These results received widespread attention in academia and in the media, and people found them fascinating. Why were these results so attention-getting? First, they showed clearly and dramatically that learning does take place prenatally. An infant need not wait until the moment of birth to begin learning about the world. This makes the learned vs. innate dichotomy unnecessary.

Even more interesting, this study underlines the fact that there is always an "environment" that serves as the context for development, meaning (a) "the environment" does not only exist after the moment of birth, so it is senseless to juxtapose things that are influenced by the environment and things that develop before birth, and (b) we do not always know what elements of the environment might be factors in development, so experiments that demonstrate that some particular cue is not influential in the development of a trait cannot be taken to mean that there is no environmental influence on the development of that trait. All development happens in one type of environment or another.

5.5 Press Pause

Infants hear in utero, and they learn what they hear. Newborns would rather listen to a story that was read to them in utero than listen to an unfamiliar, yet similar, story.

⠿ Culture and Community

Mosquito Tones

Most of what you have read in this book so far deals with early development: how infants develop into functioning children and then into functioning adults. Researchers who study lifespan development are interested in continuing maturational changes into adulthood and then into old age, including senescent decline. One developmental change that happens rather reliably is the change in auditory perception (Robinson & Sutton, 1979). Starting at the age of 18, people will gradually lose their ability to hear the highest pitches. Eighteen-year-olds can hear a 20-kilohertz pitch, whereas a 24-year-old cannot. A 24-year-old can hear a 17-kilohertz pitch, but a 30-year-old cannot. As people age, their ability to hear higher-pitched sounds decreases at a fairly predictable rate, eventually making speech perception difficult.

This gradual and normal hearing loss is due, in large part, to changes that take place deep within the inner ear in a section called the *cochlea*. Inside the cochlea, tiny hair cells are sensitive to the changes in pressure that occur when sounds enter the ear, and they relay this signal onto nerve cells. Age-related deterioration happens when hair cells are lost, when nerve cells are lost, and when connections between hair and nerve cells are lost.

Some people have taken advantage of this age-dependant hearing ability to discourage loitering. A device called a *mosquito alarm* is available to shop owners who feel that teens or young adults are intimidating paying customers by spending time in front of their shops. The device emits a loud noise (108 decibels) at a frequency of 17.4 kilohertz. Sounds of this pitch can typically only be heard by people 24 years of age or younger. This frequency is sufficiently loud enough to repel young people but goes completely undetected by customers who are 25 years of age or older.

A man named Howard Stapleton invented the mosquito alarm in 2005 after his daughter was harassed outside of a store by a group of loitering youths. Stapleton remembered that when he was a child he was irritated by the noise from a nearby factory that no one else could hear. He used his own children as subjects in order to determine what frequency would be necessary to repel young people while not annoying adults.

But young people are clever and have a tendency to be competent with respect to technology. Young people are now downloading mosquito ringtones to their cellphones. Teens and young adults may find themselves in situations where they wish to use cellphones but adult authority figures have forbidden cellphone use. Mosquito ringtones, which are high in frequency, can be heard by younger people but not by older people. Given that the decline in high-frequency hearing happens gradually and predictably, a variety of ringtones are available, so people between the ages of 18 and 30 can exclude anyone older than they are from hearing their phones ring.

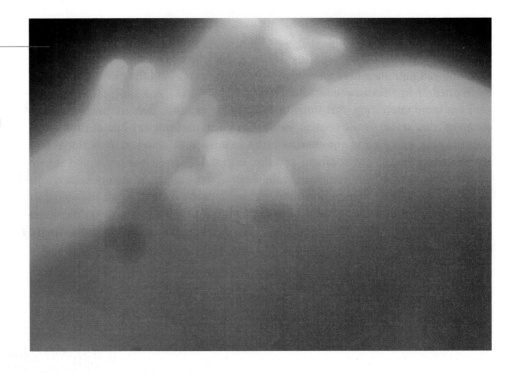

The fetus has perceptual experiences in utero. It is believed that the fetus can feel things. The developing fetus will suck its thumb and grasp the umbilical cord.

Pregnant women were asked to drink carrot juice four days a week for three weeks at the end of their pregnancies. When tested months after birth, infants exposed to carrot juice prenatally preferred carrot juice to water, clearly demonstrating that a fetus can taste and learn a taste.

Since these early experiments, we have learned that the baby hears the mother's intonation and stress patterns, even if the baby is prelinguistic and cannot decipher any words. We know this because before birth, the fetus's heart rate changes, indicating interest, when the mother starts to speak (Fifer & Moon, 1995). Also before birth, the fetus's movement patterns can change in response to other external noises (Kisilevsky, Fearon, & Muir, 1998; Lecanuet, Granier-Deferre, & Busnel, 1995; Zimmer, Chao, Guy, Marks, & Fifer, 1993).

TOUCH

A fetus can and does touch things and feel things that it touches. The developing fetus has a fairly well-developed sense of touch. We infer this, for example, from observing that a fetus can grasp the umbilical cord in utero and suck its thumb.

TASTE

There is clear evidence that a fetus has a sense of taste. A fetus will swallow the amniotic fluid that it lives in and that fluid carries flavours and tastes, including the flavours of the food that the mother has recently eaten. In fact, the very earliest evidence that a fetus can taste came when a clever clinician used a fetus's preference for sweet flavours for a therapeutic advantage: If a pregnant mother is carrying too much amniotic fluid in the amniotic sac, sweetening the amniotic fluid (e.g., with saccharin) will cause the baby to drink more of the fluid than he would if the fluid is not sweetened. The excess fluid then leaves the amniotic sac (and the fetus) via the umbilical cord. We know that the excreted fluid was the sweetened amniotic fluid because the physician injected a dye into the amniotic fluid as well and the mother's urine came out coloured with the dye. A control group was injected with only the dye and not with the sweetener, and their urine was not as deeply coloured by the dye (as cited in Liley, 1972).

Further and more contemporary evidence that a fetus can perceive tastes reveals that long-lasting preferences follow prenatal exposure to tastes. In preparation for this experiment, pregnant women were recruited. Those in the experimental group were asked to drink carrot juice four days a week for three weeks toward the end of their pregnancies when the fetus was fairly well developed, while those in the control group drank the same amount of water instead. When the infants were tested (four weeks after they were first introduced to solid food), they were fed cereal prepared with carrot juice in some sessions and cereal prepared with water in other sessions. Infants in the group who had been exposed to carrot juice prenatally, but not postnatally, enjoyed the carrot cereal more than the water cereal and showed fewer negative facial expressions to the carrot cereal compared to the water cereal. The same was not true of the infants in the control group (Mennella, Jagnow, & Beauchamp, 2001).

INNOVATIVE
RESEARCH METHOD

SMELL

It is likely that the fetus can also smell foods that the mother has ingested. We know that the amniotic fluid will smell like the foods that the mother has just eaten, particularly if the foods are flavourful. And we know that while the baby breathes (as fetuses do), the amniotic fluid comes into contact with the odour receptors (Schaal, Orgeur, & Rognon, 1995), so even though the fetus does not breathe air, he is probably experiencing smell.

Postnatal Perceptual Development

Each of the five senses develops postnatally and throughout infancy. There is even some evidence of early perception in newborns. Let us consider each sense in turn.

VISION

Vision develops quickly over the first six months of an infant's life (Kellman & Banks, 1998). At birth, neither the visual systems in the brain (the occipital cortex) nor the eye are completely developed. Even the eye movements are immature: The eyes of an infant trying to follow a moving object are slow and inaccurate (Aslin, 1993).

Acuity

A newborn baby has a very underdeveloped visual acuity of around 20/600 (Courage & Adams, 1990) meaning, roughly, that the newborn can see at 20 feet what a normal adult can see at 600 feet. At birth, the lens of the eye is inflexible so the baby cannot change its focus; objects that are in focus are those at 20 cm from the eye (Haynes, White, & Held, 1965), which is the distance that the mother's face will be from the baby's face when she breastfeeds. And unlike adults who have finer acuity for closer objects (and see farther objects as blurry), infants display similar acuity across a wider range of distances (Banks, 1980). The newborn does not see fine detail but broad patterns. A newborn's *fovea* (the central part of the retina that is dense in photoreceptors) is not fully developed, which makes inspection of fine detail impossible.

Visual acuity is better at 2 months of age but still much less clear than adult vision. The development of the visual cortex between the ages of 2 and 3 months is dramatic, resulting in great improvements in the baby's vision. At 3 months of age, however, the baby still does not have depth perception and still has not honed the skill of focussing. By 6 months of age, the baby can focus on objects at different distances. A six-month-old has a visual acuity of about 20/40; he can see at 20 feet what a normal adult can see at 40 feet (Aslin & Lathrop, 2008); motion detection is getting better, but acuity is still not adult-like. Acuity reaches adult levels around the age of 5 or even older (Leat, Yadav, & Irving, 2009), and contrast sensitivity and peripheral vision reach adult levels at around the age of 8 or older (Leat et al., 2009).

INNOVATIVE RESEARCH METHOD

The baby will orient to larger things he can see over smaller things. For example, he will look at a checkerboard made of larger squares longer than at a checkerboard made of smaller squares even if the two are held at the same distance, presumably because the larger squares are visible to him, whereas the smaller checkerboard appears to be a uniform grey field. This visual preference allows researchers to test infant acuity. In young infants, visual acuity has classically been tested using Teller acuity cards. In this procedure, an experimenter stands behind a wall and watches the infant as the infant is presented with two side-by-side cards. One card shows black and white bars (either horizontal or vertical) and the other is solid grey. The cards are presented in an order that is unknown to the experimenter, so that he or she does not know at any time what the infant is seeing. The experimenter's task is to say whether the infant has a preference between one of the two cards. If the infant does show a preference, this is evidence that the infant can discriminate between the two cards. By presenting bars of different widths, one can test the infant's acuity: The wide bars will be easy to see, and the infant will prefer these bars over the grey card; the narrow bars will be more difficult to distinguish from the grey card and the infant will show no preference (Teller, McDonald, Preston, Sebris, & Dobson, 1986). Naturally, modern researchers will use computerized presentations and recordings in the laboratory, but they still follow the logic developed by Davida Teller.

There are several reasons that a newborn does not have adult-like vision: The visual part of the infant brain (called the *occipital cortex*) is still developing after birth, and the muscles that allow the lens to focus have not yet developed (Banks & Bennett, 1988). Cells in the visual cortex have not yet myelinated and have not yet specialized to the type of visual stimuli they will be most responsive to in adulthood. As we will soon read, visual experience is necessary for this development to occur.

In the Teller acuity procedure, the infant is presented with two side-by-side cards: one with black and white bars and one that is solid grey. If the infant shows a preference, this is evidence that he can discriminate between the two cards. By presenting bars of different widths, one can test the infant's acuity.

Colour perception

A newborn does not have adult-like colour vision. While newborns' lightness perception is relatively mature, allowing them to see black and white, their colour vision (specifically the opponent-level organization (Johnson, Williams, Cusato, & Reese, 1999) is not well developed. Infants are born with some ability to discriminate between colours, but this ability is primitive and develops over time.

Newborns do not make the range of discriminations that adults do (Adams, 1989), but babies do prefer to look at coloured objects, which has allowed Russell Adams and Mary Courage at Memorial University of Newfoundland to test a newborn's ability to make colour discriminations. Adams and Courage discovered that newborns can discriminate between green and red and between green and white or red and white, but they do not seem to be able to make more subtle colour discriminations (Adams & Courage, 1998).

Why can newborns discriminate between only red and green, whereas 4-month-olds have nearly adult-like colour vision? It is because colour vision involves three different kinds of photoreceptors, or cones, and they mature at different rates. The photoreceptors that are maximally sensitive to red and to green mature early and are apparently functional at birth, whereas cones that are maximally sensitive to blue mature to functionality by 3 or 4 months of age (Suttle, Banks, & Graf, 2002).

If you have an opportunity to shop for a gift for a newborn, notice how many gifts are high-contrast black and white toys, designed to fit well with the newborn's visual abilities. By 2 months of age, infants' colour vision has developed enough that they can see bright colours including blue, red, and green. At 3 months, colour vision is quite adult-like. At 4 months of age, infant colour vision is mostly, though not completely, adult-like (Teller & Bornstein, 1987). A 4-month-old prefers to look at saturated colours, like a royal blue over a pale blue (Bornstein, 1975), just like adults do. Still, colour vision continues to develop into early childhood (Ling & Dain, 2008).

Human colour perception evolved in our terrestrial environment, and evidence shows that it evolved in the spectrum of sunlight that we see today. As mentioned earlier, our colour perception is colour constant (the visual system is able to perceive the same object as having roughly the same colour) across differences in natural terrestrial light but not across artificial light. The colours that humans see are, among others, those that would have benefitted our ancestors most in their search for berries among green foliage (Mollon, 1996). Red and green are seen as very different from each other but are common percepts of light that are quite similar in wavelength. In contrast, blue is seen when light of a very different wavelength hits the retina. Why are red and green seen as so different when they are so physically similar? One cannot be sure, but it is convenient since red berries on a background of green leaves would be striking to a visual system built like this.

The development of depth perception

The development of depth perception in infants has been assessed using what is called the *visual cliff* paradigm. The visual cliff is a large box-like apparatus. The top of the box is made of see-through glass. Under one half of this glass is a red and white checkerboard that lies just below the glass surface (the shallow side), and under the other half, the same red and white checkerboard lies several feet below the surface (the deep side).

In a classic visual cliff paradigm study (Gibson & Walk, 1960), infants were placed on the shallow side of the visual cliff and were observed as their mothers stood at the far end and tried to call them over to the deep side. Results showed that the 6- to 14-month-old babies hesitated, showing fear, when they reached the line between the

The visual cliff. If an infant hesitates to crawl onto the deep side of the visual cliff, we infer that he has depth perception.

shallow and deep sides (Walk & Gibson, 1961). From this behaviour, it is possible to infer that these crawling infants, some as young as 6 months old, perceived the difference in depth.

From there, the story gets even more interesting. It turns out that whether or not children show evidence of fear (by avoiding the deep side) is associated with their experience with self-propelled locomotion. Among infants of the same age, those infants with more experience with self-propelled motion are more likely to show fear of the deep side and thus show evidence of depth perception (Bertenthal, Campos, & Barrett, 1984; Bertenthal, Campos, & Kermoian, 1994).

The idea that self-propelled locomotion is a factor in the development of depth perception is supported by evidence from research with kittens from several decades ago. In this experiment, kittens of the same age were put in groups of two. The kittens were kept in a completely dark room except for training periods so that the experimenter could control any pairing between visual information and movement. During training, one kitten (in the normal visual-motor experience condition) wore a harness and moved about unimpeded in a brightly lit and visually interesting room while yoked to his counterpart (dissociated visual-motor condition), who moved about in a gondola and whose movement was controlled by the self-propelled kitten. Both kittens had motor experience in the darkened room but only the kitten in the normal visual-motor condition had visual experience that was coordinated with his own self-propelled motion. Those kittens that did not have the opportunity to actively explore the room showed abnormal behaviour. The kittens in the passive condition also failed to reach out a paw when being lowered to a horizontal surface and failed to blink when an object was brought right up to their faces. The authors concluded that active visual exploration was necessary for the development of the coordination between visual input and behaviour (Held & Hein, 1963).

Research with humans also reveals that depth-perception development is associated with self-propelled locomotion. In one study, 8½-month-olds were assigned membership into one of three groups: pre-locomotive (those infants who were not yet crawling), locomotive (those who were crawling), and pre-locomotive but with locomotive experience (children who had been using a walker but not yet crawling). Those who had experienced self-propelled motion, whether crawling or in a walker, performed better at object-retrieval tasks that required depth judgments (Kermoian & Campos, 1988). Together, these studies on the relationship between self-propelled movement and depth perception underline the point that when investigating the effects of experience on development, one does not always know ahead of time what kinds of experience may be relevant.

However, asking a baby to crawl over the visual cliff is not the only way to test for depth perception in infants. Infants as young as 1 month old blink when objects approach their face, indicating that they have detected a change in distance (Yonas, 1981). In addition, when you place a 2-month-old baby on the deep side of the visual cliff, his heart rate decreases (which is interpreted as a sign of interest), whereas this is not the case if you place the baby on the shallow side of the visual cliff (Bertenthal & Campos, 1990).

How does this early evidence of depth perception fit with the above evidence that pre-mobile infants do not show fear of the deep side of the visual cliff? Perhaps depth perception develops very early, but the fear of falling, or the use of depth as a cue to danger, develops relatively later. Consistent with this is the finding that 12-month-olds will cross the deep side if their parents are encouraging them and smiling but not if the parent's face shows fear (Sorce, Emde, Campos, & Klinnert, 1985).

5.6 Press Pause

The visual cliff was first used to show that babies as young as 6 months have depth perception. Recently, heart rate and blink responses have also been used to show depth perception at 1 month.

The development of motion perception

A study by Johnson and colleagues shows clear evidence that newborns detect motion and can even track a moving object (Johnson, Dziurawiec, Ellis, & Morton, 1991). Indeed, newborns show a visual preference for moving objects over static objects (Slater, 1989). That said, it is not until around 2 or nearly 3 months of age that an infant can smoothly move his eyes in order to track a moving object (Aslin, 1981). Before that, the infant tries to keep objects in sight by jerkily following them with his eyes. Infants between the ages of 2 and 5 months will orient toward the moving object in an otherwise static visual field (Dannemiller, 2000). At 3 months of age, an infant can extract enough information from movement to discriminate between a display showing a human-shaped point-light walker and an unstructured display of lights moving at equivalent velocity (Bertenthal, 1993). An infant as young as 3 months old expects an object to continue on its current trajectory: If an object in left to right motion disappears behind a screen, the infant looks not where it disappeared but toward the right, showing that she anticipates its reappearance upon the same trajectory (Haith, 1991; Haith, Wentworth, & Canfield, 1993).

HEARING

An infant's auditory system is fairly well developed right from the start (Trehub & Schellenberg, 1995). A newborn can hear a variety of sounds and prefers to listen to voices over pure tones (Bench, Collyer, Mentz, & Wilson, 1976). The newborn's hearing, however, is not as sensitive as the adult's: The quietest sound a newborn can hear is 4 times as intense as the quietest sound an adult can hear (Maurer & Maurer, 1998). Infants are less able than adults to hear very low-pitched sounds and are better at hearing high-pitched sounds (Aslin, Jusczyk, & Pisoni, 1998).

Infants can hear and discriminate among a variety of sounds but may be particularly adept at discriminating human speech sounds. Think about the sophistication of the adaptations necessary to discriminate between speech sounds, especially when sounds that are equally different physically are not so easily discriminated. Again we see evidence of functional specialization. We will talk more about the early discrimination of speech sounds in Chapter 9.

TOUCH

The sense of touch is well developed at the moment of birth and develops earliest around the mouth, the palms of the hands, and the soles of the feet (Humphrey, 1978). Some of the early reflexes that newborns show reliably are responses to touch. Just stroking a newborn on the cheek near the mouth leads to the "rooting" reflex, wherein the infant turns toward the source of touch. Placing a finger or similarly shaped object in the infant's mouth leads reflexively to sucking. Placing a finger in the infant's hand will cause him to grasp the finger tightly. And stroking the sole of the newborn's feet will cause him to fan out his toes and twist his foot, a reaction called the Babinski reflex. Newborns also respond to temperature changes, especially temperatures that are colder than body temperature (Humphrey, 1978). Newborns respond to pain, too. Exposure to intense pain can have lasting effects. When tested between 4 and 6 months of age,

This baby is showing the rooting reflex. When touched on the cheek near the mouth, the newborn infant turns toward the stimulus. This reflex demonstrates a sense of touch and facilitates breastfeeding.

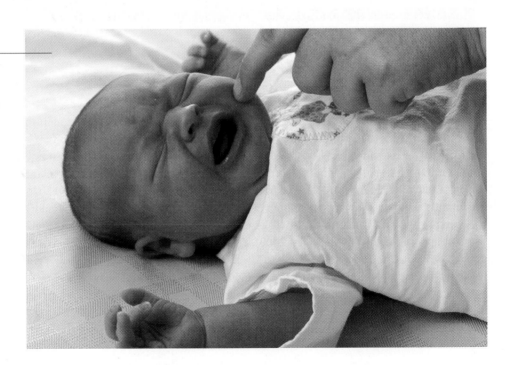

boys who had not been anaesthetized during circumcision showed a more intense pain response than boys who were anaesthetized during circumcision (Taddio, Katz, Ilersich, & Koren, 1997).

TASTE

Newborns prefer a sweet tasting liquid over water, using longer sucks with fewer pauses to consume the sweeter drink (Crook & Lipsitt, 1976). Infants respond to sweet tastes by relaxing their facial muscles and show adult-like facial expressions in response to sour and to bitter tastes (Steiner, 1979). At birth, infants are neutral toward salty tastes but come to like them by 4 months of age (Beauchamp, Cowart, Mennella, & Marsh, 1994). For this reason, they will be ready to expand their repertoire beyond breast milk when solid foods are introduced around the age of 6 months.

⠿ Developmental Milestones

Perceptual Development Milestones	
Age	**Skills**
At Birth	Interested in faces over other images Size constancy Slow and inaccurate eye movements Lightness perception well developed Can discriminate red and green but not more subtle colours Can detect motion Startle response to unexpected noise Prefers hearing mother's voice over that of a stranger's Prefers hearing a story they heard before birth over a different story Hears high-pitched sounds better than adults; low-pitched sounds worse than adults Likes sweet tastes Can discriminate smells; prefers human milk; likes the smell of bananas and chocolate Sense of touch well developed, especially around mouth, palms of hands, and bottoms of feet
1 Month	Looks mostly at the outline of faces
2 Months	Ocular dominance columns have developed Can see a variety of bright colours (blue, red, green, yellow) Shape constancy Brightness constancy (as long as the object is not too small)
3 Months	Looks mostly at the internal detail of faces Can see biological motion in a point-light walker Muscles needed to focus (by changing lens shape) are well developed Can track a moving object smoothly and accurately
4 Months	Adult-like colour vision Can discriminate more or less between saturated and unsaturated colours Colour constancy
6 Months	Visual acuity of 20/40 (can see at 20 feet what a normal adult can see at 40 feet) Consistently turns head toward direction of sound
9 Months	Depth perception develops along with self-locomotion
5 Years	Adult-like acuity

SMELL

Infants have a functioning sense of smell right from birth (Steiner, 1979) and can even discriminate between different smells. Research has shown that a newborn will relax her facial muscles in response to the smell of banana or chocolate and frown in response to the smell of rotten eggs (Steiner, 1979). She will also turn her head away from other unpleasant smells (Reiser, Yonas, & Wikner, 1976). Actually, newborns prefer the smell of human milk over all other smells (Marlier & Schaal, 2005), including the smell of amniotic fluid (Marlier, Schaal, & Soussignan, 1998). There is evidence that by the age of 4 days, breastfed infants prefer the smell of their own mothers' breast milk to that of a stranger's (Cernoch & Porter, 1985). Even a baby who is fed formula from a bottle will orient to the smell of a lactating woman over the smell of formula and over the smell of a non-lactating woman (Marlier & Schaal, 1997). Researchers also found that when placed between two breast pads, one pad from the infant's own mother and one from a stranger, infants turned reliably more frequently toward their mothers' pads by the sixth day after birth (but not the second) (Macfarlane, 1975). An infant will also turn her head toward the smell of her mother's amniotic fluid compared to a stranger's amniotic fluid (Marlier et al., 1998). When tested as early as two weeks of age, it was shown that babies also prefer the smell of their mothers in general over the smell of other women (Porter, Bologh, & Makin, 1988; Porter, Makin, Davis, & Christensen, 1992).

Intermodal Perception

Up to this point, we have talked about the development of perceptual skills within a modality, such as vision or hearing. However, we know that even from an early age infants are able to coordinate information that they perceive from multiple modalities. They may know that the pacifier they were just sucking on is the same one they are now looking at or that the drum they can see is the one they can also hear. This is called **intermodal perception**.

intermodal perception
The integration of percepts acquired via two or more modalities, or senses.

Piaget rejected the idea of intermodal perception. He thought the information from different modalities would be separate for at least the first several months after birth (Piaget, 1954). Evidence of intermodal perception is difficult to explain from a purely associationist perspective. Associationists would predict that once you have seen a pacifier you should be able to recognize it the next time you see it but not when you feel it. The discovery of intermodal perception strongly suggests that young infants possess internal representations of the objects and events that they experience.

The most obvious and simple demonstration of intermodal perception is a young baby turning toward a sound that they hear: They turn because they expect to see the object that they just heard. Multiple experiments also show that very young infants have intermodal perception. For example, if an experimenter allows an infant to suck on a pacifier without seeing it and then shows the infant two pacifiers side by side without letting him touch them, the baby will look longer at the pacifier that was just in his mouth. This is true even across trials as the experimenter counterbalances different shapes, so we know the infant is not just looking at the most visually interesting pacifier. This experimental design has revealed intermodal perception in 1-month-olds (Meltzoff & Borton, 1979) and in newborns (Kaye & Bower, 1994).

Constancies

If you look at a fly that is very close to you and look at a cow that is quite a distance away from you, the two objects might project a similarly sized image on your retina, but you have no trouble seeing them as differently sized objects. The difference is immediately apparent. Conversely, if you look at a sailboat sitting 10 feet from you on the shore and some time later see that same sailboat far out in the water, the proximal stimulus projected onto your retina is wildly different, yet you still perceive it as a full-sized sailboat. When you go shopping, a shirt that appears dark blue still looks dark, not light blue, when you bring it out of the store and into the bright sunlight despite the great difference in the illumination reaching your retina. Your visual system is capable of a great deal of size and colour constancy.

The constancies in the visual system reveal specialized functional designs. **Constancies** are strategies or heuristics used by the visual system so that a given object will appear to us as the same size, shape, brightness, or colour despite enormous differences in the characteristics of the image that actually falls on our retinas.

SIZE

Size constancy allows our visual system to see an object as the same size despite being viewed at radically different distances, and thus casting wildly different proximal images on the retina. A child standing next to you seems smaller than an adult standing a football field away in spite of casting a much larger image on the retina. Here is a demonstra-

constancy The perception of like objects as like (in terms of size, colour, lightness, and brightness) despite radically different projections on the retina.

Mechanisms in your mind let you see the man who is farther along the path as the same size as the person in the background, even though the retinal images are different and the person in the background only appears to be as tall as the near hiker's lower leg. The visual process that solves this problem is called *size constancy.*

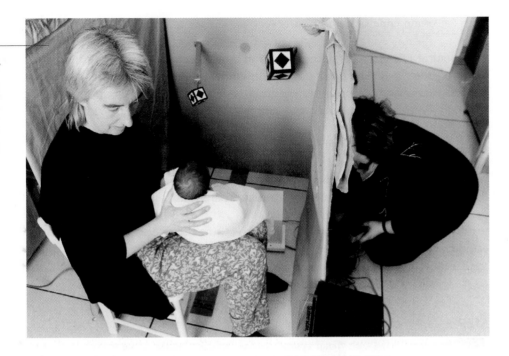

In this test of size constancy, an infant looks at two differently sized cubes that are placed so that they create the same size image on the retina. After habituation, the infant looks longer at the novel cube, indicating that even newborns have size constancy. Photo courtesy of Alan Slater, University of Exeter.

tion that you can do to test size constancy: Take a sheet of printer paper and tilt it so that one short end is about one foot from your eyes and the other short end is approximately two feet from your eyes. You know the two short ends are the same length: They are both 8½ inches. But they are casting different images on your retina, the far edge casting an image that is about 55 per cent as long as the image cast by the closer edge. What does it look like to you? Does it look like the two are the same size? Most people say no. Does it look like the closer edge is only 55 per cent longer? Most people say no. Most people say that the closer edge looks like it's about 90 or 95 per cent bigger than the far edge. This shows a lot of constancy (since it does not look like the closer edge is 55 per cent bigger than the far edge, which is the difference between the two retinal images), but it does not show perfect constancy (since it does not look like the far edge is the same size as the near edge, which it actually is). This is the case with most constancies: They are not perfect, but they are sufficient to allow us to perceive an object as the same across viewing conditions.

How would you test for size constancy in infants? Slater and colleagues used a habituation paradigm, involving two cubes, one twice as big as the other. During the habituation phase of the experiment, the infant saw only the small cube at various distances (although in another experiment, another infant would only see the large cube). Although the infant saw the small cube at a variety of distances, thus creating a variety of retinal images, she never saw the cube at the test distance. After habituation, the infant moved on to the test phase in which she saw the two cubes side by side, with the larger cube twice as far away such that the cubes projected identical retinal images. Infants now looked longer at the large cube, showing that they saw it as novel, as unlike the cube they had habituated to, even though at the test distance even the small cube projected a novel-sized retinal image. That newborns show evidence of size constancy at all (Slater, Mattock, & Brown, 1990) is remarkable.

SHAPE

Shape constancy is another example of a very complex adaptation in the visual system that is so automatic that we fail to marvel at it, or indeed to notice it. Imagine looking at an ice cream cone straight on. It is very easy to see it as an ice cream cone. Now imagine moving your head up (or the cone down) so that you see mostly a ball of ice cream with a little crescent of cone visible at the bottom. The image projected on the retina is radically different, but you have no problem still seeing the object as an ice cream cone and as the same shape. As objects in the world move and rotate with respect to your eye, the image projected onto the retina changes dramatically, but you (generally) have no problem seeing the object as the same. Can you think of a way to test for shape constancy in young infants?

In the 1960s, Bower designed an experiment to test size and shape constancy in infants. Two-month-old infants were conditioned to turn their heads to one stimulus that was presented repeatedly. Then they were shown a new stimulus that might vary from the original in terms of orientation, distance, size, or retinal size. Infants turned their head, as conditioned, if the object was the same shape and size as the original, even if orientation and distance (hence retinal size) changed, suggesting that the 2-month-old had size and shape constancy (Bower, 1966).

BRIGHTNESS

Our visual system has a remarkable ability to perceive an object as the same brightness across an incredible range of illuminations. A piece of coal in direct sunlight reflects far more light onto our retina than a white piece of paper does under interior lighting conditions, yet the coal still looks black and the paper looks white. Infants show evidence of brightness constancy as early as 7 weeks of age, as long as the object is not too small (Dannemiller, 1985).

COLOUR

Earlier in this chapter, you read that your mind creates the perceptions you see; your mind creates the motion in a motion picture. Another example of a percept that our mind generates is our perception of colour. It appears to us that the world has colours in it. We open our eyes and "see" that the grass is green and the sky is blue. But there is no such thing as green or blue except for the perception that is produced by our visual system. What is physically measurable is the wavelength of light that is reflected off of an object such as the grass or a tree branch or the particles that constitute the sky. There is a strong relationship between the wavelength that reaches our eye and the colour we perceive, but the colour is not determined by the wavelength. There is not a one-to-one relationship between wavelength and the colour we perceive. In the context of different illumination or of different contrasting surfaces, we can see vastly different wavelengths as the same colour. Our visual system is built to discount the illumination and see the grass as green even though the light that reaches our eyes will be very different when we view the grass by the morning sunrise compared to viewing it by the afternoon sun (Rutherford & Brainard, 2002).

Similar to brightness constancy, colour constancy refers to our ability to perceive an object as the same colour despite tremendous changes in the wavelength of light reflected from it. The range of wavelengths that reach the earth from the sun differ from sunrise to dusk, and the light reflected onto our retinas from objects therefore differs a great deal, but we still see objects as a constant colour, whether red or blue or green. Our colour constancy even works in some, but not all, artificial lighting situations. Colour constancy apparently develops

From the Classroom to the Lab

Animals of different species can discriminate between different colours; some hues that look the same to us are distinct for them, and vice versa. How would you test whether a non-human animal can discriminate between a pair of hues?

even later than brightness constancy; infants show evidence of colour constancy as early as 4 months of age (Dannemiller & Hanko, 1987).

Within the possible range of terrestrial light, our visual system is capable of colour constancy: perceiving an object as the same colour despite the wavelength of the light reflecting off of it. However, we are not able to achieve colour constancy in artificial light that differs too dramatically from natural terrestrial light. This is why, although our car appears blue at sunrise, noon, and sunset, it may appear yellow in a parking garage.

> **5.7** **Press Pause**
>
> Our visual system is designed to create colour constancy in the environment of evolutionary adaptedness (EEA), not in a modern parking garage.

Nobel Prize winners David Hubel and Torsten Wiesel did revolutionary work in visual development between the 1950s and the 1970s. As a result of their work, we now understand the crucial role of species-typical stimuli on normal development, what we call *experience-expectant development*.

The Nobel Prize-Winning Work of Hubel and Wiesel: Experience-Expectant Development

Torsten Wiesel of Uppsala, Sweden, and David Hubel of Windsor, Ontario, worked together at Johns Hopkins University School of Medicine in the late 1950s and at Harvard University in the 1960s and 1970s to describe the development of the visual system. Early in their collaboration, they were able to determine that some cells in the

visual system respond to lines that are oriented vertically and others to lines that are oriented horizontally. Here is how they did it: They placed a recording electrode into the visual cortex of a cat such that it was recording the activity of a single cell. Then they displayed for the cat an image that had either horizontal or vertical lines at a specific location in the visual field. Some cells responded only to horizontal lines, others to vertical lines. Hubel and Wiesel called these visual cortex cells, which responded preferentially to one type of line or the other, *simple cells*. Other cells, called *complex cells*, receive input from a number of simple cells and integrate the information received. Because of these inputs, a complex cell might respond to a line of a particular orientation in a number of different locations in the visual field, or it might respond to a line that is in motion in a particular direction. At the time of this research, these were ground-breaking discoveries illustrating the hierarchical relationship between information-processing layers in the brain.

But the real developmental story is Hubel and Wiesel's later Nobel Prize-winning work. They studied the development of **ocular dominance columns** in the visual systems of kittens. An ocular dominance column, just as it sounds, is a column of neurons in the visual system including neurons that all respond to input from either the right eye or the left eye. They are called *ocular dominance columns* because within a particular column, one eye is dominant. Neurons carry signals from the rods and cones in your right eye to specific cells in your visual cortex, and neurons carry signals from the rods and cones in your left eye to different specific cells in your visual cortex. The cells that respond to the right eye group together in a column, as do the cells that respond to the left eye, so that the visual cortex is organized into columns of equal width, and the columns alternate: One column responds to the right eye, the neighbouring column responds to the left eye, and so on. If a person, or a cat, develops in species-typical circumstances, then the amount of tissue devoted to each eye is roughly equal.

Ocular dominance columns do not exist in the visual cortex of the newborn. Instead, cells in the newborn's visual cortex receive information from both eyes. Ocular dominance columns begin to appear in the first month and develop to completely segregated columns within the first two months after birth. But there is an implication: Ocular dominance columns do not form because new connections grow between the retina and the visual cortex; they form because existing connections are eliminated. The axon of a cell that had a synaptic connection with the visual cortex retracts back to its origin.

We know this because of a series of experiments in which Hubel and Wiesel tested the results of selective visual deprivation on the development of these columns in young cats. If the kitten was deprived of input from one eye, the entire visual system would become devoted to processing information from the other eye. The columns that would otherwise have been devoted to, say, the left eye, would come to receive and process information from the right eye. And this switchover was irreversible. If the developing kitten received no input from the left eye during the critical period, it would lose the ability to respond normally to input from that eye.

Now let us put this in the context of our understanding of nature, nurture, and the environmental inputs that serve as resources for development. Hubel and Wiesel's experiments illustrate the phenomenon of experience-based selective synaptic death, known as *synaptic pruning*. This is essentially a competitive process: Some synapses will remain after others' demise. Normal development of ocular dominance columns is dependent upon experience, but notice, and this is very important, that before this outlandish manipulation was performed by Hubel and Wiesel, one would not have known that experience was important. All kittens developing in an environment that supplied visual stimuli to both eyes developed ocular dominance columns. If every

ocular dominance column
A column of neurons in the visual system that responds to input from either the right eye or the left eye.

figure 5.5   Ocular dominance columns

The visual system is organized into ocular dominance columns: One column of cells gets information from the right eye; the neighbouring column gets information from the left eye. Hubel and Wiesel discovered that species-typical visual stimuli were necessary for this organization to develop.

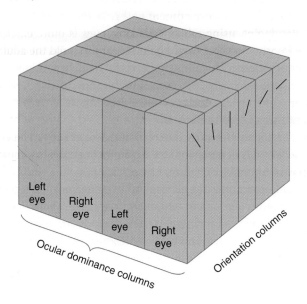

individual develops the same way, one might erroneously infer that experience makes no difference. Lowly street cats living in the slums and posh domestic companions living in the most brilliantly appointed apartments would develop the same ocular dominance columns. But we now know that experience does matter and that the specific experience that is relevant is reliably present in a species-typical environment. Because the developing visual system can rely on just the right kind of experience present, Greenough called it an experience-expectant process, that is, developmental processes that rely on experience by capitalizing on dependable regularities (Greenough, Black, & Wallace, 1987). This phenomenon is common in development: Greenough and colleagues explain that these processes use "environmental information that is ubiquitous and has been so throughout much of the evolutionary history of the species. Since the normal environment reliably provides all species members with certain experiences . . . many mammalian species . . . take advantage of such experiences to shape developing sensory and motor systems," (p. 187). Because these experiences occurred so reliably, the developmental process can depend on them and indeed require them.

It is clear that this example would be hard to understand with a very rigid expectation of nature in opposition to nurture. What would it mean to say that the development of the visual system is driven by nature when it is clear that manipulating the environmental input by depriving visual input from one eye permanently changes the visual system? Development is not determined, let alone genetically determined. At the same time, one does not want to say that the development of the visual system is driven entirely by nurture or by environmental factors. Every cat reared in species-typical circumstances with normal visual input to each eye shows a predictable pattern of alternating left-eye and right-eye dominant columns. Development is not chaotic; indeed it is species-typical given the right circumstances. This example makes clear that the nature vs. nurture question is the wrong question to ask. Instead, we want to know how the psychological process (in this case the visual system) was designed to develop. If species-typical input is reliably present in the developmental environment, as visual input available to each eye is reliably available to the visual system in species-typical circumstances, then the development of the system may rely on the input. From an engineering standpoint, using reliably available cues is more efficient than trying to store all of the information that would be necessary to build the adult visual system in the genome. Furthermore, the ability to use available cues in development allows for adaptive idiosyncratic development: An infant who sustains an eye injury early in development is benefitted by the early plasticity of the visual system.

Another point that is illustrated by this example is the concept of critical periods of development. Hubel and Wiesel discovered that there needed to be visual input into each eye at a critical time in development or the normal development of the visual system would never be possible. Evolution by natural selection has selected for critical periods because they are an efficient method for building an adult organism. During a specific period in the individual's development, they have the machinery necessary to learn from the environment, to have specific environmental cues aid in the organization of the brain. Once the individual is through that developmental period, the expensive learning mechanisms are dismantled.

5.8   Press Pause

Thanks to the work of Hubel and Wiesel, we now know how nature and nurture work together by design in the development of ocular dominance columns.

Visual Deprivation and Development in Humans

The discovery of critical periods in visual development had some practical implications for human development. As mentioned before, what is interesting about development is not just knowing that genes and the environment interact to guide the process but knowing how the various developmental resources interact. Here, let us explore two examples of visual development in which researchers have considered carefully how the developing organism interacts with the environment: What information in the environment is necessary for normal development, and what are the consequences of being deprived of this information during critical periods? We have learned quite a bit about the environment's impact on development from these studies.

THE CASE OF VISION RESTORATION IN ADULTHOOD

This chapter opened with a discussion of Michael May whose sight was restored in adulthood with only partial success. There are a few known cases of vision restoration in adulthood, including a near flurry of them in the 1960s and 1970s due to advances in clinical techniques at that time. One well-known but tragic story is that of Sidney Bradford whose sight was restored via corneal transplant by Richard Gregory, a British psychologist, when Bradford was 52 years old. Like Michael May, Bradford had been born sighted. He lost his sight at the age of 10 months.

figure 5.6   This is a Necker cube

After becoming blind at the age of 10 months and having his sight restored when he was 52, Sidney Bradford was unable to see the Necker cube as three dimensional or to see depth in paintings. His experience highlights the importance of critical periods in visual development.

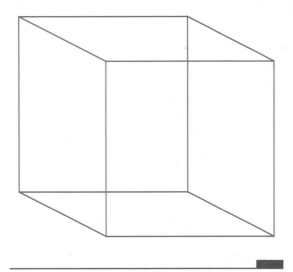

Based on Gregory's report of Bradford's visual perception after the restoration procedure, he was unable to see any depth in two-dimensional paintings, and he was unable to resolve the Necker cube, which just looked flat to him. Bradford was, however, able to read the time from a clock immediately after his operation, presumably transferring the skill he had used to read his own watch by touch. He was also able to report the distance between objects that he saw in the room, but again he had become familiar with these distances before regaining sight. Sadly, Bradford was unable to adjust to his new vision. Like Michael May, he was unable to perceive faces. Prior to the operation he had been a skilled machinist but after regaining vision he was unable to recognize by sight the tools he had used before. Ultimately he was unable to do his work, and he was scared and disturbed by sights that he could not understand. Finally, he committed suicide, just two years after regaining sight (Gregory & Wallace, 1963).

Michael May, as noted earlier in the chapter, had some markedly abnormal vision but also had some preservation of function. He could see colour immediately after his surgery. He could see motion, and he could identify simple shapes. However, he could only identify 25 per cent of the common objects he was tested on. His inability to use faces to identify familiar people, emotions, or gender was accompanied by a marked lack of activation in the fusiform face area (FFA), the part of the brain that usually responds to faces (Fine et al., 2003).

What can we conclude from these cases? They demonstrate that early visual input is important for normal visual development. Furthermore, these cases highlight the idea of critical periods. These adults with restored vision were unable to use facial information, presumably because they were blind during the critical period. Researchers who studied Michael May suggested "Motion processing develops early in infancy compared to form processing and might therefore have been more established, and consequently robust to deprivation, by the age of three" (Fine et al., 2003, p. 916).

THE EFFECT OF EARLY CATARACTS ON VISUAL DEVELOPMENT IN HUMANS

The experiments of Hubel and Wiesel, described above, were conducted on cats and lead us to infer that visual development might proceed similarly in humans. Obviously, conducting experiments in which the experimenter selectively deprives a developing human of visual input would be prohibited by ethical considerations. However, scientists can make inferences from a **natural experiment**: a situation in which atypical development exists through no action of the experimenter, allowing a comparison between two naturally occurring groups.

In this instance the natural experiment is created by the existence of cataracts in developing children. Daphne Maurer and colleagues studied young children who were born with bilateral cataracts (cataracts in both eyes) that were so dense they completely blocked visual access in the centre of the visual field. Maurer and her collaborators reported that early visual deprivation resulting from cataracts had an effect on the development of face perception. They tested a group of people who

natural experiment A situation in which two or more groups exist through no action of the experimenter, allowing a comparison between these naturally occurring groups.

had been treated for congenital cataracts and therefore had experienced complete early visual deprivation. They compared this group to a control group and found that the previously deprived group (even though they currently had unobstructed vision) were significantly worse in face recognition tasks. They had trouble recognizing a face that they had seen early in the session. However, they performed as well as the control group at matching facial expressions and eye direction, suggesting that these are different psychological processes with different developmental courses. The researchers concluded that early visual experience is necessary for the normal development of face perception (Geldart, Mondloch, Maurer, de Schonen, & Brent, 2002).

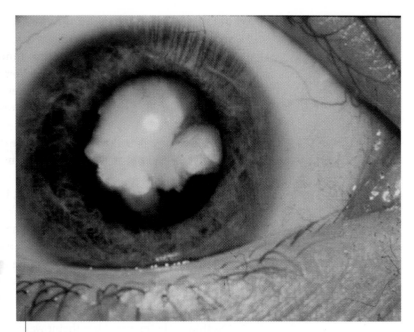

This infant has a cataract. Very early visual deprivation caused by cataracts can affect processes that develop long after the cataract is removed, a developmental process known as a *sleeper effect*.

Then they found something really surprising: a phenomenon they called a **sleeper effect**. In this study, the researchers again looked at children born with a dense central cataract in each eye, such that no patterned visual input entered the retina. Although these individuals had their cataracts removed early in their lives (between 1 month and 1 year of age), restoring access to the complete visual field, they later showed deficits in holistic face processing (Le Grand, Mondloch, Maurer, & Brent, 2004). Holistic face processing describes the way people usually see faces: The face is perceived as a whole, with the visual system encoding relationships among features (how far apart the eyes are, how far the mouth is from the nose) as well as the shapes of the features. This is unique to the perception of faces; most objects are not processed that way by the visual system. But what is really surprising about this finding is that holistic face processing does not typically develop until around 6 years of age (Carey & Diamond, 1994; Mondloch, Pathman, Maurer, Le Grand, & de Schonen, 2007), that is, years after the visual deprivation in these individuals.

sleeper effect A developmental effect that is evident only some time after exposure to a particular environmental cue.

5.9 Press Pause

The effects of experience can manifest years later in the development of the individual.

Think about the implications of this kind of process. The sleeper effect clearly shows that early experience can set up or maintain the neural architecture that will underlie some perceptual ability much later. Similar effects are found in the development of visual acuity, so the case of face processing is not an isolated case of a sleeper effect. The discovery of sleeper effects does not seem to fit with a traditional view of learning or with the Greek empiricists' idea of acquiring knowledge by being exposed to something in the environment. It does, however, illustrate that those processes that are called *learning* are varied; a developmental psychologist can ask interesting and specific questions about what learning is, and the answer will be vastly different in various domains such as visual development, language development, and motor development, to name just a few.

And again, it also illustrates that those who are asking a question about nature vs. nurture are asking the wrong question. The visual system was designed by natural selection to interact with the environment in a very specific way and with aspects of the environment that are specific to just this developmental process. And unlike the traditional view of "learning," the effects do not have to be immediate. Maurer and her colleagues speculate that "sleeper effects may arise because early visual input is necessary to preserve or establish the optimal neuronal architecture for each task" (Maurer, Mondloch, & Lewis, 2007, p. 45).

Associationist Accounts of Visual Development

In the most classic tradition of the empiricist, general-purpose learning mechanisms should lead to development. The classic empiricist Thomas Hobbes famously claimed "Nothing is in the mind but that it was first in the senses" (Hobbes, 1651/2006). Ironically, in this classic view of empiricism, you get perception for free, as there is no explanation offered for the computational processes necessary to bring about perception. Hobbes recognized the existence of perceptual experiences independent of learning. The instinct blindness that makes it difficult for any of us to appreciate the complexity of perception led the classic empiricists to overlook perceptual development entirely, causing traditional empiricist claims about perception to be entirely nativist. This view clearly bypasses the question of the development of the senses themselves.

Since we have come to understand that perception develops, contemporary associationists have contributed to the field. As with other fields, in the area of perception, associationists seek to explain the observed development with simple, associationist, learning mechanisms (e.g., a child learns to associate one stimulus with another). The most thorough current attempts to describe this developmental process come from Dale Purves and his colleagues. Even very low-level processes like shape, size, and lightness constancy are results of the visual system learning about the statistical regularities of the world according to Purves (Purves & Lotto, 2003; Purves, Lotto, Williams, Nundy, & Yang, 2001). For example, as a child develops lightness constancy, he will adjust his perceptual response to whether his past percepts were correct in predicting whether two objects were the same or different. None of this happens consciously: The visual system does a statistical analysis of how things have actually turned out compared to how things have appeared and adjusts the percepts to maximize one's perceptual accuracy with respect to size, shape, lightness, and brightness constancy.

In describing the learned ability to see objects' colours as constant, despite differences in illumination, Purves draws our attention to the inherent ambiguity in the light that arrives at the eye: It could have been caused by any of a huge number of possible illumination-by-surface reflectance combinations. (A red light on yellow paper or a yellow light on red paper might cause the same light to arrive at the eye.) Purves suggests "the visual system solves this problem by using feedback from the success or failure of [previous] responses to progressively instantiate patterns of neural connectivity that promote ever more appropriate reactions to the stimuli" (Purves et al., 2001, p. 290). The percept generated is the one that was the most useful in the past.

Purves and his colleagues are strongly committed to a functional view. They argue that visual (and generally perceptual) psychology is not for the purpose of allowing one a true representation of the world but rather of allowing one to behave in ways that are useful. However, they are not entirely clear on why the developing individual should rely only on information he or she has encountered in a single lifetime. Indeed, despite referring to their own view as empiricist, they acknowledge that "each member of the species must incorporate the experiences of the species as a whole, as well as the experience accumulated by the individual (Purves et al., 2001, p. 295).

Although this empiricist view is still being pursued, you have read about some phenomena in this chapter, such as critical periods, early competencies, and sleeper effects, that are hard to explain with general-purpose learning mechanisms. Can you think of other evidence and arguments from this chapter that challenge the associationist view?

EXPECT SOME PERCEPTION TO BE AVAILABLE PRIOR TO EXPERIENCE

Let us re-examine the extreme empiricist view. Imagine that developing infants only had a few general-purpose learning mechanisms such as classical and operant conditioning. This extreme empiricist view would suggest that a developing child would not know a priori to be cautious around a tiger until that child encountered a tiger and indeed until a tiger scared (or perhaps injured) the child. This seems a dangerous design, and we will see in Chapter 6 that children have surprisingly sophisticated knowledge about biology, including early concepts of predators and prey, but in this chapter, let us just consider the claim from the point of view of visual perception.

A classic empiricist would suggest that a baby need not be born with a fear of tigers because one unfortunate encounter with a tiger will lead the baby to "learn" that tigers are dangerous or scary and thus to stay away from them in the future. This view fails to appreciate what a complex problem the baby would have to solve just to understand that a tiger seen on one day should have the same properties as a tiger seen on a different day. The infant would first have to see the tiger (in spite of its stripes, which are designed to make it blend in to the background when viewed by a primate visual system). The baby would then have to orient to the tiger (accomplished by mechanisms that draw attention to motion cues), see the tiger as an object (accomplished by the object-parsing mechanisms described in Chapter 6), and recognize that the tiger is an animate being (motion cues signal animacy in the visual system, as you will read in Chapter 7). And the baby would also have to survive the unfortunate event that provided the education about the danger of tigers.

In order to learn about a coyote from experience, and apply this learning usefully, one has to recognize two coyotes across changes in lighting, distance, and orientation. This requires very specialized machinery that is sculpted to precision by the process of evolution by natural selection.

But now, it gets really tricky: The baby has to link this incident to a future moment when he sees a tiger. Likely the lighting will be different (yet the colour constancy mechanism will allow the baby to see the orange and black stripes), the distance will be different (yet the size constancies described above allow for the perception of a tiger that is approximately the same size), and the orientation will be different (yet the mechanisms that represent a visually inspected object allow us to recognize that object, even when seen from a wildly different angle). Perceiving the tiger through all of these variables requires very specialized machinery that is sculpted to precision by the process of evolution by natural selection. This could not be accomplished from a blank slate perspective. Although the intuitively simple claim that a baby who sees a tiger once and fears it can later recognize and avoid a different tiger is not a simple operation but an intricate set of very complex operations. Some perception needs to be reliably developing in infants.

5.10 Press Pause

The visual system has work to do prior to learning from experience.

SUMMARY

In this chapter you learned about the development of our perceptual abilities starting from before birth. A major theme of this chapter is that the function of our perceptual systems is to allow us to behave sensibly in the world, not, as you might imagine, to absorb information from the world around us. Indeed, our percepts are constructed by our brains, and percepts will be different from species to species, depending upon the adaptive pressures faced by that species.

You learned about constancies, the tricks that your perceptual systems use to perceive an object as the same despite radically different viewing conditions. The ability to see a red berry as red, even though the wavelength of light striking the retina is radically different at different times of the day, is clearly functional. The difference in light hitting the eye is not information that will allow you to behave functionally in the world; the fact that the berry is the same berry will.

You also learned about prenatal perceptual development and the fact that since babies prefer their mothers' voices over strangers' voices and even a story that they heard before birth over one they heard after birth, the innate vs. learned dichotomy does not make any sense.

You learned about postnatal perceptual development and saw that different elements of perception have different developmental trajectories, even within, say, the visual system. And different elements of the perceptual system need different and specific input in order to develop normally. Because this perceptual experience is available to all members of the species who develop in species-typical circumstances, people failed to appreciate that experience was important to development until the right experiments were performed.

Next you read about two in-depth studies into areas that have enlightened our thinking about perceptual development. The groundbreaking research of Hubel and Wiesel revealed for the first time the importance of early species-typical experiences in the normal development of the visual system.

Finally, you learned about sleeper effects, effects that are measurable only much later than the experience that contributes to their development, illustrating once again the varied and interesting ways that psychological mechanisms develop.

PRESS PAUSE SUMMARY

- The function of perception is to allow us to behave sensibly in the world with respect to survival and reproductive interests.
- Instinct blindness makes it hard to appreciate perception and hence the complexity of the adaptations underlying vision.
- Our brain and visual system construct the things we see.
- An infant's interests are adaptive: Very young infants will orient to social information allowing them to observe just what they need to learn about the world.
- Infants hear in utero, and they learn what they hear. Newborns would rather listen to a story that was read to them in utero than listen to an unfamiliar, yet similar, story.

- The visual cliff was first used to show that babies as young as 6 months have depth perception. Recently, heart rate and blink responses have also been used to show depth perception at 1 month.
- Our visual system is designed to create colour constancy in the environment of evolutionary adaptedness (EEA), not in a modern parking garage.
- Thanks to the work of Hubel and Wiesel, we now know how nature and nurture work together by design in the development of ocular dominance columns.
- The effects of experience can manifest years later in the development of the individual.
- The visual system has work to do prior to learning from experience.

KEY TERMS AND CONCEPTS

constancy, 165

instinct blindness, 149

intermodal perception, 164

natural experiment, 172

ocular dominance column, 169

sleeper effect, 173

QUESTIONS FOR THOUGHT AND DISCUSSION

1. What is the function of perception? Be as specific as possible. List some alternative functions that have been suggested. Why don't those suggestions work as an explanation for the evolution of perception?

2. What is instinct blindness? What is an example within the area of perception? Speculate on another example of instinct blindness from a different area of psychology.

3. Are aesthetics functional? Explain.

4. What are constancies? Give an example. What is the problem that the visual system has to solve? How does it solve it?

5. What is a sleeper effect? Give an example. How does this evidence challenge the nature vs. nurture dichotomy?

From the Classroom to the Lab: Follow Up

Consider the experiment you designed in response to the "From the Classroom to the Lab" challenge earlier in this chapter.

Describe your design.

Describe the procedure.

How does this procedure differ from a procedure you might use with human adults? With human infants?

What is your dependent variable?

What is your independent variable?

Is the experiment you've designed useful with a variety of animals? Could it be conducted underwater, for example? How would you have to adapt it?

Imagine you have run your experiment. What results would indicate to you that the animal tested can discriminate between two hues? What results would indicate to you that the animal cannot discriminate between two hues?

chapter 6

Concepts, Categories, and Essences

Opening Vignette: Concepts

Imagine visiting a zoo. You come to the front gate, and you are asked to pay a fee for admittance. You are able to make sense of this request because you have the concepts of exchange, money, and private property. You enter the zoo and see many animals that are familiar to you: prairie dogs and American buffalo, which are native to North America, and giraffes and elephants, which have been imported for display in the zoo. You have a concept of these animals, so you know what to expect from each: what they might eat, whether they will be active in the midday sun, and whether they will approach visitors. Then, you see a bongo.

Imagine that you have never before seen, or heard of, a bongo. Therefore, you don't have a category for it. You have read that it is a kind of antelope, and you see that it has horns, cloven hoofs, and is shaped like other antelope you have seen. Even though you don't have a concept of bongo, you do have a concept of antelope, and you therefore expect this new animal to be herbivorous, and you expect the female to nurse her offspring. Your broader concept allows you to make some pretty good predictions.

Now imagine a person from a faraway place visiting this zoo. Regardless of what culture they are from, they will have the concept of exchange and will have the concept of private property. They may or may not have the concept of money. Once inside the zoo, they, like you, may see animals that they recognize and animals that they do not recognize. They will certainly have the concept of animals and so will have some clear expectations about animals, even ones that are very unfamiliar: They expect that animals need to eat and drink and that animals try not to get too hot or too cold, etc. The more defined the concept category (animal, mammal, primate, etc.), the better their ability to make predictions about the animals. Notice that some concepts are universal to all human cultures. You could not, however, expect any non-human mind to have these same concepts.

Chapter Outline

- What Are Categories and Concepts?
- Instinct Blind to Concepts
- Universality of Categories and Concepts
- The Classic View of Categories
- A Prototype and Family Resemblance View
- What Would Piaget Say about Children's Categorization?
- The Function of Categories and Concepts
- Early Concept Formation: Function Matters
- Basic Levels and Hierarchical Categorization
- Natural Kinds
- Concept Development
- Essences and Essentialism
- Special Design
- What Would Associationists Say about Children's Categorization?

- In this chapter you will learn about concepts, categories, and the cognitive strategy that children develop, called *essentialism*, that allows them to see members of special natural categories as having an unchanging "essence."

- You will learn to understand why our concepts and categories need an explanation: Category formation happens so naturally, and so universally, that people fail to think of it as something that needs explaining. But you will learn that many of the concepts that we have are universal to us but not to other species because they increased fitness in our ancestral past.

- You will obtain a clear view of what developmental psychologists have historically said about categories and concepts. You will read the classic view of categories, the prototype view, and Piaget's thoughts about children's concepts and categories. You will learn what kinds of concepts and categories young children do (and do not) have and what Piaget thought the developmental trajectory of concepts and categories was.

- Next you will read a functional account of concepts and concept formation that is consistent with evolutionary psychology. You will come to understand the function of concepts, including what functions concepts and categories served in the EEA as well as the functions at different ages throughout childhood. You will read evidence that adults' concepts are functional and that children most easily acquire concepts when they are functional.

- You will also read about the hierarchical organization of categories and the child's acquisition of basic-level categories. You will become familiar with the research on children's concept formation, including the induction and transformation experiments that reveal children's essentialist thinking. An understanding of *natural kinds* will help you to understand the child's thinking about essentialism.

- Finally, you will read an associationist account of concept formation and a reply to it.

Imagine you go for a walk and encounter a dog that you have never seen before. Without the concept of "dog" or an ability to include this new dog in your concept, you would have no information and no expectations regarding this new dog. But you are not, in fact, encountering a completely foreign and mysterious entity. Even though you have never met that particular dog, you know a lot about it because it belongs to your concept of dogs, and everything you know about dogs generally, you infer about that particular dog. Young children and even infants also have concepts and categories and the ability to include or exclude novel objects. They use these cognitive abilities to make sense of a world in which they frequently encounter novel entities.

Everyone categorizes: We group objects and events into classes of like kinds. That said, there are developmental changes in categorization. The groupings themselves change in age-related, predictable patterns (Bruner, Olver, & Greenfield, 1966; Inhelder & Piaget, 1964; Smith & Kemler, 1977; Vygotsky, 1962). The rules that younger children use to categorize are more likely than those of older children to refer to perceptual features, the features of an object that you can easily see (Flavell, 1963, 1985). And younger children are more likely to rely on global perceptual characteristics, the similarity of the broad shapes of objects, rather than a feature-by-feature comparison that older children prefer (Kemler, 1982, 1983; Smith, 1979, 1985).

6.1 **Press Pause**

Concepts and categories are very useful: They allow us to make predictions about what to expect from individual entities that we have never seen before.

What Are Categories and Concepts?

As we begin this chapter, it will be very useful to define categories and concepts. The definitions offered here will be those that are used throughout the book and will be most useful when thinking about developmental psychology and when thinking about the functional perspective that evolutionary psychology encourages us to take. These are not the only definitions that are used either currently or historically. Be aware that the definitions may vary, especially if you study the issue from the perspective of adjacent fields like linguistics or philosophy, both of which have extensive literature on the topic of categorization.

PERCEPTUAL CATEGORIES

A **perceptual category** is an implicit classification of perceptual stimuli into discrete sets in spite of a lack of physical discontinuity in the stimuli (e.g., colours, facial expressions, and consonant sounds). In the last chapter we learned about perception, about the function of perception, and about perceptual development. Even at the earliest level of information processing, there is evidence that our mind organizes at least some of the stimuli that arrive via the sense organs into perceptual categories. Colour is a good example. We learned in the last chapter that colour is not actually something that is real; it is something that our mind creates. Our perception of various colours corresponds roughly to the physical wavelength of the light that reaches our eye, reflected from a particular object, but there is no one-to-one correspondence between wavelength and perceived colour. We perceive colours categorically: Even if the wavelength

perceptual category An implicit classification of perceptual stimuli into discrete sets in spite of a lack of physical discontinuity in the stimuli (e.g., colours, facial expressions, and consonant sounds).

figure 6.1   Perceptual category

We perceive colours categorically: As the light changes in wavelength, we see the colour as one category, say blue, right up until it suddenly appears to be green.

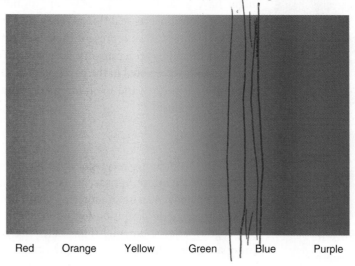

Red   Orange   Yellow   Green   Blue   Purple

of the stimulus that meets our retina changes gradually from shorter to longer, our perception does not change gradually. Rather, we see the colour as one category, say blue, and although we see that the colour blue has changed slightly, it is still blue right up until it is (relatively) suddenly perceived as green.

Experimentally, we can test for (and demonstrate) categorical perception because we more easily perceive differences in two colour patches that cross our category boundary (e.g., what we would call a *green* and a *blue*) than we perceive differences of equal physical magnitude (the difference in wavelength is the same) within our perceptual category (e.g., two different greens). Another example of perceptual categorization is the perception of speech sounds: As the physical stimulus changes gradually from "ba" to "pa," we only hear a sudden categorical change (Eimas, 1963; Liberman, Harris, Hoffman, & Griffith, 1957). The perception of emotional facial expressions is also categorical. For example if a facial expression changes from happy to surprised, the perception of a happy face changes rather quickly to the perception of a surprised face, relative to the physical change in the stimulus (Calder, Young, Perrett, Etcoff, & Rowland, 1996; Etcoff & Magee, 1992).

CATEGORIES

category A mentally represented collection of entities (objects, people, actions, or events).

For our purposes here, we define a **category** as a mentally represented grouping of entities (objects, people, actions, or events). Notice that we are defining it in psychological terms: We are talking about a psychological entity (the representation of the group) that is classified together for psychological reasons (some apparent similarity). This definition of a category is different from traditional definitions of categories, in particular the classically defined category that specifies a list of features that members of the category must have, such as red circles or an asymmetric shape, for example.

Our definition of a category also distinguishes it from an ideal category, in the tradition of Plato, which is assumed to be something real that really exists in the world. Our categories may refer to real entities that really exist but may refer to things that do not really exist. We might have a category of "dreams" or "months" without relying on those as real things. They may be real or they may not, but if we represent them as a categorical grouping, then they are a category, according to our definition. We are interested in the psychological representation of the category and in children's development of that representation.

According to the theory view of concepts, the concept of solid objects would include an understanding of causal relationships, such as a launch event that happens when one object strikes another.

CONCEPTS

In addition to defining a category, we have a working definition of a concept in order to explore the development of concepts. As with other terms in this book, finding an agreed-upon definition for a concept is difficult. One cognitive developmentalist has called the task of defining a concept "a lexicographer's nightmare" (Flavell, 1970, p. 983). Those of you who know the word have an intuition about what it means. You have the concept of a concept, but it is hard to say, exactly, what it is.

In science, one needs at least a working definition of one's object of study: A **concept** is a psychological grouping together of entities, objects, events, or even characteristics on the basis of some more or less functional commonality, including some understanding of their interrelationship. Concepts are usually associated with a word or short phrase (dog, honesty). That is, they are lexicalized, whereas a category can be a more arbitrary grouping (items that spilled out of my backpack on Tuesday). In some ways, concepts are more powerful than categories because entities that are included in a concept are, in some way, functionally related. For this reason, concepts can be powerful sources of inference and prediction. For a developmental psychologist, then, the interesting questions are "What are the concepts that develop in young children? What is the functional commonality that a child will use to delineate a concept?" Philosophers and other troublemakers can create untold numbers of artificial and awkward categories (e.g., things that Germans have a word for and that are blue), but here we are primarily interested in the concepts that infants and children form themselves, and those tend to be **natural-kinds categories**: psychological groupings of the classes of entities that are seen to be natural categories or objects grouped together as they are perceived to be in nature.

> **concept** A psychological grouping together of entities, objects, events, or even characteristics on the basis of some more or less functional commonality, including some understanding of their interrelationship.

Some authors think about concepts as theories, and some developmental psychologists liken concepts to theories. Let us explore this metaphor: A concept, like a theoretically delineated topic of study has three components: (a) a distinct set of items that are included, (b) phenomena involving members of the set of items, and (c) a set of causal relationships that apply within the domain, and explain observations within the domain, but do not apply to other domains.

An example might be the concept of solid objects. That concept includes (a) an understanding of items that are included, such as rocks and animals but not clouds and beliefs; (b) phenomena involving members of the set, such as collisions, falls, and breaks; (c) causal relationships, such as a launch event that happens when one object strikes another. According to the theory view of concepts, the concept of solid objects would include all of this information, just as a theory of solid objects would.

> **natural-kind category** A psychological grouping of the classes of entities that are seen to be natural categories or objects grouped together as they are perceived to be in nature.

Certainly, explanatory theories are the central organizing force in at least some domains of knowledge—probably for the natural-kinds categories more than for artificial categories (Carey, 1985; 1988; Carey & Spelke, 1996; Wellman and Gelman, 1992). Is the child as a theoretician a useful metaphor, each developing theories and testing hypotheses in an attempt to explain the world around them? Perhaps, but it has its shortcomings and need not be taken literally, just as with most metaphors.

Instinct Blind to Concepts

There is remarkable (though not absolute) uniformity of concepts between individuals and between human cultures. Humans everywhere have similar understandings of many natural things (water, plants, animals, food, metals, rocks) as well as a remarkable number of concepts regarding social and mental phenomena (deception and integrity, love and loyalty, empathy and vengeance). The fact that people seem to have all the right concepts to allow them to function effectively both in the physical world and in social interactions makes it hard to imagine not having them. We do not think about the fact that our very useful concepts are just a small subset of all possible concepts. We do not marvel over the fact that we do not have a concept for things that are both hairy and hollow, for things that have been set on a table at some point, or for things that weigh less than our dog. These concepts would not be useful to us. Although they might be perfectly logical categories, they would not be functional in the sense of ultimately conferring an evolutionary advantage.

We fail to marvel at the remarkable similarity between the concepts that various people have. In part we fail to appreciate this universality because we fail to appreciate the unfathomable number of concepts that are, in principle, possible. Our mental organization of animals could be determined by colour or size or how close they live to water, for example; instead they are organized into remarkably (though not perfectly) standard biological taxonomies. Our failure to appreciate the uniformity and the usefulness of our concepts is an example of what Cosmides and Tooby call *instinct blindness*

6.2 Press Pause ————————————————————————

We do not notice the uniformity in the concepts people have, in part because we fail to imagine the myriad of other logically possible categories.

(Cosmides & Tooby, 1994). As they describe it, we are sometimes utterly unable to appreciate how well designed, automatic, and adaptive our mental machinery is precisely because it *is* well designed and automatic. Like a fish that fails to notice water or a land mammal that fails to notice air, it is so easy for us to take the concepts that allow us to move through the world so effectively for granted because they do not trouble us. Our instinct blindness prevents us from noticing that there are commonly held concepts (it does not occur to us that we would not have them) and equally logically possible but absent concepts (it does not occur to us that we might have had them).

Universality of Categories and Concepts

There is remarkable uniformity in the concepts and categories that children create. Children are exposed to an enormous array of different kinds of experiences, a huge range of stimuli in the world, and yet they come to have a surprisingly uniform set of

table 6.1 Instinct blind to the uniformity of concepts

UNIVERSAL CONCEPTS	CONCEPTS WE DO NOT HAVE
Water	Things that are less than 2 feet tall
Plants	Things that are yellow
Animals	Things that have been set on a table at some point
Metal	Things that are hollow and hairy
Rocks	Things that weigh less than our dog
Deception	Things that are animals or rocks
Integrity	
Loyalty	
Vengeance	

A number of concepts come naturally to us and are universal across human populations. Because of our instinct blindness, we fail to notice all of our shared concepts, and even more so, we fail to notice all of the logically possible concepts that we do not have.

Like a fish that fails to notice water or a land mammal that fails to notice air, we tend to take the concepts that allow us to move through the world so effectively for granted because they do not trouble us.

concepts, both among individuals within a culture and between cultures. Conceivably, animals could be classified by any number of dimensions (size, colour; whether they have tails, legs, etc.), but people's classification systems are regular, develop predictably, and ignore many features that are logically permissible. (Can you think of other logically possible but unused features for categorizing animals?) An early and compelling distinction that children make is between animals that are predators and animals that are prey, and this is true cross-culturally (Barrett, 2005). Clearly, this distinction was functional in the EEA.

This uniformity of development suggests that the developmental process of categorization must be constrained, privileging some hypotheses over others. An individual

An early and compelling distinction that children make is between animals that are predators and animals that are prey, and this is true cross-culturally, even in environments where children rarely witness a predator–prey interaction other than on television.

child's experiences are unique to that child, and yet the set of concepts developed are not unique. Instead, children develop a species-typical, universal set of concepts such as animals, plants, living things, physical objects, mothers, water, faces, and countless other natural categories. To be sure, individuals can and do develop culture-specific concepts as well: iPods, prime time, and HOV lanes as well as idiosyncratic concepts like Aunt Gladys, the family cabin, and great-grandma's home canning. But it is surprising how universal the concepts that organize information about natural kinds are.

The Classic View of Categories

classic category A category that can be defined by a list of necessary and sufficient features.

In the classic view of categorization, any category is a **classic category**, which is to say that any category can be defined in terms of its necessary and sufficient features. In other words, if there was an artificial "white squares" category, then anything that is both white and square would be sufficient for inclusion in the category. However, anything that is white but not square, or square but not white, would not be sufficient for inclusion in the category. This is equally true of natural-kinds categories like "raccoon," according to the classic view.

For the category "raccoon," there should be a list of necessary and sufficient features, and if all of the features are present, you have a raccoon, according to the classic view. These features might include being four-legged, a mammal, native to North America, and furry with a dark facial mask, for example. The list of features may be more comprehensive than this, but according to the classic view, there should be some list that is comprehensive enough to serve as the definition of raccoons, such that any entity that has all of the features should be included in the category and any entity that lacks one or more of the features should not be included in the category.

In the classic view, this is not just an idealized description of categories rather, concepts are actually believed to be mentally represented as definitions (Smith & Medin,

---

figure **6.2** **Classic categories**

Classic categories can be defined in terms of their necessary and sufficient features. The category "white squares" includes anything that is both white and square.

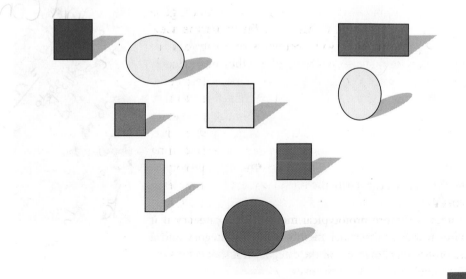

1981). According to this view, because categories are represented as a list of necessary and sufficient features, it is always possible to say whether a particular item is or is not a member of a given category. There should never be any ambiguity. If you want to know whether an item is a white square, either it is or it is not. If you want to know whether something is a raccoon, or a prime number, either it is or it is not. Furthermore, according to the classic view, everything that is in the category is an equally good example. There are not better examples of birds and not-so-good examples of birds; rather, a bird is a bird is a bird. Similarly, everything that is not in the category is equally disqualified.

As you might guess, there are problems with the classic view (why else would we call it the classic view?), and the idea that this is how the mind represents categories and concepts is now universally rejected by developmental psychologists. The first critical blow to the classic view came when Wittgenstein (1953) challenged the idea that most real-world categories have a classic definition. Can you think of a list of necessary and sufficient features that define the concept "game" and that also exclude non-games such as hunting, juggling, or kicking a ball around by oneself? No one could, and Wittgenstein suggested that for most categories and concepts, it will be similarly impossible to define them with a list of necessary and sufficient features.

More devastating to the classic view is the empirical evidence suggesting that people do not represent categories in terms of their necessary and sufficient features. First, the human mind does not view all members of a category as equally good examples or all excluded entities as equally good exclusions. Second, research shows that there are ambiguous items: Is a tomato a fruit? Is a sandal a shoe? People do have indecision with respect to some items: If you ask someone whether an olive is a fruit, or whether curtains are furniture, they may flip-flop and give you a different answer to the same question two weeks later (McCloskey & Glucksberg, 1978). The classic view cannot accommodate these results, which clearly leads to the conclusion that the human mind does not represent concepts as classic categories.

A Prototype and Family Resemblance View

A seemingly viable response to Wittgenstein's challenge to the classic view of categorization is the prototype view. According to this view, some members of a category are more central to that category than others; they more closely resemble the prototype. Think for a moment about a piece of furniture. What did you picture? You are more likely to have thought of a chair than of a bookcase, although you would probably agree that both are members of the category "furniture." Picture a fruit. It is more likely that you are picturing an orange or apple than a watermelon. The more prototypical item is not necessarily the most frequently encountered item (Barsalou, 1985; Mervis, Catlin, & Rosch, 1976). Rather, an item is a more prototypical member of a category if it shares features with other members of the category and a less prototypical member of the category if it shares features with members of other categories.

Wittgenstein challenged the classic view of categories when he proposed that most real-world categories do not have a classic definition.

This view was pioneered by Eleanor Rosch, who offered a strong empirical challenge to the classic view of categorization. If you give a number of different people a list of, say, fish and ask them to rate the typicality of each on a scale from 1 to 10, agreement among people is very high: 97 per cent in one study (Rosch, 1975). Rosch and Mervis have shown that the more features a member shares within a category, the more typical it is rated, and the more features it shares with other categories, the less typical it is rated, even when the categories and features are created artificially so that the study can be experimental, not just correlational (Rosch & Mervis, 1975). People are faster at affirming that a typical item is a category member than a non-typical item. For example, people will more quickly agree that a robin is a bird than that a chicken is a bird (Murphy & Brownell, 1985; Smith, Balzano, & Walker, 1978). If given a category, such as "furniture" or "precious stone" and then asked to produce names of members of that category, people are more likely to produce the names of typical rather than atypical items (Mervis et al., 1976).

The empirical evidence reviewed above certainly refutes the classic view that the mind would either include or exclude an item from a category and that all inclusion is equal and that all exclusion is equal. It also offers a compelling alternative view: The more features in common with the category and the fewer features in common with other categories the more proto-typical it is. But hold on to these ideas as you read about children's essentialist ideas about natural-kinds categories later in this chapter. The prototypic view of category representation cannot explain why a child will still view a raccoon as a raccoon, even when you have shaved away its mask, dyed the raccoon black, bleached a single white strip down its back, and added a skunk's stink sac, such that the resulting animal is indistinguishable from a skunk.

But first, you will read two approaches to explaining development in categorization and concept formation. In the traditional approach, exemplified by Piaget, researchers took a classic view of categories: Any category should be definable in terms of necessary and sufficient features. Given this view, researchers felt justified creating artificial categories (like blue circles, the item on the far left, or the item not chosen on the last trial) and testing children's abilities to represent these categories. Following the sections on Piaget's work, you will read about contemporary research on child concept formation, which focuses on natural categories, including natural-kinds categories. Contemporary researchers also rely on new and innovative methods, which you will also read about.

What Would Piaget Say about Children's Categorization?

Piaget subscribed to the classic view of categories: He believed that any category could be seen as a classic category and could be defined in terms of its necessary and sufficient features (Markman, 1989), whether arbitrary (red triangle) or natural (bird).

He used a free-classification method in order to test children's understandings of categorization. Children were tested to see if they could sort a number of items into a pre-specified number of groups. A simple task, for example, would be to sort red cards and blue cards into a red stack and a blue stack, starting with a mixed-up pile of cards. The experimenter would not tell the child on what basis to sort the cards (e.g., by colour), so the subject was free to create the rule for categorization. The number of groups was sometimes given by the experimenter and sometimes left up to the child. Piaget

Piaget subscribed to the classic view of categories: He believed that any category could be seen as a classic category and could be defined in terms of its necessary and sufficient features.

believed that the experimenter could infer the categories that were in the child's head from the groupings that they created.

Children do not show evidence of representing categories in a way that is consistent with the classic view of categorization. Piaget discovered this and suggested that mature categorization meant that (a) a person could identify which items were included and excluded from the category, (b) a person understood that membership in one category disqualified membership in another category at the same level (one cannot be both a dog and a cat), and (c) categories are organized hierarchically, so that members of the "bird" category and members of the "bat" category are also members of the "animal" category.

In fact, results from Piaget's research on categorization showed that children in the preoperational (2 to 7 years old) and concrete operational (7 to 11 years old) stages were **perceptually bound**: They based their categorization exclusively on visually per-

perceptually bound
Compelled to categorize objects based on visually perceivable features, as Piaget thought children were.

figure 6.3   Thematic and taxonomic grouping

Given these items to sort, a taxonomic grouping would put the horse and dog together (in the category "animals") and the dog and doghouse together and the horse and stable together (in the category "shelters"). Piaget found that children used thematic groupings and concluded that they were categorizing immaturely.

ceivable factors. This meant that if a red triangle and a red circle were near each other, colour might become the feature to sort by, but if the red circle was near the blue circle, shape might become the important feature. However, young children were more likely than older children to change criteria in the middle of the sorting task (Inhelder & Piaget, 1964), a sign of immaturity according to Piaget.

He observed that children did not group the objects into classic categories and concluded that children did not have categories. What did the children do in Piaget's task if not conform to adult categories? They grouped things thematically: A horse goes with a stable; a dog goes with a doghouse. The major finding resulting from the free-classification method was the use of **thematic associations**: Objects might be grouped together because they are used together (a stable and a horse or a dog and a doghouse) or because they appear in a story together (a cow and the moon) (Inhelder & Piaget, 1964). This thematic grouping was seen as an error.

With respect to the development of categorizations and concepts, Piaget thought that children were primitive. Categorization was a developmental phenomenon, and there were real changes from young children to older children as they moved through the stages of development. Piaget did not believe that children had proper concepts as adults did but rather that children had **complexes**: groupings that were more fluid and less well defined than a category and that did not rely on classic definitions.

thematic association The grouping of items based on their use together or their prior association in a story rather than on category membership.

complex A grouping that is more fluid and less well defined than a category and that did not rely on classic definitions. Piaget thought young children had complexes, not proper categories.

6.3   Press Pause

Piaget saw categories as classic categories and tested whether infants and children had these classic categories. They did not, he concluded.

VYGOTSKY'S VIEW

Vygotsky (1962) reached a similar conclusion when he tried to teach children classic categories that he had designed such as "large red or blue block." Children had quite a bit of difficulty with this task. Vygotsky also found evidence of children's reliance on thematic associations rather than what he considered a mature use of classic categories. Generally consistent with Piaget's thinking, Vygotsky (essentially a stage theorist) believed that there was a qualitative shift from a young child who was perceptually bound in their categorical thinking to an older child who was conceptual (meaning that things belonged to the same category if and only if there was a perceptual resemblance; i.e., things had to look alike to be in the same category). In Vygotsky's view, children younger than 7 are considered preconceptual, not yet having categories, and children 7 and older are considered conceptual. Their decisions on sorting tasks are now dictated by category membership and its implications, not just perceptual or thematic grouping.

In addition to Piaget's and Vygotsky's classic research, there is some contemporary evidence that young children are reliant upon perceptual features when creating categories, at least compared to older children and adults. Young children are more likely to refer to perceptual attributes when explaining their categorizations (Flavell, 1963). The perceptual features that they rely on changes over time as well: Colour and shape are used for categorization at a younger age than are height and width, for example (Odom, 1978).

6.4   Press Pause

Piaget, Vygotsky, and others have found that young children sort objects thematically, rather than taxonomically, and rely on perceptual features in their sorting.

The Function of Categories and Concepts

Why does our species-typical human psychology create categories? A consideration of evolutionary psychology leads one to expect that traits that have costs must confer benefits, and there is a cost to developing and maintaining the cognitive systems that create categories. Thus, one would expect there to be a function for categorization, and a function for the universal categories that our minds create, or else silly and arbitrary classifications (things that are both hairy and hollow, things that have been set on a table at some point, or things that weigh less than our dog) would be just as common as the natural categories that our minds create. What is the function of this specialized psychology?

The very broad explanation is that, like other evolved cognitive faculties, categories allow people to behave adaptively in the world in a way that ultimately increases survival and reproductive success. But you probably want a more direct answer: How do categories help us? One often-repeated suggestion is that the reason we categorize is because our cognitive and memory capacity would be swamped by information if we did not categorize. According to this view, we are unable to hold all of the individual objects and events we encounter in memory, so we categorize for storage efficiency. But this explanation does not hold water for two reasons. First, we often do remember individual items even though they have been categorized. You remember all the individuals in your close circle in spite of them being in categories such as "family" and "school friends." You remember individual months and continents, in addition to having categories such as "months" and "continents," so having categories does not relieve the memory load, it actually challenges it further (Pinker, 1997).

Second, there is no known reason that the human mind would not be able to record every event and every object it encounters. The features and factors of a particular event that need to be recorded would certainly be numerous but not astronomical, especially compared to our approximately 100 billion neurons and possibly 10^{15} synapses. As Steve Pinker points out, "people live for a paltry two billion seconds, and there is no known reason why the brain could not record every object and event we experience if it had to" (Pinker, 1997, p. 306).

Why, then, does our mind naturally and efficiently create categories and concepts? The big payoff of categorization is inference. Creating a category and then knowing that a particular object belongs in that category allows us to make inferences and thus provides a rich source of information for a species that uses information as heavily as humans do. When we encounter a brand-new, never-before-seen object, we do not immediately see everything about it that might be important to know, such as whether it is useful or dangerous. We only have immediate access to a few of its most apparent features. But categorizing it (e.g., as a house cat or a cougar) allows us to know much more about it: what we can expect from it, how we might use it, and whether it is dangerous.

When we see the world in terms of natural "real-world" categories (and not arbitrary categories such as "things that are white and spiky"), that categorization allows us to make inferences about the things in that category. If we know that mammals have lungs and that a bongo is a mammal, then we know that a bongo has lungs, even upon our first encounter with a bongo. We can make broad predictions when we have large categories (if we know that the being we just encountered is an animal, we know it will move about to seek food) and more precise predictions with smaller categories (if we know that the being we just encountered is a bongo, we know it will grow horns, that it is a herbivore, and that its offspring will be a bongo). We can make these inferences without having to conduct an experiment and wait for or observe the outcome. Conversely, in order to assign a new object that we encounter to a broad category such as "animal," we need to know relatively little about it, but in order to assign a new object to a very specific category, more information is needed (see Pinker, 1997, pp. 306–308 for more on this).

> **6.5 Press Pause**
>
> Categories and concepts allow for inference.

CATEGORIES ARE FUNCTIONAL

There is evidence to support the idea that the categories adults have are functional: They allow people to behave in a way that confers a survival and hence reproductive advantage. There is also evidence that natural categories are especially functional. Let us consider an experiment with adults: Max Krasnow proposed that concepts are organized by our minds according to the value of objects, where value means biological utility (e.g., food). The value of an item should be a stronger factor in categorization than any other statistical regularity, such as how typical it is or how common or how frequently occurring it is. Krasnow asked participants in his study to imagine that they were visitors to an alien planet and to compose a report on what they found. He taught participants two categories by presenting exemplar after exemplar and then testing how fast and accurate they were at recognizing an example. He wanted to know if people create categories by looking for those items that are the most typical of the group or those that are the most useful or functional. He found that if people were told that the category was a fruit, they were the fastest and most accurate at identifying a group member when the group member was ripe (as opposed to unripe). If people were not told that the category was fruit, then they showed the pattern that proponents of the prototype view of categorization would predict: They quickly and accurately recognized items that were the most typical of the group. Krasnow concluded that an estimate of the value of items in evolutionary terms is part of what the mind uses to create categories (Krasnow, 2008).

Early Concept Formation: Function Matters

Although children's categories may be immature, they are organized around function. The categories that children have allow for functional action contingent upon what they see and how they categorize what they see. Some research illustrates that children's categories are functional. Krascum and Andrews (1998) created two imaginary categories: wugs and gillies. They told 4- and 5-year-old preschool children about these wugs and gillies. Half of the children were given just a physical description: Wugs have claws, spikes at the end of their tails, horns, and armour on their backs;

figure 6.4

If participants were told that this was a fruit, they were the fastest at identifying it when the fruit was ripe. If they were not told that it was a fruit, they were the fastest at identifying it when it was most prototypical. (Adapted from Krasnow, 2008.)

figure 6.5 **Wugs and gillies**

Children who were given functional information about wugs and gillies were better able to categorize them and were better at remembering the two categories when tested the next day. (Adapted from Krascum & Andrews, 1998.)

"Wug"   "Gillie"

gillies have big ears, wings, long tails, and long legs. The other half of the children were also given these physical descriptions but were given functional reasons for these features as well: Wugs have claws and armour because they like to fight; gillies have big ears so they can listen for approaching wugs and flee from them rather than fight them. The children who were given functional information were better able to categorize wugs and gillies when they saw pictures of them. They were also better at remembering the two categories the next day.

6.6 Press Pause

Young children's developing categories are functional.

How would you ask a pre-verbal baby what categories it has? One way to test a young child's understanding of categories is to see which objects they think can perform a given action. As discussed above, category membership may have some functional implications. McDonough and Mandler (1998) used this strategy to show that 14-month-olds understand that animals, as a category, drink. These researchers showed a 14-month-old subject a toy dog, and the experimenter gave the dog a pretend drink from a cup, saying "Sip, sip, umm, good!" Then they let the child manipulate the cup, another toy animal, and a toy that was not an animal. The child gave a pretend drink to the animal and not the other toy, revealing an appreciation of function.

Another test is to use a habituation paradigm. If you show a baby a picture of a cat, he will look at it for a while with great interest. If you show the baby another picture of a cat, he will again show interest for a while. The baby will look at subsequent pictures of a cat for shorter and shorter durations, apparently telling you that he has seen enough cats. Now what if you show him a picture of a dog? If he distinguishes dogs from cats, if he has different categories for dogs and cats, then he may look at the dog longer. If he has only a broader category of "animal," then he will be just as bored by the dog as by the cat, having previously seen lots of "animals." In fact, Quinn and Eimas (1996) did just this experiment and discovered that babies as young as 3 and 4 months old dishabituated (as evidenced by an increased looking time) when dogs, lions, or other animals were shown instead of the cats that they had habituated to (as evidenced by decreased looking time with successive cat pictures). This suggests that cats were members of a category for these babies and that the other animals were not in that same category.

6.7 Press Pause

As early as 3 months of age there is evidence that infants have some categories.

By 3½ months of age, babies have higher-level categories. Behl-Chadha showed babies at this age pictures of mammals of various shapes and sizes, including cats, dogs, deer, elephants, and tigers, for example. They viewed these mammals until they habituated to them (indicated by shorter looking times). Next, the babies saw animals that were not mammals, such as fish or birds, as well as novel mammals that they had not seen before. Babies dishabituated to the non-mammalian animals and looked significantly longer at the non-mammals than at the novel mammals, suggesting that they have the category "mammal" and distinguish others that are not in that category (Behl-Chadha, 1996). Other studies using a habituation paradigm have shown that infants as young as 12 months can categorize different kinds of foods, different kinds of animals, and different kinds of furniture in a way that indicates that they have these categories (Ross, 1980).

FUNCTIONS OF CATEGORIES IN EVERYDAY LIFE

Our categorical knowledge helps us perform all kinds of tasks in our everyday life. If we pick up a tool that we have never seen before, we may be able to use it if we have experience with a category of similar artifacts. Conversely, if we believe that the tool belongs to a particular category, we may be unable to think of using it for a different purpose. This phenomenon is known as **functional fixedness**.

The classic experiment demonstrating functional fixedness involved giving adult subjects the task of affixing a candle to a vertical corkboard so that the candle could burn. Subjects were given a candle, a book of matches, and a box of tacks. Subjects were very slow to come to the solution (if they solved the problem at all) of tacking the tack box to the board and using it as a candle holder. Since the tack box served the function of a container, people had a hard time thinking of it as a candle holder: They showed functional fixedness. In contrast, if they were provided with the tacks in a pile and the box empty, they were much faster to arrive at the solution (Duncker, 1945). Recently, researchers have discovered evidence that functional fixedness exists even in technologically sparse cultures, that is, cultures that are living in situations more like the EEA (German & Barrett, 2005).

Recent evidence suggests that the pattern of functional fixedness looks different in younger children. Specifically, 5-year-olds did not show a facilitation of performance when the tack box was provided on its own. That is, they did not show the classic pattern of functional fixedness. Not only that, but in the most difficult situation (where the box had been used as a container), the 5-year-olds performed better than 6- and 7-year-olds and better than adults (German & Defeyter, 2000).

These results are a bit counterintuitive since we expect that problem-solving abilities will increase, and never decrease, with age. But these experiments seem to reveal that young children use categories differently than slightly older children and adults. The explanation suggested by the authors of the study, German and Defeyter, is that young children have a broader category regarding an artifact's function. For example, they might be encoding the tack box as being useful for people to reach their goals rather than being useful for holding tacks (German & Defeyter, 2000). Therefore, their reasoning about the problem is actually more flexible than that of older children.

Basic Levels and Hierarchical Categorization

Our human psychology organizes the concepts and categories in our minds into hierarchies. A category of objects or events (e.g., apples) belongs to a more general category (fruit), which in turn belongs to a broader category (food), which in turn

functional fixedness The psychological phenomenon wherein identifying an item as belonging to one category makes it difficult for a person to think of using it for a function that is not associated with that category.

figure 6.6 Duncker's candle problem

Five-year-olds do not show the classic pattern of functional fixedness. In the most difficult situation (where the tack box was used as a container), the 5-year-olds performed better than 6- and 7-year-olds and better than adults. German and Defeyter (2000) suggest that young children have a broader category regarding an artifact's function.

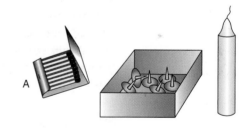

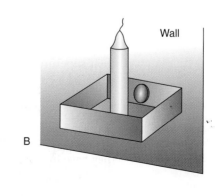

An apple (a basic-level category) belongs to superordinate categories of "fruit" and "food." The particular apple in question is a member of a more specific category, like "Braeburn"; the individual apple can be identified specifically: the apple Emerson ate for lunch on Tuesday.

belongs to an even broader category (organic matter), etc. (Can you think of broader and broader categories that the apple belongs to?) These broader categories are called *superordinate level categories*. In the other direction, "apple" is itself a divisible category. The particular object in question is a member of a more specific category, perhaps "Braeburn," which in turn belongs to an even more specific category such as "Washington Braeburn," a Braeburn apple from a particular orchard in Washington, and so on, until you get down to an individual apple. These more specific categories are called *subordinate level categories*. Almost any category you can think of is both subordinate to some other category and superordinate to yet another category. Moreover, a particular object such as an individual apple can be conceptualized at any one of multiple levels of categorization: apple, fruit, the apple Emerson ate for lunch on Tuesday.

WHAT WOULD PIAGET SAY ABOUT THE HIERARCHICAL ORGANIZATION OF CATEGORIES?

Piaget was interested in children's understandings of the hierarchical relationships of classes. He reported research focussing on the relationships between categories and their superordinate or subordinate classes. Adults usually understand that there can never be a greater number of members of a subclass than of the superordinate class since the members that count in the subclass also count in the superordinate class. For example, there cannot be more poodles than there are dogs because every entity that counts as a poodle must also count as a dog. If there are seven poodles, there have to be at least seven dogs, but there could be more. When Piaget requested children's explicit report, they did not behave as if they understood this rule.

In **class-inclusion experiments**, the experimenter presents the child with two sets of objects, each a subset of a larger set. For example, the child might see apples and oran-

class-inclusion experiment An experiment used by Piaget and others in which children were tested to see if they would include a subset in a broader grouping.

ges, where the two sets are included in a superordinate category: "fruit," in this case. One subset contains more objects than the other: Let us say there are seven apples and four oranges. The child is then asked whether there are more apples (the larger subset) or more fruit (the overarching set). If the child answers correctly, "fruit," then it is inferred that she understands the hierarchical relationship of the categories.

Even children in middle childhood have trouble with this type of problem. If an 8-year-old is made to understand that there are 16 flowers, 10 of which are red and 6 of which are blue, and the child is asked if there are more red flowers or more flowers, the child is likely to respond "more red flowers," presumably because they are mistakenly comparing the number of red flowers to the number of blue flowers instead of answering the question that has been put to them (Inhelder & Piaget, 1964). More recent studies agree with this finding (Winer, 1980). Even when a child of this age correctly reports that in this case there are more flowers than red flowers, they fail to appreciate that it must necessarily be the case that the superordinate category is equal or greater in number to the subordinate category. If asked "Could you make it so that there will be more red flowers than flowers," they may claim that this is a possibility (Markman, 1978).

In a class-inclusion experiment, a child might see seven apples and four oranges. The child would then be asked whether there are more apples or more fruit. Answering correctly, "fruit," suggests that she understands the hierarchical relationship of the categories.

6.8   Press Pause

Piaget's class-inclusion experiments led him to conclude that children were unable to reason about subordinate and superordinate classes.

BASIC AND CHILD-BASIC CATEGORIES

Not only are categories nested hierarchically (this apple, apples from Washington, apples, fruit, food, etc.), but there is a level of categorization among those levels that is psychologically basic. Conversations usually start with **basic-level categories** rather than subordinate or superordinate categories. We speak of a chair before we speak of furniture or a recliner; we speak of apples before we speak of produce or Braeburns. Eleanor Rosch and her colleagues (Mervis & Rosch, 1981; Rosch, Mervis, Gray, Johnson, & Boyes-Braem, 1976) thought that there was a basic level at which categories and concepts are most easily processed, most easily brought to mind, most easily pictured, and most easily discussed.

According to her and her colleagues, basic-level categories have just the right blend between within-category similarity and between-category differences to allow for easy mental grouping. Basic-level categories also keep between-category exemplars mentally distinct. To adults, a basic-level category intuitively seems like a mid-level category, such as "dog" (as opposed to "animal" or "poodle"), "tree" (as opposed to "oak" or "plant"),

basic-level category A category that is most easily processed at a basic level, first learned by children, and within which inferences are more generously drawn.

or "chair" (as opposed to "furniture" or "recliner"). In addition, the words that we use to label basic-level categories are shorter (compare "dog" and "chair" to "animal" and "furniture").

Developmentally, the first words that children learn are basic-level words (Anglin, 1977; Horton & Markman, 1980). Furthermore, in free-sorting tasks, children are more likely to group objects by basic-level categories than by other sorting schemes such as subordinate or superordinate categories (Rosch et al., 1976). However, although the basic-level categories children create and the basic-level categories that adults use are very similar, the specific basic-level categories that children use may be slightly different; these groupings have been called the *child-basic level* (Mervis, 1987; Dromi, 1987). Child-basic categories are slightly more general than adults' basic-level categories. Furthermore, earlier studies show that at the age of 3 months, infants more easily discriminate entities that belong to different basic-level categories than they discriminate entities within a basic-level category (Mandler, 1998). This suggests that the organization around basic-level categories develops between infancy and early childhood.

Importantly, there is also evidence that the nested hierarchy of categories confers greater inferential power than a collection of unrelated categories. By the age of 3, the primacy of basic-level categories affects how children draw inferences. Not surprisingly, children are more likely to draw inferences within the basic-level categories than

A child is more likely to make an inference from a basic-level object to a member of the subordinate category than the reverse. If he learns that birds have gizzards, he is willing to infer that robins have gizzards, but learning this about robins, he hesitates to apply this fact to all birds.

from a basic-level item to a superordinate-level item. In other words, if a child is taught that a bird has a spleen, she might be happy to say that a new, different bird has a spleen but hesitate to say that a new animal also has a spleen (Gelman, 1988; Gelman & O'Reilly, 1988). Even more cleverly, a child is more likely to make an inference from a basic-level object to a member of the subordinate category than the reverse. In other words, if he learns a new fact about birds (birds have gizzards), he is willing to infer that this fact is true about robins, but learning this fact about robins, he hesitates to apply it to all birds (Johnson, Scott, & Mervis, 1997).

6.9 Press Pause

A hierarchy of nested category relationships allows for even greater inferential power.

Notice that our intuition tells us that there is really something basic about basic-level objects. It seems that the world is actually created and organized in such a way that some things are just more basic than others. In fact, our minds create basic-level categories. They are basic because they are basic to us. There are basic-level categories because it has been adaptive for our minds to organize them as such, not because the whole world is organized that way for our convenience. Furthermore, you likely have the perception that the superordinate category is the most general category. For example, "animal" is a superordinate category, at least with respect to "dog," and may seem to be just about as broad as you can get. But think back to the thought experiment with the apple. Was there a broader category for apple than "organic matter?" If you think about it, it would be very hard to know when to stop. A broader category would be "objects," but is that as broad as you can go? How about "things that have names" or "things that reflect light?" If you think that is broad, how about "things that we can think about?" How is that for a broad category? Again, the point is that the world does not supply us with categories and hierarchies of categories; our minds do.

Natural Kinds

Naturally occurring categories such as "dogs," "water," "gold," and "trees" are among the categories that philosophers have called *natural kinds* (Schwartz, 1977). These are just the sorts of categories that allow for rich inferences because members of a group have predictable characteristics in common. Knowing that something is a rock warrants an inference that it will sink in water. Knowing that something is a mammal warrants an inference that it was born live from its mother, not hatched from an egg. Notice that although there are entities in the real world that violate both of the above conclusions, this does not mean that the categories are not functional or that the inference is not valuable. On average, these inferences conferred a benefit in our evolutionary history.

A natural-kind category is the sort of category the human mind appears to develop an interest in and an impressive competence with, even without explicit tutoring. Although Vygotsky had no luck teaching children arbitrary categories such as "large red or blue block," a child easily learns the categories "animal" and "water." They are also just the sort of categories that come so naturally to us that our instinct blindness makes it hard to see that our mind is very well prepared to perceive them. It looks like the world made them, and we could not possibly see it any other way. These categories contrast with "nominal categories," which are categories that exist because humans have named and described them (e.g., circles, even or odd numbers, bachelors, and holidays). A third type of category is "artifacts": things that are made by people (Keil, 1989).

Concept Development

We know that concepts become more refined and more precise as children get older. A very young child might have the category "horse," which includes horses, goats, cows, etc. Indeed, an even younger child might have the category "dog," which includes all of the above along with all other four-legged animals (Gibson, 1969). As the child grows older, the broad category divides and more subtle distinctions among smaller categories develop. At the same time, however, the category is also changing to accommodate unusual category members; penguins and ostriches become acknowledged birds, for example.

INNOVATIVE
RESEARCH METHOD

If the function of concepts is to allow for inference and induction, then one possible way to test the extent of a child's concept is to query what inductions the child will make from one entity to another. Susan Gelman and Ellen Markman (1986) reported a clever experiment that illustrates concepts in 4-year-olds. First, Gelman and Markman showed 4-year-olds pairs of pictured objects (e.g., a fish and a dolphin or a bat and a flamingo). They then taught the young participant some new information about the objects. For example, the child might have been told "This fish stays underwater to breathe," or "This bird's legs get cold at night, but this bat's legs stay warm at night." Following the briefing on the pictured objects, the test of induction began. The experimenter showed the child a new picture of an animal that was very perceptually similar to one of the two original pictures but that shared a category label with the other. For example, the experimenters might have shown a shark rendered to appear perceptually similar to the dolphin but labelled it "fish" or shown a blackbird in the same perspective as the bat but labelled it "bird." The child was then asked which of the newly learned properties could be applied to the new animal. According to Piaget, children at this age are still in the preoperational period and only make inferences on the basis of perceptual similarity. If he was correct, then the properties of the dolphin, not the fish, would apply to the shark, and the properties of the bat, not the bird, would apply to the blackbird. Indeed, much Piagetian research shows children making errors driven by an overreliance on perceptual similarity. But children are actually surprisingly adult-like in their categorically driven inferences. Gelman and Markman found that children's responses were not perceptually driven; they made inferences based on category membership (Gelman & Markman, 1986). Children expect the shark to breathe underwater like a fish, not above water like the similar-looking dolphin. The blackbird would have cold legs at night like the flamingo, not warm legs like the bat. A later study showed that 4-year-old children would make category-based inferences even when the category was not labelled (Gelman & Markman, 1987). Not only that, but by simplifying their method in order to make it accessible to younger children, researchers have shown that children at the age of 3, even the age of 2½ (Gelman & Coley, 1990), use category membership, not perceptual similarity, to make category-specific inferences (Gelman & Markman, 1987).

6.10 Press Pause

Children as young as 2½ years of age have rich natural-kinds categories and can make inferences or inductions from one category member to another.

As children mature, their categories change to accommodate unusual category members; penguins and ostriches become acknowledged birds.

This study and others show that children do have concepts, that the concepts they develop are relatively consistent from one child to the next, and that these concepts are not just reliant on perceptual similarity (Gelman, 2000; Scholnick, Nelson, Gelman, & Miller, 1999; Wellman & Gelman, 1998). As an experimental control, when children were asked to judge the weight of each animal, they made judgments based on perceptual characteristics, not on category membership (Gelman, 1988). It is not that children avoid using perceptual similarity in general (in this respect Piaget was right); rather, they do not rely on perceptual similarity to assign category membership or to make inductions about biological properties. Inferences are tailored to the domain.

This is problematic for the Piagetian perspective that would predict perceptual fixedness. It is also problematic for a purely empiricist account, which would predict that children would only have knowledge about things they have had an opportunity to observe. These and similar studies make it evident that the child actually has an informationally rich category in his or her mind; the child has an understanding of those entities that are members of various categories and of what kinds of inferences are appropriate to make within specific categories. Like adult categories, children's categories are deeply functional, permitting inferences and generalizations from one category to the other.

6.11 Press Pause

Recent experiments show that children are not perceptually bound when forming categories as Piaget would have predicted.

Although children as young as 4 years old use category membership to draw a variety of appropriate inductions, not all category types lend themselves to rich inferences the way natural-kinds categories do. We know this, for example, from the Gelman and Markman experiments described above (Gelman & Markman, 1986, 1987). Children are selective, and usually appropriately selective, about the inferences they will and will

figure 6.7　The blackbird, the flamingo, and the bat

Counter to Piaget's prediction that children would be perceptually driven, they actually make category-based inferences. Children inferred that a blackbird would have cold legs at night like the flamingo, not warm legs like the bat. (Adapted from Gelman & Markman, 1987.)

not make. For example, if a child is told that a dog has a spleen, she is likely to infer that other animals have spleens; but learning that a chair contains polyurethane, she is not likely to make a similar inference to other chairs. Natural kinds support rich inferences in part because natural-kinds categories are seen as having an essence.

Essences and Essentialism

essentialism The view that for any given entity there is an essence—some property that every member of that kind must possess—which gives it its category membership and its category-specific features.

Essentialism is the view that for any given entity there is an essence, or some property that every entity of a given kind must possess in order for it to belong to a given category. Moreover, our essentialist psychology leads us to expect that an essence does not change no matter how we dress up or disguise that entity. We have a strong sense that a dog is a dog, even if we dress him up as a lion for Halloween. Similarly, a rock is a rock and cannot be transformed into water or metal.

This essentialism defies classic definitions that rely on a defining set of features. A classic definition of a dog might be a domesticated, hairy mammal with four legs. But if we meet a dog with just three legs, we do not regard him as a non-dog. Our essentialist psychology still leads us to view him as a dog: he still has the essence of doghood. Likewise, we think of dogs as having hair, one of the features listed in our classic definition, but even a hairless, three-legged dog is a dog. Another part of the classic definition of a dog is a domesticated animal, but if we were to run into a feral, hairless, three-legged dog, we would know him to be a dog because we have a strong intuitive essentialist view of what it is to be a dog. And we cannot quite put our finger on what that essence is; we just know it is there.

We have talked about categories (which might be natural or arbitrary), we have talked about concepts (which arise in the minds of people, including children), and we have talked about natural kinds (which are categories that we perceive to be based on real and natural categories such as "dogs," "water," or "thunder"). There is a strong association between natural-kinds categories and essentialist beliefs: We have an intuitive sense that natural kinds have an essence, something inside of it that gives it its category membership. There is something inside a dog that gives it its dogness, and no matter what you do to change the dog's appearance, it is still a dog. Whatever that essence is that gives it its dogness is shared among all dogs (see, for example, Gelman & Wellman, 1991).

The concept of an essence was discussed in philosophical literature by the school of British philosophers that included Locke, a group we have already talked about, but the idea dates as far back as Aristotle and Plato. Locke suggested that objects, especially natural kinds, such as animals, plants, and even minerals, have essences and that these essences derive from the identity of the object and determine its properties. Notice, however, that Locke was not suggesting, as we are, that human psychology is designed to perceive essences; rather, he was suggesting that natural kinds really had essences, an important distinction to understand.

We have a strong sense that a dog is a dog, even if we dress him up as a lion for Halloween. We have a strong essentialist view of what it is to be a dog, and although we cannot quite put our finger on what that essence is, we know it is there.

Gelman (1988) found that children as young as 4 seem to have a different way of thinking about natural kinds and artifacts that reveals essentialist thinking with respect to natural kinds. In Gelman's study, 4-year-olds could answer questions about which objects are made by people and which objects are not made by people, for example. And by the age of 7 or 8, children could regard natural-kinds categories as more elaborately structured than categories of artifacts, and their essentialist view of natural kinds allows for a greater number of inferences among basic-level natural-kinds categories (like plants) than basic-level categories of artifacts (like crockery) (Gelman, 1988). Still, the capability of making this distinction develops over time, maturing between the ages of 4 and 7 as the essentialist view of natural kinds becomes more adult-like.

Some of the experiments that best illustrate the child's essentialist understanding are Frank Keil's experiments, which relied on his "transformation method" of querying a young child's understanding. Keil's series of experiments (Keil, 1979, 1989, 1991) show that children have a very strong essentialist perspective toward animals.

In a **transformation experiment**, the child is asked to consider an object that starts out as a member of one category (a raccoon or a coffeepot) but after a series of transformations has the outward appearance of something else (a skunk or a

transformation experiment An experiment in which a child is asked whether an item can change category membership given the appropriate manipulation of features. It is used to test a child's intuitions about essentialism.

birdfeeder). The child is asked what the object is: Is it a raccoon or a skunk? A coffeepot or a birdfeeder? The question is meant to probe the child's essentialist understanding of the category: Is there an essence, something inside that prevents a change in category membership whatever the changes are to the object's outward appearance?

Here is an example of a transformation experiment. In a natural-kind trial, the experimenter tells the child

> The doctors took a raccoon (show picture of raccoon) and shaved away some of its fur. They dyed what was left all black. Then they bleached a single strip all white down the center of its back. Then, with surgery, they put in its body a sac of super smelly yucky stuff, just like a skunk has. When they were all done, the animal looked like this (show a picture of a skunk). After the operation was this a skunk or a raccoon? (Keil, 1986, p. 143)

And here is what the experimenter tells the child in one example of an artifact trial:

> The doctors took a coffeepot that looked like this (show picture of coffeepot). They sawed off the handle, sealed the top, took off the top knob, sealed closed the spout, and sawed it off. They also sawed off the base and attached a flat piece of metal. They attached a little stick, cut a window in it, and filled the metal container with bird food. When they were done it looked like this (show picture of birdfeeder). After the operation was this a coffeepot or a birdfeeder? (Keil, 1986, p. 144)

The results show a developing essentialist understanding. First, children of all ages accept the transformation of the artifacts, as do adults. If someone has completely changed the form and function of a coffeepot so that it now functions as a birdfeeder, we all call it a birdfeeder. Why not? Other artifact transformations that were easily accepted by children were tire to boot, garbage to chair, and tie to shoelace.

In contrast, older children and adults reject the idea that natural kinds can change category membership. No matter what you do to a raccoon and what it looks like when you are finished, it is still a raccoon, and that is final. Other natural-kinds transformations that are rejected by older children and adults are tiger to lion, diamond to pearl, and grapefruit to orange. Younger children, that is, the 4-year-olds, are relatively tolerant of the idea of an object changing category membership: It looks so much like a skunk and acts like a skunk, I guess it is a skunk, consistent with the perceptually driven psychology that Piaget would expect. Still, even a 4-year-old requires that the transformation be sufficiently convincing. Putting a skunk costume on a raccoon does not make it a skunk, even if it looks just like one. Children also have a much harder time with a transformation across greatly dissimilar categories, from animal to plant, for example, and especially across the animate–inanimate boundary. So the pattern of results shows the development of an essentialist understanding of natural kinds. As early as 4 years of age, there is some understanding of the distinction between natural kinds and artifacts and that understanding develops until 7 years of age when it is nearly adult-like. Other research has also revealed children's essentialist thinking about biological kinds (Gelman & Wellman, 1991; Guntheil & Rosengren, 1993; Keil, 1989).

Transformation experiments show children's resistance to category changes and thus reveal their essentialist thinking with respect to natural kinds.

Just to be clear, the idea of essentialism, especially as the term is used by cognitive developmentalists, is not that there *is* an essence of a dog or a raccoon or a diamond. We are talking about the idea that a perceived essence is part of human psychology. People act as if there is an essence for each natural kind. This is as true for adults as it is for children, and it is easy to map this concept of essence onto things that are now known, specifically DNA. Since the discovery of DNA, it is easy for people to think that the dogness that makes dogs dogs, or the raccoonness that makes raccoons raccoons, is in the animal's DNA. Following our discussion of DNA in Chapter 3 and what DNA does, it should be clear that DNA does not, in fact, hold an essence. It is just a really large molecule that can be transcribed to make a protein. It is nothing more magical or essential than that.

From the Classroom to the Lab

You have read that young children treat natural-kinds categories differently than they treat categories of artifacts, or things that are "man-made." But consider this: Modern domestic breeds of dogs have been created by a long history of natural selection followed by a period of artificial selection. Imagine you want to know whether children think of these dogs as if they were natural kinds with essences or as if they were artifacts, like teapots. How would you design an experiment? What would your procedure be? What age groups would you recruit for your study? What would your outcome measures be? How would you interpret your results?

What are the features of the mental structure that would allow for essentialism? Essentialism is just a strong case of our concepts that we discussed earlier. We have talked about the fact that concepts allow for inferences. Our essentialist views of natural-kinds categories make them particularly powerful concepts, rich with inferential potential. We can infer a lot about an entity if we can assign it to a natural kind. Once we know that something is a rabbit, we know that its parents were rabbits and that its offspring will be rabbits. We know that it likes to eat carrots and lettuce, that it drinks water, that it moves about and breathes, and that someday it will die. Furthermore, without inspection, we know it has blood, a stomach, intestines, and a heart, and these are just a few of the inferences we can make when we know that the object is a rabbit because we know this to be true of other members of the category. And really, no modification of this rabbit will change our belief that it is a rabbit. If you kill it, it is just a dead rabbit; if you shave it, it is just a bald rabbit; if you feed it dog food, it is just a dissatisfied rabbit; if you sterilize it so that it cannot reproduce, it is just a sterile rabbit, but it is always a rabbit, nonetheless. Our essentialist view will not allow us to let go of that perception because the perceived essence of the rabbit is immutable.

DIFFERENT RESEARCH APPROACHES, DIFFERENT FINDINGS

Results from studies in the tradition of Gelman, Carey and Keil suggest that children have rich concepts, whereas early Piagetian research suggested that children

Conceptual Development Milestones

Age	Skills
3 Months	Infants distinguish cats from dogs (Quinn & Eimas, 1996). Infants more easily discriminate between basic-level categories than other levels (Mandler, 1998).
3½ Months	Infants appear to have the category "mammal" (Behl-Chadha, 1996).
14 Months	Infants understand that animals, as a category, drink (McDonough & Mandler, 1998).
2 Years	Children start learning basic-level words first.
2½ Years	Children are more likely to make inferences within a natural-kind category than within a perceptually similar pair (Gelman & Coley, 1990).
3 Years	Children are more likely to draw inferences within basic-level categories than across other levels (Gelman, 1988).
4 Years	Children use functional components to help them categorize (Krascum & Andrews, 1998).
5 Years	Children do not show adult functional fixedness (German & Defeyter, 2000).
7 Years	Children regard natural-kinds categories as more complex than artifacts. Children reject the idea that natural kinds can be transformed into a different category (Springer & Keil, 1989).
8 Years	Children still make errors on Piaget's class-inclusion problems (Inhelder & Piaget, 1964).

inductive method A research method in which a researcher asks a child what kinds of inferences he can make from one entity to another in order to probe the child's categories in terms of membership and internal structure.

INNOVATIVE RESEARCH METHOD

relied very heavily on perceptual, especially visual, similarity. What differences between the studies account for the differing results? Broadly, two major differences in approach.

First, the methodologies differed dramatically and therefore measures that resulted from the tasks were different: Piaget and others whose work preceded the innovative work of Gelman and Carey and others asked participants to sort or to tell "which ones go together." This task was likely to yield thematic groupings as categorization and may not have mapped onto any of the child's cognitive facilities. It may not have been clear to the child what the experimenter was asking him to do. More contemporary cognitive psychologists like Gelman, Carey and Keil use the transformation method or the **inductive method**, which can reveal what categories children hold and, importantly, what inferences are warranted within a category. For instance, all birds may have gizzards, but not all birds weigh the same. These researchers essentially ask children what kinds of inferences or generalizations they can make from one entity to another. If the function of concepts is to allow generalizations, then this is a more naturalistic question for the child to consider.

A second difference between these two generations of studies is the nature of the specific category that was being studied. Contemporary studies show that natural-kinds categories are rich sources of inference and even compare the inferences children make within natural-kinds and artificial categories. Traditional, Piagetian research assumed that all categories were classic categories, completely describable by a list of necessary and sufficient features, and thus researchers used arbitrary, artificial categories. These categories did not support inference, nor were they easy categories for the children to acquire.

Special Design

In this book we are interested in identifying and examining psychological processes that were designed by natural selection. In this chapter, you have probably inferred that the psychological processes underlying the formation of categories and concepts in children were selected for by natural selection. Categories are surprisingly uniform from person to person and from culture to culture. Certainly categories are not completely uniform since artifacts and events might be unique to one culture, making that particular concept absent in other cultures, but categories regarding living things and other natural kinds are remarkably uniform compared to the infinite number of possible arbitrary categories.

In order to determine whether a trait is an adaptation, evolutionary psychologists look for evidence that the trait in question is well engineered for its job: Does it show signs of precision, economy, efficiency, constancy, and complexity in service of its function (Dawkins, 1986; Williams, 1966, 1985)? Given these accepted criteria, the mental structures that support categories, concepts, and essentialism in developing children provide evidence of specialized design. Experiments described in this chapter, such as Krasnow (2008) and Krascum and Andrews (1998) show that categories are functional, not arbitrary. Evidence from transformation and induction studies also show that concepts are reliably developing following functional, not arbitrary or perceptually driven, criteria.

Evolutionary thinkers who are interested in the question believe that design by natural selection can be demonstrated via comparative studies (i.e., studies that compare humans to other animals) that show the convergence and divergence of a trait (Curio, 1973; Dawkins, 1986). Certainly we would expect other species to have different categories that are functional for them: Fruit is categorized as food for a fruit bat but not for a vampire bat. The categories that humans have are the categories that were functional (and increased reproductive success) in the EEA, whereas the categories that other animals have would likely be those that increased their fitness in evolutionary history.

What Would Associationists Say about Children's Categorization?

Essentialism in children is very difficult for associationist models to explain. The associationist perspective relies heavily on perceptual similarity. But studies show that children's categories allow for rich inferences that cannot be explained by perceptual similarity (Gelman, 2000; Scholnick, Nelson, Gelman, & Miller, 1999; Wellman & Gelman, 1998). When you show a child a picture of a prototypical bird, a picture of a bat that looks a lot like that bird, and a picture of an unusual bird (say a flamingo) that has an entirely different shape, the child is more likely to attribute new facts that you tell him about the bird to the penguin than to the bat. For example, if you tell the child that the target bird has a spleen (and the child has never heard of a spleen before) and then ask the child which other animal has a spleen—the bat, which looks very similar to the bird, or the penguin, which looks altogether different from the target bird—the child will pick the penguin.

THE PROBLEM WITH SIMILARITY

When Eleanor Rosch and her colleagues talk about categories, they are talking about psychological entities, not ideal or hypothetical groupings, as Plato did. The items in the category may or may not be a real-world grouping. Similarly, when Rosch talks about basic-level categories, she is talking about a level of thinking that is created by the human mind: She is not implying that there is actually anything more basic about apples than about fruit. The basic quality is in the mind of the beholder, not a property of the category. In the real world a dog is not more of a dog than it is an animal. A category is basic because the human mind uses the category as a basic category, not because the world is made of some categories that are more basic than others.

Rosch describes basic categories as the categories in which exemplars are the most similar to each other and most dissimilar to exemplars of other categories. Be aware here of your own instinct blindness because when Rosch talks about the similarity (or dissimilarity) between any two things, she is not talking about properties of the actual objects; she is talking about our perceptions. They are similar with respect to features that we see, that we notice, that are important to us, and that we use to categorize objects (Goodman, 1972). In order to categorize two things as the same, the child has to perceive similarity. But that which constitutes similarity and that which constitutes difference depends on our functional relationship with these objects in the EEA. It depends upon the biological significance of the objects in question.

> **6.13 Press Pause**
>
> Similarity is in the mind of the beholder.

The first part of this chapter introduced you to the idea that concepts and categories are formed by our human psychology and that there are other possible and logical ways to classify the things we see, but the way humans classify them is largely universal. Hopefully this chapter allowed you to get beyond your instinct blindness and appreciate that the commonality of concepts across people and across cultures needs an explanation.

In this chapter you read some possible explanations for why our human psychology generates concepts and categories. Some people have suggested that we have to categorize because we are cognitively incapable of representing everything we encounter individually. This view is plausible but does not explain why the concepts and categories children create are so ubiquitous and logical. Perhaps a more fruitful view of categories and concepts is that they are functional because they allow for inference. If we know a lot about a fish, when we encounter one that we have never seen before, we already have a lot of information about it because we make inferences based on its category membership.

You also read about Piaget's view of categorization in children. First, Piaget approached the question with the classic definitions of categories, wherein every category had a list of necessary and sufficient features that qualified or disqualified items for inclusion. His research was focussed on discovering whether children had this kind of category, and he concluded that they did not: Children had complexes that were more fluid and less well defined than classic categories.

Finally, you read about a more contemporary, functionalist view of concepts and categories and their development in young children. There is good evidence that children develop natural-kinds categories, categorizing things into natural groupings that allow for maximal inference. Children often view members of these categories as having an essence, that special something that confers category membership no matter how many of the usual features are missing. You also read about important innovations in methods in this area, techniques such as the inductive method and the transformation experiment, that allow developmental psychologists to discover the nature of the categories and concepts that children have.

PRESS PAUSE SUMMARY

- Concepts and categories are very useful: They allow us to make predictions about what to expect from individual entities that we have never seen before.
- We do not notice the uniformity in the concepts people have, in part because we fail to imagine the myriad of other logically possible categories.   *instinct blindness*
- Piaget saw categories as classic categories and tested whether infants and children have these classic categories. They did not, he concluded.
- Piaget, Vygotsky, and others have found that young children sort objects thematically, rather than taxonomically, and rely on perceptual features in their sorting.
- Categories and concepts allow for inference.
- Young children's developing categories are functional.
- As early as 3 months of age there is evidence that infants have some categories.

- Piaget's class-inclusion experiments led him to conclude that children were unable to reason about subordinate and superordinate classes.
- A hierarchy of nested category relationships allows for even greater inferential power.
- Children as young as 2½ years of age have rich natural-kinds categories and can make inferences or inductions from one category member to another.
- Recent experiments show that children are not perceptually bound when forming categories as Piaget would have predicted.
- Transformation experiments show children's resistance to category changes and thus reveal their essentialist thinking with respect to natural kinds.
- Similarity is in the mind of the beholder.

KEY TERMS AND CONCEPTS

basic-level category, 199
category, 184
classic category, 188
class-inclusion experiment, 198
complex, 192
concept, 185
essentialism, 204

functional fixedness, 197
inductive method, 208
natural-kind category, 185
perceptual category, 183
perceptually bound, 191
thematic association, 192
transformation experiment, 205

QUESTIONS FOR THOUGHT AND DISCUSSION

1. What is a classic category? What evidence is incompatible with the idea that the human mind stores categories as classic categories?
2. How does a functional view of children's concepts differ from a Piagetian view of children's concepts?
3. What two methods did Piaget use to test for an understanding of category membership and categorical hierarchies? Describe each method.
4. What methodological innovations, developed since Piaget's time, allowed for a deeper understanding of children's concepts?
5. What is a natural kind? What is essentialism? Describe experiments that show an association between natural kinds and essentialism.
6. In this chapter, you read that "similarity is in the mind of the beholder." What does that mean? Why must that be so?

From the Classroom to the Lab: Follow Up

Consider the experiment you designed in response to the "From the Classroom to the Lab" challenge earlier in this chapter.

What age group did you choose? Why? How would you expect the results to differ with a different age group?

Describe the design and procedure. Why do you think this procedure will answer the question you want to ask?

What is your dependent variable?

What are your independent variables?

Describe what you expect the results to be. What conclusions would you draw from these results?

Describe at least one possible alternative outcome. How would you interpret the results in this case?

chapter 7

Core Knowledge Part I
Physics, Space, Biology, and Number

Opening Vignette: Core Knowledge

A young baby reaches out to grasp a toy rattle, picks it up by the handle, and watches the round rattle move toward her face. This simple and common action on the part of the developing infant actually relies on a great deal of knowledge about the physical world. She knows that the rattle is a physical object. The shape of her hand as she approaches the rattle reveals her knowledge of the size of the object. And she knows that the object is coherent, such that if she moves the handle toward her, the interesting part of the rattle will come too. In fact, recent research shows that even very young infants have a surprising understanding of some core domains of knowledge. Babies have an understanding of objects and an intuitive understanding of physics. They also have an understanding of numbers and simple addition. And children in early and middle childhood seem to have a precocious understanding of biology. These areas of early understanding have come to be known as *core knowledge*, and researchers in the field believe that these understandings had a functional, adaptive role in our EEA.

Chapter Outline

- The Acquisition of Knowledge
- Framing the Question of Knowledge Acquisition
- Core Knowledge
- Areas of Core Knowledge
- A Cross-Species Comparison

Learning Objectives, Outcomes

- In the first part of this chapter, you will read about the problem of knowledge acquisition and learn a bit about the history of the problem. Moreover, you will be asked to think about knowledge acquisition from an engineering perspective and how knowledge acquisition would proceed much more efficiently with *constraints on learning* and *domain specificity*. Then you will read about the idea of core knowledge and examine research in areas that illustrate this concept.

- The first core domain you will learn about deals with *intuitive physics* including knowledge about objects. You will read some of the groundbreaking evidence that shows that infants have expectations about how objects in the world will move and how gravity influences those objects.

- You will also read about Piaget's thoughts on *object permanence* and recent methodological innovations that have changed what we know about it. You will learn about the *violation of expectancy* paradigm and the lessons about the early intuitive physics that this method has revealed.

- The second domain you will be introduced to is a child's understanding of space. What cues do children use and what cues do they ignore when locating a hidden object? When navigating through space, children have some cognitive tricks in common with rats and even ants!

- The third domain of core knowledge that you will learn about is a child's understanding of biology. Experiments in this area have focussed on children who are slightly older, and the development of intuitive biology appears to happen later than the development of intuitive physics. Nonetheless, children show an impressive understanding of biology, inheritance, growth, and death. You will read about how this early sophistication contrasts with Piaget's expectations, and you will read some evidence that children develop this understanding of biology cross-culturally.

- The last domain you will read about is the area of mathematics. Again you will learn about the violation of expectancy paradigm and, in this case, how it has revealed that very young infants have expectations about numbers. Five-month-olds know if small sets are equal or different. They know that if you add one to one, there should be two. You will also read that as children grow older and learn to count, they follow reliably developing rules for counting.

The Acquisition of Knowledge

For centuries, philosophers and developmental theorists have pondered how people come to have knowledge. The ancient Greek branch of philosophy known as *epistemology* is concerned with questions about knowledge acquisition. One debate in epistemology is whether knowledge is created within a person or whether it is a product of experience. As we have seen in previous chapters, the Greek empiricists, and later the British empiricists, believed that knowledge was based on experience, that it could only occur as a result of experience, and that it must be perceived via the five senses in order to enter the child's mind. However, this view is archaic, and no contemporary developmental psychologist believes that a child's mind is truly a blank slate.

7.1 Press Pause

Since ancient times, philosophers have been wondering how people acquire knowledge, usually framing the debate in terms of nature (infants know things without training) and nurture (all knowledge must be acquired).

How do people come to have knowledge? The ancient Greek branch of philosophy known as *epistemology* is concerned with questions about knowledge acquisition.

Early rationalists believed that at least some knowledge is provided *a priori* or without having to be taught. That is, at least some concepts develop in people via a process of maturity and are not entirely dependent upon perceived observations. According to this view, one could know something—say, that a rock in mid-air will fall if not supported or that if a family has two pieces of food to share and they eat one piece, only one remains—without ever having observe it. So again, we find ourselves facing the nature vs. nurture debate. But let us think about this old problem from a new vantage point.

An assumption in both the nativist and the empiricist views, perhaps especially the empiricist view, is that knowledge acts in some key ways like physical "stuff": Knowledge is some kind of substance that either has to get in your brain or is some-

If someone emails a text document to you, nothing physical has left their computer and nothing physical has entered yours. Rather, there is new organization among the bits and bytes in your computer that represent the sent text. This is a metaphor for knowledge.

how already there. Another approach is to put aside the notion that knowledge is some sort of stuff that has to "get in there" and think about it in terms of information processing. In order for a text document (a reasonable metaphor for knowledge) to be transmitted from your computer to another computer, nothing physical needs to be taken from yours and given to the other. After the transfer, your computer does not weigh less; the other does not weigh more. But bits and bytes are now organized on the other computer in such a way that they represent the text; their organization represents knowledge, if you will.

To say that a young child knows that a rock will fall in mid-air if not supported is a claim (however remote) about the organization of neurons and how they communicate with each other. We know that the connections among neurons are the result of the developmental processes, a result of the species-typical development of a normal human child with a complete genome and the benefit of the resources of a species-typical environment. In this case, we do not have to ask a nature vs. nurture question but can instead explore what knowledge young infants and children demonstrate and how it comes to be represented in their brains.

Framing the Question of Knowledge Acquisition

Let us start by being mindful of three related considerations:

1. From an engineering point of view, how would you build a baby that could have knowledge?
2. What are the kinds of inheritance a baby receives reliably in a species-typical environment?
3. What informational priorities were there in the EEA?

> **7.2 Press Pause**
>
> Considering our evolutionary history can help frame the problem of knowledge acquisition.

CONSTRAINTS ON LEARNING ALLOW KNOWLEDGE ACQUISITION

Imagine that you are a computer programmer and that you have to write the code that is installed into a developing baby early in prenatal development (since we know that learning takes place before birth) that will lead him or her to function appropriately at various ages, ultimately resulting in a well-functioning adult. Assume that you get to take advantage of a species-typical environment. How do you approach this problem? Work in artificial intelligence (AI) reveals that the acquisition of knowledge requires some kind of preparedness. For many years now, computer scientists working in the field of AI have tried to create perception and learning in machines. One very clear take-home message that has come from this enterprise is an understanding that in order to learn, indeed in order to be sensitive to the right kinds of cues in the machine's environment (the problem of perception), the machine would need to have a lot of initial structure (Rumelhart & McClelland, 1985), something people in the field of development refer to as *constraints on learning*.

The sight of a male stickleback can be used to condition another male stickleback to bite a glass rod but not to swim through a hoop, whereas the sight of a female stickleback can be used to condition a male stickleback to swim through a hoop but not to bite a glass rod.

Constraints on learning are the biased heuristics and privileged hypotheses that an animal uses when acquiring information about the world. The discovery of such constraints were a surprise to people studying psychology and animal behaviour who expected that animals (people included) learned by operant conditioning: that a behaviour (any behaviour) paired with a reinforcement would be learned and repeated. Evidence shows that any arbitrarily chosen behaviour is not equally trainable using operant conditioning: The "reward" of seeing a male stickleback fish can be used to condition another male stickleback to bite a glass rod but not to swim through a hoop. Conversely, the "reward" of seeing a female stickleback fish can be used to condition a male stickleback to swim through a hoop but not to bite a glass rod (Sevenster, 1973). Furthermore, a pig or a raccoon can be taught to carry a token (the way one might use a coin) to exchange for food. But if the distance the token has to be carried is too long, the pig may stop and try "rooting" and the raccoon may start washing his tokens, both species-typical behaviours associated with food (Breland & Breland, 1961, 1966), whereas a chimpanzee trained to perform for food may begin making food calls that interfere with its performance (Gardner & Gardner, 1985). All of these examples show that the minds of these animals are not blank slates; the mind comes with prior hypotheses about what behaviours may be paired with which outcomes. It came to be recognized that most or all animal learning that occurs naturally is a result of constraints on learning (Shettleworth, 1972). People working with computers that are designed to learn have also realized that constraints on learning do not just make learning faster; they are actually necessary to make learning possible (Rumelhart & McClelland, 1985).

We know that constrained knowledge acquisition is rapid because the number of hypotheses that have to be tested is limited. (For example, if you are trying to learn who your mother is, it is best to focus on the people in your environment and save time by ignoring the furniture, appliances, and pets.) The more constrained knowledge acquisition is, the faster the learning. At the other extreme, the fewer constraints there are, the slower learning becomes until it is practically and then theoretically impossible. In order for you to build a baby that could have knowledge, what kinds of preparedness

constraints on learning Biased heuristics or privileged hypotheses that an animal uses when acquiring information about the world.

A pig or raccoon can be taught to carry a token to exchange for food. But if the distance is too long, the pig may stop and try "rooting" and the racoon may start washing his tokens (both food-associated behaviours), whereas a chimpanzee trained to perform for food may begin making food calls that interfere with its performance. Operant conditioning is not unfettered by species-typical behaviours.

would you have to build? What kinds of structures, concepts, or learning mechanisms would you like to endow the child with?

> **7.3 Press Pause**
>
> People working in artificial intelligence know that some prior assumptions and constraints on learning are necessary for knowledge acquisition. Animal studies reveal constraints on learning.

REMEMBER THE SYSTEMS VIEW OF INHERITANCE

As you engineer this developing child, think of the means of inheritance you can use to communicate from one generation to the other. The infant will inherit genes from her parents and inherit her parents' environment. This will include information that is reliably recurring, such as the day–night cycle, the seasons' cycle, and the wavelength composition of terrestrial sunlight, and it will include information that is developmentally relevant but that changes from environment to environment, such as the local native language. (Remember, however, that many aspects of human language are unchanging from one language to the next.)

INFORMATIONAL PRIORITIES IN THE EEA

When you are designing this baby who is to learn and develop knowledge to behave appropriately as a child and later as an adult, it is very important to consider the environment in which we evolved and the informational priorities of a human child or adult in that environment. In essence, what are the areas of expertise with which you want to equip this developing child? Before you read on, stop here for a moment and see if you can think of the kinds of knowledge that would have been relevant to a developing child in the EEA and the kinds of information that would have been reliably available during development in the EEA.

Core Knowledge

One possible solution to the knowledge acquisition problem, and perhaps a good model for how knowledge develops in human children, is to endow certain biologically relevant core domains with sufficient reliably developing structures to provide useful concepts for the child, relying only on experience that is very likely to occur in a

What were the informational priorities in the environment in which we evolved? In this image, the !Kung, a current hunter–gatherer society, gather water at Tsodilo Hills in Botswana.

core knowledge Privileged domains of knowledge that children learn easily by virtue of developing cognitive preparedness that is specific to those domains. These domains reflect a fitness advantage in our evolutionary history.

species-typical environment. Developing children may have **core knowledge**: privileged domains of knowledge that they learn easily by virtue of developing cognitive preparedness that is specific to those domains. These domains reflect a fitness advantage in our evolutionary history.

One area in which there is clearly a rich endowment of specialized learning mechanisms is language acquisition. We will discuss the hypothetical "language acquisition device" in Chapter 9. Other related terms that are sometimes used by developmentalists who think along these lines are *privileged domains* (Siegler & Crowley, 1994) or *innate domains* (Carey, 1995), but throughout our discussion, we will use the term *core knowledge*.

DOMAIN SPECIFICITY

domain specificity The idea that many aspects of adult and child psychology are processed by specialized psychological processes that have been shaped by natural selection and focus on areas of knowledge that were fitness-relevant in the EEA.

One implication of the considerations described above, and an idea embraced by core-knowledge theorists, is that knowledge should be domain-specific. **Domain specificity** is the idea that many aspects of adult and child psychology rely on specialized psychological processes that have been shaped by natural selection and focus on areas of knowledge that were fitness-relevant in the EEA.

One early and clear explanation of domain specificity and the logic that compels it comes from Noam Chomsky (1980). A set of core domains of knowledge is part of the human psychological endowment. These domains include knowledge about language, knowledge about physical objects, and knowledge about number, for example. Each domain of core knowledge covers a different area of expertise, and we will work through some illustrations in this chapter and the next.

7.4 **Press Pause**

Domains of knowledge are necessary in order to create a baby (or machine) that can acquire knowledge.

Developmental psychologists who espouse the core-knowledge perspective describe a domain as a knowledge system that includes information about what entities are included in the domain as well as rules that describe how the entities in the domain behave. Human cognition, according to this view, is a collection of domain-specific systems of knowledge (Carey & Spelke, 1992).

The domain also has limits; it involves knowledge of what entities are excluded and does not offer help in making inferences outside of the domain (Spelke & Kinzler, 2007). The psychological machinery that allows one to acquire knowledge about one's native language is different from the psychological machinery that allows one to acquire knowledge about faces, which is in turn different from the psychological machinery that allows one to learn how to walk. Furthermore, each of these very specialized kinds of learning is different from domain-general knowledge acquisition.

These core domains of knowledge are thought to be human universals, akin to the universality of language acquisition in humans (Carey & Spelke, 1992). Note that this design does not exclude some relatively general knowledge acquisition. Indeed, simple learning that follows the rules of associative learning is just what has been studied in "learning" research for the past several decades. People can, indeed, learn to associate arbitrary pairs of words. However, this relatively general learning is not a very powerful kind of learning, and domain-specific learning mechanisms were powerful and important tools for the child developing in the EEA.

WHAT WOULD PIAGET SAY ABOUT CORE KNOWLEDGE?

Again, in order to clarify the point that core-knowledge theorists are making, it may be helpful to understand whom they are arguing against. Piaget's view was that children had limited cognitive sophistication with respect to knowledge, that they did not have specialized processing in different domains, and that their understanding was limited to what they could see rather than making rich inferences based on their perceptual experiences. Among developmental psychologists who have a core-knowledge perspective, research is often designed to probe Piaget's claims, in which case the Piagetian predictions become the null hypothesis in the experiment. A refutation of Piaget's stages, or Piaget's rejection of the idea of sophisticated knowledge in very young children, is, in some sense, the litmus test of an interesting contribution to the field. In this chapter and the next, we will read about research showing that very young children have knowledge about physics, space, numbers, faces, animacy (i.e., categorizing objects in the world into those objects that are alive or "animate" and those that are not), and other peoples' mental states that far exceed what Piaget would have predicted of young children's cognitive development.

WHAT WOULD ASSOCIATIONISTS SAY ABOUT CORE KNOWLEDGE?

There is another group of sceptics whose ideas we can test. Traditionally, in the field of psychology, people who have studied learning have had an associationist approach, talking about a domain-general capacity of people (and other organisms with a brain) to learn to associate one feature with another. A child is supposed to learn by making associations. Indeed, years of research with rats and pigeons make it fairly convincing that organisms do learn to associate things. According to this view, a few general learning mechanisms such as classical conditioning and operant conditioning are available. But developmental psychologists who study core knowledge are interested in more specialized learning and knowledge development. Indeed, for people studying the development of core knowledge, an associationistic explanation of an observed phenomenon may be used experimentally as the null hypothesis. Debates between whether there is domain-specific preparedness to learn a particular type of knowledge or whether there is domain-general associationist learning sometimes get framed in terms of nature and nurture: Those who favour domain-general explanations are wary of the large role of constraints on learning that were shaped by natural selection, and those who favour domain-specific explanations expect little to develop if the slate is too blank.

Notice that domain-general learning is not completely incompatible with associationist learning mechanisms such as classical conditioning and operant conditioning. Teaching a raccoon to wash a token in order to earn food is still operant conditioning. It is just that teaching behaviours that are naturally, for the raccoon, within the domain of food preparation is much easier than teaching the raccoon to sit, root, or stand on two feet in order to earn food. The learning mechanisms within the domain can operate according to the rules of classical and operant conditioning; the two ideas are not, in principle, mutually exclusive.

7.5 Press Pause

Piagetian and associationist approaches predict relatively simple learning and immature knowledge and can be used experimentally to generate null hypotheses.

Areas of Core Knowledge

There are a number of domains in which children seem to develop an understanding that cannot be explained by tutoring or mere exposure. These are the domains of core knowledge. Core knowledge is reliably developing, domain-specific, and relevant to survival in the EEA. We will explore some of these domains and the research that illustrates them in depth. The following may not be the only domains of core knowledge, but they are the areas on which researchers have focused, and they give us a clear picture of development in these areas.

OBJECTS AND A DEVELOPING INTUITIVE PHYSICS

intuitive physics
Knowledge relevant to physics and objects that develops early in human infants.

One domain of knowledge that was clearly functional in the EEA (as well as in our current environment) was physical knowledge, or a naive theory of physics. Think about what we, as adults, know and expect regarding physical objects. We know they will fall to the ground if not supported, that two of them will not pass through each other, and that they still exist even if we cannot see them. These understandings help us tremendously when we want to act and interact with the physical world, and this has been true since before the time of our hunter–gatherer ancestors.

Human babies show precocious and sophisticated understandings of their own laws of physics (which are not necessarily the same as adult laws of physics) and have knowledge about objects that greatly exceeds Piaget's estimate. Babies show developing rules about the support of objects, they show an understanding of gravity, and they show a developing understanding of object permanence: That is, they continue to understand that an object exists (is permanent) even when it is out of sight.

According to Elizabeth Spelke, who is an advocate of the core-knowledge view and has contributed substantial research to our understanding of infants' developing knowledge about objects, such early knowledge "may derive from universal, early-developing capacities to represent and reason about the physical world. These capacities may emerge in all infants whose early growth and experience fall within some normal range. They may enable children to infer how any material body will move in any situation" (Spelke, 1991, pp. 160–161).

Object permanence

Earlier in this chapter we talked about the historical context of the exploration and discovery in the area of core knowledge: Specifically, we saw that many experiments in this area are designed to refute claims that Piaget made. This is also true of the study of object permanence.

Piaget made the remarkable claim that infants younger than 8 months of age do not have object permanence (Piaget, 1952). What he meant was that those infants literally did not know that an object, say a toy doll, existed if the infant could not see or touch it: out of sight, out of mind. This claim was based on his observation that if a child was interested in a doll, and the doll was covered or concealed from the child's view, the child did not search for it.

Since Piaget's time, people have explored this remarkable claim. There is widespread agreement, and substantial evidence, that Piaget's initial claim was correct: If an infant younger than 8 months is playing with an object that is suddenly removed from their view (e.g., if it drops out of their crib or is covered by a cloth) the infant will not look for it. However, Piaget inferred from this observation that infants had no mental representation of the object and that inference has been challenged with some pretty clever experiments.

Infants start passing Piaget's object permanence task at around 8 months of age. Before this point, they will not search for an occluded object, even if it holds their interest.

First, and most simply, Piaget never tried this "out of sight" experiment by simply turning off the lights. It turns out that if a 5-month-old baby is looking at an attractive object and the whole room goes dark, the baby may indeed reach out and manually search for the object, and he explores the place he last saw the object (Hood & Willatts, 1986). Although this is a very simple experiment (try it at home!) it challenges the belief that babies younger than 8 months do not know that an invisible object still exists. Not only that, but the infant has some knowledge about the object, such as its size. If a 6-month-old hears the sound of a familiar large object, he will reach for it with two hands, but if he hears the sound of a familiar small object, he will reach for it with one hand (Clifton, Rochat, Litovsky, & Perris, 1991). Not only does the infant have a representation of the object, but the representation holds some useful details!

Piaget's underestimation of infants' object knowledge was primarily due to methodological shortcomings. He observed infants' spontaneous behaviours and concluded that there was no evidence of object permanence. But think about it: What *could* an infant do that would show evidence of object permanence? Researchers since Piaget have pursued the idea that if infants respond differently to possible events than to impossible events in any way, then that is evidence that they understand that a rule has been violated. Specifically, we can test their expectation that the rules of object permanence have been violated. (Recall from Chapter 2 that the violation of expectation paradigm predicts that infants will look longer at surprising or impossible events, but even if they looked for a significantly shorter duration, which sometimes happens in looking-time paradigms, we can still infer that the infants can tell the difference between the two presentation types.)

Spelke proposes that in addition to object permanence, infants have expectations regarding the *continuity*, the *contact*, and the rules governing *cohesion* when it comes to physical objects. Objects are expected to have continuity, meaning that if they travel from one point to another, they have to occupy every point in between rather than beaming over Star-Trek style. The rules of contact require that one object be in contact with another in order to have an influence on its movement. Objects also have cohesion, meaning they have to remain a unified whole, not scatter and re-form. Spelke and her colleagues and students have conducted a number of experiments that illustrate this early knowledge.

figure 7.1 Continuity

Four-month-olds saw the rod moving back and forth behind the occluder. Once the occluder was removed, infants who saw one solid rod were not surprised, but those who saw two disconnected segments were surprised and increased looking time.

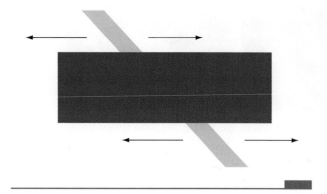

Continuity

Figure 7.1 illustrates the stimulus used in Spelke's first experiment designed to test whether infants have a sense of continuity. Two rods extend above and below a rectangle and move together back and forth. Adults see this stimulus as a single rod (even though a single continuous rod is not actually visible), occluded by the rectangle, and would be surprised to learn that the two visible bar segments were actually separate bars. In order to test how an infant represented the stimulus, Spelke and colleagues employed a habituation paradigm. After the infants viewed the stimulus until they were bored (i.e., until looking time diminished, indicating habituation), a new stimulus was presented, which they might have regarded as the same as or different than the stimulus they had been seeing. Then in a between-subjects design (comparing between subjects who were exposed to different manipulations rather than exposing each subject to two different manipulations and then comparing how they responded to each) the occluder was removed, and some infants saw one single continuous rod, and other infants saw two separate rods. Those who saw two rods dishabituated. The inference warranted by the habituation experiment is that, while watching the training trials, the infant had represented the bar as one continuous bar, just as adults do. As long as the bar is moving, the infant represents one solid bar by the time she is 4 months old (Kellman & Spelke, 1983; Spelke, 1985).

Contact

The principle of contact was explored using a violation of expectation paradigm. In one condition, infants watched a ball start to move from a stationary state after it had been hit by a moving ball and in another condition, a ball started to move just before it was

figure 7.2

After habituating to a hidden event in which an object or human actor seems to launch another, infants were surprised if the two objects *had not* come into contact, but surprised if the two human actors *had* come into contact (Adapted from Kosugi, D., and Fujita, K., 2002).

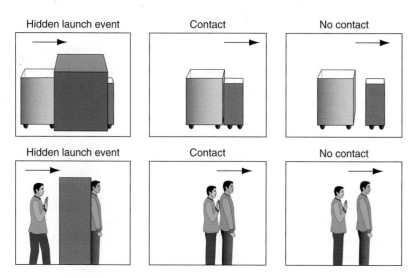

figure 7.3 Leslie and Keeble's contact experiment

Infants understand launch events at 27 months. If they habituate to one block launching the other, reversing the display leads to dishabituation. If a pause is built in at the point of contact, there is no dishabituation because no launch was perceived. (Reprinted from Leslie Keeble, 1987. With permission from Elsevier.)

Direct Launching

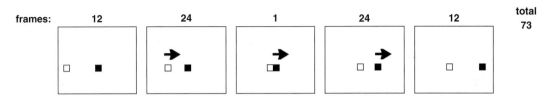

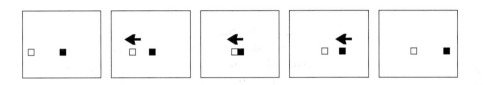

Delayed Reaction

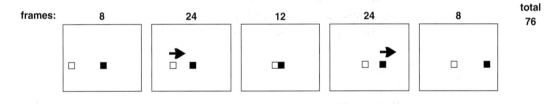

Delayed Reaction Reversed

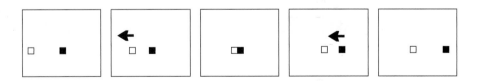

hit by a moving ball. Six-month-old infants looked at the ball that began to move with- out contact longer, indicating that they expect one object to have an effect on another only if there is contact between the two. In a control condition, infants' looking times did not increase if the stimuli were people rather than moving balls. Infants accept that people (but not balls) can affect each other's behaviour without contact (Kotovsky & Baillargeon, 1998; Spelke, Breinlinger, Macomber, & Jacobson, 1992).

In an experiment applying a habituation paradigm, 27-month-old infants watched a launch event in which a small block moved until it was in contact with another block, at which point it stopped and the second block moved off. A control group saw a "delayed launch" event in which the first block moved until it was in contact with the second, at which point it stopped and paused. After the pause, the second block moved off. The results showed dishabituation when the display was reversed only for the infants who saw the launch event, not for those who saw the delayed launch (Leslie & Keeble, 1987).

Cohesion

An object has cohesion if it stays together in one piece rather than crumbling or coming apart when it is moved. You can imagine how a violation of expectation paradigm could be used as an experimental strategy to test whether young infants expect an object to maintain cohesion. Spelke showed infants as young as 3 months of age displays in which they first saw a stationary object. Once they habituated to the display, some infants saw a hand come down and grasp the top of the object and then lift the entire object. The other infants saw the hand come down and grasp the top of the object, but instead of the complete object being lifted, part of the object came along with the hand, and part remained where it was, violating the expectation of cohesion. Infants in the later group looked longer, consistent with the idea that their expectation was violated (Spelke, Breinlinger, Jacobson, & Phillips, 1993).

figure 7.4   Spelke's cohesion experiment

As young as 3 months infants expect objects to be cohesive. If an object comes apart rather than staying connected, looking time increases in a violation of expectation paradigm. (Adapted from Spelke et al, 1993. With permission of Pion Limited, London.)

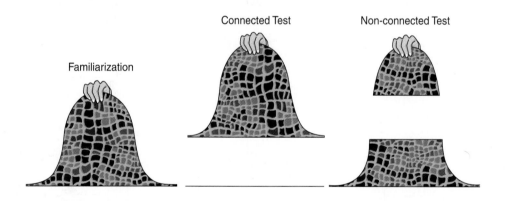

From the Classroom to the Lab

Infants have certain expectations about objects. Imagine you want to know whether infants expect an object to be defined by colour. That is, if an object is partly red but then abruptly changes to blue at some boundary point on the surface of the object, does the infant think that it is one object or two? How would you test that? Would the violation of expectation paradigm be a good method?

Support and gravity

As with object permanence, recent research has revealed that infants have a precocious and sophisticated understanding of the support an object requires so as not to succumb to gravity. Research from Baillargeon and colleagues has shown that infants go through a developmental progression of understandings of the kind of support an object needs in order to not fall down due to gravity. Infants at 3 months understand that an object needs some contact with a solid support in order not to fall, and at 5 months they understand that the contact has to be with the top of the support, not the side, or it will fall. By 6 months of age, the infant knows that most of the bottom of the object needs to be supported in order not to fall; if only a tiny corner of the object is supported, it should fall. How do we know all this when we cannot interview a pre-verbal infant about his beliefs? Baillargeon created a series of "magic shows" in which objects violated these expectations, and she used a violation of expectation paradigm in which the infants' looking times were the dependent measures.

---

figure 7.5   3-month-olds expect an unsupported object to fall

At 3 months, infants are surprised if unsupported objects do not fall.

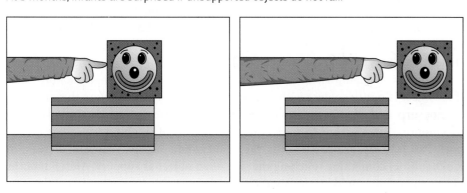

---

figure 7.6   5-month-olds expect support to come from below

At 5 months, infants expect support to come from beneath an object. After 5 months of age, they would be surprised if the object touching only the side of the support did not fall.

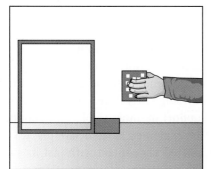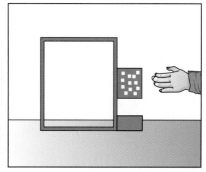

figure 7.7   6-month-olds expect most of the object to be supported

At around 6½ months, infants expect a supported object to contact most of an object's lower surface; otherwise, it should fall.

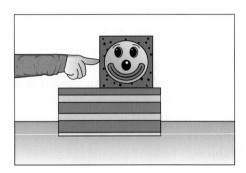 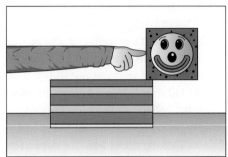

(As an aside, although we go to great lengths to test what is going on in the minds of infants, you should not assume that it is easy to know what is going on in the minds of adults. Due to instinct blindness and an inability to access one's own decision-making processes, a researcher cannot rely on verbal interviews to understand what adults know or how they think.)

At the age of 3 months, infants are "surprised" (they show a longer looking time) if an object is not in contact with a support and does not fall. Before this age, they are not surprised. That is, they do not show a longer looking time. At around the age of 5 months, infants come to accept only the support of an object *beneath* it as support. That is to say, before 5 months, the infant would "accept" (show no increase in looking time) something touching the side of an object as support. After 5 months of age, the infant would be surprised if the object touching only the side of the support did not fall.

Finally, at around the age of 6½ months, infants come to accept the support only if most of the bottom edge of the object is supported. That is to say, before 6½ months, infants "accept" (show no increase in looking time) the support of a tiny corner of the object, as shown in the right panel of Figure 7.7. After 6½ months of age, the infant is surprised if the object touching only the corner of its bottom edge does not fall (Baillargeon, 1998).

There is an important theoretical point to be made regarding this series of experiments. The results are consistent with a core-knowledge view (the reliable development of knowledge via maturation in an enriched environment) but difficult to explain from an associationist point of view. In the core-knowledge research tradition, an associationist account is often taken as the null hypothesis; an experiment whose results can be explained by weak general-purpose associationist learning is not a contribution to the core-knowledge literature. But the fact that 3-month-old infants accept a tiny corner of support or, more implausibly, contact with the side of the object as support cannot be explained by associationist learning: The infant has never seen an object supported via contact with just its side. There is clearly development unfolding, but the developmental pattern cannot be explained simply as learning.

Event categories

Baillargeon has proposed that children also develop an early understanding of specific event categories, such as *occlusion events*, *containment events*, and *covering events*. **Occlusion events** are events in which an object becomes invisible as it moves behind a nearer object, the occluder. **Containment events** are events in which an object moves into a container, possibly becoming invisible. A **covering event** is an event in which an object becomes invisible as it is hidden by a rigid cover or screen (Baillargeon, 2004).

As a result of research in the developing understanding of these events, we see evidence of domain-specific reasoning: Infants apply rules and use informative variables for each event category independently. For example, if they understand that height is important for occlusion events, they may or may not appreciate that height is important during containment events.

Research by Baillargeon and others has shown that as early as 2½ months of age, babies are responsive to violations in occlusion, containment, and covering events, although the variables they respond to differ. For example, 2½-month-old infants watched a Minnie Mouse puppet disappear behind one screen (so that the puppet was occluded) and then reappear behind a different screen that was some distance away. In this violation of expectation paradigm, the infant was surprised that the puppet was not ever visible between the screens (Aguiar & Ballargeon, 1999). It is as if the infant thinks objects behind occluders should be invisible and objects that are not behind occluders should be visible.

Similarly, at 2½ months of age, infants have some understanding of containment events. If the infant watches the experimenter place an object into a container and then move the solid container leaving the hidden object behind, the infant is surprised. A solid container that holds an object should carry the object with it (Hespos & Baillargeon, 2001). These findings are consistent with contemporary ideas about continuity (Kellman & Spelke, 1983; Spelke, 1985) and object permanence (Baillargeon, Spelke, & Wasserman, 1985).

Infants start using the informative variables independently. For example, at around 3½ months of age, infants come to recognize height as an important variable in occlusion. If a tall object goes behind a short occluder, it is not expected to disappear entirely (Baillergeon & DeVos, 1991). By 7½, infants appreciate that transparency is a variable that should be considered in occlusion: Objects should remain visible if they go behind an occluder that is transparent (Baillargeon, 2004).

Although 3½-year-olds use height as an informative variable in occlusion events, it is not until 7½ months of age that it is seen as informative in

---

occlusion event An event in which an object becomes invisible as it moves behind a nearer object, the occluder.

containment event An event in which an object moves into a container, possibly becoming invisible.

covering event An event in which an object becomes invisible as it is hidden by a rigid cover or screen.

---

figure 7.8 Expectations of the occluder

The 3½-month-old infant shows surprise in the low-window but not the high-window event when the mouse disappears behind the occluder, remains unseen, and then reappears from the far side. It is as if the infant expects the mouse to be visible when it passes between the screens. (Adapted from Baillargeon & DeVos, 1991.)

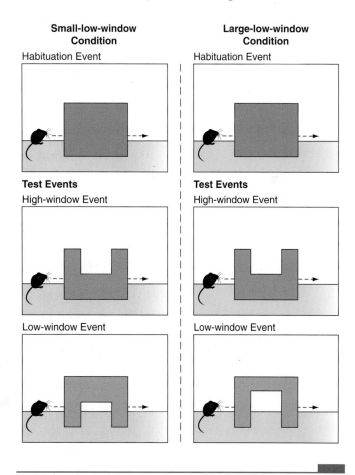

containment events. What is surprising is that the variables that infants will consider when making predictions about objects vary between event categories: An infant can start using a variable for one event category weeks or even months before they use it as informative in terms of another event category. Using a violation of expectation para-

---

figure | 7.9   What infants know about containment

This figure shows a containment event. Although 3½-month-olds use relative height as a factor in occlusion events, it is not until 7½ months that they use height in containment events, showing surprise if a short container contains a tall object. (Adapted from Hespos & Baillargeon, 2001.)

Test Events

Tall Event

Short Event

---

figure | 7.10   What infants know about covering

This figure shows a covering event. Even after infants use height as a factor in occlusion events at 3 months, and as a factor in containment events at 7½ months, it is not until 12 months that they use height as a factor in covering events. (Adapted from Wang, Baillargeon & Paterson, 2004.)

Tall-Cover Event

Short-Cover Event

digm, infants watched as an experimenter lowered a cylinder into a tube. The cylinder was taller than the tube, so should not have been hidden within the tube, but when it was hidden, infants did not reveal any surprise until 7½ months of age (Hespos & Baillargeon, 2001).

Even more surprising, the same cylinder and tube props reveal different results depending upon whether the event is a containment event or a covering event. If the tube is lowered onto the cylinder, so that the infant is seeing a covering event rather than a containment event, it is not until 12 months of age that the infant is surprised when the taller cylinder is completely hidden by the shorter tube. At ages younger than 12 months, infants do not appreciate height as an informative variable in a covering event (Wang, Baillargeon, & Paterson, 2004).

These studies illustrate how infants' concepts in the area of intuitive physics are applied very narrowly. Domain specificity, in this case, refers to very specific domains indeed. These studies also show the power of the violation of expectation paradigm in revealing what young infants know at what age.

The perspectives of Spelke, Baillargeon, and core developmentalists in general are not that infants are developing generally well-informed theories of physics. These researchers are interested in, and are succeeding in, mapping out the developmental trajectory of these cognitive skills. But infants lack some specific physical concepts such as ideas about inertia, momentum, and the expected effects of gravity on objects in motion (Spelke, 1991). This specificity of understanding brings into doubt the idea that physical knowledge is acquired by domain-general observational learning mechanisms.

Furthermore, the above knowledge is about objects and not about non-objects. Presumably, infants have had as much opportunity to observe the characteristics of non-object substances such as liquids and piles of debris (think rice or sand). If infants had learned their object concepts by opening their eyes and seeing what happens in the world, they would surely have learned about these classes of solids as well. But the developing infant does not apply the above rules, or any rules, to reasoning about those kinds of things. If an object is lowered behind a screen, an 8-month-old infant expects the object to be there when the screen is removed, but if an equivalent amount of sand is poured behind the screen, the infant is not, apparently, surprised if no sand is there when the screen is moved (Huntley-Fenner, Carey, & Somimando, 2002). This special thinking about objects does not go away: Even adults can keep track of moving objects better than they can keep track of the dynamic movement of substances (vanMarle & Scholl, 2003).

7.6   Press Pause

Babies know more about objects than Piaget thought although they only use this knowledge in very specific ways.

What would Piaget say about developing intuitive physics?

First, Piaget claimed that our adult understanding of objects, including the basic idea that they exist when we are not looking at them, is not available to infants, since it needs to be learned. Not only that, but Piaget's model of this particular learning process had infants taking a surprisingly long period to learn the object permanence concept: It was not until 18 months of age that this concept reached adult form. Finally, Piaget held that the development of the concept of object permanence progressed through stages, stages that fit into his theory of cognitive development and spanned the sensorimotor period.

To be more specific, during Sub-stages 1 and 2, that is, from birth to about 4 months of age, the infant will try to fixate and track a moving object. If the object disappears from view, the infant loses interest rather immediately. If she persists by continuing to look at the spot where the object disappeared, it is only for a moment. In other words, there is no clear evidence that the infant holds a representation of the object after it is out of view.

During Sub-stage 3, which spans 4 months to 8 months of age, the infant is quite skilled at tracking moving objects with her eyes. She even shows anticipatory eye movements, "predicting" the soon-to-be location of a moving object. In this stage, an infant can and will reach for an object that is partly occluded (e.g., a favourite bear whose ear is showing from beneath a blanket) but will still not reach for an object that is totally covered by a blanket. Here is an astonishing observation about kids this age: If the object is occluded while the baby is in the middle of reaching for it, the baby will likely drop her hand and appear to have completely forgotten the object. Even more surprising, the infant will not lift an object toward herself even if she already has it in her grasp when it becomes occluded by a blanket (Gratch, 1972; Gratch & Landers, 1971). She will, however, reach for the object if it is covered by a transparent covering, such that she can still see the object (Harris, 1983). These observations are so outlandish that we cannot blame Piaget for falsely concluding that the infant has no concept that an object continues to exist when it is out of sight.

In Sub-stage 4, which corresponds to 8 to 12 months of age, the child has developed significantly beyond the limitations of Sub-stage 3. She can now grasp and retrieve hidden objects. Unfortunately, the child now develops what developmental psychologists call the A-not-B error. Here is how it happens: You hide an attractive toy under one of two washcloths. The infant grasps and retrieves it. Again, you hide it under the same washcloth; again, the infant finds it. You repeat this a couple more times. Now, while the infant is watching you and watching the attractive toy, you put that toy under the other washcloth. The infant does not, and apparently cannot, find the toy that was hidden in plain sight. Instead she looks under the other washcloth again and again. Piaget concluded that although the infant has a representation of the object (which allows the initial successful searches), that representation is somehow not clear, conscious, and adult-like. By the way, this A-not-B error is a persistent puzzle in cognitive development; no one is sure why it happens (but see Diamond, 1991).

In Sub-stage 5, that is, from 12 to 18 months of age, the A-not-B error is resolved, and infants will search for an object in its most recently observed location. Piaget believed that in this stage the infant is developing a distinction between the object as an object and her own actions upon it. Up to this point, the object only existed insofar as it was an object of the infant's own actions. There is still one limitation, at least as defined by an adult-like understanding of objects, and that is that the child can understand "visible displacement," as she does when she sees you move the object from one hiding place to another, but not "invisible displacement." If you hide an object while she is watching and then secretly move the object from that spot, she will persist in looking for the object where she last saw it. Faced with clear evidence that the object is not there anymore, she is incapable of expanding her search. She just looks at the last location, over and over, as if thinking "no way!"

In Sub-stage 6, that is, ages 18 to 24 months, all of the above difficulties are resolved. By 2 years of age, most children can search systematically through a series of possible hiding places for a hidden object. Finally, Piaget credits the child with having a persisting representation of the object.

AN INTUITIVE UNDERSTANDING OF SPACE

Human babies show early development of an understanding of space. There is evidence that 5-month-old babies use spatial location, not appearance, shape, or colour, to define an object. Here is how we can make that conclusion from experimental results: A 5-month-old watches while an experimenter digs a hole in a sandbox and buries an object. Ten seconds later, the experimenter digs in the same location and retrieves the object. This happens four times. On the fifth trial, something different happens. In some conditions, the experimenter digs up the item from a different location in the sandbox. The infant shows surprise, measured by increased looking time, even if the new location was only 6 inches away. In contrast, the infant does not show surprise if a completely different object is dug out from the original location (Newcombe, Huttenlocher, & Learmonth, 1999).

Indeed, babies universally show a non-arbitrary strategy for navigating in space that takes advantage of some cues but not others. Humans and other animals commonly use two strategies to encode spatial information: They encode the location of an object either with respect to themselves or with respect to other landmarks in the world. Right from the start, infants seem to have an egocentric strategy when it comes to spatial knowledge. For example, young babies presented with two attractive toys will reach for the object that is closer to them (von Hofsten & Spelke, 1985).

Babies can and will use the geometry of a room as a spatial cue but will not, and apparently cannot, use other cues such as colour. Imagine an experimenter hides a toy

| figure | 7.11 | Location as object identity |

If the experimenter buries a toy and digs it up from a different location in the sandbox, the infant shows surprise. In contrast, the infant does not show surprise if a completely different object is dug out from the original location. (Adapted from Newcombe, Huttenlocker, & Learmonth, 1999.)

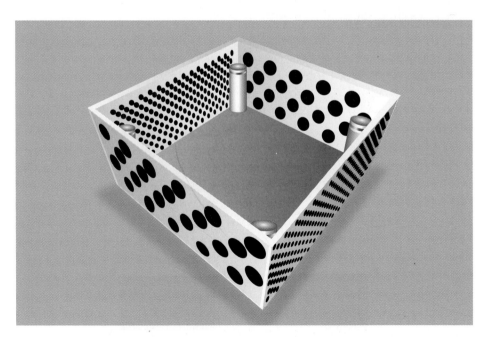

figure 7.12 The spin before the search

In the spatial navigation experiments described here, toddlers are disoriented before they search for an object. First they are shown the location of an object, then they are spun around with their eyes covered, then they are allowed to search for the hidden object. Using this method, researchers can make inferences about what cues young children use in navigation.

figure 7.13 Finding hidden toys

Babies will use the geometry of a room as a spatial cue but will not, and apparently cannot, use other cues such as colour. If a toy is hidden under a box in one of the corners of the room, the geometry of the room will be a clue, so the baby will correctly look to the right of the shorter wall, for example, but will never reliably use the only blue wall in the room as a cue (Hermer-Vazquez, Spelke, & Katsnelson, 1999).

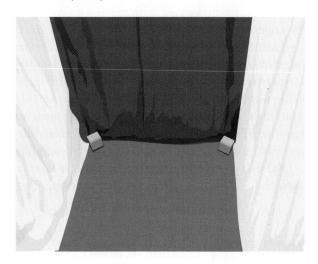

figure 7.14 Spatial navigation

Hermer & Spelke (1996) found that adults but not toddlers can use colour to navigate a room. Toddlers use only the geometry of the room to find a hidden object.

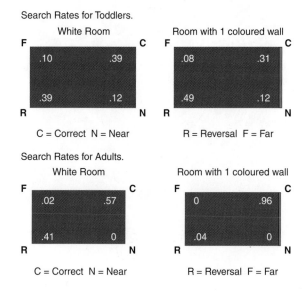

Search Rates for Toddlers.

White Room: F .10, C .39, R .39, N .12

Room with 1 coloured wall: F .08, C .31, R .49, N .12

C = Correct N = Near   R = Reversal F = Far

Search Rates for Adults.

White Room: F .02, C .57, R .41, N 0

Room with 1 coloured wall: F 0, C .96, R .04, N 0

C = Correct N = Near   R = Reversal F = Far

in one of four corners of a rectangular room in which all of the walls are the same colour. Adults who know where the object is hidden and who are then disoriented before being allowed to search for the object will search the correct corner just over 50 per cent of the time, and when they make an error are almost certain to search the corner directly opposite the hidden toy. Infants, too, are more likely to search the correct corner or the corner opposite rather than the two other corners, suggesting that they are using the geometry of the room to inform their search. Now imagine that the same experiment is done in a rectangular room in which one of the walls is painted a different colour than the other three. For adults, this one distinct wall disambiguates the problem: Success rates go up to 96 per cent. For toddlers, the coloured wall does not help at all; therefore success rates do not change (Hermer & Spelke, 1996; Hermer-Vazquez, Spelke, & Katsnelson, 1999).

In spite of using the geometry of the room to navigate space, a human infant cannot use the geometric shape of an array of objects for navigation. This universal, non-arbitrary use of some cues but not others would be hard to explain using associationist or domain-general learning.

Children develop the ability to use landmarks to locate objects as early as 6 months of age; however, the landmark must be both obvious and located close to the hidden object (Lew, Foster, Crowther, & Green, 2004).

What is even more surprising is that children show some degree of *dead reckoning* (or deductive reckoning). **Dead reckoning** is the ability to continuously keep track of one's location relative to the starting point and thus to go back to it. This is how some ant species navigate space: They can meander in any direction to find food, but when they find it, they beeline back to the nest, taking the most direct route regardless of

dead reckoning The ability to continuously keep track of one's location relative to the starting point and thus return directly to it.

figure 7.15 **Dead reckoning**

In this experiment, 2-year-old toddlers sat with a parent on one side of a sandbox, watching the experimenter hide a toy in the sand. The toddlers were then led to a different location in a room with no landmarks. Their return to the toy was better than chance, showing evidence of dead reckoning (Adapted from Newcombe, Huttenlocher, Drummey, & Wiley, 1998).

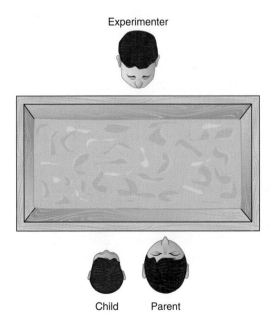

Experimenter

Child   Parent

how intricate, indirect, or long their search was (Gallistel, 1990). Two-year-old toddlers were shown an attractive toy that was then hidden in sand. The toddlers were then led to a different location, following an indirect route, in a room with no landmarks. Their return to the toy, although not perfect, was better than chance (Loomis et al., 1993; Newcombe, Huttenlocher, Drummey, & Wiley, 1998).

One thing that research has revealed about the development of spatial cognition is that self-locomotion matters. In one experiment, toddlers were allowed to watch through Plexiglas as someone hid a toy in one of two holes. Toddlers could only reach the toy by moving to the opposite side of the Plexiglas enclosure. Those who moved on their own (either crawling, walking, or using a walker) to the open side of the apparatus were more likely to reach for the correct location than were peers who were carried (Benson & Uzgiris, 1985).

7.7 Press Pause

Babies have some intuitive knowledge about space, and this knowledge shows the characteristics of domain specificity.

CHILDREN'S UNDERSTANDINGS OF BIOLOGY

Although there is no evidence that infants and toddlers have an intuitive understanding of biology, there is evidence of a precocious and non-tutored understanding of biology by early childhood and that it develops into middle childhood. Children seem to develop both an understanding of the types of objects (plants and animals) that are included in the domain of biological knowledge and some understanding of biological processes such as inheritance, growth, nourishment, and death.

Learning about a child's understanding of biology can be tricky for a researcher. Obviously, the easiest thing to do would be to ask the child. Unfortunately, that is unlikely to be a fruitful research approach since children are not usually able to describe the things that they know (Karmiloff-Smith, 1988). As we will see in this section, researchers have developed clever ways to uncover what a child knows in the biological domain. These researchers proceed with this assumption: If a child's knowledge in the domain of biology is rule-governed because they have an understanding about biological processes, then the rules should show in their behaviour toward and inferences about biological entities such as plants and animals.

One method of learning about children's understandings of biology is through the method of induction. In this method, the researcher asks what inferences (inductions) the child makes about biological entities and the relationships among them with a mind to discovering whether those inferences are law-governed. To make an induction is to generalize to an entire class or category from a single instance. What is tricky, from a cognitive point of view, is figuring out what properties can and cannot be generalized and what objects one can generalize to. As you will see in the following experiments, the fact that children can and do make inductions from one animal to another animal reveals some underlying core knowledge that informs their decisions about what features to generalize to what other animals. For example, if a child learns that baby horses drink milk from their mothers and then infers that baby mice, deer, and dogs also drink milk from their mothers, the child is revealing that he can generalize a fact within a category. If he then asserts that baby lizards, snakes, and birds do not drink milk from their mothers, he is revealing his category boundary by not extending his inference past the category of mammals.

Another technique, which we considered in our discussion of essentialism in Chapter 6, is the transformation technique in which the researcher asks children what sort of transformations they will accept. Could a cat become a skunk if we painted a stripe down its back and gave it a stink pouch? Could a toaster become a birdfeeder if we made the appropriate modifications?

A third technique is to ask children about their understanding of biological processes, such as respiration, growth, eating, and death. Let us see what has been discovered using these methods.

7.8   Press Pause

Young children have some knowledge about biology; for example, they know about inheritance, growth, and death.

Preschoolers have a theory of inheritance

Children understand that unlike artifacts, which are made by people, living things come from other living things that resemble them. They inherit characteristics of the species and characteristics of the parent. Even preschoolers know that baby dogs come from dogs and baby cats come from cats. Even if children do not have a complete idea of the laws that govern inheritance, they understand that offspring (dog, cat, or even flowers) inherit properties (like colour) from their parents and that this inheritance is lawful.

Through a very clever series of experiments, Ken Springer and his collaborator Frank Keil demonstrated that young children have a theory of inheritance. Specifically, they found that children believe that a child will resemble a parent with respect to biological traits but not with respect to social characteristics (Springer, 1992; Springer & Keil, 1989). Springer (1996) told children stories about a character who was born into one family and adopted by another. The children were asked about whether the character in the story would resemble his adoptive or his biological family. Children aged 4 to 7 tended to predict that with respect to physical traits such as hair colour and height, the character would resemble his biological family, while with respect to psychological or behavioural traits, he would resemble his adoptive family (Springer, 1996).

What would happen if a baby kangaroo was adopted and reared by goats? Children who were 7 and older in these animal adoption studies tended to base their answers on nature: Being reared by goats does not make a kangaroo any less of a kangaroo. Children around the age of 4 were more likely than older children to base their answers on nurture: Whoever is reared by a goat is a goat.

Solomon, Johnson, Zaitchik, and Carey (1996) further illustrated the difference between children's understanding of social vs. biological phenomena. In their experiments, a child was told a story about a boy who had a biological father and an adoptive father. The biological father had one characteristic, say green eyes, and the adoptive father had a different characteristic, say brown eyes. The child was asked which colour eyes the boy would have, green or brown. Results showed that children younger than 7 predicted that the boy would have the same eye colour as his adoptive father. Starting at around age 7, children predicted that the boy would have the characteristics of his biological father. Both younger and older children, then, had an understanding of inheritance: Children will resemble their fathers, but their understanding of the processes of inheritance changed (Solomon, Johnson, Zaitchik, & Carey, 1996).

The Ugly Ducking is a children's story about a young swan who accidentally finds herself in a duck family, with a duck for a mother and ducks for siblings. She struggles to fit in but ultimately cannot because she is a swan, in spite of her duck upbringing. Gelman and Wellman (1991, e.g.) conducted a series of inheritance experiments in which animals were "adopted" by other animals. In these nature vs. nurture designs, children were asked to consider what would happen if a baby kangaroo was adopted and reared by goats. Would it grow up to be a kangaroo? Would it hop? Would it have a pouch? Older children in these animal adoption studies tended to base their answers on nature: Being reared by goats does not make a kangaroo any less of a kangaroo (Gelman, 2000). The younger children in the study, around the age of 4, were less sure and more likely than older children to base their answers on nurture: Whoever is reared by a goat is a goat.

Growth

Children appreciate that living things grow and that non-living things do not. Indeed this distinguishes animals and plants from non-living things (Inagaki, 1993). Children are pretty good (not perfect) at identifying which things grow and which things do not (Inagaki & Hatano, 1996; Inagaki & Sugiyama, 1988). Even preschool children understand that living things grow larger but that artifacts do not (Rosengren, Gelman, Kalish, & McCormick, 1991). Their understanding of growth is not adult-like since young children reject the idea of qualitative change (as from a caterpillar to a butterfly) as well as the idea that very small animals such as worms also grow (Gelman, 1990).

In one study, children between 4 and 6 years of age saw a picture of either a flower, a baby animal, or a brand new artifact. Then they were asked to choose a picture that showed what that target object would look like several months or years later. The children chose the image of the same-size object in the artifact condition but chose a larger image in both the animal and the plant condition, results which the authors took as evidence that the children understood that young living things will grow (Inagaki, 1993). Similarly, another study showed that children as young as 4 years old understand that re-growth is expected after a living thing (but not an artifact) is damaged (Backscheider, Shatz, & Gelman, 1993). Children also understand that a prerequisite of growth is food for animals and water for plants (Hatano & Inagaki, 1994). Not only that, but young children ages 4 and 5 understand that growth is beyond intentional control. You do not have to want to grow in order to grow, and wanting not to grow will not keep you from growing. They even understand that the desire for growth on the part of the person providing the food (e.g., a farmer or a parent) does not create or accelerate growth (Inagaki & Hatano, 1987).

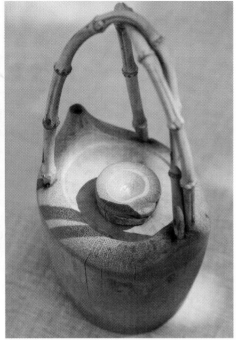

Children between 4 and 6 years of age expect the animal and the plant to be bigger after some time has passed, but not the artifact. They understand that young living things will grow.

An intuitive understanding of death

Some evidence suggests that young children develop an understanding of death before the age of 4. In one study, children as young as 4 were able to make a distinction between animals that were asleep and animals that were dead. What is more, these findings were similar when the experiment was conducted in Europe with children growing up in a contemporary industrialized culture and when it was conducted in a Shuar group, a small group of people living in South America in low-technology conditions more similar to the EEA (Barrett & Behne, 2005).

According to the core-knowledge perspective, intuitive knowledge about biology was functional for young children in the EEA. Clearly our ancestors needed to have some knowledge of the biological entities around them. For one thing, plants and animals were our ancestors' food sources. Further, knowledge about biology would have helped our ancestors understand and control their own bodily processes. You will notice that experiments examining the development of core biological knowledge focus on children who are older than those who are described as having core physical knowledge. It is possible that infants are not yet in a position to make use of any biological knowledge, being dependent entirely upon their parents and caregivers to manage their biological needs.

Universal intuitive biology

It is very likely that there are commonalities across cultures in terms of young children's understandings of biology (Atran, 1990). Comparing urban North American children to Yukatek Mayan children who live a close-to-Aboriginal lifestyle in a rainforest in Guatemala, Atran found that across cultures, children have a concept of species and apply essentialist thinking to species by the age of 4 to 5 years (Atran, 2002). He also showed that this understanding is not a result of thinking about people, or borrowing social cognitive competencies, but rather, it is specific to thinking about non-human biological entities. The younger Mayan children have a sophisticated understanding of biology without anthropomorphizing animals. They understand animals as animals, not as people or quasi-people. Atran contends that "folk psychology can't be the initial source of folk biology" (2002, p. 42). (We will talk more about folk psychology, the early developing knowledge that children have about social psychology, in the next chapter.)

Even more surprising, Atran's research with these two populations showed that in both groups, children used the same categories and the same levels (i.e., the same taxonomies) to make inferences between animals. Both populations of children used species-

These Yukatek Mayan children have an early understanding of species and of biology. This early understanding does not result from thinking of animals as people but is an understanding applied uniquely to animals.

level groupings to make biological inferences, and this preference overrides perceptual similarities. Atran argues that experience cannot account for these results since the North American children have such relative deprivation with respect to experience with biology and that the experience they do have would predict perceptual groupings, which is not what his results show. He concludes that children have biological preparedness, or core knowledge, with respect to the development of biological knowledge. There is a human universal cognitive architecture that includes species which we view as having essences, the organization (taxonomy) that describes the relationship between the species, which Atran refers to as "domain-specific cognitive universals" (Atran, 2002, p. 42).

7.9 Press Pause

As in other core-knowledge domains, a developing intuitive biology is universal across human cultures.

⁘ Culture and Community

Cultural Differences in the Intuitive Understandings of Biology

A lot of recent research interest has focussed on the kinds of understandings of biology that children in all cultures develop, including similarities in understandings of inheritance, relatedness, growth, illness, and death. But are there interesting differences in children's untutored understandings of biology as you look across different cultures? What if you look at children who have radically different experiences with biology: those who live in an urban environment and know about animals mostly from books and those whose livelihood actually depends on animals, either by breeding and raising them or by hunting them?

One early experiment suggests that experience with a living creature has an influence on a child's knowledge about that creature, knowledge about similar creatures, and the ability to make predictions about living creatures in general. Kayoko Inagaki, working at Chiba University in Japan, created two experimental groups: children who raised goldfish and children who did not. After some experience, children who raised goldfish knew more about goldfish, both in terms of their visible and their invisible characteristics. Furthermore, they also knew more about frogs and were able to make reasonable predictions about what goldfish and frogs would do in novel, hypothetical situations. These children used goldfish to make analogies about frog behaviour (Inagaki, 1990).

Scott Atran and his colleagues Norbert Ross, Douglas Medin, and John Coley working at Northwestern University near Chicago, compared early biological understandings between three groups of children: children living in urban areas, Caucasian children living in rural areas, and children in a Native American rural community (in this case the Menominee of Wisconsin). The urban group was said to have impoverished experience with respect to biological entities, while the latter two groups dealt with living things on a daily basis. The experimenters told the children novel facts, things they did not know before, about animals (e.g., humans or bees), plants (e.g., goldenrod), and non-living things (e.g., water). The interesting question is whether they would then generalize these new properties to other animals, plants, and non-living objects.

First, the authors found that only the urban children showed a developmental change in terms of seeing animals as alive: The two rural groups viewed animals as alive from a very young age. In other words, the rural children showed a more mature understanding of biology at a younger age. With respect to making inferences among entities, the two rural groups showed an earlier understanding of the affinity among biological kinds than the urban group did. In the rural groups, the youngest children were willing to make inferences about new facts, applying their learning from one biological entity to another. The older urban children (and the older rural children) also showed this tendency, but the younger urban children did not (Ross, Medin, Coley, & Atran, 2002). Experience living in nature had an effect on the development of biological understandings.

When these researchers also studied a group of Yukatek Mayan children from south-central Mexico, they found that the children's willingness to generalize new facts was a function of the relatedness between the living things. A new fact learned about a mammal was more likely applied to another mammal than to a bird, and vice versa (Atran et al., 2001).

⇛ Developmental Milestones

Cognitive Development Milestones

Age	Skills
3 Months	Infant is surprised if an object disappears while unseen (Baillargeon, 1987). Infants expect "cohesion" in an object: It should not come apart when someone picks it up. Infants understand that an object has to be in contact with a support or it will fall.
3½ Months	Height is important in occlusion events: An object that is taller than an occluder is still visible. Height is not considered in containment events.
4 Months	Infant expects "continuity" if a partly occluded object moves behind a screen (Spelke, 1985).
5 Months	Infants will manually search for a previously seen object in a dark room. Infants understand that an object has to be in contact with the top of a support or it will fall. Infants use location over shape and colour to identify an object (Newcombe et al., 1999). Infants have a sense of numbers and can habituate to a specific number of (one, two, or three) objects. Early addition: Infants who see one puppet added to another expect to see two puppets.
6 Months	Infants expect that contact is needed for objects (but not people) to have an effect on each other. Infants can use landmarks to remember object locations if the landmark is obvious and close to the hidden object.
7½ Months	Infants appreciate that height is important in a containment event: Tall objects cannot be completely hidden by a shorter container.
8 Months	Infants show object permanence, according to Piaget. Infants understand that an object has to have most of its lower surface on the top of a support or it will fall.
1 Year	Infants appreciate that height is important in a covering event: Tall objects cannot be completely hidden by a shorter container.
2 Years	Children use the shape of a room, but not the colour of its walls, to encode spatial location within the room.
4 Years	Children have beliefs about the kinds of traits that are inherited. Children expect living things, but not artifacts, to grow. Children can distinguish an animal that is asleep from one that is dead.
7 Years	Children start to expect that traits such as eye colour will resemble genetic rather than adoptive parents.

What would Piaget say about children's understandings of biology?

Much of the above research that sheds light on children's understandings of biology is at odds with Piaget's perspective (Piaget, 1929). Piaget believed that preschoolers' understanding of the world was perceptually dominated: Things that look alike are alike. Piaget would have predicted that a child categorizes animals that appear similar, such as a bat and a hummingbird (drawn with wings outspread such that they have the same shape) and that a flamingo (appearing to have a different shape when drawn) would be in a different category than either the bat or the hummingbird. Contrary to Piaget's prediction, preschool children categorize the birds together, not the bat and the hummingbird (Wellman & Gelman, 1988).

Furthermore, Piaget would expect that preschool children are pre-causal. The children should not, if Piaget was correct, be able to reason about cause and effect in any domain, nor should they be able to distinguish physical causes (food) from intentional causes (wanting to grow) for any process (growth). It would seem that digestion, growth, and death should be incomprehensible to young children, but they are not.

NUMBER UNDERSTANDING IN BABIES

You may be surprised to know that babies show an early understanding of numbers and arithmetic. When you think about math, what comes to mind may be the arduously acquired formal mathematics that you learn in school, including algebra and calculus. But we have a much more intuitive, untutored understanding of math and numbers available to us. All cultures have ways of discussing, comparing, and adding and subtracting at least small quantities. Moreover, children in every known culture acquire some understanding of numbers and basic arithmetic at about the same age, regardless of formal education (Geary, 1994). Mathematical understanding appears to be a domain of core knowledge for developing humans, resulting from evolved, domain-specific cognitive processes (Geary, 1995).

Numerosity

Infants as young as 5 months appear to have a sense of numerosity, or the equality or difference of small sets of one, two, or three objects. How do we know this? Again, we know from experiments that use looking time as a dependent measure in a habituation paradigm. Infants look at displays of a small number of objects (say two). The display changes, but the number stays the same. They see two yellow stars, then two green circles, and so on. The colour changes, the spacing changes, and the size of the objects changes, but there are always two. The infants watch these displays until they are habituated. Then the number of objects changes. Does the infant dishabituate? Yes. Looking time increases as the number of objects changes from one, two, and three (Feigenson, Carey, & Spelke, 2002; Starkey, Spelke, & Gelman, 1990). Even infants *in the first week of life* can discriminate between sets of up to three entities (Antell & Keating, 1983).

Not only that, but the infant can habituate to a small number of events or actions (say a puppet jumping two times) and then dishabituate when the number of events changes (Wynn, 1995). And by 6 months, infants can apparently represent numbers abstractly as to match across modalities: Infants who heard two drumbeats looked significantly longer at an array of two objects, whereas those who heard three drumbeats looked significantly longer at an array of three objects (Starkey, Spelke, & Gelman, 1983; Starkey et al., 1990).

It is worth noting that people who think about this area of research are not all in agreement about whether the very young infant is really representing a number. Some believe that it is possible that there is some non-numeric representation of amount or magnitude that accounts for the above-described experimental results, even in the cross-modal case.

In addition, infants possess an approximate sense of larger numbers. Again, using a habituation paradigm, Spelke and colleagues have shown that infants can discriminate between 8 and 16 dots (or 8 and 16 sounds) but not between 8 and 12 dots (or sounds) (Lipton & Spelke, 2003).

Ordinality

After the development of numerosity comes the development of ordinality: the understanding of greater than and less than, and ordinality seems to develop by 18 months. In order to study ordinality in infants, Strauss and Curtis (1984) used a touch screen and taught infants to touch the side of the screen showing the greater number of dots (or the fewer number of dots). Once the infants showed that they were reliably trained, they saw a new array on the touch screen showing a novel number of items (e.g., two dots on one side and three dots on the other). Had they learned the number, rather than the ordinal relationship, they should touch the familiar number. In contrast, had they learned the ordinal relationship, they should touch the side with the greater number of dots (or fewer number of dots, depending upon their training condition). Results were consistent with the idea that they had represented the ordinal relationship (Strauss & Curtis, 1984).

Arithmetic

What is even more surprising is that very young infants are able to do arithmetic! Karen Wynn pioneered the research in infant arithmetic using a violation of expectation paradigm. Five-month-old infants saw a single object (e.g., a Minnie Mouse doll) on a stage. A screen then rose in front of the object, occluding it completely. Then, a hand carried a second same object behind the screen and exited empty-handed, leaving the infant to infer that the second object was deposited behind the screen. When the screen dropped, infants showed surprise (measured in looking time) if they saw the wrong number of objects, in this case one. They looked for a significantly less amount of time if the screen was dropped and two objects were revealed (Wynn, 1992). Again, this finding is hard to explain without invoking arithmetic on the part of the infant since the infant has only ever seen one doll at a time: Seeing one object should be less surprising than seeing two if perceptual similarity were the driving expectation. Now that is precocious arithmetic!

7.10 Press Pause ────────────────────────────

Babies have some knowledge about numbers and even about arithmetic.

Two systems of numbers

Evidence suggests that infants psychologically represent numbers using two different core systems as if there are two separate psychological domains for numbers. The first system represents large numbers but represents them very approximately, as orders of magnitude. The second represents precise values but only represents very small numbers, perhaps only one, two, and possibly three (Feigenson, Dehaene, & Spelke, 2004).

Infants as young as 6 months old show some competency with numbers. A study using a habituation paradigm showed that infants discriminate an array of 8 items from an array of 16 items. That is, when habituated to an array of 8 or 16 items, they looked at the numerically novel test array of 8 or 16 items longer (Xu & Spelke, 2000). But there are severe limits to the precision of infants' understandings of numbers: 6-month-olds can discriminate 8 items from 16 items (a 1:2 ratio) and can discriminate 16 items from 32 items (also a 1:2 ratio) but cannot discriminate 8 items from 12 items or 16 items from 24 items (ratios of 2:3) under the same conditions (Xu & Spelke, 2000). Better precision comes with time: 10-month-olds can discriminate 8 items from 12 or 16 items from 24 (ratios of 2:3) (Xu & Arriaga, 2007), and adults are even more precise (Barth, Kanwisher, & Spelke, 2003; van Oeffelen & Vos, 2003). Oddly, infants as young as 6 months fail to discriminate the same ratios if the number of items is very small. Given the same conditions used in the studies just described, infants failed to discriminate an array of 1 from an array of 2 items, or 2 from 4 (Xu,

figure 7.16   **What infants know about arithmetic**

One doll is placed on a stage, a screen comes up, and another doll is placed behind the screen. If the screen drops revealing only one doll (but not two) then the infant is surprised, as revealed by looking time. Five-month-olds can add! (Adapted from Wynn, K., 1992.)

Sequence of events 1 + 1 = 1 or 2

1. Object placed in case	2. Screen comes up	3. Second object added	4. Hand leaves empty

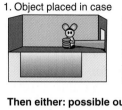 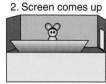 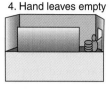 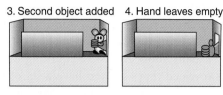

Then either: possible outcome   **or: impossible outcome**

5. Screen drops...	revealing 2 objects	5. Screen drops...	revaling 1 object

 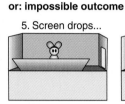 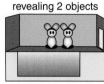 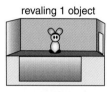

Sequence of events 2 − 1 = 1 or 2

1. Objects placed in case	2. Screen comes up	3. Empty hand enters	4. One object removed

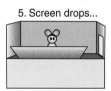 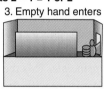  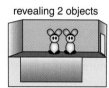

Then either: possible outcome   **or: impossible outcome**

5. Screen drops...	revealing 1 object	5. Screen drops...	revealing 2 objects

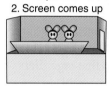  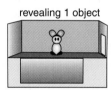

2003). Thus, the authors of these studies believe that infants in these experiments used the first of two core number systems, the one that represents large numbers as approximate magnitudes.

A distinct system represents small, exact numbers. This system represents items as individuals and can keep track of a small number of items. For example, in one experiment infants were offered to choose one of two containers of crackers after they had watched the experimenter put one cracker into one container and two crackers into another container. Ten- and 12-month-olds always chose the container with the greater number of (now invisible) crackers, even though they only saw them one at a time. They also chose three crackers over two crackers under the same conditions, but they made errors with any greater numbers, failing to choose the container with more crackers in the three vs. four, two vs. four, and even one vs. four conditions (Feigenson, Carey, & Hauser, 2002)!

Similarly, another experiment also found this upper limit of three in young infants' numerical representations. In this experiment, attractive items were hidden sequentially in a box and then infants were allowed an opportunity to search for the items. If one item went into the box, the infant retrieved one item and then stopped. If two went into the box, the infant retrieved two and then stopped. The infant was similarly successful if three items went into the box, but if four items went into the box, the infant would likely retrieve just one item and then stop (Feigenson & Carey, 2003).

Counting

Young children around the world start practising counting almost as early as they can talk, using the words for small numbers in their language, although children do not usually show adult-like counting until late in their preschool years. Research has revealed that children have a set of rules that they follow for counting, rules that are apparently part of their developing psychology (Gelman & Gallistel, 1978). These rules are

1. *The one-to-one principle*. This means that each item in the array gets a unique number label.
2. *The stable-order principle*. The number labels should be spoken in the same order each time one counts.
3. *The cardinal principle*. Whatever number label you give to the last item in the array is the total; that is how many items you have counted.
4. *The abstraction principle*. This means you can count anything, whether it is big (elephants) or small (peas). You can even count actions (jumps) or something abstract (ideas).
5. *The order-irrelevant principle*. This means that regardless of what order you count things in, you should end up with the same total.

Gelman and Gallistel found evidence that children are beginning to understand and use these rules as early as 2½ years of age, and by 5 years of age, children mostly follow the first two rules. They may not, however, come up with the correct number of items once they are done counting because they may not be using the correct sequence of number words. A child may have his own idiosyncratic number list ("one, two, five") and use that list consistently when he counts (Geary, 1994; Gelman & Gallistel, 1978).

Here is an example of how some researchers study whether children follow these rules. An array of objects are displayed in front of the child, and the child watches as a puppet counts the items. Using this method, researchers have discovered that 3-, 4-, and 5-year-olds are beginning to use the one-to-one principle and the stable-order principle. Consistent use of these principles increases over these years from 30 per cent to 90 per cent to 100 per cent (Briars & Siegler, 1984).

A Cross-Species Comparison

Another way to test the idea that domains of knowledge are evolved, species-specific, and specialized is to compare them across species. We know that other species have domain-general associationist learning mechanisms. So if a domain of knowledge is learned just by these weak associations, then any animal we pick should be smart enough to learn them if they are just exposed to the right stimuli. Even better, people tend to hold the belief, consciously or subconsciously, that humans are the smartest animals, which leads to the expectation that anything that another species is able to learn, humans should be able to learn too, save for differences in perceptual abilities that might limit our actual exposure to stimuli that are present.

table 7.1	The Rules that Children Count By
PRINCIPLE	**DESCRIPTION**
The one-to-one principle	This means that each item in the array gets a unique number label.
The stable-order principle	The number labels should be spoken in the same order each time one counts.
The cardinal principle	Whatever number label you give to the last item in the array is the total; that is how many items you have counted.
The abstraction principle	This means you can count anything, whether it is big (elephants) or small (peas). You can even count actions (jumps) or something abstract (ideas).
The order-irrelevant principle	This means that regardless of what order you count things in, you should end up with the same total.

Non-human animals show some competence with numbers and, interestingly, have some of the same characteristic limits in thinking about numbers, suggesting a possible link in our evolutionary heritage. Rats who are trained to press a lever a certain number of times will subsequently make responses that are near that number, and the error (number of presses over or under the target) increases as the target number increases (Platt & Johnson, 1971), suggesting that they represent an approximate magnitude, similar to the first core number system described above. Rhesus monkeys also show evidence of this core number system representing approximate magnitudes. In one experiment, rhesus monkeys were trained to touch a number of items in ascending order: first an array of one item, then an array of two items, etc. Once they knew that their task was to touch the arrays of items in ascending order, they were presented with two novel arrays with a differing number of items between five and nine. Monkeys were very good at touching these two arrays in ascending order even though they had never seen them before. Furthermore, the monkeys' reaction times and accuracy were a function of the ratio between the two arrays: The bigger the ratio, the faster and more accurate they were, consistent with the infant research showing a representation of approximate magnitude (Brannon & Terrace, 1998).

There is also evidence that rhesus monkeys have the second core number system representing a small number of individual items. In an experiment designed to be similar to the infant experiment described above, monkeys watched as the experimenter placed one to four apple slices in a hiding place sequentially. Monkeys always selected the larger quantity of apple slices with any number up to three but were at chance with three vs. eight or four vs. eight, like infants had been with their crackers. This is taken as evidence of the second, precise core number system in monkeys (Hauser & Carey, 2003).

Earlier, we reviewed evidence that young infants have a concept of ordinality, correctly identifying arrays of greater or fewer items and that they do so apparently without any formal training. In contrast, other mammals and some birds can acquire this concept but only after hundreds of trials and sometimes years of training (Boysen, 1983; Gallistel, 1990; Pepperberg, 1994). This contrast suggests that human cognition is different from these animals with respect to the concept of ordinality; humans are prepared to develop this concept.

With respect to the adaptive problem of dealing with real-world objects, many species face essentially the same problems. The cognitive solutions might be expected to be the same, at least for terrestrial animals. Indeed, there is evidence that many land vertebrates show cognitive development that is similar to the object understandings of human infants (Hauser, 2000). Land animals seem to have object permanence (Dore & Dumas, 1987). This stands in contrast to the social cognitive skills that we will read about in the next chapter, which are largely unique to humans.

Ants show deductive reckoning but do not show a use of landmarks for navigation. Their navigational skills are specific to their species, and other species that navigate well use cues that are peculiar to their species. Some birds use the stars, while bats, sea turtles, and some birds use the magnetic poles of the earth to guide their migration. Starlings and ants use the sun to navigate. Salmon use scents to get back to their spawning grounds. Within each species, the navigational strategy is universal, but between species a reliable cue used by one species can be completely ignored by another. Clearly, this cannot be explained by the same weak general-purpose learning mechanisms in each species. Each species is equipped with a specific, well-designed learning mechanism with which it learns navigation.

SUMMARY

This chapter offers a perspective on the age-old question of knowledge acquisition that is consistent with evolutionary psychology. Although instinct blindness makes the problem seem easy (it seems like you just "know" information because you are exposed to it), knowledge acquisition is actually a difficult computational problem. In order for a person to learn something about a topic, that person has to bring a lot of assumptions and cognitive readiness to the table.

The core-knowledge perspective offers a solution to start solving the problem of knowledge acquisition. Because certain domains of knowledge were particularly important to a developing child in the EEA, there is some specialized cognitive support for knowledge acquisition in these areas. The areas highlighted in this chapter are knowledge about objects, space, biology, and number. The idea behind the core-knowledge theory is that children are prepared to easily learn what the objects in these domains are and what the lawful relationships between objects in these domains are.

In this chapter you read about research that shows evidence that infants and young children have a surprising amount of knowledge in these core areas. In the first year, babies know that an object will fall if it is not supported. Four-year-olds know that parents pass traits to offspring, but only heritable, not psychological or acquired, traits. Infants in their first year have strategies for navigating in space. They know that if you add one to one, you should have two.

These findings may be surprising to you. They would also be surprising to Piaget. Until people started thinking in terms of evolutionary psychology and core knowledge, Piaget's cognitive model prevailed, and his view of cognitive development stressed categorization based on perceptual similarity. He would not have predicted a young child's understanding of inheritance. Furthermore, recent evidence of a child's understanding of object permanence directly contradicts Piaget's claims regarding the relatively late development of this cognitive skill.

PRESS PAUSE SUMMARY

- Since ancient times, philosophers have been wondering how people acquire knowledge, usually framing the debate in terms of nature (infants know things without training) and nurture (all knowledge must be acquired).

- Considering our evolutionary history can help frame the problem of knowledge acquisition.

- People working in artificial intelligence know that some prior assumptions and constraints on learning are necessary for knowledge acquisition. Animal studies reveal constraints on learning.

- Domains of knowledge are necessary in order to create a baby (or machine) that can acquire knowledge.

- Piagetian and associationist approaches predict relatively simple learning and immature knowledge and can be used experimentally to generate null hypotheses.

- Babies know more about objects than Piaget thought although they only use this knowledge in very specific ways.
- Babies have some intuitive knowledge about space, and this knowledge shows the characteristics of domain specificity.
- Young children have some knowledge about biology; for example, they know about inheritance, growth, and death.
- As in other core-knowledge domains, a developing intuitive biology is universal across human cultures.
- Babies have some knowledge about numbers and even about arithmetic.

KEY TERMS AND CONCEPTS

constraints on learning, 219
containment event, 231
core knowledge, 222
covering event, 231

dead reckoning, 237
domain specificity, 222
intuitive physics, 224
occlusion event, 231

QUESTIONS FOR THOUGHT AND DISCUSSION

1. What problem does "constraints on learning" solve? What would happen to the process of knowledge acquisition if there were no constraints on learning?
2. What problem does "domain specificity" solve? How?
3. Describe the problem of knowledge acquisition. What were the approaches of the ancient Greeks? How do contemporary views of knowledge acquisition differ?
4. What did Piaget believe about the development of object permanence? What do Baillargeon's results suggest? What explains the difference?
5. What specialized knowledge do children have in the domain of biology? How is this different from what Piaget would expect?
6. Describe what young infants know about numbers and arithmetic. At what age? What experimental design allowed for this discovery?

From the Classroom to the Lab: Follow Up

Consider the experiment you designed in response to the "From the Classroom to the Lab" challenge earlier in this chapter.

What age group(s) would you choose to participate? Why?

Describe your stimuli.

Describe your procedure.

What is your dependent variable?

What is your independent variable?

Imagine you have run your experiment. What results would indicate to you that the babies tested use colour as part of their object concept? What results would indicate that they do not?

chapter 8

Core Knowledge Part II
Face Perception, Animacy Perception, and Theory of Mind

Opening Vignette: Social Isolation and Hallucination

In 1986, David Adams was racing his yacht in the Trans-Tasman Challenge, sailing solo across the 2,000 or so kilometres between Australia and New Zealand and spending days at sea alone. On his eighth day out alone, he started hallucinating. "I still remember it vividly. There was a full crew on board with me. I didn't recognize any of the faces, and I wasn't quite sure how they got there, but there they were, sailing the boat." Adams let this phantom crew manage and sail the boat for a while. Then, he says, "I was just about to start yelling at them when a rubber duckie [an inflatable raft] appeared alongside and all these blokes piled in and sped away" (Adams, 1997).

Hallucinations are a surprisingly common effect of solo sailing, of sensory deprivation (Zuckerman & Cohen, 1964), of solitary prison confinement (Haney, 2003), and of the bereavement of a spouse (Hofer, 1984; Grimby, 1998), and one of the most common hallucinations in circumstances of social isolation is the hallucination of another person or people. If you saw the movie *Castaway* starring Tom Hanks, you may remember that after months of isolation on an island, the main character created a social companion by painting a face onto a volleyball and naming it "Wilson."

Chapter Outline

Learning Objectives, Outcomes

- This chapter expands on the idea of core knowledge introduced in Chapter 7 and focusses on research that reveals that humans have a psychology specialized for processing social information.

- First, you will learn why social knowledge is core knowledge for humans. You will read about pressures in our evolutionary past that made social information processing imperative. You will learn about the *social brain hypothesis* and read evidence in support of this hypothesis.

- You will then read about Piaget's thoughts on social development. You will learn about the research he did regarding children's perspective-taking. You will learn how Piaget's view of early social development was consistent with his stage theory. You will also read about Harry Harlow's early work with rhesus monkeys that suggested that social contact is a compelling need, even when other physical needs are being met.

- You will then learn about early developing social cognitive skills in infants. Infants are attracted to social information very early in life. You will also learn about important social cognitive skills that develop in the first year of life, such as *joint attention* and *social referencing*. You will read about pretend play and learn that it requires specialized cognitive machinery to understand others' minds.

- Then, you will explore face processing. You will learn that faces are special: The visual system processes faces like no other objects. A special brain area is even devoted to face perception. You will learn about research, including research about the *inversion effect* and *holistic processing*, that shows how faces are processed uniquely.

- The chapter then deals with animacy and intentionality perception in infants and young children. An understanding of animacy is a very early developing social cognitive skill. You will read evidence that young infants appreciate animacy and even perceive intentions while looking at very simple displays of geometric figures. You will also read evidence of the development of intentionality perception into childhood.

- You will then read about a vibrant field of research regarding *theory of mind* development. Children perceive other people's mental states (beliefs, desires, etc.) and use these mental states to explain and predict behaviour. You will learn about some classic research that shows that children use others' perceived beliefs to predict what they will do, and you will read what scientists think about how the theory of mind process develops.

- In the final section of this chapter you will read about autism as an example of the development of children who do not have typical social cognitive and social perceptual skills.

obligate social species
Species that *must* be with others in order to survive and who are co-evolved in order to interact with others.

Humans are an example of what biologists call an **obligate social species**: species that must be with others in order to avoid the risk of maldevelopment or even death. Obligate social species are evolved in order to interact with others. Humans have co-evolved adaptations that are appropriate to solve adaptive problems on multiple sides of a relationship: For example, we can all read facial expressions and produce facial expressions; we all seek maternal attachment as infants and provide parental security as adults.

The human mind is not designed for social isolation, and people find extended periods of isolation extremely aversive. The examples of hallucination in the opening vignette illustrate the psychological consequences of being in social isolation for a lengthy amount of time. The need for other people is so compelling that a person will create social contact via hallucination if real companions are not present for extended periods. Experimental work with rhesus monkeys shows that total social isolation can even result in death (Harlow, Dodsworth, & Harlow, 1965).

People seek social contact and enjoy spending time with others. People have specialized cognitive machinery designed to help them identify, interact with, and remember other people.

Consider this in terms of the environment in which our ancestors lived. Even in adulthood social skills were crucial in the EEA in order to live among other people. One had to solicit friendships, monitor allegiances, be aware of insults and exploitation, avoid offence, and fulfill obligations. Failure to do so could result in ostracism, which would have been deadly in ancestral conditions: A lone human might have been extremely vulnerable to predation, starvation, or exposure. In the EEA, living in a community was not just fun; it was a matter of life or death.

For infants and young children, the social imperative is even greater. Humans are born immature compared to most other species and are completely dependent upon care from others. There is early evidence of an attraction to social information. Starting at the age of 6 weeks, newborn infants smile interactively with caregivers. From then on an impressive series of developing social skills unfolds, including face perception, face identification, emotion perception in both visual and auditory domains, reciprocal interaction, attachment, and, in young childhood, mind reading. These cognitive skills are not just pleasurable, they do not just feel good, but they are actually critical for infants to secure and elicit the investment they need from their caregivers.

8.1 Press Pause

In the EEA, living in a community was not just fun; it was a matter of life or death. Our cognitive adaptations reflect this imperative from our past.

Infants depend entirely on other people to meet their needs, and they have social skills designed for just such a purpose. Starting at the age of 6 weeks, infants smile interactively with caregivers.

Social Contact as a Need: Harry Harlow's Social Experiments

An individual who is a member of an obligate social species must be with others, but how can we test the effects of isolation on humans? Clearly experimental work on humans involving social isolation is not feasible for ethical reasons. Much of our understanding of the effects of extreme isolation come from experiments conducted in the late 1950s and early 1960s by Harry Harlow, who used rhesus monkeys as a model for early social development.

ISOLATION EXPERIMENTS

One early series of experiments conducted by Harlow involved the partial or complete social isolation of infant monkeys in order to see what effects social isolation would have. The results were dramatic.

In partial isolation, infant monkeys lived in wire cages where they could hear, smell, and see other monkeys but were never in physical contact with them. In total social isolation they lived in an isolation chamber and had no experience at all of other monkeys (i.e., they could not even hear or smell them). In either case, the isolated monkeys were given adequate access to food and water and were kept clean such that all non-social needs were met.

Months of partial isolation resulted in abnormal behaviours, including self-mutilation, catatonia, and stereotyped

This photo shows an infant rhesus monkey who has been in total isolation. After being isolated for a year, infant rhesus monkeys no longer played or explored and rarely moved. Some monkeys in extended complete isolation stopped eating and died.

pacing or circling (Harlow, 1964). Results of total social isolation were even more severe. After 30 days in total isolation, the monkeys were "enormously disturbed." After being isolated for a year, they no longer played or explored and rarely moved. One of six monkeys who had been isolated for three months stopped eating and died (Harlow et al., 1965).

The effects of isolation were long-reaching: When these monkeys were impregnated and became mothers, they were incapable of effective parenting behaviour and were either neglectful or abusive to their infants. Most mothers ignored their infants, but some were actively violent toward them (Harlow & Suomi, 1971).

Harlow attempted to rehabilitate those monkeys that had been in total social isolation, but rehabilitation was not very successful. He placed monkeys who had been in total social isolation for six months with monkeys who had been reared normally and found "severe deficits in almost every aspect of social behaviour" (Harlow & Suomi,

theory of mind The part of our psychological processes that allows us to understand another person's mental states.

⠿ Research in Action

Imaginary Friends

Do you remember having an imaginary friend when you were a kid? If so, you are in good company. Imaginary friends are normal: More children have them than not. In fact, 63 per cent of children have played with an imaginary friend at some point in childhood (Taylor, 1999). Past notions of children who had imaginary friends were rather negative. The assumption was that a child with an imaginary friend must be odd, or at least so socially unskilled as to be unable to make friends with real children. Marjorie Taylor, a developmental psychologist at the University of Oregon, has been studying children with imaginary companions for over two decades and has found that having an imaginary friend is healthy, normal, and sometimes quite interesting.

One of the most surprising findings is that children who have imaginary companions are less shy, not more shy, than other children. It could be that these children are particularly social and have enough interest in social others to have both real friends and imaginary friends.

Other apparent developmental strengths are also associated with imaginary companions. Children with imaginary companions have greater attention spans than their peers. Do you recall long, involved play sessions or conversations with your imaginary friend? Such focussed play is an example of focussed attention, a developmental skill that eludes some children. On measures such as personality, creativity, and intelligence, children with imaginary companions do not differ, as a group, from children without them (Taylor, 1999).

There were, however, some measurable and reliable differences between groups of children with and without imaginary friends in Taylor's studies. Those with imaginary friends were more likely to be firstborn or "only" children, watched significantly less television, were more

verbally mature, and had a more mature **theory of mind** (Taylor, 1999; Taylor & Carlson, 1997; Taylor, Carlson, Maring, Gerow, & Charley, 2004).

The preschool years are generally associated with *pretend play,* and other than sleeping, preschool children spend more time pretending than anything else. Taylor has also found that older children have imaginary companions as well. In one study, 31 per cent of a group of 6- to 7-year-olds had imaginary companions compared to 28 per cent of a group of 3- to 4-year-olds (Taylor et al., 2004).

Most commonly, imaginary companions take the form of friends who are about the same age as the child, and often the same sex. But some imaginary companions take a different form. The imaginary companion could be an animal, like Joshua the possum or Pooreffu, a schipperke who walked on two legs. Sometimes the imaginary companion is a person of a different age, such as Nobby, the 160-year-old businessman or Derek, a 91-year-old who, though only 2-feet tall, could hit bears. Sometimes the imaginary companion resembles a real person, as was the case with "Fake Rachel," who was, in many respects, just like the child's friend Rachel.

Some imaginary companions were not actually *friends* with the child, which is why Taylor prefers the term *imaginary companion.* Some children created an individual whose purpose was to take the blame for negative events. Some children were rather abusive to their imaginary companions, using them to vent their frustration and anger in a socially acceptable way. Some used the companion to communicate about their feelings indirectly (e.g., by telling adults that the companion was afraid of the dark).

So do not worry if your child or a child you know has an imaginary companion. Not only is it normal and healthy; in some cases, it is quite useful as well.

1971). Some of the former isolates were given to surrogate mothers and showed some improvement but still had lasting social deficits. The most successful therapy for these former isolates appeared to be pairing them with a normally reared monkey who was younger than they were. The former isolates who had been in total social isolation for six months who were then placed with 3-month-old monkeys developed socially, to the point where any remaining deficits were not measureable given the research methods used by Harlow and his colleagues (Suomi, Harlow, & McKinney, 1972).

> **8.2**   **Press Pause**
>
> Studies with young rhesus monkeys show that, for that species, social contact is imperative. Social isolation can result in maldevelopment and even death.

Why the Big Brain?

Humans have large brains compared to other species—even correcting for body size— so big in fact that, as we learned in Chapter 3, a human baby is born 9 months early (relative to maturity at birth in other primates) so that the baby's head can still fit through the mother's pelvis at birth. But why is the human brain so big? Brains are costly, not just from an evolutionary point of view and a developmental point of view but also in terms of metabolic cost. Brain tissue is very expensive energetically and is prioritized above other kinds of tissue when resources are scarce. One unavoidable rule in natural selection is that the cost has to be justified by a benefit. Natural selection does not select a feature that is costly just because it would be nice to have around in case you might need it someday. What pressure, in our evolutionary past, was so strong as to lead to the evolution of our enormous brain? Two possibilities have been considered and compared: ecological pressures and social pressures.

ecological pressures
Evolutionary pressures that derive from ecological circumstances, including the availability of resources and the presence of risks or dangers.

Were the evolutionary pressures that demanded a big brain **ecological pressures**? Did our ancestors have a need for a big mental map to navigate the home range, the ability to forage, or gather, creatively (to solve problems like getting nutritional flesh out of hard nutshells and capturing fish in a moving stream), or a huge memory (because remembering where flowers and fruit trees were would lead them to future sustenance)? Alternatively, was the information-processing demand that led to our big human brain social in nature? We live in large groups, we form alliances; we remember favours and grudges; and we negotiate, scheme, manipulate, bluff, and convince. Are these the selective forces that led to the evolution of our big brain? They are, according to proponents of the *social brain hypothesis* (Barton & Dunbar, 1997; Brothers, 1990; Dunbar, 1998b; Jolly, 1966).

THE SOCIAL BRAIN HYPOTHESIS

social brain hypothesis
The idea that the large brains of humans, as well as the general intelligence of humans, has evolved in response to social conflicts and challenges that are an inherent part of group living.

The **social brain hypothesis** suggests that the large brains of humans, as well as the general intelligence of humans, has evolved in response to social conflicts and challenges that are an inherent part of group living. Allison Jolly discussed the possibility that human and other primate intelligence is a result of the social problems that individuals have to solve by virtue of living in complex social groups. Speaking of social primates, she suggests that "Since their dependence on the troop both demands social learning and makes it possible, social integration and intelligence probably evolved together, reinforcing each other in an ever-increasing spiral" (Jolly, 1966, p. 504). She

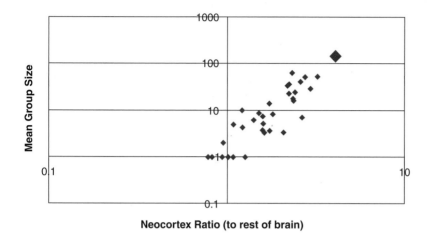

| figure | 8.1 | Primate neocortex size vs. social group size |

The social brain hypothesis suggests that the social cognition needed to understand social complexity explains our big brains. Across primate species, the neocortex ratio (how much of the brain is neocortex) is strongly related to group size. (Adapted from Dunbar, 1992.)

goes on to point out that humans' intelligence outpaced other animals, including other mammals and even other primates, in the context of, and as evolutionary results of, a complex social life. Primate society made primate intelligence possible, according to this view.

There is compelling evidence that supports the social brain hypothesis over the ecological hypothesis. Robin Dunbar (Dunbar, 1998a; Dunbar & Spoors, 1995) suggests that humans tended to congregate in groups of about 150. Indeed, research suggests that even in current environments we are most adept at interacting with about 150 or 200 people, and after that, we are less able to maintain intimacy. This is a very large number of conspecifics (organisms of the same species) to be hanging out with compared to other primate species (e.g., baboons) whose groups range from a few individuals (i.e., 5–10) to as many as 100. We are certainly an exception among primates. Even great apes—chimpanzees, bonobos, orangutans, and gorillas—rarely live in groups larger than 50. Two hundred is a relatively large number of people to individuate, remember, have mental impressions of, track favours and insults from, and follow what is important to (what else would you have to mentally track?) so that we can use these values to our advantage in negotiations. But we have evolved the cognitive capacity to do just that.

Among primates, the size of a species' neocortex (the "newest" part of the brain, associated with relatively high-level cognitive processing) correlates with the size of the group that they live in, but it does not correlate with any measure of ecological demands, such as the size of the home range (Barton & Purvis, 1994; Dunbar, 1998b). This is true of old world and new world primates, of anthropoid and prosimian primates, and of nocturnal and diurnal primates (Dunbar, 1998b). Furthermore, this relationship holds across a number of non-primate orders that vary by species in group size: bats (Barton & Dunbar, 1997), carnivores (Gittleman, 1986), and cetaceans (the order that includes porpoises, dolphins, and whales) for example (Marino, 1996).

table 8.1	Primates Group Size	
SPECIES	GROUP SIZE	REFERENCES
Orangutan (*Pongo pygmaeus*)	1	Mackinnon, 1974
Gorilla (*Gorilla gorilla*)	6	Fossey & Harcourt, 1977
Ring-tailed Lemur (*Lemur catta*)	12	Sussman, 1977
Brown Lemur (*Lemur fulvus*)	15	Sussman, 1977
Bonobo Chimpanzee (*Pan paniscus*)	28	White, 1992
Rhesus Monkey (*Macaca mulatta*)	32	Teas et al., 1980
Baboon (*Papio hamadryas*)	51	Nagel, 1973
Common Chimpanzee (*Pan troglodytes*)	59	Wrangham, 1977

Primates vary in group size. Here are some estimates of the group sizes of various primates. The social brain hypothesis suggests that the large group size in humans and the cognitive complexity of our many relationships explains our big brains.

8.3 Press Pause

According to the social brain hypothesis, the large brains in humans support the complex social cognitive processing required in large complex groups.

The social brain hypothesis predicts that brain size will correlate, across species, with group size. Although there has been evidence found in favour of this prediction (Barton, 1996; Dunbar, 1992; Dunbar, 1998b), there is more to the story than this. The human species is very social in more than one sense of the word. First, we live in groups, as do many other species, but unlike sheep, for example, we have rich social relationships. We have cognitive adaptations that are specifically designed to solve the social problems that were posed to our species in the environment in which we evolved. What does it mean to be a social species? In part, it means that in the EEA, humans spent their time in groups.

Some animals, like sheep, live in groups without having complex social structures and relationships, and thus without the corresponding social cognition. Other animals live socially, develop hierarchies, alliances, pair bonds, and thus have the social cognitive processes to support these relationships. Our social cognitive demands are greater than, say, fish, birds, sheep, or other herding animals that spend their time in large groups. These are animals that congregate in order to protect themselves from predators. Indeed, these groups do not "know" each other as individuals, save perhaps for mother and offspring.

Shultz and Dunbar (2007) suggest that it is not just the size of the group but also the nature and longevity of social relationships that should predict brain size. In some groups, such as birds, an individual may come and go without any apparent social imperative interfering with its mobility. In primate groups, in contrast, membership is stable over time, and belonging to a group has a value to an individual: One would not be equally welcome in a different group should they choose to abandon the current group. Neocortex size compared across species also correlates with clique size, that is, the individuals you hang out with on a day-to-day basis (Kudo & Dunbar, 2001). Even more intriguing, when comparing across primate species, the rates at which tactical deception is used is correlated with neocortex size (Byrne, 1995). More specific mea-

figure 8.2 Clique size and neocortex ration

The neocortex ratio is related not just to the overall group size but also to the size of the smaller clique, the small group that are our core best friends. Sheep and fish may spend time in extremely large groups, but without friends, alliances, and hierarchies, they do not have the same social cognitive problems to solve (Adapted from Dunbar, 1998).

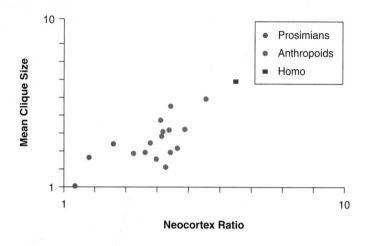

sures of social complexity also predict brain size, including deception rates (Byrne & Whiten, 1988), grooming clique size (Kudo & Dunbar, 2001), and coalition size (Dunbar & Shultz, 2007). Even more detailed analyses show that brain size (controlled for body size) is related to the amount of time spent in social activity during the day and the extent to which a species has a "bonded social structure," meaning the extent to which two individuals develop a committed relationship (Shultz & Dunbar, 2007). Again, among primates who have a complex social structure, larger group size was correlated with larger brain size, and in non-primate species that hang out in herds to reduce the risk of predation, there was no such relationship. In addition, among primates, brain size increased with the complexity of the social group, progressing from solitary to pair-bonded (a male–female couple), to a sole-male, multi-female harem to a multi-male group (Shultz & Dunbar, 2007).

The Big Brain and Long Childhood

Primates in general and humans in particular do not have big brains because they have large complex diets or live in a complex habitat. Humans have large brains because we have large, complex social groups. Another evolutionary result of our complex social lives, in addition to brain size, is our prolonged childhood or period of dependence. Compared to other species, humans spend an inordinate amount of time in development. Other species are much faster at growing up and getting right to the task of reproducing. Humans have an extremely protracted developmental period, including a prolonged period of adolescence. Again, traditional theorists who tried to figure out what took humans so long to learn looked at non-social possibilities: Were human youths trying to learn tool use, the technology of their culture, or food gathering and

Human children have an extended period of dependence and are unique in having an adolescent period. One explanation for the evolution of the lengthy period of adolescence in humans is the social cognitive demands of our species. Teenagers are maturing socially.

preparation? Again, the best explanation for the evolution of the lengthy period of adolescence in humans is the social cognitive demands of our species. Across a number of species, neocortex size correlates with the length of the juvenile period rather than with gestational period, or lactation period, or the reproductive lifespan (Bennett & Harvery, 1985; Marino, 1997).

Chapter 7 introduced the idea of core knowledge. According to the core-knowledge account, infants and children should be especially adept at acquiring knowledge in domains that have an impact on reproductive success in the EEA. In addition to easily developing knowledge in physics, space, biology, and number, as described in the last chapter, infants and young children show evidence of specialized aptitude in social domains. Social cognitive development was, indeed, a biologically significant domain in the EEA. Some of these domain-specific cognitive tools are used, even early in life, to process social information, and developmental psychologists have posited that we have, indeed, evolved domain-specific modules for the purpose of processing social information (Leslie, 1994).

8.4 Press Pause

The best explanation for humans' long juvenile period is our species' disproportionate need (given our group size) to acquire social expertise.

What Would Piaget Say about Social Cognitive Development?

Again, recent research in social cognitive development is unfolding in the wake of Piaget's research and theoretical work, which laid the foundation for contemporary thinking about social cognitive development. Piaget was particularly interested in perspective-taking. He discussed social cognitive limitations in the preoperational stage: importantly, the child's **egocentrism**. An egocentric child, according to Piaget, understood the world from her own point of view, unable to consider other views.

Piaget's early perspective-taking experiments involved creating situations in which a child saw two protagonists that had different vantage points (literally), and the child was tested to see whether he understood that different vantage points would provide access to different information (Piaget & Inhelder, 1967). For example, in the classic three mountain task, the child faced a model landscape that included three mountains. A doll served as the protagonist (in other conditions a human confederate served as the protagonist), and the child was asked whether the doll, from various vantage points, could see certain objects. When asked to select pictures of what the doll could see, young children typically selected the photo showing their own vantage point. Children younger than 9 or 10 years old were poor at appreciating that viewpoint mattered in terms of what visual information was available, and Piaget took this as evidence of their extreme egocentrism.

Younger children's failure to respond as adults would in the three mountain task showed, Piaget believed, their failure to appreciate that other people had their own mental states. The child did not understand that another person could have different knowledge and have visual access to different objects, a sign of social cognitive immaturity. This evidence of egocentrism was also considered diagnostic of the preoperational period.

egocentrism Piaget's term for a child's inability to appreciate other points of view besides their own.

figure 8.3 Piaget and Inhelder's three mountain task

In this experiment, when asked to select pictures of what the doll could see, the child was unable to predict the doll's vantage point, choosing instead pictures that showed what the child could see. Piaget took this as an example of the child's egocentrism. (Adapted from Papalia, Wendoks, and Fieldman, 1998.)

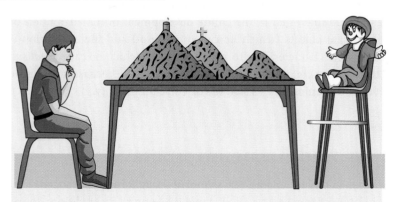

Children are more likely to hit a doll if they have just seen an adult do so. According to Albert Bandura, this illustrates the central idea of social learning theory: that children learn by observing and imitating those in their social environment.

8.5   **Press Pause**

Preoperational children are egocentric; they cannot see beyond their own point of view, according to Piaget.

Egocentrism is also evident in children's speech. Preschool-aged children routinely report events without enough information for the listener to understand. The child may tattle, "He broke it before I finished making it," when the adult does not know who "he" is or what "it" is. Even more amusing is watching two children of this age group have a "parallel" conversation, which sounds like a regular conversation until you realize that they are not responding to each other's content. A child may respond to "We went to the beach yesterday" with "My grandma has three cats."

Piaget was also interested in the child's development of the attribution of mental states to inanimate objects (which he called *animism*) and the attribution of physical and mechanical characteristics to mental entities (which he called *realism*). Piaget observed that his own child thought the moon was animate because it moved across the sky. Piaget took this animism as a sign of cognitive immaturity.

What Would Associationists Say?

As we have seen in other domains, one school of thought regarding social development is the associationist perspective. Following the empiricist tradition, John Watson believed that children's personalities and temperaments were determined by their social environments, primarily via simple but general learning mechanisms like conditioning.

The most prominent contemporary example of this empiricist tradition is the social learning theory. Social learning theory emphasizes observation and imitation rather than reward and punishment (Bandura, 1977). For example, children know quite a lot about driving a car (insert key, turn key, change gears, stop at a red light, accelerate at a green light, etc.) long before they have any experience, and hence any feedback about, driving. In one experiment, children who watched an adult hit a doll with a hammer were more likely to do so than children in a control condition (Bandura, Ross, & Ross, 1961).

Social Domains of Core Knowledge

What cognitive capacities do we have that are unique to humans? A recent study provides compelling and important evidence that humans have species-specific cognitive skills, even compared to our closest relatives. Researchers gave a battery of cognitive tasks, some involving physical problem-solving and some involving social problem-solving, to three groups: adult orangutans, adult chimpanzees, and 2½-year-old children who could not yet read and who had not yet attended school. The physical cognitive tests included object permanence, memory for object location, discriminating quantities, and using a stick to retrieve a reward, for example. The social cognitive tests included understanding someone's cue regarding the location of food, communicating to receive food, considering another's attentional state, and following eye gaze,

| figure 8.4 | **Social cognition in humans** |

Adult chimps and adult orangutans are just as good as 2½-year-old humans at non-social tasks such as location memory and using a tool to retrieve a treat, but the human toddler outperformed the apes at social tasks such as following eye gaze and understanding someone's cue regarding food location. (Adapted from Herrmann, Call, Hernandez-Lloreda, Hare, & Tomasello, 2007.)

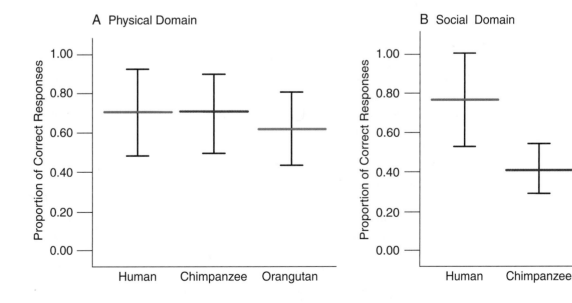

for example. Researchers found that the three groups were equal on performance on the physical cognitive tasks, but the human children outperformed adult orangutans and adult chimpanzees on the social cognitive tasks (Herrmann, Call, Hernandez-Lloreda, Hare, & Tomasello, 2007).

Humans are expert at social psychology in a number of ways, including recognizing faces, perceiving emotion, holding grudges, feeling gratitude, forming alliances and coalitions, and understanding others' mental states, to name a few. Some of the outcomes of our uniquely human social cognition, such as altruism and moral reasoning, will be examined in later chapters. Here we will look at evidence of core knowledge in social domains. There are important specific demands of social cognition that follow from the adaptive pressures in the EEA. Here you will read about several social cognitive adaptations that are thought to be core knowledge and a description of their developmental trajectories. Now that we have briefly reviewed some thinking on the social evolutionary pressures that prevailed in the EEA and their effects on the evolution of human psychology, we will discuss imitation, joint attention, social referencing, pretend play, face perception, the perception of animacy and intentionality, and theory of mind. Each of these social cognitive skills is thought to be dependent upon dedicated cognitive machinery that is reliably developing in our species.

From the Classroom to the Lab

Given that experimental work on the effects of social isolation in humans would not be feasible for ethical reasons, how might you approach research on the relationship between social isolation and other psychological factors? What variables could you measure? How would you analyze the relationship between variables?

Social Cognitive Development in Infancy

Human infants are born extremely immature (compared to other species at birth) and are extremely dependent upon the care of conspecifics to meet their needs. As a consequence, evolution by natural selection has designed the very young infant to be able to attract the attention of adults, to summon and keep adults nearby, and to manipulate adults to their own purposes.

Since Piaget, and as a reply to his research, others have explored the question of infants' egocentrism, challenging the idea that infants and young children are completely perceptually bound and that they do not understand that others may be able to see things that they cannot see themselves, or vice versa. Consider the behaviour of an 18-month-old infant who has been asked to show an adult something when that adult is covering her eyes with her hands. The infant will often try to remove the adult's hands from her face, or to insert the object between the adult's hands and face, evidence that the infant understands that there needs to be a direct line of vision between the adult's eyes and the object (Lempers, Flavell, & Flavell, 1977).

Following this discovery, John Flavell elaborated that at the age of 2 and 3 years, young children have what he calls a Level 1 understanding of perspective: They know whether or not you can see something but do not know that you may be looking at it differently than they are (Flavell, 1992). At this age, children know that in order to see something, a person's eyes have to be open and that there has to be a clear line of sight

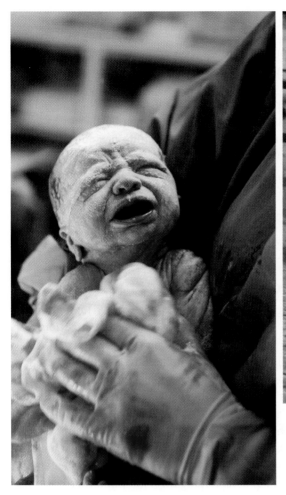

Here are two newborns: a human and a horse. Compared to other species at birth, human newborns are extremely helpless. They depend on others entirely to fulfill their needs and keep them safe. From birth, social cognitive skills, including crying, are designed to elicit help from others.

in order for the person to see an object. If the child sees a picture on a two-dimensional card that is held between himself and an adult, the child understands that the person seated opposite does not see the picture. At the age of 4 or 5 years the child comes to have what Flavell calls a Level 2 understanding: She gets that another person might see an object but see it differently. A picture that lays flat on a table between the two appears right-side up to one person and upside-down to the other (Masangkay et al., 1974).

> ### 8.6 Press Pause
>
> Contrary to Piaget's early claims, young children are not completely egocentric: They have some understanding that others may be prevented from seeing what they can see themselves.

IMITATION

Researchers have seen imitation as an early social skill for several decades. For the infant, the ability to imitate, even if in a very rudimentary way, creates an interactive relationship with an adult that the adult finds rewarding and that thus facilitates the infant's resource acquisition. By the age of 5 or 6 weeks, infants imitate adults' facial behaviours such as mouth opening and tongue protrusion. Developmental psychologists are fairly sure that this is, indeed, a social behaviour since babies do not imitate non-animate objects (e.g., robotic faces) producing similar behaviours (Legerstee, 1991).

Infants at 14 months of age prefer to look at an adult who is imitating their facial expressions and gestures. In one study, a 14-month-old sat at a table with two adults; each person had the same toy. If the baby picked up the toy and manipulated it, the adults each picked up their toy. One adult imitated (as precisely as possible) what the infant did, while the other adult manipulated the toy in some other way. The baby smiled more and looked more at the imitating adult than at the other adult. Babies can discriminate between imitative and non-imitative activity (Meltzoff, 1990).

8.7 **Press Pause**

Imitation is an early developing social cognitive skill.

JOINT ATTENTION AND SOCIAL REFERENCING

joint attention An individual's ability to tell when he shares an object of attention with another person.

Another early developing social cognitive skill is called *joint attention*. **Joint attention** refers to an individual's ability to tell when he shares an object of attention with another person. Babies develop the ability to follow an adult's eye gaze between 2 and 12 months (Scaife & Bruner, 1975) and follows her pointed index finger starting at around 9 months (Murphy & Messer, 1977). Infants respond to an adult's bid to create joint attention (responsive joint attention) and issue bids to create joint attention (initiated joint attention).

There is a broad consensus in the field that evidence of joint attention means that the child is aware of mental processes in others. In particular, it shows that children have some understanding of attention, intention, and affect. Therefore, joint attention behaviours are thought to be evidence of a developing theory of mind (Baron-Cohen, 1989a; Rochat & Striano, 1999).

social referencing A young child looking at a trusted authority in situations that are ambiguous with respect to the appropriate response.

Another social cognitive skill that develops early in life is called **social referencing**: A young child will look at a trusted authority in situations that are ambiguous with respect to the appropriate response starting at around 9 or 10 months. If, for example, an unknown furry animal enters the room, an infant may need input from an experienced authority to know whether to pet the animal or to run away from it. If the adult

---

figure **8.5** **Joint attention**

These two people share joint attention. They are both attending to the plant, and they *know* they are both attending to the plant. A baby follows his mother's line of sight as early as 9 months of age.

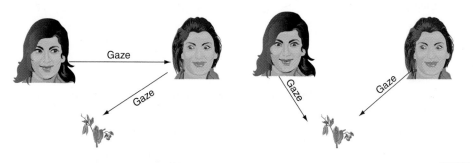

smiles, or looks pleased and interested, the baby will approach the animal; if the adult looks fearful, the baby will avoid the object and approach the adult instead (Campos & Sternberg, 1981; Klinnert, 1984; Sorce, Emde, Campos, & Klinnert, 1985). This skill implies that young children can discriminate among different emotional facial expressions and can put them to good use.

Both social referencing and neonatal imitation are phylogenetically ancient skills, present in both monkeys and rats. Both of these social cognitive skills are adaptive in highly social animals. Conversely, they would serve no function, and thus would not evolve, in solitary species.

> **8.8 Press Pause**
>
> Imitation, joint attention, and social referencing are early social cognitive skills in humans; imitation and social referencing appear to have evolved in other species as well.

Pretend Play

Play is how a child spends most of his or her time awake (Sutton-Smith, 1976). Children do not need any explicit instruction in order to engage in play activity; rather, they create play for themselves and watch and imitate play behaviour in peers (Garvey, 1991; Moyles, 1994). Piaget (1952) distinguished two different types of play: **sensorimotor play**, which involves the manipulation of objects, presumably in order to master the

sensorimotor play Child's play involving object manipulation as a means for the practice and mastery of action schemas.

figure 8.6 Pretend play requires theory of mind

To engage in pretend play with someone else or to understand pretend play, one must understand mental states. Here, the child understands that Mommy is pretending the banana is a telephone while understanding that Mommy knows it is really just a banana.

pretend play Play that involves the use of actions or objects to represent real life or imagined actions, objects, or characters.

skills associated with tool use; and **pretend play**, which involves creating representations of imagined actions, objects, or characters. Piaget saw pretend play as practice as well, practice for events in the child's social world. Pretend play has been defined by contemporary developmental psychologists as simulative or non-literal play (Fein, 1981) or as acting as if something is the case when it is not (McCune-Nicolich, 1981). In other words, a child is pretending if she is using one object to substitute for an imagined object, attributing imagined properties to an object (pretending a towel is wet, e.g.), or attributing agency to a doll or another object.

Some people who study theory of mind see pretend play as evidence that the child is developing theory of mind (Leslie, 1987). Leslie suggests that pretend play involves the same kind of cognitive processing that understanding other minds takes. Here is the logic behind this claim: When a child engages in pretend play, the child simultaneously understands the primary, real-world reality (the banana is just a banana) and the new, pretend interpretation of the situation (the banana is a telephone). Understanding the pretend interpretation of the scenario is the same social cognitive trick as understanding another person's mental states. This is true whether the child is producing pretend play or just observing and understanding someone else's pretend play.

This child is engaged in sensorimotor play. This kind of play involves the manipulation of objects in order to explore them and master skills that are associated with them.

It would be easy to miss the fact that pretend play is a sophisticated and complex cognitive accomplishment: Pretend play is child's play. But in order to pretend that the banana is a telephone, one must have two simultaneous representations (banana as banana and banana as telephone), and one must understand another person's mental states: We are pretending that the banana is a telephone, where "pretending" is a mental state. Pretend play begins to emerge by the age of 18 months, and it becomes more elaborate and sophisticated over the preschool years (McCune-Nicolich, 1981).

8.9   Press Pause

Engaging in pretend play and understanding others' pretend play requires an understanding of others' mental states.

Pretend play is simulative or non-literal play, or as acting as if something is the case when it is not. It involves creating representations of imagined actions, objects, or characters.

Face Perception

Faces are certainly special visual objects for us and are perceived unlike any other visual stimuli. For most adults, there is an area of the brain that is dedicated to face perception (Tong, Nakayama, Moscovitch, Weinrib, & Kanwisher, 2000). This area is referred to as the **fusiform face area**, or FFA. There is evidence that this area of the brain is specialized for face processing, although it may occasionally be used for processing objects that are associated with special areas of expertise for certain individuals.

Not only are we very interested in faces, and likely to be looking at faces whenever they are in the same room with us, but we see them even where there are none: in the moon, clouds, and rock formations. Experimentally, there are a couple of hallmarks of face processing that we take as evidence that people process faces differently than any other stimuli they see: the inversion effect and holistic processing.

The **inversion effect** is the disruption in face processing that is observed when a face is inverted. A typical demonstration of the inversion effect involves a task in which a participant has to say which of two pictures is identical to a third. If the pictures are inverted, people are slower to choose and less accurate in their choices. But the "cost" of inversion is much higher if the pictures are of faces: People are about 10 per cent less accurate if the pictures show cars, houses, or furniture, but 25 per cent less accurate if the pictures show faces. This is taken as evidence that faces are processed somehow differently than other objects and that the perceptual mechanisms that process faces are so specialized that they do not work when faces are inverted.

Other evidence also reveals how face processing is special: In **holistic processing**, we see faces as a whole, as a gestalt, not as separate parts put together. That holistic processing is mandatory is illustrated by the composite face task (Carey & Diamond, 1994; Le Grand, Mondloch, Maurer, & Brent, 2004). In this task, participants are asked to tell whether the upper half (or in other trials just the lower half) of a face is the same in two images that show the upper halves of the faces aligned with different bottom halves. If the two top halves are identical, people find it very difficult to see that they are the same because they see each face as a whole, and the difference in bottom halves makes the two faces seem different. Based on this task, recent evidence has revealed holistic face processing as early as 6 years of age (Mondloch, Pathman, Maurer, Le Grand, & de Schonen, 2007).

fusiform face area The area of the brain that is dedicated to face perception.

inversion effect The disruption in face processing that is observed when a face is inverted.

holistic processing The integration of visual information from the whole of the perceived visual region of interest, usually the face region, in contrast to the perception and representation of component parts.

figure 8.7 **Fusiform face area**

The fusiform face area is active during face perception.

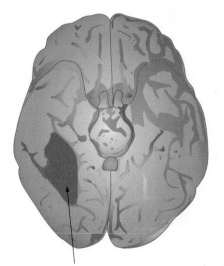

FUSIFORM FACE AREA

8.10 Press Pause

Faces are special visual objects, as evidenced by the inversion effect and holistic processing.

THE EARLY DEVELOPMENT OF FACE PERCEPTION

Recall that in Chapter 4 you were asked to consider that what people call *learning* is, in fact, not a singular type of event. There are many kinds of learning (learning to walk, learning to talk, learning who one's mother is, etc.), and each kind of learning relies on a different learning mechanism; each mechanism is designed for its own purpose. To say that something is learned, therefore, does not answer the developmental question. As curious developmental psychologists, we want to know everything we can about the nature of that learning. Here, we will consider the story of the development of early face recognition as a special kind of learning.

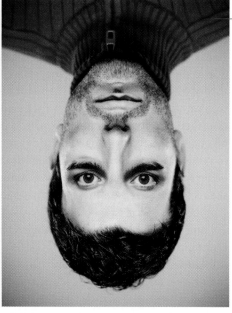

Our ability to process a face is disrupted when the face is presented upside-down. This is the inversion effect.

Humans become face experts early in development. We know that very young children are interested in faces as early as 2 months of age (Morton & Johnson, 1991) and, when scanning a face, are particularly interested in eyes (Farroni, Johnson, Brockbank, & Simion, 2000; Hains & Muir, 1996; Vecera & Johnson, 1995). How do we know this? Because babies would rather look at images of faces than non-faces.

Initially, people thought that the story of face recognition was going to be just another straightforward story about learning: As infants had more and more exposure to faces, they learned what faces looked like. Some evidence supported this idea: Experiments showed that although 1-month-old infants had no preference for

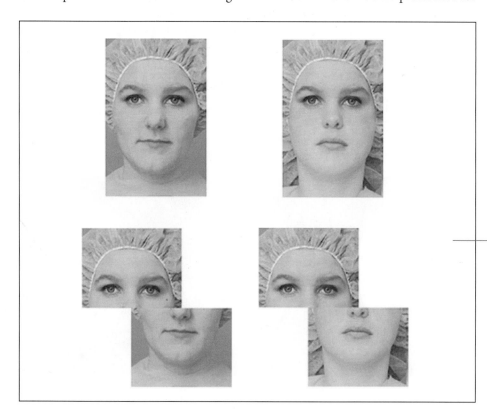

The top halves of all the photos are identical. It is hard for people to see that when the bottom halves are different because we automatically process faces as a whole. Holistic processing creates the impression that the top halves are different.

faces, babies would preferentially look at face-like schematic pictures compared to other equally complex pictures (usually scrambled face parts) as early as 4 months (Wilcox, 1969), 3 months (Fantz & Nevis, 1972), and even 2 months (Maurer & Barrera, 1981). The difference in the age at which the infant showed a preference is likely due to differences in methodology. Here, let us consider the most sensitive method, that of Maurer and Barrera's. Their stimuli consisted of a cartoon-like face compared to scrambled schematic faces, which had the same features but were arranged in a non-face-like configuration. The experimenter showed a 2-month-old infant a slide of one of the images and that slide stayed up until the infant looked away. That looking time was recorded and then the next slide was presented. Most researchers believed that this infant-controlled stimulus presentation was very sensitive, and it seems to be the reason these authors found such early evidence of face preference at 2 months.

But here is the perplexing thing: One experiment already existed that showed that newborns (yes, newborns) prefer to look at faces. Goren, Sarty, and Wu tested 9-minute-old newborns and showed that they were willing to turn their eyes and their heads farther to keep a schematic face in view than to see a scrambled or blank stimulus.

The experiment placed the infant lying on his back on the experimenter's lap. The infant would turn his head and his eyes farther in order to track a moving image of a face compared to control images. But this did not make any sense! People in the field were quite satisfied that young infants knew nothing about faces, and that they slowly learned of faces due to exposure, until they finally showed evidence of a face preference as early as 2 months. Because the findings did not fit what people believed to be true, this experiment was largely ignored for many years.

Finally, these results were replicated (Johnson, Dziurawiec, Ellis, & Morton, 1991) 16 years later, and people started to take seriously the possibility that they were seeing something very interesting. This pattern of results is called a **U-shaped curve**: Infants show a competence, then at a later age fail to show it, then at an even later age show it again. If you graphed this skill by age, the results would be shaped like a *U*, hence the name. This pattern of results is very difficult to explain if the face preference the

U-shaped curve
A graph depicting a developmental time course over which an individual displays a competence, then fails to display that same competence, and then displays it again at a later stage.

figure 8.8   Face and control stimuli

One of these three images was shown to a 2-month-old until they looked away. They looked longest at the face image. (Adapted from Maurer & Barrera, 1981.)

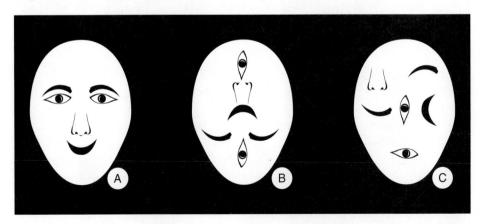

figure 8.9 Very early attention to faces—experiment

In an experiment by Goren, Sarty, and Wu (1975), the experimenter placed a newborn on his lap and measured how far the baby would turn his head and eyes to follow face and non-face images. The finding that babies preferred faces was so astonishing that scientists ignored it for 16 years.

figure 8.10 Very early attention to faces—results

The dependent measure in Goren, Sarty, and Wu's (1975) experiment was the number of degrees the newborn would turn his head or eyes. This figure shows that infants turned their head and eyes more to follow the image of the face compared to scrambled face features or a blank paddle.

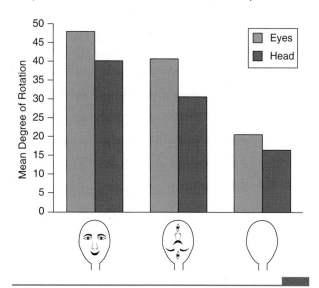

infant shows is the result of a single mechanism, so Johnson and Morton have proposed that the early face preference and the later face preference are mediated by different psychological processes, indeed, processes that were designed to work together (Morton & Johnson, 1991).

Johnson and Morton proposed a two-process development plan wherein an early system orients the baby to things in the environment that are likely to be faces, and the second process takes advantage of this visual orientation to build its adult-like face template that will be used for face recognition throughout life.

8.11 Press Pause

Babies orient to faces at birth and at 2 months, but not at 1 month. This U-shaped curve may require two different psychological processes to explain it.

Babies show other evidence of orienting to social information as well. In Chapter 5 we discussed the infant's very early preference for orienting visually to faces. Even visual preferences that seem non-social may very well have evolved because of their social utility: Babies prefer to look at objects that have oval contours, objects that are relatively large, objects that move, objects that have high light–dark contrast, and objects that are either brightly coloured or light in colour. As it turns out, orienting to objects that fit that description in a species-typical environment usually means orienting to a face. Even very young babies prefer human speech over other sounds; they are attentive to human voices and are very adept at parsing speech sounds. As we discussed in Chapter 5, infants even seem to learn something about their own mothers' voices prenatally.

PERCEPTUAL NARROWING: FACE PERCEPTION BECOMES MORE SPECIALIZED

perceptual narrowing
A developmental process in which perceptual mechanisms become more specialized such that infants lose the ability to discriminate between categories that are irrelevant.

Some research in early face perception illustrates the idea of **perceptual narrowing**, a finding that underlines our thesis that nature and nurture are inextricably linked. Infants are good at discriminating between two faces. But what might be surprising is the experimental finding that human 6-month-olds were good at discriminating two human faces and were also good at discriminating two monkey faces. Nine-month-olds had apparently specialized: They were good at discriminating two human faces but not two monkey faces. The authors think these results suggest that there is early developing psychological machinery specialized for processing information about faces and that this machinery undergoes a process of "perceptual narrowing" as it is exposed to a subset of possible faces; in most cases that subset would be human as opposed to monkey faces (Pascalis, De Haan, & Nelson, 2002).

Apparently the specialization in human faces could have gone the other way, based on recent research with Japanese monkeys. Infant monkeys were deprived of exposure to any faces during a period of 6 to 24 months. They were then exposed either to only human faces or to only monkey faces. They became specialists in the subset they saw: They were good at discriminating human faces if exposed to human faces but poor at discriminating monkey faces, or vice versa if exposed only to monkey faces (Sugita, 2008).

Animacy and Intentionality Perception

Very young infants distinguish between animate and inanimate entities and know that the behaviour of others is purposeful and goal-directed. Indeed, this "animacy perception" ability may be developmentally fundamental to all social cognition and social understanding. The first step in understanding the social world is to categorize objects with which one can have a social understanding or social relationship. One must first figure out what in the world has intentions, agency, or mental states. In that sense, animacy perception may be a fundamental developmental building block. Animacy perception would have to precede other kinds of social cognitive development, and a child who did not develop animacy perception would fail to develop typical social cognition. A child cannot reason about another person's mental state or perspective if that child is not aware that the other has psychological goings-on. Now, do not fail to appreciate the enormity of this problem: The very young child comes to perceive, reason about, and make predictions based on other people's mental states, when mental states themselves are completely intangible (indeed they may not *really* exist; who knows?).

Young infants expect that people can do things but objects cannot. An infant is unimpressed (as measured by looking time) if a person walks across a stage in front of him but surprised (inferred from increased looking time) if a chair moves entirely on its own across the platform in front of him (Spelke, Phillips, & Woodward, 1995). In another study, 1-year-old infants were similarly unimpressed if a person knocked a ball into a doll but surprised if a ball knocked another ball into the doll, again all indicated by the infant's looking time (Poulin-Dubois & Shultz, 1988). We conclude, then, that not only can infants distinguish between people and other objects but they also have an expectation of the kinds of behaviour in which a person would engage in but that an object would not. Impressive for such a young baby, no?

8.12 Press Pause

One-year-olds have different expectations of the behaviour of animate vs. inanimate objects.

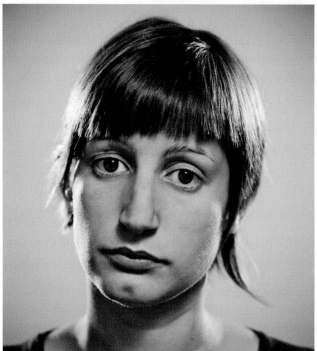
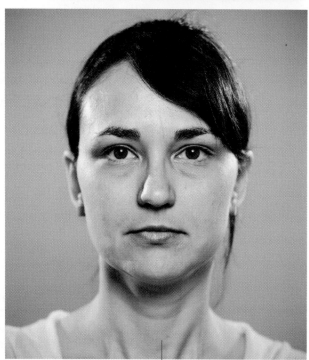

You might find it easy to distinguish the two human faces and relatively harder to distinguish the two monkey faces. Nine-month-olds would agree with you, but 6-month-olds find it just as easy to discriminate the monkey faces as the human faces, a developmental phenomenon called *perceptual narrowing* (Pascalis, De Haan, & Nelson, 2002).

INTENTIONALITY DETECTION IN ONE MODEL OF SOCIAL DEVELOPMENT

One prominent model of social cognitive development that includes an animacy perception component is that developed by Simon Baron-Cohen. On the way to developing adult-like social cognition, Baron-Cohen proposes that the infant must first develop an "intentionality detector." This intentionality detector is a mechanism that interprets the movement of an object in terms of volitional mental states. That is, based on just the movement of an object, one can tell not only that it is an agent but that it has goals or "intentionality" (Baron-Cohen, 1995).

EVIDENCE OF EARLY ANIMACY PERCEPTION

Central to the development of core social knowledge is the ability to discriminate animate from inanimate objects. Recent studies strongly suggest that even very young children appreciate an animate–inanimate distinction. Preschoolers explicitly distinguish animate from inanimate objects based on an object's ability to move by itself (Gelman, 1990).

Even very young infants can distinguish objects that show autonomous movement from those that do not (Golinkoff, Harding, Carlson, Sexton, 1984). Young children's understanding of the mind–body distinction (Inagaki & Hatano, 1993) shows that they distinguish modifiable traits (running speed) from mental traits (memory) and from traits that are beyond the influence of one's intentions (heartbeat).

Some early research that showed infants categorize objects as animate or inanimate came from the laboratory of Phillipe Rochat. In his study, adults, 3-month-olds, and 6-month-olds looked at two side-by-side computer displays. On one computer monitor, two balls moved around on the screen as if they were following, or "chasing," one another. On the other screen, two balls moved around and remained about the same distance from one another but did not seem to be interacting with one another. Each of the subject groups looked at the two displays differently, suggesting that for each group, the two displays showed something different. The observers could discriminate the displays. The youngest infants (the 3-month-olds) spent more time looking at the display that showed the "chase" scene, suggesting that these very young infants have some interest in a social display over a non-social display even though this social information is conveyed only by the movement patterns of dots on a computer screen. One could take this result to suggest that 3-month-olds see these dots as "alive" based on their movements (Rochat, Morgan, & Carpenter, 1997).

8.13 **Press Pause** ─────────────────────────────

Infants as young as 3 months can distinguish animate from inanimate objects based on the object's movements.

Another important and exciting experiment that showed an early understanding of social information was performed by Gergely and colleagues. These researchers showed that not only do infants categorize objects as animate and inanimate, but by 12 months

---

figure **8.11** **Animacy perception**

Three-month-old infants were shown two side-by-side monitors, one with balls that were chasing each other and the other with balls that were moving independently. At 3 months of age, infants spent more time looking at the monitor displaying the balls that were chasing each other, showing a perception of animate motion. (Adapted from Rochat et al., 1997.)

Balls Chasing Each Other

Balls Moving Independently

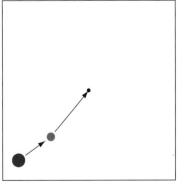
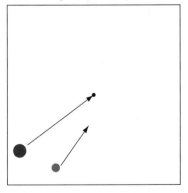

| figure | 8.12 | **Attribution of Dispositional States** |

If a 12-month-old saw the yellow triangle helping the red ball up the hill and the blue square hindering the ball from getting up the hill, he would be surprised (look longer) if the red ball later approached the blue square rather than the yellow triangle. (Adapted from Kuhlmeier, Wynn, & Bloom, 2003).

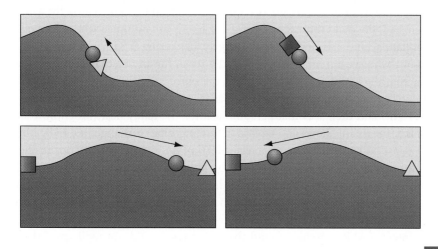

---

of age, they also expect rational behaviour from intentional objects. This was a habituation experiment. The babies in this experiment watched as the following scenario played out: A smaller black ball jumped over a barrier to reach a larger black ball. Once the baby habituated to this movement pattern, the barrier was removed. Would the babies still expect the smaller ball to jump to reach the larger ball because this was the trajectory the baby had habituated to? (This would be a reasonable prediction if you thought the baby had no expectation of rational behaviour.) Or would the baby expect the smaller ball to take a direct path to the larger ball now that this path was available with no barrier? In a between-subjects design (one group of babies saw one option, the other group saw the other option), babies dishabituated more to the "irrational" display of the ball jumping (even though jumping was now unnecessary) even though this was the trajectory they had habituated to. It appears that as early as 12 months of age, infants expect animate objects, or agents, to behave rationally (Gergely, Nadasdy, Csibra, & Biro, 1995).

Another interesting study shows that, like adults, 12-month-olds also seem able to attribute dispositional states to agents and use those dispositions not only to predict the behaviour of the agent in question but also to predict how attracted others will be to that agent. In this experiment, infants watched a film that adults interpret as a ball "trying and failing" to get up a hill as it is being "helped" by a triangle and being "blocked" by a square. Subsequently, with just the three shapes on the screen, infants' looking behaviours indicated that they expected the ball to approach the helpful triangle while avoiding the hindering square (Kuhlmeier, Wynn, & Bloom, 2003).

INTENTION PERCEPTION

A few classic experiments have strongly indicated that young children have an understanding of other people's intentions. One experiment showed that a toddler understands a person's intentions even if their intention fails. If a child as young as 18-months-old watches an adult attempt, but fail, to complete a task such as hanging a ring on a hook or pulling a block off of a stick, the child will complete the task. The fact that the child will complete the task, when the completion of the task was never modelled, suggests that the child understands the intention. This is not true if the child watches a machine complete essentially the same physical movements as the adult model. Watching the machine approximate the task, the child does not infer intention or goal and does not pick up the objects and complete the task (Meltzoff, 1995).

In addition, 14-month-old infant might imitate an actor who uses her forehead to turn off a light if her hands are not occupied (there must be some reason the actor used her forehead, the child thinks) but not if her hands are occupied (the actor could not use her hands, but I can, and so I will; Gergely, Bekkering & Kiraly, 2002).

Infants who see a human arm repeatedly reach for an object in the same location assume that the action is directed toward the object, not the place. If a 9-month-old infant looks at a person who repeatedly reaches for a ball on the left (not a teddy bear on the right) and then sees that person reach for the teddy bear, which now appears on the left, the infant shows an increase in looking time (dishabituate), indicating that she is surprised by the change in object selection despite the consistency in the location. This is true in spite of the fact that the physical trajectory has not changed. The habituated child does not dishabituate if the person's arm reaches for the ball on the right, even though the physical trajectory has changed, and this is presumably because the child appreciates that the goal has not changed. The 9-month-old understands the actor's intentions. Researchers found that these results did not replicate if the "arm" looked so mechanical that the child was not able to read a mental state into its actions (Woodward, 1998).

Even infants as young as 7 months of age seem to understand a person's intentions, even if the actor's goal is not fulfilled. If a 7-month-old infant watches an experimenter reach for one of two toys that are just out of reach, the baby will more likely pick up the toy that the actor was reaching for than the other, equally attractive, toy. This result is not explained simply by the infant's attention having been drawn to that toy because if the experimenter points to, but does not reach for, the toy, the infant selects the toy by chance, apparently not affected by the experimenter's actions (Hamlin, Hallinan, & Woodward, 2008).

INNOVATIVE
RESEARCH METHOD

Another experiment suggests very strongly that young children understand the intentions of others based on the finding that infants parse other people's actions. What does that mean? Imagine you are watching someone pick a dishtowel off of the floor, hang it up, and then pick up a glass of water from the counter. These are three discrete acts, but the person who performs these three acts is likely in constant fluid motion and does not pause once each small goal is achieved. As adults, we can appreciate that we have watched the completion of three small goals and thus three separate acts, but would an infant know this, given that the physical motion is uninterrupted? How would we know? In a very clever habituation study, infants were shown a movie of a series of actions like those described above. The 11-month-old infants saw the same movie until they thought it was boring. Then, in a between-subjects design, infants saw either a movie in which pauses were artificially inserted just as the actor completed an act or inserted in the middle of an act. The placement of the pauses should not make much difference to the viewer—since the physical motion was continuous in the original movie—unless the viewer appreciates that the actor had a goal and that that goal was achieved. Infants dishabituated to the movie in which a pause appeared in mid-act (which seemed inexplicable) but not to the movie in which the pause appeared at the completion of an act (as if they had already imagined a pause there). It would be hard to make sense of this result except to suggest that the infant understood the actor's intention (Baldwin, Baird, Saylor, & Clark, 2001).

8.14   **Press Pause**

Infants in their first year of life can infer someone's intentions just by watching their actions.

Theory of Mind

Recall that *theory of mind* is a term that is used by developmental psychologists to describe our human ability to understand another person's mental states. By watching people's behaviours, we can understand their beliefs, desires, and goals, and we can determine if they are pretending. When we understand people's mental states, we can use our knowledge of these mental states to understand and predict people's behaviours.

DEVELOPMENT OF THEORY OF MIND

By 12 months of age, infants know a great deal about how people's behaviours are related to their goals and intentions, suggesting very early precursors of theory of mind. Young children have a naive psychology, a common-sense level of understanding of other people and themselves. Fifteen-month-olds can make inferences about what a person will do based on the knowledge of what the person knows. At the centre of naive psychology are three constructs that people commonly use to understand human behaviour: desires, beliefs, and actions. Infants think about other people in terms of invisible constructs by 12 months of age and possibly earlier.

Early studies of a child's understanding of mental states focussed on the appearance–reality distinction. If a child could understand that something was a sponge but appeared to be a rock, then they understood that someone's point of view could be independent of what was true.

THE APPEARANCE–REALITY DISTINCTION

An early empirical attempt to test children for an understanding of the existence of mental states was to see if they could appreciate that an object could *look* like one thing but actually *be* something else. Could the child appreciate that there could be a difference between appearance and reality? A child might be shown a sponge that looks very much like a rock. When only allowed to look at the object, the child might report that it is a rock. When allowed to feel, lift, and squeeze the object, the child realizes that the object is a sponge. The critical question, then, is whether the child can now report that the object appears to be a rock, or is that representation completely overwritten by knowing that the object is a sponge? Most 3-year-olds are baffled by this task: They cannot appreciate both the appearance and the reality simultaneously. Once the object is revealed to be a sponge, it is no longer a rock; they will report that it is a sponge and has always appeared so. They are resistant to any teaching, demonstration, or attempt to make them understand both appearance and reality at the same time (Flavell, Green, & Flavell, 1986). Children ages 6 to 7 "get" the distinction and recognize that there can be a difference between what something really is and what it appears to be. This parallels the development of skills on perceptual perspective-taking tasks such as the three mountain task. Still, at this age children find it difficult to discuss and describe what that difference is. It is hard for them to talk about how something "looks different from the way it really and truly is." By 11 or 12 years of age, children are pretty adept at discussing the appearance–reality distinction (Flavell et al., 1986).

Although the appearance–reality distinction was an early and easy measure of a child's understanding of mental states, some have argued that this test may underestimate theory of mind competence. Hansen and Markman have argued that the question "What does this look like?" is confusing because it could query mere resemblance, "Peter looks like Jim," or actual equivalence, "That looks like Jim" (Hansen & Markman, 2005). Indeed, other methods have revealed evidence of theory of mind development at earlier ages.

FALSE-BELIEF TASKS

As theory of mind was originally conceived and measured in developing children, researchers relied on some version of the false-belief task, a task in which a child must appreciate a character's false belief in order to predict or explain their behaviour. A classic demonstration of this task involves an experimenter showing a child a box of Smarties. The experimenter asks the child what she thinks is in the box, and the child invariably replies "Smarties!" Next, the experimenter reveals that the box contains nothing but pencils. Now the experimenter refers to a friend of the child who is waiting outside of the room. "If we show Bobby this box, what will he think is in the box?" If the child is a typical 5-year-old, she will reply "Smarties" because she understands that Bobby will have a false belief. However, a 3-year-old will reply "pencils" (Gopnik & Astington, 1988; Perner, Leekam, & Wimmer, 1987). The 3-year-old fails to appreciate that Bobby has not had access to the information about the pencils and does not appreciate that Bobby will have a false belief. Indeed, unlike the 5-year-old, the 3-year-old has not shown evidence of understanding that Bobby has mental states at all. The child's theory of mind is still immature.

Another false-belief task is called the Sally–Anne task. In this task, a child is asked to consider two puppets or dolls: Sally and Anne. Sally puts her ball in a basket while Anne is watching. Sally leaves the room. Then "naughty Anne" moves the ball from the basket to a box. The critical question is "Where will Sally look for her ball first?" If the child answers "the basket," this indicates that the child appreciates that Sally has a false belief, an indication that the child understands mental states and uses them to predict behaviour. According to these standard measures, typically developing children show evidence of theory of mind development when they are nearly 4 years old, or older. Three-year-olds almost uniformly fail standard false-belief tasks. Does this mean theory of mind develops at around 4 years, or are these tasks just not sensitive enough to measure theory of mind development in younger children?

With new and innovative methods, researchers have been able to find evidence of theory of mind development in much younger children. Kristine Onishi (now of McGill University in Montreal) and Renée Baillargeon (working at the University of Illinois) used the violation of expectation paradigm to test theory of mind understanding in 15-month-olds. These infants watched an actor place a toy in a green box. Next, the toy was revealed and placed back in the green box or revealed and moved to a yellow box. This action happened either while the actor was looking or while the actor was not looking. Thus, four conditions were created: two in which the actor had a true belief and two in which the actor had a false belief, crossed with two in which the toy had moved and two in which the toy had been placed back in the original position.

INNOVATIVE
RESEARCH METHOD

During test trials, the infants saw the actor reach into either the green or the yellow box. Results clearly showed evidence of an appreciation of the actor's belief and the role belief plays in predicting the actor's behaviour. No matter whether the toy had been placed back in its original position or moved, the infants expected the action to be guided by the belief, whether the belief was true or not. In cases where the actor had a true belief, looking time was greater if the actor looked in the wrong location, but in cases where the actor had a false belief, looking time was greater in cases where the actor looked in the right location (Onishi & Baillargeon, 2005).

Does this mean that theory of mind understanding develops first at 15 months of age? Again, innovative research reveals evidence of theory of mind reasoning at an even younger age. Luca Surian, Stefania Caldi, and Dan Sperber, working at the University of Trento, Italy, had 13-month-old infants watch as an actor first established a preferred food item: The actor consistently chose either an apple or a piece of cheese when each was hidden behind a screen. In the test trial, the locations of the apple and the cheese were reversed. If the screen was high and occluded the food, the infant was surprised if the actor reached for the preferred food (how did she know it was there when its location had been switched?). But if the screen was low and the food was visible, the infant was surprised if the actor reached for the non-preferred food. Using looking time as a measure, researchers found evidence that infants as young as 13 months expect one's beliefs to guide one's actions (Surian, Caldi, & Sperber, 2007).

8.15 Press Pause

Classic theory of mind measures suggested theory of mind development around 4 years of age, but contemporary theory of mind tasks suggest some development as early as 13 months.

figure 8.13 Belief-induction trial

In Onishi and Baillargeon's (2005) experiment, 15-month-old infants watched an actor place a toy in a green box. Next, the toy was revealed and placed back in the green box or revealed and moved to a yellow box while the actor was or was not looking. During test trials, the infants saw the actor reach into either the green or the yellow box. The results, measured by looking time, clearly showed evidence of the infants' appreciation of the actor's belief and the role belief plays in predicting the actor's behaviour. (Adapted from Onishi & Baillargeon, 2005.)

A True Belief-green condition

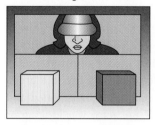 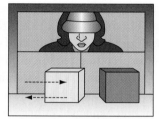 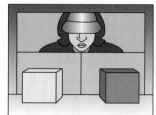

B True Belief-yellow condition

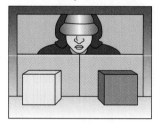 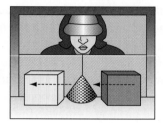 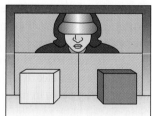

C False Belief-green condition

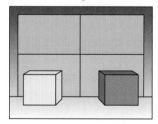 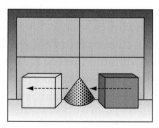 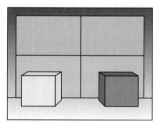

D False Belief-yellow condition

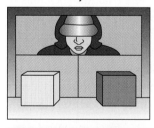 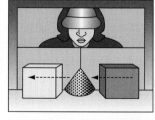 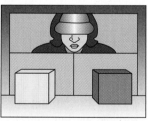

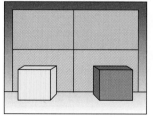 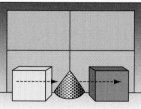 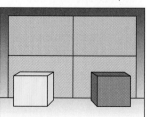

THEORY OF MIND IN NON-HUMANS?

Is the theory of mind mechanism uniquely human? This has been a point of some controversy. Imagine what kind of experiment you might do to convince yourself that a non-human animal, say a chimpanzee or your pet dog, has theory of mind. What experimental results could convince you that the animal is mentalizing and has not just made an association? People have tried to create experiments that test for this. For example, if a dog is forbidden to take food, that dog will attempt to take the food less often if a person is looking at him than if the person is looking away, has her back turned, or is involved in a different activity. This suggests that a dog understands what a person is paying attention to (Call, Brauer, Kaminski, & Tomasello, 2003).

Similarly, chimpanzees might have some theory of mind ability. If a chimp can request food from one of two experimenters, one who knows where the food is and one who does not know where the food is, they are much more likely to request food from the experimenter who knows where the food is. This finding suggests that chimps can understand some mental states (Povinelli, Nelson, & Boysen, 1990). So, we know that animals have some ability to use mental states to predict behaviour. Whether this ability is the same as the human theory of mind is an open question, but recent research seems to suggest that non-human primates do not have some human-like theory of mind abilities (Povinelli & Eddy, 1996; Povinelli & Vonk, 2004).

Do dogs have theory of mind? If a dog is forbidden to take food, that dog will attempt to take the food less often if a person is looking at him than if the person is looking away, has her back turned, or is involved in a different activity.

Autism: What If There Were No Theory of Mind?

Autism is a developmental disorder that is defined and characterized by three classes of abnormal processing: a deficit in social cognition, a delay in the development of communication, and an adherence to routine or repetitive behaviours (American Psychiatric Association, 1994). Arguably, the most clinically debilitating of these deficits is the deficit in social cognition, and the social cognitive delays are among the earliest to develop.

Simon Baron-Cohen first proposed that a deficit in theory of mind development was a defining feature of autism (Baron-Cohen, Leslie, & Frith, 1985). According to his model of theory of mind development (Baron-Cohen, 1995), typical children develop the ability to identify objects that are animate as a precursor to the theory of mind mechanism (TOMM). Children with autism spectrum disorder ASDs have a deficit in the development of this capability, measurable by a relative inability to distinguish objects engaged in animate and inanimate motion (Rutherford, Pennington, & Rogers, 2006). Similarly, Klin (2000) has shown that adults with ASD are less likely than a control group to attribute social and personality characteristics to simple geometric shapes that are "acting" out a social scenario.

The most common deficits in children with ASD are those in social areas including joint attention and imitation. The single most reliably measurable deficit in children with ASD is a deficit in joint attention (Baron-Cohen, 1989a, 1989b, 1995; Buitelaar, van Engeland, de Kogel, de Vries, & van Hoof, 1991; Mundy & Sigman, 1989; Mundy, Sigman, Ungerer, & Sherman, 1986), and it is possible to see this difference in the development of a child with ASD as early as 18 months (Baron-Cohen & Cross, 1992) and

autism A developmental disorder that is defined and characterized by a deficit in social cognition, a delay in the development of communication, and an adherence to routine or repetitive behaviours.

maybe even as early as 12 months (Osterling & Dawson, 1994). Children with ASD are impaired both in the production of and in the comprehension of joint-attention gestures such as pointing (Curcio, 1978; Ricks & Wing, 1975) and in their ability to follow an adult's eye gaze (Leekam, Hunnisett, & Moore, 1998).

8.16 Press Pause

Children with autism spectrum disorder (ASD) show deficits in performance on false-belief tasks and other milestones of theory of mind development.

Evidence shows that children with ASD have trouble with false-belief tests such as the Sally–Anne task and the Smarties task described above (Baron-Cohen et al., 1985). A clever test, called the *false-photo test* (Zaitchik, 1990), was devised to test whether those children with ASD who failed the false-belief task were really having trouble understanding mental states specifically or whether they had trouble with the logical structure of the problem. In the false-photo task, the experimenter uses a Polaroid camera to take and quickly develop a picture of a room in some configuration (e.g., with a teddy bear lying on a bed). Then, without showing the child the photograph, the experimenter changes the configuration of the room, say by moving the teddy bear to a chair. Do you see the analogy? The experimenter has created a false photograph that is not visible to the child, just as in the Sally–Anne task where the experimenter created a false belief that was not available to the child for direct inspection. The experimenter can then probe the child's understanding by asking whether the photograph shows the current configuration or the past configuration. Children with ASD have specific difficulty with the false-belief task, but that deficit does not extend to the false-photograph task. Indeed their performance on the false-photograph task tends to exceed that of age-matched controls (Leslie & Thaiss, 1992; Peterson & Siegal, 1998).

FACE PERCEPTION IN AUTISM

Children with ASD have trouble with face recognition (Boucher & Lewis, 1992; Braverman, Fein, Lucci, & Waterhouse, 1989; de Gelder, Vroomen, & van der Heide, 1991; Klin et al., 1999; Tantam, Monaghan, Nicholson, & Stirling, 1989) and the identification of emotional facial expressions (Celani, Battacchi, & Arcidiacono, 1999; Hobson, 1986; Hobson, Ouston, & Lee, 1988; Pelphrey et al., 2002). Differences in face processing appear early in life in those with ASD, as we know from both behavioural and neuroimaging studies (Behrmann, Thomas, & Humphreys, 2006; Dawson, Carver, Meltzoff, Panagiotides, & McPartland, 2002; Dawson, Webb, & McPartland, 2005). Although children with ASD may be able to perceive basic emotions much like other people do (Adolphs, Sears, & Piven, 2001; Baron-Cohen, Wheelwright, & Jolliffe, 1997; Grossman, Klin, Carter, & Volkmar, 2000; Ogai et al., 2003), they may be doing so using atypical strategies (Rutherford & McIntosh, 2007). In addition, there may be ASD-specific impairments in the recognition of some emotional expressions, specifically anger and disgust (Ellis & Leafhead, 1996) and surprise (Baron-Cohen, Spitz, & Cross, 1993), and impairments in the recognition of fear (Howard et al., 2000; Pelphrey et al., 2002). Humphreys and colleagues (2007) found greater impairments in lower-functioning ASD individuals in recognition of fear and (less reliably) disgust, happiness, and, to some extent, anger.

⇒ Developmental Milestones

Social Skills Milestones

Age	Skills
At Birth	Prefers faces to other visual stimuli Prefers voices to other sounds
6 Weeks	Smiles in response to others
3 Months	Prefers to watch two balls chasing each other vs. two balls moving independently (Rochat, Morgan, & Carpenter, 1997)
6 Months	Just as good at discriminating between two people's faces and two monkey's faces (Pascalis et al., 2002)
9 Months	Now specialize in human faces, discriminating between people more easily than monkeys (Pascalis et al., 2002) Joint attention Social referencing
By 12 Months	Knows that people, but not objects, do things (Poulin-Dubois & Shultz, 1988) Responds to own name
18 Months	Perceive goals (Gergely, Nadasdy, Csibra, & Biro, 1995; Meltzoff, 1995) Imitates goal-directed behaviour and play behaviour Pretend play begins and continues for many years
2 Years	Has a sense of ownership and defends own possessions
By 3 Years	Plays alongside other children, in "parallel play"
4 Years	Passes the false-belief task, showing evidence of theory of mind processing Plays interactively with other children Spontaneously shares toys with other children Pretend play grows more elaborate and includes storylines
5 Years	Interacts with whole groups and can participate in group decision-making, rule-making, and enforcement

The results regarding emotion recognition in ASD has tended to follow a pattern. When studies have matched ASD and non-ASD children on non-verbal IQ, ASD children tend to show impairments in recognition of emotions; however, when the groups are matched on verbal IQ, deficits in emotion perception are not found (Braverman, Fein, Lucci, & Waterhouse, 1989; Ozonoff, Pennington, & Rogers, 1991). In addition, complex social emotions that require mentalizing or identifying with the mental state of others, such as arrogance and flirtatiousness, are difficult for those with ASD to recognize (Baron-Cohen et al., 1997).

When most of us look at a face, we look at the eyes first. But an individual with autism does not; the eyes are not attended to preferentially (Baron-Cohen, Wheelwright, & Jolliffe, 1997; Klin, Jones, Schultz, Volkmar, & Cohen, 2002; Pelphrey et al., 2002). The eyes are important for processing information that is available on a person's face and particularly important for understanding complex mental states (Baron-Cohen, Campbell, Karmiloff-Smith, Grant, & Walker, 1995; Baron-Cohen & Cross, 1992). Baron-Cohen and colleagues (1997) wanted to know which areas of the face are important for a person to look at in order to perceive emotions. They showed participants images of just the eyes, just the mouth, and the whole face. Participants were asked to choose which emotion described the face. Simple emotions and complex emotions were presented, and results showed that for complex emotions, seeing just the eyes is as informative as seeing the whole face for the control group (i.e., for people who did not have autism). In contrast, people with ASD were not as able to use information from the eye region to correctly identify the emotion if the emotion was a complex one that required thinking about a person's mental state. This deficit in processing complex emotions may be a key factor in the impaired social interaction and the theory of mind impairment associated with autism.

It is possible that those with ASD develop strategies to compensate for the difficulty in the recognition of emotional expressions—that is, a less intuitive, more time-consuming strategy in which individual features are examined (Bormann-Kischkel, Vilsmeier, & Baude, 1995; Hobson, Ouston, & Lee, 1988; Joseph & Tanaka, 2003; Klin et al., 2002). Rutherford and McIntosh (2007) found that those with ASD are more tolerant of extremely exaggerated basic facial expressions than typical individuals, consistent with the idea that they are using a rule-based strategy for emotion recognition rather than a template-based strategy, which is used by individuals with a history of typical development. When Jim Carrey, renowned facial contortionist, became the stepfather of Jenny McCarthy's son (who has autism), McCarthy reported that her son "came alive."

A SOCIAL ORIENTING VIEW OF AUTISM

One of the most important puzzles surrounding autism is to figure out how social development gets off track, when social development gets off track, and whether there is any intervention or treatment that can correct social cognitive development in autism. Of course, even though the social cognitive deficit in ASD is profound, this deficit is not the only characteristic that defines autism, and a description of the social development of autism is not an explanation of it. Nonetheless, a look at social development in autism may be interesting for its own sake.

Children with autism spectrum disorders do not show the same social developmental trajectory as other children. In their first year of life, they orient to social information less than other children do and, subsequently, do not show the same theory of mind development as other children.

The social orienting view (Dawson, Meltzoff, Osterling, Rinaldi, & Brown, 1998; Mundy & Neal, 2001; Rutherford, 2007) suggests that, in autism, the cause of social cognitive deficits is an early failure to orient normally to social stimuli. Specifically, the theory predicts less attention to the eyes, eye gaze, emotional facial expressions, animate and biological motion, tone of voice, and pointing, all of which result in differences in social development. This view makes a lot of sense when you consider what we have learned in this book: Not only do nature and nurture work together, but nature relies on all developmental resources. In many domains there is evidence that psychological processes are designed to develop in response to and in coordination with environmental inputs. Natural selection stores information in the environment and it is efficient to do so. But if there is a deficit in processes that orient to and gather social information, then the developing social cognitive processes do not get what they need for typical development and thus do not develop typically. Conceptually, this is not unlike what happened to kittens deprived of visual information during development, as we read in Chapter 5.

We study autism for both practical and theoretical reasons. Clearly, research into autism will have clinical applications. Knowing more about the development of autism will help us identify it earlier (Rutherford, 2009) and create effective treatments for children who are developing with it. (Notice how the social orienting theory of autism suggests an obvious intervention?) In addition, research into autism can help test some hypotheses about typical development. Because children with ASD have specific, circumscribed deficits and also preserved areas of cognitive development, one could test whether specific cognitive skills are developmental precursors to later-developing cognitive skills. For example, you could measure whether early signs of joint-attention development predict later pretend play skills, which they do (Rutherford, Young, Hepburn, & Rogers, 2007; Rutherford & Rogers, 2003).

SUMMARY

In this chapter you read about the specialized adaptations designed for social cognition that develop in infants and children. First, you read that social cognition is one of the core domains of development. Humans have, apparently, evolved sophisticated social cognitive skills as a result of the intense social demands that our ancestors faced in the EEA. Social interactions, intimate long-term relationships, competition, and negotiations led to the evolution of a new kind of intelligence. Humans are an obligate social species: In the EEA, an individual could not have survived alone, and the legacy of this history is a mandatory social cognition. Psychologically, we need others and will create companions via hallucination if necessary.

You also read that early in development infants and children develop improbably sophisticated social cognitive skills. In the first year, infants look at faces and eyes and use adults' eye directions to direct their own attention. By late in the first year, young children can appreciate and use other people's mental states, as evidenced by imitation, joint attention, social referencing, and pretend play. And evidence suggests that the perceptual processing of faces is unlike any other kind of visual processing. Instinct blindness makes these infantile skills seem easy, but they are computationally sophisticated nonetheless.

Next, you read about infants' abilities to perceive animacy and intentions. Based on nothing but motion cues, infants are able to attribute animacy to simple objects and even to see them as helpful or harmful. Infants know when a person is behaving in a goal-directed manner. These skills are precursors to a child's maturing theory of mind: the ability to use another person's mental states to explain and predict other people's behaviours.

Finally you read about children developing with autism and the profoundly different way that social cognition develops in these children. Deficits in the development of theory of mind is characteristic of autism, and children with autism show deficits in joint attention, social referencing, pretend play, and the perception of intentionality. The fact that these skills are all delayed or absent in these children is consistent with the idea that these are all components of a developing theory of mind.

PRESS PAUSE SUMMARY

- In the EEA, living in a community was not just fun; it was a matter of life or death. Our cognitive adaptations reflect this imperative from our past.

- Studies with young rhesus monkeys show that, for that species, social contact is imperative. Social isolation can result in maldevelopment and even death.

- According to the social brain hypothesis, the large brains in humans support the complex social cognitive processing required in large complex groups.

- The best explanation for humans' long juvenile period is our species' disproportionate need (given our group size) to acquire social expertise.

- Preoperational children are egocentric; they cannot see beyond their own point of view, according to Piaget.

- Contrary to Piaget's early claims, young children are not completely egocentric: They have some understanding that others may be prevented from seeing what they can see themselves.

- Imitation is an early developing social cognitive skill.

- Imitation, joint attention, and social referencing are early social cognitive skills in humans; imitation and social referencing appear to have evolved in other species as well.

- Engaging in pretend play and understanding others' pretend play requires an understanding of others' mental states.

- Faces are special visual objects, as evidenced by the inversion effect and holistic processing.

- Babies orient to faces at birth and at 2 months, but not at 1 month. This U-shaped curve may require two different psychological processes to explain it.

- One-year-olds have different expectations of the behaviour of animate vs. inanimate objects.

- Infants as young as 3 months can distinguish animate from inanimate objects based on the object's movements.

- Infants in their first year of life can infer someone's intentions just by watching their actions.

- Classic theory of mind measures suggested theory of mind development around 4 years of age, but contemporary theory of mind tasks suggest some development as early as 13 months.

- Children with autism spectrum disorders (ASDs) show deficits in performance on false-belief tasks and other milestones of theory of mind development.

KEY TERMS AND CONCEPTS

autism, 287

ecological pressures, 260

egocentrism, 265

fusiform face area, 274

holistic processing, 274

inversion effect, 274

joint attention, 270

obligate social species, 256

perceptual narrowing, 278

pretend play, 272

sensorimotor play, 271

social brain hypothesis, 260

social referencing, 270

theory of mind, 259

U-shaped curve, 276

QUESTIONS FOR THOUGHT AND DISCUSSION

1. What does it mean to be an obligate social species? What circumstances in the EEA led to strong pressures favouring social cognition? What experimental evidence suggests that social contact is crucial, possibly even mandatory?

2. What is the social brain hypothesis? What evidence supports this idea?

3. What evidence suggests that face processing is special? What evidence suggests that face perception is important very early in life? Is face perception different for those with autism? Explain.

4. What is theory of mind? How is its development measured? What social cognitive skills may be precursors to theory of mind? What evidence is there suggesting that people with autism may have theory of mind difficulties?

From the Classroom to the Lab: Follow Up

Consider the experiment you designed in response to the "From the Classroom to the Lab" challenge earlier in this chapter.

What kind of design does your experiment have (e.g., experimental, correlational)?

Would your experimental method meet the ethical standards expected by the field?

What variables would you measure?

What are your dependent variables?

What are your independent variables?

Imagine you have run your experiment. How would you interpret your results? How would you know if there is a reliable relationship between social isolation and other psychological measures?

chapter 9

Language Development

Opening Vignette: The Sparrow, the Vervet Monkey, and the Chimpanzee

The white-crowned sparrow has regional dialects that are passed from generation to generation. The young male has to learn his region's dialect from older males during a critical learning period, even though that learning period comes months before his ability to produce songs (Marler & Tamura, 1964). Peter Marler, who made these discoveries in the late 1960s and early 1970s, described the young bird as having an "instinct to learn." At the time, the idea was preposterous since instinct and learning were regarded as mutually exclusive processes.

The vervet monkey utters sounds that symbolize specific referents. For example, the vervet has three acoustically distinct alarm calls that it emits: one when it sees a snake, a different one when it sees a leopard, and a third when it sees an eagle. Each strategy could be life-saving or deadly, depending on whether a snake or an eagle has been spotted (Cheney & Seyfarth, 1990). As impressive as this small, yet functional, vocabulary is, vervets never combine these calls to generate new ideas.

In the 1930s, a psychologist couple who wanted to see if chimpanzees could acquire human language adopted a chimpanzee named Viki. Unlike the human children in the family, Viki got intense language training, including having her lips and tongue manually moulded into place by her adoptive parent. With thousands of hours of practice, Viki learned to speak three words, which (if you were very generous) could be heard as "papa," "mama," and "cup" although she got the three words mixed up when she was excited (Tartter, 1986).

Chapter Outline

- After reading this chapter, you should be able to describe the arguments in favour of the idea that humans have a uniquely human psychology, which includes powerful and specially designed learning processes that support language. You should understand the alternative explanations for language (associationist learning in the Skinnerian tradition) and their limitations.

- You should have an understanding of the areas of the brain that support language production and understanding for most people. You should have an idea of what results when one of the areas associated with language is damaged.

- Once you have read this chapter, you will know what steps children take on their way to adult language use.

You should know what perceptual skills young infants have to prepare them for language learning, and you should also know what special rules young children use in language learning that allow them to achieve what would otherwise be an impossible task.

- Toward the end of the chapter you will read about rare instances in history when children are raised together without an adult language model. In these cases, the children invented a fully grammatical human language. Finally you will read something about attempts to teach language to non-humans. You will learn what methods people have used, the success they have had, and you will understand the limits of their success.

Language Is Part of Our Psychology

The ability to speak and understand a spoken language is part of human nature. Everyone, save the severely disabled, learns language regardless of IQ or any other measure of general intelligence. Every known culture and every known group of humans has a spoken language. If young children are raised without a native language but raised in community with other children, they will invent a native language, and the language they invent will be every bit as complex and human as any other human language. Furthermore, the language of a modern or industrialized culture is in no way more complex or sophisticated than the language of a pre-industrialized or technologically sparse culture. Unlike agriculture, fire, and written language, spoken language is not an innovation. We know (more or less) when and where agriculture was invented and how it spread through human civilizations. Not so with language: Not only does every human culture have language, but as far as we know, every human culture has always had language. It is part of human psychology, just as bat echolocation is part of bat psychology and colour vision is part of chimpanzee psychology.

9.1 Press Pause

Language is part of our human psychology, just as bat echolocation is part of bat psychology.

Language is part of the environment that a developing child has access to. It is, therefore, a developmental resource in the perspective of developmental systems theorists. It would have been available to the developing child in the EEA as well. The mind of the developing child is designed to interface with existing adult language in order to learn language with surprisingly little guidance. The child has specialized psychological mechanisms designed to orient to, perceive, and analyze human speech as well as language acquisition mechanisms designed to learn language.

Language as a Case Study in Evolutionary Psychology

Language development is clearly a significant part of child development. As you will see, it is also a good case study to illustrate some of the broader points we have made about development throughout this book. A detailed look at language development makes it clear that the nature vs. nurture question is misleading. Instead, language development illustrates what has been called the *instinct to learn* (Marler & Tamura,

Every known culture and every known group of humans has a spoken language.

The saddle quern, shown here, was an ancient agricultural tool. Unlike agriculture, fire, and the wheel, spoken language is not an innovation. Language was not invented and then spread through human civilizations. Every human culture has language.

1964) or the *language instinct* (Pinker, 1994). Considering language development reveals that asking whether something is learned or evolved is nonsensical: Language is clearly learned, and it is clearly learned using an intricate, complexly designed, evolved learning mechanism. Examining language acquisition in detail illustrates that the interesting and relevant question is never about nature or nurture (both are essential) but rather "What is this mechanism designed to do?"

In addition, a consideration of language acquisition shows why the question of domain-specific learning devices vs. domain-general learning is important. Animals that are operating without a well-designed *language acquisition device*, though they have functioning classical and operant conditioning processes as described by associationist psychologists, never learn language. The fact that human children acquire language so reliably underlines that operant conditioning and classical con-

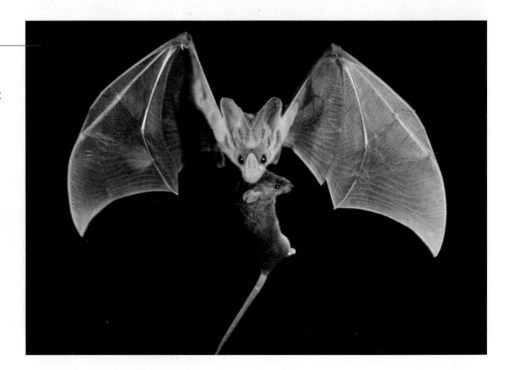

Language is part of our human psychology, just as bat echolocation is part of bat psychology.

ditioning cannot explain all learning in humans since rats, cats, and dogs clearly have operant and classical conditioning but not language acquisition, even though domestic animals that live in human homes are exposed to as much human language as a developing baby.

9.2   Press Pause

The study of language development makes it clear that nature is not opposed to nurture. Rather, the developing child interacts with the environment by design.

Is language the result of experience? Clearly, since Japanese babies grow up to speak Japanese and Portuguese babies grow up to speak Portuguese, experience plays a big part in the spoken language of adults. But only the developing human mind is able to respond to the environmental inputs by learning language. There is a rich, evolved, and prepared set of psychological mechanisms that are designed for language learning. Your dog, your hamster, or indeed your bowl of oatmeal will not learn language no matter how frequently and persistently each is exposed to it. Even a chimpanzee raised in a human household and exposed to language just as frequently as a baby will never acquire human language (Hayes, 1951). Human infants, even those with extremely low IQ, will learn their native language through mere auditory exposure: No explicit tutoring is required. Clearly there is something special about the developing human mind that is designed for language acquisition.

Noam Chomsky and the Language Acquisition Device

Noam Chomsky is a linguist and cognitive scientist who is known as the Father of Modern Linguistics (though you may know him as an anarchist and political dissident). Chomsky's contribution redirected the field of linguistics and language acquisition because before his work the field was dominated by the associationist belief that children learned language via available general-purpose learning mechanisms: classical and operant conditioning and imitation. The behaviourist B. F. Skinner was an extremely influential psychologist at one time and argued in his book *Verbal Behavior* (Skinner, 1957) that language, like all other behaviours, was acquired via simple operant principles.

Chomsky was the first to argue that these general-purpose learning principles were inadequate for the acquisition of language. Primarily, his argument rested on the fact that human language relies on using very complex, abstract rules governing word formation and sentence formation and that children learn language at an astonishingly fast pace during a period of time when their other cognitive capacities are still quite immature (Chomsky, 1957, 1959, 1965). Most of us are unaware of the rules that we use to form spoken language, another example of instinct blindness, and adults certainly do not teach children these rules.

Noam Chomsky introduced the idea that developing children had powerful learning mechanisms designed to acquire language. He showed that general-purpose learning mechanisms were not powerful enough to explain children's rapid language learning.

language acquisition device The learning mechanisms that young children have that allow them to analyze the language they hear, imperfect as it is, and to acquire and produce their own native language.

deep structure Chomsky's term for the wordless structure that is common to utterances with the same meaning that must be mapped onto the actual surface structure in order for children to understand and learn language.

universal grammar The set of principles and adjustable parameters that are common to all known and presumably undiscovered human languages.

Chomsky proposed that developing children have a **language acquisition device,** the learning mechanisms that allow them to analyze the language they hear, imperfect as it is, and to acquire and produce their own native language. Imitation did not work as a proposed method of child language learning for two reasons. First, the adult language that is modelled for children is very imperfect, full of stammering, hesitating, incomplete sentences, and various errors. Second, children produce novel sentences that they have never heard before, a phenomenon that cannot be explained by simple mimicking.

Chomsky noticed that there was **deep structure** in human language that was common to, for example, the sentences "The dog chased the cat" and "The cat was chased by the dog," as well as to any sentence in other languages expressing the same idea. Children have to learn the rules that connect the deep structure to the surface structure. That is, they have to decipher what people actually mean based on the surface structure.

Universal grammar is the term that Chomsky uses to describe the underlying plan for all human languages that babies have even prior to learning a language and that allows them to learn language. The **universal grammar** is the set of principles and adjustable parameters that are common to all known and presumably undiscovered human languages. Language has an underlying plan and that plan is part of our human psychology. This structure is how infants get language learning started: According to Chomsky it allows young children, after mere exposure, to acquire the language of their language community.

One recent experiment, which focussed on the "home signs" generated by deaf children, has uncovered what might be evidence of this universal grammar in development. Home signs are a system of communication that is developed by deaf children of hearing parents in cases where the children are not regularly exposed to adult sign language. Despite these home signs being specific to an individual, rather than shared by a group, the signs are distinct from the manual gestures that hearing children and adults use to accompany spoken language (Frishberg, 1987).

Susan Goldin-Meadow (2003) studied and compared the home signs of Chinese and American deaf children of hearing parents. These children were not being taught sign language and did not have access to their parents' spoken languages, and so they generated their own idiosyncratic home signs. In spite of the different grammatical structure of their parents' spoken languages (Mandarin and English), the home signs generated by these children had remarkable similarities. They included subjects, actions, and objects and tended to keep them in that order, regardless of the order their parents used (Goldin-Meadow, 2003).

9.3 Press Pause

There is a regularity or universal grammar common to all human languages.

The Brain Basis of Human Language

We know that the functions of language are largely controlled by specific and identifiable brain areas. This means that generally, and on average, we know where in the brain language-related operations take place. Note, however, that there will be individual differences. Some differences arise spontaneously with language processing as with species-typical organs. For example, you might know where in the human body the spleen is located, but for no particular reason, its location in one person may differ

| figure | 9.1 | **Language centres of the brain** |

The left hemisphere is, for most people, where language is processed. Broca's area is near the motor cortex, and Wernicke's area is near the auditory cortex.

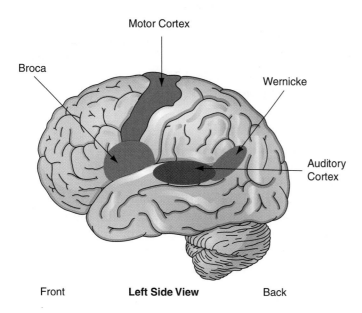

from its location in another person by only a few millimetres. Also, if someone suffers from an injury early in life to the brain area that controls speech, there is enough neural plasticity that the person may develop normal language and that language may be mediated by an entirely different brain area.

That said, there are, for most people, two areas that are known to be important for language functions. For 90 per cent of people who are right-handed, language processing occurs primarily in the left hemisphere. This was first described in 1961 by Paul Broca, who, after observing various patients with various injuries, noticed that damage to the left hemisphere was much more likely than right-hemisphere damage to result in language malfunction. Since then, EEG studies have shown that children, adults, and even young infants listening to language show more activity on the left side of the brain (Molfese & Betz, 1988; Molfese, Freeman, & Palermo, 1975). This specialization, that is, the difference in participation between the right and left hemispheres in language processing, increases with age (Witelson, 1987).

Within the left hemisphere, just at the lower edge of the motor cortex, there is an area known as *Broca's area*. People who suffer from damage to Broca's area will show **Broca's aphasia**, a condition that results in "telegraphic" speech—or single-word, halting, laboriously produced word strings—lacking in grammatical organization (Goodglass, 1979). Their speech is almost exclusively content words and lacks grammatical morphemes entirely. In response to a question about what they did today, a person with Broca's aphasia might say "buy bread store." People with Broca's aphasia show good, almost unaltered, language comprehension, unless the sentence is grammatically complex.

Another area in the left hemisphere, seen in Figure 9.1, is called *Wernicke's area*. It may be relevant that Wernicke's area is located very near the auditory cortex,

Broca's aphasia
A condition resulting from damage to Broca's area that involves single-word speech, or short word strings, lacking in grammatical organization.

and people who have damage to this area have an inability to understand other people's speech. These people have **Wernicke's aphasia**, a condition that results in very fluent speech that includes grammatical morphemes, seemingly used correctly, although the speech is nonsensical. A person with Wernicke's aphasia may say something like "Nothing the keeserez the, these are davereez, and these and this one and these are living. This one's right in and these are . . . uh . . . and that's nothing, that's nothing . . ." (Schwartz, 1987), which is fluent, so it sounds like it should mean something, but it does not. When speaking, the Wernicke's aphasic has trouble producing labels for people, objects, and actions and so speaks using pronouns and nonsense words instead.

Infant Speech Perception

Human babies learn human languages while cats, dogs, and the most sophisticated computer programs designed for language acquisition do not. Why? A human infant is able to analyze or parse a human speech stream. Babies can perceive speech sounds, can perceptually isolate words, and can discern the rules that tell them what order words (nouns, verbs, subjects, objects) in their native language should come in. The human baby has "programmes," if you will, that are designed by natural selection to decode the speech stream. The human brain is unique in this ability to perceive and acquire human language.

There is ample evidence that infants come into the world prepared to perceive speech sounds. Newborns are most sensitive to (i.e., best able to hear) sounds that fall within the frequency range of the human speaking voice. Newborn infants can hear a variety of sounds but prefer to listen to human speech over pure tones (Bench, Collyer, Mentz, & Wilson, 1976).

Different languages use different subsets of speech sounds, taken from the available human speech sounds. You might wonder, as researchers have, whether a developing child must be exposed to a particular language (e.g., English or Hindi) in order to learn to discriminate between two different speech sounds used in one's own language. The alternative is that infants are already prepared to discriminate between human speech sounds prior to any language experience and that this ability declines with age as a function of exposure to their own native language.

Very young infants can make distinctions between different human speech sounds. In an auditory adaptation of the habituation paradigm, researchers gave infants a pacifier fitted with an electrode so that the researcher could record the frequency of the infant's sucking. The researcher would present the infant with a given speech sound, say "ba," and the baby would suck vigorously. As the researcher continued to present this sound, the baby habituated to it and sucking slowed down. Now the researcher could present a new sound and, in essence, "ask" the baby if he was hearing the same old sound or a new sound. If the researcher played a / ga/ sound, the sucking picked right back up; the baby dishabituated, showing that he had perceived a different speech sound (Jusczyk, 1995). What we know from research using this method is that young infants discriminate between a huge number of speech sounds and that they do so from all known (and tested) languages. They can discriminate between sounds that adults in their language community cannot. In other words, it appears that human infants are prepared to hear speech in any human language community.

In the conditioned head-turn procedure, if the infant turns his head toward the loudspeaker when he hears a speech sound change, then he is rewarded by a toy that illuminates and begins to move. Once trained in this procedure, researchers can "ask" infants whether they can discriminate between any pair of sounds.

One pair of researchers set out to test when this ability to discriminate between non-native-language speech sounds declines, and they did this by using a visually reinforced infant speech discrimination paradigm known as the *conditioned head-turn procedure* (CHT). In this paradigm, infants are trained to indicate when they hear different speech sounds by rewarding their behaviour following the principles of operant conditioning. A continuous stream of speech sounds emanates from a loudspeaker. If the infant turns his head away from the experimenter and toward the loudspeaker when he hears the speech sound change, then he is rewarded with an electrically activated toy that illuminates and begins to move, the toy having been previously invisible in a cabinet behind a smoked-Plexiglas screen. If the infant turns his head when there is no change in the speech sound, nothing happens; there is no reward. When the infant indicates that he has been trained in this paradigm, by making three successful head-turns in a row in response to a change in speech sound, then he is ready to go on to the test phase of the experiment. Once trained in this procedure, researchers can "ask" infants whether they can discriminate between any pair of sounds.

INNOVATIVE RESEARCH METHOD

In this particular experiment, three groups were compared: English-speaking adults, infants who were acquiring English as a native language, and adults whose native language was Salish, a language from coastal British Columbia. Adults indicated that they had perceived a difference in speech sound by pressing a key rather than turning their heads. Participants were tested to see if they could discriminate between a pair of speech sounds taken from the Salish language.

The results indicated, not surprisingly, that all native adult speakers of the Salish language could discriminate between Salish speech sounds. Only 30 per cent of English-speaking adults could hear the difference. Critically, 80 per cent of the 7-month-old infants could discriminate between the two speech sounds despite having no experience listening to the Salish language (Werker & Tees, 1984).

A second experiment tested children ranging in ages from 8 months to 4 years in order to test when the decline in the ability to discriminate happened. Researchers determined that the decline happened during the first year of life. They compared three groups of infants, defined by age. The first group was aged 6 to 8 months, the second aged 8 to 10 months, and the third 10 to 12 months. There was no statistically significant difference in performance between the first two groups, but the third group performed significantly worse on the speech sound discrimination task (Werker & Tees, 1984).

9.4 Press Pause

Young infants can discriminate between speech sounds in any human language. Older infants and adults can only discriminate between speech sounds in their own language.

Does this ability decline gradually or suddenly? In order to tell, the researchers looked at the performance of just those infants that were, eventually, able to make the discrimination to see if they needed more trials in order to hear the difference. Their thinking was that if the ability disappeared gradually with age, infants who succeeded may need more trials to succeed as they got older. This is not the pattern they saw: Among the infants who successfully made the discrimination, age did not affect the number of trials to criterion. These results were consistent with the idea that the ability to discriminate between non-native speech sounds disappears quickly, not gradually, with experience (Werker & Tees, 1984).

INNOVATIVE RESEARCH METHOD

In addition to the above, other careful experimental work reveals infants' perceptual categorization of human speech sounds. One experiment used the habituation paradigm adapted for use with auditory stimuli. A baby heard one sound over and over while sucking on a pacifier. The pacifier was rigged so that the experimenter could tell how much the baby was sucking; when the baby sucked, the stimulus was presented (Eimas, Siqueland, Jusczyk, & Vigorito, 1971). The baby sucked on the pacifier while the first sound was presented over and over. When the baby was bored with the first sound, sucking diminished, and the speech sound was switched. If the baby could not tell the difference between the two sounds, he would continue to be bored. If he started sucking faster after the sounds changed, this was evidence that he could distinguish the two sounds. He had taken an interest again.

categorical perception
The perception of stimuli that differs continuously as being categorically or qualitatively different.

voice onset time
The time that passes between when a stop-consonant is released and when the vocal folds begin to vibrate and thus voicing begins.

Using this technique, Eimas and colleagues (1971) discovered that 1-month-old infants can tell the difference between "ba ba ba ba" and "pa pa pa pa." But here is an even more intriguing finding: Infants show **categorical perception**. The speech sounds /ba/ and /pa/ are produced nearly identically, the only difference being the amount of time between when air is passed through the lips (or as linguists would say, when the stop-consonant is released) and when the vocal cords start vibrating (what linguists call *voicing*). The technical term for this interval is the **voice onset time** or VOT. When you say "ba," the VOT is about 15 ms, which is perceived as being essentially simultaneous. When you say "pa," the VOT is about 100 ms. Try it. What is interesting experimentally is that this difference is just quantitative, and using a voice synthesizer, you could create a continuum of artificial speech sounds all the way from a good /ba/ to a good /pa/ and see what people think they sound like.

figure 9.2   Categorical perception of speech by adults

Adults perceive speech sounds categorically. As the physical characteristics of the speech sounds change gradually, the perception changes suddenly from one category (/ba/) to another (/pa/).

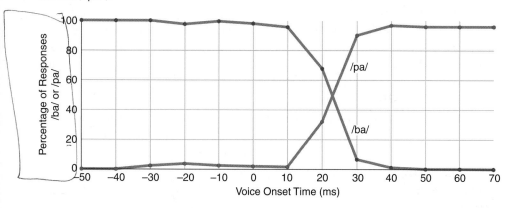

figure 9.3   Categorical perception of speech sounds by infants

In a habituation paradigm, 1-month-old infants were presented with pairs of speech sounds that were equal in their physical dissimilarity. Infants did not dishabituate if the two speech sounds fell within an adult category (/ba/ or /pa/) but did if the pair spanned the category boundary.

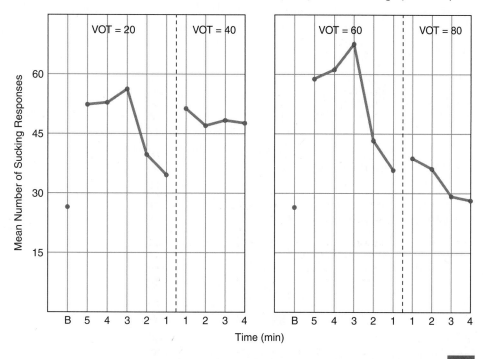

Adults perceive these speech sounds categorically: That is, the sounds with a VOT of less than about 25 ms are heard unambiguously as "ba," and those sounds with a VOT of more than 25 ms are heard unambiguously as "pa." If perception were not categorical, then there would be sounds in between 15 ms and 100 ms (the usual /ba/ and /pa/ VOTs) that adults thought sounded kind of like "ba" and kind of like "pa," or as a mixture. But people do not perceive this mixture as they are presented with the gradually changing continuum, and this is what we mean by categorical perception.

In the Eimas et al. study, 1- to 4-month-old babies were habituated to a /ba/ or /pa/ sound (we know this because their sucking declined and the sucking was causing the consonant sound to play). Next, one group of infants heard a /ba/ sound and one group of infants heard a /pa/ sound, but both groups heard sounds that were equally physically dissimilar to the one they had habituated to. Because each group heard a new sound that was different from the sound they had habituated to, and equally physically different, each group should have dishabituated equally if speech perception was not associated with these sounds. Instead, the group that heard a sound from a different speech category (using the adult categories as a guide) dishabituated more than the infants whose new sound was within the same category they had habituated to.

All the /ba/ sounds were categorized by the babies as one type of sound, and all the /pa/ sounds were another. These 1-month-old babies were unresponsive to physical changes within the /ba/ category or within the /pa/ category but started sucking faster when physically different sounds that crossed the category boundary were presented (Eimas et al., 1971).

9.5 Press Pause

One-month-old infants perceive speech sounds categorically, just as adults do.

By the way, this is another example of our instinct blindness. As human experimenters, we are not capable of comparing the physical difference of two /ba/ sounds with the physical difference between a /ba/ and a /pa/ sound. We need to use specialized sound equipment to tell us what these differences are because our perception of the auditory stream is automatically run through our language processing device, which collapses these sounds into their respective categories.

Researchers do not believe that the ability of these 1-month-olds to distinguish speech sounds is learned via exposure to their native language. Indeed, it is thought that infants can hear more (not fewer) speech sounds than their native language will require (as described in the preceding CHT experiments). Infants have the ability to distinguish speech sounds in any known human language, even if they will not need that sound to speak or understand their own language. Speech sounds that are distinct in some languages may be collapsed in others. An example that will be familiar to English-speaking people and to Japanese-speaking people who have tried to learn English is the clear distinction that English speakers make between "r" and "l." These sounds are collapsed in Japanese. At 1 month old, an infant can make this distinction, as well as distinctions that are not made in English. The infant could not have learned these distinctions because he is making distinctions that he does not hear in his own language environment. These are distinctions that English-speaking adults cannot hear, even with a fair bit of training. The infant loses the ability to make distinctions outside of his native language after the age of 6 months, as discussed above. By 10 months, he distinguishes only the phonemes that are distinguished in his native language. Now if he tries to learn a foreign language in university, his pronunciation may be imperfect. Notice this development is not likely to be dependent upon an understanding of word meanings since babies at 10 months old are just beginning to comprehend. Indeed, it is unlikely that this distinction is dependent upon the parsing of words at all.

Interestingly, it is not that the younger infant has no knowledge of his native language. Even a 4-day-old baby, given an opportunity to suck on a pacifier rigged with a sensor that plays an audiotape when sucked, will suck faster when hearing his mother's language than when hearing a foreign language (Mehler et al., 1988). Further, the babies still prefer their native language if the sounds are filtered such that clear speech sounds are not distinguishable and only the inflection or melody is audible. The baby does not prefer his native language if the sounds are played backwards, and he does not demonstrate a preference between two different foreign languages.

Proto-Babbling and Babbling

Well before babies say their first words, they are preparing for language. As mentioned earlier, they pay close attention to adult voices and the language that adults are producing. At around 2 months, babies begin to make "cooing" noises that sound like vowels. At around the age of 4 or 5 months, babies start to "babble," adding consonant sounds to their cooing as they explore the sounds they can make. That is to say, they do not just use the sounds to communicate needs and discomfort; they produce sounds just to see what the sounds sound like. Indeed, they produce sounds that are more and more like adult speech sounds. Babies, including deaf babies, in various language communities begin to babble at about the same time and produce a similar set of speech sounds during babbling (Stoel-Gammon & Otomo, 1986).

Then, around 7 or 8 months, they begin to babble in earnest. They begin producing real adult speech sounds and repeating the same consonant for a short sequence. At first, they produce sounds that are common across all or many languages, such as "ba ba ba ba," rather than producing sounds that are derived from their own native language. At this point, hearing is a necessary part of the language development process. The production of speech-like sounds is delayed in hearing-impaired babies and absent in deaf babies (Eilers & Oller, 1994). By the end of their first year, babies are producing series of sounds that combine syllables rather than series that repeat just one syllable (Petitto & Marentette, 1991). Indeed, they are, by that age, producing the consonant–

  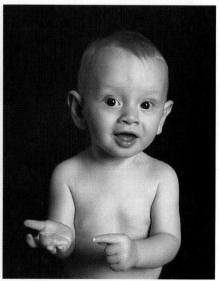

Infants whose parents are deaf and cannot speak to their babies in auditory language will still babble, but they do so with their hands, producing the identical linguistic structures observed in spoken language babbling. In each case, babbling involves repeated, rhythmic strings of syllables.

From the Classroom to the Lab

Babies that are hearing impaired develop speech-like babbling late, and babies that are deaf do not develop speech-like babbling at all (just the manual babbling described above). From this we can conclude that hearing is an important part of early language development. But, does the baby need to hear adult language or does the baby need to hear his or her own babbling in order to progress in the development of speech-like babbling? How would you design an experiment to sort out these possibilities?

vowel patterns and the intonation patterns of their own language (Levitt & Utmann, 1992). Infants whose parents are deaf and cannot speak to their babies in auditory language will still babble, but they do so with their hands, producing the identical linguistic structures observed in spoken language babbling. In each case, babbling involves repeated, rhythmic strings of syllables (Petitto, Holowka, Sergio, & Ostry, 2001).

If you point toward this animal and say "bunny," how is a child to know if the word *bunny* means the animal, the colour brown, fur, furriness, that particular bunny, all bunnies, mammals, animals, or any part of the bunny: ears, tail, feet, eyes, face? A child must come to word learning with assumptions and rules.

Word Learning

And then come words. Most babies' first real words come right around or slightly before their first birthday, the first word being spoken anywhere from about 8 months to about 18 months. (That means that a 16-month-old who still has not spoken his first word may still be within the normal developmental time course.) Sometime between 18 months and 2 years of age, toddlers will start to combine words, so they now have two-word phrases available (Bloom, 1998). By the age of 6, an average child has a vocabulary of about 10,000 words, which they put together in elaborate, mostly grammatical, sentences.

Consider the difficulty of word learning. Children are confronted with what philosopher Willard Quine (1960) called the *problem of reference*. If you get the attention of a young child and point to a furry brown rabbit and say "bunny," what will the child learn? Instinct blindness makes it difficult to see the problem: The child will learn that the cute little creature is called a *bunny*. Leaving aside the perceptual and categorical issues that we discussed in Chapters 5 and 6 (the child has to visually distinguish the creature from the background, see that it is an independent object, somehow categorize it with other bunnies seen in the past and future, etc.), how does the child know what you are referring to? Quine pointed out that there are literally an infinite number of possible "referents." You could, logically, be referring to the colour brown, fur, furriness, that particular bunny, all bunnies collectively, mammals, animals, objects, things that are smaller than a bread box, things that have mass, etc. You could be referring to any part of the bunny: ears, tail, feet, eyes, face. You could even be referring to all the parts of the bunny together. Why not?

Quine was a philosopher, so he got even crazier with his suggestions: There is no logical reason that you could not be referring to a conjunctive category like bunnies *or* lions or even bunnies *or* the month of December. These suggestions certainly sound weird, and likely it did not occur to you that the baby might think that the word *bunny* referred to any of these things, but that is because you are human and have many of the same word-learning assumptions that the baby does, another instance of instinct blindness. The point is that even word learning strongly demonstrates that babies come into the world prepared, prepared with some very powerful, well-designed machinery and a number of rules for acquiring words.

9.6 Press Pause ─────────────────────────────

> Word learning (another case of instinct blindness) is much more difficult than you might think.

THE TWO-WORD PHRASE

Around the time that children have a vocabulary of 200 words, somewhere around their second birthday, give or take, they begin to put two words together. They say things like "daddy go" or "more juice" or "doggy kiss." (This type of speech is called *telegraphic speech* because it sounds like the kind of language people used to use when sending a telegram: Small and expendable words were left out because the cost of using them was too high.) Although the child at this point is not using adult grammar, he or she uses an idiosyncratic, systematic set of rules and formulas. Children might consistently generate phrases like "want *something*" or "more *something*" for example.

TOOLS AND RULES OF WORD LEARNING

Children learn a half a dozen or so words a day between the ages of 2 and 6. During this period children are able to connect a word with the concept that it represents after very few (and sometimes only one) encounters with the word. Developmental psychologists call this phenomenon *fast mapping*. How do kids do it?

Around the age of 18 months, children learn words at an astonishing rate (Bloom, Lifter, & Broughton, 1985; Corrigan, 1983; Dromi, 1987; Goldfield & Reznick, 1990; Halliday, 1975; McShane, 1979; Nelson, 1973). Indeed, children at this age learn several new words every day and need to keep up this pace in order to eventually acquire an adult-sized vocabulary. Psychologists who study language acquisition in children have argued that this fast pace of word learning must be accomplished by a constrained (i.e., specific) kind of learning and not by a more general associationist learning device (see, e.g., Markman, 1991).

Children who are acquiring word meanings follow "rules." That is to say, they will consider some hypotheses about a word's meaning preferentially before considering other possible meanings. According to Ellen Markman, children use many rules, three of which include (a) the whole-object assumption, (b) the taxonomic assumption, and (c) the mutual exclusivity assumption.

The **whole-object assumption** is the assumption that young children make that a novel word they hear refers to a whole object and just the whole object. In the example

whole-object assumption
The assumption that children make that novel words will refer to whole objects to narrow the set of possible meanings that might be associated with a novel word.

| figure 9.4 | **The taxonomic assumption** |

If asked to sort these items freely, children will likely put the bone with the dog. However, if the dog is referred to as a *dax* and the child is asked to identify another "dax," they will very likely pick the cat and not the bone.

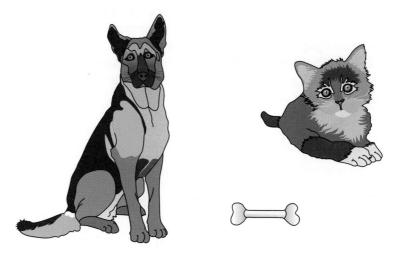

above, the adult pointing to the bunny and saying "bunny" could have been referring to any part, feature, or aspect of that bunny or to a larger category of which the bunny is a member. But the baby does not wait until she collects enough information to exclude these other hypotheses; she simply makes the assumption that you are talking about the bunny as a whole (Macnamara, 1982; Markman, 1990; Soja, Carey, & Spelke, 1992).

The **taxonomic assumption** tells children how to generalize their new word. What else is a bunny? Children will use the word to describe other "like kinds." Again, this may seem so obvious that you would not think it would need a name. The reason it is remarkable is that people who study categorization in children have documented and described the way that children group objects together. When asked to put things together, they use thematic relationships, not taxonomic relationships, to group objects. They will pair a cat with a dog, or a dog with a bone, or a bird with a nest. They group people with the objects they use (e.g., momma with a book). Children explicitly and implicitly find a variety of thematic relationships interesting and compelling (Gelman & Baillargeon, 1983; Markman, 1989; Markman & Callanan, 1983). However, they do not ever make the mistake of using the new word to describe another object with a thematic relationship. Instead, they apply the word to other objects within the taxonomic category "like kinds."

Here is an experiment that illustrates this rule. Children were presented with two objects (say a cat and a dog) and then a third object that was thematically related to one of the two objects (say a bone). If no new label was introduced, the child usually picked the two thematically related objects to go together: the dog and the bone. During trials, the child was given a new word to describe one of the original objects. For example, if the dog was referred to as a *dax* and the child was told to find another "dax," they were very likely to pick the cat and very unlikely to pick the bone. The bone is not the same kind of thing. That is, it is not an object in the same taxonomic category, although it has a thematic relationship (Markman & Hutchinson, 1984). Believing they were learning

taxonomic assumption
The assumption that children make that novel words will refer to objects that are grouped conceptually or categorically rather than thematically.

a new label made all the difference in what they picked to go with the dog, changing their selection from thematic to taxonomic.

The third assumption, also following the work of Ellen Markman, is the **mutual exclusivity assumption**. Following this assumption, the child rejects the notion that a novel word is a synonym of a word that they already know. If an adult gets the attention of a child who knows the word *cup*, points to a cup and says the unfamiliar word "handle," the child rejects the hypothesis that this new word refers to the whole cup. He already has a word for cup. The mutual exclusivity assumption allows him to override the whole-object assumption and learn the referent of the word *handle*. Constraints on hypotheses are necessary if a child is to solve the inductive problem of word learning. The same would be true if you were trying to program a computer to learn the meanings of words based solely on the kind of input a child is exposed to.

> **mutual exclusivity assumption** The assumption that children make that novel words applied to a known object will refer to a novel property rather than to the whole object or a known property. A novel word does not duplicate a known word but means something else.

9.7 Press Pause

A set of word-learning rules allows children to learn the meanings of words, something that would otherwise be impossible.

Other, higher-level "pragmatic cues" are known to be available to young children for the purpose of word learning. Children can perceive adults' focus of attention and use it in word acquisition. Psychologist Dare Baldwin showed 18-month-olds two novel objects, the labels for which were unknown to the child. She then put the objects into separate opaque containers and then peered into one and said "there's a modi in here." When she later asked the child to give her the modi, the child was more likely to hand her the object she had been peering at when she used the label *modi* (Baldwin, 1993).

Children use an adult's focus of attention as a cue to word learning. If an adult shows an 18-month-old two novel objects, puts the objects into separate containers and then peers into one container saying "there's a modi in here," the child will infer that *modi* is an object label for the object the adult was looking at.

Children can and do use adults' emotional reactions in word learning as well. An experimenter told an 18-month-old that she wanted to find a "gazer." She then looked into one container and expressed disappointment and then looked into another container and expressed joy. The child applied the label *gazer* to the second object (Tomasello, Strosberg, & Akhtar, 1996). Similarly, there is evidence that a child's perception of an adult's intentionality affects what label he is willing to give an action. When the experimenter said "Let's dax Mickey Mouse" and then performed two actions on the doll, one that looked deliberate and was followed by the exclamation "there!," while the other looked accidental and was followed by "whoops!," the child thought the action label *dax* applied to the first, intentional, action (Tomasello & Barton, 1994).

If an adult uses a novel word that is unknown to a child while looking back and forth between an object and the child in a playful, animated manner, the child is likely to understand the new word to be an invitation to "come" or "play" rather than a label for the object (Tomasello & Akhtar, 1995).

What Would Associationists Say about Language Acquisition?

B. F. Skinner (1957) proposed that language acquisition, like any other developing behaviour, was acquired via operant conditioning. According to his view, a baby has no specialized learning machinery that facilitates language learning but is reinforced for language behaviour: The baby makes a sound, and if the sound happens to sound like a speech sound in its native language, the parent smiles or somehow reinforces the speech behaviour. More recently, some behaviourists have also proposed that imitation is part of the language acquisition process: That is, children acquire a complex grammatical sentence because that very sentence has been modelled for them by an adult (Whitehurst & Vasta, 1975).

Explanations that propose no role for psychological structures designed to acquire language cannot explain the rapidity and efficiency of language learning as well as the language production of young children. Children routinely and commonly put together idiosyncratic utterances that they have never heard before. Anyone who has had a conversation with a child knows that children clearly generate novel sentences that they have never heard before. Imitation and operant conditioning may play a very small role in the development of language, but these psychological tools are not nearly strong enough to explain the language acquisition that actually takes place in every healthy member of our species.

Adults' Roles in Children's Language Learning

You might be thinking that teaching a child a language must surely be a tedious, laborious task and that it probably takes hours of rote repetition, practice, editing, and carefully designed demonstration to teach a baby to speak its native language, right? Actually, adults do not do as much active teaching as you would think.

Parents do not explicitly teach the rules of language. Furthermore, children do not learn the complex rules of grammar from school or from explicit correction when they write essays. The surprising fact is that the grammar of spoken language, the grammatical rules that we all acquire without being taught, are much more complex and nuanced than the grammar rules that are explained to us in school. Indeed the complex grammar rules of our spoken language that we acquire and follow implicitly cannot be taught to all children because they are not explicitly known and explicable by most adults. They are really only known to several dozen psycholinguists, who had to derive them by laboriously studying spoken and written language, and as far as we know those psycholinguists may not be finished discovering all of the rules we use when we speak.

The rules of language that we all know are far more sophisticated than the rules we learn in school (e.g., rules that dictate word order, that allow us to encode and decipher meaning based on word order, and that allow us to make nouns plural and change the tense of verbs). We unconsciously know that we can use the auxiliary *is* at the beginning of a sentence to make it a question ("A unicorn is in the garden" becomes "Is a unicorn in the garden?"), and we also unconsciously know that we cannot just take any *is* in a sentence to make it a question ("A unicorn that is eating a flower is in the garden" cannot be changed to "Is a unicorn that eating a flower is in the garden?") (Pinker, 1997).

Some sort of interaction seems to be necessary judging by the fact that a child cannot learn to speak his native language just by watching television or listening to the radio. There was a time when deaf parents of hearing children were told to let their children watch as much television as possible so that they would learn their spoken language from the television broadcasts. A nice theory, but it did not work (Ervin-Tripp, 1973). Just hearing the broadcasts did not expose children to the right kind of language input. So what are parents doing that a television broadcast cannot?

To give them credit, adults do use **infant-directed speech**, also sometimes called *motherese* or *baby talk*, when talking to an infant. The pitch is higher; there is extreme, exaggerated intonation; and the speech is slower than in adult-directed speech. Infant-directed speech is typically accompanied by exaggerated facial expressions and is also more grammatically pure. People do not produce grammatical errors when talking to infants. This is not because infant-directed speech is so grammatically simple. It is not (Pinker, 1994). Furthermore, when speaking to infants, adults talk about concrete and current topics, rather than discussing abstract, hypothetical, or future topics (Fernald, 1992). And there is evidence that infants find it easier to parse words when an adult is using infant-directed speech. However, infant-directed speech, though common to many cultures, is not a human universal. It seems to be used in all cultures in which adults talk to infants (Falk, 2004; Fernald, 1992), but there are cultures in which adults never speak to children at all until the child is conversational. Adults simply talk in front of the child but never to the child.

Adults use infant-directed speech when talking to babies. They also often use exaggerated facial expressions and do not produce many grammatical errors when talking to infants.

infant-directed speech
The kind of speech, or "baby talk," adults use when talking to an infant.

9.8 **Press Pause**

Adults use infant-directed speech (baby talk) when talking to infants, but this is not the case in every culture.

In addition, there is evidence that the intention encoded in a mother's utterance is understood by adults, even if the content of the utterance is not understandable to the hearer. Greg Bryant and Clark Barrett recorded North American mothers producing one of four intentions: prohibitive, approval, comfort, or attention. When they played these recordings to the Shuar, a group of South American hunter-horticulturalists who could not understand the English words spoken in the recordings, the adults correctly categorized the recordings by intention. What is more, they could distinguish infant-directed from adult-directed speech, and they were faster and more accurate at identifying the intention in recordings of infant-directed speech compared to adult-directed speech (Bryant & Barrett, 2007).

Infant-directed speech does tend to emphasize words for concrete objects, apparently making it easier for children to acquire these labels (Bloom, 1998; Menyuk, Liebergott, & Schultz, 1995). So there is some evidence that parents, with their infant-directed speech, are in the game, but what is really surprising is how little parents tutor their children in language learning and how little they correct their children when they make language errors. Roger Brown examined conversations between children and their parents and showed that parents were no more likely to correct grammatically incorrect sentences than grammatically correct sentences. And this is not because parents were worried about their children's developing self-esteem. Parents did correct children's utterances that were factually incorrect, just not sentences that were grammatically incorrect. He also found that the children's non-grammatical sentences were perfectly understandable to the parent. Parents responded appropriately (by following the conversational thread) just as frequently when the sentence was non-grammatical as when it was grammatical (Brown & Hanlon, 1970).

Remember that babies are adapted to the EEA, and the environment in which they evolved includes the language environment, the language modelled by the people around them. Adult language is a part of the environment that was reliably present in the EEA.

Critical Periods for Language Learning

A critical period is a finite period during development (or more generally during the life cycle) during which the developing organism can learn something (or develop a skill, or mature in a content-specific way, depending upon what you want to call it). We know of many examples of critical periods. You read in Chapter 5 that there must be specific kinds of visual inputs at particular times in order for the perception of vertical and horizontal lines to develop normally. The young white-crowned sparrow needs to hear his region's dialect from older males during a specific critical period or he will never be able to learn it. Why should there be critical periods? Simply put: because computation does not come for free. Brain material is very expensive tissue, and brain activity is very, very expensive metabolically. If language learning can be accomplished once, early in life, then the individual should not bear the cost of having a language acquisition device sitting around doing nothing. In our EEA, people were not emigrating from Asia to North America in a single lifetime; these migrations took thousands

figure 9.5 Test of the critical-period hypothesis

The performance of Korean- and Chinese-born adults on an English grammar test was directly related to the age at which they came to the United States and were exposed to English. (Adapted from Newport, 1990).

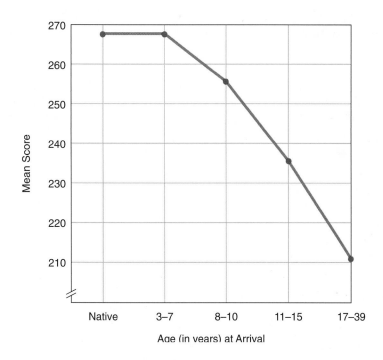

of years. Indeed, during an individual's lifetime in the EEA, one would rarely, if ever, have encountered a person who spoke a language that was unintelligible to them.

One could create a computer simulation, inputting reasonable assumptions about the costs and benefits of maintaining a language acquisition device at various ages and use that simulation to predict when a developing child should be within his critical period for language. This is just what James Hurford has done, and it turns out that language acquisition in early childhood is ideal. That is the only time period that the benefits justify the cost (Hurford, 1991).

Learning your native language is easy. Learning a second language may be harder, depending upon the age you are exposed to that language. Immigrants who move to a new language community after puberty may never be able to eliminate the accent of their native language. And yes, puberty seems to be critical in the timing of one's ability to effectively acquire a second language: Elissa Newport tested Korean- and Chinese-born members of the University of Illinois community on their ability to detect small grammatical errors like "The little boy is speak to a policeman," for example. People who relocated to an English-speaking community before the age of 7 performed just as native speakers did, but those who relocated between the ages of 8 and 15 caught errors less frequently than native speakers, and those who arrived after the age of 17 did worse still (Newport, 1990).

The story is even more dire if a child is not exposed to any native language. Clearly such a situation is rare, but there are cases of "wild children" who, usually due to extreme abuse, are not exposed to their native language with sufficient con-

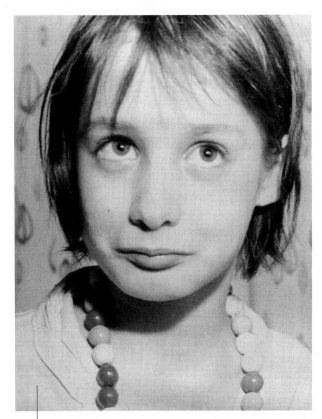

"Genie," who was rescued from isolation at the age of 13, never successfully acquired a fully grammatical language. Cases of "wild children" illustrate the importance of critical periods in language acquisition.

sistency to acquire it. There are also less sinister instances in which deaf children born to hearing parents are not exposed to sign language until adulthood and as a result never acquire their native (sign) language to the same level of fluency as other deaf children (Newport, 1990).

Cases of wild or feral children who are deprived of language input should not be interpreted as good scientific evidence of the effect of early language exposure on language production since clearly these children were abused, neglected, and deprived of a lot more than just language. That said, there seems to be some evidence that the age of their rescue and subsequent introduction to language makes a difference. "Genie," who was rescued from isolation at the age of 13 (after puberty), never successfully acquired a fully grammatical language (Curtiss, 1977). Isabelle, who had never been exposed to language before she was rescued from isolation at the age of 6½, was speaking grammatically complex and correct English by the time she was 8 (Tartter, 1986).

Another recent case may have more value because it does not involve physical or emotional abuse. "Chelsea" was born deaf but was not diagnosed with deafness when she was a child. Doctors thought she was intellectually disabled or emotionally disturbed. She was raised by loving and protective parents. Finally, when she was 31 years old, she was diagnosed as deaf and began intensive language therapy; she never successfully acquired grammatically complex language (Curtiss, 1989).

9.9 **Press Pause**

Cases involving children who did not get early language exposure demonstrate the importance of the critical periods of language learning.

Other evidence of a critical period for language development is the plasticity that is seen in an individual who acquires brain damage early in life compared to the relative lack of plasticity in persons who acquire brain damage in adulthood. As previously mentioned, for most people language is centred in the left hemisphere of the brain. A child who sustains damage to the left hemisphere will still learn language. Indeed even in cases where the left hemisphere of a young child has been removed, the child eventually acquires adult language. However, adults who suffer brain damage to the left hemisphere often show language deficits, and those deficits are permanent (Curtiss, 1989; Lenneberg, 1967).

SECOND-LANGUAGE ACQUISITION

Another area of research that lends strong support to the idea that there are critical periods for language acquisition is bilingualism. People who are bilingual, that is, who speak and understand two languages fluently, may have learned their second language at various points in development. One might learn a second language simultaneously with their first language, hearing both in their immediate environment from infancy, or one might be introduced to a second language later in childhood or adolescence. It turns out that the age at which a bilingual person was introduced to his or her second language has an effect on which hemisphere of the brain is used in language processing.

Researchers asked Chinese–English bilingual participants to identify grammatical errors while the researchers measured electrical signals indicating brain activity. For most monolingual people, the left hemisphere is primarily used in language processing; there is very little concurrent activity in the right hemisphere during this time. Similarly, in this study, people who had learned English as a second language earlier than the age of 3 used the left hemisphere almost exclusively for grammatical processing, like monolingual speakers do. Those who had been exposed to English between the ages of 4 and 6 showed significantly more right-hemisphere use during the grammatical task, and those who had not learned English until they were 11 to 13 years of age showed almost equal left- and right-hemisphere activation while completing the task (Weber-Fox & Neville, 1996).

These results are consistent with the idea that those people who were exposed to their second language during the critical period were able to make use of specialized language acquisition processes that are located in the left hemisphere. Those who were

figure 9.6   Bilinguals: Grammatical processing

Adults who learned a second language at 1 to 3 years of age showed greater left-hemisphere activity in a grammar test, just as most people do. Learning a second language later was associated with increased right-hemisphere activity. This illustrates that language exposure must happen during a critical period in order to acquire typical language.

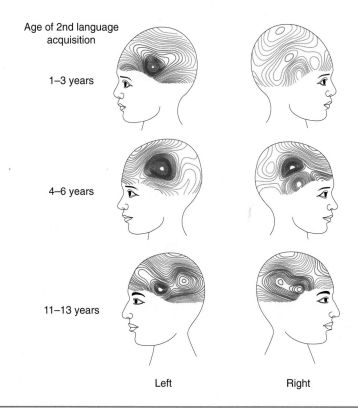

Age of 2nd language acquisition

1–3 years

4–6 years

11–13 years

Left   Right

exposed to their second language when their critical period had passed had to rely on alternative processes in order to achieve language acquisition, and these alternative processes were just as likely to be in the right hemisphere as the left.

Learning Grammar

In language learning, perception precedes comprehension, and comprehension precedes production. Babies who are still speaking predominantly single words already understand some complex grammatical constructions. One experiment had these

⠿⠿ Assessing Social Impact

Bilingual Education

Nearly half of the children in the world today are exposed to more than one language as they grow up, some as a result of immigration and many because their parents have different native languages. More than ever before, large numbers of children are growing up bilingual (speaking two languages proficiently) or even multilingual (speaking more than two languages proficiently). Bilingualism has increased across Canada by 12 per cent since the 1990s. Researchers wonder what the effects of bilingualism will be, and educators wonder how best to approach bilingual education. So far, the news is mostly good.

A classic, now no longer supported, view of bilingual education was that learning more than one language at once could impede learning in general. The theory was that young children approach all the linguistic information in the environment equipped only with cognitive machinery designed to learn one language. Thus, children approached the two languages as if they were learning one, and they then had to laboriously learn to separate the two. This theory predicted delay in cognitive development in bilingual children, and indeed there was evidence to support this prediction. Children learning two languages at home learn each language more slowly than monolingual children. They reach various language milestones at later ages than do monolinguals. But this lag disappears with age, and the children are eventually as proficient in each of the two languages as the monolingual children are in one language (Oller & Pearson, 2002).

Currently, researchers favour a multi-system view of bilingual language learning (Bialystok, 2001). In this view, children learn each language using dedicated cognitive systems, minimizing interference between the languages. As early as 4 months of age, infants who live in a bilingual home can distinguish the speech sounds of the two languages (Bosch & Sebastian-Galles, 2001). Furthermore, to the extent that young children engage in

"code-mixing," that is, using vocabulary and grammatical constructions from each language in a single sentence, they may be responding to parental modelling. Parents in bilingual households often use more than one language in a single child-directed utterance and respond positively to the child's code-mixing rather than trying to correct it (Goodz, 1989; Lanza, 1997).

Clearly there are economic and cultural advantages to speaking more than one language: Employment and travel opportunities open up to speakers of multiple languages. In addition, there may be some real cognitive advantages to bilingualism. Bilingual children outperform monolingual children on a variety of cognitive tasks (Bialystok, Shenfield, & Codd, 2000). Ellen Bialystok, a developmental psychologist working at York University in Toronto has found that bilingual children have greater executive control than monolingual children. That is to say, they are better able to control their own attention, to disregard irrelevant stimuli, and to focus their own cognitive processes. Bialystok explains that bilingual speakers have to use this kind of control constantly: Whenever they form a sentence, they have to inhibit the use of one word in favour of another word for the same concept. Bialystok also shows that this cognitive advantage is evident throughout adulthood and even serves as a buffer against cognitive decline in old age (Bialystok, 2007).

How is an educator to provide the best possible bilingual education? Canadian language immersion programs have been very successful. In these programs, young children are schooled in their non-dominant language: Children living in English-speaking households learn all of their classes in French; those in French-speaking households learn in English. Crucially, the programs also support the child's dominant language. Children spend a class period each day studying language skills in their native language. By Grade 6, children in immersion programs score as well as monolingual counterparts in reading, writing, and math (Holobow, Genesee, & Lambert, 1991).

single-word producers sit in front of two computer screens. One showed Cookie Monster tickling Big Bird, and one showed Big Bird tickling Cookie Monster. When the voice came over the audio saying, "Oh look! Big Bird is tickling Cookie Monster! Find Big Bird tickling Cookie Monster!," the baby, at around 27 months of age, was more likely to look at the picture of Big Bird tickling Cookie Monster and not at the picture of Cookie Monster tickling Big Bird. What could explain this non-random response? The child can decode the meaning encoded in the grammar of the sentence even though the child is only producing single words (Hirsh-Pasek & Golinkoff, 1996). Another experiment similarly revealed that the 2-year-olds can use word order to understand the meanings of new verbs (Gertner, Fisher, & Eisengart, 2006).

Between the ages of 2 and 3, children begin to produce word order that is appropriate for their native language. For example, in English-speaking communities, children will begin to construct sentences with a subject–verb–object word order consistently. Children in other language communities adopt the word order of the adults around them (Maratsos, 1998). At about this same time, they begin to use the conventions of their language that are necessary to convey plural in nouns or tense in verbs, and they begin to use prepositions (e.g., *in* and *on*). All of these grammatical markers that are mastered by young children are acquired in a predictable (though language-specific) order (Brown, 1973; de Villiers & de Villiers, 1973). Once they master these grammatical tools, they are notorious for over-applying them in a phenomenon known as *over-regularization*: "I have two feets, and you have two feets!" (Marcus, 1995; Marcus et al., 1992). By the end of preschool, children use most of the grammatical conventions of their native language competently and consistently (Tager-Flusberg, 1997).

Although it seems clear that practice and feedback are necessary in order for a baby to produce speech sounds (babbling), the same is not true for the development of grammatical structure. Karin Stromswold (1994) reported on a child who was unable to speak but nonetheless had complex grammatical understanding. This 4-year-old, who had never spoken a word, could choose the correct picture when told "the dog was bitten by the cat" as opposed to "the cat was bitten by the dog" and other similarly complex sentences.

One thing to notice about the errors that children make is that they are, in and of themselves, evidence that children are generating language, not just learning language by association. If the languages that children produced were just imitation, then they could never produce errors such as "goed" as a past tense for go or "don't giggle me" because they would never have heard them from adults (Pinker, 1994).

Children Generate Language

One misconception about language is that parents teach their children to speak. Surprisingly, this is not so. You read above about the minimal role that adults play in teaching and correcting children's developing languages. In fact, children who have deaf parents who only speak to them via sign language, or indeed children who grow up without hearing language from their parents at all, can and do learn spoken language from their peers. Children are also influenced much more by peers than by parents when acquiring accents and local vocabulary and speech mannerisms.

One phenomenon that illustrates child-generated language is the language that emerges in situations where children do not have adult models from whom to learn a native language. We learned earlier that human languages in every culture, at every level of technological advance, and in every historical period are equally complex and

Language Development Milestones

Age	Skills
At Birth	Cries Shows evidence of hearing; is startled by noise Prefers mother's language to a foreign language
1 Month	Already perceiving speech sounds categorically
3 Months	Different needs are expressed with audibly different cries Responds to speech with focus of attention and smiling Makes vowel sounds, called *cooing*
6 Months	Babbles by repeating sounds /ba ba/ or /pa pa/ for example Still good at discriminating speech sounds of all human languages
9 Months	Uses voice to attract attention Enjoys own voice Makes a variety of different speech sounds that are recognizable as adult speech sounds Babbles sound musical
By 1 Year	Understands several words Can comply with simple instructions Babbles Has specialized in discriminating speech sounds of own language
15 Months	Jabbers freely Can communicate needs using vocalization
18 Months	Echoes adult speech
2 Years	Speaks 50 or more words Learning several new words every day Combines two words together Receptive language is much more advanced than expressive language (they understand more than they can say)
By 3 Years	Speaks in sentences Produces word order that is appropriate for their native language Talks a lot, both to self and to others Uses past tense verbs
4 Years	Speech is mostly grammatical but with errors Consistently uses prepositions
5 Years	Sophisticated sentence structure Can refer to past, present, and future Almost all of the child's speech is understandable

equally good examples of human language. However, in situations of historical anomaly when two (or more) adult language communities come into contact for the first time, adults may create what is called a *pidgin language*.

The adults in these communities are well past the critical period for learning and creating language. One historical example of this occurred during the early days of the slave trade in the southern United States. Africans were being kidnapped from various language communities in West Africa and were being mixed together in a single workforce, either intentionally (some slave traders tried to prevent communication and organization among those they enslaved) or accidentally (the slave trader purchased whoever was available). These adults from different language communities had to communicate in order to work together day-to-day and presumably because they wanted to share experiences, but they did not have a common language. In such circumstances, the adults created a pidgin language. Pidgin languages are choppy and non-standardized, their word order may vary from speaker to speaker, inflections that carry grammatical information are not shared (often not even used), and they typically borrow vocabulary from each of the adult language communities. Also, these slaves would have likely borrowed words from their captor's language as well. So a pidgin language is not a complex human language of the sort we have been discussing.

What happens next is amazing. Children are born into the community (finally someone shows up who is not past the critical period for language acquisition). These children do not acquire a choppy non-grammatical language as their native language; they actually create the grammar *de novo*. Yes, small children, who do not have an adult model teaching them what is grammatical, create the grammar that a native human language ought to have, one that is of equal complexity to, say, the Queen's English. The children do not speak a pidgin language but now speak what is called a *creole language*.

9.10 Press Pause

> Adults from different language communities who come together create a pidgin language. Young children brought together from different languages can create a bona fide language called a *creole language*.

Notice that this only happens in very unusual historical circumstances: The children have to be born into a community that uses the pidgin language exclusively, or at least primarily. If they are spending most of their time with parents who are speaking the home language to them, then they will acquire the home language as their native language and will continue to speak the pidgin language with peers who speak a different home language.

A somewhat recent example of this—recent enough to have been studied by a contemporary linguist—happened in the late 1800s in Hawaii when there was a rapid, economically motivated expansion in the sugar plantation industry. There was not enough local labour to meet the demand, so workers were brought to Hawaii from China, Japan, Korea, the Philippines, Portugal, and Puerto Rico. Derek Bickerton, a linguist, studied the languages that resulted from this amalgamation. His research took place in the 1970s, and many of the pidgin and creole languages, that were created during this period still existed for his study. The adults who were brought to Hawaii as workers developed a pidgin language. Bickerton was able to document this language by interviewing the retirees in their late 60s and 70s. They spoke without grammatical conventions, leaving the listener to do a lot of the work figuring out which word was meant to serve which role in the sentence. Their children were a different story. The children of these workers created Hawaiian creole, which is—you guessed it—a fully complex, fully grammatical human language. These children were born in Hawaii, went through their linguistic critical periods in a pidgin language community, and were not going to put up with having a non-grammatical language as a native language. The children (yes children) created auxiliaries, prepositions, case markers, and relative pronouns. They standardized the word orders and created grammatical markers. The only thing they took from their parents was vocabulary (Bickerton, 1981).

In the late 1800s, workers were brought to Hawaii from China, Japan, Korea, the Philippines, Portugal, and Puerto Rico. The children of these workers created Hawaiian creole, a fully grammatical language.

Another natural experiment in our more recent history involves the creolization of sign language by a community of deaf children in Nicaragua. Contrary to what you might believe, sign languages are bona fide human languages, complete with their very own grammatical rules. Sign languages are not just signs people make that represent English. American Sign Language is not even related to English; indeed, American Sign Language and British Sign Language are different, mutually unintelligible languages, neither of which is derivative of English. In Nicaragua, before the 1970s, there was no sign language in use among the deaf because they had never been organized into a community. Each deaf person was at home with his or her hearing family, perhaps using some idiosyncratic manual signs but with no actual language. The first elementary school for the deaf was opened in Managua in 1977, and a vocational school for the deaf was opened in 1981. The students who came to these schools were largely older children who were past their linguistic critical period. There was no encouragement from teachers for the students to develop a sign language; the teachers wanted them to lip-read and learn to speak Spanish. But the students spent time together on the playground, during breaks, and after school, and by doing so and trying to communicate with one another, they developed Nicaragua's first sign language (Kegl, 1994). This was really a pidgin language; people contributed signs that they had been using at home or developed new ones, but no grammar or consistent word order developed.

As younger cohorts, children who were not yet past their critical periods, joined the community and were exposed to the pidgin language that was in use, they created a bona fide language, which is now called Idioma de Signos Nicaragüense (ISN) or, in English, Nicaraguan Sign Language (NSL). As in other known instances of creolization, the younger children added grammatical conventions and standardized word order to the pidgin language. Again, the children created this language. They did not learn it from adults; no adults had a sign language to teach them.

9.11 Press Pause

Children with no adult-modelled language create a human language, but they must begin before they are past their critical period.

An experiment that illustrates the difference between the pidgin language used by older children and the creole language created by younger children examined participants' hand movements while they were describing an action-packed movie that they had just watched. (It involved a cartoon cat eating a bowling ball and then wobbling around a steep street.) The researchers compared the hand movements of deaf people who began communicating with sign language when they were older, deaf people who began communicating with sign language when they were younger, and Spanish speakers who were not hearing impaired. Those who were not hearing impaired often used their hands to accompany speech. People all over the world accompany speech with manual gestures (Goldin-Meadow, 1999) even if the speaker and listener are both blind (Iverson & Goldin-Meadow, 1998). The hand movements that the later signers used were similar to those of the Spanish speakers. As they talked about the cat rolling and descending down the street, their hands simultaneously represented rolling and descending. In contrast, the earlier signers used segmented and sequenced signs to talk

When previously isolated deaf children were brought together in Nicaragua for the first time in 1977, they began to communicate with each other via signs. The younger children developed a fully grammatical sign language despite there being no adult to teach it to them.

figure 9.7 Nicaraguan sign language experiment

These people are telling a story about a cat who, after having swallowed a bowling ball, proceeded rapidly down a steep street in a wobbling, rolling manner. In Example A, a Spanish-speaker wiggles his fingers while moving his hand to the right. The type of motion the cat makes and the path the cat follows are expressed together in a single movement. In Example B, the type of motion and path are expressed in two separate signs assembled into a sequence: first a circular motion and then a movement to the right. Sign language is different from the gestures that accompany spoken language.

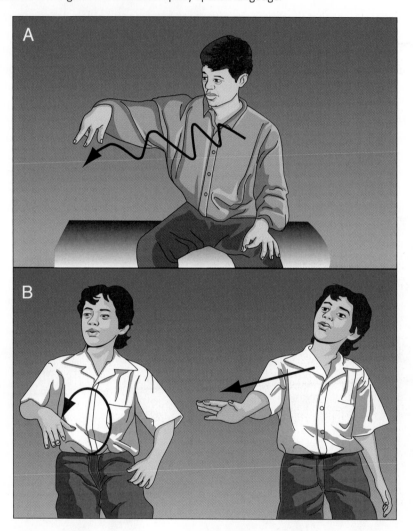

about rolling and descending. They were using language and following its grammatical rules and were not using their hands to emphasize what they were saying (Senghas, Kita, & Özyürek, 2004).

Language Is Species-Specific

What is unique about human language? Do non-human animals have language? It turns out that that depends on how you define *language*, which makes the question fairly uninteresting. Non-human animals certainly have communication and arguably have some limited symbolic vocabulary, but whether they have language depends on whether you want to call their communication *language*. What *is* clear is that human language is unique; it is far more complex than that of any other animal, and only humans have an infinitely generative language. Other animals do not have human language because, unlike humans, they do not have a generative grammar, meaning they cannot combine words in an infinite number of ways to produce an unlimited number of new ideas.

We have seen several examples throughout this book where it has been informative to compare human psychology to that of other animals. This comparison can help us understand what humans are actually doing. It helps to clear our instinct blindness and bring to light what is unique to human psychology. So it is with language, so let us look at differences between the easy and automatic development of language in humans and the arduous attempts to teach human language to other species.

ATTEMPTS TO TEACH NON-HUMANS LANGUAGE

The communication of non-human animals is characterized by either a small and finite number of calls, such as that of the vervet monkey's alarm calls, or a continuous signal, the duration of which conveys the magnitude of some feature of the world. An example of the latter is the bee's waggle dance, which, as it becomes more animated, tells of richer and richer food sources. Human language is infinitely generative because

---

figure 9.8 Animals have methods of communication

The bee's waggle dance becomes more animated to communicate richer food sources. Non-human communication is distinct, psychologically, from human language.

our rules of grammar allow us to generate untold novel sentences, each conveying meaning (Pinker, 1994).

A final clue that the communication of other primates is not, psychologically, the same thing as human language is that the calls and vocalizations that are a part of a non-human primate's repertoire are not controlled by brain areas that are analogous to those that control human language in humans. Instead, they are controlled by older brain structures, specifically those associated with emotions, such as the limbic system and the brain stem. These are the very brain areas that, in humans, control non-linguistic vocalizations such as laughing, crying, exclaiming in pain, or moaning (Deacon, 1989).

9.12 Press Pause

Other species have communication systems but not human language psychology.

In the last century, some very determined linguists tried very hard to teach language to non-humans, usually targeting apes. Earlier in the chapter you read about attempts, with remarkably limited success, to teach the chimpanzee Viki to speak. But perhaps the mistake was trying to make Viki use her vocal apparatus, which is clearly not human-like. More recent attempts to teach chimpanzees human language have employed manual sign languages or symbolic systems that can be manipulated, acknowledging that chimpanzees cannot vocalize as humans do.

In the 1960s and 1970s it seemed as if it were going to be possible to teach human language to chimps. Their trainers were claiming success. Allen and Beatrice Garder were the first to have the insight that a manual sign language might help teach language to a species whose vocal apparatus is not designed for speech production or entirely available to voluntary control. They attempted to teach a chimpanzee named Washoe sign language and claimed success: Washoe responded to novel combinations of words and, on at least one occasion, generated a novel word combination. In 1972, Francine (Penny) Patterson began teaching a manual sign language to a gorilla named Koko. She succeeded in teaching Koko over 300 manual signs and is still working with him today. By the early 1970s there were more than a dozen apes receiving intensive language training. Despite their popularity, their influence on the scientific community was hindered by the trainers' failure to publish results and their apparent unwillingness to share raw data.

9.13 Press Pause

Although apes trained in human language have captured popular attention, the scientific community has not been convinced that they can acquire human language.

Kanzi, a bonobo chimpanzee got more attention from the scientific community and was the subject of peer reviewed publications. Sue Savage-Rumbaugh, Kanzi's handler and trainer, believed that Kanzi had advanced language aptitude. Kanzi communicated by pointing to representational pictures on a keyboard. Savage-Rumbaugh tells the story of Kanzi, on an outing into the woods, pointing to the symbols for "marshmallow" and "fire." When provided with a marshmallow and a match, he constructed a fire

Nim Chimpsky underwent extensive language training. Despite his trainers setting out to show that language was not unique to humans, they had to conclude that Nim's language was vastly dissimilar from human language.

and toasted his marshmallow. Kanzi eventually learned a vocabulary of around 200 of these symbolic pictures (Savage-Rumbaugh & Lewin, 1994).

These "experiments" were followed up by some scientists who were more willing to share data and more willing to be sceptical. Herbert Terrace spearheaded a project involving the chimpanzee, "Nim Chimpsky," and included collaborator Laura Ann Petitto and others. Following a careful analysis of what Nim was doing, these scientists came to different conclusions than their predecessors. First, crediting Washoe and other chimps with a vocabulary of about 125 words depended upon a very generous reading. If the chimp pressed the button that turned the computer on, the button was taken to symbolize the word "please" and the word credited to his vocabulary. If the chimp tickled, scratched, kissed, or hugged, he might be credited with using the sign for tickle, scratch, kiss, or hug. A deaf research assistant, who actually spoke ASL as a first language, noticed that the hearing research assistants were very generous with crediting words to Washoe, noting that "When the chimp scratched itself, they'd record it as the sign for scratch" (Neisser, 1983, p. 215). These researchers concluded that the smartest of chimps probably had a vocabulary of about 25 words (Petitto & Seidenberg, 1979). Chimps do not comment on things, do not take conversational turns, and do not frequently use language spontaneously. When they do, it is almost always a request: They name something they want.

A persistent issue was the length of the chimp's utterances: While human children start to construct long and intricate sentences shortly after the age of 2, a chimp's utterance is likely to be only two words long or extremely repetitive. For example, to quote a chimp, he might say: "Give orange me give eat orange me eat orange give me eat orange give me you" (Terrace, 1979). And this would be after thousands of training attempts. The human child, by contrast, has learned language without any explicit attempts at training. For human children, just hanging out with humans is enough to start understanding and producing language. Terrace, who initially thought he would find language use in chimps, burst the field's bubble when he concluded that the apes had not learned language but that their apparent language was the result of repetitive drills and responses to the researchers' prompting (Terrace, 1979). Although attempts to teach chimps language persist and still get occasional attention in the popular press, they fail to capture the attention of the scientific community.

9.14 **Press Pause**

Chimpanzees and other apes lack human language learning psychology.

Not only do chimpanzees lack the psychological processes necessary to acquire and comprehend language, they also lack the vocal tract anatomy necessary to produce speech. But there is a price that humans pay for our language-ready anatomy: Tens of thousands of people choke to death every year because their larynxes are positioned low in their throats.

Charles Darwin famously commented on the dangerous human vocal tract, noting "the strange fact that every particle of food and drink which we swallow has to pass over the orifice of the trachea, with some risk of falling into the lungs" (Darwin, 1859, p. 191). Chimpanzees and all other terrestrial animals have a larynx that rises up like a periscope and can be sealed off, watertight, so that non-human animals can breathe while they eat or drink. We cannot. The human larynx (you will know where yours is by feeling your Adam's apple) is so low it does not reach the opening of the nose. In humans, a common pathway transports air, food, and drinks, such that food and drinks pass over the larynx, while air travels into the larynx. If food accidentally falls into the larynx, it obstructs the passageway to the lungs and a person can choke and die.

Interestingly, this language-ready vocal tract develops after the first several months of life. Human newborns have a tract similar to non-human primates (Lieberman, Crelin, & Klatt, 1972; Negus, 1949). At birth, the newborn does not articulate speech sounds, so there would have been no selection pressure in favour of the more precarious vocal tract configuration. Instead, the non-human type configuration reduces the newborn's risk of choking. Starting at around 3 months of age, the vocal tract begins to shift to an adult-like configuration. In fact, it continues to change to be more adult-like until puberty, so a developing child has to continuously relearn to articulate speech sounds.

Can a Gene Cause the Development of Grammar?

There is a family living in England (known in the field as the KE family) who are affected by specific language impairment and who have been studied intensely. Very close to half of the 30 family members, spanning three generations, have a characteristic set of language deficits, including an inability to speak fluently or produce complicated speech sounds, and difficulty generating as many words as possible starting with a given letter. The other family members speak normally, showing no common deficits with their affected family members.

The other thing that the affected family members have in common with each other is a mutation on Chromosome 7 (Vargha-Khadem, Watkins, Alcock, Fletcher, & Passingham, 1995). Furthermore, one unrelated individual has been identified who has the same mutation and, similarly, a deficit in the acquisition of speech and language (Lai, Fisher, Hurst, Vargha-Khadem, & Monaco, 2009). A single dominant gene apparently affects one's ability to learn grammar.

Certainly, the revelation that a gene can selectively disturb grammar development is clearly devastating to the idea that language is acquired via general-purpose learning mechanisms in an associationist manner. But this discovery led to unwarranted claims: It was reported in the popular press, and to a lesser extent the scientific literature, as the discovery of a "grammar gene." Reporters and columnists were claiming that a single gene set apart those students in a classroom who easily learned grammar from those who struggled, and the *Associated Press* reported "Ability to Learn Grammar Laid to Gene by Researcher" (Pinker, 1994, p. 441).

This provides us with a great opportunity to revisit our discussion about causality and the role of a gene in development. Recall from our discussion in Chapter 4 that any event has multiple causes. Statistically, when you compare the group of family members with this developmental anomaly to those family members without it, there is a strong (100 per cent) association between having the gene mutation and having difficulty in the development of grammar. This should not be taken to mean that this gene alone is the cause of grammar. In typical development, many, many genes as well as non-genetic factors from the chemical level to the social and emotional level have an impact on language development. All of these developmental resources working together result in typical language development, whereas the perturbation of any of these developmental resources results in atypical development. There is not a single gene that codes for grammar, much less grammar development. There is no grammar gene.

Moreover, this is an opportunity to revisit our discussion about the universality of complex adaptations. Language development, or the language acquisition device, is an extremely complex adaptation; its development depends on many, many genes, and its evolution almost certainly happened when one beneficial mutation spread throughout the population to universality followed at some later time by a new mutation spreading to universality and so on. The discovery of the KE family has tempted some (did it tempt you?) to imagine that at some point in our evolutionary history a single mutation led to complex human grammar. An infinitely more likely possibility is that after the very slow evolution of the complex psychological machinery underlying complex grammar, a single deleterious mutation messed it up.

SUMMARY

In this chapter you read about children's acquisition of language. Early in the chapter you learned that spoken language is a part of human nature and not a human innovation that was invented and then spread from there. The acquisition of language, or the instinct to learn language, is a great example to help you understand why the learned vs. evolved dichotomy does not work. Language is clearly learned: People who grow up in Japan speak Japanese, not Portuguese, because they were exposed to Japanese when they learned language. And language acquisition clearly relies on evolved learning mechanisms: Perfectly intelligent non-human animals that have the associationist learning tools do not learn human language no matter how many hours of careful tutoring they are exposed to.

You also read about the brain basis for speech. You learned about Broca's area and Wernicke's area and the kind of disability that results if those areas are damaged. You learned about the kind of evidence that people use to infer that a specific part of the brain is involved in a specific kind of processing.

Next you read about infant speech perception. Infants seem to be ready to attend to and learn language right from the start. Infants are really good at discriminating one speech sound from another, even better than discriminating other equally physically dissimilar auditory stimuli. They can discriminate between sounds in any human language: Only later do they specialize in their own native language.

You learned about some of the steps young children go through on the way to language use: First they coo and then they babble. Then they learn words, a process that is much more difficult than it seems. Children have a set of rules that help them narrow down the possibilities when learning words. You learned about adults' roles in language acquisition, which was perhaps not as involved as you thought, although some tricks like infant-directed speech may help young language learners.

You also learned about critical periods, a concept that should be familiar from Chapter 5 when you read about perceptual development. Studies of children who immigrate to a new language community provide us with some information about critical periods, and so do stories of children who were language deprived.

The studies that you read about in this chapter regarding deaf children who were raised without exposure to a learnable language also shed light on the question of critical periods. More fascinating, these stories provide compelling evidence that children who are in a community with each other have the cognitive capacity to create a fully sophisticated, fully human language, even without learning that language from an adult language community. Adults who come together with no common language do not.

Finally, you read about attempts to teach non-human animals human language. Several scientists have committed themselves to hours upon hours of training, and the results have been impressive, considering these animals do not have human language acquisition capacities. But ultimately, these studies with animals have revealed that human language learning and use is unique to humans. The comparatively small vocabularies and language use seen in other animals are no comparison to humans' cognitive sophistication.

PRESS PAUSE SUMMARY

- Language is part of our human psychology, just as bat echolocation is part of bat psychology.
- The study of language development makes it clear that nature is not opposed to nurture. Rather, the developing child interacts with the environment by design.
- There is a regularity or universal grammar common to all human languages.
- Young infants can discriminate speech sounds in any human language. Older infants and adults can only discriminate speech sounds in their own language.
- One-month-old infants perceive speech sounds categorically, just as adults do.
- Word learning (another case of instinct blindness) is much more difficult than you might think.
- A set of word-learning rules allow children to learn the meanings of words, something that otherwise would be impossible.
- Adults use infant-directed speech (baby talk) when talking to infants, but this is not the case in every culture.
- Cases involving children who did not get early language exposure demonstrate the importance of the critical periods of language learning.
- Adults from different language communities who come together create a pidgin language. Young children brought together from different languages can create a bona fide language, called a *creole language*.
- Children with no adult-modelled language create a human language, but they must begin before they are past their critical period.
- Other species have communication systems but not human language psychology.
- Although apes trained in human language have captured popular attention, the scientific community has not been convinced that they can acquire human language.
- Chimpanzees and other apes lack human language learning psychology.

KEY TERMS AND CONCEPTS

Broca's aphasia, 303
categorical perception, 306
deep structure, 302
infant-directed speech, 315
language acquisition device, 302
mutual exclusivity assumption, 313

taxonomic assumption, 312
universal grammar, 302
voice onset time, 306
Wernicke's aphasia, 304
whole-object assumption, 311

QUESTIONS FOR THOUGHT AND DISCUSSION

1. Do domain-general learning mechanisms, including classical conditioning, operant conditioning, and imitation, explain language acquisition? Why or why not? Which authors are associated with each side of this debate?

2. Why is learning a word hard? Explain this in terms plain enough for someone who has never thought about it before. How do children learn language?

3. Under what circumstances do a group of people who share no common language create a sophisticated human language? Under what circumstances do they not, and what happens then? What do these facts reveal about language development?

4. Do non-human animals learn language? Describe what a scientist on either side of this debate might argue in defence of his or her position.

From the Classroom to the Lab: Follow Up

Consider the experiment you designed in response to the "From the Classroom to the Lab" challenge earlier in this chapter.

Would your experimental method meet the ethical standards expected by the field?

What is your dependent variable?

What is your independent variable?

Describe the procedure of your experiment. What stimuli is the infant exposed to? What task does the infant have to perform?

Imagine you have run your experiment. What results would indicate to you that the babies tested need to hear adult speech in order to engage in speech-like babbling? What results would indicate to you that the baby need only hear themselves in order to babble?

chapter 10

Social Contexts for Development

Opening Vignette: Three Different Families

B ob spent three years interviewing experts, visiting schools, and even moving his son from school to school in order to find just the right academic fit. He knew that his son, Roberto, was an academically gifted child, and he was determined to see just how great Roberto could be if given the right kind of support. Finally, Bob enrolled Roberto in a private boarding school that served the needs of the profoundly gifted.

Elverda was a single mom living on a modest income. She enrolled her 5-year-old son, Jeff, in swimming. It seemed like a modest and inexpensive hobby. It cost her $5 to get him a membership at the local swimming pool, and later, when he began competing, it cost her 75¢ per event. Then it became evident that he had some talent. She enrolled him in a more elite swimming club that cost $200 a month. She spent the next decade and a half supporting his developing swimming career, spending thousands of dollars and every minute of her spare time getting him to competitions.

Christopher was born to poor, hard-working parents. As a 9-year-old, he got up every weekday at 4:30 a.m., started the family fire, and started boiling water for breakfast before the other family members got up. When he returned from school at around three o'clock in the afternoon, his parents were still at work. It was up to Christopher to start the dinner preparations, perhaps peeling and cutting yams, preparing meat from a pig that his parents had raised and slaughtered, going to the river to fill the pot with water and hauling it back, and having coffee ready for his parents when they returned from work. His parents loved him, he knew, but there was rarely time for cuddling or even kind words.

Chapter Outline

- Learning about One's Own Context
- Psychological Adaptations for Culture
- Life History Theory
- Attachment
- Emotional Development More Generally
- Parents, Alloparents, Siblings, and Peers
- Differences in Parenting Make Little Difference
- Peer Influence
- Step-Parents
- Birth Order

Learning Objectives, Outcomes

- This chapter describes some of the effects of social context on development. After reading this chapter, you should have a better understanding of some of the facultative adaptations that allow developing children and adolescents to learn about their own social contexts and their own social positions in relation to others'. You should understand why facultative adaptations are sometimes the best evolutionary strategy and what kind of information relies on a learning mechanism in order to achieve an optimal behavioural strategy.

- You should understand the concept of attachment. You should know what function it serves and what function it may have served in the EEA. You should understand how researchers measure and categorize attachment and what developmental outcomes are predicted by each attachment style.

- You should understand the life history strategy and its implications. You will read about the strategic decisions that developing individuals have to make and the social and ecological factors that influence the payoffs of each strategy. These are complex decisions influenced by ecological and economic factors and by what other men and women in the developing child's environment are doing.

- You should also understand some of the influences of parents, peers, and siblings. Are parent's efforts to be "super parents" effective in creating "super kids"? Who socialized a developing child: his parents or his peers? And how are the effects of developing with older siblings different from the effects of developing with younger children?

Learning about One's Own Context

Developmental psychologists agree that early experience influences development and can contribute to individual differences in later development and in adulthood. There is certainly debate over specifics: how strongly early experience affects development, what specific inputs are necessary to have measurable effects on later development, and the timing of influence and the outcomes of exposure to various inputs. Nonetheless, it is widely recognized that early experience contributes to individual development. Why? Why should the developing child be designed such that early information input affects development?

You have already read about facultative adaptations: adaptations that are designed to respond to specific cues in the environment in order to optimize the fit between the developing organism and the environment. Facultative adaptations were functional in the EEA since they prepared organisms for the varying conditions that were possible.

As you learned in Chapter 4, learning mechanisms are facultative adaptations. Furthermore, learning is not a result of a unitary psychological process but is a result of a broad set of psychological processes, each one designed to accomplish a particular kind of learning: learning a face template, learning language, learning to walk, for example. We have talked about the idea that different selection pressures, created by specific adaptive problems, led to the evolution of each specific kind of learning mechanism. In this chapter we will read about the learning mechanisms that support the acquisition of culture, as well as learning mechanisms designed to take other social information as input.

Learning in this context serves a different function from the learning we have read about in previous chapters (e.g., regarding perceptual or language development). From an engineering point of view, there may be more than one reason to build a learning mechanism rather than structures that are ready to use without specific inputs. In our discussion of visual development in Chapter 5, we saw cases where the visual system requires exposure to particular input (e.g., horizontal lines and vertical lines made available to both eyes equally) in order for typical development to result. This is a case where regularities in the environment were virtually certain to be available, and it was easier to engineer a developing visual system that took advantage of the reliably present visual input rather than to build the system to its adult form without such input. In natural settings, the developing organism could hardly fail to encounter the appropriate stimuli, so such developmental disasters were not frequent enough to provide the selection pressure against this kind of learning. In some sense, developmentally reliable information is "stored" in the environment and can be exploited.

There is a second engineering problem that learning might solve: Learning gives one an opportunity to assess their circumstances before choosing a strategy, and this is the kind of learning that is the focus of this chapter. Instead of the developing organism relying on regularities in the environment in order to develop typically, in this case, the individual needs to learn about his or her specific circumstance. In some cases this is as specific as learning the identity of and attaching to one's own mother or a small set of caregivers. In other cases, it is learning one's circumstances in order to "choose" (unconsciously) one's best life strategy (e.g., choosing a mating strategy and behaving appropriately with respect to one's position in the status hierarchy). We will see that ecological and economic circumstances tell a person whether their best strategy is to reproduce young with many partners or to first find a stable pair bond. Some authors believe that birth order, being the eldest or youngest in the family, tells one whether sticking with the status quo or innovating and rebelling is the better strategy. Sometimes parents have to make difficult decisions: Ecological circumstances may affect whether coddling and indulging a child or toughening him up is the better strategy. In this chapter, we are going to learn about a set of **social facultative adaptations**: adaptations that are designed to respond to specific cues in the social environment, allowing one to pursue the most advantageous social strategy.

Here is an example of a facultative adaptation believed to allow a developing child to "calibrate" to existing circumstances, circumstances that could not be predicted before conception: Recent research has revealed that access to nutrition in utero affects physical health and growth throughout the lifespan. Nutritional deprivation before birth can result in glucose intolerance and reduced sensitivity to insulin (Phillips, 1998), problems with the immune system (McDade, Beck, Kuzawa, & Adair, 2001), and earlier senescence (Sayer et al., 1998). It is as if early exposure to nutrition informs the

Early exposure to nutrition informs the developing individual about the local circumstances, thus calibrating the individual's physiology (e.g., glucose tolerance and sensitivity to insulin) to make the best of the circumstances. This is an example of a functional adaptation.

social facultative adaptation An adaptation designed to respond to specific cues in the social environment, allowing one to pursue the most advantageous social strategy.

developing individual about the circumstances into which he or she is being born, thus calibrating the individual's physiology to make the best of the circumstances. It is clear why designing these systems to be open to information would be adaptive. So, too, has it been adaptive that some psychological domains are open to being calibrated early in life in order to optimize fitness in the current environment, and we will explore some examples in this chapter.

> **10.1 Press Pause**
>
> Learning one's circumstances allows one to calibrate behaviour that is optimal for one's life circumstances. Some learning mechanisms are designed to do just that.

Psychological Adaptations for Culture

Culture is unique to humans. Certainly, social transmission of behaviour has been observed in many species, and examples of social learning are abundant. One scientist observed an old female vervet monkey dip an Acacia pod into a pool of water that had gathered in a dead tree. After several minutes, the pod was soft and pliable, and the monkey was able to open it and eat the seeds. Within nine days, four other monkeys were doing this, and eventually 10 of the monkey's group members were using this strategy although no vervet monkey, in any group, had been seen doing this before (Hauser, 1988). In other examples, chimpanzees in only one part of the Ivory Coast use stones to open nut shells, and chimpanzees in only one area of Tanzania use twigs or blades of grass to extract and eat termites and ants (Whiten, Goodall, & McGrew, 1999). Some of the best known examples of social learning in animals are the learned songs of male songbirds (Marler, 1970).

Even simple human tools are far more complex than anything any other animal makes because humans are able to accumulate innovations on top of innovations.

Despite examples of social learning in various animals, only humans have cumulative culture because only humans have the cognitive machinery to permit and support the evolution and transmission of culture. Consider a simple human tool: a spear that might be used for hunting. As simple as it is, to build it requires several individuals and an accumulation of innovation on top of innovation: one or more people to design the aerodynamic shaft, others to design the stone point, others to design the system for lashing the two together, and others to design the tools used to shape and sharpen the point. Innovations built on innovations create an artifact that is far more complex than anything any other animal makes (Richerson & Boyd, 2005). To offer a comparison, a chimpanzee strips a twig and pokes it into a termite hole. Cumulative culture has allowed humans, and humans alone, to design artifacts as complex as written language, jet airplanes, microwave ovens, and the Internet.

At the heart of cognitive adaptations that allow for culture is imitation. Humans have the unique ability to observe other behaviours, infer their goals, and reproduce the behaviour in other contexts across a time delay. We have discussed this and other social cognitive mechanisms in humans in Chapter 8. Notice that instinct blindness may prevent you from wondering what it is about our psychology that makes culture possible, but a comparison with other species makes it clear that we are unique in having a psychology that creates and conveys culture. The effects of this ability would be difficult to overstate.

THE HADZA, THE !KUNG, AND ECOLOGICALLY DEPENDENT PARENTING STRATEGIES

Culture, which is influenced by local ecology, has an effect on parenting. As illustrated in the opening vignette of this chapter, the extent of parental investment can vary greatly depending on the resources the parent has available. Consider the !Kung and the Hadza.

The Hadza are a group of hunter–gatherers who have been subjects of anthropological study for nearly a century. They live in Tanzania, Africa, southeast of Lake Eyasi, and are travelling foragers who cover a 2,500 km² area, move seasonally, and in total number about 750 people (Hawkes, O'Connell, & Blurton Jones, 1995). They live in a savannah woodland, where they can hunt large game like zebra and impala and can in turn be hunted by lions, leopards, and hyenas. Hadza marry and raise children co-operatively, although they also practise divorce and serial monogamy (Marlowe, 1999).

The !Kung are a group of hunter–gathers who live in northern Botswana and who also live and forage in the African savannah. They hunt big game with poison-tipped spears and live in one spot until hunting opportunities are depleted, at which point they settle in a new area. Compared to the Hadza, the !Kung live in a relatively harsher climate, having to concentrate more of their time finding food and drinkable water.

Unlike the !Kung, who live in harsher conditions, in the Hadza culture, adults discipline their children less, pay more attention to their children, and do not expect their children to contribute significantly to the work of the group until a later age.

table 10.1	**Ecologically Situated Parenting**	
!KUNG	**HADZA**
Harder to find food	Easier to find food
Harder to find water	Easier to find water
Less attentive to children	More attentive to children
Longer birth intervals	Shorter birth intervals
More discipline	Less discipline
Children expected to work more and at an earlier age	Children not expected to work until a later age

The !Kung find fewer calories for a given amount of time spent foraging compared to the Hadza.

There are several respects in which parenting practices differ between the !Kung and the Hadza. The birth interval is shorter for Hadza women than for !Kung women, implying that !Kung women either devote more resources to each child or simply have fewer resources to devote to child rearing. Hadza women have an average of 6.2 children in their lifetime (Blurton Jones, Smith, O'Connell, Hawkes, & Kamuzora, 1992), whereas !Kung women have 4.7 (Howell, 1979).

The !Kung and the Hadza also differ with respect to their responsiveness to their children. Those studying the !Kung see less interaction between parent and child. Parents are less responsive to children's behaviour, children's speech, and children's bids for attention. !Kung parents are also are more likely to use physical punishment and child-directed commands and prohibitions compared to the Hadza (Blurton Jones, Hawkes, & O'Connell, 1996).

The !Kung people are known to be a gentle people, but nonetheless are strict with respect to safety rules for their children. They are relatively intolerant of their children taking risks in order to acquire food or water, instead allowing their children to have complete dependence on their parents. Hadza children both forage for food and retrieve water.

Paternal investment is different between these two groups as well. Hadza men invest less in their own children both directly (holding the child, feeding the child) and indirectly (defending the territory, hunting for large game) compared to !Kung men. Hadza men are more likely than !Kung men to divorce, leaving a single mother to raise their children. They are also relatively more likely to have an extramarital affair (Blurton Jones et al., 1996).

Anthropologists Nicholas Blurton Jones and Kristen Hawkes, who have lived among and studied savannah hunter–gatherer groups, think that differences in parenting styles can be explained by differences in the immediate ecological circumstances rather than being explained by culture or tradition. Because the Hadza live in an environment in which food and water are easier to find, compared to the !Kung environment, a Hadza woman can use her resources to refuel her body and begin her next pregnancy. Her child will be fine without her full-time foraging efforts since the environment is so fertile that the child can forage as well.

The fact that young children can find their own sources of food also lowers the penalty on fathers who desert their families. Thus, the ecological conditions explain the relatively smaller paternal investment in the Hadza. Generally, Blurton Jones and Hawkes make the point that evolutionary considerations, situated in a specific ecological context, can shape behaviours that we might otherwise think of as mere cultural differences. People's behaviours change as costs and benefits change, where costs and benefits are defined with respect to the number of offspring one contributes to the next generation. Therefore, these differences are consistent with an adaptationist interpretation: The parent is optimizing reproductive success by allocating parental investment in the context of the ecological conditions.

Life History Theory

Life history theory is a theory that has recently been applied to humans but was originally conceived to apply generally across animal and even plant species. It is a theory meant to account for and predict the timing of major life events across development, especially dealing with the trade-off in allocating resources to growth and reproduction (Charnov, 1993; Ellis, 2004; Stearns, 1992).

An individual has to allocate a finite supply of resources, time, and energy across the competing goals of physical growth, physical and energetic maintenance, and reproduction. Efforts toward reproduction are further subdivided into mating efforts and parenting efforts. Most species, humans included, have to decide when to switch their life strategies from growth to reproduction. Once one has begun the reproductive period in the life cycle, one must make strategic decisions between allocating resources to existing offspring (parenting) and seeking new mating opportunities. Facultative adaptations in humans are designed to allow people to calibrate their reproductive strategy during development.

Each person must choose whether to mate and reproduce earlier in life or defer reproduction until life circumstances are propitious. Each person must decide whether to commit to monogamy and invest all of his resources in a mate and that mate's

figure 10.1   Life history theory

Life history theory examines how individuals optimally allocate their resources toward their own growth, energetic needs, and reproduction. Reproductive efforts are divided between pursuing new mates and investing in offspring.

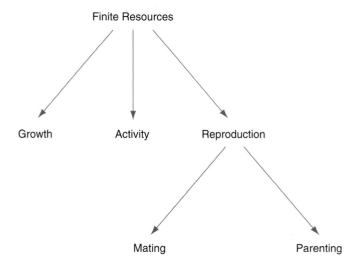

Human societies vary greatly with respect to how much time and other resources fathers invest in their offspring. Which is the best mating strategy to pursue? It depends on what others in your society are doing.

paternal investment
A father's investment in his offspring. Paternal investment does not occur in all species and varies across human societies.

children or to try to maximize the number of mates and children he has. These resource allocation choices are not necessarily conscious; as we will see, the strategy employed involves unconscious physical and physiological changes as well as behavioural changes.

One strategy is to mate relatively later in life, commit to monogamy, and raise children in partnership with one's mate; the other strategy is to mate relatively earlier and more frequently as is beneficial. What is the best strategy? It depends on what everyone else is doing.

Human cultures vary with respect to how much **paternal investment** is common. For humans, paternal investment is not obligatory; it is facultative, which means it is not always necessary for the child's survival (as it is in some species) and thus can vary from culture to culture based on the local conditions (Westneat & Sherman, 1993). If paternal investment has little or no benefit to offspring's survival and quality of life, male abandonment (in pursuit of other mating opportunities) will be favoured as a strategy (Clutton-Brock, 1991). The decision point is described by Hamilton's rule: Paternal investment can occur only in situations where a father can deliver enough resources to his mate and children to make a difference (Trivers, 1972; Westneat & Sherman, 1993; Williams, 1966). In circumstances that are extremely impoverished, where dad cannot hold a job or deliver the resources a family might need, males are less likely to be family men.

Whether one is in a high-investing or a low-investing society affects each person's optimal reproductive strategy. In a high paternal-investment society, a woman's optimal mating strategy is different than it would be in a low paternal-investment society. The fact that women follow different strategies in these two types of societies in turn affects men's optimal reproductive strategies. First let us work through the logic and see how men's and women's strategies are affected and then we will look at the psychological mechanisms (and the evidence for such mechanisms) that would be predicted from this way of thinking.

10.2 Press Pause

Human societies differ with respect to the amount of paternal investment that is common, and this affects women's and men's optimal reproductive strategies.

Here is the logic from a woman's point of view: If you are a woman of reproductive age, you could hold out on reproduction until you have secured the commitment and investment of a man who promises to be a good producer and committed father or you could get started on reproduction as soon as possible, taking advantage of more of your available reproductive years and perhaps securing short-term investments from a number of men. Should you commit to and remain monogamous with your long-term mate, or should you have liaisons which may result in the acquisition of resources that you can use for child rearing and your own maintenance? (Remember, we are not asking a moral question; we are asking which strategy has the maximum payoff in evolutionary terms.)

If a woman is in a society in which paternal investment is the norm, in which men are willing and able to invest in offspring, and in which men tend to marry and remain with their families, a woman's best reproductive strategy is to secure an investing mate. Children in this high-investing society commonly receive biparental care, so a woman would need to secure paternal care for her child in order for that child to be competitive among his peers. A woman is vulnerable to being abandoned by a mate and left with the sole responsibility of raising the children, so she must be careful about choosing a man with whom to bear children. She very much needs to have a mate who believes in her sexual fidelity and thus believes that her children are his children. Straying from the marriage, or doing anything that might create doubt in her mate's mind, is a risk that women in this kind of society cannot, strategically, take.

In contrast, if a woman lives in a society where men do not tend to invest in their offspring or make long-term commitments to their sexual partners, then a woman need not wait for a committed partner in order to begin reproducing (indeed, if she were to do so, she may completely squander her reproductive opportunities). In this situation a woman is better off focussing on the resources that can be harvested from a short-term sexual liaison. She may, overall, garner more resources by having more sexual partners in this kind of society compared to a woman who tries to secure the investment of a monogamous partner. Notice, however, that doing so reduces her attractiveness as a marriage partner, so correctly assessing which society she is in is extremely important to maximizing her reproductive success.

For a woman living in a high-investing society, the optimal strategy may be to postpone reproduction until she secures an investing mate. In other societies, the best strategy may be to take advantage of reproductive opportunities.

10.3 Press Pause

Whether men in a given society are willing and able to invest in offspring affects a woman's optimal life strategy.

Now let us look at the decision from a man's point of view. Is a man's best strategy to be a family man, commit to one woman, and allocate all of his resources to rear her children? (Again, this is a question about evolutionary strategy, *not* a question about morals.) For a man, the family-man strategy can be a very fruitful strategy if his wife's children are also his children. In a society in which women are likely to choose a mate who is a family man and then commit to sexual fidelity, women are likely to be very discriminating, saving themselves for men who really and truly are good husbands and fathers. A man in this society may have to spend considerable time and effort in courtship and may find that his best strategy is to actually commit to and raise the children of his mate. The greatest danger to a man in this situation is to be cuckolded. If he contributes his reproductive efforts to his wife and her children, but there is some significant likelihood that his wife's children are not his children, he is (from an evolutionary point

For a man living in a high-investing society, his best strategy is to enter a committed relationship with the mother of his children. His children will need his contribution to be successful. In a promiscuous society, committing to investing in one woman's children may be too risky.

of view) squandering his resources to promote someone else's genetic interests, and he cannot get those resources back. In a society in which there is relative promiscuity, a man may have greater reproductive success by being a playboy instead of a committed father. In this case, a man might maximize his reproductive success by maximizing his number of sexual partners. In such a society, most of the children (his child's competitors) have only maternal care as they mature, so withholding paternal care from his own children will not be a severe handicap for them compared to their peers.

10.4 Press Pause

A man's optimal life strategy depends on what strategies the women in his environment are following.

EVIDENCE UNCOVERED BECAUSE OF THE LIFE HISTORY PERSPECTIVE

Depending on their social contexts, developing children and adolescents select one strategy or another and develop behaviours, emotions, and physiologies that promote that strategy. Recent research suggests that individuals choose a strategy and that from a very early age children are receptive to information about their social environment that tells them how stable the families, mate-ships, and social relationships around them are. Indeed, there is apparently a critical period in developing children for learning what kind of society, high-investing or low-investing, they are growing up in.

Whether a child's father is absent or present during early to mid-childhood informs them of whether they are likely to be in a high paternal-investment or low paternal-investment society and thus influences their own sexual strategy (Draper & Harpending, 1982). If a father is not in the household, this is a good indication to the developing child that in this local environment a stable adult pair bond is relatively unlikely and therefore not the best strategy. In contrast, if a father is present in the

table 10.2	Women whose fathers were absent or present

WOMEN	
FATHER ABSENT	**FATHER PRESENT**
Likely a low-investing society	Likely a high-investing society
Sexually active earlier	Later puberty
Have more sexual partners	More securely attached
More dominant	Smile more frequently
Better liars	Lower androgen levels

table 10.3	Men whose fathers were absent or present

MEN	
FATHER ABSENT	**FATHER PRESENT**
Likely a low-investing society	Likely a high-investing society
More manipulative	More stable romantic relationships
More competitive	

Whether there is a father present in one's childhood household has implications and developmental consequences. The specific developmental influences are different for men and women.

household, this is a cue that in the local environment enduring adult mate-ships are possible and therefore appear to be a viable life strategy (Kanazawa, 2001).

Males who grow up in father-absent homes show more manipulative behaviour and strive toward dominance more than young men who are raised in a family with the father present (Draper & Harpending, 1982). Dominance is more rewarding in a society in which males can have multiple partners, and in such societies, most males have no children, so failing to show dominance could be costly.

Women who grow up in father-absent homes are sexually active earlier in life, have more sexual partners, and have less stable relationships with their partners compared to women who were reared by both parents in the same home (Draper & Harpending, 1982). Those who have a more promiscuous socio-sexual strategy have less securely attached relationships, and vice versa.

Elizabeth Cashdan (1995) conducted an experiment with young women housed in a dormitory in a North American university and discovered that each could be placed in one of two categories and that a whole suite of personality and physiological traits measured the differences between these categories. One group of women had more sexual partners, were more dominant, had higher self-esteem, had higher androgen levels, and smiled infrequently. The other group of women had fewer sexual partners, displayed traits thought of as more feminine, were more popular, and had lower androgens.

In another study, Cashdan also showed that there was a relationship between people's explicit expectations of the likelihood of securing paternal care and their own reproductive strategy. She found that those women and men who expected that paternal investment was scarce showed a more promiscuous sexual strategy. For example, she would probe men's expectations by creating a continuum. On one end was Bob, who says "A woman can raise children successfully on her own." On the other end of the continuum was Don, who says "Children need to have their father present when they are growing up." (Cashdan, 1993, p. 10). Participants indicated where, along the continuum, their own beliefs lay, and after a series of such questions, Cashdan had a measure of whether this participant was likely to be an investing male. Women participants were asked to respond to a similar questionnaire designed for women in order to assess whether the participant was likely waiting to secure the commitment of an investing male before reproducing. Subsequently, Cashdan gave participants a questionnaire that was designed to measure which sexual strategy the person was actually employing. They had to rate (on a 5-point scale) how often they used various strategies to attract and secure a mate, such as "wore sexy clothes," "paid for dinner," or "showed I wasn't interested in anyone else" (Cashdan, 1993).

The results were clear: Women's expectations about the likelihood of finding an investing male predicted their sexual strategy. If they believed they were likely to secure an investing male, they showed that they had eyes only for their dates, downplayed sexuality, and postponed sexual activity within a relationship. Women who thought it unlikely to secure the commitment of an investing male were more likely to wear sexy clothes, and they generally used more overt sexual strategies to attract the attention of their dates. Conversely, males who thought that high paternal investment was expected tried to attract mates by investing and courting. Men who thought that low paternal investment was expected were more overtly sexual in their mating strategies. In either case, they were maximizing their chances for success in the society they believed themselves to inhabit.

> **10.5 Press Pause**
>
> Once a life strategy is "selected", a whole suite of traits develop together including physiological, personality, and behavioural characteristics.

Girls who grow up in a home with a father experience puberty later than girls who grow up in a home with no father. Later sexual maturation may be one part of the life strategy that is optimal for women in high paternal-investment societies.

PUBERTAL TIMING

Puberty in humans marks the beginning of the end of growth for an individual entering the reproductive years. As is true for other animals, and even plants, humans could either allocate resources to growth for an extended period of time or curtail the growth period in favour of earlier sexual maturation. Human pubertal timing varies between societies and between individuals within a society. Life history theory (Charnov, 1993;

Roff, 1992; Stearns, 1992) describes and explains differences in people's life strategies with respect to the timing of sexual maturation and the conception of offspring.

Following the discovery that father-absent and father-present childhoods lead to differences in a young woman's early sexual behaviour came the prediction that one proximate factor that would mediate these differences was a difference in pubertal timing: Girls who grow up in a home with a father experience puberty later than girls who grow up in a home with no father (Belsky, Steinberg, & Draper, 1991; Moffitt, Caspi, Belsky, & Silva, 1992; Quinlan, 2003), and the earlier in the girl's life her father leaves, the earlier her puberty (Moffitt et al., 1992; Quinlan, 2003; Surbey, 1990).

Furthermore, this prediction framed the different courses of development in terms of a set of factors that would inform a developing child about the social and ecological circumstances she was growing up in: family dynamics, father presence, and the quality of the parent–child relationship. These early factors, in turn, influence the girl's subsequent social development, sexual behaviour, pair-bonding, parenting skills, as well as the timing of first menarche (Belsky et al., 1991).

Researchers suggest that there are evolved psychological mechanisms in the child's first five to seven years of life designed to assess the environment in terms of how easily and predictably available resources are (Belsky et al., 1991). These resources might be very broadly defined to include the reliability of social and familial relationships. This information then guides the child into one reproductive life strategy or the other. In other words, there is a sensitive period for acquiring this kind of information which informs the child's strategy from that point on. Childhoods that includes family stressors such as the frequent or unpredictable scarcity of food, coercive family relationships, and the absence of a father (meaning the father does not live in the home, not that the father works long hours) will lead to earlier puberty, earlier sexual relationships, and more sex partners. Children who have high levels of support in their family and have a father present will show later sexual maturation (Belsky et al., 1991). These authors explain the commitment to one strategy or the other as a decision about resource allocation in terms of information that is available to the child during development. Since these early findings, we now know that a warm and supportive family environment is associated with later puberty (Ellis, McFadyen-Ketchum, Dodge, Pettit, & Bates, 1999; Graber, Brooks-Gunn, & Warren, 1995) and that more frequent interactions with parents during that critical time period also leads to later puberty (Ellis et al., 1999).

Just as men and women are two different morphs of the human genome committed to a particular lifetime strategy of sexual reproduction, so too are these early sexual-maturing and later sexual-maturing people committed to a lifetime strategy. For each group, a whole suite of morphological, physiological, and cognitive adaptations work together toward the same end.

10.6 Press Pause

Social context in early childhood can affect the timing of puberty and sexual maturation.

From the Classroom to the Lab

Some people have suggested that the evidence linking father presence to later puberty does not eliminate a genetic explanation: Those whose fathers are present in early childhood are more likely to be carrying a gene (or genes) that makes the whole suite of behaviours more likely. Design an experiment that could compare the influence of these two factors on later puberty in girls whose fathers are present in early childhood.

LOCAL MORTALITY RATES

Another prediction of life history theory is that local mortality rates may have an affect on a child's development with respect to decisions about growth and reproduction. Any organism has to choose between investing in growth and allocating scarce resources toward the business of reproduction. Any decision to delay reproduction and invest instead in growth carries an inherent risk: The individual might die and leave no off-spring. Human societies vary with respect to local mortality; so the risk of delaying reproduction, while never zero, can vary across human populations (Chisholm, 1999; Stearns, 1992). Might developing children be sensitive to this variable and respond with strategic changes in reproductive timing?

In a large Chicago-area sample, mortality risk and local resource availability pre-dicted the age of first reproduction and number of children born per woman: As local

Mortality rates vary, not just between nations but between neighbourhoods in a given city. These very local mortality rates predict the age at which women have their first child, which is consistent with predictions of life history theory.

mortality rates increased across neighbourhoods, so did the probability of a woman having her first baby before the age of 30 (Wilson & Daly, 1997). In another study, young women in Gloucestershire who had their first baby in their teens were more likely to report a shorter expected lifespan than women who had their first baby after their teenage years (Johns, 2003).

Attachment

SURROGATE NUTRITIVE AND SOFT MOTHERS

In a groundbreaking series of experiments conducted between 1957 and 1963, Harlow compared a baby rhesus monkey's reaction to a wire monkey mother and a terry-cloth monkey mother. As a result of events surrounding World War II, it was becoming clear that a baby separated from his parents would suffer immediate discomfort and lasting effects in terms of social development. Harlow's experiments allowed one to directly compare the effects of the nutritional contribution of the mother and the comforting features of the mother in terms of social development.

Rhesus monkey infants were taken from their mothers shortly after birth and housed with two surrogate mothers. In the first experimental group, the "terry-cloth mother," which was a wire monkey-sized frame covered with soft terry cloth and topped with

Do infants bond with their mothers just because she meets their nutritional needs, or is there something else that infants need from their mothers? Harlow tested infant rhesus monkey's reactions to a wire and a terry-cloth mother.

an artificial monkey-like face, delivered no nutrition, while the "wire mother," which was a hollow, bare wire frame affixed with a very stylized face and a bottle, provided the baby monkey with all of its nutrition. In the second experimental group, the terry-cloth mother provided nutrition via an affixed bottle, while the wire mother did not. Results showed that regardless of the source of nutrition, the baby preferred to spend time close to or on the terry-cloth mother, moving onto the wire mother (in the group where she provided nutrition) only to feed.

Furthermore, if a frightening stimulus was introduced (e.g., a mechanical toy monkey that banged cymbals together), the baby ran to the terry-cloth mother for comfort, regardless of the source of nutrition. If placed in a novel environment with their terry-cloth mothers, the babies would cling to the mother until they felt secure enough to explore. If similarly placed in a new room with the wire mother, they would fail to explore, instead rocking themselves, screaming, or sucking their thumbs.

Later experiments in which a group of baby monkeys would be provided with only a wire mother or a terry-cloth mother showed that those with the wire mother had trouble digesting what they ate and frequently had diarrhea. The results of these studies were important and informative in the context of the prevailing beliefs of the time. The results were a challenge to the empiricist view, espoused by the behaviourists who controlled the field at the time, since their perspective was that food was the reward that animals worked for and the reason that children loved their parents. According to the behaviourist view, the need for food was the primary drive, and the need for a mother's soft comfort and warmth was secondary learned only when the primary drive was satisfied while paired with these features. These experiments showed that there was something about comfort that was different from nutrition. The results were hard to explain without invoking some need for social contact (Harlow, 1962).

attachment The emotional bond a young child feels with another specific person.

John Bowlby was a British psychoanalyst who started thinking about attachment just after World War II. There were a great number of children in England who had been orphaned, and these children were the subject of Bowlby's research.

10.7 Press Pause

Contrary to behaviourist predictions, young rhesus monkeys prefer the comfort of a soft furry mother over a wire mother who provides food.

IMPRINTING AND ATTACHMENT THEORY

Attachment is the word we use in developmental psychology to describe the emotional bond a young child feels with another specific person. Traditionally, attachment has referred to the bond that an infant develops with his or her primary caregiver, but recent research has focussed on the emotional bonds adults have in adult relationships, and this research has used the term *attachment* to describe this adult bond. Is this, in fact, the same psychological process? This is an empirical question that is approachable by research, and so far research suggests that infant attachment and adult attachment may be related and that an individual's experience with infant attachment has an effect on adult relationships.

Attachment theory was developed by John Bowlby, one of the first to write about developmental psychology from an evolutionary perspective. He thought about attachment in terms of function, which at the time was a novel perspective to take, especially when studying something involving emotions. He

Konrad Lorenz studied imprinting in the greylag goose. The imprinting mechanism was designed to allow the baby animal to imprint on its mother, just as attachment in humans allows infants to stay close to their mothers.

even thought about the function of attachment in our ancestral environments and, recall from Chapter 1, coined the term *environment of evolutionary adaptedness*. This was a perspective that advanced his thinking and led to many years of successful and interesting research.

Let us first consider Bowlby's historical context. Bowlby was a British psychoanalyst who started thinking about attachment just after World War II. At this time, there were a great number of children in England who had been orphaned or separated from their parents due to the war, and these children were the subject of Bowlby's research. He observed that these children were depressed, listless, emotionally disturbed, and cognitively delayed. They were aimless and lacked *joie de vivre*. Most significantly, these children did not have normal attachments to anyone (Bowlby, 1953).

Bowlby's thinking about attachment was influenced by ethologists, who understood imprinting in some bird species such as the greylag goose (Lorenz, 1952). Konrad Lorenz studied imprinting, the developing attachment between an offspring and (typically) its mother, seen in specific species. In the bird species that Lorenz studied, the imprinting mechanism was designed to allow the baby animal to imprint on its mother, and this was accomplished by drawing its attention to nearby movement, among other features likely to identify the chick's mother.

Some commentaries on this mechanism have noted that this means that the mechanism is not really designed to imprint on the baby's mother but is designed to imprint on the first thing that moves. Think about this for a moment: The imprinting mechanism was selected for because its result is that the infant stays near its mother. How could this come about in the environment in which the developing chick evolved? The chick would need to use a cue that was available in that environment. Clearly a DNA test was out of the question as a source of information on maternal identity. What cues might have been available to identify the mother? In the environment in which the greylag gosling evolved, "mother" and "the first thing I see move" were almost always one and the same, and that is why the mechanism was selected for. This heuristic is not infallible, especially in laboratory situations where an experimenter tries to find a way to trick the mechanism, but this does not mean that the imprinting mechanism is not designed to imprint on the mother: It was selected for because the design allowed the chick to stay close to its mother.

Ethologists had a tradition of thinking of behaviour in functional terms and in an evolutionary context, and Bowlby followed this tradition. Attachment psychology, according to Bowlby's theory, serves the two functions of keeping the infant safe and allowing for exploration. Infants use their caregiver (usually their mothers but possibly a grandparent, aunt, father, or other reliable adult) as a secure base. Because the caregiver is there, the infant feels secure and can explore the environment. The infant will return to the caregiver if he is hurt, scared, or disoriented. Just like imprinting, attachment was selected for because it increased the safety and hence survival of its bearer.

10.8 Press Pause

Attachment is functional: It calibrates the balance between a child's exploration and his or her safety. Attachment is analogous to imprinting seen in some species.

Bowlby was thinking of attachment in functional terms and in terms of the evolutionary context of the species. He considered how attachment would have served the developing child and hence how attachment might have been selected for in our ancestors' environment.

Mary Ainsworth began her collaboration with Bowlby in 1950, as his student. She thought deeply about attachment theory, set out to find a way to test and do research on attachment theory, and developed the strange situation task to study the development of attachment. This task is still one of the tools used to study and measure the development of attachment. Based on Bowlby's idea that an attached infant uses his parent as a secure base, and on her observations of infants and mothers together, Ainsworth concluded that two factors were key in assessing the quality of the child's attachment:

table 10.4 The Strange Situation Task

EPISODE	DESCRIPTION	DURATION	OF INTEREST
1	Caregiver, experimenter, and baby enter experiment room. Caregiver sits. Experimenter leaves while baby plays with toys.	30 seconds	
2	Caregiver and baby are in experiment room. Baby can explore. Caregiver is not to initiate contact but can respond to baby.	3 minutes	Baby's exploration and use of parent as secure base
3	Stranger enters the room, sits quietly, then talks to caregiver, then tries to interact with baby.	3 minutes	Reaction to stranger
4	Mother leaves baby alone with stranger. Stranger may try to comfort baby if needed.	Up to 3 minutes	Reaction to separation; reaction to stranger's attempts to comfort
5	Caregiver returns. Stranger leaves. Caregiver may try to comfort baby if needed.	Up to 3 minutes	Reaction to reunion and caregiver's attempts to comfort
6	Parent leaves infant alone.	Up to 3 minutes	Reaction to separation
7	Stranger returns and greets the infant. Stranger may try to comfort baby if needed.	Up to 3 minutes	Whether the infant can be quieted and comforted by stranger
8	Caregiver returns. Stranger leaves. Caregiver may try to comfort baby if needed.	3 minutes	Reaction to reunion and caregiver's attempts to comfort

Source: Reprinted from *Ethnology and Sociobiolgy*, Vol. 6/Issue 4, Martin Daly, Margo Wilson, Child abuse and other risks of not living with both parents, page 14, Copyright 1985, with permission from Elsevier.

(a) how effectively the baby used his caregiver as a home base and (b) how the infant behaved when the caregiver was separated from and then reunited with the infant. This was the basis of the strange situation task.

In the strange situation task, the infant comes into the unfamiliar laboratory room with his parent. The new room is full of interesting toys. After the experimenter leaves the child and caregiver alone together, the experimenter observes (e.g., via a one-way mirror) the mother and infant together to see whether the infant uses the parent as a secure base. Next, a "stranger" (the experimenter or confederate) enters the room and chats with the caregiver. The experimenter is interested in the infant's reaction to the stranger. Then the caregiver leaves, and the experimenter notes whether the child is distressed by this and how the infant reacts to this separation and to the stranger's attempts to comfort him. Next the parent returns and the stranger leaves. At this point the experimenter is very interested in how the infant reacts to being reunited with his parent. Then the parent leaves and the infant is all alone in the room. The experimenter notices how the infant reacts to this separation. Then the stranger re-enters the room and tries to comfort the infant; the experimenter observes the infant's reaction. Finally the caregiver returns, and the experimenter observes the infant's reaction to this final reunion (Ainsworth, 1973).

INNOVATIVE RESEARCH METHOD

10.9 Press Pause

Mary Ainsworth created the strange situation task, a standardized way for researchers to assess attachment in developing children.

More recently, an instrument called the Attachment Q-sort has been developed in order to improve versatility when gathering data. A researcher can use this tool in an in-home observational situation, which makes more families accessible to research and increases the age-range of eligible children. The researcher has a set of cards and, during the observation, sorts them into piles ranging from "most like" to "least like." The cards describe behaviours associated with secure attachment, such as "Child readily shares with mother or lets her hold things if asked to," and behaviours associated with insecure attachment, such as "When child returns to mother after playing, he is sometimes fussy for no clear reason." Results are concordant with the results from the strange situation task, so the Attachment Q-sort is considered a reliable and versatile alternative to the strange situation task for assessing attachment styles (Vaughn & Waters, 1990).

Based on observations during one of these assessments, children are assigned an attachment style. They are said to have one of the following: secure attachment, insecure/resistant attachment, insecure/avoidant or disorganized/disoriented attachment. A securely attached child is one who explores the toys while his mother is in the room, reacts with distress when his mother leaves, and is happy and consolable when she returns. The insecurely attached child is clingy and unwilling to separate from his mother in order to explore the new environment. The child is deeply distressed when his mother leaves and is inconsolable when his mother returns. He will either solicit and then reject his mother's comfort (insecure ambivalent) or avoid his mother altogether upon her return (insecure avoidant). A disorganized/disoriented child shows behaviour that is confusing and contradictory. This category was not defined by Ainsworth but was described by researchers who followed her work and could not categorize these children with Ainsworth's original categories (Main & Hesse, 1990; Main & Solomon, 1990). These children did not seem to have a strategy for dealing

table 10.5	Attachment Types
TYPE	**DESCRIPTION**
Secure	High-quality, positive relationship with caregiver. In the strange situation task, the baby may be upset when the caregiver leaves and quickly comforted when she returns. The caregiver, when present, is used as a secure base for exploring the new environment.
Insecure / Resistant	This infant is clingy, staying close to the caregiver rather than exploring the new environment. In the strange situation task, this baby is very upset when left alone with the stranger and not easily soothed when the caregiver returns.
Insecure / Avoidant	The infant is indifferent to the caregiver or may avoid them. In the strange situation task, the baby does not use the caregiver as a secure base, is not upset when the caregiver leaves, and is indifferent when the caregiver returns. The baby can be as easily comforted by caregiver or stranger.
Disorganized	This baby has no consistent way to cope with novelty. The baby may appear confused or disoriented.

with the distress of being separated from their mothers. They may have even appeared to be disoriented.

In much of the Western world, children who are securely attached as infants grow into adults who have secure adult relationships and are more socially skilled than children who are insecurely attached. Those who were securely attached infants have better, more stable peer relationships as children too (Troy & Sroufe, 1987). And compared to insecurely attached infants, those who are securely attached will grow to have better peer relationships and romantic relationships as adolescents (Collins, Henninghausen, Schmit, & Srouf, 1997).

10.10 Press Pause

> Measures of attachment early in life predict some adult outcomes, especially the quality of adult relationships.

Emotional Development More Generally

Attachment theory touches on the development of fear and anxiety. Some research has revealed the developmental trajectory of fear and anxiety as well as the development of other positive and negative emotions. In the first few months of life, there is no clear evidence that infants feel fear (Witherington, Campos, & Hertenstein, 2001). The earliest evidence of fear in infants appears at 6 or 7 months of age: As infants' attachment to their primary caregivers grow, their fear of strangers becomes evident (Camras, Malatesta, & Izard, 1991). In the first few months of life, an infant can be comforted by a stranger, but once the child is attached to his mother, the arrival of a stranger scares him rather than comforts him (Bronson, 1972). This fear of strangers continues to intensify until about the age of 2 years. Separation anxiety, which is related to performance in the strange situation paradigm, emerges around the age of 8 months. This fear increases between 8 and 15 months, and then decreases thereaf-

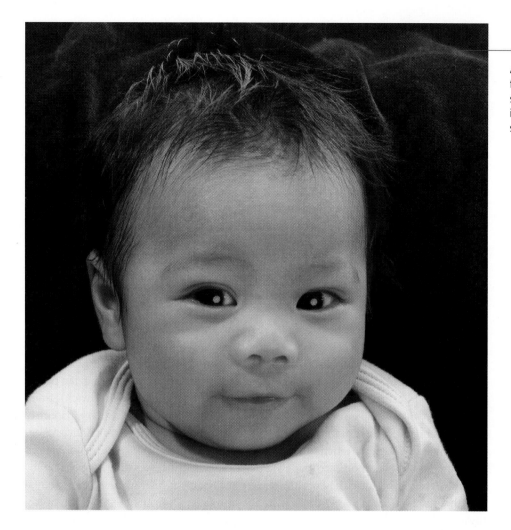

At 6 weeks of age, a baby finally gives her first true social smile: a smile that is actually directed at someone else.

ter, and this pattern of development of separation anxiety has been observed cross-culturally (Kagan, 1976).

Very young infants apparently feel positive emotions and wish to share these positive emotions with others. Social smiles, that is, smiles directed at other people, are evident as early as 6 weeks of age (Sroufe, 1995). Clearly, this exchange is rewarding to the caregiver, who has been attending to the infants' every need for 6 weeks; the adult who is the recipient of a social smile reacts with delight (Camras et al., 1991). Infants smile at people much more than they smile at other objects, but they do smile at objects that capture their interest (Ellsworth, Muir, & Hains, 1993). Infants also smile if they can influence their world: Compared to infants who hear music that starts on its own, infants who can pull a string to start music smile more (Lewis, Alessandri, & Sullivan, 1990). By 7 months, infants smile more at familiar people than unfamiliar people and indeed respond with delight when their parents show playfulness and joy (Weinberg & Tronick, 1994).

Finally, negative emotions similarly show significant development over the first year of life. First, infants show general distress, primarily in response to hunger, pain, or discomfort. This distress results in a grimaced face and loud cry. At the age of 2 months, infants show distinct facial expressions of sadness and anger in some contexts (Izard, Hembree, & Huebner, 1987). Researchers in the area tend to believe that early nega-

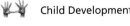

tive emotions are not differentiated: Distress, pain, and anger are not distinct but are expressed and perhaps experienced as the same in very young infants (Camras, 1992; Oster, Hegley, & Nagel, 1992). This appears to be adequately functional as it is effective in eliciting a parental response to alleviate the discomfort.

Parents, Alloparents, Siblings, and Peers

PARENTAL LOVE AND INVESTMENT

Believe it or not, until relatively recently, psychologists did not have a good theory about why parents love their children. Parental investment occurs cross-culturally. It is a human behaviour that is deeply consuming, as a parent will make a tremendous investment in a child, whether that investment is measured in terms of calories, time, or money. However, this clearly costly behaviour did not attract the research efforts of psychologists. Apparently instinct blindness made parental love seem so right, so natural, that it did not need an explanation.

parental investment
An investment by a parent in an individual offspring that increases that offspring's chance of surviving and reproducing at the cost of the parent's ability to invest in other offspring.

Parental-investment theory (Trivers, 1972) is a theory that stresses the evolutionary basis of many aspects of parental behaviour, including the extensive investment parents make in their offspring. Trivers defined **parental investment** as an investment by a parent in an individual offspring that increases that offspring's chance of surviving and reproducing at the cost of the parent's ability to invest in other offspring. If a parent gives her child calories (whether via lactation or by handing him a sandwich), those calories are not available for the parent to give to another child or for the parent to consume and use in later mating or parenting efforts. Allocation of parental investment is, for any individual, a tremendously important strategic decision in terms of natural selection, and the decisions are made via psychological processes that were shaped by natural selection because they optimized our ancestors' *inclusive fitness*. The parental love that humans feel, as well as the irritation and frustration that a parent might feel toward a child, are parts of psychological processes that calibrate the level of parental investment a parent is willing to give a particular child.

Contemporary environments with higher resources and less risks are associated with more warmth and higher levels of care on the part of both mothers and fathers compared to environments with low or unpredictable levels of resources (MacDonald, 1992). Parents with low socio-economic status (SES) are more likely than higher SES parents to use an authoritarian and punitive child-rearing style. Higher SES mothers are more likely to use a style that is accepting and democratic, and they use more language with their children. In other words, the psychological mechanisms that calibrate the level of parental investment, possibly mediated by parental love, are responsive to resource levels in contemporary societies as well.

PARENT–OFFSPRING CONFLICT AND ITS IMPLICATIONS FOR CHILD REARING

inclusive fitness
One's evolutionary fitness (number of viable offspring) plus the number of viable relatives one has, discounted by the relatedness of those relatives. For example, one gets full credit for oneself, half credit for offspring or siblings, and a quarter credit for nieces or nephews.

Robert Trivers, writing in the neo-Darwinian tradition in the 1960s and early 1970s, described an inherent conflict between parent and offspring. From a parent's point of view, the parent is equally related to each offspring and would like to share resources equally among them. This equality is overridden only by differences in the extent to which parental investment will translate to greater **inclusive fitness**. For example, one offspring may show greater need: If one child is hungry and the last piece of food would save her life, then the parent would prefer to feed that child instead of the child who has just eaten. Alternatively, if one of the parents' children is old enough, able-bodied, and

Until relatively recently, psychologists did not have a good theory about why parents love their children. Instinct blindness obscured the fact that there was a phenomenon that needed to be explained.

can secure his own meal, the parent would rather feed the child who is more dependent on parental investment.

Conflict arises because the child's point of view is different from the parents' with respect to the favoured course of action. The child's relatedness to his sibling is only 0.5, which means that for any gene is his body, the probability of that same allele being in his sister's genome by virtue of common descent (having the same parents) is 0.5. The child would agree that if his sister is at death's door and a sandwich would save her, the sandwich should go to her, but the point at which his hunger becomes more urgent than hers differs between the parent and the offspring. The offspring would keep more for himself and share less with his sister than a parent would prefer. This conflict applies to hypothetical siblings who are not yet born or conceived. The parent would like to stop investing in the existing child and start working on the next child (which could mean building up one's own fat stores, or courting, depending on the parent's circumstances) before the existing child is ready to forgo parental resources. **Parent–offspring conflict** results from the fact that the ideal point for decreasing parental investment is not the same from the point of view of the parent and the point of view of the child.

parent–offspring conflict
Conflicts between parents and their offspring that results from the fact that, in our evolutionary history, maximizing each offspring's inclusive fitness would have resulted from different, mutually exclusive, courses of action.

table 10.6	Genetic Relatedness
Self	1.0
Parent, Full Sibling, or Offspring	0.5
Aunt, Uncle, Niece, or Nephew	0.25
Cousin	0.125

Relatedness has an effect on whether altruistic behaviour increases inclusive fitness.

10.11 Press Pause

The optimal moment for a parent's investment to end is different from the points of view of the parent and the offspring.

figure 10.2   Zone of parent–offspring conflict

If Shane is extremely hungry, his brother Billy will agree with their parents that the resources should go to Shane. If Billy is hungrier than Shane, Billy will agree with their parents that the resources should go to him. But the point at which their relative need dictates this switchover differs from Billy's and his parents' point of view, creating the zone of parent-offspring conflict.

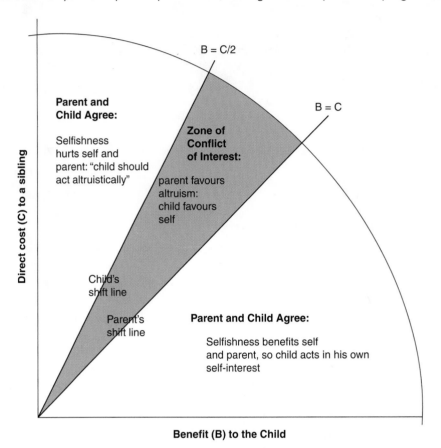

Benefit (B) to the Child

Hamilton's rule

This discrepancy can be quantified when you consider Hamilton's rule, named after British evolutionary biologist W. D. Hamilton, who first articulated the idea. According to this rule, altruistic behaviour toward close family members, including direct parental investment as well as investment in a younger sibling, is favoured by natural selection when the benefit to the recipient discounted by the relatedness between the recipient and the actor is greater than the cost to the actor (Hamilton, 1963).

$$rB > C$$

In the equation above, "B" stands for benefit to the recipient and "C" stands for cost to the actor. These refer to the costs and benefits in terms of reproductive success: how many additional viable offspring the act affords the recipient and how many fewer offspring the act costs the actor. For practical purposes, researchers would need to find a proxy measurement for costs and benefits, so a researcher might measure how many calories (of food or of activity) the action costs the actor and how many calories are delivered to the recipient. Calories can be translated into reproductive success.

figure | 10.3   **Hamilton's rule**

Altruistic behaviour is favoured when the benefit to the recipient discounted by the relatedness between the recipient and the actor is greater than the cost to the actor.

The variable "r" in the equation refers to relatedness. It is mathematically defined as the probability that a gene picked at random from the actor's genome would be the same allele as that of the gene at the same locus in the recipient's genome and that they will be the same because they inherited the gene from a common ancestor (not because that locus is universally the same throughout the species). This probability can be easily estimated for humans: Your relatedness to yourself is 1.0; your relatedness to a parent, full sibling, or your own child is 0.5; your relatedness to an aunt, uncle, niece, or nephew is 0.25; and your relatedness to a cousin is 0.125, for example. This set of relationships was captured by J. B. S. Haldane, who supposedly said "I would lay down my life for two brothers, or eight cousins."

Imagine Mom has a hungry 4-year-old, Billy, a hungry 1-year-old, Shane, and a small pizza. Who should eat the pizza? Mom's relatedness to each of her children is 0.5. If the benefit to each is the same (they are both equally hungry), she will want the pizza to be split equally. If Billy is only slightly hungry but Shane is very hungry, she will give the pizza to Shane because the benefit to him is so much greater than the benefit to Billy. Billy has a different opinion: His relatedness to himself is 1.0, while his relatedness to his brother is only 0.5, so all else equal, he will want to eat pizza until he is not hungry anymore and give Shane whatever is left. This could change if the benefit (B) to Billy and Shane is different. If Billy is only slightly hungry but Shane has been without food for so long that his health is threatened, then the benefit of sharing the pizza with Shane, discounted by his relatedness to Billy, is greater than the cost to Billy: rB > C. So, for both Mom and Billy, there is a point where Billy will sacrifice the pizza to benefit Shane, but the critical thing here is that the point where they reach that position is different, and it is different because Mom is equally related to Billy and Shane, but Billy is twice as "related" to himself as he is to Shane.

IMPLICATIONS FOR THE PSYCHOLOGY OF CHILD REARING

Parents and their children do not have identical best interests and that creates conflict in the household even when children are young: A parent may want his child to share with a sibling when the child would prefer to consume more herself. Trivers pointed out that although children essentially have to comply with their parents' wishes when they are young (because parents are bigger, stronger, and control the food supply), the offspring should not adopt or internalize the parents' wishes and values. Parents are encouraging behaviours that further their own interests, and those interests are different from the child's. If the offspring were "to continue to act out parental wishes that were not in harmony with its own self-interest, it would continue to lower its own inclusive fitness" (Trivers, 1985, p. 164).

Let us step back and consider the implications of this concept, which applies broadly to sexually reproducing species, on human cognitive development. Imagine a cognitive design in which a child has to learn everything—values, tastes, preferences, goals—primarily from his parents, but also from other adults, using a domain-general learning mechanism. It is not outlandish to think that a respected developmental psychologist would suggest this. This idea is at the heart of social learning theory (Bandura, 1977) and gender socialization theory (Bandura & Walters, 1963). But if parents could teach their children to absorb whatever values and motivations they wanted, as these theories predict, there would never be any conflict between parent and child. The parent would simply teach the child to sacrifice everything for his younger sibling and that would be that.

10.12 Press Pause

> An implication of Trivers's theory is that parents should not be able to socialize children to adopt the parents' values.

Differences in Parenting Make Little Difference

Up to this point we have discussed the tremendous contribution that parents make in the upbringing of human children. Clearly, parents make a sizeable investment to the development of children. A child's very survival is completely dependent on the contribution of his or her parents. A separate but related question is whether differences in parenting, given species-typical circumstances, make a big difference. Can a parent create a particularly advantaged child by providing early exposure to reading, gymnastics, or music? Can a parent instill values of hard work or generosity by example and explication? If we exclude extreme circumstances outside of normal parenting, such as cases of abuse and neglect, then recent evidence suggests that parenting within a broad range of normal parenting makes little difference in terms of the child's development, including personality traits, political values, and language.

According to Sandra Scarr, this finding should be expected. Evolution should not permit environmental factors that are easily modified to have an effect on traits that are important for survival and reproductive success (Scarr, 1992; Scarr, Weinberg, & Waldman, 1993). Aspects of emotional, social, and cognitive development that are important for an individual's success should be resilient to differences in the environment as long as those differences are more or less within a normal, species-typical range of environments, and this includes parental input. It would be detrimental if a very specific, narrow range of parental behaviours were necessary for the viability of the child, according to this view. Based on this perspective, Scarr proposes the idea of **good-enough parenting**. She suggests that it is not necessary to be a super parent in order to bring up a healthy, functional child. Moreover, it is not even clear that extraordinary parental contributions make a measureable difference.

good-enough parenting
Parenting that is sufficient to rear viable children. The term is based on Scarr's idea that extraordinary parenting makes little difference to the child's outcome compared to good-enough parenting.

WHO SOCIALIZES CHILDREN?

Parental influence on the socialization of personality traits and values is almost negligible. Decades ago, Eleanor Maccoby and John Martin reviewed the research on **socialization**, that is, the process believed to lead a child to acquire the beliefs, values, language, skills, and, in essence, the "culture" of his parents in order to become a member of that culture himself. They realized that parental effects were small or absent and concluded that "there is very little impact of the physical environment that parents provide for the children and very little impact of parental characteristics (Maccoby & Martin, 1983, p. 82). Since that time, others have also failed to find evidence that differences in parenting have an effect on individual differences in offspring. As adults, adoptive siblings will be no more similar than strangers, and biological siblings reared in the same home will not be very similar but will still be more similar than adoptive siblings. Even monozygotic twins reared together will not be noticeably more similar than identical twins reared apart (Bouchard, Lykken, McGue, Segal, & Tellegen, 1990; Plomin & Daniels, 1987; Scarr, 1992). Judith Harris (1995) made the startling claim that kids would turn out essentially the same if they had different parents but the same school and neighbourhood.

This failure to find evidence that parents are the agents of socialization flies in the face of socialization theory but makes sense following Trivers's idea of parent–offspring conflict. A developing child should not be infinitely malleable and open to internalizing whatever values his parents want him to. He has aspirations that are different from theirs, and he should have cognitive mechanisms that preserve his self-interest.

Although her work is still considered controversial within the field of developmental psychology, Harris proposed that in addition to acquiring information about how to conform to one's culture, developing children have to learn about their relative status and relative attractiveness. This information, Harris argues, is much more reliably delivered from peers than from family. A boy cannot judge his relative status by the fact that he can physically dominate his younger brother or that his older brother and father can physically dominate him; he relies on peer interactions to judge his own relative status.

One longitudinal study revealed personality differences between early maturing boys (who were larger than their peers during adolescence) and late maturing boys (who were smaller relative to their peers): The early maturing boys were less anxious and more poised than their peers, and they scored higher on measures of dominance even as adults, when the relative size of the two groups had equalized. In fact, these early maturers were more likely to have executive positions in their professions, regardless of their ultimate adult height (Jones, 1957). Similarly, although we have known for some time that, for males, adult height is associated with salary, recent evidence suggests that height during adolescence is a better predictor of adult salary than either adult height or childhood height (Persico, Postlewaite, & Silverman, 2004). The idea is that, at least for males, the critical period for the development of personality traits associated with dominance is adolescence (Harris, 2005).

socialization The process believed to lead a child to acquire the beliefs, values, language, skills, and, in essence, the "culture" of his parents in order to become a member of that culture himself.

Judith Harris proposes that children are socialized in their childhood and adolescent peer groups and that parental influence is minimal. This surprising claim is consistent with Trivers' parent–offspring conflict theory.

Peer Influence

Harris suggests that although children need and depend on both parents and peers for normal social development, the absence of peers would be a greater challenge to normal development than the absence of parents (assuming that physical and nutritional needs are taken care of). As an example, experiments with rhesus monkeys show that the social behaviour of individuals raised without peers is more abnormal than that of individuals raised without parents (Harlow & Harlow, 1975). Harris also cites the example of six Jewish children who spent their first three years together in a concentration camp with no stable adult caregiver. After their experience in the camp, the children came to England to live and were studied by Anna Freud. They reportedly grew to be typical adults, leading functional lives, presumably because they had the stability of each other as peers in their earliest years (Hartup, 1983).

Trivers's insight regarding parent and offspring conflict led him to some pretty radical predictions regarding peer influence. At the time, the conventional wisdom and widespread belief was that a developing child received their personality traits and values from their parents via some form of "learning" or "socialization." (People did not really spell out what that process was, believing that socialization was self-evident.) But Trivers realized that this was unlikely since the child and the parent have somewhat conflicting goals, and the child should not absorb the parent's values or let these behaviours shape his or her personality, precisely because the parent's and child's interests are in conflict. The parent could compel the child to serve the interests of his younger siblings at the cost of his own reproductive success, or the child might allow the parent

⠿⠿ Developmental Milestones

Social Context Milestones

Age	Skills
Birth to 5 Years	Stability of early social relationships and food availability affect later life strategies (Belsky et al., 1991).
6 Weeks	Infants produce the first "social smile" in response to another person.
2 Months	Infants show some distinct facial expressions: sadness, happiness, and anger.
6 Months to 3 Years	This is the critical period in the development of attachment. Fear of strangers grows as attachment to caregivers grows.
7 Months	Infants smile more at familiar than unfamiliar people.
8 Months	Separation anxiety begins to be evident and increases to the age of 2 years.
9–18 Months	The strange situation task is an effective assessment of attachment style.
1–5 Years	The Attachment Q-sort is an effective assessment of attachment style.
Early to Mid-Childhood	A father's presence or absence can inform the developing life strategy.
10–14 Years	Pubertal timing can be affected by the presence or absence of a father in earlier childhood.
Teen Years	These are important years for peer socialization, according to Judith Harris.

to broker his marriage to further a political aim or make a profit instead of seizing the right to pick his own mate.

Harris instead proposes "group socialization theory" in which peers and siblings, especially acting in groups, have a measurable effect on the personality development of children. According to this view, socialization takes place in peer groups, especially sex- and age-segregated peer groups that form from middle childhood through adolescence. In adolescence these groups are also segregated by ability and interest. Once children identify with such a peer group, they adopt the group's attitudes and norms of behaviour. Behaviours learned at home will only be transmitted to the group if that behaviour is shared by and approved by most of the group members. Ultimately, the

⫸ Assessing Social Impact

Facebook: Good or Bad?

If Facebook were a country, it would be the third largest country in the world, after China and India. Facebook has hundreds of millions of active users. Adolescents and college and university students make up about 40 per cent of users. How often do you visit Facebook? About half of its active members visit every day. The average user has 130 friends and spends 55 minutes on Facebook each day. The amount of time people spend on social-networking sites is increasing at three times the rate of Internet use generally.

Is this new and heavily used social platform a great opportunity for building self-esteem and alleviating loneliness or a tempting trap leading to isolation, addiction, and social dysfunction? Research psychologists have recently become interested in finding ways to answer this question. Danah Boyd of Microsoft Research New England and Nicole Ellison of Michigan State University define social-networking sites for us: (a) they provide a forum where users create a public (or semi-public) profile, (b) they create a list of "friends" or other users who have privileged access to their information, and (c) they can view information and follow links, rapidly moving about the information pages that their friends list gives them access to. And thoughts on whether social networking is good or bad has changed in the ever-so-brief history of the phenomenon (Boyd & Ellison, 2007).

Initially, psychological research was suggesting that online social time might be harmful. As social psychologist John Cacioppo at the University of Chicago observes, early research regarding Internet use showed a correlation between time spent on the Internet and loneliness (Cacioppo & Patrick, 2008). The early view was that online socializing was somehow not real socializing. One was unlikely to meet someone they met online in person, and they probably did not have accurate information about who that person actually was to begin with.

More recently, researchers have published a study that considers more factors. Kaveri Subrahmanyam and Gloria Lin,

working at California State University, interviewed 192 high-school students about their online social behaviour. These students also completed psychological tests, including an assessment of loneliness. They found that just considering time spent socializing online would not allow you to predict loneliness, social anxiety, or depression (Subrahmanyam & Lin, 2007).

Shima Sum at the University of Sydney looked at the use of social networks among older adults. She found that using social networking was an effective way to diminish loneliness and isolation but only if one's online relationships were also offline relationships. In contrast, when people in her study attempted to use social networking in order to make new connections and create new friendships, the result was more loneliness, not less. Similarly, Laura Freberg at the California Polytechnic State University, who studied college students' use of social networking, found that those who had face-to-face relationships with their online "friends" became more socially connected, while students who attempted to alleviate loneliness on these sites became more lonely. The best use of social networks, according to this research, was in support of real social connections (Sum, Mathews, Hughes, & Campbell, 2007).

Charles Steinfield, Nicole Ellison, and Cliff Lampe at Michigan State University recently completed a study suggesting that the advantages of Facebook use might extend beyond virtual socializing. They followed 477 Facebook users for a year and discovered that Facebook time was positively correlated with an increase in social benefits. These benefits were measureable even offline: People became more socially skilled and felt more socially confident when interacting in person (Steinfield, Ellison, & Lampe, 2008).

Social networking technology is new, and its rapid emergence into people's daily social lives has created an unprecedented new kind of socializing. The truth is, hundreds of millions of people are engaging in the largest social psychology experiment ever. It may be some time before we understand the effects on our social psychology.

child's peer group creates the children's culture by selecting and rejecting elements of adult culture and by inventing novel elements (Harris, 1995). Peers influence the development of everything from personality traits to children's culture (songs and stories) to accents and speech mannerisms.

Notice, however, that this does not mean that culture is lost and created anew with each generation. Children's traditions can be passed on for centuries. Indeed, British children today play games that children were playing in the same location during the time of the Romans, but children's culture is passed not from parent to child but from slightly older children to slightly younger children (Opie & Opie, 1969). Nyansongo children in Africa have a vocabulary used to describe intimate body parts although the entire vocabulary is forbidden for adults to use or for children to use in front of adults. The vocabulary passes from older children to younger children, never from adults to children (LeVine & LeVine, 1988).

ALLOPARENTS

Alloparents are all of the people who contribute to the upbringing of a child other than the child's parents. You might be familiar with the African proverb "It takes a village," recently popularized by former United States First Lady (now Secretary of State) Hillary Clinton. Alloparenting has likely been a significant factor in child-rearing in humans (Hrdy, 1999). In traditional societies today, mothers rely on the help of others, especially female family members and close female friends, in order to provide their children with consistent childcare. There is also evidence of indirect support on the part of non-family members for mothers with young children: Among the Ache, who are hunter–gatherers in the forests of Paraguay, mothers of young children forage less, but their deficit is made up for by the foraging of other women, especially relatives (Hill & Hurtado, 1996). In traditional societies, most of the childcare responsibilities fell on the mother and her female relatives, and this pattern is true today (Hetherington, Henderson, & Reiss, 1999) although in the information age, fathers are playing an increasing role (Cabrera, Tamis-LeMonda, Bradley, Hofferth, & Lamb, 2000; Collins, Maccoby, Steinberg, Hetherington, & Bornstein, 2000).

GRANDPARENTS

Also important to the upbringing of children, today and in the EEA, are grandparents. Several theorists have even proposed that older women have specialized adaptations (such as menopause) that allow for an extended lifespan and increased reproductive success via grandparental investment (Alexander, 1974; Hamilton, 1966; Hawkes, O'Connell, & Blurton Jones, 1997; O'Connell, Hawkes, & Blurton Jones, 1999). Childbirth is dangerous and risky, and the probability of successful pregnancy and childbirth decreases as a woman ages: Pregnancy in older women is associated with higher miscarriage rates, low birth weight, stillborn birth, and maternal death in child-

alloparents All of the people who contribute to the upbringing of a child other than the child's parents.

A woman who is past her own reproductive years can increase her fitness by grandparenting. The presence of a grandmother does, indeed, contribute to the success of grandchildren.

birth (Kline, Stein, & Susser, 1989). Menopause marks a shift in strategy from parenting to grandparenting. Most women in contemporary and traditional societies can expect to live more than 20 years beyond their last childbirth and can increase their inclusive fitness by investing in genetic relatives, including grandchildren. Research focussing on the Hadza, a traditional foraging society in Africa, provides evidence that the presence of a grandmother does, indeed, contribute to the success of grandchildren (Hawkes et al., 1997; O'Connell et al., 1999). In particular, a grandmother's foraging provided crucial nutrition for young children who were no longer nursing but who were not yet eating adult food. In families in which the mother was still nursing a younger sibling, the health of the weaned child was predicted by the foraging of the grandmother (Hawkes et al., 1997). Clearly this would increase the inclusive fitness of the grandmother since it would reduce the birth interval of the mother. She was free to wean her older child at a younger age, trusting that his grandmother would contribute to his nutrition, allowing the mother to become pregnant with her next child.

Step-Parents

A family that includes a step-parent would not have been uncommon in the EEA. Mortality rates were high due to famine, warfare, and disease, so losing one parent during childhood would not have been terribly uncommon. If a woman with young children lost her mate, finding a new mate who might invest in her and her offspring would have been a good strategy.

figure 10.4 **Child homicide committed by genetic fathers vs. stepfathers**

Stepchildren are more likely to be abused than children in families with no step-parent, whether we are talking about battery, sexual abuse, or even murder. Step-parents incur tremendous costs with no gain in inclusive fitness.

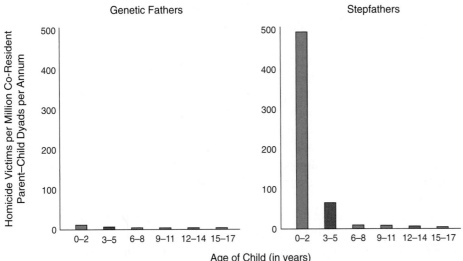

Parenting is difficult: It involves the tremendous sacrifice of resources to an individual who will never reciprocate in kind. A step-parent would not be expected to invest in stepchildren to the extent that the child's biological parent invests since investing in this unrelated child does not advance the step-parent's reproductive interests directly. As might be expected from this perspective, a study focussing on middle-class stepfamilies in the United States revealed that only 53 per cent of stepfathers and 25 per cent of stepmothers report feeling any "parental feelings" for their stepchildren (Duberman, 1975). Stepfathers spend significantly less time with their stepchildren, about three hours a week less, than with their biological children (Anderson, Kaplan, & Lancaster, 1999) and are less likely to help their stepchildren with homework than they are their biological children (Anderson et al., 1999).

The pattern is paralleled in traditional societies: A study conducted among the Hadza showed that stepfathers cared for biological children more than stepchildren, as measured by the amount of time spent together: Biological fathers spent more time near their children; communicated with their children more; and held, fed, and cleaned their children more than stepfathers did. And although biological fathers spent more time playing with their children, in this study, a stepfather was not once seen to play with a stepchild. Stepfathers also reported weaker feelings for stepchildren than for their own children (Marlowe, 1999).

The cognitive machinery that allows us to subjugate our interests completely to another individual's are, in fact, adaptations that will be passed to the next generation by the genes that underlie these cognitive adaptations. But from here it is easy to see that trouble would be predicted in step-parent and stepchild relationships, and indeed, such trouble is found in studies of stepfamilies. Research motivated from this evolutionary analysis has revealed that the rate of murders committed by stepfathers against children residing with them is hundreds of times higher than the rate for fathers against their biological children (Daly & Wilson, 1988, 1996), and children are 40 times more likely to be abused if they live with a step-parent than if they live in a home with two biological parents (Daly & Wilson, 1985). Children under the age of 2 are 100 times more likely to be killed if they live in a home with a step-parent compared to children living with two biological parents (Daly & Wilson, 1988). Stepchildren are more likely to be abused than children in families with no step-parent, whether we are talking about battery, sexual abuse, or even murder (Daly & Wilson, 1988). Furthermore, when step-parents are physically abusive in the home, they are likely to be abusive only to their stepchildren and not to their own offspring. One study, for example, showed that abuse was directed toward the stepchild exclusively in 19 out of 22 abusive families (Daly & Wilson, 2005).

It is worth noting that this research, which is largely based on data that are part of the public record, benefitted greatly from an evolutionary perspective. Originally, the public record seemed puzzling because it seemed to say that the greatest risk of violence that a child faces is from his parent, which, if true, would be a critical challenge to our beliefs about evolution by natural selection. In fact, because evolutionary psychologists Martin Daly and Margo Wilson looked at these data from an adaptationist perspective, they discovered that it was not genetic relatives who were doing violence to children; it was step-parents.

Please note that it is not the case that most step-parents are doing violence to their stepchildren; rather it is the case that most children who are suffering violence in their homes are suffering at the hands of step-parents. The distinction is important. Furthermore, Daly and Wilson do not propose that people have any adaptations that are designed for harming stepchildren. (This is in contrast to male lemur monkeys and lions, who systematically kill all existing infants when they join a female.) Rather, abuse by step-parents may be triggered by the demands, complaints, and ingratitude that all children manifest and that would otherwise irritate the biological parent to the point of aggression if not for their adaptation compelling nurturing parenting behaviours. When step-parents do invest in stepchildren and form an emotional bond with them, it is likely due to deliberate attempts on the part of the step-parent to create that relationship rather than due to the naturally occurring relationship that forms between biologically related parents and children.

10.13 **Press Pause**

Children who have step-parents are at far greater risk of abuse than those who do not.

LETTING DAD KNOW HE IS NOT A CUCKOLD

An infant's first job is to attract the investment of caregivers by being cute and sometimes loud. As mentioned earlier, one of the most serious dangers to a man in a high paternal-investment society is to be cuckolded: to unknowingly raise another man's children when he invests in his wife's offspring. One job that an infant has is to solicit parental care at least from the mother and, if possible, from the father as well. Consistent with this concern, research shows that newborn babies are said to resemble their

At the age of 1 year, photos of babies can be matched with photos of their fathers more easily than they can be matched with photos of their mothers.

fathers more than they are said to resemble their mothers. Furthermore, it is the mother who is more likely than the father to allege that the newborn baby looks like the father, presumably in order to reassure the father that he is, indeed, the baby's father. Maternal relatives are also twice as likely to say that the baby resembles his or her father than his or her mother (Daly & Wilson, 1982). Surprisingly, one study suggests that babies might be making a special effort to solicit resources from dad, who might be uncertain about his relationship to the baby, as opposed to mom, who is certain of her relationship to the baby. At the age of 1 year, photos of babies can be matched with photos of their fathers more easily than they can be matched with photos of their mothers (Christenfeld & Hill, 1995).

Recent research also provides evidence that men are sensitive to their own resemblance to a child, which might be expected if men have psychological mechanisms designed to monitor their own risk of cuckoldry. This research was accomplished through the use of morphing technology. Researchers assembled a set of electronic pictures of young children. Then they had men and women participants come to the lab. Each participant was photographed digitally, and then, without the participant's knowledge, researchers morphed the photograph of the participant with photographs of children selected at random. Then researchers presented the participants with pictures of children who looked a bit like them and children who did not.

During the test phase for each trial the participant would be presented with five photographs of children, four of which were unmodified and one that resembled the participant. The participant was asked questions such as "Which child would you punish more severely if he damaged something valuable of yours?" and "Which child would you be more likely to adopt?" Men were biased: They were more likely than chance to choose the child that resembled them in response to the positive questions and less likely than chance to choose the resembling child in response to the negative questions. Women did not show any bias with respect to the children who resembled them (Platek, Burcg, Panyavin, & Wasserman, 2002). This finding is consistent with the idea that men, and not women, may have evolved psychological processes designed to protect them against cuckoldry.

10.14 **Press Pause**

> Babies and moms may have adaptations designed to convince dads that they are not cuckolds.

Birth Order

Birth order is one's age rank (eldest, youngest, middle) among siblings. Birth order may be a significant social contextual factor that has an effect on the developing personality. Although his conclusions are quite controversial in the field of psychology, historian Frank Sulloway used different methods to research and test hypotheses on the relationship between birth order and personality.

Sulloway proposes that birth order has an enduring and formative effect on a person's personality. In humans, as in several bird species, the first-born child (or in some cases the first-born son) will inherit many or all of the parents' resources. This is because the home territory or the family home is a resource that is practically indivisible: If you split the family farm in two, its value decreases by more than half. But if your children then take their halves and split them up for your grandchildren, you

Sulloway proposes that birth order has an enduring and formative effect on a person's personality.

soon have parcels that are too small to sustain a family unit. Whatever family fortune has been amassed will dwindle to a negligible benefit. It turns out to be a better strategy (for ancestral humans and for territorial birds) to keep the homestead as an indivisible unit, give it to your first-born, and let him pass it undivided to his first-born. As you can anticipate, this creates a situation in which there are different optimal strategies for first-born children and later-born children.

Sulloway's research did, indeed, reveal a relationship between birth order and the personality that a person develops consistent with the hypothesis that children of different rank develop different life strategies in order to optimize their success. The oldest child, who is likely to inherit the parents' home as well as their status, identifies most strongly with the parents and with authority figures generally. That child grows up being conservative, a supporter of tradition and the status quo. A surprising number of presidents and heads-of-state are first-born children.

The younger child has a different optimal strategy because that child has to seek his or her fortune elsewhere. The younger child, therefore, is more of a risk-taker and, out of necessity, thinks outside of the box. The title of Sulloway's book *Born to Rebel* is a nod toward that developmental propensity. Sulloway gives examples of revolutionaries in history, both in science and in politics, who were later-born children within their families. Indeed, Charles Darwin is one example! Harriet Tubman, who led hundreds of fugitive slaves from the southern United States to their freedom in Canada, was also a later-born child.

10.15 Press Pause

First-born and later-born children fill different niches and may develop differently in order to take optimal advantage of their specific niche.

THE NON-SHARED ENVIRONMENT

Research by Sulloway and others on the effects of birth order illustrate the power of the non-shared environment on an individual's development. Recall that when we discussed the heritability statistic, we looked at the statistically measurable contributions of differences in genes and differences in the environment to differences in some trait in the population. For our current discussion, let us say we are talking about some measure of rebelliousness that reveals quite a bit of variance throughout a large population. Prior to considering the effects of birth order, you may have thought that some amount of variance would be explained by genes so that people who were more similar genetically would be more similar on a measure of rebelliousness, and those less similar genetically would be less similar on this measure of rebelliousness. This would predict that family members, at least those who were genetic relatives, should be similar. Another source of variance, you may have thought, would be a result of environmental factors; perhaps you would have thought about socioeconomic status, exposure to television, parents' education levels, or even nutrition and exposure to local water sources. In terms of all of these environmental factors, factors of the *shared environment*, children reared in the same family would be

| figure | 10.5 | **Receptivity to scientific innovation by birth order** |

According to Frank Sulloway's research, later-born children are more receptive to scientific innovation than first-born children. He suggests that later-borns have to be more open to change since only the first-born will inherit the parent's position.

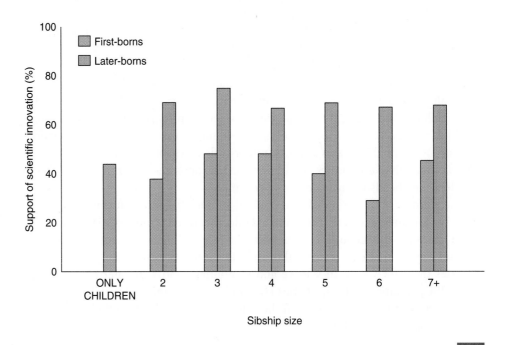

expected to be the same. Again, the prediction would be that family members would be more similar on this measure than strangers. But notice what birth order research reveals: a variable (birth order), which leads to an increased difference between family members. Siblings are more different, not more similar, than strangers on the measures of interest such as rebelliousness or adherence to the status quo. This is because within a family, there are non-shared environmental factors among siblings. The most obvious is birth order: Each child has his or her own rank within the family. Another is gender: Watch for interactions between gender and some of the common variables such as parents' education levels, religion, parents' involvement with extended family, or exposure to television. Non-shared environmental factors can lead to siblings that are more different than strangers, as is the case with birth order. As evolutionary psychologist Matt Ridley has said of *Born to Rebel*, "Sulloway's argument demolishes all simplistic notions of nature and nurture."

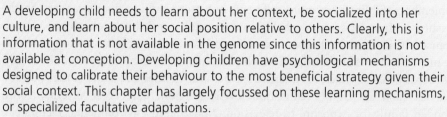

SUMMARY

A developing child needs to learn about her context, be socialized into her culture, and learn about her social position relative to others. Clearly, this is information that is not available in the genome since this information is not available at conception. Developing children have psychological mechanisms designed to calibrate their behaviour to the most beneficial strategy given their social context. This chapter has largely focussed on these learning mechanisms, or specialized facultative adaptations.

In this chapter you read about life history theory and the facultative adaptations thought to calibrate a person's reproductive strategy. Boys and girls growing up in their own ecological and economic circumstances have to learn about those circumstances. They affect whether dads can and will invest in their children, which in turn influences the best mating and dating strategies of both developing girls and boys as they come into sexual maturity.

The beginning of the chapter also illuminates parental love and parental investment from a functional, evolutionary perspective. Until the question was considered from this perspective, no one had an explanation for why parents love their children with such devoted, selfless love. Indeed, no one had noticed that it was a mystery that needed explaining. Trivers's parental-investment theory and parent–offspring conflict theory are capable of explaining, in terms of inclusive fitness, why parents love their offspring so much and why parents and offspring do not see eye to eye about when unrestricted investment should end: Weaning earlier means having another baby, which is good for the parent before it is good for the offspring.

Attachment theory is a good example of a mechanism designed to learn one's own context: A child has to learn which adult can be trusted to be a safe home base. Bowlby described attachment in terms of the function it served in the EEA: It allowed children to have a secure base from which to explore the world. Bowlby also coined the term *EEA* and, influenced by ethologists, was one of the first psychologists to think seriously about the function of psychological mechanisms in the environment in which they evolved.

Next you read about differences parents can make and the unique challenges of step-parenting. You may have been surprised to read that differences in parenting, at least within a normal range, make very little difference to the child's outcome, an observation that led Sandra Scarr to coin the term *good-enough parenting*. Furthermore, evidence suggests that a child is socialized (i.e., acquires values and behaviours appropriate for his or her culture and his or her relative status) not from parents or family but from interactions with peer groups. And finally you read about the effects that birth order seem to have on the development of an individual.

PRESS PAUSE SUMMARY

- Learning one's circumstances allows one to calibrate behaviour that is optimal for one's life circumstances. Some learning mechanisms are designed to do just that.
- Human societies differ with respect to the amount of paternal investment that is common, and that affects women's and men's optimal reproductive strategies.
- Whether men in a given society are willing and able to invest in offspring affects a woman's optimal life strategy.
- A man's optimal life strategy depends on what strategies the women in his environment are following.
- Once a life strategy is "selected," a whole suite of traits develop together including physiological, personality, and behavioural characteristics.
- Social context in early childhood can affect the timing of puberty and sexual maturation.
- Contrary to behaviourist predictions, young rhesus monkeys prefer the comfort of a soft furry mother over a wire mother who provides food.
- Attachment is functional: It calibrates the balance between a child's exploration and his or her safety. Attachment is analogous to imprinting seen in some species.
- Mary Ainsworth created the strange situation task, a standardized way for researchers to assess attachment in developing children.
- Measures of attachment early in life predict some adult outcomes, especially the quality of adult relationships.
- The optimal moment for a parent's investment to end is different from the points of view of the parent and the offspring.
- An implication of Triver's theory is that parents should not be able to socialize children to adopt the parents' values.
- Children who have step-parents are at far greater risk of abuse than those who do not.
- Babies and moms may have adaptations designed to convince dads that they are not cuckolds.
- First-born and later-born children fill different niches and may develop differently in order to take optimal advantage of their specific niche.

KEY TERMS AND CONCEPTS

alloparents, 366
attachment, 352
good-enough parenting, 362
inclusive fitness, 358
parental investment, 358

parent–offspring conflict, 359
paternal investment, 344
social facultative adaptation, 339
socialization, 363

QUESTIONS FOR THOUGHT AND DISCUSSION

1. What is a facultative adaptation? Give some examples from this chapter and other chapters. Explain why facultative adaptations are a good strategy for acquiring information about one's social context.

2. Describe two different strategies available to men and women according to the life history theory. In what circumstances would each be the most rewarding strategy in terms of fitness?

3. What does it mean for a child to become socialized? Do parents socialize their children? Do peers? What evidence supports your answer?

From the Classroom to the Lab: Follow Up

Consider the experiment you designed in response to the "From the Classroom to the Lab" challenge earlier in this chapter.

What is your independent variable?

What is your dependent variable?

Describe the design and procedure. Why do you think this procedure will answer the question you want to ask?

Describe possible results. How would you interpret these results with respect to your original question? That is, what would each possible outcome tell you about developmental influences on pubertal timing?

chapter 11

Sex and Gender

Female Genes

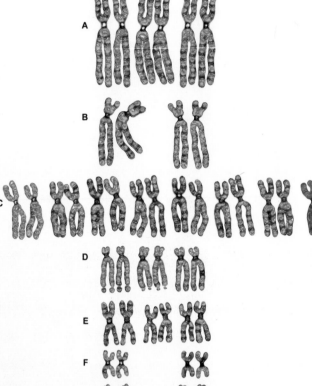

Male Genes

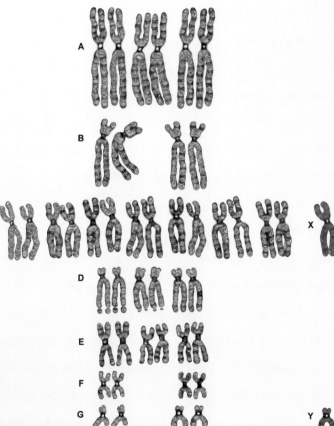

Opening Vignette: Androgen Insensitivity Syndrome

In the early 1960s, a baby with both an X and a Y chromosome was born in a Chicago county hospital. Cosmetic surgeries to normalize this baby's external genitalia were performed right away, and after a couple of days, the baby went home with parents who had been told that they had a boy. They named their baby Steven Lenell. Steven had a fairly normal childhood except that he played jump rope and dolls with the girls and was so feminine that all the boys in the neighbourhood teased him, including his own brothers.

At the age of 14, when other boys were developing facial hair and deeper voices, Steven developed breasts. His mother and his doctor stood by their story: This unusual development was a result of a pituitary malfunction, and Steven was a boy. Although Steven believed himself to be a girl, and actually wanted to be a girl, he took the male hormones that his doctor prescribed for three years, being told by his doctor that he could still become a normal male. Because Steven was enrolled in school as a boy, he took gym class with the boys, even showering with them, in spite of developing no body hair and developing breasts. He found these classes to be excruciating.

It was not until she was in her thirties that she learned that she had androgen insensitivity syndrome, changed her name to Lynnell Stephani, and began living as a woman. Although her karyotype is XY, her body is insensitive to androgens, so she was not masculinized by the testosterone that was in her system during prenatal development or the testosterone that was prescribed to her in early adolescence. Although she was reared as a boy, and no one ever told her that there was anything unusual about her birth, she always believed herself to be female. Indeed, prior to learning about her condition, she even identified as a male-to-female transsexual for some time.

Chapter Outline

Learning Objectives, Outcomes

- This chapter describes sex and gender development in humans while examples from non-human development are offered for contrast and illustration. Once you have read this chapter, you should have an idea of how different cognitive and social-psychological adaptations work together in each sex and why there is sex-based cognitive specialization. You should know what psychological adaptations men and women have and also understand that there are many psychological adaptations that are common to both sexes.

- After reading this chapter you will understand some of what is known about sex and gender development. You will know that there are events that happen in utero that are associated with male or female prenatal development, including the functions of the Y chromosome and of hormones. You will also know

about developing sex differences in preschool, in young children, and in adolescents.

- With this understanding of typical development, you will read about the experience of intersex and transsexual children. As you read about intersex conditions, you will understand how each differs from typical development. After reading the section covering intersex and transsexual experiences, you will understand the challenges these cases pose to socialization theories of gender development.

- The case of the Reimer twins, discussed later in this chapter, is a particularly telling test of the socialization theory of gender. It is also a "history of science," look into the changing views about gender and gender development, the power of the idea of the socialization of gender, and the difficulty that people have had looking critically at that theory.

Lynnell Stephani as an adult and as a child.

Why Look at Gender?

In addition to the fact that the development of sex and gender are interesting topics, there are three primary reasons for a chapter focussing on gender. First, the sexual dimorphism in our species provides a good "natural control group" for some interesting cognitive adaptations. By examining the cognitive differences between males and females, we can appreciate that some output is a result of an evolved cognitive process. Without that contrast, the phenomenon could be lost to instinct blindness. For example, men who navigate by reference to their cognitive map, which they do in terms of Euclidean coordinates, or inferring the most direct route back to a starting point in spite of a winding path (Moffat, Hampson, & Hatzipantelis, 1998; Sandstrom, Kaufman, & Huettel, 1998), might feel their navigational adeptness is so easy that they are unaware of the cognitive adaptations allowing such navigation. Women navigating the same environment but relying on landmarks, as they more often do (Galea & Kimura, 1993; Sandstrom et al., 1998), might similarly find their navigational strategy so natural that they do not even realize it is a cognitive strategy. Only by comparing typical male and female navigation does it become clear that there are complex cognitive adaptations underlying human navigation.

Second, it is a good opportunity to put our commitment to viewing nature and nurture as working together, not in opposition, to the test. There is a politically motivated fear that sometimes keeps people from seriously considering the development of boys and girls differently. People who otherwise adamantly insist on setting aside the nature vs. nurture issue will fall into bad habits when talking about gender development, suggesting that sex differences must be "learned" or "cultural" rather than "biological." We will work our way through what is known about the development of the two genders, and the developing sexual dimorphism of humans, while upholding our commitment to thinking of nature and nurture as working together in development.

Third, looking at the adaptations of men as a group and of women as a group allow us an opportunity to consider the fit between adaptations and the adaptive problems they solve. Although this relationship is not fully understood for every sex difference you will read about here, it is interesting to consider what adaptive problems were presented to men and women, and boys and girls, in the EEA. Each sex has a suite of adaptations that work in concert to maximize fitness by pursuing either the male or the female reproductive strategy.

Gender Roles in the EEA

Anthropological evidence from hunter–gatherer cultures, as well as evidence of sex differences in human psychology, indicates that men and women experienced different selection pressures in the EEA. In some cases those pressures meant solving adaptive problems that were specific to one sex; in most cases they meant answering to different priorities. The cost of some problems was worth incurring from the point of view of one sex or the other.

---

figure 11.1   Overlapping distributions

Many of the sex differences we talk about describe a difference in the average performance of men and women although there is great overlap between men and women as a group. A graph of height, running speed, or verbal fluency would show such an overlap, for example.

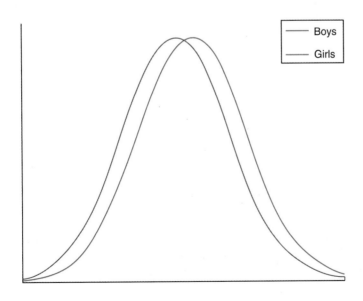

The hunting that our ancestors did required specialized cognitive adaptations to support navigation. Hunters travelled long distances to track animals and then had to efficiently return home. This man is using a GPS, but his grandfather did not.

It is likely that the biggest sex differences in terms of selection pressures were rooted in the social and familial division of labour described in the last chapter. In addition, men and women had different specialties when it came to providing. Archaeological and paleontological evidence, gathered from sites that represent a variety of time periods in our evolutionary history, strongly suggest that hunting was mostly done by males and that foraging was mostly done by females (Tooby & DeVore, 1987). Among our hunter–gatherer ancestors in the EEA, women contributed calories to their household by gathering fruits and vegetables. Based on a survey of contemporary hunter–gatherer societies, it seems clear that women contributed substantially, although the female contribution to the household varies considerably across societies, from fairly minimal to up to 60 per cent of the family's calories (Marlowe, 2003). (In addition, women were the exclusive source of calories for a newborn baby who was breastfed exclusively for several months, and in the EEA breastfeeding typically lasted for years longer than it does in modern North America.) Women gathered foods close to home. They needed to find fruit-bearing plants and remember the location of those plants across time when their fruits were in season (Silverman & Eals, 1992). They needed to make fine perceptual discriminations, including colour and texture, as they selected ripe fruit from unripe fruit.

Men were the hunters. Males contribute food in all known foraging societies (Marlowe, 2003), but the extent to which they contribute to their mates and offspring varies greatly across societies (Marlowe, 2003). In the EEA, hunting had some specific task demands. Because of the challenge of hunting game, as well as the risk of encountering rival human groups, males hunted in coalitions, evolving a coalitional psychology that is different from the psychology of women. Hunting required the use of projectile weapons, that is, throwing things at moving targets. You may not think of throwing a weapon at a target as a cognitive task, but this skill shows a relationship to other spatial-cognition tasks (Jardine & Martin, 1983; Kolakowski & Molina, 1974). Hunting required travelling across a much larger range than did gathering, thus creating selection pressures for some relatively sophisticated spatial-cognition and navigational skills. Successful hunters needed to orient themselves in a novel environment, conceptualize their locations across distances, and perform mental rotations of their environments as they travelled (Silverman & Eals, 1992). There is cross-cultural data supporting the idea that boys have a larger range of exploration than girls and that boys explore farther from home, starting in early childhood (Gaulin & Hoffman, 1988).

But it is important to note that this navigational talent is not inherently masculine: Navigation abilities will be greater in males only for those species in which greater navigational abilities were selected for. When a species of polygynous voles, whose males travel great distances to seek females, was compared to a species of monogamous voles, researchers found male superiority in the ability to navigate a maze only in the polygynous species (Gaulin, FitzGerald, & Wartell, 1990). Furthermore, only in the polygynous species do the males have a larger hippocampus, the brain area associated with spatial navigation, than the females (Jacobs, Gaulin, Sherry, & Hoffman, 1990; Sherry, 2000).

Adaptive Sex Differences

In earlier chapters of this book, we learned that we should expect complex adaptations to be universal. If the adaptation is beneficial, it will spread throughout the species (Tooby & Cosmides, 1990). Remember from Chapter 3 that complex designs are built when one very small change, mediated by one beneficial mutation, becomes universal in the species and that, at some point in the future, a new change, caused by a new beneficial mutation, becomes universal in the population. The implication is that people everywhere have the same adaptations, whether they originate in Africa, Asia, or the Americas, at least when talking about any adaptation complex enough to involve multiple genes. Some adaptive genetic differences that do not require numerous genes working in tandem might vary regionally across the globe, such as genes underlying malaria susceptibility and sickle-cell anemia. Most variation in human genomes can be accounted for by genes that have little or no effect on the phenotype or are relatively recent (usually deleterious) mutations.

The sexes are an interesting exception to this rule but only to an extent. Males and females are two different morphs of the same species. We will focus our discussion upon men and women, the males and females of the human species. To say that men and women are

Men and women both have the complete set of human genetic information, just as both the butterfly and the caterpillar have the genetic information that supports each other's morphologies.

two morphs of the human species means there are two different phenotypes (man and woman), each of which shows a coherent set of complex adaptations, and the genes that underlie the complex adaptations are universal to every individual in the species. A man has all of the genes that underpin the development of ovaries, fallopian tubes, and a uterus; he got these genes from his mother *and father*, and he will pass these genes on to his daughters *and sons*. Men and women both have the complete set of human genetic information, just as both the butterfly and the caterpillar have the genetic information that supports each other's morphologies.

11.1 Press Pause

In addition to many shared complex adaptations, men and women will also have some different complex adaptations—a rare exception to the rule that complex adaptations are universal.

When thinking about sex differences in any species, including the human species, one must realize that sex differences result from each sex having a complete set

 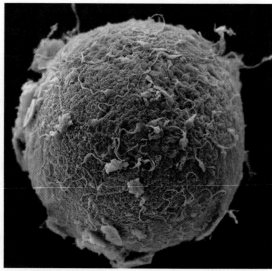

To a biologist, sex is defined by gamete size. Whoever has the larger gamete (egg) is female; whoever has the smaller gamete (sperm) is male. Although human eggs are microscopic, they are far larger than human sperm.

of adaptations that optimize one reproductive strategy or another. Men have a suite of adaptations that all work in tandem to optimally take advantage of the male reproductive strategy, and women have a different suite of adaptations that are designed to optimize the female reproductive strategy. These adaptations include morphological (internal and external genitalia), physiological, endocrinological, cognitive, and emotional adaptations. To the extent that men and women differ on any of these factors (from testosterone level to verbal ability) is by design, and the design is a package deal.

Sex is defined, biologically, in terms of gamete size. In any species that produces two gamete sizes, males produce the smaller gamete (which we call *sperm*), and females produce the larger gamete (which we call the *egg*). For many species that have male individuals and female individuals, especially if fertilization is internal to the female, the female becomes the choosier sex since making the larger gamete means making a larger investment, and internal fertilization leads to a larger investment in offspring. She is making a substantial contribution to reproduction and is in a position to use that as a bargaining chip to hold out for better gene quality or a larger investment on the part of the male. A male in this type of species, because he makes such a small mandatory investment (he need only produce some sperm), can theoretically make many more offspring than the female can. This influences a male's reproductive strategy: He would like to maximize the number of his offspring, is willing to invest if necessary, and is very motivated to avoid accidentally investing in another male's offspring. Strategies will vary from species to species, and certain behaviours will differ in different species, but the point is that the suite of adaptations that a male has and the suite of adaptations that a female has work together to optimize a given strategy. One could not arbitrarily select some cognitive adaptations, with some morphological adaptations, and package them with either gamete size for the same reproductive fitness.

11.2 Press Pause

Each sex has a suite of adaptations that work together. These adaptations include morphological, physiological, endocrinological, cognitive, and emotional adaptations.

The Development of Sex and Gender

In typical human development, development is set in motion toward one sex or the other when the sex chromosome from the father is delivered to the mother's egg, creating the complete genome. A fertilized egg (and every subsequent cell except gametes in that developing individual) has 46 chromosomes, comprising 23 pairs. Twenty-two of those pairs are **autosomes**: They match and apparently have the same set of loci on the mother's and father's chromosomal contribution. The twenty-third pair of chromosomes is the pair of sex chromosomes. These chromosomes are commonly referred to as X and Y, X being the larger of the two. The developing offspring receives an X chromosome from the mother, because X is all she has to contribute: Every cell in her body has two X chromosomes, and her sex cells (eggs) carry an X chromosome. (In fact, each carries a unique X chromosome that she created earlier via meiosis.) The father may contribute an X chromosome or a Y chromosome via the sperm that fertilizes the egg. Father has one X and one Y chromosome in every cell in his body and creates sex cells (sperm) that have either an X or a Y cell. If the fertilized egg, now a conceptus, gets a Y chromosome from Father, then that offspring has an XY genome and is on his way to developing into a boy. If the conceptus gets an X chromosome from Father, then that offspring has an XX genome and begins to develop into a girl. Remember, this is the story of typical development. Some other interesting developmental trajectories will be described later in this chapter.

The default development of external genitalia is female: Without androgens influencing development, the baby will have the external appearance of a female. The Y

autosome Any pair of chromosomes that are not sex chromosomes.

Every cell in your body (except sex cells) has 46 chromosomes, comprising 23 pairs. Twenty-two pairs are autosomes, and the twenty-third pair is your sex chromosomes.

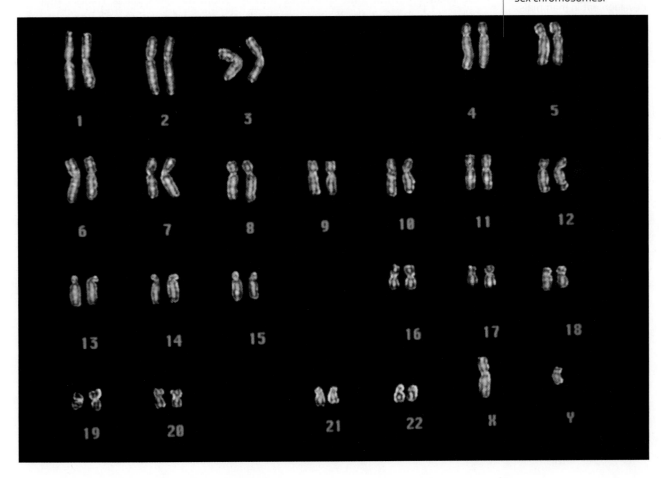

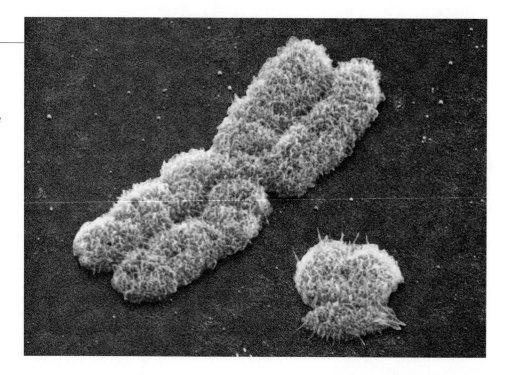

Sex chromosomes are commonly referred to as *X* and *Y*, X being the larger of the two. The developing human receives an X from the mother, while the father may contribute an X chromosome or a Y chromosome.

SRY gene The gene on the Y chromosome usually associated with male development in mammals, SRY is an acronym for sex-determining region Y.

testis determining factor A protein that will likely trigger the development of the fetus's testes in typical male development.

chromosome typically changes this by putting the developing fetus on the path to masculine development, and this is just about the only thing the Y chromosome does. It is the smallest chromosome so it does not have room for many genes. (Notice that this leaves each gene on the X chromosome in the unusual position of being without a complementary allele on its partner chromosome. For a gene on the male's X chromosome, there is no dominant or recessive.) The Y chromosome has a gene, called the **SRY gene**, that starts a whole cascade of events. When transcribed, it leads to the creation of the **testis determining factor**, a protein that triggers the development of the fetus's testes. The testes then produce and release androgens, including testosterone. These

The sex chromosome system used by humans and other mammals is not the only way that sexes develop. Male birds have two of the same sex chromosomes, while the females have the unmatched set.

androgens masculinize the body (leading to the development of male external genitalia), and they also masculinize the brain. Sex hormones, both androgens and estrogens, can affect neurons by manipulating the onset and rate of growth of axons and dendrites (Toran-Allerand, 1976). Of course, in order to be so affected, the neuron in question has to have the right receptors. Receptors for androgens and estrogens are found in the hippocampus, the hypothalamus, the amygdala, the limbic system, and the cerebral cortex, presumably because all of these areas are optimized differently in each sex (Geary, 1998; Kimura, 1999).

11.3 Press Pause

In humans, the presence of the SRY gene on the Y chromosome usually leads to the development of the suite of masculine adaptations.

androgen insensitivity syndrome A condition in which a person has a mutation in the gene associated with the development of androgen receptors. Without functioning androgen receptors, a person with an XY karyotype can develop a female phenotype.

Now, this does not mean that the Y chromosome "determines" sex. First of all, even though the SRY gene starts a series of events that lead to masculinization, lots of genes on lots of chromosomes are involved in the development of the penis, testes, dense musculature, deep voice, facial hair, receding hairline, and suite of cognitive adaptations that are characteristic of men (just as many genes underlie the suite of female adaptations). Moreover, there are human conditions, such as **androgen insensitivity syndrome**, described in more detail later in this chapter, in which a person has an SRY gene but instead develops female morphology and a female psychology.

So far we have been talking about sex development in humans, and this developmental system is used in most mammals as well. But there are different schemes of sex development in different species. In birds, for example, the female has two different chromosomes, and the male has two copies of the same kind of chromosome. A worm called *Bonellia* will develop into a male if it spends its embryonic period in another worm's mouth, but otherwise it will be female. In some species of reptiles, such as turtles and alligators, chromosomes are not different in the two sexes. Instead, in many turtle species, females hatch from eggs that develop at temperatures warmer than 32 degrees, and males, who have the same chromosomes as females, hatch from eggs that develop at temperatures cooler than 28 degrees (Bull, 1980). Again, do not think of this as nurture over nature: The temperature "determines" sex only in concert with the turtle's complete complement of genes and only because the developing organism was designed to develop this way in response to temperature.

There are sex differences right from the moment of conception. Males are more likely than females to suffer from a spontaneous miscarriage. They are more vul-

Some animals do not rely on chromosomal differences for sex development. Female turtles hatch from eggs that develop at temperatures warmer than 32 degrees and males from eggs that develop at temperatures cooler than 28 degrees.

nerable to physical and mental forms of developmental abnormalities and are more likely to die shortly after birth as well (Hartung & Widiger, 1998; Jacklin, 1989). Also, boys are more active in utero than girls, moving and kicking more (Almli, Ball, & Wheeler, 2001).

In humans, as in mammals generally, the default external genitalia are female, and masculinization relies on the production of relatively high concentrations of male hormones. We know this because if you remove the gonadal tissue of a fetal rabbit, the rabbit develops a visibly female body complete with vagina, uterus, and cervix, regardless of its chromosomes (Jost, 1953). (Note, however, that internal development is not completely typical of female development, as you will read more about later in this chapter.) The masculinization of the genitals occurs in the middle of the second trimester and is dependent upon a surge in androgens at that point. The masculinization of the brain, and apparently the concurrent masculinization of gender identity, takes place just prior to and around the time of birth and relies on a new surge of androgens at that time.

figure 11.2　Differentiation of the external genitalia

Male and female genitalia differentiate in the middle of the second trimester. Androgen typically leads to the masculinization of the external genitalia, whereas in the absence of androgen, female external genitalia will develop.

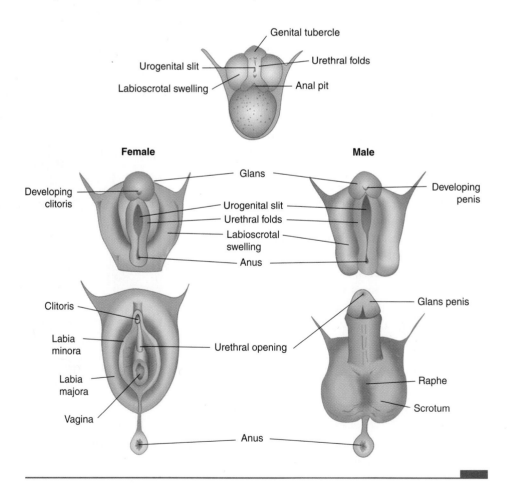

POSTNATAL DEVELOPMENT

In humans, sex differences in development continue after birth. Differences in behaviour emerged because they offer reproductive advantages. For example, males are known to use different navigating strategies than women and to have specialized spatial reasoning skills. This is thought to be due to selection pressures resulting from the task of hunting: Hunters who could track animals over long distances and then return home easily and safely could increase their fitness. Similarly, women's gathering tasks in the EEA may be associated with better colour and texture discrimination, fine motor skills, and memory for landmarks. Studies of play behaviour in boys and girls suggest that children practise the sex-specific skills they are developing: Boys are more likely to engage in rough-and-tumble play, while girls are more likely to participate in pretend parenting (Geary, 1998; Maccoby & Jacklin, 1987). Here you will read about postnatal development in physical size and strength, motor skills, various cognitive skills (verbal, quantitative, social, and spatial), sex differences in aggression, how developing children use their free time, and their understanding of gender.

11.4 Press Pause

Sex differences arose because men and women solved a slightly different set of adaptive problems in the EEA.

Physical size and strength

Early in life, males and females appear similar in size, and there is tremendous overlap between girls and boys, but as a group, girls are measurably smaller, lighter, healthier, more mature, and less muscular right from birth (Garai & Scheinfeld, 1968; Lundqvist & Sabel, 2000; Tanner, 1990). During childhood, boys and girls have similar growth rates, but boys continue to be measurably stronger (Sartario, Lafrotuna, Poglaghi, & Trecate, 2002).

Motor skills

There are early sex differences in motor development too. At birth, girls are generally more coordinated than boys (Sartario et al., 2002). On average, boys have an advantage on measures that require strength and power: By the age of 5, boys jump farther and run faster than girls, and they can throw a ball substantially farther than girls. Girls at this age are superior in fine motor skills and balance. For example, they are better at skipping and hopping. Notice that these sex differences occur long before puberty. Furthermore, these skills develop as a result of everyday play; there seems to be little formal instruction for many of these childhood motor skills. Indeed, exposure to formal training seems to have little impact on motor development for typically developing children (Robertson, 1984). The sex differences in motor skills increase with age, and physical differences between boys and girls greatly increase after puberty. In middle childhood, girls are still better at fine motor skills, a difference that shows up in penmanship and drawing. Girls still have superior skills in balance and agility, which serve them in their preferred activities of jumping rope and skipping. Boys are superior on gross motor skills and strength, such as throwing and kicking. This gender gap increases through middle childhood (Cratty, 1986).

Verbal skills

Boys and girls have tested nearly identically on IQ tests, but items that differed systematically across the genders were dropped in early test construction. Other accepted measures of general intelligence show no consistent sex differences. Girls as a group tend to be slightly stronger in language development. Even as infants, girls produce more speech sounds than boys (Harris, 1977), and young girls perform better than boys on verbal skills tests (Feingold, 1992, 1993). Girls use words earlier, have larger early vocabularies (Huttenlocher, Haight, Bryk, Seltzer, & Lyons, 1991), and show more grammatical complexity (Koenigsknecht & Friedman, 1976) than boys. During the school years, girls also have superior verbal memories (Kimura, 2002, 2004).

Quantitative skills

Despite perceptions to the contrary, girls receive higher grades in mathematics than boys, although on average, boys perform better on high-stakes tests of mathematics achievement such as the SAT (Snyder & Hoffman, 2000). Males, as a group, tend to be stronger than females in some aspects of visual-spatial processing. This difference emerges between 3 and 4 years of age and becomes more substantial during adolescence. Boys and girls do particularly well on different kinds of math problems: From early to middle childhood, girls do better on computational problems; boys do better on mathematical reasoning (Hyde, Fennema, & Lamon, 1990; Kimura, 2002).

Social skills

As early as infancy there are sex differences in social orienting. Shortly after birth, girls orient toward people by turning toward both faces and voices more than boys do (Haviland & Malatesta, 1981); as babies, girls smile more at other people than boys do (Cossette, Pomerleau, Malcuit, & Kaczorowski, 1996); girls maintain eye contact longer than boys do (Connellan, Baron-Cohen, Wheelwright, Batki, & Ahluwalia, 2000); and at 3 months, girls participate in more face-to-face communication than boys do (Lavelli & Fogel, 2002). Girls who were studied between the ages of 12 and 20 months showed more empathy (measured by concern for the feigned distress of a confederate), showing more facial expressions, orienting, and gestures, compared to the relatively nonresponsive boys (Zahn-Waxler, Radke-Yarrow, Wagner, & Chapman, 1992).

These findings are consistent with sex differences in adulthood: Except for anger, women experience emotions more intensely (Kimura, 1999), have more intimate friendships, and are more empathetic toward their friends than males are (Blum, 1997; Geary, 1998; Kimura, 1999). They make eye contact more, smile more, and laugh more (Provine, 1993).

Spatial skills

Preschool boys are better than preschool girls at tasks that require spatial rotation (Baenninger & Newcombe, 1995; Casey, 1996), and this male spatial rotation superiority continues through childhood and adulthood (Geary, 1998; Halpern, 2000; Kimura, 1999). Boys outperform girls on tasks involving spatial transformations (LeVine, Dixon, Taylor, & Langrock, 1999) and three-dimensional spatial reasoning such as duplicating a Lego model (McGuiness & Morley, 1991). Sex differences on spatial tasks increase through adolescence and into adulthood (Voyer, Voyer, & Bryden, 1995), especially for spatial rotations tasks (Kimura, 2002, 2004).

Compared to girls, boys are better at navigating both real and virtual environments (Moffat, Hampson, & Hatzipantelis, 1998; Silverman et al., 2000), at making maps (Matthews, 1987), and at interpreting a map in order to navigate (Dabbs, Jr., Change,

figure	11.3	**Spatial rotation**

Preschool boys are better than preschool girls at tasks that require spatial rotation. Sex differences on spatial tasks increase through adolescence and into adulthood. (Adapted from Shepard and Metzler, 1970.)

Standard

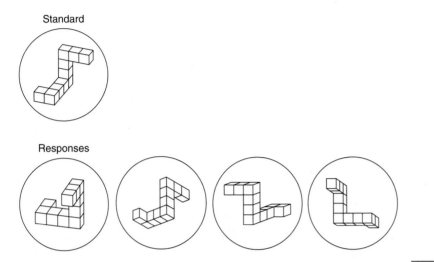

Responses

figure	11.4	**Spatial skills**

When shown an array of objects and later asked to recall which objects appeared where, girls were better than boys at recalling the identity and location of the missing object. Evolutionary thinking led to this discovery. (Adapted from Silvermann and Eals, 1992.)

Strong, & Milun, 1998). Again, these differences appear as early as preschool. A study that examined children in kindergarten, second grade, and fifth grade found that, at every age, boys outperformed girls on tasks that required them to re-create a town's layout after a walk through the town (Herman & Siegel, 1978). Interestingly, girls who have abnormally high prenatal androgen levels show superior performance on spatial rotation tasks (Collaer & Hines, 1995).

Girls are better than boys at remembering the locations of specific objects among an array of various objects, and these differences are evident as early as 8 years of age (Eals & Silverman, 1994; Kail & Siegel, 1997; Silverman & Eals, 1992). When shown an array of objects as in Figure 11.4 and later asked to recall which objects appeared where, girls were better at recalling the identity of the objects and their locations. Silverman and Eals make the connection between this cognitive skill and the selection pressures that girls and women faced during the EEA. As gatherers, they would have had to make fine perceptual discriminations and remember the location of objects they had observed.

Aggression

One area that has received a lot of research attention is aggression and the sex differences in aggressive behaviour. Boys and girls are aggressive in different ways. Boys are far more physically aggressive than girls, and this is true cross-culturally, according to a study involving 4,640 preschoolers across eight countries (LaFreniere et al., 2002). From early childhood on, boys are more likely than girls to be physically aggressive, including kicking, punching, and pushing, compared to same-aged girls. As adults, men commit 89 per cent of murders and 79 per cent of assaults in the United States (U.S. Department of Justice, 2007) with similar numbers reported cross-culturally (Kenrick & Trost, 1993).

relational aggression
The attempt to harm others by damaging social relationships. This type of aggression may take the form of gossip, spreading rumours, or ostracism.

In contrast, girls are more likely than boys to engage in relational aggression. **Relational aggression** is the attempt to harm others by damaging social relationships, and it may take the form of gossip, spreading rumours, or ostracism (Crick et al., 2001). Relational aggression is the preferred form of aggression for girls from preschool (Ostrov & Crick, 2007) through high school (Cillessen & Mayeux, 2004; Murray-Close, Ostrov, & Crick, 2007).

Boys are more physically aggressive than girls, cross-culturally and throughout development. Girls are more likely to use relational aggression, attempting to harm others by damaging social relationships.

Given a choice between toys, vervet females spent more time playing with the girl-preferred toys, while vervet males played more with boy-preferred toys.

Interests and free time

There are behavioural differences between boys and girls early in preschool. Walk into any typical preschool class, and you will see that the boys tend to interact with other boys, and they tend to play with more active and constructive toys like blocks and toy vehicles.

Girls tend to spend time among other girls and tend to play with quieter toys associated with fine motor skills, such as drawing, reading, and pretend housekeeping (including pretend child care). At age 4, children spend three times as much time with same-sex playmates compared to opposite sex playmates; by the age of 6, they spend 11 times more time with same-sex playmates than those of the opposite sex (Benenson, Apostoleris, & Parnass, 1997; Maccoby & Jacklin, 1987).

These effects are not confined to humans. Research involving vervet monkeys has shown similarities in sex-defined preferences for toys. Young vervets had the opportunity to play with toys that human boys usually prefer (a police car and a ball), toys that human girls usually prefer (a doll and a pan), and neutral toys that are typically preferred equally (a book and a plush dog). The vervet females spent more time playing with the girl-preferred toys, the males showed the opposite pattern, and there was no sex difference in playing time for the neutral toys. The study's authors suggested that this is evidence that sex differences in toy preferences develop even in the absence of human culture (Alexander & Hines, 2002).

Early sex differences are seen cross-culturally. All over the world, girls spend more time doing household chores and contributing to child care, and boys spend more time unsupervised by adults (Larson & Verma, 1999). Boys' activities take them farther from home, and girls are more likely to be found close to home (Weisner, 1996; Whiting & Edwards, 1988).

11.5 Press Pause

Early sex differences in cognition reveal adaptive sex differences. Each sex has adaptations specialized for gender-specific tasks in the EEA.

So, boys and girls have different areas of cognitive expertise consistent with the cognitive demands of the EEA as we understand them. Let us consider the development of these differences. What is known about the developmental factors that contribute to the sex differences in spatial-cognitive skills is interesting. Recall that boys and girls play differently and seem to have different preferences in terms of the activities they choose during free time. Boys spend more time in active play and girls in quiet, focussed play. In ordinary playground play, boys cover more territory than girls. Indeed, in a wide range of cultures, boys have larger territories of exploration than do girls. One study showed that the activities that boys select in their free time involve more visual-spatial skills than the activities the girls choose (Connor & Servin, 1977).

It is possible that this sex difference in play facilitates the development of spatial cognition in boys. Children who play with manipulative activities, such as blocks or construction toys, score higher on spatial-cognition tasks (Baenninger & Newcombe, 1995). It is known, for example, that in adult females, there is a relationship between spatial-cognitive abilities and the frequency with which an individual engages in activities that demand spatial-cognitive skills (Newcombe, Bandura, & Taylor, 1983). One rather intricate and involved study actually undertook to equalize the amount of exposure children had to spatial play in their environment, at least to an extent, and, indeed, found reduced sex differences in spatial-cognitive abilities (Hazen, 1982). Another study found a relationship between visual-spatial play (more common in boys) and performance on standardized measures of spatial cognition (Connor & Servin, 1977).

Recall that in Chapters 3 and 4 we talked about interactions between genes and the environment. We discussed the fact that just saying that there was an interaction between genes and the environment in the development of a trait is relatively uninteresting since it is true for every trait. What is more interesting is to know something about what that interaction is. Here again, we see an example of an interaction that we know something about. Boys and girls are attracted to different types of play in early childhood, and those different types of play contribute to sex differences in cognitive development that were adaptive, given the sex-specific tasks of our ancestors living in the EEA.

Be careful not to fall into the trap of asking nature vs. nurture questions in this instance. Recall from Chapter 3 that to claim that a trait is adaptive, or shaped by natural selection, is NOT a claim that such a trait has no developmental story. All traits must have a developmental story. And we have seen multiple examples of evolved learning mechanisms, from perceptual development to language development to attachment. We know that natural selection is free to use multiple resources, including environmental and experiential input, during development. Do not be tempted to dismiss our evolutionary history simply because we know something about the developmental trajectory and that development involves experience. An evolved mechanism can involve both learning and experience: Boys learn more about spatial cognition (if indeed our current beliefs about its development are correct) because boys are attracted to the kinds of activities that lead to its development. This is good engineering, designed by natural selection.

11.6   Press Pause

Natural selection has multiple avenues of development available, including the active participation of the developing individual.

Children's understanding of gender

Infants appear to be able to tell the difference between the sexes using multiple perceptual cues although the capacity to make this distinction does not reveal what they understand about what it means to be male or female. Shortly after entering toddlerhood, children begin showing distinct patterns of gender development. By the latter half of their second year, children begin forming gender-related expectations about the kinds of objects and activities that are typically associated with males and females. Between their second and third birthdays, most children come to know which gender

Between the ages of about 9 and 12, boys increasingly adhere to gender expectations during a time when girls relax their adherence to feminine expectations. This period of gender freedom for girls ends in early adolescence, a period of intensifying attitudes toward gender norms.

⇢ Developmental Milestones

Milestones in the Development of Sex and Gender

Age	Skills
Conception	A sperm cell joins an egg cell, combining genetic material. The sperm contributes either an X or a Y sex chromosome. The X chromosome is associated with the development of a girl and the Y chromosome with the development of a boy.
10 Weeks Post-Conception	Male fetus produces testosterone and other androgens. External genitals begin to differentiate by sex.
In Utero	Boys are more active than girls. Masculinization of the brain (and gender identity) takes place just prior to birth and relies on a surge of androgens at that time.
At Birth	From birth, girls are more coordinated than boys. Girls orient to people's faces and voices more than boys.
3 Months	Girls participate in more face-to-face communication than boys.
12 Months	Girls show more evidence of empathy than boys.
3 Years	Children categorize people by gender and identify themselves as "girl" or "boy."
4 Years	Sex differences in visual-spatial processing emerge. Boys are better at navigation and map-making than girls. Children spend three times as much time with same-sex compared to opposite-sex playmates. Boys are more physically aggressive.
5 Years	Boys jump farther, run faster, and throw a ball farther than girls.
9 to 12 Years	Boys become more rigid in rules about masculinity, while girls relax their adherence to feminine expectations.
12 Years	Girls return from the period of gender freedom and again adhere to feminine expectations.

group they belong to, and by age 3, they use gender terms (e.g., "boy") in their speech. Children begin to categorize and label their own, and others', sex around the age of 2, a process that increases with accuracy and determination until around the age of 4. Children at this age quickly become adept at categorizing the gender cues of their local culture, associating toys, tools, activities, occupations, and colours with one sex or the other (Ruble & Martin, 1998). Even at this age, girls are more compliant, sensitive, relationally aggressive, fearful, and dependent, whereas boys are more active and physically aggressive (Brody & Hall, 1993; Feingold, 1994). These differences appear cross-culturally (Whiting & Edwards, 1988).

Gender stereotypes become stronger until around the age of 4, when children actually act as gender enforcers, telling children and adults what they can and cannot wear, and what occupations they can and cannot hold, based on gender (Biernat, 1991; Martin, 1989). They will demonstrate the gender-appropriate response to peers (Langlois & Downs, 1980), and boys are particularly intolerant of cross-gender behaviour (Fagot, 1984): A boy who repeatedly engages in cross-gender behaviour is eventually excluded from social activities.

During the school years, children have a set of expectations regarding the characteristics of each sex. They think girls are "gentle," "sympathetic," and "dependent," and boys are "tough," "aggressive," and "rational" (Best et al., 1977; Serbin, Pow-

⠿ Research in Action

Infants' Understandings of Gender Stereotypes

According to traditional gender-schema theory, gender schemas and accompanying expectations about male and female behaviour did not develop in children until their own gender identity had developed. That is, until a child could label themselves as "girl" or "boy" at around the age of 2½ or 3, they were not expected to know anything about gender-specific interests, roles, or activities (Martin, 1993; Martin & Little, 1990).

In spite of this prediction, there is clear evidence that very young children categorize male and female. Infants discriminate between male and female voices as early as 6 months (Miller, 1983) and between male and female faces between 9 and 12 months (Poulin-Dubois, Serbin, Kenyon, & Derbyshire, 1994). More surprising is the evidence that toddlers and infants have expectations about gender-related behaviours and stereotypes.

Diane Poulin-Dubois and her colleagues at Concordia University in Montreal have recently found evidence of very early gender-defined expectations. In one study, toddlers as young as 2 years old were asked which of three dolls would act out various activities. One of the dolls was male, one was female, and one was a monkey, meant to be a gender-neutral option. The activities were typically male activities, typically female activities, or activities that both men and women are likely to do. Examples were shaving, fixing a car, holding a baby, vacuuming, and sleeping. Two-year-old girls, but not 2-year-old boys, preferred the male doll to perform masculine activities and the female doll to perform the feminine activities. In other words, 2-year-old girls, but not boys, revealed an understanding of gender stereotypes (Poulin-Dubois, Serbin, Eichstedt, Sen, & Beissel, 2002).

These researchers also used a looking time measure, which we have seen can be more sensitive, in order to reveal an understanding of gender-typed behaviour at an even younger age. This time, Julie Eichstedt and colleagues, again at Concordia University, tested infants as young as 18 months old. The infants looked at a computer screen and saw feminine items (a tiara, a heart, a dress, e.g.) and masculine items (a fire hat, a hammer, a tree, e.g.). They also viewed male and female faces. While looking at one of the gendered objects, infants heard a gender-neutral voice (it had been digitally altered to reveal no male or female characteristics) say "This is the one I like. Can you look at me? Here I am! Look at me!" Then two faces, one male and one female, appeared. Infants looked longer at the female face when they had seen a feminine object on that trial and looked longer at the male face when they had seen a masculine object on that trial (Eichstedt, Serbin, Poulin-Dubois, & Sen, 2002).

Most surprising, the Concordia University group, this time led by Lisa Serbin, found that 2-year-olds have expectations regarding the actions and behaviours men and women might perform. These researchers used the violation of expectation paradigm: Two-year-olds sat looking toward two computer screens. On one screen a man (wearing a shirt and tie) performed an activity while on the other screen a woman (wearing a blouse and skirt) performed the exact same activity. Activities were masculine (fixing a toy car or hammering, e.g.), feminine (putting on makeup or feeding a baby, e.g.), or neutral (turning on a light or putting on shoes, e.g.). Two-year-olds looked significantly longer when a man performed activities that were considered feminine, indicating that their expectations had been violated (Serbin, Poulin-Dubois, & Eichstedt, 2002).

lishta, & Gulko, 1993). They see mathematics, athletics, and mechanics as masculine academic areas and reading, art, and music as feminine (Eccles, Jacobs, & Harold, 1990; Jacobs & Weisz, 1994).

In middle childhood, children can be fairly tolerant of a girl who crosses gender lines by, say, playing sports or excelling at math but are harsh critics of a boy who crosses gender lines by playing with dolls or cross-dressing, often responding with moral outrage as if a moral rule has been violated (Levy, Taylor, & Gelman, 1995). Between the ages of about 9 and 12, boys increasingly adhere to gender expectations during a time when girls relax their adherence to feminine expectations (Serbin, Powlishta, & Gulko, 1993). However, girls do not experiment with masculine sex roles in cultures where the division of sex roles is greater than in, say, North America. This period of gender freedom for girls ends in early adolescence, a period of intensifying attitudes toward gender norms (Galambos, Almeida, & Petersen, 1990). Girls especially experience an increase in gender-typed attitudes and behaviours after adolescence (Huston & Alvarez, 1990).

Puberty

Puberty is a coordinated set of changes that lead to sexual maturation and entry into the sexually reproductive years. A series of dramatic bodily transformations are associated with puberty in early adolescence. These changes include **menarche** in girls (the onset of menstruation) and **spermarche** in boys (the onset of ejaculation). In our modern society, hormonal increases that underlie puberty, such as the increase in growth hormone (GH) and thyroxine, begin as early as 8 or 9 years of age. As puberty begins, a boy's testes release testosterone in unprecedented amounts, leading to the development of primary and secondary sexual characteristics: increased muscle mass, facial hair, and a deepened voice, for example. A girl's ovaries begin to release large amounts of estrogen, leading to the development of breasts, the uterus, and a feminine pattern of fatty deposits. In girls, androgens released from the adrenal glands (above each kidney) lead to increased height and the growth of pubic and underarm hair. The growth spurt, leading to a dramatic increase in height, is underway at age 10 for girls and age 12½ for boys in a North American sample (Malina, 1990). The average girl is taller than the average boy between the ages of 10 and 14. Girls are typically through growing in height at age 16 and boys at age 17½ (Malina, 1990; Tanner, 1990). During this growth spurt, body proportions change in the two sexes: boys' shoulders grow wider than their hips, while girls' hips grow wider than their shoulders. During puberty, body fat increases in girls, deposited on the arms, legs, and trunk, while it decreases in boys.

Of course, the big story in puberty is sexual maturation. For girls, a three- to four-year period of development is characterized by the beginning of breast growth, the growth spurt, menarche, pubic and underarm hair development and the completion of breast maturation, in that sequence. Menstruation, then, does not occur until the girl's body is large enough to carry a pregnancy. Her capacity is further ensured by a 12- to 18-month period of sterility following first menstruation during which ovaries are not is not producing eggs with each cycle. The age of first menstruation varies from society to society and has changed over historical periods. In North America, the average age is about 12½. Women who are menstruating experience cyclical fluctuations in hormonal levels, and when their estrogen levels are at their highest, they perform better on cognitive tasks typically associated with superior female performance, such as verbal fluency tasks. When their estrogen levels are at their monthly low, women are better on tasks usually associated with male superior performance, such as spatial-rotation tasks (Blum, 1997).

In boys, the first sign of puberty is the growth of the testes. This is followed by the emergence of pubic hair and then, close to the age of 12, the growth of the penis. It is not until the development of these primary sexual characteristics is complete that a boy starts his growth spurt. The masculinization of the boy's voice (as the larynx enlarges and the vocal cords lengthen) begins during the growth spurt and is not typically complete until puberty is complete. Spermarche occurs around the age of 13, although the boy is still sterile for several months, producing semen that contains no sperm.

menarche The point in female puberty at which the first menstrual bleeding occurs.

spermarche The point in male puberty at which sperm is first ejaculated. It typically occurs around the age of 11 to 15 and is an early pubertal event, occurring before secondary sexual characteristics are fully developed.

> **11.7** **Press Pause**
>
> Girls are not sexually mature until after their growth spurts, when their bodies are big enough to carry a pregnancy. Boys sexually mature before growth is complete.

Views of Gender Development

Boys and girls differ physically, cognitively, and behaviourally, and theorists across academia are far from reaching a consensus regarding the reasons for this. As in other topics in this book, we will look at various perspectives on development. In some chapters, when we were discussing the development of perception, concepts or core knowledge for example, Piaget provided an important point of contrast. Here we also consider some prevailing views, examining whether general-purpose learning mechanisms might underlie development in both boys and girls, paying particular attention to the social learning theory of gender known as *gender socialization theory*.

GENDER SOCIALIZATION THEORY

Within psychology, some have tried to explain gender development in terms of more general, associationist psychological processes. Some have proposed that gender roles, norms, and behaviours are "learned" via the same general learning principles that underlie, according to them, other types of social learning: observation, imitation, and reinforcement (Bussey & Bandura, 1999, 2004; Lott & Maluso, 2001).

The crux of this view is that gender develops when children are "socialized" by parents, peers, and culture at large (Bandura, 1977; Bandura & Walters, 1963). One mechanism by which children are said to be socialized is by observing and then imi-

One study conducted in a science museum showed that parents were three times more likely to explain the science exhibits to their sons than to their daughters.

tating role models of one sex or the other. There is some laboratory research that supports this idea: When watching adult models perform various activities, children watched the same-sex model more, they remembered the actions of the same-sex model, and they were more likely to imitate the same-sex model (Bussey & Bandura, 1984; Perry & Bussey, 1979).

Another mechanism through which gender is socialized, according to this view, is the explicit and implicit way in which parents convey their expectations regarding gender-appropriate behaviour. North American parents tend to provide gender-appropriate toys (trucks and tools for boys, dolls and kitchen sets for girls) before their children are even old enough to verbally request these toys (Fisher-Thompson, 1993). Parents assign different household chores to boys and girls, again consistent with gender expectations (Leaper & Friedman, 2007). And parents may express their own gender expectations in conversation: One naturalistic observation study conducted in a science museum showed that parents were three times more likely to explain the science exhibits to their sons than to their daughters (Crowley, Callanan, Tenenbaum, & Allen, 2001).

According to the gender socialization perspective, boys behave like boys because they are rewarded for masculine behaviour and punished for feminine behaviour; girls learn to behave like girls because they are rewarded for doing so and punished for masculine behaviour. Both boys and girls are said to imitate a variety of gender models, including teachers, parents, and television characters (Leaper & Friedman, 2007). These theorists see these general learning mechanisms as the cause of differing behaviours and gender-defined roles in girls and boys.

> **11.8 Press Pause**
>
> A common view in psychology and throughout academia is that gender is "socialized," that it is not a result of our biological history, and that it is completely malleable.

Compared to other topics such as the development of visual perception, the development of language, or the development of animacy perception, the question of how sex differences develop is politically charged. There is a fear among some that if biology plays a role in sex differences, if boys and girls are different from each other by design, then this will justify discrimination against women. This fear is not entirely unfounded. Some authors have noted that, in the past, social commentators have argued that women should stay home, marry, have lots of babies, and avoid professional work on the grounds that, more or less, biology is destiny (Crittenden, 1999; Shalit, 1999). Realize, however, that to create moral prohibitions based on what is usually seen in nature is to commit the naturalistic fallacy that confuses "is" with "ought." There is no moral imperative to enforce the patterns and characteristics that we tend to see in nature.

From this perspective, a school of thought called *gender feminism* (Sommers, 1994) has emerged in the hope of protecting and promoting the rights of women. It is the strong contention of this school of thought that differences between men and women, other than the obvious anatomical differences, are not at all a result of biology or our biological history but are entirely "socially constructed." Anne Fausto-Sterling (1985) contends that "The key biological fact is that boys and girls have different genitalia" (p. 152). From there, she argues, parents label the child pink or blue so that they can be socialized appropriately (Fausto-Sterling, 1985). Gender feminists emphasize the complete gender plasticity of each infant, viewing newborn infants as "bi-sexual," which is to say "equipotent," with respect to gender. According to this view, infants are then transformed into male and female by those around them.

It would be precarious to make the argument that men and women should have, say, equal access to professional opportunities or equal access to education because they are cognitively indistinguishable. Politically, the problem with making this argument is that as soon as cognitive differences are documented (and many are) then the argument fails, and one is no longer obliged to ensure equal access to men and women. A more robust argument appeals to justice: Each person should be treated justly, regardless of demographics such as sex or race. This argument is not vulnerable to scientific discovery, and proponents of this argument need not feel motivated to thwart scientific discovery.

The Reimer Twins: A Natural Test of the Socialization Theory of Gender

Imagine that you were trying to design an experiment to test the hypothesis that, at birth, babies' minds are blank slates with respect to gender. One really excellent design for testing this hypothesis would be to take a baby boy, surgically reconstruct his genitals so that they are believably female; tell him he is a girl; tell everyone in his peer group, teachers, and family friends that he is a girl; and see how he turns out. If he grows up feeling and acting like a girl, it is good evidence that gender is socialized. If he grows up feeling and acting like a boy, in spite of all attempts to socialize him as a girl, then gender development is not left up to societal whim. The only thing that would make this experiment more perfect is to give this child an identical twin brother and let the twin grow up as a boy. Eerily, this experiment has been done. Not by some mad scientist but by accident.

Bruce Reimer was born a healthy, typical boy, with no physical or psychological anomalies whatsoever. He was born with an identical twin brother, Brian. At the age of 8 months, Bruce's penis was destroyed by a doctor during an attempted circumcision. The prevailing belief at the time was that children learn what they are socialized to learn by the adults around them. This was believed to be true of children's values, beliefs, attitudes, aggression, and their gender identities. In other words, a baby's mind was a blank slate with respect to gender, and the baby could be raised as either a boy or a girl. Dr. John Money, a psychologist who was known for his groundbreaking work within the field of sexual development and gender identity, not only held this belief, but he was also determined to prove that it was true. To this end, he jumped at the chance to work with the Reimer family, recommend Bruce's course of treatment, and—most importantly—report and interpret his findings to the world.

Dr. John Money, a psychologist who was known for his groundbreaking work within the field of sexual development and gender identity, believed in the gender socialization theory. He recommended raising Bruce Reimer as a girl and named her Brenda.

Brenda was miserable. She never felt like a girl. She hated being raised as a girl. She was ostracized and bullied as her peers rejected her as a girl. She was far too aggressive to fit in as a girl in her social milieu.

Money convinced the Reimer parents to raise Bruce, now called Brenda, as a girl. The Reimers were naturally concerned about doing the best they could for their child, and they were not educated in medicine or child development, so they found Money's forceful arguments persuasive. He convinced the Reimer parents that a normal life would be impossible for Bruce if they did not follow his recommendation and that, otherwise, the child would "live apart." Bruce's testes were removed at the age of 22 months, a vagina was surgically fashioned, and the baby was raised as a girl. (This was done because it was believed that a realistic vagina was easier to fashion surgically than a penis, not because anyone was trying to design an experiment.) Brenda was given estrogen treatments at puberty to induce breast development. Money pressured the family to continue with more surgery and with regular visits to his office where he could "treat" and observe the twins (Colapinto, 2000).

Money was in a position to tell the world his interpretation of the twins' development, and because of his clinical relationship with them, he could always claim that he was preserving their privacy and confidentiality and thus prevent any other researcher from independently evaluating their progress. Because Money was eager to prove that gender was socialized, and many academics, clinicians, and developmental theorists were eager to hear that this was true, Money reported that Brenda was a happy child with completely typical female gender development: "The child's behaviour is so clearly that of an active little girl and so different from the boyish ways of her twin brother" (Money, 1975). Academics had no reason to question his reports, as it agreed with all expectations, and moreover, no ability to challenge the reports since no one else had access to the family. As far as everyone in academia and medicine was concerned, the case "proved" that gender was socialized.

As Brenda grew up, the Reimer family was completely unaware of the impact of Money's reports on their case, or even that he was reporting on their case. But Brenda was miserable. She never felt like a girl. She hated being raised as a girl. She was ostracized and bullied as her peers rejected her as a girl. She was far too aggressive to fit in as a girl in her social milieu. In 1997, Reimer's harrowing story was finally revealed to the academic audience by Dr. Milton Diamond, who realized the impact that Money's misleading report was having. Diamond's intention was primarily to ensure that this infant sex-reassignment was not seen as a viable strategy and, secondarily, to weigh in on the theoretical claim that gender was completely socially constructed.

When the twins were 13, their parents told them the whole story. Brenda almost immediately decided to live as a male and chose the name David. Money never recanted or said anything to suggest that the sex reassignment was anything but completely successful. Separately, David and Brian both took their own lives.

Intersex

Above we discussed the typical pattern of prenatal development for male and female genitalia, which is paralleled by prenatal male and female brain development. It is interesting to consider that there are, in some cases, fetuses that develop differently and end up with some combination of chromosomal, genital, and brain development that is not typically male or female. These people are **intersex** people. A person might have genitals that are not clearly male or female, might have female-appearing external genitalia but internal male reproductive organs, or might have a genetic "mosaic" pattern such that some body tissues have male (XY) chromosomes and some tissues have female (XX) chromosomes. Here we will look at four of the known intersex conditions in detail although there are many more.

5-ALPHA-REDUCTASE DEFICIENCY

Also known as *guevedoche*, **5-alpha-reductase deficiency** is a disorder caused by the failure of the body to produce sufficient levels of 5-alpha-reductase, which in turn is caused by a mutation in the gene that normally carries out that function. This condition affects people with male genotypes, or an XY chromosome configuration. Five-alpha-reductase is an enzyme that is necessary for the conversion of testosterone, which is produced in the testes, to dihydrotestosterone (DHT), which is the form that is usable in the body.

Babies with this condition are born with male internal reproductive organs (testicles and **Wolffian structures**) but typically have female-appearing external genitalia. Thus, they are identified by their parents as female, given girls' names, and reared as girls. At puberty, these individuals produce sufficient concentrations of testosterone to prompt some masculinization (either due to direct effects of the testosterone, the effects of the small amounts of DHT that exist in the body, or the effects of a nongonadal type of DHT in the body). As a result, a person who has been raised as a girl up to this point may grow facial and body hair, his voice may lower, and his testes may descend from the abdomen into the scrotum. Some people with 5-alpha-reductase deficiency go on to assume male identities and live as men in spite of spending the first 12 or so years of their lives living as girls. This developmental trajectory is especially likely in the Dominican Republic because there are, by chance, enough cases of the disorder on that island that the changing of genders at puberty has become a social possibility.

Although not everyone with this condition changes gender at puberty, the fact that some do is again a challenge to the idea that gender development is a product of general-purpose learning mechanisms responding to the differences in the way boys and girls are treated. Individuals with this disorder are believed to be girls by their parents, siblings, teachers, and peers. However people treat girls is how these individuals would be treated. The fact that some of them go on to identify as male, believe themselves to be male, and successfully fulfill a male social role is counter to the predictions of the socialization theory of gender.

CONGENITAL ADRENAL HYPERPLASIA

Congenital adrenal hyperplasia (CAH) is a developmental condition that occurs in people with an XX chromosomal configuration and is the most common intersex condition in XX people. During prenatal development, the adrenal gland produces not just cortisone (which is typical) but also (again due to a mutation in a gene that produces a particular enzyme) an unusually large concentration of androgens (specifically, androstenedione). In some cases, the concentrations are high enough to produce masculinized external genitalia: a large clitoris and sometimes a partial scrotum. In most cases, parents are advised to raise the child as a girl, and in 90 per cent of the cases, the individual develops a female gender identity: That is, she thinks of herself as a girl (Houk, Hughes, Ahmed, & Lee, 2006).

intersex An umbrella term describing conditions in which an individual has some combination of chromosomal, genital, and brain development that is not typically male or female.

5-alpha-reductase deficiency A developmental condition caused by the failure of the body to produce sufficient levels of 5-alpha-reductase. Babies with male genotypes, or an XY chromosome configuration, will be born with typical internal male reproductive organs but female-appearing external genitalia.

Wolffian structures The internal male reproductive structures.

congenital adrenal hyperplasia A condition, in which the excessive production of androgens results in the masculinization of primary or secondary sex characteristics in developing girls.

This condition affects not just physical development but cognitive development as well. Children with this condition are more likely than other girls to engage in rough and tumble play and to choose toys that boys tend to prefer, like trucks and construction blocks. In fact, girls with CAH show significant masculinization compared to non-affected girls in their play activities, playmate preference, spatial ability, aggression, and even their adolescent activities (Berenbaum, 2002). Girls with CAH have less interest in the kinds of activities that typical girls do: Compared to their unaffected sisters, girls with CAH have less interest in infants. This finding led researchers to conclude that early exposure to androgens can reduce female-typical behaviour (Leveroni & Berenbaum, 1998).

Again, there are some interesting conclusions that can be drawn from this research. And again, these findings are a challenge to domain-general learning explanations of gender development since these studies focus on girls who were identified as female at birth, were raised as girls, and yet who show masculinized behaviour and cognition as a result of exposure to androgens. It also serves as an illustration of an interaction. We see that genes interact with hormonal milieu to lead to masculinized behaviour. Genes do not determine masculine (or feminine) behaviour.

ANDROGEN INSENSITIVITY SYNDROME

Androgen insensitivity syndrome (AIS) is an X-linked recessive trait associated with a gene on the X chromosome that is involved in the development of androgen receptors. It affects people with an XY karyotype who would otherwise develop as male but whose bodies do not respond to androgens. Their androgen receptors do not bind to androgens the way other people's (men's and women's) do, so the hormone has no mechanism allowing it to have its effect on the body. Because the fetus has a Y chromosome, the baby's body forms testes prenatally, and the testes produce both testosterone and a Mullerian-inhibiting hormone. In typically developing babies, the Mullerian-inhibiting hormone causes the Mullerian ducts to atrophy so that the fetus does not develop ovaries, fallopian tubes, or a cervix; this is true for individuals with androgen insensitivity syndrome as well because their bodies are only insensitive to androgens, not to the Mullerian-inhibiting hormone. However, the development of the external male genitalia is dependent on testosterone, and external male genitalia do not develop in these individuals whose tissues do not respond to androgens. The external genitalia in those with complete AIS develop according to the default plan, which appears as female.

Although there are varying degrees of androgen insensitivity, people with complete androgen insensitivity will typically appear completely female, will be identified from birth as female, and will be raised female, despite their XY karyotype. These girls do go through puberty, as the hypothalamus and pituitary signal the testes to increase hormonal production, but it occurs later than most girls. Levels of androgens and estrogens increase, and although the body does not respond to the androgens, it does respond to estrogens, resulting in breast development and hips. At this point the only overt clue of atypical development might be very sparse pubic hair. Most often in these cases, there is no reason to suspect that the child is experiencing any unusual development until she fails to menstruate, which in typical development would occur a couple of years after the onset of puberty. She cannot menstruate since she has no uterus or cervix, and her vagina is a relatively short, closed cavity. At this point the condition can be diagnosed by a blood assay of hormone levels, which will reveal that this young girl has adult male levels of androgens in her blood. Ironically, the visual appearance of an adult with complete androgen insensitivity may be more feminine than the average woman because women without the condition do respond to the androgens in their system and, compared to women with AIS, will have more hair on their arms, legs, and upper lips and less hair atop their heads as a result.

Clearly the existence of women with complete androgen insensitivity who have an XY karyotype and a female identity shows a disconnect between genes and gender. Gender is not genetically determined. It also gives us a chance to see that hormones can act independently of one another, and their action depends on their ability to bind to their own receptors: The developing AIS girl's body responds typically to the Mullerian-inhibiting hormone.

TURNER'S SYNDROME

Finally, let us consider **Turner's syndrome**. A person who has Turner's syndrome has only one sex chromosome, and it is an X chromosome. Will this person appear to be male or female? Think about this for a second. Remember that the default developmental plan for the human body is female. Remember that genetic information on the Y chromosome triggers a cascade of development that leads to masculinization. A person who has Turner's syndrome looks female because in order to develop a female body plan, you do not need to have two X chromosomes; you need only lack a Y chromosome. People who have Turner's syndrome are raised as and live as girls.

A person with Turner's syndrome is usually shorter than the average woman. She may also experience abnormal gonad development and subsequently abnormal levels of sex hormones. In some individuals, the ovaries actually degenerate and thus cannot produce normal levels of estrogen. In these cases, the development of secondary sex characteristics at puberty depends on exogenous estrogen therapy. Those affected with Turner's syndrome have typical female genitalia: clitoris, labia, and vagina, but other abnormalities are associated with this condition, including heart problems. One thing that this condition makes clear, that we might not have known otherwise, is that the second X chromosome is necessary for typical female development.

But Turner's syndrome is even more interesting. A person who has Turner's syndrome has only one X chromosome, and she may have received that chromosome from either her mother or her father. You know from Chapter 3 and our discussion of Mendelian inheritance that the alleles that mothers and fathers pass on to their children do not differ by the sex of the parent: They vary across individuals but not in any way that is associated with the sex of the parent. However, it turns out that the parental source of the X chromosome (mother vs. father) makes a difference due to a process called *genomic imprinting*, which the parent uses to prepare the X chromosome for a daughter or a son.

Genomic imprinting is a chemical alteration, or chemical tagging, of an allele that alters the likelihood that it will be expressed in the phenotype. (For example, an allele might be tagged by chemically bonding a methyl group to the DNA, and this "tag" can be taken off in the next generation.) Imprinting is reversible: The imprinting of an allele can be erased in one gen-

Turner's syndrome
A condition in which an individual has only one sex chromosome, always an X chromosome.

genomic imprinting The chemical tagging of an allele that alters the likelihood that it will be expressed in the phenotype.

figure 11.5   From Mom or Dad?

A person who has Turner's syndrome has only one X chromosome, and she may have received that one chromosome from either her mother or her father.

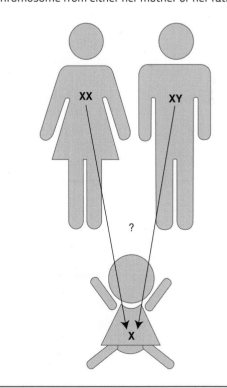

eration and then re-established again in a later generation. Imagine that you are taking a physiology course. In the psychology textbook that you are using for this course, certain passages have already been marked with Post-it Notes so that you can make best use of the book. Later, you give the book to someone who plans to use it for a cognition course, so you go through and replace the original Post-it Notes with new notes that will highlight the most useful information in a cognition course. The book is handed from person to person; all the information is still in the book even when it is not needed, and the Post-it Notes can be removed as easily as they are placed.

Recall that for an autosomal gene (a gene that is not on an X or Y sex chromosome), there will be a pair of alleles, one from the father and one from the mother. As far as we currently know, most autosomal alleles are not imprinted, and both the allele from the mother and the allele from the father might be expressed, either according to our understanding of Mendel's dominant and recessive genes or according to other interactions with each other. In mammals, less than 1 per cent of the alleles are imprinted such that either the father's or the mother's allele is expressed, and the other is suppressed in a manner independent of the dominant and recessive genes described by Mendel and discussed in Chapter 3. In mammals, an example of this effect is the relative involvement in embryonic and placental development: Alleles contributed from the mother contribute more to embryonic development, while alleles contributed from the father contribute more to placental development (Barton, Surani, & Norris, 1984). In fact, this arrangement has become mandatory, and a conceptus that was created from all female contributions would not have enough placental development to live, while one created from all male contributions would not have sufficient embryonic development to be viable.

Genomic imprinting allows each parent to make alleles more or less active in the offspring. The parent can custom tailor the chromosome for a child in ways that are known to affect both body and brain development, and we know that parents do, in fact, prepare their X chromosomes to optimize performance for either a son or a daughter.

Remember that a father is going to give his offspring the chromosome that triggers sex-specific development. Typically, if he gives his offspring an X chromosome, that child will have an XX karyotype and develop to be a girl, and if he gives his offspring a Y chromosome, that child will have an XY karyotype and develop to be a boy. If he gives an X, the baby will be a girl, and so he prepares his X chromosome for a daughter, ready to optimize a female life strategy. Any X chromosome that the father makes is an X chromosome made for a girl, Turner's syndrome girls included.

Conversely, an X chromosome that comes from a mother is an X chromosome made for a boy. This is because if the mother's X is paired with a Y chromosome, alleles on her X will act unopposed. The Y chromosome is very small and does not have all of the alleles to complement those on the X chromosome. There is no dominant and recessive interaction between alleles with respect to alleles on the X chromosome of a boy since he just does not have those alleles on the Y chromosome he got from dad. The sex of the parent that donates the X chromosome does not affect which alleles are

From the Classroom to the Lab

Imagine you wanted to test the hypothesis that girls with Turner's syndrome with a maternally derived X chromosome would be better at "male superior" cognitive skills. How would you test that?

passed down or which alleles are available for the offspring to pass on to his or her off-spring, but the relative activation of some alleles is affected by genomic imprinting. So for a particular generation, genetic expression is affected by the genetic imprinting the mother or father did before she passing the X chromosome on to the offspring.

So you can divide people with Turner's syndrome into two groups: those who have an X chromosome optimized for boys and those who have an X chromosome opti-mized for girls. And guess what? It matters. Those with girl-optimized X chromosomes (from Dad) are better at cognitive skills that females are better at (Skuse et al., 1997): reading body language and facial expressions, recognizing faces, verbal fluency, and social skills, broadly, compared to those with boy-optimized X chromosomes (from Mom). Clearly, this shows that something more interesting than the socialization of gender underlies sex differences in these studies since most parents (and teachers and peers) were unaware of whether a girl with Turner's syndrome had her father's X chro-mosome or her mother's X chromosome.

The Transgender Experience

Another challenge to gender socialization theory is the experience of transgender indi-viduals. Children begin to identify with one gender or the other around 3 years of age. For most children, their gender identity is consistent with their parents' views of their gender, but some children may identify with, indeed insist on, an identity that is not consistent with others' evaluations. This transgender expression begins early in life. What is more, the gender identity is extremely resilient and resistant even to intensive

Some children may have a gender identity that is not consistent with others' evaluations. Once old enough, these individuals may choose to transition in order to live as the gender that fits with their gender identity, as was the case with one of these identical twins.

therapy (Zucker & Bradley, 1995). Once old enough, these individuals may choose to transition in order to live as the gender that fits with their gender identity.

How do the examples of anomalous gender development bear on gender socialization theory? The case of the Reimer twins shows how a stubborn adherence to gender socialization theory did a great deal of damage to one developing child and his family. The case of 5-alpha reductase deficiency is interesting because some of the individuals with this condition live as adult men with a male identity in spite of being "socialized" to be female before puberty. With both CAH and Turner's syndrome, there are cases of cognitive and behavioural sex differences that occur within a group of girls, all of whom were identified as girls, given girls' names, and again "socialized" to be girls from birth. Finally, the experience of transgender individuals (just as in David Reimer's case) shows that gender identity is robust and is not easily changed no matter how insistent and consistent parents and doctors are.

Relative Life Expectancy

As is true in many species, human males die at a younger age than females, and for humans the difference is five years on average. Females live longer than males in a wide range of species, so the reason cannot be something that is specific to humans (such as societal pressures on men to live a stressful life). In order to understand what is going on here, recall that the variance in reproductive success is greater for males than it is for females. Males can potentially have lots and lots of children, but if some men are having lots and lots of children, then other men are not. Women have an upper limit in terms of the number of children they can have: They are compelled to gestate each child for nine months and then nurse the child for many more.

There is evidence consistent with the idea that men have a much greater variance than women in reproductive success. Everyone has mitochondrial DNA, which is DNA that is not in the nucleus of the cell organized into chromosomes but in the extra-nuclear organelle of each cell. This DNA comes to you only from your mother; there is no sexual recombination and no contribution from your father. Conversely, men have Y chromosomes that they always get from their fathers only. Women do not have a Y chromosome to give. So in the human population, we have DNA that is inherited only from our mothers that we can compare directly to DNA that is inherited only from our fathers. Guess what? There is greater diversity of DNA in the mitochondrial DNA (mom's DNA) than in Y chromosome DNA (dad's DNA), which is consistent with the idea that there is greater variance in reproductive success in males than females. The human population has more grandmothers than grandfathers (Gibbons, 2000).

Furthermore, an examination of 18 different data sets (including historic genealogies covering recent centuries) from 17 different countries revealed that for contemporary human populations, there is more variance in the number of offspring males have than the number of offspring females have. That is, compared to women, more men have a greater number of children, and more men have none, while women tend to stay closer to the average. Note, however, that this difference changed a lot cross-culturally. More importantly, there is a positive correlation between the number of mates a man has and the number of offspring he has (Brown, Laland, & Borgerhoff Mulder, 2009). A man can increase his reproductive success by having more mates, but men in general run the risk of losing the game completely by having no offspring. The implication is that, in many domains, risk-taking is worth it for males but not for females.

This means that there is a greater potential payoff for any male strategy that might attract a mate, and therefore males are willing to accept the risk commensurate with this greater payoff. The "strategy" that might attract a mate could be behavioural or physiological. The derring-do of male displays of physical acumen (think extreme sports) may have been attractive to females in the EEA or may have impressed other males enough to raise an individual's status, indirectly leading to greater mate value, but it also leads to fatal accidents. Accidents are the leading cause of death in young males aged 1–24 and the second highest cause of death in adult males aged 25–44. Even if daredevil behaviour is not attractive in our current environment, it is a result of a psychology formed by a high payoff awarded to males in the EEA who were willing to accept high risks in order to win mates. Males with higher testosterone levels are more attractive to females (Feinberg, 2008), but testosterone suppresses their immune system, leaving them open to the risk of exposure to pathogens.

In addition to the greater risk associated with male behaviour and male hormones, another very important contributor to the sex difference in life expectancy results from pleiotropy. Recall from Chapter 3 that pleiotropy occurs when a single gene has effects on more than one phenotypic trait. Pleiotropy is thought to be a good explanation for senescence in general and for the sex difference in senescence. If a single gene affords a great advantage to someone (in terms of reproduction) at the age of 20 but causes a breakdown of some system at age 80, that gene will be selected for more strongly than it is selected against, regardless of how damaging it is at age 80. Because males stand to gain more from a possibly beneficial change at age 20, they are more resistant to the "weeding out" of deleterious effects that occur after the age of reproduction. Men are more vulnerable than women to the senescent effects of pleiotropic genes.

As you might predict from this argument, if you examine a polygynous species living in a zoo (in which males have the potential of mating with many females and in which variance in male reproductive success is consequently greater than female variance in reproductive success), where all hazards of death due to risk-taking are reduced and you have all the medical care you could hope for, males still die younger than females. Compare that to monogamous species in which male and female variance in reproductive success is more equal, and you do not see the same sex difference in life expectancy (Daly & Wilson, 1983).

Cultural Differences in Mating and Parenting

Greater male variance in reproductive success has implications for child rearing. We know that when polygynous species are compared to monogamous species, there are greater sex differences. Often, males in polygynous species are larger and more aggressive, reflecting the greater payoff available to those who successfully out-compete other males.

Human societies vary in the extent to which they are polygynous versus monogamous, so similar cross-cultural comparisons are possible with humans. One might expect that greater polygyny in a society would lead to greater sex differences measured behaviourally. Indeed, in an ambitious cross-cultural survey, the more polygyny (measured as the per cent of males who were married to more than one woman), the more boys were taught to exhibit aggression, fortitude, and industriousness (Low, 1989). There is also a correlation between maximum harem size (the greatest number of wives a man can have) and training boys to be competitive (except in stratified societies where caste systems prevent successfully striving for success).

Meanwhile, in polygynous societies, girls are taught to be responsible and to show sexual restraint. Training for industriousness and responsibility, for girls, increases with the degree of polygyny. The author of the study concludes that boys and girls are trained differently than each other and trained differently in different societies in a pattern that is consistent both with evolutionary theory and with findings across other species (Low, 1989).

SUMMARY

Males and females, in humans as in many other species, have a suite of adaptations that are designed to work together and are designed to execute the male reproductive strategy or the female reproductive strategy most effectively. One strategy will lead to maximum reproductive success for a man and a different reproductive strategy will lead to the highest payoff for a woman.

Many psychological adaptations are the same in boys and girls, but because the best male strategy differs from the best female strategy, there is evidence of different performance on some cognitive and social tasks. Males tend to perform better on different types of spatial tasks than females do. Girls and women are more verbally fluent than boys and men. Temperament and toy preferences also differ, beginning at an early age.

The examples you read about people whose sex and gender development differ from the norm are interesting stories on their own but can also help shed light on typical development. The effects of genomic imprinting in Turner's syndrome are particularly interesting: Those women who have genes that were meant to be expressed in a girl are more feminized, on social and cognitive tests, than those women who have genes that were meant to be expressed in a boy.

The story of the Reimer twins is a story about gender development in one family as well as a story about a deeply held belief about gender development being challenged. At the time that the Reimer twins were born, scientists (and many academics across disciplines) believed that gender was completely malleable and that either femininity or masculinity could be socialized. The experiment falsified the idea that gender was completely a result of socialization.

PRESS PAUSE SUMMARY

- In addition to many shared complex adaptations, men and women will also have some different complex adaptations—a rare exception to the rule that complex adaptations are universal.

- Each sex has a suite of adaptations that work together These. adaptations include morphological, physiological, endochrinological, cognitive and emotional adaptations.

- In humans, the presence of the SRY gene on the Y chromosome usually leads to the development of the suite of masculine adaptations.

- Sex differences arose because men and women solved a slightly different set of adaptive problems in the EEA.

- Early sex differences in cognition reveal adaptive sex differences. Each sex has adaptations specialized for gender-specific tasks in the EEA.

- Natural selection has multiple avenues of development available, including the active participation of the developing individual.

- Girls are not sexually mature until after their growth spurt, when their bodies are big enough to carry a pregnancy. Boys sexually mature before growth is complete.

- A common view in psychology and throughout academia is that gender is "socialized," that it is not a result of our biological history, and that it is completely malleable.

KEY TERMS AND CONCEPTS

5-alpha-reductase deficiency, 403

androgen insensitivity syndrome, 387

autosome, 385

congenital adrenal hyperplasia, 403

genomic imprinting, 405

intersex, 403

menarche, 398

relational aggression, 392

spermarche, 398

SRY gene, 386

testis determining factor, 386

Turner's syndrome, 405

Wolffian structures, 403

QUESTIONS FOR THOUGHT AND DISCUSSION

1. Describe some sex differences in cognitive and social performance. What is the relationship between the tasks that boys perform better on and the tasks that girls perform better on? Put this in the context of the sex roles that likely existed in the EEA.

2. What is genomic imprinting? What cognitive tasks reveal an effect of genomic imprinting in women with Turner's syndrome? What do the results of these tasks suggest about the development of cognitive sex differences?

3. What is socialization? What does the socialization theory of gender development propose? Provide evidence for and against this theory of gender development.

4. Describe how nature and nurture work together to contribute to gender development. Why do you think people continue to discuss nature vs. nurture when they talk about the area of gender development?

From the Classroom to the Lab: Follow Up

Consider the experiment you designed in response to the "From the Classroom to the Lab" challenge earlier in this chapter.

What is your independent variable?

What set of tasks did you choose to compare to test your hypothesis?

Are there control tasks? If so, what are they? What would be the danger of not including any control tasks?

Imagine you have run your experiment. If the group with a maternally derived X chromosome performs better on your experimental tasks but not on your control tasks, what do you conclude?

If the group with a maternally derived X chromosome performs better on your experimental tasks and on your control tasks, what do you conclude?

chapter 12

Moral and Prosocial Development

Opening Vignette: Morals

Xander is 3 years old. He asks his dad if he can drink the bottle of juice he found in the refrigerator. Dad says, "No! Go put that back." Xander understands that there is a "rule" against drinking the juice and that because Dad said so, it is "wrong" to drink the juice. Therefore he hides behind the couch, where no one can see him, and drinks the bottle of juice.

Madison is 7 years old. She is playing a game with her friends. One rule of the game is that everyone plays on their own: Teams are not allowed. One of her friends has a cousin visiting from out of town, and the cousin doesn't know how to play the game. She wants to play on a team. Madison says, "Well, the rule is that you can't play as a team, but I guess if everyone agrees to change the rule, you can play as a team today."

Andrew is 16 years old. His neighbour Ben got caught stealing Andrew's bike, but the bike was returned unharmed. Ben says he meant no harm and was going to return the bike later that day. He wouldn't have taken it, but his own bike was in the shop. Ben's dad said that as a punishment for stealing Andrew's bicycle, Ben had to give Andrew his own bike. Ben is devastated. Andrew tells Ben that since the bike wasn't harmed and since it was returned right away, he didn't have to give up his own bike.

Chapter Outline

- Morality and Prosocial Behaviour
- Traditional Views on Moral Development
- What Evolutionary Thinking Adds to Moral and Prosocial Development
- The Function of Morality
- Social Behaviour and Fitness
- Getting Altruism off the Ground
- Kin-Selected Altruism
- Co-operation among Non-Kin
- Moral Intuition or Rational Moral Decision-Making?
- Specialized Cognitive Machinery Underlying Morality
- The Development of Social Exchange Reasoning
- The Development of Sexual Morals
- Universal Rules vs. Conventions
- Teaching Morals: Over-Reward or Internalize?

- In this chapter you will read about moral development and the development of prosocial behaviour. After reading this chapter you should be familiar with the ideas of the ancient philosophers and the Enlightenment-era British philosophers with regard to the acquisition of morality.

- You should understand the foundation of contemporary thinking on moral development laid out by Piaget and Kohlberg. You should also understand how their theories were common to each other, how they differed from each other, and how they differ from evolutionary thinking about moral psychology.

- You will learn about altruism in this chapter. Importantly, you should understand why altruism was a puzzle for evolutionary psychologists. You should understand three major solutions to the altruism puzzle: kin selection, reciprocal altruism, and by-product mutualism.

- One of the cognitive prerequisites for reciprocal altruism is a mechanism for excluding cheaters. You should understand why that is, and you will read evidence of cheater detection in children. You should understand why people would need psychological mechanisms to avoid incest and how the proposed incest avoidance mechanisms work in humans.

- This chapter describes two specific cases of moral development in detail. The first case deals with reciprocal altruism and the ability to detect cheaters. The second case addresses the development of moral judgments relating to incest.

- You will also read about morality in other cultures. You should understand why certain moral rules seem to be human universals, while others differ from culture to culture. You should understand the concept of moral inclusion and the psychology that makes even the universal rules of morality only nominally universal.

morality The intuitive sense of right and wrong that guides our own behaviour and leads us to judge and possibly condemn others' behaviours.

prosocial behaviour All the nice things we do for, and to, others, including altruism, friendship, coalitional behaviours, and even parental behaviours.

Morality and Prosocial Behaviour

Morality is the intuitive sense of right and wrong that guides our own behaviour and leads us to judge and possibly condemn others' behaviours. Although other animals may have a sense of right and wrong, especially with respect to behaviours that may lead to punishment from others, humans' morality is unique. Although other animals have prosocial and altruistic behaviours, humans are unique in holding some behaviours as obligatory and others as prohibited. For the purposes of this chapter, we will take morality to be all of the psychological processes governing prosocial behaviour and regulating obligatory or forbidden behaviours and exchanges between individuals.

12.1 Press Pause

Morality is the intuitive sense of right and wrong that guides our behaviour and leads us to judge others' behaviours. It is part of our human psychology.

Prosocial behaviour is the broad term that refers to all the nice things we do for, and to, others. It includes altruism, friendship, coalitional behaviours, and even parental behaviours. You will read in this chapter why prosocial behaviour is a mystery that demands an explanation against a backdrop of our evolutionary perspective of competing alleles.

Traditional Views on Moral Development

As in fields we have discussed previously, from conceptual development to language development, traditional debates about the development of morality have predominantly been framed in terms of nature vs. nurture. Psychologists in the last several decades and philosophers centuries before them have wondered whether morality was part of human nature, unfolding inevitably during development, or whether it was something that had to be carefully taught.

English philosopher Thomas Hobbes stated in his 1651 field-establishing book *Leviathan* that "Justice and Injustice are none of the Faculties neither of the Body, nor Mind." In other words, Hobbes was very much of the opinion that our minds were blank slates. Morality, and any thinking or reasoning about morality, was learned. The human mind needed to provide nothing in order for a person to develop morally; rather, explicit tutoring was necessary, according to this Hobbesian view. John Locke, as you can imagine, also held this empiricist view of morality.

British philosopher John Stuart Mill (1806–1873) advanced his view of morality: *utilitarianism*. According to this view, one could and should make deliberate moral decisions based on what is best overall for the greatest number of people. One could, theoretically, sum up the advantage or "utility" conferred by a given course of action distributed across everyone, and whichever course of action conferred the greatest utility was the morally correct path. An individual could be injured, even killed, if a sufficient number of people benefitted a sufficient amount to justify the injury.

> ### 12.2 Press Pause
> Traditional discussions of moral development have been framed in terms of the nature vs. nurture question.

In 1903, British philosopher George Edward Moore offered a critique of the prevailing view, still pertinent today, by pointing out what he called the *naturalistic fallacy*. The naturalistic fallacy is the error of equating what is good with what is natural, akin to the "is–ought" fallacy (Moore, 1903). In more recent support of this view, philosopher Wolfgang Wickler argues that what is good for evolution is good ethically: "The ethologist is . . . justified in criticizing many of the existing ethical norms . . . both positive and negative. He is, also, I believe, fully entitled to suggest, on

In 1651, Thomas Hobbes wrote that "Justice and Injustice are none of the Faculties neither of the Body, nor Mind." In other words, Hobbes was very much of the opinion that our minds were blank slates with respect to morality.

John Stuart Mill believed that one could sum up the advantage or "utility" conferred by a given course of action distributed across everyone; whichever course of action conferred the greatest utility was the morally correct path.

the basis of his scientific knowledge, where and how norms should be changed" (Wickler, 1972, pp. 141–142).

Defining what is good in terms of what occurs in nature, or conversely what is bad in terms of what does not occur in nature, does not work. Violence, including domestic violence and infanticide, occurs in nature. Polygamy is more common worldwide than monogamy. Women worldwide spend more of their time engaged in child care than men do. Is it correct to conclude that these naturally occurring human behaviours are therefore moral imperatives? To draw that conclusion is to make the naturalistic fallacy.

In the contemporary field of psychology, moral psychology and assumptions about moral development in particular have been sculpted by the thinking of Jean Piaget and later by Lawrence Kohlberg. Piaget and Kohlberg both held the view that morality and moral judgments are delivered to the developing child from society and that processes such as reward and punishment are an integral part of moral development. Moral judgment, according to both of these psychologists, was dependent upon sufficient cognitive development so that a child could think through the dispassionate logic that Piaget and Kohlberg believed constituted moral thinking. For Piaget and Kohlberg, morality is not based on intuition but on deliberate cognitive reasoning.

George Edward Moore pointed out what he called the *naturalistic fallacy*. The naturalistic fallacy is the error of equating what is good with what is natural.

12.3 Press Pause

Piaget and Kohlberg have laid the foundation of contemporary thinking in moral development.

WHAT WOULD PIAGET AND KOHLBERG SAY ABOUT MORAL DEVELOPMENT?

Historically, Piaget was the first to lay the foundation of the cognitive development of moral understanding in 1932 when he wrote *The Moral Judgment of the Child*. Piaget's view of moral development is a stage theory and is consistent with his model of cognitive development generally. In his view, a child's understanding changed from a concrete acceptance of rigid, unchangeable rules to an understanding of rules as a social contract and was, therefore, negotiable and changeable. According to Piaget, this change came about largely as a result of struggles and interactions with peers rather than as a result of interactions with adults.

Piaget employed a couple of different methods in his study of moral development. His earlier work on moral development used an observational method in which he observed children playing games together. He watched how they negotiated their games and dealt with the creation of and violation of rules.

Subsequently, he devised another method wherein he interviewed children about their reaction to rules being broken and rules being followed. He was interested in whether it made a difference if breaking a rule was intentional or accidental and what factors affected what the children thought about appropriate punishments. Piaget developed a standardized interview method in which he told a child a short story and had them identify the more serious of two transgressions. For example, the child would be asked which of two children was naughtier: a child named Augustine who accidently knocked over a large glass of juice while helping set the table or a child named Julian who knocked over a small glass of juice while running in the house, a forbidden act. From these interviews, he was able to map developmental change in the seriousness of the "crime." Children younger than 6 considered only the amount of damage, whereas older children also considered the intentions of the actor.

Piaget's stages of moral development

Piaget described stages of moral development, including the morality of constraint stage, the transitional period, and the stage of autonomous morality.

Morality of constraint

The morality of constraint stage is the earliest stage and typically involves children younger than 7 or 8 years old who have not yet reached the stage of concrete operations. In the morality of constraint stage, children take rules as unchangeable and non-negotiable. A rule is a rule because an authority figure (parent, teacher, or other adult) says it is. Punishment, likewise, is justified because the authority figure says it is. Good and bad are clear and easy to define: Following the rules is good, and violating the rules is bad. According to Piaget, children in this stage overlook the intention of the actor; the consequence of the action, not the intention, determines whether the act was good or bad. The child in this stage evaluates morality in terms of objective consequences: A child who breaks several cups but does so unintentionally is naughtier than a child who breaks one cup but does so maliciously. (However, during this stage, children ages 2 to 4 do not have a concept of morality. They often play without rules and do not follow others' rules consistently. Although they may or may not follow a rule, it does not occur to them that they might question or negotiate a rule given by an authority figure.)

Is it worse to spill a small glass of juice while being naughty or a large glass of juice while trying to be helpful? To Piaget, a child's answer to this question would reveal his stage of moral development.

In Piaget's view, there were two reasons for the child's acceptance of rules as unalterable. First, because they were in an early stage of cognitive development, they could only understand rules as "things" like any other object whose existence could not be disputed. The second reason was more practical: Parents are bigger than kids and have power over kids, so small children are not in a position to enter into negotiations.

From the Classroom to the Lab

Imagine that you want to test the hypothesis that the changes described here that take place during the transitional period show a different course of time depending on whom the child interacts with. Perhaps rules become flexible with peers before they become flexible with adults. Design an experiment to test this hypothesis.

| figure | 12.1 | **Piaget's theory of moral judgment** |

Piaget's view of moral development is a stage theory. Children younger than 7 or 8 years are in the *morality of constraint* stage and take rules as unchangeable and non-negotiable. After the age of 10, children are in the *autonomous morality* stage and believe that rules are social contracts that can be negotiated and renegotiated.

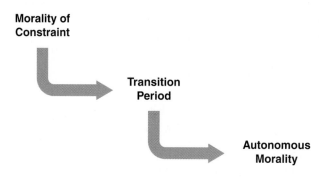

The transitional period

Between the ages of 7 and 10, children are in the transitional period with respect to moral development. During this period, children spend an increasing amount of time with peers and are therefore in more relationships that are equal with respect to power status. They have more opportunities to negotiate and have input into what the rules are and how they are enforced. They learn, therefore, that rules can change. For example, the rules in a game of marbles could be changed to adapt to a current situation, like an unusual number of players present or an unusual number of marbles available. Children in this stage also learn how to appreciate another person's perspective and take it into account, and they consider intentions when deciding on punishments: An accident does not call for the same punishment as a malicious deed, even if the damage is the same. In the example above with the spilled juice, Julian's behaviour is seen as naughtier, even though the damage is less, because he was violating a prohibition.

Autonomous morality

The stage of autonomous morality (also called *moral relativism*) is actually the second stage of moral development since the transitional period is not a stage in Piaget's view. Children enter the stage of autonomous morality after the age of 10 and believe that rules are social contracts that can be negotiated and renegotiated. They understand that rules have to meet the needs of multiple people, and they are able to consider multiple perspectives when proposing fair rules. They believe that punishment is a product of social agreement and should be fair to everyone involved. They also believe that sometimes authority figures impose rules and punishments that are not fair.

| 12.4 | **Press Pause** |

Piaget's model of moral development was a stage theory, and it paralleled his views on more general cognitive development.

KOHLBERG

Lawrence Kohlberg (1927–1987) is the most well-known name in the field of moral development, and he is widely recognized to be the biggest contributor to the foundation of the field. Kohlberg worked on moral development later than Piaget and was influenced by his framework and his methods, especially the technique of presenting children with vignettes and asking them to evaluate them. Kohlberg gave children fictional stories that ended in a dilemma and asked them to tell him what the right thing to do would be and, very importantly for Kohlberg, why.

Like Piaget, Kohlberg was a stage theorist and was interested in describing and sequencing the stages that children went through on their way to mature moral reasoning. A famous story, and a good example of the method he used to approach moral development research, is the story about Heinz:

Lawrence Kohlberg is widely regarded as the biggest contributor to the foundation of the field of moral development. He was influenced by Piaget, adopting his stage perspective, cognitive perspective, and interview method. Kohlberg created scenarios, like the famous "Heinz" story, to probe moral development.

> A woman was near death from a special kind of cancer. There was one drug that the doctors thought might save her. It was a form of radium that a druggist in the same town had recently discovered. The drug was expensive to make, but the druggist was charging ten times what the drug cost him to make. He paid $200 for the radium and charged $2,000 for a small dose of the drug. The sick woman's husband, Heinz, went to everyone he knew to borrow the money, but he could only get together about $1,000 which is half of what it cost. He told the druggist that his wife was dying and asked him to sell it cheaper or let him pay later. But the druggist said: "No, I discovered the drug and I'm going to make money from it." So Heinz got desperate and broke into the man's store to steal the drug for his wife. Should the husband have done that? (Kohlberg, 1963, p. 19)

Kohlberg listened to the child's thoughts on whether this was right or wrong and encouraged the child to explain why he answered the way he did. Is the husband prevented from stealing because doing so is forbidden, or is the husband obliged to do so because of his responsibility for his wife's well-being? The child's stage of moral development was determined not by whether he (all of Kohlberg's subjects were boys) thought it was right or wrong to steal the drug but by the reasoning behind the choice. If the child appealed to authority, the law, and law enforcement, the child was at a lower level of moral development than a child who mentioned concern for the wife's health and well-being.

INNOVATIVE
RESEARCH METHOD

Kohlberg described three levels of moral reasoning: pre-conventional, conventional, and post-conventional. Within each level, there are two stages. This means that there are theoretically six stages of moral reasoning, but according to Kohlberg it was exceptionally rare for anyone to reach the sixth stage. In fact, Kohlberg eventually stopped scoring that stage (Kohlberg, 1978).

Pre-conventional reasoning is self-centred, concrete, and immediate. In this stage, children are focussed on punishment and, in particular, how to avoid it. This level encompasses the first two stages. Stage 1 is the "punishment and obedience orientation" in which children suggest that the person should follow the law in order to avoid punishment. Stage 2 is "instrumental and exchange orientation" in which children might suggest bargaining in order to mitigate punishment. If Heinz gets caught stealing, he should just give the medicine back, and things should be okay.

Conventional reasoning recognizes that rules are social contracts, and people who are in this stage follow rules and laws in order to preserve and promote social relationships and social order. This level includes Stages 3 and 4. In Stage 3, the "mutual interpersonal relationships" stage, relationships are the focus. The actor should do what is expected of him by virtue of his role in his relationships, as a good citizen or a good husband. The focus of Stage 4 is on "social systems." People behave as they do in order to preserve social systems such as the legal system, marriage, or "law and order."

Post-conventional reasoning, according to Kohlberg, is reasoning according to ideals or moral principles. At this level, breaking a rule might be called for if breaking the rule involved behaviour that was consistent with the higher principle and obeying the rule involved behaviour that was inconsistent with that principle. Stage 5 is included in this level. In Stage 5, the "social contract and individual rights" stage, the focus is on the greatest good for the greatest number. At this stage people can reason hypothetically. They can imagine how their own society might be even better than it is. Stage 6, the "universal principles" stage, involves reasoning in a way that is consistent with one's own moral principles, such as equality or respect for all, even if adhering to these principles means breaking the law. The development from Stage 5 and Stage 6 can be thought of as shifting from a social, communal perspective to a more personal perspective, with an emphasis on the value of each person regardless of his or her ideas.

Kohlberg believed (following Piaget's tradition) that these stages were achieved and completed in the same order by children all over the world. However, Kohlberg was very clear that not all people reached the same stage. No one, as it turns out, reached Stage 6. Kohlberg eventually abandoned his sixth level because too few people achieved it.

Stage 5 was only attained by less than 10 per cent of people. The majority of people reached and stayed in Stage 4 reasoning. There is a small but positive relationship

table 12.1   **A Summary of Kohlberg's Stages of Moral Development**

COGNITIVE FOCUS	DESCRIPTION
Stage 1: Obedience	One must obey authority to be moral.
Stage 2: Exchange	Following a tit-for-tat strategy is moral.
Stage 3: Relationships	Fulfilling the expectations of one's social role is moral.
Stage 4: Law and Order	Uphold the law and conform to societal expectations.
Stage 5: Social Contracts and Individual Rights	Laws can be violated if they violate individual rights or harm society.
Stage 6: Universal Moral Principles	There are universal moral principles that do not change regardless of context or majority opinion.

Kohlberg believed that these stages were achieved in the same order by children all over the world, but not all people achieved the same final stage.

figure 12.2 Age trends in moral reasoning in Kohlberg's longitudinal sample

Kohlberg believed that these stages were achieved in the same order, but his data show that not all people achieved the same final stage. Most people end up in Stage 4, fewer than 10 per cent achieve Stage 5, and no one makes it to Stage 6.

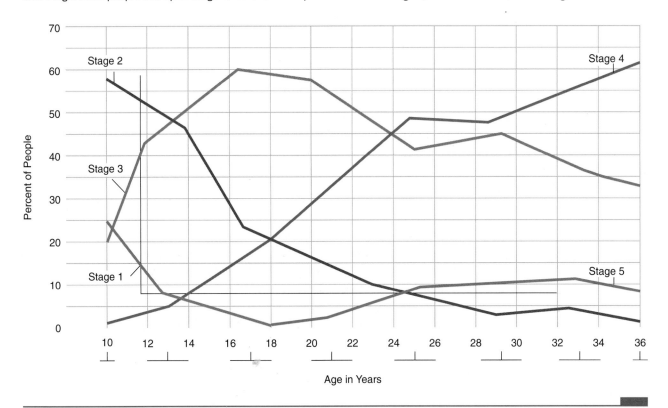

between moral reasoning (as measured by Kohlberg's methods) and moral behaviour (Kohlberg & Candee, 1984). People who have a higher stage of moral reasoning are more likely to provide assistance to others in need (Blasi, 1980) and less likely to engage in immoral behaviours (Jurkovic, 1980; Lee & Prentice, 1988; Palmer & Hollin, 1998). However, the relationship between Kohlberg's level of reasoning and people's behaviours is weak, as people actually act more impulsively or more intuitively and then use moral reasoning to justify their decisions rather than to guide them (Krebs & Denton, 2005; Krebs et al., 2002).

12.5 Press Pause

Kohlberg told children stories that presented a moral dilemma and then evaluated their thought processes. According to Kohlberg, children everywhere passed through the stages in the same order but not every person made it to the same level.

SHORTCOMINGS OF KOHLBERG'S RESEARCH

Although Kohlberg's work set the stage for the study of moral development, and it did show that there were systematic and predictable changes in children's moral thinking as they aged, Kohlberg's work has been critiqued rather strongly over the years. First, note that all of Kohlberg's subjects were male. Carol Gilligan (1977) and others have suggested that testing girls on research measures that were normed exclusively on males will produce skewed results. Kohlberg's measures of moral development were based on his work with boys and reflect the kinds of answers boys give at various ages. If girls give different answers at different ages (research suggests that they do) then they will be judged to be less mature than boys their ages, which Gilligan suggests is unfair. Gilligan specifically suggests that boys are taught to value ideal principles and societal rules and so score relatively high on Kohlberg's scales, while girls are taught to value responsibility for others and avoiding hurting others, which yields a lower score according to Kohlberg's scales (Gilligan & Attanucci, 1988).

Another significant critique of Kohlberg's body of work was the idea that although he posits his stages as universal stages of child development, his results could not be generalized cross-culturally. Children in non-Western cultures do not usually climb as high in terms of Kohlberg's levels compared to children in Western cultures. Complex urban societies are favoured, and middle-class populations are favoured insofar as they attain higher levels on Kohlberg's scales (Snarey, 1985). This bias has been seen as unfair: In more traditional societies where conflicts are more likely to be worked out face to face among people who have a lifelong relationship (as opposed to in a court of law), adherence to ideal principles may not be highly valued, or even useful. Furthermore, there are cross-cultural differences in terms of the balance between individual rights and obedience to authority, and Kohlberg does not equally allow for either to be more important than the other (Simpson, 1974).

AN EVOLUTIONARY COMMENTARY ON KOHLBERG'S WORK

An important contribution to the discussion regarding Kohlberg's stages of moral development is the evolution-motivated commentary offered by Richard Alexander (1987). He interprets Kohlberg's six stages in terms of the priorities a child has at different life stages.

Alexander likens Stage 1, in which the child obeys rules just in order to avoid punishment, to the juvenile stage, experienced in many species, in which the developing individual is focussed on its own growth and development. The fact that the child is at liberty to disregard every other person's point of view, including close relatives, reflects the fact that the extremely altricial, helpless state of human infants makes parental tolerance necessary. Parents tolerate a very young child's focus on his own interests. The child is not really paying attention to anything but his own needs, all in service of physical growth.

Stage 2 sees the child develop the ability to make a fair deal, to execute a concrete exchange. The child here develops the tolerance of others' needs and interests while still primarily pursuing his own needs and interests. Here Alexander sees a life stage dominated by physical growth but now employing a mix of direct (fulfilling immediate hunger, e.g.) and indirect efforts, where indirect efforts involve engaging other people in fulfilling one's needs. The child can strike bargains but is still negotiating in order to see that his needs are met.

In Stage 3 the child begins to be concerned with others' feelings and to cultivate relationships. Loyalty and trust become factors. Morality is defined in terms of fulfilling the expectations of those close to you, or "being good." Here Alexander sees the development of the ability to engage in indirect reciprocity. An exchange can be negotiated, and the reciprocation can be delayed and may not even be explicitly identified as reciprocation for a certain past act. Although Kohlberg emphasized good feelings and good relationships, Alexander sees these as a means to an end: These tools are the most effective way for the individual to see that his needs are met.

Stage 4 is the stage of social systems and conscience maintenance. What is morally right is maintaining one's duty to society, to maintain the welfare of the society or group. One does right by the whole. At this stage, and even more so at Stage 5, where moral decisions are to be made in terms of the explicit principles of the society, Alexander sees a change in life stage. A person is now concerned for his reproductive efforts. He has engaged, perhaps, in social contract with a mate (whom he now hopes will remain monogamous in conformity to societal principles) and has or will soon teach his offspring to buy into this society's rules. He is now invested in this society, and upholding its values furthers his reproductive interests, according to Alexander. The individual is now not just a rule follower but also a rule enforcer.

Stage 5 involves upholding the values and principles of the society, even when they conflict with explicit laws and rules. One is concerned with the greatest good for the greatest number of people. Alexander sees here a "complete commitment to the notion of rule-enforcement" (1987, p. 135). He thinks of Stage 6 as purely hypothetical, rejecting the idea that anyone "explicitly favours a system in which everyone (including himself) behaves so as to bring the greatest good to the greatest number" (1987, p. 135). It is, however, beneficial to shepherd others toward this goal, even if persuading them to do so requires one to appear to be embracing the goal himself.

Stage 6 is the stage of universal ethical principles. In this stage, one is to assume that universal ethical principles exist and that all people, in all cultures, in all circumstances, should follow these ideal principles. Laws that are in violation of these principles need not be followed or enforced. Alexander sees this as an extension of people becoming preoccupied with rules (making and enforcing) as they become increasingly concerned with their own reproductive efforts.

Although the final stages seem more moral, more civilized, Alexander emphasizes that they are every bit as self-serving if interpreted in terms of the individual's life stage. The individual has now made a reproductive investment, and enforcing societal rules secures that investment. Alexander also sees here an opportunity to explain why some people do not reach the final stages. If one has not been given the opportunity to reproduce, to invest in mate and offspring, then it serves one's interests to resist becoming a rule enforcer. Rule enforcement carries a cost, and one who has no reproductive investment does not benefit from carrying that cost.

> **12.6 Press Pause**
>
> According to Alexander, each of Kohlberg's stages of moral development is functional, and changes with age reflect changes in the adaptive problems children and adults face.

What Evolutionary Thinking Adds to Moral and Prosocial Development

Just as we have done with other topics of psychological development, let us consider what we could gain by considering the evolutionary history of moral psychology. Many evolutionary thinkers have proposed and described ways in which evolution by natural selection has led to cognitive adaptations that give rise to human morality and moral thinking (Alexander, 1979; Darwin, 1871; Dawkins, 1976; Hamilton, 1975; Williams, 1966). Our moral psychology is part of what allows us to live in large social groups and thus to develop culture. Evolutionary psychologists regard morality as cognitively complex and well designed for the complex adaptive problem of getting along with a large group of others.

According to evolutionary psychologists, complex cognitive adaptations underlie our morality and allow us to live co-operatively in large groups. Our moral psychology leads to strong intuitions about which behaviours are obligatory and which are prohibited.

The view of moral development that is forwarded by evolutionary psychology has been summarized thus:

1. The learning mechanisms of humans include learning mechanisms specialized for solving the adaptive problems of the EEA.
2. These specialized learning mechanisms include content that led to learning that would have been adaptive in the EEA.
3. Developing children can "learn" their culture or become socialized to the extent that these specialized learning mechanisms were designed for this purpose (Lieberman, Tooby, & Cosmides, 2003; Tooby & Cosmides, 1992).

The implication of this view is that there will be universals in the development of morality, and the culture-specific or individual differences from the universal "template" should deviate from the template in predictable ways based on relevant factors in the developing individual's life (Lieberman et al., 2003). In other words, this view explicitly rejects the blank slate idea, the idea that a developing child is capable of absorbing any moral norms that any hypothetical culture may have to offer; moral learning is constrained by our cognitive learning mechanisms, which were in turn designed by natural selection.

12.7 Press Pause

The evolutionary psychology perspective rejects the idea that the acquisition of morality should be left to general-purpose learning mechanisms. Moral learning is constrained by learning mechanisms designed by natural selection.

The Function of Morality

Let us turn now to the function of morality or, more specifically, the function of our evolved psychologies underlying our moral judgments. It is always helpful to consider evolved function as this will shed light on the likely structure of the psychological processes. Recall when we discussed the function of perception in Chapter 5. Most generally, the function of perception is to allow us to behave sensibly in the world with respect to our reproductive interests. So it is with our moral psychology. The function of our perceptual systems is not to see the world as it really is or to learn the truth about what is out there. Similarly, the function of our moral psychology is not to allow us access to some ideal truth that is real and exists in the world. The function of our moral psychology is to enable us to behave in the world in a way that maximizes our evolutionary fitness. Like our perceptual systems, our moral psychology functions so well that it creates a veneer of instinct blindness. Our sense that some things are morally obligatory and some things are morally forbidden is so powerful that we are unable to notice that these moral judgments are a product of our psychology and not facts that are true about the world. Notice this perspective stands in contrast to Piaget's and Kohlberg's perspective: They believed that there were real, ideal moral judgments that should be unchanging across situations or points of view.

> **12.8 Press Pause**
>
> In general terms, the function of morality is to enable us to behave in the world in a way that maximizes our evolutionary fitness, not to give us access to some real-world moral truths.

Notice how much this is similar to our discussion of the function of our perceptual systems. When we were talking about our evolved visual systems, we learned that our instinct blindness made us oblivious to the psychological processes that gave rise to our percepts, instead making it seem like the colour red was something real in the world and that everything we saw was just there waiting for us to observe it. Likewise, our well-designed moral psychology works so well that it seems that there are really moral rights and wrongs in the world waiting for us to learn about and reason with.

In general, cognitive adaptations that support moral behaviour are part of a suite of social cognitive adaptations that allow us to be a large-group social species. That said, there are specific kinds of morality that are designed to affect behaviour in specific domains, each with its own evolutionary history, each with its own cognitive underpinnings, and each with its own developmental story. In the next section we consider moral psychology as social psychology and look at some of the specialized psychological processes underpinning moral cognition.

Social Behaviour and Fitness

Our human psychology is chock full of processes and mechanisms designed to solve the adaptive problems of our ancestral past. Different psychological machinery solved different kinds of adaptive problems. As we discussed in Chapter 8, a whole suite of psychological adaptations are designed to solve the adaptive problems of dealing with other people: We have a complex social psychology that is unique to humans.

In the EEA, it was not possible to store food in a refrigerator. By giving excess food to a hungry friend, you could "store" it in the form of an obligation.

The importance of social cognition to our ancestors cannot be overstated. In the stark and brutal living conditions of the EEA, being a member of a group was crucial. Humans living alone in most EEA types of environments would not have the ability to protect themselves from the elements or from predators. They would be at risk of depleting food, water, and other resources and would always be vulnerable to attack and exploitation by other human groups. Living alone was not an option. Living in a group and creating alliances and friendships provided protection and insulated one somewhat from the fluctuations of resource availability. In the EEA, it was not possible to store food in a refrigerator, but by giving it to a hungry friend, you could "store" it in the form of an obligation, increasing the likelihood that someone might feed you at a time when you became hungry. The social skills afforded by one's human social psychology that allowed alliances and friendships and avoided offences were a matter of life and death in the EEA.

12.9 Press Pause

It would be hard to overstate the importance of getting along with others in the EEA. Ostracism would mean isolation and very likely lead to death. Moral psychology allowed people to remain living within the community.

Getting Altruism off the Ground

For a long time, altruism was a puzzle for those concerned with evolution by natural selection. Likewise, altruistic behaviour was an early puzzle in evolutionary psychology. Remembering the discussion of evolution by natural selection in Chapter 3, it is easy to see why altruistic behaviour was considered problematic. From Darwin's earliest conception of natural selection, we have known that in order for an allele to spread throughout the population, that allele has to out-compete other alleles for scarce resources, allowing it to out-reproduce other alleles and thus become a larger proportion of all alleles in the population until it becomes universal. Alleles are spread throughout a population if they "win," which is to say, if they acquire more resources so as to produce more and healthier offspring than other members of the population.

From this point of view, one could easily predict and explain aggressive behaviour and the psychology that underlies it but not the psychology underlying altruistic, kind, and generous behaviour. If an allele is associated with generosity, such that having such an allele makes a person more likely to share meat from a recently killed wildebeest, how could that allele be competitive? It costs the individual meat (he now has fewer calories to invest in his own growth, reproduction, and reproductive pursuits), and possibly even worse, his competitor now has more calories to dedicate to passing his alleles onto the next generation. How can such an allele ever spread?

If a person is being nice to others, sharing or enabling access to scarce resources, it seems obvious that such a "nice" design, especially if infrequent in the population, will be beaten out by other, more selfish, designs. The behaviour seemed inexplicable in humans as well as in other species where altruistic behaviour is observed.

12.10 **Press Pause**

The fact that humans and other animals behave altruistically was a puzzle for biologists: How could you explain an individual incurring a fitness cost in order to provide another a fitness benefit?

An early, now largely refuted, attempt to explain altruistic behaviour was an appeal to group selection (Wynne-Edwards, 1962). Maybe individuals could be self-sacrificing for the good of the group. Maybe if a weaker individual sacrifices for the benefit of an individual who has a better chance of creating and raising healthy offspring, that act will better the group, and such behaviour may be rewarded by natural selection. Or if a well-fed individual shares resources with a hungry individual, then the group as a whole is better off. Group selection theory regards the group, not the individual or the gene, as the unit of selection.

Group selection theory did not work as an explanation for altruism. Once evolutionary thinkers understood that the unit of selection was particulate (involving alternate competing alleles, rather than a blending inherited fluid, as discussed in

If the hallmark of natural selection is competition, as these elephant seals are displaying, then how could altruism ever evolve?

Chapter 3), following the re-discovery of Mendel's work, it became clear that groups were not the relevant unit of selection. Indeed, individuals were not even the important level of selection to consider—the gene was (Dawkins, 1976; Williams, 1966). Richard Dawkins wrote the book *The Selfish Gene*, which led to a much wider understanding of the idea that complex adaptations could be understood only as the product of eons of natural selection at the level of the gene (Dawkins, 1976). Evolutionary thinkers prefer to regard the gene, not the individual, as the level of selection because the genome of an individual, for reasons that we need not get into here, includes various genes whose fitness will not be maximized by the same outcome (Cosmides & Tooby, 1981; Dawkins, 1982; Haig, 1993). What maximized the fitness of one gene may not necessarily maximize the fitness of another.

Kin-Selected Altruism

The first well-established theory to explain why one organism would accept a cost to benefit another is **kin-selected altruism**. Hamilton originally described the idea of inclusive fitness, the idea that one's behaviour could increase the likelihood that a gene in one's own genome is represented in the next generation either because it increases the likelihood that one will produce healthy offspring or because it increases the likelihood that another individual who also carries that allele will produce healthy offspring. Behaviours that enhance the reproductive success of genetic relatives can enhance inclusive fitness. An allele spreads if an individual who has that allele out-competes and out-reproduces other individuals, but it can also spread if that person *promotes* the fitness of people who are closely related. Others who are closely related by common descent (i.e., they have the same parents or grandparents) share some genes. The probability that any given gene, including the one that promotes altruistic behaviour toward kin members, is in those individuals is greater than the probability that it is in the general population (Hamilton, 1964; Trivers, 1971).

> **kin-selected altruism** Altruism that was shaped by the fitness advantage provided by increasing the frequency of one's genes via the fitness success of genetic relatives.

> **12.11 Press Pause**
>
> The most straightforward way to get altruistic behaviour off the ground is kin-selected altruism. An allele can spread if an individual with that allele promotes the fitness of others who are closely related.

Consider a classic example of an animal exhibiting kin-selected altruism: When a ground squirrel sees a predator approaching, instead of immediately heading for cover, the squirrel makes itself more conspicuous when it stands on its hind legs and emits a loud alarm call. Why would an individual ground squirrel issue an alarm call when a predator was near and when doing so would attract the attention of the predator? The classic explanation as it is now understood is that those who would benefit from the alarm call would be individuals who were likely to share genes with the squirrel making the call. Like ground squirrels, people in the EEA were likely to be living in communities that had a high density of kin (Hinde, 1980). Within these relatively stable groups, psychological mechanisms for prosocial and altruistic behaviour could evolve.

Clearly, there is a limit here. You cannot throw down your life to save a third cousin, can you? According to the inclusive fitness theory, the probability of prosocial behaviours such as co-operation and altruism will increase with the relatedness between the actor and the recipient. Relatedness has an effect on the benefits of kin-selected altru-

figure 12.3 An early attempt to explain altruism was a group selection theory

Individuals acted for the good of the group. Unfortunately, a group of individuals acting for the group good could be exploited by a selfish individual, and the theory could not account for this vulnerability.

ism because it affects the probability that an allele that the actor has in his genome will also be in the genome of the recipient. Additional factors are how much the act benefits the recipient and how much the act costs the actor. Recall from Chapter 10 that all together, the degree of relatedness, "r," benefit to the recipient, "B," and cost to the actor, "C," affect the probability of altruistic behaviour. Specifically, kin-selected altruism is expected to happen in cases where rB > C.

People (and other organisms) will be better co-operators with parents and full siblings than with cousins and grandparents and better co-operators with cousins and grandparents than with non-kin, according to inclusive fitness theory. Indeed, studies in Great Britain show that, consistent with this prediction, kin are a high proportion of modern adults' social networks and that in contemporary society adults are more likely to turn to kin as opposed to non-kin for help and support (Dunbar & Spoors,

One way to explain altruism is kin selection. Behaviours that enhance the reproductive success of genetic relatives can enhance inclusive fitness. This family gathers to spend time with and share with close kin.

1995). Therefore, one solution to the puzzle of altruistic behaviour is kin selection, and research examining animal and human behaviour suggests that people do behave more altruistically toward kin and look to kin for altruistic support.

12.12	**Press Pause**

> Even in contemporary societies, kin are a high proportion of adults' social networks. Adults are more likely to turn to kin as opposed to non-kin for help.

Co-operation among Non-Kin

The inclusive fitness theory is a very fruitful way to think about the evolution of altruism in humans and other animals and was a great relief to evolutionary thinkers who had struggled over why an animal would incur a cost in order to benefit another individual. But it did not explain everything because researchers found forms of altruism, co-operation, and alliances between and among non-kin individuals in humans and in a few other species. Try as they might, it was difficult to explain this phenomenon using inclusive fitness theory. They needed a viable explanation for non-kin altruism.

RECIPROCAL ALTRUISM

reciprocal altruism Helping another individual and then having the favour returned.

Reciprocal altruism is the phenomenon of helping another individual and then having the favour returned: I'll scratch your back; you scratch mine. Goods do not have the same value to every person, so if our exchange means that I give you something I do not need in exchange for something I do need, while you give up something that has little value to you while gaining something that has greater value to you, then we both have a net benefit. According to the reciprocal altruism theory, the overall benefit for both parties is greater than the cost once the altruism is reciprocated (Axelrod & Hamilton, 1981; Trivers, 1971; Williams, 1966). Altruism can be selected for if such behaviour causes reciprocation. Similar to the example above, if I give you a meal at a time when I am well-fed and you are hungry and if later you give me a meal at a time when you are well-fed and I am hungry, we have both benefitted. Our benefits exceed our costs, regardless of relatedness.

> ### 12.13 Press Pause
>
> Altruistic behaviour between non-kin can be explained by the reciprocal altruism theory. If I give you an item that is of greater value to you than it is to me, you may someday repay me with an item that is of greater value to me than it is to you.

The Tit-for-Tat Strategy

Reciprocal exchange can be beneficial to both parties, but there is a risk of exploitation: One must ensure that one is not giving away valuable resources to those who will not reciprocate. In a population in which individuals were generously donating resources to non-kin, an exploitative design, the non-reciprocating "cheater" could take advantage of everyone's kindness. Having the advantage, that design would then proliferate throughout the population via natural selection. Is the best solution then to be defensive? One could refuse to behave altruistically toward anyone who did not first donate, but although this strategy cannot be exploited, an individual playing this strategy may fail to reap the benefits of reciprocal altruism.

> **evolutionarily stable strategy** A strategy which, if played by a number of individuals in a population, cannot be invaded via natural selection by an alternative strategy that is introduced at a low frequency.

A strategy that is stable and also compatible with reciprocal altruism is a strategy often called *tit-for-tat*. Essentially, this strategy means starting out nice and repaying others' kindnesses but excluding anyone who has cheated you from further exchanges. This is an **evolutionarily stable strategy**: Once it is predominant in the population, no other (known) strategy can infiltrate the population (Axelrod, 1984).

Prisoner's Dilemma

Alternate strategies have been compared directly to one another using a game called the prisoner's dilemma. In this game, a player is to assume the role of a prisoner and select the best strategy for the prisoner given the following situation: Two prisoners are in police custody, held in separate rooms and without a line of communication, but the police do not have enough evidence for a conviction unless one of them testifies against the other. Each prisoner is offered the same deal: If you testify against the other prisoner (this is called *defecting*) but the other prisoner keeps your secret (this is called *co-operating* because the prisoner is co-operating with his partner in crime) then you will go free and your partner will go to jail for 10 years, the maximum sentence. If both remain silent (they co-operate with each

Altruism can be selected for if such behaviour leads to reciprocation. If I lend you my car when I am not using it and yours is in the shop and if later you lend me your car when you are not using it and mine is in the shop, we have both benefitted. Our benefits exceed our costs, regardless of relatedness.

Humans and vampire bats have the cognitive machinery necessary to support delayed reciprocal altruism. Very few other species do.

other), then each prisoner gets a six-month jail term for the only minor charge that police do have enough evidence for. If both agree to testify against each other, then both get a five-year sentence. You will not know what your partner chose before the trial ends, and he will not know what you chose. What do you do?

In the simple case, where you only get to play the game with a given partner once, the best strategy is always to defect. If your partner defects, your sentence will be lighter if you defect; if your partner co-operates, your sentence will be even lighter if you defect. But the more interesting case is the iterated prisoner's dilemma in which you play repeatedly with the same partner. In this case, continuous co-operation can be greatly beneficial to each party over time. This iterated prisoner's dilemma was the format of the "tournament" organized by Robert Axelrod. People were invited to submit whatever strategy they thought would be most competitive, and Anatol Rapoport's submission, the tit-for-tat strategy, was shown to be an evolutionarily stable strategy: No other strategy submitted could infiltrate the tit-for-tat strategy.

The iterated prisoner's dilemma is taken as a model for reciprocal altruism: Each person has an opportunity to take advantage of the other person's kindness, but you do not get a second chance to exploit someone. Conversely, you can be generous with someone once, testing the relationship to see if each person may have an ongoing advantage resulting from the affiliation, but the initial kindness needs to be reciprocated or the relationship will be abandoned.

In species that practise reciprocal altruism, cognitive mechanisms are necessary to ensure that the tit-for-tat strategy is enforced. An individual must ensure that his generosity is not taken advantage of. For example, vampire bats practise reciprocal altruism. They live in stable social groups and have a long lifespan: up to 20 years. Thus they have multiple opportunities to interact with the same individual. If an individual bat has not hunted successfully for more than 60 hours, it will die, unless another bat shares food with it. And bats frequently do share with each other; they even share with non-relatives. These bats seem to practise a tit-for-tat strategy: They share food with those who have shared with them in the past (Wilkinson, 1984).

Humans, too, participate in reciprocal altruism. Shortly you will read about a cognitive adaptation in humans, a "cheater detection" skill, that allows for reciprocal altruism, and you will also read evidence that young children have this skill as well.

BY-PRODUCT MUTUALISM AND EVOLUTION OF FRIENDSHIPS

Reciprocal altruism is a now widely accepted explanation for social exchanges that take place between non-relatives, and it explains why we are adept at executing exchanges that take place with a long delay between delivery of goods and even between relative strangers.

However, there may be another type of altruism in humans that does not involve the reciprocation of equally valued goods and services but rather takes place within a friendship. Friends often find it awkward to keep track of exact exchange values and prefer to return favours in a more casual, less exact way.

Because a person's time was limited in the EEA, they had to choose friends wisely: One could not simultaneously cultivate friendships with everyone. Tooby and Cosmides argue that there are a number of factors that influence the selection of friends. One is by-product mutualism. It is possible that spending time with some people will confer benefits to you at a very low cost or possibly no cost to you at all. In the EEA, spending time with someone who knew how to navigate the local area, knew how to speak the neighbouring dialect, or knew the seasonal patterns of game would confer a benefit and cost the actor little. Other factors also influenced the choice of one's friends: who was good at reading minds, who had similar goals, and who reciprocated the friendship were also considerations.

Once a person became a friend, they were of greater value. Because they were of greater value, it was worth behaving altruistically toward them when they were in need: feeding them if they were hungry, helping them if they were injured or sick, etc. This situation created what Tooby and Cosmides called a *runaway friendship*: Since one person valued another to the extent that they were willing to make great sacrifices for them, they, in turn, became more valuable to their friend and would benefit from extraordinary aid in their own times of need. Because one did not have time to be everyone's special friend, when one did create a deep bond, the friendship was of value and worth incurring some cost to keep. This created a situation in which great acts of altruism could take place without strict accounting in terms of how much was reciprocated (Tooby & Cosmides, 1996).

This theory is useful in explaining a perplexing observation: The closer and more intimate relationships get, the less people ensure that exchanges are equal. Indeed, to

table 12.2	**Three Evolutionary Pathways to Altruism**
EVOLUTIONARY PATHWAY	**DESCRIPTION**
Kin-Selected Altruism	Behaviours that enhance the reproductive success of genetic relatives are selected for.
Reciprocal Altruism	Individuals can trade goods and services, and both increase fitness if a commodity has greater value to the recipient than to the donor.
By-Product Mutualism	There can be benefits to hanging around others, perhaps because of their status or knowledge. As the friendship grows, each person values the other more.

These theories describe three different evolutionary routes to altruism.

According to the by-product mutualism idea, there are benefits to being around some people, perhaps because they have high status, know how to navigate the local terrain, or have extra resources. This may lead some to try to be near high-status people, even without an invitation.

make an exchange explicit and equal is offensive in an intimate relationship: If a good friend invites you over to their home for dinner, it would be an insult to pull out your wallet and offer to pay for your portion of the food. Instinct blindness makes it seem very natural that the closer the friendship the more relaxed we are about keeping an exact balance of give and take in a relationship, but nothing about the theory of reciprocal altruism allows for this. The by-product mutualism idea may fill in where reciprocal altruism falls short.

Moral Intuition or Rational Moral Decision-Making?

On 10 June 2003, same-sex marriage became legal in Ontario, Canada, following a provincial supreme court ruling, and on 20 July 2005, it became legal nationwide. In the United States, the issue was dealt with on a state-by-state basis, and during this tumultuous time, an Attorney General in one of the states, which briefly offered same-sex marriage, explained how the decision was formulated in his office. First, he decided whether to allow same-sex marriage. Then he informed his staff of this outcome. The staff then went to work, searching past decisions and legislation that would not only justify but also compel the final decision. The outcome of this process was a document that read as if the issue and past case law had been carefully considered and the final verdict rendered because the research revealed that the stated outcome was the only possible path.

Some psychologists think that this is quite analogous to how moral decisions are made by the human mind. That is, decisions about how to act are fast, spontaneous, and automatic. Next our cognitive machinery goes to work, like the staff in the Attorney General's office, to look up principles, precedents, and reasons in support of our decisions. Finally, a coherent moral reason is assembled, like the final document from the Attorney General's staff that reads as if the reasons compelled the decision. Instinct blindness obscures the fact that our decisions precede our explanations, and as we consider the outcomes, analogous to the Attorney General's final document, it appears that the reasons compel our decisions.

Contrast this with the classic view of morality, which is captured by this quote from a text on moral philosophy: "Morality is, first and foremost, a matter of consulting reason. The morally right thing to do, in any circumstance, is whatever there are the best reasons for doing" (Rachels, 2003, p. 12).

Furthermore, this is how our moral reasoning seems to unfold. We explain our moral decisions, even to ourselves, in terms of the reasons that seem to compel, not jus-

---

figure | **12.4** | **Laws regarding same-sex marriage in Canada before 2005**

Before same-sex marriage became legal across Canada, it was legal in some provinces but not others. When people make moral decisions, such as the morality of legalized same-sex marriage, do they rely on intuition or rational decision-making?.

Same-sex marriage
illegal before 2005

Same-sex marriage
legal before 2005

tify, the decisions we have adopted. But this may be another example of instinct blindness. Consider an alternative process, similar to the process that the Attorney General's office employed to arrive at a decision statement: First, the verdict is made very quickly and intuitively. Then the deliberate work of finding the reasons, principles, and precedents to motivate that decision are retrieved and amassed.

Marc Hauser, a modern psychologist, has proposed that the revolution in thinking about language development can inform the way we think about morality and its development. Hauser points out that prior to Chomsky's work, people interested in language and language development focussed on differences between languages and failed to notice the commonalities in languages and in the psychology underlying language acquisition. Similarly, Hauser suggests, the study of moral development could benefit from refocussing on the cognitive similarities that universally underlie human moral reasoning, similarities he calls the *human grammar of morality*.

moral grammar The rules, heuristics, and intuitions that are a part of our human psychology and allow us to make moral decisions quickly and automatically.

Hauser emphasizes that this **moral grammar** allows people, cross-culturally and without explicit tutoring, to make moral judgments quickly and automatically. Contrary to Piaget's and Kohlberg's view that we use dispassionate reasoning to draw moral conclusions, Hauser contends that we make instantaneous judgments and then use reasoning and logic to explain and advocate our decisions. Experimental evidence for this proposal is the finding that once a participant makes a moral judgment, if the experimenter logically counters (thus dismissing) each proposed justification, the participant sticks with her moral decision, but without a logical justification she is left "morally dumbfounded" (Haidt, 2001).

12.14 Press Pause

Marc Hauser proposes that a "moral grammar" is acquired by specialized cognitive machinery, analogous to language acquisition. This moral grammar allows people everywhere to make moral judgments quickly and automatically.

Just as we use language without deliberation and without explicitly knowing the rules of the grammar we are using, so do we have a reliably developing moral grammar that allows us to make instantaneous moral decisions without awareness of the principles guiding those decisions. The study of morality in humans would be more fruitful than Piaget's and Kohlberg's work if we were to see the cognitive machinery underlying morality as an organ and study it as a biological entity derived from evolution by natural selection.

Noam Chomsky would likely not mind us thinking of morality the way we think of language (thanks to him). Chomsky once said,

> Why does everyone take for granted that we don't learn to grow arms, but rather, are designed to grow arms? Similarly, we should conclude that in the case of the development of moral systems, there's a biological endowment which in effect requires us to develop a system of moral judgment and a theory of justice, if you like, that in fact has detailed applicability over an enormous range. (as cited in Hauser, 2006)

Specialized Cognitive Machinery Underlying Morality

If the moral intuition idea is correct, that deliberate reasoning follows moral decision-making rather than preceding moral decision-making and driving the outcome, then perhaps Kohlberg's method of measuring moral development is not an appropriate gauge of moral behaviour. In fact, there is evidence from patients who have had damage in the orbit frontal region of the brain that deliberate reasoning on Kohlberg's problems is dissociable from the ability to respond to potential punishment for the purposes of guiding one's actions.

Antonio Damasio studied a group of adults who had suffered from orbit frontal brain damage in adulthood. Anecdotally, these patients seem to have a very difficult time making and implementing socially acceptable plans of behaviour. One patient frequently uses profanity and off-colour humour, although he did not characteristically do so before his brain injury. One patient is described as always making decisions in pursuit of immediate payoffs, oblivious to long-term consequences. Experimentally, Damasio created a card game designed to measure the effects of future punishment on decision-making. To play the game, subjects had to draw a card from one of four decks. Cards may "reward" the subject by awarding points or "punish" the subject by costing points. Two of the decks are winning decks, awarding more points than they cost, and two are losing decks, costing more on average over time than they award. The trick is that the winning decks award and cost relatively small amounts, while the losing decks deal with larger amounts. The only way to reap a really big reward is to draw from the losing decks, although one will lose over time by playing with those decks.

Control subjects quickly learn to avoid the losing decks and draw only from the winning decks. Patients with orbit frontal damage do not. Furthermore, the experimenter measures the sweat on their skin as an index of emotional response. While learning which decks are dangerous, control subjects unknowingly sweat more when picking the losing decks, while orbit frontal patients show no differential sweat responses to the four decks.

The patient group and the control group perform about the same on a whole variety of cognitive tasks, and, here is the kicker, the patients show no difference in performance on Kohlberg's moral dilemma tasks. In other words, these patients show no deficits in moral reasoning, where moral reasoning is the deliberate, slow, logical part of morality. But their physiological responses and behavioural responses to the artificial punishments of the card game show that they ignore information about punishments that control participants respond to. This is consistent with the patient group's real-world behaviour in which they make poor and impulsive decisions. It is also consistent with the idea that our moral behaviour is guided by quick and automatic decision-making, not the deliberate logical moral reasoning measured by Kohlberg. The premise of the evolutionary perspective on morality is that there is specialized

figure 12.5   Orbitofrontal cortex

People with orbitofrontal damage behave as if they are not guided by normal moral intuitions. People who acquired this brain damage early in life showed abnormal performance on Kohlberg's measures of moral reasoning.

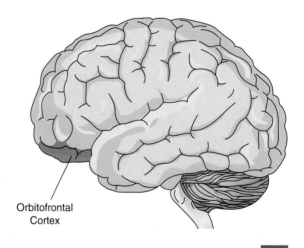

Orbitofrontal
Cortex

cognitive machinery underpinning our moral thinking. There is evidence that brain damage affects moral reasoning (Damasio, 2000).

The above describes patients who acquired orbit frontal brain damage in adulthood. What patterns would a person show if they suffered or developed such brain damage in childhood? Damasio and his colleagues have tested people who acquired frontal lobe damage either as infants or as young toddlers. These individuals showed what could be described as impaired moral development. The two patients with the earliest brain damage had repeated convictions for minor crimes as adults. The fact that they were repeatedly caught and convicted of the same types of minor crimes suggested that they were having trouble considering the consequences of their actions, even when those consequences should be known to them. Damasio and colleagues gave these people a battery of Kohlberg's moral reasoning problems, and these patients, unlike those who had acquired brain damage as adults, showed abnormal performance on Kohlberg's tests. They had developed neither the quick, automatic component nor the slow, deliberate component of moral decision-making (Anderson, Bechara, Damasio, Tranel, & Damasio, 1999; Anderson, Damasio, Tranel, & Damasio, 2000).

EMBODIED MORALITY

Piaget and Kohlberg thought about moral reasoning in terms of passionless reasoning about using ideal principles. In their way of thinking, there actually is right and wrong, and as children become more cognitively mature, they become better able to reason about moral ideals. However, the purpose of our psychological processes is not to conceive of and understand any ideal or actual truth; it is to cause us to behave in ways that maximized fitness in ancestral environments. In Chapter 5, we discussed the fact that our perceptual systems are not there so that we can perceive the world as it really is. We perceive things that have (or had in the EEA) a bearing on our fitness, and we perceive them because in our evolutionary past perceiving them enhanced fitness. So it is with moral reasoning. Our moral beliefs and impulses, our moral grammar if you will, cause us to perceive, make decisions, and act in ways that maximize our fitness. Unlike Piaget's and Kohlberg's view, then, this leaves room for some moral relativism. People in different positions, with respect to power or strength, may believe and behave differently regarding moral decisions. Morality may be embodied.

In one study, researchers examined prosocial behaviour in individuals 7 to 18 years of age. They played what economists call the *dictator game* and the *ultimatum game*. In the dictator game, a player is given a resource (tokens that can be exchanged for cash) and gets to decide how the tokens are shared with their partner, another player. In the ultimatum game, they are again given a resource and get to propose a division of the tokens, but the second player can accept or reject the proposal. If accepted, the tokens are divided as proposed. If the proposal is rejected, neither player gets anything. In the dictator game, individuals' proposals became more equitable with age, as their expectations of fairness developed. A really interesting finding was that taller players kept more for themselves than shorter players. Indeed height was a better predictor of dictator proposals than gender, although the authors had expected girls to be more equitable (Harbaugh, Krause, Liday, & Versterlund, 2003). In other words, although the players were developing in terms of their expectations of fairness and their fair behaviours, what they saw as fair may have been influenced by relative height and thus relative power.

12.15   Press Pause

Piaget and Kohlberg had an ideal view of morality: It was something real, something "out there" in the world to be learned. More recent thinkers see morality as a creation of the human mind; it can differ from situation to situation.

Notice that thinking about embodied morality allows for more hypotheses than either Piaget or Kohlberg considered. Specifically, Piaget observed that young children reasoned about morality almost exclusively in terms of authority. If an authority figure articulated a rule, that rule defined what was moral. For Piaget, a young child's inability to consider other approaches to morality was due to a lack of cognitive development (Piaget, 1932). Thinking about this phenomenon functionally, mindful of embodied morality, lends another approach. A young child is small, and his behaviour can be effectively controlled by an authority figure, a parent or teacher, who is much larger and much stronger. Moral reasoning that involved negotiable rules and reciprocity would not serve this child functionally and may, indeed, be maladaptive.

Research with adults has built a convincing case that adults have dedicated cognitive processes that allow for altruism and reasoning about moral judgment, including the ability to recognize individuals, the ability to detect cheaters, and the ability to ostracize those who do not conform to social requirements. What is known about the development of these psychological processes? Is it possible that children have different requirements for negotiating the social world and therefore different cognitive processes? In fact, recent research suggests that children as young as 3 are particularly good at excluding cheaters.

The Development of Social Exchange Reasoning

The reciprocal altruism described above requires specialized cognitive machinery. Very few species show delayed social reciprocation, where you give your altruistic act and have to trust that your social exchange partner will reciprocate in the future. In order

figure 12.6   Cheater detection

In this task, subjects must evaluate the rule "If there is a 'D' on one side of the card, then there is a '3' on the other side of the card." Which card or cards would you have to turn over to see if the rule has been violated? (Adapted from Cosmides & Tooby, 1992.)

figure 12.7 **Cheater detection**

Now identify the cards that you need to turn over to see if the following rule has been violated: "If a previous employee gets a pension from the firm, then that person must have worked for the firm for at least 10 years." If this task is easier than the last, it is due to your cheater detection mechanism. (Adapted from Girgerenzer & Hug, 1992.)

Got a pension

Worked for 10 years

Did not get a pension

Worked for 8 years

for reciprocal altruism to evolve in a population, it is necessary that individuals be able to recognize and exclude cheaters. If they cannot, an individual may offer his act of altruism to another individual never to have the favour returned. Too many of these errors could deplete one's resources. Indeed, evidence suggests that people are good at the ability to recognize cheaters and have specialized cognitive processes designed to do so (Cosmides & Tooby, 1992).

There is evidence that people have just the kind of specialized machinery that one would need in order for reciprocal altruism to evolve: People are particularly good at detecting cheaters. Research studies have used the Wason four-card selection task to support this idea (Wason, 1966), revealing that if a rule in the format "If P, then Q" involves a "social contract" or an agreement that two parties have made, then it is easy to tell when the rule has been violated, but if the rule does not involve such a social contract, then detecting a violation involves some deliberate reasoning.

To illustrate, first, here is the hard problem, involving no social contract. You have a special deck of cards, in which each card has a letter on one side and a number on the other side. Out of this deck of cards, an experimenter places four cards in front of you. You are then told a rule and told to test whether this rule has been violated: "If there is a 'D' on one side of the card, then there is a '3' on the other side of the card." In order to see if this rule has been violated, which card or cards do you have to turn over?

Now, here is a problem that is logically the same but that involves a social contract. You work in the personnel department, where information about employees is recorded on cards. Each card represents one person. On one side of the card, it tells how long the person was employed before retiring, and on the other side it tells whether that person is being paid a pension. You are told a rule and told to test whether this rule has been violated: "If a previous employee gets a pension from the firm, then that person must have worked for the firm for at least 10 years" (Gigerenzer & Hug, 1992). In order to see if this rule has been violated, which card or cards do you have to turn over?

Did you find these two problems equally easy? The answer to the first problem is the "D" card and the "7" card. The answer to the second problem is the "Got a pension" card and the "Worked for 8 years" card. Most people find the second problem very easy, but the first problem takes some thinking. Research results show that most people get the second problem correct and get the first problem incorrect. Evolutionary psychologists have taken this as evidence that humans have specialized cognitive processes for detecting cheaters, just the sort of thing a species would need in order for reciprocal altruism to evolve (Cosmides & Tooby, 1992; Gigerenzer & Hug, 1992).

Young children show evidence of having access to adult-type cognitive machinery for cheater detection (Cummins, 1996; Harris & Núnez, 1996). In one experiment, children heard a short story. In one condition, the story involved a character who broke a rule, while in the other condition, the same character was involved in the same scenario, but no rule was broken. For example, in the cheater condition, the participant is told that "One day Carol wants to do some painting. Her Mum says if she does some painting she should put her apron on." In the control condition, the participant is told that "One day Carol wants to do some painting. Carol says that if she does some painting she always puts her apron on." Then the children are shown four drawings while the experimenter describes what is shown in each drawing. The child would see a drawing of Carol painting with her apron on, a drawing of Carol painting without her apron on, a drawing of Carol not painting and not wearing her apron, and a picture of Carol not painting but wearing her apron. In the cheater condition, children were asked "Show me the picture where Carol is doing something naughty and not doing what her Mum said," while in the control condition they

Children were asked to tell when a child was painting without wearing an apron. The results were better if painting with an apron on was described as a rule rather than a habit, revealing a young cheater detection mechanism.

were asked "Show me the picture where Carol is doing something different and not doing what she said." Both 3- and 4-year-olds performed significantly better (actually twice as well) in the cheater condition than in the control condition. In other words, although the logic of the two problems was the same, performance differed, which is consistent with the idea that our cognitive machinery is designed to detect cheaters (Harris & Núnez, 1996).

12.16 **Press Pause**

Specialized cognitive machinery for "cheater detection" is required in order for reciprocal altruism to evolve. Recent evidence suggests that children as young as 3 years of age are good at cheater detection.

According to some evolutionary thinkers, performance on the social exchange version of this task is facilitated by cognitive processes that are designed to detect cheaters (Cosmides & Tooby, 1992; Cummins, 1996). Cummins argues that in the social milieu that existed in the EEA, people needed to understand what one was and was not permitted to do in order to navigate the social world. This is why children as young as 3 show evidence of cognitive machinery specialized for reasoning about permissions and obligations (Cummins, 1996).

In the final sections of this chapter we will examine topics for which relatively more is known in terms of moral development. You will read about the development of sexual morals, reviewing empirical research in that area; then we will look at the difference between universal rules and conventional rules, particularly what is known with respect to developmental differences between the two; finally, you will read about teaching and learning moral values.

The Development of Sexual Morals

In many (but not all) species, incest is a bad evolutionary strategy. This is because incest (e.g., sex between a brother and a sister) leads to a greater chance that any resulting offspring will inherit the same harmful recessive alleles that could lead to maldevelopment. This phenomenon, called *inbreeding depression*, occurs not just in humans but also in many other sexually reproducing species. A better strategy is to pair your genetic contribution with someone who is not closely related and thus reduce the risk of pairing deleterious recessives in your developing offspring. Some species have mechanisms that reduce the probability that individuals will mate with close kin. In most social primate species, one sex or the other leaves the home group and joins another group prior to becoming sexually active (Owens & King, 1999). In humans there would be a need for psychological machinery leading to incest avoidance. People spend so much time with close kin that in the absence of such incest-avoidance mechanisms, a sibling or other close relative would be a convenient mate.

Anthropologists have discovered that incest is taboo cross-culturally. However, until recently, they have been committed to explaining these incest-avoidance taboos in a blank slate, empiricist framework: that children are taught by their cultures to avoid incest and are rebuffed in their attempts at incest (Arens, 1986; Levi-Strauss, 1969). In contrast, evolutionary thinkers have suggested that incest avoidance is part of the human cognitive architecture; such an important problem would have applied substantial selection pressure in favour of incest avoidance. One requirement in avoiding incest is to first categorize individuals according to relatedness. It is thought that people have such strategies for kin recognition for the purpose of allocating altruistic acts toward close genetic relatives as discussed above (Hamilton, 1964). Similarly, kin-recognition mechanisms may be employed for the purpose of incest avoidance.

There are many ways that an individual might recognize his or her close kin. (Can you think of any?) But evidence suggests that humans, for the purpose of incest avoidance, identify close kin as those who live in our homes in early life. Those people who live with you and are raised with you, especially in your younger years, are not interesting potential mates. This psychological phenomenon is called the **Westermarck effect,** named after the Finnish anthropologist who conceived of the psychological mechanism that leads to incest avoidance in humans (Westermarck, 1921). It prevents a person from being sexually attracted to individuals who lived in the same household as them when they were children.

Westermarck effect A psychological process that makes sexual attraction unlikely between two people who lived together as young children. This process is thought to be designed to avoid incest.

12.17 Press Pause

Incest avoidance is part of the human cognitive architecture. One will not be sexually attracted to individuals who lived in the same household as them when they were children.

A few studies involving unusual child-rearing practices have provided evidence for Westermarck's ideas that children who are raised together will develop a sexual disinterest toward one another. In China and Taiwan, there has occasionally been a practice of "adopting" one's son's bride as an infant or young child, a practice called *minor marriage*. In other words, the parents of a young son select his bride early in his life and then bring that girl into their homes, raising her from infancy. Arthur Wolf found, as a result of studying over 40 years worth of data, that contrary to the parents' hopes, but consistent with Westermarck's predictions, these couples who were raised together as children have higher divorce rates (three times higher) and produce fewer children (40 per cent fewer) than contemporaries who were not raised together. Couples who were raised together as children were also more likely to have extramarital affairs. The woman in particular was likely to object to the marriage, especially if she joined the family prior to 30 months of age (Wolf, 1995). These are the measurable results of the couple's sexual disinterest in one another.

Similarly, children reared together in Israeli kibbutzim had difficulties creating fertile marriages (Shepher, 1971). In this recent, unusual child-rearing practice, children were reared communally from a very young age and so spent much of their time together rather than in nuclear family units. After puberty, sexual intercourse between members of a kibbutz was rare, even though these people were not close genetic relatives. Marriage between members of the same kibbutzim was also rare. It is telling that frequent sexual play between boys and girls did occur in the kibbutzim but only when the children involved were pre-pubescent. As soon as the child became fertile, sexual behaviour among children reared together stopped (Shepher, 1971).

Evidence in favour of the Westermarck effect comes from studies of minor marriages. Couples who were raised together as children have higher divorce rates and produce fewer children, results of the couple's sexual disinterest in one another.

The experiences of children raised in kibbutzim also illustrate the Westermarck effect. Unrelated children reared together grew up to be uninterested in marrying each other.

Furthermore, there is recent evidence that the moral imperative that leads to righteous repugnance at the thought of other people having sexual relationships with close kin may be mediated by the same cognitive processes. People who are raised with opposite-sex siblings are more horrified at the idea of siblings having sex than are people who were raised without opposite-sex siblings. In fact, the length of time that one spent in the same household with an opposite-sex sibling predicted the strength of the "moral wrongness" judgment regarding sibling sex, and the number of years of co-residence was a stronger predictor of this judgment than actual genetic relatedness (Lieberman et al., 2003). Although the function of these processes is the avoidance of inbreeding, they do not prevent the sexual attraction of people who are closely related unless those people were frequently together during childhood. Genetic siblings who were not reared in the same household are much more likely than siblings reared together to have sexual intercourse with each other as adults (Bevc & Silverman, 2000).

Universal Rules vs. Conventions

Some moral imperatives, whether prohibitions, permissions, or obligations, are cross-culturally universal. They are a part of our human nature and apparently develop reliably in environments that are similar to the EEA in relevant respects. Examples are prohibitions of cheating, stealing, harming, and murdering. Other moral rules vary from culture to culture. The design of our human psychology is such that we can adjust our own morality in response to specific cues in our social environment. Think about how what counts as cheating, stealing, or even murdering differs from culture to culture. This is adaptive, given that local demands differ from culture to culture and differences in ecologies actually lead to different equilibrium strategies for the group. These equilibrium strategies translate to moral norms.

12.18   Press Pause

Some moral rules are cross-culturally universal; other rules, called *conventions*, vary from culture to culture.

One nice illustration of different possible developmental trajectories is the difference between universal and conventional moral rules. Universal moral rules, such as "do not kill" and "do not steal" (or perhaps "do not get *caught* killing or stealing"), seem to be important moral guidelines in all known cultures. These rules were likely important to all environments of evolutionary adaptedness, and the cognitive processes that

Moral rules, which are universal across cultures, are psychologically and developmentally different from conventions, which vary widely across cultures. These women live in a culture where extreme modesty is the convention; they are dressed for a swim.

underlie these rules do not require information about the specific ecological or cultural conditions in which a person is situated in order to develop reliably. In contrast, conventions are rules that are not universal but that in some cultures can be very serious. Examples of such conventions are rules about nudity and rules about familiarity with people of various sexes, ages, and status levels. Cultures differ with respect to the morality of the age of sexual consent, marriage between first cousins, polygamy, the treatment of animals, the killing of unhealthy newborns, and the ownership of other humans. The cognitive processes that underlie these rules do seem to need specific inputs in order to develop, but they seem to have critical or sensitive periods such that those who are raised to be modest may always feel uncomfortable with nudity even if they move to a new culture where nudity is permitted.

Previous work using such a task shows that, typically, people distinguish moral rules ("do not hit another person") from conventions ("Do not stand up while a speaker is reading a story to an audience"). Children recognize that these types of rules are different, seeing the moral rules as impermissible without exception, more serious if violated, and more likely to be true in other countries as well. Children usually explain moral rules in terms of harm to others but explain conventions in terms of what is socially acceptable, using words like *rude* or *impolite*. The two types of rules are also distinct for children because conventional rules can be overturned by an authority figure, but moral rules cannot (Turiel, Killen, & Helwig, 1987).

Oddly, psychopaths make no distinction between universal and conventional rules (Blair, 1997). Blair administered a moral/conventional instrument to a number of psychopaths and a number of control subjects. For example, children diagnosed with psychopathy are likely to say that moral prohibitions against hitting are not in effect if there is no explicit rule against hitting, whereas control subjects would regard

⁜ Developmental Milestones

Moral and Prosocial Development Milestones

Age	Skills
3 Years	Children solve the "cheater detection" problem (Cummins, 1996; Harris & Núñez, 1996).
Birth to 30 Months	Sensitive period for the Westermarck effect. People who live together in early childhood are unlikely to find each other sexually attractive.
Early Childhood	Sensitive period for culture-specific rules such as modesty and comfort with nudity.
Birth to 7 Years	Piaget's morality of constraints stage. Children take rules as unchangeable and non-negotiable.
7 to 10 Years	Piaget's transitional period. Children spend more time with peers and have more opportunities to negotiate. They learn that rules can change.
10 and Older	Piaget's stage of autonomous morality. Children believe that rules are social contracts that can be negotiated and renegotiated.
Mid-Childhood	Children may consider height as a factor in fairness. Taller children are expected to, and do, keep larger portions of resources when given the option of sharing those resources (Harbaugh et al., 2003).

Parents who employ more authoritarian parenting styles have children who are less morally mature. Constructive parenting is associated with greater prosocial behaviour. The best parenting strategy is to ask the child to consider the effect of her behaviour on others.

hitting as prohibited with or without a stated rule. Whereas typical children explain moral rules in terms of harm, those diagnosed with psychopathy are more likely to explain them in terms of social convention: Why don't you hit others? Because it just isn't done (Blair, 1997). Of course, psychopaths also behave abnormally with regard to moral judgments, and their inability to correctly categorize moral and conventional rules has been taken as further evidence that specialized cognitive machinery underlies moral thinking.

Teaching Morals: Over-Reward or Internalize?

Parents usually hope that their children will come to internalize the values of sympathy and prosocial behaviour, but strong-arm tactics do not have the desired effect. Greater parental punishment and authoritarianism are associated with less maturity in terms of moral reasoning and moral behaviour (Hoffman, 1983). A parenting style that relies on physical punishment and coercion is associated with children who lack sympathy and display little prosocial behaviour (Asbury, Dunn, Pike, & Plomin, 2003; Hastings, Zahn-Waxler, Robinson, Usher, & Bridges, 2000; Kochanska, Forman, & Coy, 1999; Krevans & Gibbs, 1996). If the goal is the internalization of prosocial values, a supportive and constructive parenting style is more effective (Strayer & Roberts, 2004). In order to encourage prosocial behaviour in children, the most effective strategy seems to be asking the child to reflect on the effect of her behaviour on others (Krevans & Gibbs, 1996).

The Effect of Parenting Styles on Moral Development

Most parents want their children to grow up to be kind, fair, and sociable. In a word, parents want their children to be *moral*. But what would be the best parenting strategy toward that end? Should we let children find their own way and learn from the consequences? Should we strictly control their behaviours in order to ensure that they never stray from moral behaviour? What is a parent to do?

The answer comes, in part, from the research of Diana Baumrind, working at the University of California at Berkeley. Baumrind described three (now classic) parenting styles: authoritarian, permissive, and authoritative. Authoritarian parents are rigid, harsh, and demanding. Not all authoritarian parents are abusive, but abusive parents are authoritarian. Permissive parents, in contrast, allow children to have and to do whatever they please. They indulge their children and do not set and enforce rules and guidelines. Baumrind described the "just right" parenting style as authoritative. Authoritative parents are relatively responsive but not indulgent and set rules that they enforce consistently but not rigidly; they can make exceptions when necessary.

Both authoritarian and permissive parenting styles can lead to poor outcomes with respect to moral development. Children who are subjected to authoritarian parenting, complete with high demand and rigid regulation, are more likely to show physically aggressive behaviour in childhood and juvenile delinquency and criminal behaviour later on (Gershoff, 2002). Perhaps children who are constantly monitored and controlled do not have enough freedom, or motivation, to develop their own moral directions. This parenting style is also associated with low self-esteem and depression.

Perhaps surprisingly, permissive parenting is not the answer. Children whose parents are so inattentive that they are not monitoring their children's behaviours, or parents who are inconsistent with respect to feedback and the enforcement of rules, also have poor outcomes. Inconsistent enforcement of the rules is associated with delinquency and aggression later in childhood (Frick, Christian, & Wooten, 1999; Laub & Sampson, 1988). Inattentive parents are not available to monitor their children's behaviours and may not be aware when they are spending time with peers who do not uphold the parents' values. Peers are powerful influences, especially in adolescent development.

The above research is intriguing, but keep in mind that it is not experimental. Children have not been randomly assigned to be parented by authoritative, permissive, or authoritarian parents. Baumrind reminds us to keep in mind other factors, such as socioeconomic status, when interpreting the data. For example, although there is a statistical relationship between spanking in early childhood and later criminal involvement, it is also true that parents in lower socioeconomic situations are both more likely to spank and more likely to raise children who later have trouble with the law. This could explain the association between spanking and criminal activity entirely (Baumrind, Larzelere, & Cowan, 2002). Can you think of a study that would clarify the relationship between early spanking and later anti-social behaviour?

12.19 **Press Pause**

Greater parental punishment and coercion are associated with children who lack sympathy and display little prosocial behaviour. The most effective strategy for teaching moral behaviour is asking the child to reflect on the effect of her behaviour on others.

PEERS AS THE AGENTS OF SOCIALIZATION

In Chapter 10 we read about Judith Harris and her view that peers, not parents, socialize a child. This view is relevant to our discussion about teaching morality since Harris argues in *The Nurture Assumption* that children learn moral rules and behave morally as a result of interactions with peers, not as a result of teaching and admonishment from parents (Harris, 1998). Let us look at the evidence:

First, Harris describes a study conducted in the 1930s by Hartshorne and May, who were studying what they called *character* but what might be called *moral development*. These researchers set up situations in which children would be tempted to cheat, lie, or steal. They found that "character" was situation-specific: Children who were willing to cheat in one situation were not more or less likely to do so in another. Those who resisted temptation at home did not show more "character" outside of the home (Hartshorne & May, 1971). However, across a variety of contexts, children made the same moral decisions as their peers or siblings (though they were not in the presence of other children). Harris concludes that children who lived in the same neighbourhood and attended the same school shared a "children's culture" (Harris, 1998, p. 216) and thus had internalized the same norms of moral behaviour.

The other study that Harris highlights in terms of moral development is a study from Denmark. With the kinds of thorough records that are kept in Denmark, it was possible to do a comprehensive study on the criminal behaviour of adopted children and their biological and adoptive parents, including over 4,000 adopted men (Mednick, Gabrielli, & Hutchings, 1987). Results of this study did show that if the biological father had a criminal record, then there was a relationship between the child's criminal behaviour (which Harris takes as an index of moral development) and the criminality of the adoptive father but only in the case where the child grew up in the capital city of Copenhagen. There was no statistical relationship between criminality of adoptive parent and child when the child grew up in a rural area. Harris (1998) concludes, "It wasn't the criminal adoptive parents who made the biological son of criminals into criminals: it was the neighborhood in which they reared him" (p. 298). In other words, nothing the parent did at home made criminal behaviour more or less likely, but if the parent reared the child in a high-crime neighbourhood, a child with criminal biological parents was relatively likely to engage in criminal activity. Because the association with peers, their local cultures, values, and behaviours influenced the developing child more than the parents who raised them, Harris concludes that peers, not parents, socialize children.

SUMMARY

It is clear that a child's understanding of moral expectations and their compliance with these expectations changes with age. It is also clear that there are cross-cultural commonalities with respect to moral expectations. Our morality and our moral reasoning are part of our human psychology.

This chapter reviewed traditional views of moral development, most notably those of Piaget and Kohlberg, who had a realist view of morality: Morality is something real, something "out there," in the world that children learn. This view of morality does not permit moral relativism: Changing the point of view should not change the morally correct outcome. Both Piaget and Kohlberg believed in a stage theory of moral development: Children all over the world were believed to move from one stage to the next, never varying the order of the stages or moving backwards.

An evolutionary perspective on morality invites a functional analysis: What is our moral psychology designed for? Most generally, we can say that our moral psychology facilitates behaviour that maximizes reproductive success. More specifically, our moral psychology, like the rest of our social cognitive adaptations, allows us to live with other people and benefit from living in a community.

One of the great puzzles in modern evolutionary biology was altruism. How can evolution by natural selection create organisms that benefit others while incurring an expense for themselves? Two answers are now commonly accepted: Kin-selected altruism is consistent with what we know about natural selection because an allele in the actor is also likely to be in the beneficiary due to their close relationship, and reciprocal altruism can evolve because both parties benefit when they exchange items that are valued differently by each actor.

In this chapter, we considered two in-depth examples of developing psychological machinery for moral decision-making. Some sexual prohibitions, specifically incest avoidance, are governed by the Westermarck effect. Children are less likely to develop a sexual attraction for individuals who reside in their homes in early childhood. And young children show evidence of a developing "cheater detection" mechanism, psychological machinery that would be necessary in any species to evolve delayed reciprocal altruism.

Finally, you read about universal rules and conventional rules. Some rules, such as prohibitions against killing, develop universally, whereas conventions, such as modesty in clothing, develop in cultures where those conventions are common. Once learned, however, those conventions may be difficult for an individual to ignore.

PRESS PAUSE SUMMARY

- Morality is the intuitive sense of right and wrong that guides our behaviour and leads us to judge others' behaviours. It is part of our human psychology.
- Traditional discussions of moral development have been framed in terms of the nature vs. nurture question.
- Piaget and Kohlberg have laid the foundation of contemporary thinking in moral development.
- Piaget's model of moral development was a stage theory, and it paralleled his views on more general cognitive development.

- Kohlberg told children stories that presented a moral dilemma and then evaluated their thought processes. According to Kohlberg, children everywhere passed through the stages in the same order but not every person made it to the same level.

- According to Alexander, each of Kohlberg's stages of moral development is functional, and changes with age reflect changes in the adaptive problems children and adults face.

- The evolutionary psychology perspective rejects the idea that the acquisition of morality should be left to general-purpose learning mechanisms. Moral learning is constrained by learning mechanisms designed by natural selection.

- In general terms, the function of morality is to enable us to behave in the world in a way that maximizes our evolutionary fitness, not to give us access to some real-world moral truths.

- It would be hard to overstate the importance of getting along with others in the EEA. Ostracism would mean isolation and very likely lead to death. Moral psychology allowed people to remain living within the community.

- The fact that humans and other animals behave altruistically was a puzzle for biologists: How could you explain an individual incurring a fitness cost in order to provide another a fitness benefit?

- The most straightforward way to get altruistic behaviour off the ground is kin-selected altruism. An allele can spread if an individual with that allele promotes the fitness of others who are closely related.

- Even in contemporary societies, kin are a high proportion of adults' social network. Adults are more likely to turn to kin as opposed to non-kin for help.

- Altruistic behaviour between non-kin can be explained by the reciprocal altruism theory. If I give you an item that is of greater value to you than it is to me, you may someday repay me with an item that is of greater value to me than it is to you.

- Marc Hauser proposes that a "moral grammar" is acquired by specialized cognitive machinery, analogous to language acquisition. This moral grammar allows people everywhere to make moral judgments quickly and automatically.

- Piaget and Kohlberg had an ideal view of morality: It was something real, something "out there" in the world to be learned. More recent thinkers see morality as a creation of the human mind; it can differ from situation to situation.

- Specialized cognitive machinery for "cheater detection" is required in order for reciprocal altruism to evolve. Recent evidence suggests that children as young as 3 years of age are good at cheater detection.

- Incest avoidance is part of the human cognitive architecture. One will not be sexually attracted to individuals who lived in the same household as them when they were children.

- Some moral rules are cross-culturally universal; other rules, called *conventions*, vary from culture to culture.

- Greater parental punishment and coercion are associated with children who lack sympathy and display little prosocial behaviour. The most effective strategy for teaching moral behaviour is asking the child to reflect on the effect of her behaviour on others.

KEY TERMS AND CONCEPTS

evolutionarily stable strategy, 433

kin-selected altruism, 430

moral grammar, 438

morality, 416

prosocial behaviour, 416

reciprocal altruism, 432

Westermarck effect, 444

QUESTIONS FOR THOUGHT AND DISCUSSION

1. What method did Kohlberg use to study moral development? How did he evaluate a child's response? What were the similarities between Kohlberg's and Piaget's thinking about moral development?

2. What is the function of our moral psychology? In what ways are the instinct blindness to our moral psychology and the instinct blindness to our visual processes similar?

3. Why was altruism a problem for evolutionary psychologists? What was (were) the solution (or solutions) to the problem?

4. Which comes first, the moral verdict or the explanation? What evidence supports your answer?

5. What specialized cognitive machinery is necessary for a species to have reciprocal altruism? What evidence is there that people have such machinery? Is there evidence that children have it?

6. Why is incest avoidance important? What specialized psychological processes do humans have to accomplish incest avoidance? What evidence supports that idea?

From the Classroom to the Lab: Follow up

Consider the experiment you designed in response to the "From the Classroom to the Lab" challenge earlier in this chapter.

Would your experimental method meet the ethical standards expected by the field?

What is your independent variable?

What is your dependent variable?

What age group would you select? Why?

Describe the procedure the participants would experience once they are in the lab.

What results would support your hypothesis? What results would refute your hypothesis?

Glossary

5-alpha-reductase deficiency A developmental condition caused by the failure of the body to produce sufficient levels of 5-alpha-reductase. Babies with male genotypes, or an XY chromosome configuration, will be born with typical internal male reproductive organs but female-appearing external genitalia.

accommodation The process of changing one's current theory, understanding, or knowledge in order to cope with new information.

adaptation A trait that is designed and preserved by the process of natural selection because that trait confers a reproductive advantage in the environment in which it evolved.

adoption studies Heritability studies in which the correlation of a trait between adopted children and their adoptive parents is compared to the correlation of the trait between biologically related parents, children, and siblings living in different households.

allele One possible form of a gene that may occupy a particular locus (location) on the chromosome.

alloparents All of the people who contribute to the upbringing of a child other than the child's parents.

androgen insensitivity syndrome A condition in which a person has a mutation in the gene associated with the development of androgen receptors. Without functioning androgen receptors, a person with an XY karyotype can develop a female phenotype.

assimilation The process of interpreting new information in terms of previously understood theories and knowledge.

associationist perspective An approach that encompasses learning theories in general and social learning theory as well. This perspective suggests that people have only general-purpose learning mechanisms, allowing them to associate one stimulus with another. Other than these associationist learning mechanisms, the newborn mind is a blank slate.

attachment The emotional bond a young child feels with another specific person.

autism A developmental disorder that is defined and characterized by a deficit in social cognition, a delay in the development of communication, and an adherence to routine or repetitive behaviours.

autosome Any pair of chromosomes that are not sex chromosomes.

axon The long fibre that runs the length of a neuron, conducting the electric signal from the cell body to the terminals.

baby biography An intensive study first developed by Charles Darwin that describes the activities of an individual baby, typically the scientist's own child or a close relative.

basic-level category A category that is most easily processed at a basic level, first learned by children, and within which inferences are more generously drawn.

between-subjects design An experimental design in which each participant is included in only one group, and variables of interest are compared across groups.

bottleneck A situation in which the population is drastically reduced for at least one generation such that genetic diversity is lost.

Broca's aphasia A condition resulting from damage to Broca's area that involves single-word speech, or short word strings, lacking in grammatical organization.

by-product A trait that has come about as a result of natural selection, although it was not itself selected for.

categorical perception The perception of stimuli that differs continuously as being categorically or qualitatively different.

category A mentally represented collection of entities (objects, people, actions, or events).

chromosome A single molecule comprising a very large DNA helix. A single chromosome may include thousands of genes.

classic category A category that can be defined by a list of necessary and sufficient features.

classical conditioning A learning process in which a neutral stimulus comes to be associated with a naturally motivating stimulus so that each evokes the same response.

class-inclusion experiment An experiment used by Piaget and others in which children were tested to see if they would include a subset in a broader grouping.

clinical method A research method involving a semi-structured interview. The researcher approaches the interview with a planned set of questions but may have followed up on or probed areas of interest depending upon the child's responses.

complex A grouping that is more fluid and less well defined than a category and that did not rely on classic definitions. Piaget thought young children had complexes, not proper categories.

concept A psychological grouping together of entities, objects, events, or even characteristics on the basis of some more or less functional commonality, including some understanding of their interrelationship.

conditioned response In classical conditioning, the response to the conditioned stimulus once training has taken place.

conditioned stimulus In classical conditioning, the stimulus with which the unconditioned stimulus has been associated and which elicits a response after training has taken place.

congenital adrenal hyperplasia A condition in which the excessive production of androgens results in the masculinization of primary or secondary sex characteristics in developing girls.

constancy The perception of like objects as like (in terms of size, colour, lightness, and brightness) despite radically different projections on the retina.

constraints on learning Biased heuristics or privileged hypotheses that an animal uses when acquiring information about the world.

containment event An event in which an object moves into a container, possibly becoming invisible.

core knowledge Privileged domains of knowledge that children learn easily by virtue of developing cognitive preparedness that is specific to those domains. These domains reflect a fitness advantage in our evolutionary history.

correlation The relationship between two variables. Reports of correlation include direction and strength.

correlation coefficient A number between -1 and +1 that describes the correlation between two variables in terms of direction and strength.

correlational design A research design in which the researcher will observe the relationship between two variables in a group of subjects without manipulating either variable.

covering event An event in which an object becomes invisible as it is hidden by a rigid cover or screen.

critical period The time period in development during which a specific kind of learning can take place if the necessary stimuli are present.

cross-sectional design A type of developmental study in which children of different ages are measured at the same time and compared in order to infer age-related change.

cross-sequential design A type of developmental study in which different-aged groups of children are studied at the same time, once initially and then later after a set period of time, in order to observe age-related changes.

dead reckoning The ability to continuously keep track of one's location relative to the starting point and thus return directly to it.

deep structure Chomsky's term for the wordless structure that is common to utterances with the same meaning that must be mapped onto the actual surface structure in order for children to understand and learn language.

dendrite One of the fibres extending from the cell body of a neuron, designed to receive a signal from a nearby neuron.

dependent variable In an experiment, the variable that is expected to be affected by, or dependent on, the experimental manipulation.

developmental psychology The scientific study of recurrent psychological changes across the human lifespan, focussing on development from the prenatal period to early, but sometimes middle and late, adulthood.

developmental systems theory A perspective that emphasizes that when it comes to complex systems, the whole is more than the sum of its parts. This perspective reminds us to consider all of the resources contributing to development, genetic and environmental, rather than emphasizing the contribution of one over the other.

dialectical process A process of shared problem-solving.

dizygotic twins Twins that develop from two completely different zygotes and thus have different genomes.

DNA Deoxyribonucleic acid can store information because it is made of sequences of four types of nucleotides. Two strands of DNA zip together to form a double helix.

domain specificity The idea that many aspects of adult and child psychology are processed by specialized psychological processes that have been shaped by natural selection and focus on areas of knowledge that were fitness-relevant in the EEA.

ecological pressures Evolutionary pressures that derive from ecological circumstances, including the availability of resources and the presence of risks or dangers.

EEA The "environment of evolutionary adaptedness" is the condition under which our ancestors lived, and to which our morphological and psychological features are adapted.

egocentrism Piaget's term for a child's inability to appreciate other points of view besides their own.

empiricist One who believes that all knowledge depends upon direct experience or empirical observation. The newborn's mind is a blank slate and requires exposure to information in order to gain knowledge.

equilibration The process of balancing assimilation and accommodation in order to maintain a stable understanding of the world while still allowing for development.

essentialism The view that for any given entity there is an essence—some property that every member of that kind must possess—which gives it its category membership and its category-specific features.

ethology The study of fitness-enhancing behaviours that were shaped by natural selection.

evolutionarily stable strategy A strategy which, if played by a number of individuals in a population, cannot be invaded via natural selection by an alternative strategy that is introduced at a low frequency.

evolutionary psychology An approach to the study of psychology that holds that being well informed about the process of evolution as well as the circumstances in which our ancestors lived during our evolutionary history will aid us in understanding the function and design of the human mind.

experience-dependent learning mechanism A learning mechanism that responds to individual, specific information.

experience-expectant learning mechanism A learning mechanism that is designed to respond to species-typical environmental input, usually during a critical period, in order for normal brain development to result.

experimental design A research design in which the researcher carefully controls one or more variables and observes the effect on another variable. Subjects are randomly assigned to conditions.

facultative adaptation An adaptation that is designed to respond to specific cues in the environment, thus preparing organisms for the varying conditions that were possible in the EEA.

family studies Studies designed to estimate the heritability of a trait in which the concordance of a trait between people is compared to their genetic relatedness. Researchers then estimate how much of the variance of the trait in the population is accounted for by genetic relatedness.

founder effect A special case of genetic drift in a small "founder" population.

functional fixedness The psychological phenomenon wherein identifying an item as belonging to one category makes it difficult for a person to think of using it for a function that is not associated with that category.

fusiform face area The area of the brain that is dedicated to face perception.

gamete One of two sex cells, egg or sperm, that fuse together during fertilization.

gene A functional sequence of DNA that remains across a large number of generations, potentially for long enough for it to function as a significant unit of natural selection.

generative entrenchment A phenomenon that slows the evolution of developmental processes. Because early perturbations in development can have catastrophic effects later in development, random mutations that affect early development are unlikely to be beneficial.

genetic drift The change in gene frequency that results from the fact that genes passed from parent to offspring are selected randomly.

genetic epistemology Genetic epistemology, according to Piaget, describes the process of cognitive development from birth through late adolescence.

genomic imprinting The chemical tagging of an allele that alters the likelihood that it will be expressed in the phenotype.

good-enough parenting Parenting that is sufficient to rear viable children. The term is based on Scarr's idea that extraordinary parenting makes little difference to the child's outcome compared to good-enough parenting.

habituation paradigm An experimental design that takes advantage of an infant's declining response to (habituation to) a repeatedly presented stimulus. If a new stimulus elicits a recovery in response, the experimenter infers that the infant can discriminate between the old and the new stimulus.

heritability statistic The estimate of the proportion of the measured variance in a trait among individuals in a given population that is attributable to genetic differences among those individuals.

holistic processing The integration of visual information from the whole of the perceived visual region of interest, usually the face region, in contrast to the perception and representation of component parts.

imprinting The psychological process by which newborns first identify their mother and then strongly attach to her psychologically.

inclusive fitness One's evolutionary fitness (number of viable offspring) plus the number of viable relatives one has, discounted by the relatedness of those relatives. For example, one gets full credit for oneself, half credit for offspring or siblings, and a quarter credit for nieces or nephews.

independent variable In an experiment, the variable that is systematically manipulated to test its relationship to the dependent variable.

inductive method A research method in which a researcher asks a child what kinds of inferences he can make from one entity to another in order to probe the child's categories in terms of membership and internal structure.

infant-directed speech The kind of speech, or "baby talk," adults use when talking to an infant. It involves a higher pitch; extreme, exaggerated intonation; and slower speech.

instinct blindness Our inability to appreciate the complexity of our mental processes because they seem automatic and inevitable to us.

interactionism The perspective in developmental science that development unfolds as a result of the interaction between genes and all other "developmental resources."

intermodal perception The integration of percepts acquired via two or more modalities, or senses.

intersex An umbrella term describing conditions in which an individual has some combination of chromosomal, genital, and brain development that is not typically male or female.

intuitive physics Knowledge relevant to physics and objects that develops early in human infants.

inversion effect The disruption in face processing that is observed when a face is inverted.

joint attention An individual's ability to tell when he shares an object of attention with another person.

kin-selected altruism Altruism that was shaped by the fitness advantage provided by increasing the frequency of one's genes via the fitness success of genetic relatives.

language acquisition device The learning mechanisms that young children have that allow them to analyze the language they hear, imperfect as it is, and to acquire and produce their own native language.

longitudinal design A type of developmental study in which a group of children are studied first at one age and later at another age, or many ages, in order to observe age-related changes.

meiosis The process by which sex cells—eggs and sperm—are produced.

menarche The point in female puberty at which the first menstrual bleeding occurs.

messenger RNA A molecule that serves as an intermediate step when DNA is transcribed to make a protein. The sequence of the messenger RNA is read from the DNA molecule, and the messenger RNA is then translated into a protein.

modern synthesis The modern understanding that the gene, Mendel's particulate mechanism of inheritance, was the heritable matter that Darwin's theory of evolution relied upon.

monozygotic twins Twins that form from one zygote and thus have identical genomes.

moral grammar The rules, heuristics, and intuitions that are a part of our human psychology and allow us to make moral decisions quickly and automatically.

morality The intuitive sense of right and wrong that guides our own behaviour and leads us to judge and possibly condemn others' behaviours.

mutation A spontaneous error to create a true replica in the process of DNA replication, resulting in a novel sequence.

mutual exclusivity assumption The assumption that children make that novel words applied to a known object will refer to a novel property rather than to the whole object or a known property. A novel word does not duplicate a known word but means something else.

myelination The development of a fatty sheath around the axon. This sheath serves as insulation, allowing for signals to travel faster.

nativist One who views development as being driven primarily or exclusively by internal forces. The information needed for development is assumed to exist within the developing child. Often this information is thought to be preserved in the genes.

natural experiment A situation in which two or more groups exist through no action of the experimenter, allowing a comparison between these naturally occurring groups.

naturalistic observations A study in which data are collected in everyday settings.

natural-kind category A psychological grouping of the classes of entities that are seen to be natural categories or objects grouped together as they are perceived to be in nature.

neuron A nerve cell. A cell specialized for conducting information between the brain and other body parts or within the brain.

norm of reaction The relationship between a specific environmental factor and a measurable phenotypic expression.

normative approach The study of development in which norms or averages are computed over a large population and individual development is compared to these norms.

nucleotide One of the compounds constituting the basic building blocks of DNA and RNA. In the structure of DNA, the four nucleotides are guanine, adenine, cytosine, and thymine.

object permanence A child's understanding that an object still exists even when it can no longer be observed directly. A major development in the sensorimotor period, according to Piaget.

obligate social species Species that must be with others in order to survive and who are co-evolved in order to interact with others.

observational learning The learning process by which an actor's behaviour changes as a result of observing a model.

occlusion event An event in which an object becomes invisible as it moves behind a nearer object, the occluder.

ocular dominance column A column of neurons in the visual system that responds to input from either the right eye or the left eye.

operant conditioning A type of learning in which a specific behaviour becomes more or less likely as a result of rewards or punishments.

parental investment An investment by a parent in an individual offspring that increases that offspring's chance of surviving and reproducing at the cost of the parent's ability to invest in other offspring.

parent–offspring conflict Conflicts between parents and their offspring that results from the fact that, in our evolutionary history, maximizing each offspring's inclusive fitness would have resulted from different, mutually exclusive, courses of action.

paternal investment A father's investment in his offspring. Paternal investment does not occur in all species and varies across human societies.

perceptual category An implicit classification of perceptual stimuli into discrete sets in spite of a lack of physical discontinuity in the stimuli (e.g., colours, facial expressions, and consonant sounds).

perceptual narrowing A developmental process in which perceptual mechanisms become more specialized such that infants lose the ability to discriminate between categories that are irrelevant.

perceptually bound Compelled to categorize objects based on visually perceivable features, as Piaget thought children were.

Piaget's theory of cognitive development Piaget described children's development through stages, which predicted that children attained a certain set of cognitive skills at a certain stage. Children were thought to be limited to the skills characterized by that stage until they reached the next stage, at which point a whole new set of cognitive skills were available to them.

pleiotropy The phenomenon of a single gene having effects on more than one phenotypic trait.

practice effects Participants in a longitudinal study performing differently over time as a result of prior exposure to the test or testing situation.

preferential-looking paradigm An experimental design in which an infant is presented with two visual stimuli at the same time. If the looking time differs reliably between the two, the experimenter infers that the infant can discriminate between the two stimuli.

prepared learning Learning that is easier to induce than a random paired association would be because of its importance in our evolutionary history.

pretend play Play that involves the use of actions or objects to represent real life or imagined objects, characters, and actions.

prosocial behaviour All the nice things we do for, and to, others, including altruism, friendship, coalitional behaviours, and even parental behaviours.

protein A sequence of amino acid that combines and folds in specific shapes in order to accomplish specific functions.

punisher In operant conditioning, any consequence that makes a behaviour less likely to occur.

random assignment A procedure that ensures that each participant in a study has an equal chance of being assigned to any group in the experiment.

reciprocal altruism Helping another individual and then having the favour returned.

reinforcer In operant conditioning, any consequence that makes a behaviour more likely to occur.

relational aggression The attempt to harm others by damaging social relationships. This type of aggression may take the form of gossip, spreading rumours, or ostracism.

reliability The consistency in repeated measures of the same variable using the same measurement method.

selective attrition Attrition in which the subjects who quit a study or move away from a study location are different from the remaining subjects in some way that is relevant to the object of the study.

sensitive period The time period in development during which a specific kind of learning takes place most easily.

sensorimotor play Child's play involving object manipulation as a means for the practice and mastery of action schemas.

sleeper effect A developmental effect that is evident only some time after exposure to a particular environmental cue.

social brain hypothesis The idea that the large brains of humans, as well as the general intelligence of humans, has evolved in response to social conflicts and challenges that are an inherent part of group living.

social facultative adaptation An adaptation designed to respond to specific cues in the social environment, allowing one to pursue the most advantageous social strategy.

social referencing A young child looking at a trusted authority in situations that are ambiguous with respect to the appropriate response.

socialization The process believed to lead a child to acquire the beliefs, values, language, skills, and, in essence, the "culture" of his parents in order to become a member of that culture himself.

sociobiology The study of the biological basis of social behaviour, popularized by E. O. Wilson in the 1970s.

species-typical environment The environment that provides the features that the genome needs or "expects" in order to develop typically.

spermarche The point in male puberty at which sperm is first ejaculated. It typically occurs around the age of 11 to 15 and is an early pubertal event, occurring before secondary sexual characteristics are fully developed.

SRY gene The gene on the Y chromosome usually associated with male development in mammals, SRY is an acronym for sex-determining region Y.

SSSM The standard social science model is a summary of current thoughts about human nature, including the assumptions that underlie most undergraduate curriculum and popular press reports on human issues.

synapse The gap between two neurons, across which a chemical signal is transmitted.

synaptic pruning The developmental process by which synapses are eliminated.

synaptogenesis The growth of synapses between neurons.

taxonomic assumption The assumption that children make that novel words will refer to objects that are grouped conceptually or categorically rather than thematically.

testis determining factor A protein that will likely trigger the development of the fetus's testes in typical male development.

thematic association The grouping of items based on their use together or their prior association in a story rather than on category membership.

theory of mind The part of our psychological processes that allows us to understand another person's mental states.

transformation experiment An experiment in which a child is asked whether an item can change category membership given the appropriate manipulation of features. It is used to test a child's intuitions about essentialism.

Turner's syndrome A condition in which an individual has only one sex chromosome, always an X chromosome.

twin studies A special type of family study in heritability. Concordance of a trait among monozygotic twins is compared to the concordance of the trait among dizygotic twins, allowing for the estimate of genetic relatedness contributing to the variance of the trait in the population.

unconditioned response In classical conditioning, the response that follows the presentation of the unconditioned stimulus.

unconditioned stimulus In classical conditioning, the stimulus that elicits a response before any training has taken place.

universal grammar The set of principles and adjustable parameters that are common to all known and presumably undiscovered human languages.

U-shaped curve A graph depicting a developmental time course over which an individual displays a competence, then fails to display that same competence, and then displays it again at a later stage.

validity The extent to which a measuring technique measures the attribute that it is designed to measure.

violation of expectation paradigm An experimental procedure in which an infant is expected to look longer at an event that violates a belief or expectation that the infant holds.

voice onset time The time that passes between when a stop-consonant is released and when the vocal folds begin to vibrate and thus voicing begins.

Wernicke's aphasia A condition resulting from damage to Wernicke's area that involves fluent, nonsensical speech.

Westermarck effect A psychological process that makes sexual attraction unlikely between two people who lived together as young children. This process is thought to be designed to avoid incest.

whole-object assumption The assumption that children make that novel words will refer to whole objects to narrow the set of possible meanings that might be associated with a novel word.

within-subjects design An experimental design in which participants are exposed to multiple experimental treatments, and measures taken from the same individuals are compared.

Wolffian structures The internal male reproductive structures.

zone of proximal development The tasks a child can complete with and without adult support.

zygote The fertilized egg, which is still in the single-cell stage.

References

Chapter 1

American Psychological Association. (2002). Ethical principles of psychologists and code of conduct. *American Psychologist, 57,* 1060–1073.

Barkow, J., Cosmides, L., & Tooby, J. (1992). *The adapted mind.* New York, NY: Oxford University Press.

Canadian Psychological Association. (2000). *Canadian Code of Ethics for Psychologists 3* [Monograph]. Ottawa, ON.

Fox, N. A., & Card, J. A. (1998). Psychological measures in the study of attachment. In J. Cassidy & P. Shaver (Eds.), *Handbook of attachment: Theory, research, and clinical applications* (pp. 226–245). New York, NY: Guilford.

Hall, G. S. (1904). *Adolescence: Its psychology and its relations to physiology, anthropology, sociology, sex, crime, religion, and education* (Vols. 1–2). New York, NY: D. Appleton & Co.

Ledingham, J. E. (1981). Developmental patterns of aggressive and withdrawn behaviour in childhood: A possible method for identifying preschizophrenics. *Journal of Abnormal Child Psychology, 9,* 22.

Mayr, E. (1985). *The growth of biological thought: Diversity, evolution and inheritance.* Cambridge, MA: Harvard University Press.

Moskowitz, D. S., & Schwartzman, A. E. (1989). Painting group portraits: Studying life outcomes for aggressive and withdrawn children. *Journal of Personality, 57,* 723–746.

Moskowitz, D. S., Schwartzman, A. E., & Ledingham, J. E. (1985). Stability and change in aggression and withdrawal in middle childhood and early adolescence. *Journal of Abnormal Psychology, 94,* 30–41.

Pinker, S. (1997). *How the mind works.* New York, NY: W. W. Norton.

Society for Research in Child Development. (1993). Ethical standards for research with children. In *Directory of Members* (pp. 337–339). Ann Arbor: MI: Society for Research in Child Development.

Urberg, K. A., Degirmencioglu, S. M., Tolson, J. M., & Halliday-Scher, K. (1995). The structure of adolescent peer networks. *Developmental Psychology, 33,* 834–844.

Watson, J. B. (1930). *Behaviorism* (Rev. ed.). Chicago, IL: University of Chicago Press.

Watson, J. B., & Raynor, R. (1920). Conditioned emotional reactions. *Journal of Experimental Psychology, 3,* 1–14.

Wimsatt, W. C., & Schank, J. C. (1988). Two constraints on the evolution of complex adaptations and the means of their avoidance. In M. H. Nitecki (Ed.), *Evolutionary Progress* (pp. 231–275). Chicago, IL: University of Chicago Press.

Chapter 2

American Psychological Association. (2002). Ethical principles of psychologists and code of conduct. *American Psychologist, 57,* 1060–1073.

Baillargeon, R., Spelke, E. S., & Wasserman, S. (1985). Object permanence in 5-month-old infants. *Cognition, 20,* 191–208.

Bandura, A. (1977). *Social learning theory.* Upper Saddle River, NJ: Prentice-Hall.

Bandura, A., & Walters, R. H. (1963). *Social learning and personality development.* New York, NY: Holt, Rinehart & Winston.

Barkow, J., Cosmides, L., & Tooby, J. (1992). *The adapted mind.* New York, NY: Oxford University Press.

Bower, T. G. R. (1974). *Development in infancy.* San Francisco, CA: Freeman.

Bowlby, J. (1969). *Attachment and loss: Vol 1. Attachment.* New York, NY: Basic Books.

Buss, D. M. (1995). Evolutionary psychology: A new paradigm for psychological science. *Psychological Inquiry, 6,* 1–30.

Canadian Psychological Association. (2000). *Canadian code of Ethics for Psychologists 3* [Monograph]. Ottawa, ON.

Charlesworth, W. R. (1966). *Development of the object concept: A methodological study.* Paper presented at the annual meetings of the American Psychological Association, New York, NY.

Cook, M., & Mineka, S. (1989). Observational conditioning of fear to fear-relevant versus fear-irrelevant stimuli in rhesus monkeys. *Journal of Abnormal Psychology, 98,* 448–459.

Daly, M., & Wilson, M. (1983). *Sex, evolution and behavior* (2nd ed.). Boston, MA: Willard Grant Press.

Darwin, C. (1859). *On the origin of species by means of natural selection, or the preservation of favoured races in the struggle for life.* London: John Murray.

DeCasper, A. J., & Fifer, W. P. (1980). Of human bonding: Newborns prefer their mothers' voices. *Science, 208,* 1174–1176.

Eibl-Eibesfeldt, I. (1975). *Ethology: The biology of behavior* (2nd ed.) New York, NY: Hold, Rinehart & Winston.

Eibl-Eibesfeldt, I. (1989). *Human ethology.* New York, NY: de Gruyter.

Ellis, B. J., McFadyen-Ketchum, S., Dodge, K. A., Pettit, G. S., & Bates, J. E. (1999). Quality of early family relationships and individual differences in the timing of pubertal maturation in girls: A longitudinal test of an evolutionary model. *Journal of Personality and Social Psychology, 77,* 387–401.

Fox, N. A., & Card, J. A. (1998). Psychological measures in the study of attachment. In J. Cassidy & P. Shaver (Eds.), *Handbook of attachment: Theory, research, and clinical applications* (pp. 226–245). New York, NY: Guilford.

Garcia, J., Kimeldorf, D. J., & Koelling, R. A. (1955). Conditioned aversion to saccharin resulting from exposure to gamma radiation. *Science, 122,* 157–158.

Jones, M. C. (1924). A laboratory study of fear: The case of Peter. *Pedagogical Seminary, 31,* 308–315.

Karmiloff-Smith, A. (2009). Nativism versus neuroconstructivism: Rethinking the study of developmental disorders. *Developmental Psychology, 45,* 56–63.

Ledingham, J. E. (1981). Developmental patterns of aggressive and withdrawn behaviour in childhood: A possible method for identifying preschizophrenics. *Journal of Abnormal Child Psychology, 9,* 22.

Lickliter, R., & Berry, T. D. (1990). The phylogeny fallacy: Developmental psychology's misapplication of evolutionary theory. *Developmental Review, 10,* 348–364.

Lickliter, R., & Honeycutt, H. (2003). Developmental dynamics: Toward a biologically plausible evolutionary psychology. *Psychological Bulletin, 129,* 819–835.

Lorenz, K. Z. (1935). Companions as factors in the bird's environment. *Journal of Ornithology, 83,* 137–213.

Lorenz, K. Z. (1952). *King Solomon's ring.* New York, NY: Crowell.

Miller, N. E., & Dollard, J. (1941). *Social learning and imitation.* New Haven, CT: Yale University Press.

Miller, P. H., & Coyle, T. R. (1999). Developmental change: Lessons from microgenesis. In E. K. Scholnick, K. Nelson, S. A. Gelman, & P. H. Miller (Eds.), *Conceptual development: Piaget's legacy.* Mahwah, NJ: Erlbaum.

Molfese, D. L., & Molfese, V. J. (1979). Hemispheric and stimulus differences are reflected in the cortical responses of newborn infants to speech sounds. *Developmental Psychology, 15,* 505–511.

Moskowitz, D. S., & Schwartzman, A. E. (1989). Painting group portraits: Studying life outcomes for aggressive and withdrawn children. *Journal of Personality, 57,* 723–746.

Moskowitz, D. S., Schwartzman, A. E., & Ledingham, J. E. (1985). Stability and change in aggression and withdrawal in middle childhood and early adolescence. *Journal of Abnormal Psychology, 94,* 30–41.

Oyama, S. (2000). *The ontogeny of information.* Durham, NC: Duke University Press.

Oyama, S. (2001). Terms and tensions: What do you do when all the good words are taken? In S. Oyama, P. E. Griffiths, & R. D. Gray (Eds.), *Cycles of contingency: Developmental systems and evolution* (pp. 177–193). Cambridge, MA: MIT Press.

Oyama, S., Griffiths, P. E., & Gray, R. D. (2001). Introduction: What is developmental systems theory? In S. Oyama, P. E. Griffiths, & R. D. Gray (Eds.), *Cycles of contingency: Developmental systems and evolution* (pp. 1–11). Cambridge, MA: MIT Press.

Piaget, J. (1954). *The construction of reality in the child.* New York, NY: Basic.

Serbin, L. A., Cooperman, J. M., Peters, P. L., Lehoux, P. M., Stack, D. M., & Schwartzman, A. E. (1998). Inter-generational transfer of psycho-social risk in women with childhood histories of aggression, withdrawal or aggression and withdrawal. *Developmental Psychology, 34,* 1246–1262.

Serbin, L. A., Peters, P. L., McAffer, V. J., & Schwartzman, A. E. (1991). Childhood aggression and withdrawal as predictors of adolescent pregnancy, early parenthood, and environmental risk for the next generation. *Canadian Journal of Behavioural Science, 23,* 318–331.

Skinner, B. F. (1953). *Science and human behavior.* New York, NY: MacMillan.

Society for Research in Child Development. (1993). Ethical standards for research with children. In *Directory of Members* (pp. 337–339). Ann Arbor: MI: Society for Research in Child Development.

Symons, D. (1979). *The evolution of human sexuality.* New York, NY: Oxford University Press.

Thelen, E., & Smith, L. B. (2006). Dynamic systems theories. In R. M. Lerner (Ed.), *Handbook of child psychology: Vol. 1. Theoretical models of human development* (6th ed.). New York, NY: Wiley.

Tooby, J., Cosmides, L., & Barrett, H. C. (2003). The second law of thermodynamics is the first law of psychology: Evolutionary developmental psychology and the theory of tandem, coordinated inheritances: Comment on Lickliter and Honeycutt (2003). *Psychological Bulletin, 129,* 858–865.

Urberg, K. A., Degirmencioglu, S. M., Tolson, J. M., & Halliday-Scher, K. (1995). The structure of adolescent peer networks. *Develomental Psychology, 33,* 834–844.

Watson, J. B. (1928). *Psychological care of infant and child.* New York, NY: Norton.

Watson, J. B., & Raynor, R. (1920). Conditioned emotional reactions. *Journal of Experimental Psychology, 3,* 1–14.

Wilson, E. O. (1975). *Sociobiology: The new synthesis.* Cambridge, MA: Belknap Press of Harvard University Press.

Chapter 3

Amara, S. G., Jonas, V., Rosenfeld, M. B., Ong, E. S., & Evans, R. M. (1982). Alternative RNA processing in calcitonin gene expression generates mRNAs encoding different polupoptide products. *Nature, 298,* 240–244.

Anderson, M., & Rutherford, M. D. (2008, June). *Remembering faces: How pregnancy impacts cognition.* Paper presented at Canadian Society for Brain, Behaviour and Cognitive Science 18th Annual Meeting, London, ON.

Beekmans, K., Thiery, E., Derom, C., Vernon, P. A., Vlietinck, R., & Derom, R. (1993). Relating type of placentation to later intellectual development in monozygotic (MZ) twins. *Behavior Genetics, 23,* 547–548.

Brett, M., & Baxendale, S. (2001). Motherhood and memory: A review. *Psychoneuroendocrinology, 26,* 362.

Burmeister, S. S., Kailasanath, V., & Fernald, R. D. (2007). Social dominance regulates androgen and estrogen receptor gene expression. *Hormones and Behavior, 51,* 164–170.

Caspi, A., Sugden, K., Moffitt, T. E., Taylor, A., Craig, I. W., Harrington, H., . . . Poulton, R. (2003). Influence of life stress on depression: Moderation by a polymorphism in the 5-HTT gene. *Science, 301,* 386–389.

Cole, S. W., Hawkley, L. C., Arevelo, J. M., Sung, C. Y., Rose, R. M., & Cacioppo, J. T. (2007). Social regulation of gene expression in human leukocytes. *Genome Biology, 8,* R189.

Corballis, M. C. (1991). *The lopsided ape: Evolution of the generative mind.* New York, NY: Oxford University Press.

Cowan, W. M. (1979). The development of the brain. *Scientific American, 241,* 112–133.

Cziezel, A. E., & Puho, E. (2004). Association between severe nausea and vomiting in pregnancy and lower rate of preterm births. *Paediatric and Perinatal Epidemiology, 18,* 253–259.

Dawkins, R. (1976). *The selfish gene.* Oxford, England: Oxford University Press.

Fagan, B. (2004). *The long summer: How climate changed civilization.* New York, NY: Basic Books.

Fessler, D. M. T. (2002). Reproductive immunosuppression and diet. *Current Anthropology, 43,* 19–61.

Flaxman, S. M., & Sherman, P. W. (2000). Morning sickness: A mechanism for protecting mother and embryo. *Quarterly Review of Biology, 75,* 113–148.

Golombok, S., Cook, R., Bish, A., & Murray, C. (1995). Families created by the new reproductive technologies: Quality of parenting and social and emotional development of the children. *Child Development, 66,* 285–298.

Golombok, S., MacCallum, F., & Goodman, E. (2001). The "test-tube" generation: Parent–child relationships and the psychological well-being of in vitro fertilization children at adolescence. *Child Development, 72,* 599–608.

Gould, S. J. (1980). *Ever since Darwin.* Harmondsworth, England: Penguin Books.

Gould, S. J. (1985). *The flamingo's smile: Reflections in natural history.* New York, NY: Norton.

Gould, S. J. (1991). Exaptation: A crucial tool for an evolutionary psychology. *Journal of Social Issues, 47,* 43–65.

Gould, S. J., & Lewontin, R. C. (1979). The spandrels of San Marco and the Panglossian paradigm. *Procedings of the Royal Society of London, B, 205,* 581–598.

Gould, S. J., & Vrba, E. S. (1982). Exaptation: A missing term in the science of form. *Paleobiology, 8,* 4–15.

Haig, D. (1993). Genetic conflicts in human pregnancy. *Quarterly Review of Biology, 68,* 495–532.

Hook, E. B. (1976). Changes in tobacco smoking and ingestion of alcohol and caffeinated beverages during early pregnancy: Are these consequences, in part, of feto-protective mechanisms diminishing maternal exposure to embryotoxins? In S. Kelly (Ed.), *Birth defects: Risks and consequences* (pp. 173–183). New York, NY: Academic Press.

Hook, E. B. (1978). Dietary cravings and aversions during pregnancy. *American Journal of Clinical Nutrition, 31,* 1355–1362.

Huttenlocher, P. R. (1990). Morphometric study of human cerebral cortex development. *Neuropsychologia, 28,* 517–527.

Johnston, T. D. (1987). The persistence of dichotomies in the study of behavioral development. *Developmental Review, 7,* 149–182.

Jones, B. C., Perrett, D. I., Little, A. C., Boothroyd, L., Cornwell, R. E., Feinberg, D. R., ... Moore, F. R. (2005). Menstrual cycle, pregnancy and oral contraceptive use alter attraction to apparent health in faces. *Proceedings of the Royal Society, B, 272,* 347–354.

Kolb, B. (1995). *Brain plasticity and behavior.* Hillsdale, NJ: Erlbaum.

Krogman, W. M. (1972). *Child growth.* Ann Arbor, MI: University of Michigan Press.

Lewontin, R. C. (1983). Gene, organism, and environment. In D. S. Bendall (Ed.), *Evolution from molecules to men.* Cambridge, England: Cambridge University Press.

Maynard Smith, J. (1993). *The theory of evolution.* (Canto ed.) Cambridge, England: Cambridge University Press.

Melnick, M., Myrianthopoulos, N. C., & Christian, J. C. (1978). The effects of chorion type on variation in IQ in the NCPP twin population. *American Journal of Human Genetics, 30,* 425–433.

Molfese, D. L., & Molfese, V. J. (1979). Hemispheric and stimulus differences are reflected in the cortical responses of newborn infants to speech sounds. *Developmental Psychology, 15,* 505–511.

Nachman, M. W., & Crowell, S. L. (2000). Estimate of the mutation rate of the nucleotide in humans. *Genetics Society of America, 156,* 297–304.

Navarrete, C. D., Fessler, D. M. T., & Eng, S. J. (2007). Elevated ethnocentrism in the first trimester of pregnancy. *Evolution and Human Behavior, 28,* 60–65.

Neumann-Held, E. M. (1998). The gene is dead—Long live the gene: Conceptualizing genes the constructionist way. In P. Koslowski (Ed.), *Sociobiology and bioeconomics: The theory of evolution in biological and economic theory.* Berlin, Germany: Springer-Verlag.

Pinker, S. (1997). *How the mind works.* New York, NY: W. W. Norton.

Pohorecky, L. A., Blakley, G. G., Kubovcakova, L., Krizanova, O., Patterson-Buckendahl, P., & Kvetnansky, R. (2004). Social hierarchy affects gene expression for catecholamine biosynthetic enzymes in rat adrenal glands. *Behavioural Neuroendocrinology, 80,* 42–51.

Profet, M. (1988). The evolution of pregnancy sickness as protection to the embryo against Pleistocene teratogens. *Evolutionary Theory, 8,* 177–190.

Raff, R. (1996). *The shape of life: Genes, development, and the evolution of animal form.* Chicago, IL: Chicago University Press.

Rakic, P. (1995). Corticogenesis in human and nonhuman primates. In M. S. Gazzaniga (Ed.), *The cognitive neurosciences* (pp. 127–145). Cambridge, MA: MIT Press.

Rutherford, M. (2002). It's adaptations all the way down. *Behavioral and Brain Sciences, 25,* 526.

Scarr, S. (1992). Developmental theories for the 1990s: Development and individual differences. *Child Development, 63,* 1–19.

Scarr, S. (1993). Biological and cultural diversity: The legacy of Darwin for development. *Child Development, 64,* 1333–1353.

Smith, C. W. J., Patton, J. G., & Nadal-Ginard, B. (1989). Alternative splicing in the control of gene expression. *Annual Review of Genetics, 23,* 527–577.

Sokol, D. K., Moore, C. A., Rose, R. J., Williams, C. J., Reed, T., & Christian, J. C. (1995). Intrapair differences in personality and cognitive ability among young monozygotic twins distinguished by chorion type. *Behavior Genetics, 25,* 457–465.

Tanapat, P., Hastings, N., & Gould, E. (2001). Adult neurogenesis in the hippocampal function. In C. A. Nelson & M. Luciana (Eds.), *Handbook of developmental cognitive neuroscience.* Cambridge, MA: Bradford Books.

Tooby, J., & Cosmides, L. (1990). On the universality of human nature and the uniqueness of the individual: The role of genetics and adaptation. *Journal of Personality, 58,* 17–67.

Tooby, J., & Cosmides, L. (1992). Psychological foundations of culture. In J. Barkow, L. Cosmides, & J. Tooby (Eds.), *The adapted mind* (pp. 19–136). New York, NY: Oxford University Press.

Tooby, J., & Cosmides, L. (1996). Friendship and the banker's paradox: Other pathways to the evolution of adaptations for altruism. *Proceedings of the British Academy, 88,* 119–143.

Waddington, C. H. (1957). *The strategy of the genes: A discussion of some aspects of theoretical biology.* New York, NY: Macmillan.

Wells, S. (2002). *The journey of man: A genetic odyssey.* Princeton, NJ: Princeton University Press.

Werker, J. F., & Vouloumanos, A. (2001). Speech and language processing in infancy: A neurocognitive approach. In C. A. Nelson & M. Luciana (Eds.), *Handbook of developmental cognitive neuroscience* (pp. 269–307). Cambridge, MA: MIT Press.

Williams, G. C. (1966). *Adaptation and natural selection.* Princeton, NJ: Princeton University Press.

Chapter 4

Barkow, J., Cosmides, L., & Tooby, J. (1992). *The adapted mind.* New York, NY: Oxford University Press.

Black, J. E., & Greenough, W. T. (1986). Induction of pattern in neural structure by experience: Implications for cognitive development. In M. E. Lamb, A. L. Brown & B. Rogoff (Eds.), *Advances in developmental psychology* (pp. 1–50). Hillsdale, NJ: Erlbaum.

Block, N. (1995). How heritability misleads about race. *Cognition, 56,* 99–128.

Bouchard, T. J. Jr. (1981). Familial studies of intelligence: A review. *Science, 212,* 1055–1059.

Bouchard, T. J. Jr. (2004). Genetic influences on human psychological traits: A survey. *Current Directions in Psychological Science, 13,* 148–151.

Bouchard, T. J. Jr., Lykken, D. T., McGue, M., Segal, N. L., & Tellegen, A. (1990). Sources of human psychological differences: The Minnesota study of twins reared apart. *Science, 250,* 223–228.

Brown, D. E. (1991). *Human universals.* New York, NY: McGraw Hill.

Burchinal, M. R., Campbell, F. A., Bryant, D. M., Wasik, B. H., & Ramey, C. T. (1997). Early intervention and mediating processes in cognitive performance of children of low-income African-American families. *Child Development, 68,* 935–954.

Campbell, F. A., Pungello, E. P., Miller-Johnson, S., Burchinal, M., & Ramey, C. T. (2001). The development of cognitive and academic abilities: Growth curves from an early childhood educational experiment. *Developmental Psychology, 37,* 231–242.

Chen, C., & Stevenson, H. W. (1995). Motivation and mathematics achievement: A comparative study of Asian-American, Caucasian-American, and East Asian high school students. *Child Development, 66,* 1215–1234.

Cook, E., Hodes, R., & Lang, P. (1986). Preparedness and phobia: Effects of stimulus content on human visceral conditioning. *Journal of Abnormal Psychology, 95,* 195–207.

Cyphers, L. H., Fulker, D. W., Plomin, R., & DeFries, J. C. (1989). Cognitive abilities in the early school years: No effects of shared environment between parents and offspring. *Intelligence, 13,* 369–386.

Dolan, B. (1999). From the field: Cognitive profiles of First Nations and Caucasian children referred for psychoeducational assessment. *Canadian Journal of School Psychology, 15,* 63–71.

Duncan, G. J., & Magnuson, K. A. (2005). Can family socioeconomic resources account for racial and ethnic test score gaps? *The Future of Children, 15,* 35–54.

Elbert, T., Pantev, C., Wienbruch, C., Rockstroh, B., & Taub, E. (1995). Increased cortical representation of the fingers of the left hand in string players. *Science, 270,* 305–307.

Freitag, C. M. (2007). The genetics of autistic disorders and its clinical relevance: A review of the literature. *Molecular Psychiatry, 12,* 2–22.

Garcia, J., Kimeldorf, D. J., & Koelling, R. A. (1955). Conditioned aversion to saccharin resulting from exposure to gamma radiation. *Science, 122,* 157–158.

Goren, C. C., Sarty, M., & Wu, P. Y. K. (1975). Visual following and pattern discrimination of face-like stimuli by newborn infants. *Pediatrics, 56,* 544–549.

Greenough, W. T., & Black, J. E. (1992). Induction of brain structure by experience: Substrates for cognitive development. In M. R. Gunnar & C. A. Nelson (Eds.), *Developmental behavior neuroscience* (pp. 155–200). Hillsdale, NJ: Erlbaum.

Greenough, W. T., Black, J. E., & Wallace, C. S. (1987). Experience and brain development. *Child Development, 58,* 539–559.

Hoekstra, R. A., Bartels, M., Verweij, C. J., & Boomsma, D. I. (2007). Heritability of autistic traits in the general population. *Archives of Pediatrics & Adolescent Medicine, 161,* 372–377.

Hubel, D. H., & Wiesel, T. N. (1962). Receptive fields, binocular interaction and functional architecture in the cat's visual cortex. *Journal of Physiology, 160,* 106–154.

Hunter, J. E., & Hunter, R. E. (1984). Validity and utility of alternative predictors of job performance. *Psychological Bulletin, 96,* 72–98.

Jensen, A. R. (1973). *Educability and group differences.* New York, NY: Harper & Row.

Jensen, A. R. (1998). *The g factor: The science of mental ability.* Westport, CT: Praeger.

Johnson, M. H. (1998). The neural basis of cognitive development. In W. Damon, D. Kuhn, & R. S. Siegler (Eds.), *Handbook of child psychology: Vol. 2. Cognition, perception and language* (5th ed., pp. 1–49). New York, NY: Wiley.

Juraska, J. M., Henderson, C., & Muller, J. (1984). Differential rearing experience, gender and radial maze performance. *Developmental Psychobiology, 17,* 209–215.

Lewontin, R. C. (1970). Race and intelligence. *Bulletin of the Atomic Scientists, 26,* 2–8.

Loehlin, J. C. (2000). Group differences in intelligence. In R. J. Sternberg (Ed.), New York, NY: Cambridge University Press.

Maurer, D. (1985). Infants' perception of facedness. In T. Field & N. Fox (Eds.), *Social Perception in Infants.* New York, NY: Ablex.

Maurer, D., Lewis, T. L., Brent, H. P., & Levin, A. V. (1999). Rapid improvement in the acuity of infants after visual input. *Science, 286,* 108–110.

McCall, R. B., Applebaum, M. I., & Hogarty, P. S. (1973). Developmental changes in mental performance. *Monographs of the Society for Research in Child Development, 38.*

Meltzoff, A. N. (1995). Infants' understanding of people and things: From body imitation to folk psychology. In J. L. Bermudez, A. Marcel & N. Eilan (Eds.), *The body and the self* (pp. 43–69). Cambridge, MA: MIT Press.

Mineka, S. (1986). Animal models of anxiety-based disorders: Their usefulness and limitations. In A. H. Tuma & J. Maser (Eds.), *Anxiety and the anxiety disorders* (pp. 199–224). Hillsdale, NJ: Erlbaum.

Moore, D. S. (2001). *The dependent gene: The fallacy of "Nature vs. Nurture".* New York, NY: W.H. Freeman.

Morton, J., & Johnson, M. H. (1991). CONSPEC and CONLERN: A two-process theory of infant face recognition. *Psychological Review, 98,* 164–181.

Neisser, U., Boodoo, G., Bouchard, T. J. Jr., Boykin, A. W., Brody, N., Ceci, S. J., . . . Urbina, S. (1996). Intelligence: Knowns and unknowns. *American Psychologist, 51,* 77–101.

Nesse, R. (1990). Evolutionary explanations of emotions. *Human Nature, 1,* 261–289.

Öhman, A. (1986). Face the beast and fear the face: Animal and social fears as prototypes for evolutionary analyses of emotion. *Psychophysiology, 23,* 123–145.

Olson, J. M., Vernon, P. A., Harris, J. A., & Lang, K. L. (2001). The heritability of attitudes: A study of twins. *Journal of Personality and Social Psychology, 80,* 845–860.

Pascual-Leone, A., Cammarota, A., Wasserman, E. M., Brasil-Neto, J. P., Cohen, L. G., & Hallett, M. (1993). Modulation of motor cortical outputs to the reading hand of Braille readers. *Annals of Neurology, 34,* 33–37.

Pedersen, N. L., Plomin, R., Nesselroade, J. R., & McClearn, G. E. (1992). A quantitative genetic analysis of cognitive abilities during the second half of the life span. *Psychological Science, 3,* 346–353.

Plomin, R. (1994). *Genetics and experience: The interplay between nature and nurture.* Thousand Oaks, CA: Sage.

Plomin, R., & DeFries, J. C. (1980). Genetics and intelligence: Recent data. *Intelligence, 4,* 15–24.

Plomin, R., Fulker, D. W., Corley, R., & DeFries, J. C. (1997). Nature, nurture, and cognitive development from 1 to 16 years: A parent–offspring adoption study. *Psychological Science, 8,* 442–447.

Ramey, C. T., Campbell, F. A., Burchinal, M. R., Skinner, M. L., Gardner, D. M., & Ramey, S. L. (2000). Persistent effects of early childhood education on high-risk children and their mothers. *Applied Developmental Science, 4,* 2–14.

Rowe, D. C., Jacobson, K. C., & van der Oord, E. J. C. G. (1999). Genetic and environmental influences on vocabulary IQ: Parental education level as a moderator. *Child Development, 70,* 1151–1162.

Sameroff, A. J., Seifer, R., Baldwin, A., & Baldwin, C. (1993). Stability of intelligence from preschool to adolescence: The influence of social and family risk factors. *Child Development, 64,* 80–97.

Sattler, J. M. (1988). *Assessment of children.* (3rd ed.) San Diego, CA: Jerome M. Sattler.

Scarr, S., & Weinberg, R. A. (1976). IQ test performance of black children adopted by white families. *American Psychologist, 31,* 726–739.

Scarr, S., & Weinberg, R. A. (1983). The Minnesota adoption studies: Genetic differences and malleability. *Child Development, 54,* 260–267.

Scarr, S., Weinberg, R. A., & Waldman, I. D. (1993). IQ correlations in transracial adoptive families. *Intelligence, 17,* 541–555.

Segal, N. (2000). Virtual twins: New finding on within-family environmental influences on intelligence. *Journal of Educational Psychology, 92,* 442–448.

Seligman, M. E. (1971). Phobias and preparedness. *Behavior Therapy, 2,* 307–320.

Sternberg, R. J., Grigorenko, E. L., & Bundy, D. A. (2001). The predictive value of IQ. *Merrill-Palmer Quarterly, 47,* 1–47.

Wallman, J. (1979). A minimal visual restriction experiment: Preventing chicks from seeing their feet affects later responses to mealworms. *Developmental Psychobiology, 12,* 391–397.

Wilcox, B. M. (1969). Visual preferences of human infants for representations of the human face. *Journal of Experimental Child Psychology, 7,* 10–20.

Chapter 5

Adams, R. J. (1989). Newborns' discrimination among mid- and long-wavelength stimuli. *Journal of Experimental Child Psychology, 47,* 130–141.

Adams, R. J., & Courage, M. L. (1998). Human newborn color vision: Measurement with chromatic stimuli varying in excitation purity. *Journal of Experimental Child Psychology, 60,* 344–360.

Aslin, R. N. (1981). Development of smooth pursuit in human infants. In D. F. Fisher, R. A. Monty, & J. W. Senders (Eds.), *Eye movements: Cognition and visual perception* (pp. 31–51). Hillsdale, NJ: Erlbaum.

Aslin, R. N. (1993). Perception of visual direction in human infants. In C. E. Granrud (Ed.), *Visual perception and cognition in infancy* (pp. 91–119). Hillsdale, NJ: Erlbaum.

Aslin, R. N., Jusczyk, P. W., & Pisoni, D. B. (1998). Speech and auditory processing during infancy: Constraints on and precursors to language. In D. Kuhn & R. Siegler (Eds.), *Handbook of Child Psychology* (5th ed., pp. 147–198). New York, NY: Wiley.

Aslin, R. N., & Lathrop, A. L. (2008). Visual perception. In M. M. Haith & J. B. Benson (Eds.), *Encyclopedia of infant and early childhood development*. Oxford, England: Elsevier.

Associated Press. (2003, August 25). Man's restored sight offers new view of vision. Retrieved from www.cnn.com.

Baldwin, D. A., Baird, J. A., Saylor, M. M., & Clark, M. A. (2001). Infants parse dynamic action. *Child Development, 72,* 708–717.

Banks, M. S. (1980). The develoment of visual accommodation during early infancy. *Child Development, 51,* 646–666.

Banks, M. S., & Bennett, P. J. (1988). Optical and photoreceptor immaturities limit the spatial and chromatic vision of human neonates. *Journal of the Optical Society of America, 5,* 2059–2097.

Beauchamp, G. K., Cowart, B. J., Mennella, J. A., & Marsh, R. R. (1994). Infant salt taste: Developmental, methodological, and contextual factors. *Developmental Psychobiology, 27,* 353–365.

Bench, R. J., Collyer, Y., Mentz, L., & Wilson, I. (1976). Studies in infant behavioural audiometry: I. Neonates. *Audiology, 15,* 85–105.

Bertenthal, B. I. (1993). Infants' perception of biomechanical motions: Intrinsic image and knowledge-based constraints. In C.E. Granrud (Ed.), *Visual perception and cognition in infancy* (pp. 175–214). Hillsdale, NJ: Erlbaum.

Bertenthal, B. I., Campos, J., & Barrett, L. (1984). Self-produced locomotion: An organizer of emotional, cognitive, and social development in infancy. In R. Emde & R. Harmon (Eds.), *Continuities and discontinuities in development* (pp. 175–209). New York, NY: Plenum.

Bertenthal, B. I., Campos, J., & Kermoian, R. (1994). An epigenetic perspective on the development of self-produced locomotion and its consequences. *Current Directions in Psychological Science, 3,* 140–145.

Bertenthal, B. I., & Campos, J. J. (1990). A systems approach to the organizing effects of self-produced locomotion during infancy. In C. Rovee-Collier & L. P. Lipsitt (Eds.), *Advances in infancy research* (pp. 1–60). Norwood, NJ: Ablex.

Bhalla, M., & Proffitt, D. R. (1999). Visual–motor recalibration in geographical slant perception. *Journal of Experimental Psychology: Human Perception and Performance, 25,* 1076–1096.

Bornstein, M. H. (1975). Qualities of color vision in infancy. *Journal of Experimental Child Psychology, 19,* 401–409.

Bower, T. G. R. (1966). The visual world of infants. *Scientific American, 215,* 80–92.

Carey, S., & Diamond, R. (1994). Are faces perceived as configurations more by adults than by children? *Visual Cognition, 1,* 253–274.

Cernoch, J. M., & Porter, R. H. (1985). Recognition of maternal axillary odors by infants. *Child Development, 56,* 1593–1598.

Courage, M. L., & Adams, R. J. (1990). Visual acuity assessment from birth to three years using the acuity card procedure: Cross-sectional and longitudinal samples. *Optometry and Vision Science, 67,* 713–718.

Crook, C. K., & Lipsitt, L. P. (1976). Neonatal nutritive sucking: Effects of taste stimulation upon sucking rhythm and heart rate. *Child Development, 47,* 518–522.

Dannemiller, J. L. (1985). The early phase of dark adaptation in human infants. *Vision Research, 25,* 207–212.

Dannemiller, J. L. (2000). Competition in early exogenous orienting between 7 and 21 weeks. *Journal of Experimental Child Psychology, 76,* 253–274.

Dannemiller, J. L., & Hanko, S. A. (1987). A test of color constancy in 4-month-old infants. *Journal of Experimental Child Psychology, 44,* 255–267.

DeCasper, A. J., & Fifer, W. P. (1980). Of human bonding: Newborns prefer their mothers' voices. *Science, 208,* 1174–1176.

DeCasper, A. J., & Spence, M. J. (1986). Prenatal maternal speech influences newborn's perception of speech sounds. *Infant Behavior and Development, 9,* 133–150.

Farroni, T., Johnson, M. H., Brockbank, M., & Simion, F. (2000). Infants' use of gaze direction to cue attention: The importance of perceived motion. *Visual Cognition, 7,* 705–718.

Fifer, W. P., & Moon, C. M. (1995). The effects of fetal experience with sound. In J. P. Lecanuet, W. P. Fifer, N. A. Krasnegor & W. P. Smotherman (Eds.), *Fetal development: A psychobiological perspective*. Hillsdale, NJ: Erlbaum.

Fine, I., Wade, A. R., Brewer, A. A., May, M. G., Goodman, D. F., Boynton, G. M., . . . MacLeod, D. I. (2003). Long-term deprivation affects visual perception and cortex. *Nature Neuroscience, 6,* 915–916. doi:10.1038/nn1102

Fodor, J. A. (1983). *The modularity of mind*. Cambridge, MA: MIT Press.

Geldart, S., Mondloch, C. J., Maurer, D., de Schonen, S., & Brent, H. P. (2002). The effect of early visual deprivation on the development of face processing. *Developmental Science, 5,* 490–501.

Gibson, E. J., & Walk, R. D. (1960). The "visual cliff." *Scientific American, 202,* 64–71.

Goren, C. C., Sarty, M., & Wu, P. Y. K. (1975). Visual following and pattern discrimination of face-like stimuli by newborn infants. *Pediatrics, 56,* 544–549.

Greenough, W. T., Black, J. E., & Wallace, C. S. (1987). Experience and brain development. *Child Development, 58,* 539–559.

Gregory, R. L., & Wallace, J. G. (1963). Recovery from early blindness: A case study. *Experimental Psychology Society Monograph, 2.* London, England: Heffer.

Hains, S. M. J., & Muir, D. (1996). Infant sensitivity to adult eye direction. *Child Development, 67,* 1940–1951.

Haith, M. M. (1991). Gratuity, perception–action integration and future orientation in infant vision. In F. Kessel, A. Sameroff & M. Bornstein (Eds.), *Contemporary construction of the child: Essays in honor of William Kessen* (pp. 23–43). Hillsdale, NJ: Erlbaum.

Haith, M. M., Bergman, T., & Moore, M. J. (1977). Eye contact and face scanning in early infancy. *Science, 198,* 853–855.

Haith, M. M., Wentworth, N., & Canfield, R. (1993). The formation of expectations in early infancy. In C. Rovee-Collier & L. P. Lipsitt (Eds.), *Advances in infancy research* (pp. 217–249). Norwood, NJ: Ablex.

Haynes, H., White, B. L., & Held, R. (1965). Visual accommodation in human infants. *Science, 148,* 528–530.

Held, R., & Hein, A. (1963). Movement-produced stimulation in the development of visually guided behavior. *Journal of Comparative and Physiological Psychology, 56,* 872–876.

Hobbes, T. (1651/2006). *Leviathan.* Dover.

Hood, B. M., Willen, J. D., & Driver, J. (1998). Adult's eyes trigger shifts of visual attention in human infants. *Psychological Science, 9,* 131–134.

Hulbert, A. C., & Poggio, T. A. (1988). Synthesizing a colour algorithm from examples. *Science, 239,* 482–485.

Humphrey, T. (1978). Function of the nervous system during prenatal life. In U. Stave (Ed.), *Perinatal physiology* (pp. 651–683). New York, NY: Plenum.

James, W. (1891). *The principles of psychology.* Cambridge, MA: Harvard University Press.

Johnson, M. H., Dziurawiec, S., Ellis, H. D., & Morton, J. (1991). Newborns preferential tracking of faces and its subsequent decline. *Cognition, 40,* 1–19.

Johnson, P. T., Williams, R. R., Cusato, K., & Reese, B. E. (1999). Rods and cones project to the inner plexiform layer during development. *Journal of Comparative Neurology, 414,* 1–12.

Kaye, K. L., & Bower, T. G. R. (1994). Learning and intermodal transfer of information in newborns. *Psychological Science, 5,* 286–288.

Kellman, P. J., & Banks, M. S. (1998). Infant visual perception. In D. Kuhn & R. S. Siegler (Eds.), *Cognition, perception, and language: Vol. 2, Handbook of child psychology* (pp. 103–146). New York, NY: Wiley.

Kermoian, R., & Campos, J. J. (1988). Locomotor experience: A facilitator of spatial cognitive development. *Child Development, 59,* 908–917.

Kisilevsky, B. S., Fearon, I., & Muir, D. W. (1998). Fetuses differentiate vibroacoustic stimuli. *Infant Behavior and Development, 21,* 25–46.

Le Grand, R., Mondloch, C. J., Maurer, D., & Brent, H. O. (2004). Impairment in holistic face processing following early visual deprivation. *Psychological Science, 15,* 762–768.

Leat, S. J., Yadav, N. K., & Irving, E. L. (2009). Development of visual acuity and contrast sensitivity in children. *Journal of Optometry, 2,* 19–26.

Lecanuet, J. P., Granier-Deferre, C., & Busnel, M. C. (1995). Human fetal auditory perception. In J. P. Lecanuet, W. P. Fifer, N. A. Krasnegor & W. P Smotherman (Eds.), *Fetal development: A psychobiological perspective* (pp. 239–262). Hillsdale, NJ: Erlbaum.

Liley, A. W. (1972). The foetus as a personality. *Australian and New Zealand Journal of Psychiatry, 6,* 99.

Ling, B. Y., & Dain, S. J. (2008). Color vision in children and the Lanthony new color test. *Visual Neuroscience, 25,* 441–444.

Loomis, J. M., Da Silva, J. A., Fujita, N., & Fukusima, S. S. (1992). Visual space perception and visually directed action. *Journal of Experimental Psychology: Human Perception and Performance, 18,* 906–921.

Macfarlane, A. (1975). Olfaction in the development of social preferences in the human neonate. In *CIBA Foundation Symposium 33: Parent–Infant Interaction.* Amsterdam, The Netherlands: Elsevier.

Marlier, L., & Schaal, B. (1997). The perception of olfactory familiarity in the neonate: Differential influence of the mode of feeding? *Enfance, 1,* 47–61.

Marlier, L., & Schaal, B. (2005). Human newborns prefer human milk: Conspecific milk odor is attractive without postnatal exposure. *Child Development, 76,* 155–168.

Marlier, L., Schaal, B., & Soussignan, R. (1998). Neonatal responsiveness to the odor of amniotic and lacteal fluids: A test of perinatal chemosensory continuity. *Child Development, 69,* 611–623.

Maurer, D. (1985). Infants' perception of facedness. In T. Field & N. Fox (Eds.), *Social Perception in Infants.* New York, NY: Ablex.

Maurer, D., & Maurer, C. (1998). *The world of the newborn.* New York, NY: Basic Books.

Maurer, D., Mondloch, C., & Lewis, T. L. (2007). Sleeper effects. *Developmental Science, 10,* 40–47.

Maurer, D., & Salapatek, P. (1976). Developmental changes in the scanning of faces by young infants. *Child Development, 47,* 523–527.

Meltzoff, A. N., & Borton, R. W. (1979). Intermodal matching by human neonates. *Nature, 282,* 403–404.

Mennella, J. A., Jagnow, C. P., & Beauchamp, G. K. (2001). Prenatal and postnatal flavor learning by human infants. *Pediatrics, 107,* 88.

Mollon, J. D. (1996). The evolution of trichromacy: An essay to mark the bicentennial of Thomas Young's graduation in Göttingen. In N. Elsner & H. U. Schnitzler (Eds.), *Brain and Evolution* (pp. 125–139). Stuttgart, Germany: Springer.

Mondloch, C., Pathman, T., Maurer, D., Le Grand, R., & de Schonen, S. (2007). The composite face effect in six-year-old children: Evidence of adult-like face processing. *Visual Cognition, 15,* 564–577.

Moore, C., & Corkum, V. (1998). Infant gaze following based on eye direction. *British Journal of Developmental Psychology, 16,* 495–503.

Morton, J., & Johnson, M. H. (1991). CONSPEC and CONLERN: A two-process theory of infant face recognition. *Psychological Review, 98,* 164–181.

Phillips, W., Baron-Cohen, S., & Rutter, M. (1992). The role of eye-contact in the detection of goals: Evidence from normal toddlers, and children with autism or mental handicap. *Development and Psychopathology, 4,* 375–383.

Piaget, J. (1954). *The construction of reality in the child.* New York, NY: Basic Books.

Porter, R. H., Bologh, R. D., & Makin, J. W. (1988). Olfactory influences on mother–infant interactions. In C. Rovee-Collier & L. P. Lipsitt (Eds.), *Advances in infancy research* (pp. 39–69). Norwood, NJ: Ablex.

Porter, R. H., Makin, J. W., Davis, L. B., & Christensen, K. M. (1992). Breast-fed infants respond to olfactory cues from their own mother and unfamiliar lactating females. *Infant Behavior and Development, 15,* 85–93.

Proffitt, D. R., Bhalla, M., Gossweiler, R., & Midgett, J. (1995). Perceiving geographical slant. *Psychonomic Bulletin and Review, 2,* 409–428.

Purves, D., & Lotto, R. B. (2003). *Why we see what we do: An empirical theory of vision.* Sunderland, MA: Sinauer Associates.

Purves, D., Lotto, R. B., Williams, S. M., Nundy, S., & Yang, Z. (2001). Why we see things the way we do: Evidence for a wholly empirical strategy of vision. *Philosophical Transactions of the Royal Society of London, B: Biological Sciences, 356,* 285–297.

Querleu, D., & Renard, K. (1981). Les perceptions auditives du foetus humain. *Medicine and Hygiene, 39,* 2102–2110.

Reiser, J., Yonas, A., & Wikner, K. (1976). Radial localization of odors by human neonates. *Child Development, 47,* 856–859.

Robinson, D. W., & Sutton, G. J. (1979). Age effect in hearing: A comparative analysis of published threshold data. *Audiology, 18,* 320–334.

Rutherford, M. D., & Brainard, D. H. (2002). Lightness constancy: A direct test of the illumination estimation hypothesis. *Psychological Science, 13,* 142–149.

Salapatek, P., & Kessen, W. (1966). Visual scanning of triangles by the human newborn. *Journal of Experimental Child Psychology, 3,* 155–167.

Schaal, B., Orgeur, P., & Rognon, C. (1995). Odor sensing in the human fetus: Anatomical, functional, and chemoecological bases. In J. P. Lecanuet, W. P. Fifer, N. A. Krasnegor, & W. P. Smotherman (Eds.), *Fetal development: A psychobiological perspective.* Hillsdale, NJ: Erlbaum.

Slater, A. (1989). Visual memory and perception in early infancy. In A. Slater & G. Bremner (Eds.), *Infant development* (pp. 43–72). Hove, UK: Erlbaum.

Slater, A., Mattock, A., & Brown, E. (1990). Size constancy at birth: Newborn infant's responses to retinal and real size. *Journal of Experimental Child Psychology, 49,* 314–322.

Sorce, J. F., Emde, R. N., Campos, J., & Klinnert, M. D. (1985). Maternal emotional signaling: Its effect on visual cliff behavior of one-year-olds. *Developmental Psychology, 21,* 195–200.

Steiner, J. E. (1979). Human facial expression in response to taste and smell stimulation. In H. W. Reese & L. P. Lipsitt (Eds.), *Advances in child development and behavior* (pp. 257–295). New York, NY: Academic Press.

Suttle, C. M., Banks, M. S., & Graf, E. W. (2002). FPL and sweep VEP to tritan stimuli in young human infants. *Vision Research, 42,* 2879–2891.

Taddio, A., Katz, J., Ilersich, A. L., & Koren, G. (1997). Effect of neonatal circumcision on pain response during subsequent routine vaccination. *Lancet, 349,* 599–603.

Teller, D. Y., & Bornstein, M. H. (1987). Infant color vision and color perception. In P. Salapatek & L. Cohen (Eds.), *Handbook of infant perception: Vol. 1. From sensation to perception.* New York, NY: Academic Press.

Teller, D. Y., McDonald, M. A., Preston, K., Sebris, S. L., & Dobson, V. (1986). Assessment of visual acuity in infants and children: The acuity card procedure. *Developmental Medicine & Child Neurology, 28,* 779–789.

Trehub, S. E., & Schellenberg, E. G. (1995). Music: Its relevance to infants. *Annals of Child Development, 11,* 1–24.

Vecera, S. P., & Johnson, M. H. (1995). Gaze Detection and the Cortical Processing of Faces: Evidence from Infants and Adults. *Visual Cognition, 2,* 51–87.

Walk, R. D., & Gibson, E. J. (1961). A comparative and analytical study of visual depth perception. *Psychological Monographs, 75,* 519, 1–44.

Yonas, A. (1981). Infants' responses to optical information for collision. In R. N. Aslin, J. Alberts, & M. Petersen (Eds.), *Development of perception: Psychobiological perspectives: The visual system* (pp. 313–334). New York, NY: Academic Press.

Zimmer, E. Z., Chao, C. R., Guy, G. P., Marks, F., & Fifer, W. P. (1993). Vibroacoustic stimulation evokes human fetal micturition. *Obstetrics and Gynecology, 81,* 178–180.

Chapter 6

Anglin, J. M. (1977). *Word, object, and conceptual development.* New York, NY: W.W. Norton.

Barrett, H. C. (2005). Adaptations to predators and prey. In D. M. Buss (Ed.), *The handbook of evolutionary psychology* (pp. 200–223). New York, NY: Wiley.

Barsalou, L. W. (1985). Ideals, central tendency, and frequency of instantiation as determinants of graded structure in categories. *Journal of Experimental Psychology: Learning Memory and Cognition, 11,* 629–654.

Behl-Chadha, G. (1996). Basic-level and superordinate-like categorical representations in early infancy. *Cognition, 60,* 105–141.

Bruner, J. S., Olver, R. R., & Greenfield, P. M. (1966). *Studies in cognitive growth.* New York, NY: Wiley.

Calder, A. J., Young, A. W., Perrett, D. I., Etcoff, N. L., & Rowland, D. (1996). Categorical perception of morphed facial expressions. *Visual Cognition, 3,* 81–117.

Carey, S. (1985). Conceptual change in childhood. Cambridge, MA: Bradford/MIT Press.

Carey, S. (1988). Conceptual differences between children and adults. *Mind and Language, 3,* 167–181.

Carey, S., & Spelke, E. (1996). Science and core knowledge. *Philosophy of Science, 63*(4), 515–533.

Cosmides, L., & Tooby, J. (1994). Beyond intuition and instinct blindness: The case for an evolutionarily rigorous cognitive science. *Cognition, 50,* 41–77.

Curio, E. (1973). Towards a methodology of teleonomy. *Experientia, 29,* 1045–1058.

Dawkins, R. (1986). *The blind watchmaker.* New York, NY: W.W. Norton.

Dromi, E. (1987). *Early lexical development.* Cambridge, England: Cambridge University Press.

Duncker, K. (1945). On problem solving. *Psychological Monographs, 58,* 1–110.

Eimas, P. D. (1963). The relation between identification and discrimination along speech and non-speech continua. *Language and Speech, 6,* 206–217.

Etcoff, N. L., & Magee, J. J. (1992). Categorical perception of facial expressions. *Cognition, 44,* 227–240.

Flavell, J. H. (1963). *The developmental psychology of Jean Piaget.* Princeton, NJ: Van Nostrand.

Flavell, J. H. (1970). Concept development. In P. H. Mussen (Ed.), *Carmichael's manual of child psychology* (3rd ed.). New York, NY: Wiley.

Flavell, J. H. (1985). *Cognitive development.* Engelwood Cliffs, NJ: Prentice-Hall.

Gelman, S. A. (1988). The development of induction within natural kind and artifact categories. *Cognitive Psychology, 20,* 65–95.

Gelman, S. A. (2000). The role of essentialism in children's concepts. In H. W. Reese (Ed.), *Advances in child development and behavior* (Vol. 27). San Diego, CA: Academic Press.

Gelman, S. A., & Coley, J. D. (1990). The importance of knowing a dodo is a bird: Categories and inferences in 2 1/2 year old children. *Developmental Psychology, 26,* 796–804.

Gelman, S. A., & Markman, E. M. (1986). Categories and induction in young children. *Cognition, 23,* 183–209.

Gelman, S. A., & Markman, E. M. (1987). Young children's induction from natural kinds: The role of categories and appearances. *Child Development, 58,* 1532–1541.

Gelman, S. A., & O'Reilly, A. W. (1988). Children's inductive inferences within superordinate categories: The role of categories and appearances. *Child Development, 59,* 876–887.

Gelman, S. A., & Wellman, H. M. (1991). Insides and essences: Early understandings of the non-obvious. *Cognition, 38,* 213–244.

German, T., & Barrett, H. C. (2005). Functional fixedness in a technologically sparse culture. *Psychological Science, 16,* 1–5.

German, T., & Defeyter, M. A. (2000). Immunity to functional fixedness in young children. *Psychological Bulletin & Review, 7,* 707–712.

Gibson, E. J. (1969). *Principles of perceptual learning nd development.* New York, NY: Appleton-Century-Crofts.

Goodman, N. (1972). Seven strictures on similarity. In N. Goodman (Ed.), *Problems and projects* (pp. 437–447). Indianapolis, IN: Bobbs-Merrill.

Gutheil, G., & Rosengren, K. S. (1993). A rose by any other name: Preschoolers' concept of identity across name and appearance changes. *British Journal of Developmental Psychology, 14,* 477–498.

Horton, M. S., & Markman, E. M. (1980). Developmental differences in the acquisition of basic and superordinate categories. *Child Development, 51,* 708–719.

Inhelder, B., & Piaget, J. (1964). *The early growth of logic in the child.* New York, NY: Harper and Row.

Johnson, K. E., Scott, P., & Mervis, C. B. (1997). Development of children's understanding of basic-subordinate inclusion relations. *Developmental Psychology, 33,* 745–763.

Keil, F. C. (1979). *Semantic and conceptual development.* Cambridge, MA: MIT Press.

Keil, F. C. (1986). The acquisition of natural kind and artifact terms. In W. Demopoulas & A. Marras (Eds.), *Language learning and concept acquisition: Foundational issues* (pp. 133–153). Norwood, NJ: Ablex.

Keil, F. C. (1989). *Concepts, kinds, and cognitive development.* Cambridge, MA: MIT Press.

Keil, F. C. (1991). The emergence of theoretical beliefs as constraints on concepts. In S. Carey & R. Gelman (Eds.), *The epigenesis of mind: Essays on biology and cognition.* Hillsdale, NJ: Erlbaum.

Kemler, D. G. (1982). Classification in young and retarded children: The primacy of overall similarity relations. *Child Development, 53,* 768–779.

Kemler, D. G. (1983). Holistic and analytic modes in perceptual and cognitive development. In T. J. Tighe & B. E. Shepp (Eds.), *Perception, cognition, and development: Interactaional analyses.* Hillsdale, NJ: Erlbaum.

Krascum, R. M., & Andrews, S. (1998). The effects of theories on children's acquisition of family-resemblance categories. *Child Development, 69,* 333–346.

Krasnow, M. (2008, June). *Evolutionizing the study of conceptual knowledge.* Paper presented at Human Behavior and Evolution Society 2008, Kyoto, Japan.

Liberman, A. M., Harris, K. S., Hoffman, H. S., & Griffith, B. C. (1957). The discrimination of speech sounds within and across phoneme boundaries. *Journal of Experimental Psychology, 54,* 358–368.

Mandler, J. M. (1998). Representation. In D. Kuhn & R. S. Siegler (Eds.), *Cogntion, perception and language* (5th ed.). New York, NY: Wiley.

McDonough, L., & Mandler, J. M. (1998). Inductive generalization in 9- and 11-month-olds. *Developmental Science, 1,* 227–232.

Markman, E. M. (1978). Empirical versus logical solutions to part-whole comparison problems concerning classes and collections. *Child Development, 49,* 168–177.

Markman, E. M. (1989). *Categories and naming in children: Problems of induction.* Cambridge, MA: MIT Press.

McCloskey, M. E., & Glucksberg, S. (1978). Natural categories: Well defined or fuzzy sets? *Memory and Cognition, 6,* 462–472.

Mervis, C. B. (1987). Child-basic object categories and early lexical development. In U. Neisser (Ed.), *Concepts and conceptual development: Ecological and intellectual bases of categorizations.* Cambridge, England: Cambridge University Press.

Mervis, C. B., & Rosch, E. (1981). Categorization of natural objects. *Annual Review of Psychology, 32,* 89–115.

Mervis, C. B., Catlin, J., & Rosch, E. (1976). Relationships among goodness-of-example, category norms, and word frequency. *Bulletin of the Psychonomic Society, 7,* 283–284.

Murphy, G. L., & Brownell, H. H. (1985). Category differentiation in object recognition: Typicality constraints on the basic category advantage. *Journal of Experimental Psychology: Learning, Memory and Cognition, 11,* 70–84.

Odom, R. D. (1978). A perceptual salience account of decalage relations and developmental change. In L. S. Siegel & C. J. Brainerd (Eds.), *Alternatives to Piaget.* New York, NY: Academic.

Pinker, S. (1997). *How the mind works.* New York, NY: W. W. Norton.

Quinn, P. C., & Eimas, P. D. (1996). Perceptual organization and categorization in young infants. In C. Rovee-Collier and L. P Lipsitt (Eds.), *Advances in infancy research.* Norwood, NJ: Ablex.

Rosch, E., & Mervis, C. B. (1975). Family resemblance: Studies in the internal structure of categories. *Cognitive Psychology, 7,* 573–605.

Rosch, E., Mervis, C. B., Gray, W. D., Johnson, D. M., & Boyes-Braem, P. (1976). Basic object in natural categories. *Cognitive Psychology, 8,* 382–439.

Rosch, E. H. (1975). Cognitive representations of semantic categories. *Journal of Experimental Psychology: General, 104,* 192–233.

Ross, G. (1980). Categorization in 1- to 2-year-olds. *Developmental Psychology, 16,* 391–396.

Scholnick, E. K., Nelson, K., Gelman, S. A., & Miller, P. H. (1999). *Conceptual development: Piaget's legacy.* Mahwah, NJ: Erlbaum.

Schwartz, S. R. (1977). *Naming, necessity and natural kinds.* Ithaca, NY: Cornell University Press.

Smith, E. E., Balzano, G. J., & Walker, J. (1978). Nominal, perceptual, and semantic codes in picture categorization. In J. W. Cotton & R. L. Klatzky (Eds.),

Semantic factors in cognition (pp. 137–168). Hillsdale, NJ: Erlbaum.

Smith, E. E., & Medin, D. L. (1981). *Categories and concepts.* Cambridge, MA: Harvard University Press.

Smith, L. B. (1979). Perceptual development and category generalization. *Child Development, 10,* 705–715.

Smith, L. B. (1985). Young children's attention to global magnitude: Evidence from classification tasks. *Journal of Experimental Child Psychology, 39,* 472–491.

Smith, L. B., & Kemler, D. G. (1977). Developmental trends in free classification: Evidence for a new conceptualization of perceptual development. *Journal of Experimental Child Psychology, 24,* 279–298.

Springer, K., & Keil, F. C. (1989). On the development of biologically specific beliefs: The case of inheritance. *Child Development, 60,* 637–648.

Vygotsky, L. S. (1962). *Thought and language.* Cambridge, MA: MIT Press.

Wellman, H. M., & Gelman, S. A. (1992). Cognitive development: Foundational theories of core domains. *Annual Review of Psychology, 43,* 337–375.

Wellman, H. M., & Gelman, S. A. (1998). Knowledge acquisition in foundational domains. In D. Kuhn & R. S. Siegler (Eds.), *Handbook of child psychology: Vol. 2. Cognition, perception, and language.* New York, NY: Wiley.

Williams, G. C. (1966). *Adaptation and natural selection.* Princeton, NJ: Princeton University Press.

Williams, G. C. (1985). A defense of reductionism in evolutionary biology. *Oxford Surveys in Evolutionary Biology, 2,* 1–27.

Winer, G. A. (1980). Class-inclusion reasoning in children: A review of the empirical literature. *Child Development, 51,* 309–328.

Wittgenstein, L. (1953). *Philosophical investigations.* Oxford: Blackwell.

Chapter 7

Aguiar, A., & Baillargeon, R. (1999). 2.5-month-old infants' reasoning about when objects should and should not be occluded. *Cognitive Psychology, 39 (2),* 116–157.

Antell, S. E., & Keating, D. P. (1983). Perception of numerical invariance in neonates. *Child Development, 54,* 695–701.

Atran, S. (1990). *Cognitive foundations of natural history: Towards an anthropology of science.* Cambridge, England: Cambridge University Press.

Atran, S. (2002). Modular and cultural factors in biological understanding: An experimental approach to the cognitive basis of science. In P. Carruthers, S. Stich & M.

Siegal (Eds.), *The cognitive basis of science* (pp. 41–72). Cambridge, England: Cambridge University Press.

Atran, S., Medin, D. L., Lynch, E., Vapnarsky, V., Ek, E. U., & Sousa, P. (2001). Folkbiology doesn't come from folkpsychology: Evidence from Yukatek Maya in cross-cultural perspective. *Journal of Cognition and Culture, 1,* 42.

Backscheider, A. G., Shatz, M., & Gelman, S. A. (1993). Preschoolers' ability to distinguish living kinds as a function of regrowth. *Child Development, 64,* 1242–1257.

Baillargeon, R. (1987). Object permanence in 3.5- and 4.5-month-old infants. *Developmental Psychology, 23,* 655–664.

Baillargeon, R. (1998). Infants' understanding of the physical world. In M. Sabourin, F. Craik & M. Robert (Eds.), *Advances in psychological science* (pp. 503–529). London, England: Psychology Press.

Baillargeon, R. (2004). Infants' physical world. *Current Directions in Psychological Science, 13,* 89–94.

Baillargeon, R., Spelke, E. S., & Wasserman, S. (1985). Object permanence in 5-month-old infants. *Cognition, 20,* 191–208.

Baillargeon, R., & DeVos, J. (1991). Object permanence in 3.5- and 4.5- month old infants: Further evidence. *Child Development, 62,* 1227–1246.

Barrett, H. C., & Behne, T. (2005). Children's understanding of death as the cessation of agency: A test using sleep versus death. *Cognition, 96,* 93–108.

Barth, H., Kanwisher, N., & Spelke, E. (2003). The construction of large number representation. *Cognition, 86,* 201–221.

Benson, J. B., & Uzgiris, I. C. (1985). Effect of self-initiated locomotion on infant search activity. *Developmental Psychology, 21,* 923–931.

Boysen, S. T. (1983). Counting in chimpanzees: Nonhuman principles and emergent properties of number. In S. T. Boysen & E. J. Capaldi (Eds.), *The development of numerical competence: Animal and human models* (pp. 39–59). Hillsdale, NJ: Erlbaum.

Brannon, E. M., & Terrace, H. S. (1998). Ordering of the numerosites 1–9 by monkeys. *Science, 282,* 746–749.

Breland, K., & Breland, M. (1961). The misbehavior of organisms. *American Psychologist, 16,* 681–684.

Breland, K., & Breland, M. (1966). *Animal behavior.* New York, NY: Macmillan.

Briars, D., & Siegler, R. S. (1984). A featural analysis of preschoolers' counting knowledge. *Developmental Psychology, 20,* 607–618.

Carey, S. (1995). On the origin of causal understanding. In D. Sperber, D. Premack & A. J. Premack (Eds.), *Causal cognition: A multi-disciplinary debate.* New York, NY: Oxford University Press.

Carey, S., & Spelke, E. (1992). Domain-specific knowledge and conceptual change. In L. A. Hirschfeld & S. A. Gelman (Eds.), *Mapping the mind* (pp. 169–200). New York, NY: Cambridge University Press.

Chomsky, N. (1980). *Rules and representation.* New York, NY: Columbia University Press.

Clifton, R. K., Rochat, P., Litovsky, R. Y., & Perris, E. E. (1991). Object representation guides infants' reaching in the dark. *Journal of Experimental Psychology: Human Perception and Performance, 17,* 323–329.

Diamond, A. (1991). Neuropsychological insights into the meaning of object concept development. In S. Carey & R. Gelman (Eds.), *The epigenesis of mind: Essays on biology and knowledge* (pp. 67–110). Hillsdale, NJ: Lawrence Erlbaum Associates.

Dore, F. Y., & Dumas, C. (1987). Psychology of animal cognition: Piagetian studies. *Psychological Bulletin, 102,* 219–233.

Feigenson, L., & Carey, S. (2003). Tracking individuals via object-files: Evidence from infants' manual search. *Developmental Science, 6,* 568–584.

Feigenson, L., Carey, S., & Hauser, M. (2002). The representations underlying infants' choice of more: Object-files versus analog magnitudes. *Psychological Science, 13,* 150–156.

Feigenson, L., Carey, S., & Spelke, E. (2002). Infants' discrimination of number vs. continuous extent. *Cognitive Psychology, 44,* 33–66.

Feigenson, L., Dehaene, S., & Spelke, E. S. (2004). Core systems of number. *Trends in Cognitive Science, 8,* 307–314.

Gallistel, C. R. (1990). *The organization of learning.* Cambridge, MA: MIT Press.

Gardner, B. T., & Gardner, R. A. (1985). Signs of intelligence in cross-fostered chimpanzees. *Philosophical Transactions of the Royal Society, B, 308,* 159–176.

Geary, D. C. (1994). *Children's mathematical development: Research and practical applications.* Washington, DC: American Psychological Association.

Geary, D. C. (1995). Reflections of evolution and culture in children's cognition: Implications for mathematical development and instruction. *American Psychologist, 50,* 24–37.

Gelman, R. (1990). First principles organize attention to and learning about relevant data: Number and the animate–inanimate distinction as examples. *Cognitive Science, 14,* 79–106.

Gelman, R., & Gallistel, R. (1978). *The child's*

understanding of number. Cambridge, MA: Harvard University Press.

Gelman, S. A. (2000). The role of essentialism in children's concepts. In H. W. Reese (Ed.), *Advances in child development and behavior* (Vol. 27). San Diego, CA: Academic Press.

Gelman, S. A., & Wellman, H. M. (1991). Insides and essences: Early understandings of the non-obvious. *Cognition, 38,* 213–244.

Gratch, G. (1972). A study of the relative dominance of vision and touch in six-month-old infants. *Child Development, 43,* 615–623.

Gratch, G., & Landers, W. F. (1971). Stage IV of Piaget's theory of infants' object concepts: A longitudinal study. *Child Development, 42,* 359–372.

Harris, P. L. (1983). Infant cognition. In M. M. Haith & J. J. Campos (Eds.), *Handbook of child psychology: Vol. 2 Infancy and developmental psychobiology.* New York, NY: Wiley.

Hatano, G., & Inagaki, K. (1994). Young children's naive theory of biology. *Cognition, 50,* 171–188.

Hauser, M. D. (2000). *Wild minds: What animals really think?* New York, NY: Holt.

Hauser, M. D., & Carey, S. (2003). Spontaneous representations of small numbers of objects by rhesus macaques: Examinations of content and format. *Cognitive Psychology, 47,* 367–401.

Hermer, L., & Spelke, E. (1996). Modularity and development: The case of spatial reorientation. *Cognition, 61,* 195–232.

Hermer-Vazquez, L., Spelke, E., & Katsnelson, A. (1999). Source of flexibility in human cognition: Dual task studies of space and language. *Cognitive Psychology, 39,* 3–36.

Hespos, S. J. & Baillargeon, R. (2001). Knowledge about containment events in very young infants. *Cognition, 78,* 204–245.

Hood, B., & Willatts, P. (1986). Reaching in the dark to an objects' remembered position: Evidence for object permanence in 5-month-old infants. *British Journal of Developmental Psychology, 4,* 57–65.

Huntley-Fenner, G., Carey, S., & Somimando, A. (2002). Objects are individuals but stuff doesn't count: Perceived rigidity and cohesiveness influence infants' representations of small groups of discrete entities. *Cognition, 85,* 203–221.

Inagaki, K. (1990). The effects of raising animals on children's biological knowledge. *British Journal of Developmental Psychology, 8,* 119–129.

Inagaki, K. (1993). *Young children's differentiation of plants from non-living things in terms of growth.* Paper presented at the 60th meeting of the Society for Research in Child Development, New Orleans, LA.

Inagaki, K., & Hatano, G. (1987). Young children's spontaneous personification as analogy. *Child Development, 58*, 1013–1020.

Inagaki, K. & Hatano, G. (1996). Young children's recognition of commonalities between plants and animals. *Child Development, 67*, 2823–2840.

Inagaki, K., & Sugiyama, K. (1988). Attributing human characteristics: Developmental changes in over- and underattribution. *Cognitive Development, 3*, 55–70.

Karmiloff-Smith, A. (1988). The child is a theoretician, not an inductivist. *Mind and Language, 3*, 184–195.

Kellman, P. J., & Spelke, E. S. (1983). Perception of partly occluded objects in infancy. *Cognitive Development, 15*, 483–524.

Kosugi, D., & Fujita, K. (2002). How do 8-month-old infants recognize causality in object motion and that in human action? *Japanese Psychological Research, 44*, 66–78.

Kotovsky, L., & Baillargeon, R. (1998). The development of calibration-based reasoning about collision events in young infants. *Cognition, 67*, 311–351.

Leslie, A., & Keeble, S. (1987). Do six-month-olds perceive causality? *Cognition, 25*, 265–288.

Lew, A. R., Foster, K. A., Crowther, H. L., & Green, M. (2004). Indirect landmark use at 6 months of age in a spatial orientation task. *Infant Behavior and Development, 27*, 81–90.

Lipton, J. S., & Spelke, E. S. (2003). Origins of number sense: Large number discrimination in human infants. *Psychological Science, 14*, 396–401.

Loomis, J. M., Klatzky, R. L., Golledge, R. G., Cicinelli, J. G., Pellegrino, J. W., & Fry, P. A. (1993). Nonvisual navigation by blind and sighted: Assessment of path integration ability. *Journal of Experimental Psychology: General, 12*, 73–91.

Newcombe, N., Huttenlocher, J., Drummey, A. B., & Wiley, J. G. (1998). The development of spatial location coding: Place learning and dead reckoning in the second and third years. *Cognitive Development, 13*, 185–200.

Newcombe, N., Huttenlocher, J., & Learmonth, A. (1999). Infants' coding of location in continuous space. *Infant Behavior and Development, 22*, 483–510.

Pepperberg, I. M. (1994). Numerical competence in an African gray parrot (*Psittacus erithacus*). *Journal of Comparative Psychology, 198*, 36–44.

Piaget, J. (1929). *The child's conception of the world.* London, England: Routledge & Kegan Paul.

Piaget, J. (1952). *Play, dreams and imitation in childhood.* New York, NY: W. W. Norton.

Platt J. R, & Johnson D. M. (1971). Localization of position within a homogeneous behavior chain: Effects of error contingencies. *Learning & Motivation, 2*, 386–414.

Rosengren, K. S., Gelman, S. A., Kalish, C. W., & McCormick, M. (1991). As time goes by: Children's early understanding of growth in animals. *Child Development, 62*, 1302–1320.

Ross, N., Medin, D., Coley, J. D., & Atran, S. (2002). Cultural and experiential differences in the development of folkbiological induction. *Cognitive Development, 18*, 25.

Rumelhart, D. E., & McClelland, J. L. (1985). Distributed memory and the representation of general and specific information. *Journal of Experimental Psychology: General, 114*, 159–188.

Sevenster, P. (1973). Incompatibility of response and reward. In R. A. Hinde & J. Stevenson-Hinde (Eds.), *Constraints on learning: Limitations and predispositions* (pp. 265–283). London, England: Academic Press.

Shettleworth, S. (1972). Constraints on learning. *Advances in the Study of Behaviour, 4*, 1–68.

Siegler, R. S., & Crowley, K. (1994). Constraints on learning in nonprivileged domains. *Cognitive Psychology, 27*, 194–226.

Solomon, G., Johnson, S., Zaitchik, D., & Carey, S. (1996). Like father, like son: Young children's understanding of how and why offspring resemble their parents. *Child Development, 67*, 151–171.

Spelke, E. S. (1985). Perception of unity, persistence and identity: Thoughts on infants' conceptions of objects. In J. Mehler & R. Fox (Eds.), *Neonate cognition: Beyond the booming, buzzing confusion* (pp. 89–114). Hillsdale, NJ: Erlbaum.

Spelke, E. S. (1991). Physical knowledge in infancy: Reflections on Piaget's theory. In S. Carey & R. Gelman (Eds.), *Epigenesis of mind: Essays on biology and knowledge* (pp. 133–169). Hillsdale, NJ: Erlbaum.

Spelke, E., & Kinzler, K. D. (2007). Core knowledge. *Developmental Science, 10*, 89–96.

Spelke, E. S., Breinlinger, K., Jacobson, K., & Phillips, A. (1993). Gestalt relations and object perception: A developmental study. *Perception, 22*, 1483–1501.

Spelke, E. S., Breinlinger, K., Macomber, J., & Jacobson, K. (1992). Origins of knowledge. *Psychological Review, 99*, 605–632.

Spelke, E. S., Phillips, A., & Woodward, A. L. (1995). Infants' knowledge of object motion and human action. In D. Sperber, D. Premack & A. J. Premack (Eds.),

Causal cognition: A multidisciplinary debate (pp. 44–78). New York, NY: Oxford University Press.

Springer, K. (1992). Children's beliefs about the biological implications of kinship. *Child Development, 63,* 950–959.

Springer, K. (1996). Young children's understanding of a biological basis for parent–offspring relations. *Child Development, 67,* 2841–2856.

Springer, K., & Keil, F. C. (1989). On the development of biologically specific beliefs: The case of inheritance. *Child Development, 60,* 637–648.

Starkey, P., Spelke, E. S., & Gelman, R. (1983). Detection of intermodal numerical correspondence by human infants. *Science, 222,* 179–181.

Starkey, P., Spelke, E. S., & Gelman, R. (1990). Numerical abstraction by human infants. *Cognition, 36,* 97–127.

Strauss, M. S., & Curtis, L. E. (1984). Development of numerical concepts in infancy. In C. Sophian (Ed.), *Origins of cognitive skills: The Eighteenth Annual Carnegie Symposium on Cognition* (pp. 131–155). Hillsdale, NJ: Erlbaum.

van Oeffelen, M. P., & Vos, P. G. (2003). A probabilistic model for the discrimination of visual number. *Cognition, 86,* 201–221.

vanMarle, K., & Scholl, B. J. (2003). Attentive tracking of objects versus substances. *Psychological Science, 14,* 498–504.

von Hofsten, C., & Spelke, E. S. (1985). Object perception and object-directed reaching in infancy. *Journal of Experimental Psychology: General, 114,* 198–212.

Wang, S., Baillargeon, R., & Paterson, S. (2004). Detecting continuity violations in infancy: A new account and new evidence from covering and tube events. *Cognition, 95,* 129–173.

Wellman, H. M., & Gelman, S. A. (1988). Children's understanding of the nonobvious. In R. J. Sternberg (Ed.), *Advances in the psychology of human intelligence* (Vol. 4) (pp. 99–135). Hillsdale, NJ: Erlbaum.

Wynn, K. (1992). Addition and subtraction by human infants. *Nature, 358,* 749–750.

Wynn, K. (1995). Infants possess a system of numerical knowledge. *Current Directions in Psychological Science, 4,* 172–177.

Xu, F. (2003). Numerosity discrimination in infants: Evidence for two systems of representations. *Cognition, 89,* B15–B25.

Xu, F., & Arriaga, R. I. (2007). Number discrimination in 10-month-old infants. *British Journal of Developmental Psychology, 25,* 103–108.

Xu, F., & Spelke, E. S. (2000). Large number discrimination in 6-month old infants. *Cognition, 74,* B1–B11.

Chapter 8

Adams, D. (1997). *Chasing liquid mountains.* Sydney, Australia: McMillan.

Adolphs, R., Sears, L., & Piven, J. (2001). Abnormal processing of social information from faces in autism. *Journal of Cognitive Neuroscience, 13,* 232–240.

American Psychiatric Association (1994). *Diagnostic and statistical manual of mental disorders* (4th ed.). Washington, DC: American Psychiatric Publishing.

Astington, J., Harris, P. L., & Olson, D. R. (1988). *Developing theories of mind.* New York, NY: Cambridge University Press.

Baldwin, D. A., Baird, J. A., Saylor, M. M., & Clark, M. A. (2001). Infants parse dynamic action. *Child Development, 72,* 708–717.

Bandura, A. (1977). *Social learning theory.* Upper Saddle River, NJ: Prentice Hall.

Bandura, A., Ross, D., & Ross, S. A. (1961). Transmission of aggression through imitation and aggressive models. *Journal of Abnormal and Social Psychology, 63,* 575–582.

Baron-Cohen, S. (1989a). Perceptual role-taking and protodeclarative pointing in autism. *British Journal of Developmental Psychology, 7,* 113–127.

Baron-Cohen, S. (1989b). Joint-attention deficits in autism: Towards a cognitive analysis. *Development and Psychopathology, 1,* 185–189.

Baron-Cohen, S. (1995). *Mindblindness: An essay on autism and theory of mind.* Cambridge, MA: MIT Press.

Baron-Cohen, S., Campbell, R., Karmiloff-Smith, A., Grant, J., & Walker, J. (1995). Are children with autism blind to the mentalistic significance of the eyes? *British Journal of Developmental Psychology, 13,* 379–398.

Baron-Cohen, S. & Cross, P. (1992). Reading the eyes: Evidence for the role of perception in the development of a theory of mind. *Mind and Language, 6,* 173–186.

Baron-Cohen, S., Leslie, A. M., & Frith, U. (1985). Does the autistic child have a "theory of mind"? *Cognition, 21,* 37–46.

Baron-Cohen, S., Spitz, A., & Cross, P. (1993). Can children with autism recognize surprise? *Cognition and Emotion, 7,* 507–516.

Baron-Cohen, S., Wheelwright, S., & Jolliffe, T. (1997). Is there a "language of the eyes"? Evidence from normal adults, and adults with autism or Asperger syndrome. *Visual Cognition, 4,* 311–331.

Barton, R. A. (1996). Neocortex size and behavioural ecology in primates. *Proceedings of the Royal Society of London, B, 263,* 173–177.

Barton, R. A., & Dunbar, R. I. M. (1997). Evolution of

the social brain. In A. Whiten & R. Byrne (Eds.), *Machiavellian intelligence, Vol. II.* Cambridge, England: Cambridge University Press.

Barton, R. A., & Purvis, A. (1994). Primate brains and ecology: Looking beneath the surface. In J. R. Anderson, B. Thierry & N. Herrenschmidt (Eds.), *Current primatology* (pp. 1–12). Strasbourg, France: University of Strasbourg Press.

Behrmann, M., Thomas, C., & Humphreys, K. (2006). Seeing it differently: Visual processing in autism. *Trends in Cognitive Sciences.*

Bennett, P. M., & Harvery, P. H. (1985). Brain size, development and metabolism in birds and mammals. *Journal of Zoology, London, 207,* 491–509.

Bormann-Kischkel, C., Vilsmeier, M., & Baude, B. (1995). The development of emotional concepts in autism. *Journal of Child Psychology and Psychiatry and Allied Disciplines, 36,* 1243–1259.

Boucher, J., & Lewis, V. (1992). Unfamiliar face recognition in relatively able autistic children. *Journal of Child Psychology and Psychiatry, 33,* 843–859.

Braverman, M., Fein, D., Lucci, D., & Waterhouse, L. (1989). Affect comprehension in children with pervasive developmental disorders. *Journal of Autism and Developmental Disorders, 17,* 301–316.

Bretherton, I., & Beeghly, M. (1982). Talking about internal states: The acquisition of an explicit theory of mind. *Developmental Psychology, 18,* 906–921.

Brothers, L. (1990). The social brain: A project for integrating primate behaviour and neurophysiology in a new domain. *Concepts in Neuroscience, 1,* 27–251.

Buitelaar, J., van Engeland, H., de Kogel, K., de Vries, H., & van Hoof, J. (1991). Differences in the structure of social behaviour of autistic children and non-autistic retarded controls. *Journal of Child Psychology and Psychiatry, 32,* 995–1015.

Byrne, R. B. (1995). *The thinking primate.* Oxford, England: Oxford University Press.

Byrne, R. W., & Whiten, A. (1988). *Machiavellian intelligence.* Oxford, England: Oxford University Press.

Call, J., Brauer, J., Kaminski, J., & Tomasello, M. (2003). Domestic dogs (*Canis familiaris*) are sensitive to the attentional state of humans. *Journal of Comparative Psychology, 117,* 257–263.

Campos, J. J., & Sternberg, C. (1981). Perceptions, appraisal, and emotion. In M. Lamb & S. Shulman (Eds.), *Infant social cognition* (pp. 273–314). Hillsdale, N.J.: Lawrence Erlbaum Associates.

Carey, S., & Diamond, R. (1994). Are faces perceived as configurations more by adults than by children? *Visual Cognition, 1,* 253–274.

Celani, G., Battacchi, M. W., & Arcidiacono, L. (1999). The understanding of the emotional meaning of facial expressions in people with autism. *Journal of Autism and Developmental Disorders, 29,* 57–66.

Curcio, F. (1978). Sensorimotor functioning and communication in mute autistic children. *Journal of Autism and Childhood Schizophrenia, 8,* 281–292.

Dawson, G., Webb, S. J., & McPartland, J. (2005). Understanding the nature of face processing impairment in autism: Insights from behavioral and electrophysiological studies. *Developmental Neuropsychology, 27,* 403–424.

Dawson, G., Carver, L., Meltzoff, A. N., Panagiotides, H., & McPartland, J. (2002). Neural correlates of face recognition in young children with autism spectrum disorder, developmental delay, and typical development. *Child Development, 73,* 700–717.

Dawson, G., Meltzoff, A., Osterling, J., Rinaldi, J., & Brown, E. (1998). Children with autism fail to orient to naturally occurring social stimuli. *Journal of Autism and Developmental Disorders, 28,* 479–485.

de Gelder, B., Vroomen, J., & van der Heide, L. (1991). Face recognition and lip reading in autism. *European Journal of Cognitive Psychology, 3,* 69–86.

Dunbar, R. I. M. (1992). Neocortex size as a constraint on group size in primates. *Journal of Human Evolution, 22,* 469–493.

Dunbar, R. I. M. (1998a). *Grooming, gossip, and the evolution of language.* Cambridge, MA: Harvard University Press.

Dunbar, R. I. M. (1998b). The social brain hypothesis. *Evolutionary Anthropology, 6,* 178–190.

Dunbar, R. I. M., & Shultz, S. (2007). Understanding primate brain evolution. *Philosophical Transactions of the Royal Society B: Biological Sciences, 362,* 649–658.

Dunbar, R. I. M., & Spoors, M. (1995). Social networks, support cliques, and kinship. *Human Nature, 6,* 273–290.

Ellis, H. D. & Leafhead, K. (1996). Raymond: A study of an adult with Asperger syndrome. In P. W. Halligan & J. C. Marshall (Eds.), *Methods in madness: Case studies in cognitive neuropsychiatry* (pp. 79–92). East Sussex, England: Psychology Press.

Fantz, R., & Nevis, S. (1972). Pattern preferences and perceptual-cognitive development in early infancy. *Journal of Experimental Child Psychology, 14,* 477–492.

Farroni, T., Johnson, M. H., Brockbank, M., & Simion, F. (2000). Infants' use of gaze direction to cue attention: The importance of perceived motion. *Visual Cognition, 7,* 705–718.

Farroni, T., Menon, E., & Johnson, M. H. (2006). Factors influencing newborns' preference for faces with eye contact. *Journal of Experimental Child Psychology, 95,* 298–308.

Fein, G. G. (1981). Pretend play in childhood: An integrative review. *Child Development, 52,* 1095–1118.

Flavell, J. H. (1992). Perspectives on perspective taking. In H. Beilin & P. Pufall (Eds.), *Piaget's theory: Prospects and possibilities.* Hillsdale, NJ: Erlbaum.

Flavell, J. H., Green, F. L., & Flavell, E. R. (1986). Development of knowledge about the appearance–reality distinction. *Monographs of the Society for Research in Child Development, 51,* 1–87.

Fossey, D., & Harcourt, A. H. (1977). Feeding ecology of free ranging mountain gorillas (*Gorilla gorilla beringei*). In T. H. Clutton-Brock (Ed.), *Primate ecology: Studies of feeding and ranging behaviour in lemurs, monkeys and apes* (pp. 539–556). London, England: Academic Press.

Garvey, C. (1991). *Play* (2nd ed.). London, England: Fontana Press.

Gelman, R. (1990). First principles organize attention to and learning about relevant data: Number and the animate–inanimate distinction as examples. *Cognitive Science, 14,* 79–106.

Gergely, G., Nadasdy, Z., Csibra, G., & Biro, S. (1995). Taking the intentional stance at 12 months of age. *Cognition, 56,* 165–193.

Gittleman, J. H. (1986). Carnivore brain size, behavioural ecology and phylogeny. *Journal of Mammology, 67,* 23–36.

Golinkoff, R. M, Harding, C.G., Carlson, V., & Sexton, M. E. (1984). The infant's perception of causal events: The distinction between animate and inanimate objects. In L. L. Lipsitt & C. Rovee-Collier (Eds.), *Advances in infancy research* (Vol. 3) (pp. 145–165)*.* Norwood, NJ: Ablex.

Gopnik, A., & Astington, J. W. (1988). Children's understanding of representational change and its relation to the understanding of false belief and the appearance–reality distinction. *Child Development, 59,* 26–37.

Goren, C. C., Sarty, M., & Wu, P. Y. K. (1975). Visual following and pattern discrimination of face-like stimuli by newborn infants. *Pediatrics, 56,* 544–549.

Grimby, A. (1998). Hallucinations following the loss of a spouse: Common and normal events among the elderly. *Journal of Clinical Geropsychiatry, 4,* 65–74.

Grossman, Klin, Carter, and Volkmar, (2000). Verbal bias in recognition of facial emotions in children with Asperger syndrome. *Journal of Child Psychology and Psychiatry, 41*(3), 369–379.

Hains, S. M. J., & Muir, D. (1996). Infant sensitivity to adult eye direction. *Child Development, 67,* 1940–1951.

Hamlin, J. K., Hallinan, E. V., & Woodward, A. L. (2008). Do as I do: 7-month-old infants selectively reproduce others' goals. *Developmental Science, 11,* 487–494.

Haney, C. (2003). Long term health issues in long-term solitary and "supermax." *Crime Delinquency, 49,* 124–156.

Hansen, M. B., & Markman, E. M. (2005). Appearance questions can be misleading: A discourse-based account of the appearance–reality problem. *Cognitive Psychology, 50,* 233–263.

Harlow, H. F. (1964). Early social deprivation and later behavior in the monkey. In A. Abrams, H. H. Gurner & J. E. P. Tomal (Eds.), *Unfinished tasks in the behavioral sciences* (pp. 154–173). Baltimore, MD: Williams & Wilkins.

Harlow, H. F., Dodsworth, R. O., & Harlow, M. K. (1965). Total social isolation in monkeys. *Proceedings of the National Academy of Science, 54,* 90–97.

Harlow, H. F., & Suomi, S. J. (1971). Social recovery by isolation-reared monkeys. *Proceedings of the National Academy of Science, 68,* 1534–1538.

Herrmann, E., Call, J., Hernandez-Lloreda, M. V., Hare, B., & Tomasello, M. (2007). Humans have evolved specialized skills of cognitive cognition: The cultural intelligence hypothesis. *Science, 317,* 1360–1366.

Hobson, R. P. (1986). The autistic child's appraisal of expressions of emotion. *Journal of Child Psychology and Psychiatry and Allied Disciplines, 27,* 321–342.

Hobson, R. P., Ouston, J., & Lee, A. (1988). What's in a face? The case of autism. *British Journal of Psychology, 79,* 441–453.

Hofer, M. A. (1984). Relationships as regulators: A psychobiologic perspective on bereavement. *Psychosomatic Medicine, 46,* 183–197.

Howard, M. A., Cowell, P. E., Boucher, J., Broks, P., Mayes, A., & Farrant, A. (2000). Convergent Neuroanatomical and behavioural evidence of an amygdala hypothesis of autism. *Neuroreport, 11,* 2935.

Humphreys, K., Minshew, N., Leonard, G., & Behrmann, M. (2007). A fine-grained analysis of facial expression processing in high functioning adults with autism. *Neuropsychologia, 45,* 685–695.

Inagaki, K., & Hatano, G. (1993). Young children's understanding of the mind–body distinction. *Child Development, 64,* 1534–1549

Johnson, M. H., Dziurawiec, S., Ellis, H. D., & Morton, J. (1991). Newborns' preferential tracking of faces and its subsequent decline. *Cognition, 40,* 1–19.

Jolly, A. (1966). Lemur social behavior and primate intelligence. *Science, 153,* 501–506.

Joseph, R. M. & Tanaka, J. (2003). Holistic and part-based face recognition in children with autism. *Journal of Child Psychology and Psychiatry, 44,* 529–542.

Klin, A., Jones, W., Schultz, R., Volkmar, F., & Cohen, D. (2002). Visual fixation patterns during viewing of naturalistic social situations as predictors of social competence in individuals with autism. *Archives of General Psychiatry, 59*, 809–816.

Klin, A., Sparrow, S., de Bildt, A., Cicchetti, D., Cohen, D., & Volkmar, F. (1999). A normed study of face recognition in autism and related disorders. *Journal of Autism and Developmental Disorders, 29*, 499–508.

Klin, A. (2000). Attributing social meaning to ambiguous visual stimuli in higher-functioning autism and Asperger syndrome: The social attribution task. *Journal of Child Psychology and Psychiatry and Allied Disciplines, 41*, 831–846.

Klinnert, M. D. (1984). The regulation of infant behavior by maternal facial expression. *Infant Behavior and Development, 7*, 447–465.

Kudo, H., & Dunbar, R. I. M. (2001). Neocortex size and social network size in primates. *Animal Behaviour, 62*, 711–722.

Kuhlmeier, V. A., Wynn, K., & Bloom, P. (2003). Attribution of dispositional states by 12-month-olds. *Psychological Science, 14*, 402–408.

Le Grand, R., Mondloch, C. J., Maurer, D., & Brent, H. O. (2004). Impairment in holistic face processing following early visual deprivation. *Psychological Science, 15*, 762–768.

Leekam, S. R., Hunnisett, E., & Moore, C. (1998). Targets and cues: Gaze-following in children with autism. *Journal of Child Psychology & Psychiatry & Allied Disciplines, 39*, 951–962.

Legerstee, M. (1991). The role of person and object in eliciting early imitation. *Journal of Experimental Child Psychology, 51*, 423–433.

Lempers, J. D., Flavell, E. R., & Flavell, J. H. (1977). The development in very young children of tacit knowledge concerning visual perception. *Genetic Psychology Monographs, 95*, 3–53.

Leslie, A. (1994). ToMM, ToBy, and agency: Core architecture and domain specificity. In L. A. Hirschfeld & S. A. Gelman (Eds.), *Mapping the mind: Domain specificity in cognition and culture*. Cambridge, England: Cambridge University Press.

Leslie, A. M. (1987). Pretense and representation: The origins of "theory of mind." *Psychological Review, 94*, 412–426.

Leslie, A. M., & Thaiss, L. (1992). Domain specificity in conceptual development. *Cognition, 43*, 225–251.

MacKinnon, J. (1974). The behaviour and ecology of wild orangutan (*Pongo pygmaeus*). *Animal Behavior, 22*, 3–74.

Marino, L. (1996). What can dolphins tell us about primate evolution? *Evolutionary Anthropology, 5*, 81–86.

Marino, L. (1997). The relationship between gestation length, encephalisation and body weight in odontocetes. *Marine Mammal Science, 14*, 143–148.

Masangkay, Z. S., McCluskey, K. A., McIntyre, C. W., Sims-Knight, J., Vaughn, B. E., & Flavell, J. H. (1974). The early development of inferences about the visual percepts of others. *Child Development, 45*, 237–253.

Maurer, D., & Barrera, M. (1981). Infants' perception of natural and distorted arrangements of a schematic face. *Child Development, 52*, 196–202.

McCune-Nicolich, L. (1981). Toward symbolic functioning: Structure of early pretend games and potential parallels with language. *Child Development, 52*, 785–797.

Meltzoff, A. N. (1990). Foundations for developing a concept of self: The role of imitation in relating self to other and the value of social mirroring, social modeling, and self practice in infancy. In D. Cicchetti & M. Beeghly (Eds.), *The self in transition: Infancy to childhood*. Chicago, IL: University of Chicago Press.

Meltzoff, A. N. (1995). Understanding the intentions of others: Re-enactment of intended acts by 18-month-old children. *Developmental Psychology, 31*, 838–850.

Mondloch, C., Pathman, T., Maurer, D., Le Grand, R., & de Schonen, S. (2007). The composite face effect in six-year-old children: Evidence of adult-like face processing. *Visual Cognition, 15*, 564–577.

Moore, C., & Corkum, V. (1998). Infant gaze following based on eye direction. *British Journal of Developmental Psychology, 16*, 495–503.

Morton, J., & Johnson, M. H. (1991). CONSPEC and CONLERN: A two-process theory of infant face recognition. *Psychological Review, 98*, 164–181.

Moyles, J. R. (1994). *The excellence of play*. Buckingham, England: Open University Press.

Mundy, P., & Neal, R. A. (2001). Neural plasticity, joint attention, and a transactional social-orienting model of autism. In L. M. Glidden (Ed.), *International review of research in mental retardation: Autism* (pp. 139–168). San Diego, CA: Academic Press.

Mundy, P. & Sigman, M. (1989). The theoretical implications of joint-attention deficits in autism. *Development and Psychopathology, 1*, 173–183.

Mundy, P., Sigman, M., Ungerer, J., & Sherman, T. (1986). Defining the social deficits of autism: The contribution of non-verbal communication measures. *Journal of Child Psychology & Psychiatry & Allied Disciplines, 27*, 657–669.

Murphy, C., & Messer, D. (1977). Mothers, infants and pointing: A study of gesture. In H. R. Schaffer (Ed.),

Studies in mother–infant interaction. London, England: Academic Press.

Nagel, U. (1973). A comparison of anubis baboons, hamadryas baboons and their hybrids at a species border in Ethiopia. *Folia Primatologica, 19,* 104–65.

Ogai, M., Matsumoto, H., Suzuki, K., Ozawa, F., Fukuda, R., & Uchiyama, I. (2003). fMRI study of recognition of facial expressions in high-functioning autistic patients. *Neuroreport, 14,* 559–563.

Onishi, K. H., & Baillargeon, R. (2005). Do 15-month-old infants understand false beliefs? *Science, 308,* 255–258.

Osterling, J. & Dawson, G. (1994). Early recognition of children with autism: A study of first birthday home videotapes. *Journal of Autism and Developmental Disorders, 24,* 247–257.

Ozonoff, S., Pennington, B. F., & Rogers, S. J. (1991). Executive function deficits in high-functioning autistic individuals: Relationship to theory of mind. *Journal of Child Psychology and Psychiatry and Allied Disciplines, 32,* 1081–1105.

Pascalis, O., De Haan, M., & Nelson, C. A. (2002). Is face processing species-specific during the first year of life? *Science, 296,* 1321–1323.

Pelphrey, K. A., Sasson, N. J., Reznick, J. S., Paul, G., Goldman, B. D., & Piven, J. (2002). Visual scanning of faces in autism. *Journal of Autism and Developmental Disorders, 32,* 249–261.

Perner, J., Leekam, S. R., & Wimmer, H. (1987). Three-year-olds' difficulty with false belief: The case for a conceptual deficit. *British Journal of Developmental Psychology, 5,* 125–137.

Peterson, C. C., & Siegal, M. (1998). Changing focus on the representational mind: Deaf, autistic and normal children's concepts of false photos, false drawings and false beliefs. *British Journal of Developmental Psychology, 16,* 301–320.

Phillips, W., Baron-Cohen, S., & Rutter, M. (1992). The role of eye-contact in the detection of goals: Evidence from normal toddlers, and children with autism or mental handicap. *Development and Psychopathology, 4,* 375–383.

Piaget, J. (1952). *Play, dreams and imitation in childhood.* New York, NY: W. W. Norton.

Piaget, J., & Inhelder, B. (1967). The coordination of perspectives. In J. Piaget & B. Inhelder (Eds.) *The child's conception of space* (pp. 209–246). New York, NY: W. W. Norton.

Poulin-Dubois, D., & Shultz, T. R. (1988). The development of the understanding of human behavior: From agency to intentionality. In J. W. Astington, P. L. Harris & D. R. Olson (Eds.),

Developing theories of mind. Cambridge, England: Cambridge University Press.

Povinelli, D. J., & Eddy, T. J. (1996). What young chimpanzees know about seeing. *Monographs of the Society for Research in Child Development, 61,* 1–152.

Povinelli, D. J., Nelson, K. E., & Boysen, S. T. (1990). Inferences about guessing and knowing by chimpanzees (*Pan trodlodytes*). *Journal of Comparative Psychology, 104,* 203–210.

Povinelli, D. J., & Vonk, J. (2004). We don't need a microscope to explore the chimpanzee's mind. *Mind and Language, 19,* 1–28.

Premack, D., & Woodruff, G. (1978). Does the chimpanzee have a theory of mind? *Behavioral and Brain Sciences, 1,* 515–526.

Ricks, D. M. & Wing, L. (1975). Language, communication, and the use of symbols in normal and autistic children. *Journal of Autism and Childhood Schizophrenia., 5,* 191–221.

Rochat, P., Morgan, R., & Carpenter, M. (1997). Young infants' sensitivity to movement information specifying social causality. *Cognitive Development, 12,* 441–465.

Rochat, P., & Striano, T. (1999). Social-cognitive development in the first year. In P. Rochat (Ed.), *Early social cognition: Understanding other in the first months of life.* Mahwah, NJ: Lawrence Erlbaum Association.

Rutherford, M. D. (2007). Beyond nature and nurture: A systems approach to autism. In P. C. Carlisle (Ed.), *Progress in autism research* (pp. 167–186). New York, NY: Nova Science Publishers.

Rutherford, M. D. (2009). *Diverging social perceptual development in the autism phenotype in the first year of life.* Paper presented at the Bi-Annual Meetings of the Society for Research in Child Development, Denver, CO.

Rutherford, M. D. & McIntosh, D. N. (2007). Rules versus prototype matching: Strategies of perception of emotional facial expressions in the autism spectrum. *Journal of Autism and Developmental Disorders, 37,* 187–196.

Rutherford, M. D., Young, G. S., Hepburn, S., & Rogers, S. J. (2007). A longitudinal study of pretend play in autism. *Journal of Autism and Developmental Disorders, 37,* 1024–1039.

Rutherford, M. D., Pennington, B. F., & Rogers, S. J. (2006). The perception of animacy in young children with autism. *Journal of Autism and Developmental Disorders, 36,* 983–992.

Rutherford, M. D., & Rogers, S. J. (2003). The cognitive underpinnings of pretend play in autism. *Journal of Autism and Developmental Disorders, 33,* 289–302.

Scaife, M. & Bruner, J. (1975). The capacity for joint visual attention in the infant. *Nature, 253,* 265–266.

Shultz, S., & Dunbar, R. I. M. (2007). The evolution of the social brain: Anthropoid primates contrast with other vertebrates. *Procedings of the Royal Society of London, B, 274,* 2429–2436.

Sorce, J. F., Emde, R. N., Campos, J., & Klinnert, M. D. (1985). Maternal emotional signaling: its effect on visual cliff behavior of one-year-olds. *Developmental Psychology, 21,* 195–200.

Spelke, E., Phillips, A., & Woodward, A. L. (1995). Infant's knowledge of object motion and human action. In D. Sperber, D. Premack, & A. J. Premack (Eds.), *Causal cognition: A multidisciplinary debate.* Oxford, England: Clarendon Press.

Sugita, Y. (2008). Face perception in monkeys reared with no exposure to faces. *Proceedings of the National Academy of Sciences, 105,* 394–398.

Suomi, S. J., Harlow, H. F., & McKinney, W. T. (1972). Monkey psychiatrists. *American Journal of Psychiatry, 128,* 927–932.

Surian, L., Caldi, S., & Sperber, D. (2007). Attribution of beliefs by 13-month-old infants. *Psychological Science, 18,* 580–586.

Sussman, R. W. (1977). Distribution of Malagasy lemurs. Part 2: *Lemur catta* and *Lemur fulvus* in southern and western Madagascar. *Annals of the New York Academy of Sciences, 293,* 170–183.

Sutton-Smith, B. (1976). *The psychology of play.* New York, NY: Arno Press.

Tantam, D., Monaghan, L., Nicholson, H., & Stirling, J. (1989). Autistic children's ability to interpret faces: A research note. *Journal of Child Psychology and Psychiatry and Allied Disciplines, 30,* 623–630.

Taylor, M. (1999). *Imaginary companions and the children who create them.* London, England: Oxford University Press.

Taylor, M., & Carlson, S. M. (1997). The relation between individual differences in fantasy and theory of mind. *Child Development, 68,* 436–455.

Taylor, M., Carlson, S. M., Maring, B. L., Gerow, L., & Charley, C. M. (2004). The characteristics and correlates of fantasy in school-age children: Imaginary companions, impersonation, and social understanding. *Developmental Psychology, 40,* 1173–1187.

Teas, J., Richie, T., Taylor, H., & Southwick, C. (1980). Population patterns and behavioral ecology of rhesus monkeys (*Macaca mulatta*) in Nepal. In D. Lindburg (Ed.), *The macaques: Studies in ecology, behavior, and evolution* (pp. 247–262). New York, NY: Van Nostrand Reinhold.

Tong, F., Nakayama, K., Moscovitch, M., Weinrib, O., & Kanwisher, N. (2000). Response properties of the human fusiform face area. *Cognitive Neuropsychology, 17,* 257–279.

Vecera, S. P., & Johnson, M. H. (1995). Gaze detection and the cortical processing of faces: Evidence from infants and adults. *Visual Cognition, 2,* 51–87.

White, F. J. (1992). Pygmy chimpanzee social organization: Variation with party size and between study sites. *American Journal of Primatology, 26,* 203–214.

Wilcox, B. M. (1969). Visual preferences of human infants for representations of the human face. *Journal of Experimental Child Psychology, 7,* 10–20.

Wimmer, H., & Perner, J. (1983). Beliefs about beliefs: Representation and constraining function of wrong beliefs in young children's understanding of deception. *Cognition, 13,* 103–128.

Woodward, A. L. (1998). Infants selectively encode the goal object of an actor's reach. *Cognition, 69,* 1–34.

Wrangham, R. W. (1977). Feeding behavior of chimpanzees in Gombe National Park Tanzania. In T. H. Clutton-Brock (Ed.) *Primate Ecology: Studies of feeding and ranging behaviour in lemurs, monkeys and apes* (pp. 504–538). London, England: Academic Press.

Zaitchik, D. (1990). When representations conflict with reality: The preschoolers' problem with false beliefs and false photographs. *Cognition, 35,* 41–68.

Zuckerman, M., & Cohen, N. (1964). Sources of reports of visual and auditory sensations in perceptual-isolation experiments. *Psychological Bulletin, 62,* 1–20.

Chapter 9

Baldwin, D. A. (1993). Early referential understanding: Infants' ability to recognize referential acts for what they are. *Developmental Psychology, 29,* 832–843.

Bench, R. J., Collyer, Y., Mentz, L., & Wilson, I. (1976). Studies in infant behavioural audiometry: I. Neonates. *Audiology, 15,* 85–105.

Bialystok, E. (2001). *Bilingualism in development: Language, literacy, and cognition.* New York, NY: Cambridge University Press.

Bialystok, E. (2007). Cognitive effects of bilingualism: How linguistic experience leads to cognitive change. *International Journal of Bilingual Education and Bilingualism, 10,* 210–223.

Bialystok, E., Shenfield, T., & Codd, J. (2000). Languages, scripts, and the environment: Factors in developing concepts of print. *Developmental Psychology, 36,* 66–76.

Bickerton, D. (1981). *Roots of language.* Ann Arbor, MI: Karoma.

Bloom, L. (1998). Language acquisition in its developmental context. In D. Kuhn & R. S. Siegler (Eds.), *Handbook of child psychology: Vol. 2. Cognition, perception, and language* (5th ed.) (pp. 309–370). New York, NY: Wiley.

Bloom, L., Lifter, K., and Broughton, J. (1985). The convergence of early cognition and language in the second year of life: Problems in conceptualization and measurement. In M. Barrett (ed.), *Children's single-word speech* (pp. 149–180). New York, NY: Wiley.

Bosch, L., & Sebastian-Galles, N. (2001). Evidence of early language discrimination abilities in infants from bilingual environments. *Infancy, 2,* 29–50.

Brown, R. & Hanlon, C. (1970) Derivational complexity and order of acquisition in child speech. In J. R. Hayes (Ed.), *Cognition and the development of language.* New York, NY: Wiley.

Brown, R. W. (1973). *A first language: The early stages.* Cambridge, MA: Harvard University Press.

Bryant, G. A., & Barrett, H. C. (2007). Recognizing intentions in infant-directed speech: Evidence for universals. *Psychological Science, 18,* 746–751.

Cheney, D. L., & Seyfarth, R. M. (1990). *How monkeys see the world.* Chicago, IL: University of Chicago Press.

Chomsky, N. (1957). *Syntactic structures.* The Hague, the Netherlands: Mouton.

Chomsky, N. (1959). A review of B. F. Skinner's verbal behavior. *Language, 35,* 26–58.

Chomsky, N. (1965). *Aspects of the theory of syntax.* Cambridge, MA: MIT Press.

Corrigan, R. (1983). The development of representational skills. In K. W. Fischer (Ed.), *Levels and transitions in children's development* (pp. 51–64). San Francisco, CA: Jossey-Bass.

Curtiss, S. (1977). *Genie: A linguistic study of a modern-day 'wild child'.* New York, NY: Academic Press.

Curtiss, S. (1989). The independence and task-specificity of language. In A. Bornstein and J. Bruner (Eds.), *Interaction in human development.* Hillsdale, NJ: Erlbaum.

Darwin, C. (1859). *On the origin of species by means of natural selection, or the preservation of favoured races in the struggle for life.* London, England:John Murray.

de Villiers, J. G., & de Villiers, P. A. (1973). A cross-sectional study of the acquisition of grammatical morphemes in child speech. *Journal of Psycholinguistic Research, 2,* 267–278.

Deacon, T. W. (1989). The neural circuitry underlying primate calls and human language. *Human Evolution, 4,* 367–401.

Dromi, E. (1987). *Early lexical development.* New York, NY: Cambridge University Press.

Eilers, R. E., & Oller, D. K. (1994). Infant vocalizations and the early diagnosis of severe hearing impairment. *Journal of Pediatrics, 124,* 199–203.

Eimas, P. D., Siqueland, E. R., Jusczyk, P., & Vigorito, J. (1971). Speech perception in infants. *Science, 171,* 303–306.

Ervin-Tripp, S. M. (1973). *Language acquisition and communicative choice.* Stanford, CA: Stanford University Press.

Falk, D. (2004). Prelinguistic evolution in early hominins: Whence motherese? *Behavioral and Brain Sciences, 27,* 491–541.

Fernald, A. (1992). Human maternal vocalizations to infants as biologically relevant signals. In J. H. Barkow, L. Cosmides & J. Tooby (Eds.), *The adapted mind: Evolutionary psychology and the generation of culture* (pp. 391–428). New York, NY: Oxford University Press.

Frishberg, N. 1987. Home sign. In J. Van Cleve (Ed.), *Gallaudet encyclopedia of deaf people and deafness* (Vol. 3) (pp. 128–131). New York, NY: McGraw Hill.

Gelman R., & Baillargeon R. (1983). A review of some Piagetian concepts. In P. H. Mussen (Ed.), *Handbook of child psychology* (Vol. 3) (pp. 167–230). New York, NY: Wiley.

Gertner, Y., Fisher, C., & Eisengart, J. (2006). Learning words and rules: Abstract knowledge of word order in early sentence comprehension. *Psychological Science, 17,* 684–691.

Goldfield, B. A. & Reznick, J. S. (1990). Early lexical acquisition: Rate, content, and the vocabulary spurt. *Journal of Child Language, 17,* 171–183.

Goldin-Meadow, S. (1999). The role of gesture in communication and thinking. *Trends In Cognitive Science, 3,* 419–429.

Goldin-Meadow, S. (2003). *The resilience of language: What gesture creation in deaf children can tell us about how all children learn language.* New York, NY: Psychology Press.

Goodglass, H. (1979) Effect of aphasia on the retrieval of lexicon and syntax. In C. J. Fillmore, D. Kempler & W. S. Y. Wang (Eds.), *Individual differences in language ability and language behavior* (pp. 253–260). New York, NY: Academic Press.

Goodz, N. S. (1989). Parental language mixing in bilingual families. *Journal of Infant Mental Health, 10,* 25–34.

Halliday, M.A.K. (1975) *Learning how to mean.* London, England: Edward Arnold.

Hayes, Catherine (1951). *The ape in our house.* New York, NY: Harper.

Hirsh-Pasek, K. & Golinkoff, R. M. (1996). The preferential looking paradigm reveals emerging language comprehension. In D. McDaniel, C. MeKee & H. Cairns (Eds.), *Methods for assessing children's syntax* (pp. 105–124). Cambridge, MA: MIT Press.

Holobow, N. E., Genesee, F., & Lambert, W. E. (1991). The effectiveness of a foreign language immersion program for children from different ethnic and social class backgrounds: Report 2. *Applied Psycholinguistics, 12,* 179–198.

Hurford, J. (1991) The Evolution of the Critical Period for Language Acquisition. *Cognition, 40,* 159–201.

Iverson, J. M., & Goldin-Meadow, S. (1998). Why people gesture when they speak. *Nature, 396,* 228.

Jusczyk, P. (1995). Language acquisition: Speech sounds and phonological development. In J. L. Miller & P. D. Eimas (Eds.), *Handbook of perception and cognition: Vol. 2. Speech, language, and communication* (pp. 263–301). Orlando, FL: Academic Press.

Kegl, J. (1994). The Nicaraguan sign language project: An overview. *Signpost, 7,* 40–46.

Lai, C. S., Fisher, S. E., Hurst, J. A., Vargha-Khadem, F., & Monaco, A. P. (2009). A forkhead-domain gene is mutated in a severe speech and language disorder. *Nature, 413,* 465–466.

Lanza, E. (1997). *Language mixing in infant bilingualism: A sociolinguistic perspective.* Oxford, England: Oxford University Press.

Lenneberg, E. (1967). *Biological foundations of language.* New York, NY: Wiley.

Levitt, A. G. & Utmann, J. G. A. (1992). From babbling towards the sound system of English and French: A longitudinal two-case study. *Journal of Child Language, 19,* 19–40.

Lieberman, P., Crelin, E. S., & Klatt, D. H. (1972). Phonetic ability and related anatomy of the newborn, adult human, Neanderthal man, and the chimpanzee. *American Anthropologist, 74,* 287–307.

Macnamara, J. (1982). *Names for things: A study of human learning.* Cambridge, MA: MIT Press.

Maratsos, M. (1998). The acquisition of grammar. In D. Kuhn & R. S. Siegler (Eds.), *Handbook of child psychology: Vol 2. Cognition, perception, and language* (5th ed.) (pp. 421–466). New York, NY: Wiley.

Marcus, G. F. (1995). Children's overregularization of English plurals: A quantitative analysis. *Journal of Child Language, 22,* 447–459.

Marcus, G. F., Pinker, S., Ullman, M., Hollander, M., Rosen, T. J., & Xu, F. (1992). Overregularization in language acquisition. *Monographs of the Society for Research in Child Development, 57,* 1–182.

Markman, E.M. (1989) *Categorization and naming in children: Problems of induction.* Cambridge, MA: MIT Press, Bradford Books.

Markman, E. M. (1990). Constraints children place on word meanings. *Cognitive Science, 14,* 57–77.

Markman, E. M. (1991). *Categorization and naming in children: Problems of induction.* Cambridge, MA: MIT Press, Bradford Books.

Markman, E. M., & Callanan, M.A. (1983). An analysis of hierarchical classification. In R. Sternberg (Ed.), *Advances in the psychology of human intelligence* (Vol. 2) (pp. 325–365). Hillsdale, NJ: Erlbaum.

Markman, E. M., & Hutchinson, J. E. (1984). Children's sensitivity to constraints on word meaning: Taxonomic versus thematic relations. *Cognitive Psychology, 16,* 1–27.

Marler, P., & Tamura, M. (1964). Culturally transmitted patterns of vocal behavior in sparrows. *Science, 146,* 1483–1486.

McShane, J., 1979. The development of naming. *Linguistics* 17, pp. 879–905

Mehler, J., Jusczyk, P. W., Lambertz, G., Halsted, N., Bertoncini, J., & Amiel-Tison, C. (1988). A precursor of language acquisition in young infants. *Cognition, 29,* 144–178.

Menyuk, P., Liebergott, J. W., & Schultz, M. C. (1995). *Early language development in full-term and premature infants.* Hillsdale, NJ: Erlbaum.

Molfese, D.L. and Betz, J., 1988. Electrophysiological indices of the early development of lateralization for language and cognition of their implications for predicting later development. In D. L. Molfese & S. Segalowitz (Eds.), *Brain lateralization in children.* New York, NY: Guilford Press.

Molfese, D. L., Freeman, R., & Palermo, D. (1975). The ontogeny of lateralization for speech and nonspeech stimuli. *Brain and Language, 2,* 356–368

Negus, V. E. (1949). *The comparative anatomy and physiology of the larynx.* New York, NY: Hafner.

Neisser, A. (1983). *The other side of silence.* New York, NY: Knopf.

Nelson, K. (1973). Structure and strategy in learning to talk. *Monographs of the Society for Research in Child Development, 38,* 1–135.

Newport, E. (1990). Maturational constraints on language learning. *Cognitive Science, 14,* 11–28.

Oller, D. K., & Pearson, B. Z. (2002). Assessing the effects of bilingualism. In D. K. Oller (Ed.), *Language and literacy in bilingual children.* Clevedon, England: Multilingual Matters.

Petitto, L. A., & Seidenberg, M. S. (1979). On the evidence for linguistic abilities in signing apes. *Brain and Language, 8,* 162–183.

Petitto, L. A., Holowka, S., Sergio, L. & Ostry, D. (2001). Language rhythms in babies' hand movements, *Nature, 413*, pp. 35–36.

Petitto, L. A., & Marentette, P. (1991). Babbling in the manual mode: Evidence for the ontogeny of language. *Science, 251*, 1483–1496.

Pinker, S. (1994). *The language instinct*. New York, NY: William Morrow.

Pinker, S. (1997). *How the mind works*. New York, NY: W. W. Norton.

Quine, W. (1960). *Word and object*. Cambridge, MA: MIT Press.

Savage-Rumbaugh, S., & Lewin, R. (1994). *Kanzi: The ape at the brink of the human mind*. New York, NY: Wiley.

Schwartz, M. F. (1987). Patterns of speech production deficit within and across aphasia syndromes: Application of a psycholinguistic model. In M. Coltheart, G. Sartori & R. Job (Eds.), *The cognitive neuropsychology of language* (pp. 402–403). Hillsdale, NJ: Erlbaum.

Senghas, A., Kita, S., & Özyürek, A. (2004). Children creating core properties of language: evidence from an emerging sign language in Nicaragua. *Science, 305*, 1779–1782.

Skinner, B. F. (1957). *Verbal behavior*. New York, NY: Appleton-Century-Crofts.

Soja, N. N., Carey, S., & Spelke, E. S. (1992). Ontological categories guide young children's inductions of word meaning: Object terms and substance terms. *Cognition, 43*, 85–91.

Stoel-Gammon, C., & Otomo, K. (1986). Babbling development of hearing-impaired and normal hearing subjects. *Journal of Speech and Hearing Disorders, 51*, 33–41.

Stromswold, K. (1994). Language comprehension without language production: Implications for theories of language acquisition. Paper presented at the 19th Annual Boston University Conference on Language Development, Boston, MA.

Tager-Flusberg, H. (1997). Language acquisition: Grammar. In K. Brown & J. Miller (Eds.), *Concise encyclopedia of syntactic theories*. Oxford, England: Elsevier Science.

Tartter, V. C. (1986). *Language processes*. New York, NY: Holt, Rinehart, & Winston.

Terrace, H. S. (1979). *Nim*. New York, NY: Knopf.

Tomasello, M., & Akhtar, N. (1995). Two-year-olds use pragmatic cues to differentiate reference to objects and actions. *Cognitive Development, 10*, 201–224.

Tomasello, M., & Barton, M. (1994). Learning words in non-ostensive context. *Developmental Psychology, 30*, 639–650.

Tomasello, M., Strosberg, R., & Akhtar, N. (1996). Eighteen-month-old children learn words in non-ostensive contexts. *Journal of Child Language, 23*, 157–176.

Vargha-Khadem, F., Watkins, K., Alcock, K., Fletcher, P., & Passingham, R. (1995). Praxic and nonverbal cognitive deficits in a large family with a genetically transmitted speech and language disorder. *Proceedings of the National Academy of Science, 92*, 930–933.

Weber-Fox, C., & Neville, H. J. (1996). Maturational constraints on functional specializations for language processing: ERP and behavioral evidence in bilingual speakers. *Journal of Cognitive Neuroscience, 8*, 231–256.

Werker, J. F., & Tees, R. C. (1984). Cross-language speech perception: Evidence for perceptual reorganization during the first year of life. *Infant Behavior and Development, 7*, 49–63.

Whitehurst, G. J., & Vasta, R. (1975). Is language acquired through imitation? *Journal of Psycholinguistic Research, 4*, 37–59.

Witelson, S.F. (1987) Neurobiological aspects of language in children. *Child Development, 58*, 653–688.

Chapter 10

Ainsworth, M. D. (1973). The development of infant–mother attachment. In B. Caldwell & H. Riccuiti (Eds.), *Review of child development research*, (Vol. 3) (pp. 1–94). Chicago, IL: University of Chicago Press.

Alexander, R. D. (1974). The evolution of social behavior. *Annual Review of Ecology and Systematics,5*, 325–384.

Anderson, K. G., Kaplan, H., & Lancaster, J. (1999). Paternal care by genetic fathers and stepfathers I: Reports from Albuquerque men. *Evolution and Human Behavior, 20*, 405–431.

Anderson, K. G., Kaplan, H., & Lancaster, J. (1999). Paternal care by genetic fathers and stepfathers II: Reports by Xhosa high school students. *Evolution and Human Behavior, 20*, 433–451.

Bandura, A. (1977). *Social learning theory*. Upper Saddle River, NJ: Prentice Hall.

Bandura, A., & Walters, R. H. (1963). *Social learning and personality development*. New York, NY: Holt, Rinehart & Winston.

Belsky, J., Steinberg, L., & Draper, P. (1991). Childhood experience, interpersonal development, and reproductive strategy: An evolutionary theory of socialization. *Child Development, 62*, 647–670.

Blurton Jones, N. G., Hawkes, K., & O'Connell, J. F. (1996). The global process and local ecology: How should we explain differences between the Hadza and !Kung? In S. Kent (Ed.), *Cultural diversity among twentieth century foragers: An African perspective* (pp. 159–187). Cambridge, England: Cambridge University Press.

Blurton Jones, N. G., Hawkes, K., & Draper, P. (1994). Differences between Hadza and !Kung children's work: Original affluence or practical reason? In E. S. Burch & L. J. Ellana (Eds.), *Key Issues in Hunter–Gatherer Research* (pp.189–215). Oxford, England: Berg.

Blurton Jones, N. G., Smith, L. C., O'Connell, J. F., Hawkes, K., & Kamuzora, C. L. (1992). Demography of the Hadza, an increasing and high density population of Savannah foragers. *American Journal of Physical Anthropology, 89,* 159–181.

Bouchard, T. J., Lykken, D. T., McGue, M., Segal, N. L., & Tellegen, A. (1990). Sources of human psychological differences: The Minnesota study of twins reared apart. *Science, 250,* 223–228.

Bowlby, J. (1953). *Child care and the growth of love.* London, England: Penguin Books.

Boyd, D. M. & Ellison, N. B. (2007). Social networking sites: Definition, history, and scholarship. *Journal of Computer-Mediated Communication, 13,* 210–230.

Bronson, G. W. 1972. Infants' reactions to unfamiliar persons and novel objects. *Monographs of the Society for Research in Child Development, 37,* 1–46.

Cabrera, N. J., Tamis-LeMonda, C. S., Bradley, R. H., Hofferth, S., & Lamb, M. E. (2000). Fatherhood in the twenty-first century. *Child Development, 71,* 127–136.

Cacioppo, J. T., & Patrick, W. (2008). *Loneliness: Human nature and the need for social connection.* New York, NY: W.W. Norton.

Camras, L. A. (1992). Expressive development and basic emotions. *Cognition and Emotion, 6,* 269–283.

Camras, L. A., Malatesta, C., & Izard, C. (1991). The development of facial expressions in infancy. In R. Feldman & B. Rime (Eds.), *Fundamentals of nonverbal behavior* (pp. 73–105). New York, NY: Cambridge University Press.

Cashdan, E. (1993). Attracting mates: Effects of paternal investment on mate attraction strategies. *Ethology and Sociobiology, 14,* 1–24.

Cashdan, E. 1995. Hormones, sex and status in women. *Hormones and Behavior, 29,* 354–366.

Charnov, E. L. (1993). *Life history invariants.* Oxford, England: Oxford University Press.

Chisholm, J. (1999). *Death, hope and sex: Steps to an evolutionary ecology of mind and mortality.* New York, NY: Cambridge University Press.

Christenfeld, N. J., & Hill, E. A. (1995). Whose baby are you? *Nature, 378,* 669.

Clutton-Brock, T. H. (1991). *The evolution of parental care.*

Princeton, NJ: Princeton University Press.

Collins, W. A, Henninghausen, K. H., Schmit, D. T., & Sroufe, L. A. (1997). Developmental precursors of romantic relationships: A longitudinal analysis. In S. Shulman & W. A. Collins (Eds.), *Romantic relationships in adolescence: Developmental perspectives* (pp. 69–84). San Francisco, CA: Jossey-Bass.

Collins, W. A., Maccoby, E. E., Steinberg, L., Hetherington, E. M., & Bornstein, M. J. (2000). Contemporary research on parenting: The case for nature and nurture. *American Psychologist, 55,* 218–232.

Daly, M. & Wilson, M. (1985). Child abuse and other risks of not living with both parents. *Ethology and Sociobiology, 6,* 197–210.

Daly, M. & Wilson, M. (1988). *Homicide.* New York, NY: Aldine de Gruyter.

Daly, M. & Wilson, M. (1996). Violence against children. *Current Directions in Psychological Science, 5,* 77–81.

Daly, M. & Wilson, M. (2005). The "Cinderella Effect" is no fairy tale. *Trends in Cognitive Sciences, 9,* 507–508.

Daly, M. & Wilson, M. I. (1982). Whom are newborn babies said to resemble? *Ethology and Sociobiology, 3,* 69–78.

Draper, P. & Harpending, H. (1982). Father absence and reproductive strategy: An evolutionary perspective. *Journal of Anthropological Research, 38,* 255–273.

Duberman, L. (1975). *The reconstituted family: A study of remarried couples and their children.* Chicago, IL: Nelson-Hall.

Ellis, B. J. (2004). Timing of pubertal maturation in girls. *Psychological Bulletin, 130,* 920–958.

Ellis, B. J., McFadyen-Ketchum, S., Dodge, K. A., Pettit, G. S., & Bates, J. E. (1999). Quality of early family relationships and individual differences in the timing of pubertal maturation in girls: A longitudinal test of an evolutionary model. *Journal of Personality and Social Psychology, 77,* 387–401.

Ellsworth, C., Muir, D., & Hains, S. (1993). Social competence and person–object differentiation: An analysis of the still-face effect. *Developmental Psychology, 29,* 63–73.

Graber, J. A., Brooks-Gunn, J., & Warren, M. P. (1995). The antecedents of menarcheal age: Heredity, family environment, and stressful life events. *Child Development, 66,* 346–359.

Hamilton, W. D. (1963). The evolution of altruistic behavior. *American Naturalist, 97,* 354–356.

Hamilton, W. D. (1966). The moulding of senescence by natural selection. *Journal of Theoretical Biology, 12,* 12–45.

Harlow, H. F. (1962). Development of affection in primates. In E. L. Bliss (Ed.), *Roots of behavior* (pp. 157–166). New York, NY: Harper.

Harlow, H. F. & Harlow, M. K. (1975). Social deprivation in monkeys. In R. C. Atkinson (Ed.), *Readings from Scientific American: Psychology in progress* (pp. 225–233). San Francisco, CA: Freeman.

Harris, J. R. (1995). Where is the child's environment? A group socialization theory of development. *Psychological Review, 102,* 458–489.

Harris, J. R. (2005). Social behavior and personality development: The role of experiences with siblings and with peers. In B. J. Ellis & D. F. Bjorklund (Eds.), *Origins of the Social Mind: Evolutionary Psychology and Child Development* (pp. 245–270). New York, NY: Guilford Press.

Hartup, W. W. (1983). Peer relations. In E. M. Hetherington (Ed.), *Handbook of child psychology: Vol. 4. Socialization, personality, and social development* (4th ed.) (pp. 103–196). New York, NY: Wiley.

Hauser, M. D. (1988). Invention and social transmission: New data from wild vervet monkeys. In R. W. Byrne & A. Whiten (Eds.), *Machiavellian Intelligence: Social Expertise and the Evolution of Intellect in Monkeys, Apes and Man* (pp. 327–343). Oxford, England: Clarendon Press.

Hawkes, K., O'Connell, J. F., & Blurton Jones, N. G. (1995). Hadza children's foraging: Juvenile dependency, social arrangements and mobility among hunter–gatherers. *Current Anthropology, 36,* 688–700.

Hawkes, K., O'Connell, J. F., & Blurton Jones, N. G. (1997). Hadza women's time allocation, offspring provisioning, and the evolution of post-menopausal lifespans. *Current Anthropology, 38,* 551–578.

Hetherington, E. M., Henderson, S. H., & Reiss, D. (1999). Adolescent siblings in stepfamilies: Family functioning and adolescent adjustment. *Monographs of the Society for Research in Child Development, 64,* 1–209.

Hill, K., & Hurtado, A.M. (1996). *Ache life history: The ecology and demography of a foraging people.* New York, NY: Aldine de Gruyter.

Hrdy, S. B. (1999). *Mother nature: A history of mothers, infants, and natural selection.* New York, NY: Pantheon Books.

Howell, N. (1979). *Demography of the Dobe !Kung.* New York, NY: Academic Press.

Izard, C.E., Hembree, E.A., Huebner, R.R. (1987). Infants' emotional expressions to acute pain: Developmental change and stability of individual differences. *Developmental Psychology, 23,* 105–113.

Johns, S. E. (2003). *Environmental risk and the evolutionary psychology of teenage motherhood* (Unpublished doctoral dissertation). University of Bistol, Bristol, England.

Jones, M. C. (1957). The later careers of boys who were early or late maturing. *Child Development, 28,* 113–128.

Kagan, J. (1976). Emergent themes in human development. *American Scientist, 64,* 186–196.

Kanazawa, S. (2001). Why father absence might precipitate early menarch: The role of polygyny. *Evolution and Human Behavior, 22,* 329–334.

Kline, J., Stein, Z., & Susser, M. (1989). *Conception to birth: Epidemiology of prenatal development.* New York, NY: Oxford University Press.

LeVine, R. A., & LeVine, S. E. (1988). Parental strategies among the Gusii of Kenya. In R. A. LeVine, P. M. Miller & M. M. West (Eds.) *New Directions for Child Development, No.40* (pp. 27–35). San Francisco, CA: Jossey-Bass.

Lewis, M., Alessandri, S. M., & Sullivan, M. W. (1990). Violation of expectancy, loss of control, and anger expressions in young infants. *Developmental Psychology, 26,* 745–751.

Lorenz, K. Z. (1952). *King Solomon's ring.* New York, NY: Crowell.

Maccoby, E. E., & Martin, J. A. (1983). Socialization in the context of the family: Parent–child interaction. In E. M. Hetherington (Ed.), *Handbook of child psychology: Vol. 4. Socialization, personality, and social development* (pp. 1–101). New York, NY: Wiley.

MacDonald, K. (1992). Warmth as a developmental construct: An evolutionary analysis. *Child Development, 63,* 753–773.

Main, M., & Hesse, E. (1990). Parents' unresolved traumatic experiences are related to infant disorganized attachment status: Is disorganized and/or frightening parental behavior the linking mechanism? In M. T. Greenberg, D. Cicchetti & E. M. Cummings (Eds.), *Attachment in the preschool years* (pp. 161–182). Chicago, IL: University of Chicago Press.

Main, M., & Solomon, J. (1990). Procedures for identifying infants as disorganized/disoriented during the Ainsworth Strange Situation. In M. T. Greenberg, D. Cicchetti & E. M. Cummings (Eds.), *Attachment in the preschool years* (pp. 121–160). Chicago, IL: University of Chicago Press.

Marler, P. (1970). A comparative approach to vocal learning: Song development in white-crowned sparrows. *Journal of Comparative and Physiological Psychology, 71,* 1–25.

Marlowe, F. (1999). Showoffs or providers? The parenting effort of Hadza men. *Evolution and Human Behavior, 20,* 391–404.

McDade, T. W., Beck, M. A., Kuzawa, C. W., & Adair, L. S. (2001). Prenatal nutrition, postnatal environments, and antibody response to vaccination in adolescence. *American Journal of Clinical Nutrition, 74,* 543–548.

Moffitt, T. E., Caspi, A., Belsky, J., & Silva, P. A. (1992). Childhood experience and the onset of menarche: A test of a sociobiological model. *Child Development, 63,* 47–58.

O'Connell, J. F., Hawkes, K., & Blurton Jones, N. G. (1999). Grandmothering and the evolution of *Homo erectus. Journal of Human Evolution, 36,* 461–485.

Opie, I., & Opie, P. (1969). *Children's games in street and playground.* Oxford, England: Oxford University Press.

Oster, H., Hegley, D., & Nagel, L. (1992). Adult judgments and finegrained analysis of infant facial expressions: Testing the validity of a priori coding formulas. *Developmental Psychology, 28,* 1115–1131.

Persico, N., Postlewaite, A., & Silverman, D. (2004). The effect of adolescent experience on labor market outcomes: The case of height. *Journal of Political Economy, 112,* 1019–1053.

Phillips, D. I. (1998). Birth weight and the future development of diabetes. *Diabetes Care, 21B,* 150–155.

Platek, S. M., Burcg, R. L., Panyavin, I. S., & Wasserman, B. H. (2002). Reactions to children's faces: Resemblance affects males more than females. *Evoltuion and Human Behavior, 23,* 159–166.

Plomin, R., & Daniels, D. (1987). Why are children in the same family so different from one another? *Behavioral and Brain Sciences, 10,* 1–60.

Quinlan, R. J. (2003). Father absence, parental care, and female reproductive development. *Evolution and Human Behavior, 24,* 376–390.

Richerson, P. J., & Boyd, R. (2005). *Not by genes alone.* Chicago, IL: University of Chicago Press.

Roff, D. (1992). *The evolution of life histories.* New York, NY: Chapman & Hall.

Sayer, A. A., Cooper, C., Evans, J. R., Rauf, A., Wormald, R. P, Osmond, C., & Barker, D. J. (1998). Are rates of ageing determined in utero? *Age and Ageing, 27,* 579–583.

Scarr, S. (1992). Developmental theories for the 1990s: Development and individual differences. *Child Development, 63,* 1–19.

Scarr, S., Weinberg, R. A., & Waldman, I. D. (1993). IQ correlations in transracial adoptive families. *Intelligence, 17,* 541–555.

Sroufe, L. A. (1995). *Emotional development: The organization of emotional life in the early years.* Cambridge, England: Cambridge University Press.

Stearns, S. (1992). *The evolution of life histories.* Oxford, England: Oxford University Press.

Steinfield, C., Ellison, N., & Lampe, C. (2008). Social capital, self-esteem, and use of online social network sites: A longitudinal analysis. *Journal of Applied Developmental Psychology, 29,* 434–445.

Subrahmanyam, K., & Lin, G. (2007). Adolescents on the Net: Internet use and well-being. *Adolescence, 42,* 659–677.

Sum, S., Mathews, R. M., Hughes, I., & Campbell, A. (2007). Internet use and loneliness in older adults. *CyberPsychology & Behavior, 11,* 208–211.

Surbey, M. K. (1990). Family composition, stress, and the timing of human menarche. In T. E. Ziegler & F. B. Bercovitch (Eds.), *Socioendocrinology of primate reproduction* (pp. 11–32). New York, NY: Wiley-Liss.

Trivers, R. L. (1972). Parental investment and sexual selection. In B. Campbell (Ed.), *Sexual selection and the descent of man 1871–1971* (pp. 136–179). Chicago, IL: Aldine Publishing.

Trivers, R. L. (1985). *Social evolution.* Menlo Park, CA: Benjamin/Cummings.

Troy, M., & Sroufe, L. A. (1987). Victimization among preschoolers: Role of attachment relationship history. *Journal of the American Academy of Child and Adolescent Psychiatry, 26,* 166–172.

Vaughn, B., & Waters, E. (1990). Attachment behavior at home and in the laboratory: Q-sort observations and Strange Situation classifications of one-year-olds. *Child Development, 61,* 1965–1973.

Weinberg, M. K., & Tronick, E. Z. (1994). Beyond the face: An empirical study of infant affective configurations of facial, vocal, gestural, and regulatory behaviors. *Child Development, 65,* 1503–1515.

Westneat, D. F., & Sherman, P. W. (1993). Parentage and the evolution of parental behavior. *Behavioral Ecology, 4,* 66–77.

Whiten, A., Goodall, J., & McGrew, W. C. (1999). Cultures in chimpanzees. *Nature, 399,* 682–685.

Williams, G. C. (1966). *Adaptation and natural selection.* Princeton, NJ: Princeton University Press.

Wilson, M., & Daly, M. (1997). Life expectancy, economic inequality, homicide, and reproductive timing in Chicago neighbourhoods. *British Medical Journal, 314,* 1271–1274.

Witherington, D. C., Campos, J. J., & Hertenstein, M. J. (2001). Principles of emotion and its development in infancy. In G. Bremner & A. Fogel (Eds.), *Blackwell handbook of infant development: Handbooks of developmental psychology* (pp. 427–464). Malden, MA: Blackwell Publishers.

Chapter 11

Alexander, G., & Hines, M. (2002). Sex differences in response to children's toys in non-human primates. *Evolution and Human Behavior, 23,* 467–479.

Almli, C. R., Ball, R. H., & Wheeler, M. E. (2001). Human fetal and neonatal movement patterns: Gender differences and fetal-to-neonatal continuity. *Developmental Psychobiology, 38,* 252–273.

Baenninger, M., & Newcombe, N. (1995). Environmental input to the development of sex-related differences in spatial and mathematical ability. *Learning and Individual Differences, 7,* 363–379.

Bandura, A. (1977). *Social learning theory.* Upper Saddle River, NJ: Prentice-Hall.

Bandura, A., & Walters, R. H. (1963). *Social learning and personality development.* New York, NY: Holt, Rinehart & Winston.

Barton, S. C., Surani, M. A., & Norris, M. L. (1984). Role of paternal and maternal genomes in mouse development. *Nature, 311,* 374–376.

Benenson, J. F., Apostoleris, N. H., & Parnass, J. (1997). Age and sex differences in dyadic and group interaction. *Developmental Psychology, 33,* 538–543.

Berenbaum, S. A. (2002). Prenatal androgens and sexual differentiation of behavior. In E. Eugster & O. H. Pescovitz (Eds.), *Developmental endocrinology: From research to clinical practice* (pp. 293–312). Totowa, NJ: Humana Press.

Best, D. L., Williams, J. E., Cloud, J. M., Davis, S. W., Robertson, L. S., Edwards, J. R. et al. (1977). Development of sex-trait stereotypes among young children in the United States, England, and Ireland. *Child Development, 48,* 1375–1384.

Biernat, M. (1991). Gender stereotypes and the relationship between masculinity and femininity: A developmental analysis. *Journal of Personality and Social Psychology, 61,* 351–365.

Blum, D. (1997). *Sex on the brain: The biological differences between men and women.* New York, NY: Viking.

Brody, J. E. & Hall, J. A. (1993). Gender and emotion. In M. Lewis & J. M. Haviland (Eds.), *Handbook of emotion* (pp. 447–460). New York, NY: Guilford.

Brown, G. R., Laland, K. N., & Borgerhoff Mulder, M. B. (2009). Bateman's principles and human sex roles. *Trends in Ecology and Evolution, 24,* 297–304.

Bull, J. J. (1980). Sex determination in reptiles. *Quarterly Review of Biology, 55,* 3–21.

Bussey, K., & Bandura, A. (1984). Influence of gender constancy and social power on sex-linked modeling. *Journal of Personality and Social Psychology, 47,* 1292–1302.

Bussey, K., & Bandura, A. (1999). Social-cognitive theory of gender development and differentiation. *Psychological Review, 106,* 676–713.

Bussey, K. & Bandura, A. (2004). Social cognitive theory of gender development and functioning. In A. H. Eagly, A. E. Beall, & R. J. Sternberg (Eds.), *The psychology of gender* (2nd ed.) (pp. 92–119). New York, NY: Guilford.

Casey, M. B. (1996). Understanding individual differences in spatial ability within females: A nature/nurture interactionist framework. *Developmental Review, 16,* 241–260.

Cillessen, A. H., & Mayeux, L. (2004). Sociometric status and peer group behavior: Previous findings and current directions. In J. B. Kupersmidt & K. A. Dodge (Eds.), *Children's peer relations: From development to interventions* (pp. 3–20). Washington, DC: American Psychological Association.

Colapinto, J. (2000). *As nature made him: The boy who was raised as a girl.* New York, NY: Harper Collins.

Collaer, M. L., & Hines, M. (1995). Human behavioral sex differences: A role for gonadal hormones during development? *Psychological Bulletin, 118,* 55–107.

Connellan, J., Baron-Cohen, S., Wheelwright, S., Batki, A., & Ahluwalia, J. (2000). Sex differences in human neonatal social perception. *Infant Behavior and Development, 23,* 113–118.

Connor, J. M., & Servin, L. A. (1977). Behaviorally based masculine and feminine activity-preference scales for preschoolers: Correlates with other classroom behaviors and cognitive tests. *Child Development, 48,* 1411–1416.

Cossette, L., Pomerleau, A., Malcuit, F., & Kaczorowski, J. (1996). Emotional expressions of female and male infants in a social and nonsocial context. *Sex Roles, 35,* 693–710.

Cratty, B. J. (1986). *Perceptual and motor development in infants and children* (3rd ed.). Englewood Cliffs, NJ: Prentice-Hall.

Crick, N. R., Nelson, D. A., Morales, J. R., Cullerton-Sen. C., Cases, J. F., & Hickman, S. E. (2001). Relational victimization in childhood and adolescence: I hurt you through the grapevine. In J. Juvonen & S. Graham (Eds.), *Peer harassment in school: The plight of the vulnerable and the victimized* (pp. 196–214). New York, NY: Guildford.

Crittenden, D. (1999). *What our mothers didn't tell us: Why happiness eludes the modern woman.* New York, NY: Simon & Schuster.

Crowley, K., Callanan, M. A., Tenenbaum, H. R., & Allen, E. (2001). Parents explain more often to boys than to girls during shared scientific thinking. *Psychological Science, 12,* 258–261.

Dabbs, J. M., Change, E. L., Strong, R. A., & Milun, R. (1998). Spatial ability, navigation strategy, and geographic knowledge among men and women. *Evolution and Human Behavior, 19,* 89–98.

Daly, M., & Wilson, M. (1983). *Sex, evolution and behavior* (2nd ed.). Boston, MA: Willard Grant Press.

Eals, M., & Silverman, I. (1994). The hunter–gatherer theory of spatial sex differences: Proximate factors mediating the female advantage in recall of object arrays. *Ethology and Sociobiology, 15,* 95–105.

Eccles, J. S., Jacobs, J. E., & Harold, R. D. (1990). Gender-role stereotypes, expectancy effects, and parents' role in the socialization of gender differences in self-perceptions and skill acquisition. *Journal of Social Issues, 46,* 183–201.

Eichstedt, J. A., Serbin, L. A., Poulin-Dubois, D., & Sen, M. G. (2002). Of bears and men: Infants' knowledge of conventional and metaphorical gender stereotypes. *Infant Behavior & Development, 25,* 296–310.

Fagot, B. I. (1984). The child's expectations of differences in adult male and female interactions. *Sex Roles, 11,* 593–600.

Fausto-Sterling, A. (1985). *Myths of gender: Biological theories about women and men.* New York, NY: Basic Books.

Feinberg, D. R. (2008). Are human faces and voices ornaments signaling common underlying cues to mate values? *Evolutionary Anthropology, 17,* 112–118.

Feingold, A. (1992). Sex differences in variability in intellectual abilities: A new look at an old controversy. *Review of Educational Research, 62,* 61–84.

Feingold, A. (1993). Cognitive gender differences: A developmental perspective. *Sex Roles, 29,* 91–112.

Feingold, A. (1994). Gender differences in personality: A meta-analysis. *Psychological Bulletin, 116,* 429–456.

Fisher-Thompson, D. (1993). Adult toy purchase for children: Factors affecting sex-typed toy selection. *Journal of Applied Developmental Psychology, 14,* 385–406.

Galambos, N. L., Almeida, D. M., & Petersen, A. C. (1990). Masculinity, femininity, and sex role attitudes in early adolescence: Exploring gender intensification. *Child Development, 61,* 1905–1914.

Galea, L. A., & Kimura, D. (1993). Sex differences in route-learning. *Personality and Individual Differences, 14,* 53–65.

Garai, J. E., & Scheinfeld, A. (1968). Sex differences in mental and behavioral traits. *Genetic Psychology Monographs, 7,* 169–299.

Gaulin, S. J., FitzGerald, R. W., & Wartell, M. S. (1990). Sex differences in spatial ability and activity in two vole species (*Microtus ochrogaster* and *M. pennsylvanicus*). *Journal of Comparative Psychology, 104,* 88–93.

Gaulin, S. J., & Hoffman, H. A. (1988). Evolution and development of sex differences in spatial ability. In M. B. Betzig, M. B. Mulder & P. Turke (Eds.), *Human reproductive behavior: A Darwinian perspective* (pp. 129–152). Cambridge, England: Cambridge University Press.

Geary, D. C. (1998). *Male, female: The evolution of human sex differences.* Washington, DC: American Psychological Association.

Gibbons, A. (2000). Europeans trace ancestry to Paleolithic people. *Science, 290,* 1080–1081.

Halpern, D. (2000). *Sex differences in cognitive abilities* (3rd ed.). Mahwah, NJ: Erlbaum.

Harris, L. J. (1977). Sex differences in the growth and use of language. In E. Donelson & J. E. Gullahorn (Eds.), *Women: A psychological perspective.* New York, NY: Wiley.

Hartung, C. M., & Widiger, T. A. (1998). Gender differences in the diagnosis of mental disorders: Conclusions and controversies of the DSM-IV. *Psychological Bulletin, 123,* 260–278.

Haviland, J. J., & Malatesta, C. Z. (1981). The development of sex differences in nonverbal signals: Fallacies, facts, and fantasies. In C. Mayo & N. M. Henley (Eds.), *Gender and nonverbal behavior* (pp. 183–208). New York, NY: Springer-Verlag.

Hazen, N. L. (1982). Spatial exploration and spatial knowledge: Individual and developmental differences in very young children. *Child Development, 53,* 826–833.

Herman, J. F. & Siegel, A. W. (1978). The development of cognitive mapping of the large-scale environment. *Journal of Experimental Child Psychology, 26,* 389–406.

Houk, C. P., Hughes, I. A., Ahmed, S. F., & Lee, P. A. (2006). Summary of consensus statement on intersex disorders and their management. *Pediatrics, 118,* 753–757.

Huston, A. C. & Alvarez, M. M. (1990). The socialization context of gender role development in early adolescence. In R. Montemayor, G. R. Adams & T. P. Gullotta (Eds.), *From childhood to adolescence: A transitional period?* (pp. 156–179). Newbury Park, CA: Sage.

Huttenlocher, J., Haight, W., Bryk, A., Seltzer, M., & Lyons, T. (1991). Early vocabulary growth: Relation to language input and gender. *Developmental Psychology, 27,* 236–248.

Hyde, J. S., Fennema, E., & Lamon, S. J. (1990). Gender differences in mathematics performance: A meta-analysis. *Psychological Bulletin, 107,* 139–153.

Jacklin, C. N. (1989). Female and male: Issues of gender. *American Psychologist, 44,* 127–133.

Jacobs, J. E. & Weisz, V. (1994). Gender stereotypes: Implications for gifted education. *Roeper Review, 16,* 152–155.

Jacobs, L. F., Gaulin, S. J., Sherry, D. F., & Hoffman, G. E. (1990). Evolution of spatial cognition: Sex-specific patterns of spatial behavior predict hippocampal size. *Proceedings of the National Academy of Science, 87,* 6349–6352.

Jardine, R., & Martin, N. G. (1983). Spatial ability and throwing accuracy. *Behavior Genetics, 13,* 331–340.

Jost, A. (1953). Problems of fetal endocrinology: The gonadal and hypophyseal hormones. *Recent Progress in Hormone Research, 8,* 379–418.

Kail, R. V., & Siegel, A. W. (1997). Sex differences in retention of verbal and spatial characteristics of stimuli. *Journal of Experimental Child Psychology, 23,* 341–347.

Kenrick, D. T. & Trost, M. R. (1993). The evolutionary perspective. In A. E. Beall & R. J. Sternberg (Eds.), *The psychology of gender.* New York, NY: Guilford.

Kimura, D. (1999). *Sex and cognition.* Cambridge, MA: MIT Press.

Kimura, D. (2002). Sex hormones influence human cognitive pattern. *Neuroendocrinology, 23,* 67–77.

Kimura, D. (2004). Human sex differences in cognition: Fact, not predicament. *Sexualities, Evolution, and Gender, 6,* 45–53.

Koenigsknecht, R. A., & Friedman, P. (1976). Syntax development in boys and girls. *Child Development, 47,* 1109–1115.

Kolakowski, D., & Molina, R. M. (1974). Spatial ability, throwing accuracy and man's hunting heritage. *Nature, 251,* 410–412.

LaFreniere, P., Masataka, N., Butovskaya, M., Chen, Q., Dessen, M. A., & Atwanger, K. (2002). Cross-cultural analysis of social competence and behavior problems in preschoolers. *Early Education and Development, 13,* 201–219.

Langlois, J. H., & Downs, A. C. (1980). Mothers, fathers, and peers as socialization agents of sex-typed play behaviors in young children. *Child Development, 51,* 1237–1247.

Larson, R. W., & Verma, S. (1999). How children and adolescents spend time across the world: Work, play and developmental opportunities. *Psychological Bulletin, 125,* 701–736.

Lavelli, M., & Fogel, A. (2002). Developmental changes in mother–infant face-to-face communication: Birth to 3 months. *Developmental Psychology, 38,* 288–305.

Leaper, C., & Friedman, C. K. (2007). The socialization of gender. In J. Grusec & P. Hastings (Eds.), *Handbook of socialization: Theory and research* (pp. 561–587). New York, NY: Guilford.

Leveroni, C. L., & Berenbaum, S. A. (1998). Early androgen effects on interest in infants: Evidence from children with congenital adrenal hyperplasia. *Developmental Neuropsychology, 14,* 321–340.

LeVine, R. A., Dixon, S., Taylor, A., & Langrock, A. (1999). Early sex differences in spatial skills. *Developmental Psychology, 35,* 940–949.

Levy, G. D., Taylor, M. G., & Gelman, S. A. (1995). Traditional and evaluative aspects of flexibility in gender roles, social conventions, moral rules, and physical laws. *Child Development, 66,* 515–531.

Lott, B., & Maluso, D. (2001). Gender development: Social learning. In J. Worell (Ed.), *Encyclopedia of women and gender.* San Diego, CA: Academic Press.

Low, B. (1989). Cross-cultural patterns in the training of children: An evolutionary perspective. *Journal of Comparative Psychology, 103,* 311–319.

Lundqvist, C., & Sabel, K.-G. (2000). Brief report: The Brazelton Neonatal Behavioral Assessment Scale detects differences among newborn infants of optimal health. *Journal of Pediatric Psychology, 25,* 577–582.

Maccoby, E. E., & Jacklin, C. N. (1987). Gender segregation in childhood. In E. H. Reese (Ed.), *Advances in child development and behavior* (pp. 239–287). New York, NY: Academic Press.

Malina, R. M. (1990). Physical growth and performance during the transitional years (9–16). In R. Montemayor, G. R. Adams, & T. P. Gullotta (Eds.), *From childhood to adolescence: A transitional period?* (pp. 41–62). Newbury Park, CA: Sage.

Marlowe, F. W. (2003). The mating systems of foragers in the standard cross-cultural sample. *Cross-Cultural Research, 37,* 282–306.

Martin, C. L. (1989). Children's use of gender-related information in making social judgments. *Developmental Psychology, 25,* 80–88.

Martin, C. L. (1993). New directions for investigating children's gender knowledge. *Developmental Review, 13,* 184–204.

Martin, C. L., & Little, J. K. (1990). The relation of gender understanding to children's sex-typed preferences and gender stereotypes. *Child Development, 61,* 1427–1439.

Matthews, M. H. (1987). Sex differences in spatial competence: The ability of young children to map "primed" unfamiliar environments. *Educational Psychology, 7,* 77–90.

McGuiness, D., & Morley, C. (1991). Sex differences in the development of visuo-spatial ability in pre-school children. *Journal of Mental Imagery, 15,* 143–150.

Miller, C. L. (1983). Developmental changes in male/female voice classification by children. *Child Behavior and Development, 6,* 313–330.

Moffat, S. D., Hampson, E., & Hatzipantelis, M. (1998). Navigation in a "virtual" maze: Sex differences and correlation with psychometric measures of spatial ability in humans. *Evolution & Human Behavior, 19,* 73–87.

Money, J. (1975). Ablatio penis: Normal male infant sex-reassigned as a girl. *Archives of Sexual Behaviour, 4,* 65–71.

Murray-Close, D., Ostrov, J. M., & Crick, N. R. (2007). A short-term longitudinal study of growth of relational aggression during middle childhood: Associations with gender, friendship intimacy, and internalizing problems. *Development and Psychopathology, 19,* 187–203.

Newcombe, N., Bandura, M. M., & Taylor, D. C. (1983). Sex differences in spatial ability and spatial activities. *Sex Roles, 9,* 377–386.

Ostrov, J. M., & Crick, N. R. (2007). Forms and functions of aggression during early childhood: A short-term longitudinal study. *School Psychology Review, 36,* 22–43.

Perry, D. G. & Bussey, K. (1979). The social learning theory of sex differences: Imitation is alive and well. *Journal of Personality and Social Psychology, 37,* 1699–1712.

Poulin-Dubois, D., Serbin, L. A., Eichstedt, J. A., Sen, M. G., & Beissel, C. F. (2002). Men don't put on make-up: Toddlers' knowledge of the gender stereotyping of household activities. *Social Development, 11,* 166–181.

Poulin-Dubois, D., Serbin, L. A., Kenyon, B., & Derbyshire, A. (1994). Children's intermodal knowledge about gender. *Develomental Psychology, 30,* 436–442.

Provine, R. R. (1993). Laughter punctuates speech: Linguistic, social, and gender contexts of laughter. *Ethology, 95,* 291–298.

Robertson, M. A. (1984). Changing motor patterns during childhood. In *Motor development during childhood and adolescence* (pp. 48–90). Minneapolis, MN: Burgess.

Ruble, D. N., & Martin, C. L. (1998). Gender development. In N. Eisenberg (Ed.), *Handbook of child psychology: Vol. 3. Social, emotional, and personality development* (5th ed.) (pp. 933–1016). New York, NY: Wiley.

Sandstrom, N. J., Kaufman, J., & Huettel, S. A. (1998). Males and females use different distal cues in a virtual environment navigation task. *Cognitive Brain Research, 6,* 351–360.

Sartario, A., Lafrotuna, C. L., Poglaghi, S., & Trecate, L. (2002). The impact of gender, body dimension, and body composition in hand-grip strength in healthy children. *Journal of Endocrinological Investigation, 25,* 431–435.

Serbin, L. A., Poulin-Dubois, D., & Eichstedt, J. A. (2002). Infants' responses to gender-inconsistent events. *Infancy, 3,* 531–542.

Serbin, L. A., Powlishta, K. K., & Gulko, J. (1993). The development of sex typing in middle childhood. *Monographs of the Society for Research in Child Development, 58,* 1–99.

Shalit, W. (1999). *A return to modesty: Discovering the lost virtue.* New York, NY: Free Press.

Sherry, D. F. (2000). What sex differences in spatial ability tell us about the evolution of cogntion. In M. S. Gazzaniga (Ed.), *The new cognitive neurosciences* (2nd ed.) (pp. 1209–1217). Cambridge, MA: MIT Press.

Silverman, I., Choi, J., Mackewn, A., Fisher, M., Moro, J., & Olshansky, E. (2000). Evolved mechanisms underlying wayfinding: Further studies on the hunter–gatherer theory of spatial sex differences. *Evolution and Human Behavior, 21,* 201–213.

Silverman, I. & Eals, M. (1992). Sex differences in spatial abilities: Evolutionary theory and data. In J. H. Barkow, L. Cosmides, & J. Tooby (Eds.), *The adapted mind: Evolutionary psychology and the generation of culture* (pp. 533–549). New York, NY: Oxford University Press.

Skuse, D. H., James, R. S., Bishop, D. V. M., Coppin, B., Dalton, P., Aamodt-Leeper, G., et al. (1997). Evidence from Turner's Syndrome of an imprinted X-linked locus affecting cognitive function. *Nature, 287,* 705–708.

Snyder, J., & Hoffman, C. M. (2000). Digest of education statistics: 1999. *Education Statistics Quarterly, 2,* 123–126.

Sommers, C. H. (1994). *Who stole feminism?* New York, NY: Simon and Schuster.

Tanner, J. M. (1990). *Fetus into man: Physical growth from conception to maturity* (2nd ed.). Cambridge, MA: Harvard University Press.

Tooby, J., & Cosmides, L. (1990). On the universality of human nature and the uniqueness of the individual: The role of genetics and adaptation. *Journal of Personality, 58,* 17–67.

Tooby, J. & DeVore, I. (1987). The reconstruction of hominid behavioral evolution through strategic modeling. In W. Kinzey (Ed.), *Primate models of hominid behaviour.* New York, NY: SUNY Press.

Toran-Allerand, C. D. (1976). Sex steroids and the development of the newborn mouse hypothalamus and preoptic area in vitro: Implications for sexual differentiation. *Brain Research, 106,* 407–412.

U.S. Department of Justice (2007). Table 33: Ten year arrest trends by sex, 1997–2006. In *Crime in the United States.* Retrieved from www.fbi.gov/ucr/cius2006/data/table_33.html.

Voyer, D., Voyer, S., & Bryden, M. P. (1995). Magnitude of sex differences in spatial abilities: A meta-analysis and consideration of critical variables. *Psychological Bulletin, 117,* 250–270.

Weisner, T. S. (1996). The 5 to 7 transition as an ecocultural project. In A. Sameroff & M. M. Haith (Eds.), *The five to seven year shift: The age of reason and responsibility.* Chicago, IL: University of Chicago Press.

Whiting, B., & Edwards, C. P. (1988). A cross-cultural analysis of sex differences in the behavior of children aged 3 through 11. In G. Handel (Ed.), *Childhood socialization* (pp. 281–297). New York, NY: Aldine de Gruyter.

Zahn-Waxler, C., Radke-Yarrow, M., Wagner, E., & Chapman, M. (1992). Development of concern for others. *Developmental Psychology, 28,* 126–136.

Zucker, K. J., & Bradley, S. J. (1995). *Gender identity disorder and psychosexual problems in children and adolescents.* New York, NY: Guilford Press.

Chapter 12

Alexander, R. A. (1987). *The biology of moral systems.* New York, NY: Aldine de Gruyter.

Alexander, R. D. (1979). *Darwinism and human affairs.* Seattle, WA: University of Washington Press.

Anderson, S. W., Bechara, A., Damasio, H., Tranel, D., & Damasio, A. R. (1999). Impairment of social and moral behavior related to early damage in human prefrontal cortex. *Nature Neuroscience, 2,* 1032–1037.

Anderson, S. W., Damasio, H., Tranel, D., & Damasio, A. R. (2000). Long-term sequelae of prefrontal cortex damage acquired in early childhood. *Developmental Neuropsychology, 18,* 281–296.

Arens, W. (1986). *The original sin: Incest and its meanings.* London, England: Oxford University Press.

Asbury, K., Dunn, J. F., Pike, A., & Plomin, R. (2003). Nonshared environmental influences on individual differences in early behavioral development: A monozygotic twin difference study. *Child Development, 74,* 933–943.

Axelrod, R. (1984). *The evolution of cooperation.* New York, NY: Basic Books.

Axelrod, R., & Hamilton, W. D. (1981). The evolution of cooperation. *Science, 211,* 1390–1396.

Baumrind, D., Larzelere, R. E., & Cowan, P. A. (2002). Ordinary physical punishment: Is it harmful? Comment on Gershoff (2002). *Psychological Bulletin, 128,* 580–589.

Bender, H. L., Allen, J. P., McElhaney, K. B., Antonishak, J., Moore, C. M., & Kelly, H. O. (1997). Use of harsh physical discipline and developmental outcomes in adolescence. *Development and Psychopathology, 19,* 227–242.

Bevc, I. & Silverman, I. (2000). Early separation and sibling incest: A test of the revised Westermark theory. *Evolution and Human Behavior, 21,* 151–161.

Blair, R. J. (1997). Moral reasoning and the child with psychopathic tendencies. *Personality and Individual Differences, 22,* 731–739.

Blasi, A. (1980). Bridging moral cognition and moral action: A critical review of the literature. *Psychological Bulletin, 88,* 1–45.

Cosmides, L., & Tooby, J. (1992). Cognitive adaptations for social exchange. In J. Barkow, L. Cosmides & J. Tooby (Eds.), *The adapted mind: Evolutionary psychology and the generation of culture* (pp. 163–228). New York, NY: Oxford University Press.

Cosmides, L. M. & Tooby, J. (1981). Cytoplasmic inheritance and intragenomic conflict. *Journal of Theoretical Biology, 89,* 83–129.

Cummins, D. D. (1996). Evidence of deontic reasoning in 3- and 4-year-old children. *Memory and Cognition, 24,* 823–829.

Damasio, A. (2000). *The feeling of what happens.* New York, NY: Basic Books.

Darwin, C. (1871). *The descent of man, and selection in relation to sex.* London, England: Murray.

Dawkins, R. (1976). *The selfish gene.* Oxford, England: Oxford University Press.

Dawkins, R. (1982). *The blind watchmaker.* Essex, England: Longman.

Dunbar, R. I., & Spoors, M. (1995). Social networks, support cliques, and kinship. *Human Nature, 6,* 273–290.

Frick, P. J., Christian, R. E., & Wooten, J. M. (1999). Age trends in the association between parenting practices and conduct problems. *Behavior Modification, 23,* 106–128.

Gershoff, E. T. (2002). Parental corporal punishment and associated child behaviors and experiences: A meta-analytic and theoretical review. *Psychological Bulletin, 128,* 539–579.

Gigerenzer, G., & Hug, K. (1992). Domain-specific reasoning: Social contracts, cheating and perspective change. *Cognition, 43,* 127–171.

Gilligan, C. (1977). In a different voice: Women's conceptions of self and morality. *Harvard Educational Review, 47,* 481–517.

Gilligan, C. & Attanucci, J. (1988). Two moral orientations: Gender differences and similarities. *Merrill-Palmer Quarterly, 34,* 223–238.

Haidt, J. (*2001*). The emotional dog and its rational tail: A social intuitionist approach to moral judgment. *Psychological Review, 108,* 814–834.

Haig, D. (1993). Genetic conflicts in human pregnancy. *Quarterly Review of Biology, 68,* 495–532.

Hamilton, W. D. (1964). The genetical theory of social behavior. *Journal of Theoretical Biology, 12,* 12–45.

Hamilton, W. D. (1975). Innate social aptitudes of man: An approach from evolutionary genetics. In R. Fox (Ed.), *Biosocial anthropology* (pp. 133–155). New York, NY: Crowell.

Harbaugh, W. T., Krause, K., Liday, S. G., & Versterlund, L. (2003). Trust in children. In E. Ostrom & J. Walker (Eds.), *Trust, reciprocity and gains from association.* New York, NY: Russell Sage Foundation.

Harris, J. R. (1998). *The nurture assumption.* New York, NY: The Free Press.

Harris, P. L., & Núñez, M. (1996). Understanding of permission rules by preschool children. *Child Development, 67,* 1572–1591.

Hartshorne, H., & May, M. A. (1971). Studies in the organization of character. In H. Munsinger (Ed.), *Readings in child development* (pp. 190–197). New York, NY: Holt, Rinehart and Winston.

Hastings, P. D., Zahn-Waxler, C., Robinson, J., Usher, B., & Bridges, D. (2000). The development of concern for others in children with behavior problems. *Developmental Psychology, 35,* 531–546.

Hauser, M. D. (2006). *Moral minds: How nature designed a universal sense of right and wrong.* New York, NY: HarperCollins.

Hinde, R. A. (1980). *Ethology.* London, England: Fontana.

Hoffman, M. L. (1983). Affective and cognitive processes in moral internalization. In E. T. Higgins, D. N. Ruble & W. W. Hartup (Eds.), *Social cognition and social development: A sociocultural perspective* (pp. 236–274). Cambridge, MA: Cambridge University Press.

Jurkovic, G. J. (1980). The juvenile delinquent as a moral philosopher: A structural-developmental perspective. *Psychological Bulletin, 88,* 709–727.

Kochanska, G., Forman, D. R., & Coy, K. C. (1999). Implications of the mother–child relationship in infancy for socialization in the second year. *Infant Behavior and Development, 22,* 249–265.

Kohlberg, L. (1963). The development of children's orientations toward a moral order: I. Sequence in the development of moral thought. *Vita Humana, 6,* 11–33.

Kohlberg, L. (1978). Revisions in the theory and practice of moral development. In W. Damon (Ed.), *New directions for child development: Moral development.* New York, NY: Wiley.

Kohlberg, L., & Candee, D. (1984). The relationship of moral judgment to moral action. In L. Kohlberg (Ed.), *Essays in moral development: Vol. 2. The psychology of moral development* (pp. 498–581). New York, NY: Harper & Row.

Krebs, D., & Denton, K. (2005). Towards a more pragmatic approach to morality: A critical evalution of Kohlberg's model. *Psychological Review, 112,* 629–649.

Krebs, D. L., Denton, K., Wark, G., Couch, R., Racine, T. P., & Krebs, D. L. (2002). Interpersonal moral conflict between couples: Effects of type of dilemma, role, and partner's judgments on level of moral reasoning and probability of resolution. *Journal of Adult Development, 9,* 307–316.

Krevans, J., & Gibbs, J. C. (1996). Parents' use of inductive discipline: Relations to children's empathy and prosocial behavior. *Child Development, 67,* 3263–3277.

Laub, J. H. & Sampson, R. J. (1988). Unraveling families and delinquency: A reanalysis of the Glueck's data. *Criminology, 26,* 355–379.

Lee, M., & Prentice, N. M. (1988). Interrelations of empathy, cognition, and moral reasoning with dimensions of juvenile delinquency. *Journal of Abnormal Child Psychology, 16,* 127–139.

Levi-Strauss, C. (1969). *The elementary structures of kinship.* London, England: Eyre and Spottiswoode.

Lieberman, D., Tooby, J., & Cosmides, L. (2003). Does morality have a biological basis? An empirical test of the factors governing moral sentiments relating to incest. *Proceedings of the Royal Society of London, 270,* 819–826.

Mednick, S. A., Gabrielli, W. F. Jr., & Hutchings, B. (1987). Genetic factors in the etiology of criminal behavior. In S. A. Mednick, T. E. Moffitt & S. A. Stack (Eds.), *The causes of crime: New biological approaches* (pp. 74–91). Cambridge, UK: Cambridge University Press.

Moore, G. E. (1903). *Principia ethica.* Cambridge, England: Cambridge University Press.

Owens, K., & King, M. (1999). Genomic views of human history. *Science, 286,* 451–453.

Piaget, J. (1932). *The moral judgment of the child.* London, England: Routledge & Kegan Paul.

Palmer, E.J., & Hollin, C.R. (1998). A comparison of patterns of moral development in young offenders and non-offenders. *Legal and Criminological Psychology, 3,* 225–235.

Rachels, J. (2003). *The elements of moral philosophy.* Boston, MA: McGraw Hill.

Shepher, J. (1971). Mate selection among second generation kibbutz adolescents and adults: Incest avoidance and negative imprinting. *Archives of Sexual Behavior, 1,* 293–307.

Simpson, E. L. (1974). Moral development research: A case study of scientific cultural bias. *Human Development, 17,* 81–106.

Snarey, J. R. (1985). Cross-cultural universality of socio moral development: A critical review of Kohlbergian review. *Psychological Bulletin, 97,* 202–232.

Strayer, J., & Roberts, W. (2004). Children's anger, emotional expressiveness, and empathy: Relations with parents' empathy, emotional expressiveness, and parenting practices. *Social Development, 13,* 229–254.

Tooby, J. & Cosmides, L. (1992). Psychological foundations of culture. In J. Barkow, L. Cosmides & J. Tooby (Eds.), *The adapted mind* (pp. 19–136). New York, NY: Oxford University Press.

Tooby, J., & Cosmides, L. (1996). Friendship and the banker's paradox: Other pathways to the evolution of adaptations for altruism. *Proceedings of the British Academy, 88,* 119–143.

Trivers, R. L. (1971). The evolution of reciprocal altruism. *Quarterly Review of Biology, 46,* 35–57.

Turiel, E., Killen, M., & Helwig, C. (1987). Morality: Its structure, functions, and vagaries. In J. Kagan & S. Lamb (Eds.), *The emergence of morality in young children* (pp. 155–244). Chicago, IL: University of Chicago Press.

Wason, P. C. (1966). Reasoning. In B. M. Foss (Ed.), *New horizons in psychology* (pp. 135–151). Harmondsworth, England: Pelican Books.

Westermarck, E. A. (1921). *The history of human marriage* (5th ed.). London, England: Macmillan.

Wickler, W. (1972). *The biology of the ten commandments.* New York, NY: McGraw-Hill.

Wilkinson, G. S. (1984). Reciprocal food sharing in the vampire bat. *Nature, 308,* 181–184.

Williams, G. C. (1966). *Adaptation and natural selection.* Princeton, NJ: Princeton University Press.

Wolf, A. P. (1995). *Sexual attraction and childhood association: A Chinese brief for Edward Westermarck.* Stanford, CA: Stanford University Press.

Wynne-Edwards, V. C. (1962). *Animal dispersion in relation to social behaviour.* Edinburgh, Scotland: Oliver & Boyd.

Additional Credits

PHOTOS

page xxx: Courtesy M.D. Rutherford;

Chapter 1

page 2: ITV Granada; page 4: ©iStockphoto.com/ Jbryson; page 7: © William Manning/Corbis; page 8: © iStockphoto.com/Vasiliki Varvaki (left); page 8: Ludovisi Collection (right); page 8: ©iStockphoto.com/ Bruce Lonngren (bottom left); page 9: Wiki Commons: Collection of Sir Robert Walpole, Houghton Hall, 1779. (top); page 9: ©iStockphoto.com/Georgios Kollidas (bottom); page 10: Photo by Time Life Pictures/ Timepix/Time Life Pictures/Getty Images (top); page 10: photo by Gutekunst, Collection National Library of Medicine (bottom); page 11: © Bettmann/Corbis (top); page 11: Archives of the History of American Psychology at the University of Akron (bottom); page 12: © Bettmann/CORBIS; page 13: Archives of the History of American Psychology, The Center for the History of Psychology – The University of Akron; page 14: Courtesy M.D. Rutherford; page 16: Courtesy M.D. Rutherford; page 18: © iStock/Cathy Keifer; page 19: Rob & Ann Simpson/Visuals Unlimited, Inc.; page 22: © iStockPhotos/Mark Evans (left); page 22: © iStockPhotos/Grigory Bibikov (right)

Chapter 2

page 28: Doug Goodman / Photo Researchers, Inc.; page 30: Wellcome Photo Library/Wellcome Images; page 31: © Farrell Grehan/CORBIS; page 34: Courtesy M.D. Rutherford; page 35: Novosti / Photo Researchers, Inc; page 37: Archives of the History of American Psychology, The Center for the History of Psychology – The University of Akron; page 38: Photo by Nina Leen/Time & Life Pictures/Getty Images (top); page 38: Albert Bandura (bottom); page 41: © iStockPhotos/ Linda & Colin McKie; page 43: © iStockPhotos/Kristian Larsen (top); page 43: © Frans Lanting/Corbis (bottom); page 44: © iStockPhotos/Lucyna Koch; page 46: © iStockPhotos/Daniel Laflor (left); page 46: Horst Herget/ Masterfile (right); page 46: ITV Granada (bottom);

page 47: © iStockPhoto/Steve Debenport (left); page 47: Anders Hald/Masterfile (right); page 53: David Tanaka; page 55: University of Illinois at Urbana-Champaign News Bureau; page 56: © iStockPhotos/lvdesign77

Chapter 3

page 62: © Mary Evans Picture Library / Alamy; page 64: © iStockPhoto/mathieukor; page 65: Rob & Ann Simpson/Visuals Unlimited, Inc. (right); page 65: Leroy Simon/Visuals Unlimited, Inc. (left); page 66: © iStockPhoto/Willi Schmitz (left); page 66: © iStockPhoto/PeJo29 (centre); page 66: © iStockPhoto/ Aimin Tang (right); page 70: Adrian T Sumner / Science Photo Library; page 71: © Bill Ross/Corbis; page 75: "Rue des Archives / The Granger Collection, NYC — All rights reserved; page 76: © iStockPhoto/Jameson Weston; page 77: © iStockPhoto/felinda; page 85: (2005) Social Opportunity Produces Brain Changes in Fish. PLoS Biol 3(11): e390. doi:10.1371/journal.pbio.0030390 (top); page 85: © iStockPhoto/VanDenEsker (bottom); page 86: © iStockPhoto/Ana Abejon (left); page 86: Blend Images/Masterfile (right); page 88: © Matthias Kulka/Corbis; page 92: © Julian Winslow/Corbis; page 93: © Corbis; page 94: Ralph Hutchings/Visuals Unlimited, Inc. (top left); page 94: Dr. M.A. Ansary / Photo Researchers, Inc. (top right); page 94: © Mark Alberhasky/Science Faction/Corbis (bottom left); page 94: Mediscan/Visuals Unlimited, Inc. (bottom right);

Chapter 4

page 104: © Peter Frank/Corbis; page 106: © Ronnie Kaufman/Larry Hirshowitz/Blend Images/Corbis; page 107: © iStockPhoto/Pascal Genest; page 108: © iStockPhoto/Janis Dreosti; page 109: © iStockPhoto/ Dan Brandenburg; page 112: Kenneth Libbrecht / Photo Researchers, Inc.; page 114: © iStockPhoto/ Aimin Tang (right); page 114: © iStockPhoto/Focus_ on_Nature (left); page 115: Image by © Bettmann/ Corbis; page 118: Mark Clarke / Science Photo Library (left); page 118: © iStockPhoto/© Ekaterina

Monakhova (right); page 122: © John Lund/Drew Kelly/Blend Images/Corbis; page 124: Steve Wooster/ Dorling Kindersley/Getty Images (left); page 124: altrendo nature/Altrendo/Getty Images (right); page 126: © iStockPhoto/Debbie Lund; page 129: © iStockPhoto/Christopher Futcher (top); page 129: © Uden Graham/Redlink/Corbis (left); page 130: CW Hanley/The Image Bank/Getty Images; page 132: © iStockPhoto/Tomasz Zachariasz (bottom); page 132: Frank Greenaway/Dorling Kindersly/Getty Images (top); page 137: © iStockPhoto/Dmitry Maslov;

Chapter 5

page 144: Photo by Florence Low; page 146: Marilyn Conway/Photographer's Choice/Getty Images; page 148: Carol Farneti Foster. © photolibrary. All rights reserved (left); page 148: Charles E. Mohr / Photo Researchers, Inc.(right); page 150: © iStockPhoto/doga yusuf dokdok; page 151: BBC Films / The Kobal Collection; page 152: Hannelie Coetzee/Masterfile; page 156: Neil Bromhall. © photolibrary. All rights reserved; page 156: Topic Photo Agency/maxxImages; page 158: © Laura Dwight/Corbis; page 160: Science Source / Photo Researchers, Inc; page 162: © Bubbles Photolibrary / Alamy; page 165: © iStockPhoto/wiktor bubniak; page 166: Photo courtesy of Alan Slater, University of Exeter; page 168: © Ira Wyman/Sygma/Corbis; page 173: NIH, Department of Health and Human Services, USA ; page 175: © iStockPhoto/Michael Rubin (left); page 175: © iStockPhoto/Melissa Papaj (right);

Chapter 6

page 180: China Photos/Stringer/Getty Images; page 182: © Russ Bishop / Alamy; page 184: © iStockPhoto/ Diane Diederich; page 187: © iStockPhoto/George Clerk (top); page 187: © iStockPhoto/Graeme Purdy (bottom); page 189: Photo Researchers; page 191: Bill Anderson / Photo Researchers, Inc.; page 198: © iStockPhoto/ Jack Puccio (top left); page 198: © iStockPhoto/April Turner (top right); page 198: © iStockPhoto/Rakoskerti

(bottom left); page 198: © iStockPhoto/Zlatko Kostic (bottom right); page 199: © iStockPhoto/Natallia Bokach (top); page 199: © iStockPhoto/ZoneCreative (bottom); page 200: © Mark Tomalty/Masterfile; page 203: © iStockPhoto/Peter Cheyne; page 205: © iStockPhoto/Annette Shaff;

Chapter 7

page 214: © iStockPhoto/Kim Pin Tan; page 216: © Ghislain & Marie David de Lossy/cultura/Corbis; page 217: © iStockPhoto/Jeff Hathaway (top); page 217: Masterfile.com (bottom); page 219: © DK Limited/ Corbis; page 220: © iStockPhoto/jeff gynane (top left); page 220: © SuperStock (bottom left); page 220: Karl Amman / Photo Researchers, Inc. (right); page 221: © Peter Johnson/Corbis; page 225: Doug Goodman / Photo Researchers, Inc. (left); page 225: Doug Goodman / Photo Researchers, Inc. (right); page 239: © iStockPhoto/Dimitar Marinov (left); page 239: © iStockPhoto/William Ross-Jones (right); page 241: © iStockPhoto/Andrejs Zemdega (top left); page 241: © iStockPhoto/Eric Isselée (bottom left); page 241: © Laurence Mouton/ZenShui/Corbis (right); page 242: © Macduff Everton/Corbis;

Chapter 8

page 254: © Dorit Lombrosso/Monsoon/Photolibrary/ Corbis; page 256: © Olivier Martel/Corbis; page 257: © Jochen Tack/Maxx Images; page 258: © Blend Images / Alamy (top); page 258: Science Source / Science Photo Library (bottom); page 264: © iStockPhoto/Kai Chiang; page 266: Courtesy Albert Bandura, Ph.D. 82; page 269: © iStockPhoto/Don Bayley (left); page 269: William Munoz / Science Photo Library (right); page 271: © Frans Lanting/Corbis; page 273: Masterfile.com (top); page 273: © iStockPhoto/Andrew Rich (bottom); page 275: © iStockPhoto/Joan Vicent Cantó Roig (top); page 275: From Le Grand, R., Mondloch, C. J., Maurer, D., & Brent, H. P. (2004). 'Impairment in holistic face processing following early visual deprivation'. Psychological Science,

15 , 762 _768 (bottom); page 279: © iStockPhoto/ Exkalibur (top left); page 279: © Frans Lanting/Corbis (top right); page 279: © iStock/Joan Vicent Cantó Roig (bottom left); page 279: © iStock/Joan Vicent Cantó Roig (bottom right); page 283: © iStock/bilgehan yilmaz; page 287: © iStock/Simone van den Berg;

Chapter 9

page 296: Photo by Mark Kauffman//Time Life Pictures/ Getty Images; page 298: © iStock/Vladimir Mucibabic; page 299: © blickwinkel / Alamy (left); page 299: © Janine Wiedel Photolibrary / Alamy (top right); page 299: © Gavin Hellier / Alamy (bottom right); page 300: Saddle quern with grinding stone, from an Iron Age farm at Mingies Ditch, Oxon (stone), Iron Age / Ashmolean Museum, University of Oxford, UK / The Bridgeman Art Library International (top); page 300: ANT Photo Library / Photo Researchers, Inc.(bottom); page 301: © Dennis Van Tine/Retna Ltd./Corbis; page 305: Madeleine, performing in the conditioned head turn procedure in the Infant Studies Centre, University of British Columbia. Reprinted with permission from Current Directions in Psychological Sciences: photo courtesy of Steve Heine.; page 309: Dr. Laura-Ann Petitto/University of Toronto; page 310: © iStock/Betsy Dupuis; page 313: Courtesy M.D. Rutherford; page 315: Masterfile.com; page 318: © Bettmann/Corbis; page 324: Bain News Service, Library of Congress, Prints and Photographs Division; page 325: Reuters/Oswaldo Rivas; page 329: Susan Kuklin / Photo Researchers, Inc.;

Chapter 10

page 336: © Danita Delimont / Alamy; page 338: © iStock/Bart Coenders; page 339: © iStock/Aldo Murillo; page 340: Lawrence Migdale / Photo Researchers, Inc. (left); page 340: © Ingo Arndt/Minden Pictures (right); page 341: © Ulrich Doering/Alamy; page 344: © iStockphoto.com/digitalskillet; page 345: Getty Images; page 346: ©iStock/Elena Korenbaum; page 348: © iStock/Aldo Murillo; page 350: © iStock/Steve Geer (top); page 350: © iStock/Denis Jr. Tangney (bottom); page 351: Photo Researchers / Science Photo Library; page 353: Nina Leen /Time & Life Pictures/Getty Images

(left); page 353: Time & Life Pictures/Getty Images (right); page 357: © iStockphoto.com/Donna Coleman (357); page 359: © iStockphoto.com/gabyjalbert; page 363: Nomi Harris; page 366: Masterfile.com; page 369: © Flint/Corbis; page 371: © Blend Images / Alamy; page

Chapter 11

378: James Cavallini / Photo Researchers, Inc.; James Cavallini / Photo Researchers, Inc.; page 380: Courtesy Lynnell Stephani; page 382: Rolex; page 383: © iStock/ Cathy Keifer; page 384: © iStock/archives (left); page 384: Eye of Science / Photo Researchers, Inc. (right); page 385: CNRI / Photo Researchers, Inc.; page 386: Power and Syred / Science Photo Library (top); page 386: © iStock/Steve Byland (bottom); page 387: Mitch Reardon / Photo Researchers, Inc.; page 392: Catherine Ursillo / Photo Researchers, Inc. (left); page 392: Masterfile.com (right); page 393: Photos: Gerianne M. Alexander, Ph.D.; page 395: © Photo Media/ClassicStock/Corbis (top); page 395: © Corbis Premium RF / Alamy (bottom); page 399: © PhotoAlto / Alamy; page 401: Archives of the History of American Psychology, The Center for the History of Psychology – The University of Akron; page 402: © Reuters/CORBIS; page 407: Stewart Cook;

Chapter 12

page 414: Masterfile.com; page 416: © Michael Hall Photography Pty Ltd/Corbis; page 417: Sheila Terry / Science Photo Library (top); page 417: Wikimedia (bottom); page 418: ©Topham/ The Image Works; page 419: © iStockphoto.com/Rhienna Cutler; page 421: Lee Lockwood/Time & Life Pictures/Getty Images; page 426: © Brooks Kraft/Sygma/Corbis; page 428: © iStock/ Daniel Schweinert; page 429: © iStock/ Dave Adalian; page 432: © Celia Peterson/arabianEye/Corbis; page 433: © iStockphoto.com/diego cervo; page 434: Rexford Lord / Photo Researchers, Inc.; page 436: Photo by Samantha Appleton/White House via Getty Images; page 443: © Kim Gunkel; page 445: ©Ben Edwards / Impact / HIP / The Image Works; page 446: © Jerry Cooke/Corbis; page 447: © Mary Evans Picture Library / Alamy; page 449: © Image Source/Corbis;

FIGURES

Figures 7.5, 7.6 and 7.7: Adapted from Baillargeon, Renée. How Do Infants Learn about the Physical World? *Current Directions in Psychological Science, A Journal of the Association For Psychological Science.* Volume 3, Number 5, October 1994. p134, Fig.1.

Figure 7.8: Reprinted from *Cognitive Psychology*, Vol. 45, Issue 2, Andréa Aguiara and Renée Baillargeon, Developments in young infants' reasoning about occluded objects, pp. 267–336, 2002, with permission from Elsevier.

Figure 7.9: *Cognitive Psychology* Vol. 45, Issue 2, September 2002, pp. 267–336. Copyright © 2002 Elsevier Science (USA). All rights reserved. With permission from Elsevier.

Figure 7.10: Reprinted from *Cognition*, Vol. 78/Issue 3, Susan J. Hespos, Renée Baillargeon, Reasoning About Containment Events in Very Young Infants, p. 39, Copyright 2001, with permission from Elsevier.

Figure 7.16: *Nature* vol 358 # 27, p. 749, Addition and Subtraction from Human Infants by Karen Wynn.

Figure 8.1: Group size by neocrotex ratio from Dunbar (1992) *Journal of Human Evolution* 20, 469–93

Figure 8.2: Figure 6 from Dunbar (1998), The Social Brain Hypothesis. *Evolutionary Anthropology*, (6) p. 178–190

Figure 8.3: Based on figure in Papalia, D., Wendoks, S., & Fieldman, R. D. (1998). *Human Development*, 7th edn. USA: McGraw-Hill Companies and other sources.

Figure 8.9 and 8.10: Reproduced with permission from *Pediatrics*, Vol. 56, pages 544–9, Copyright © 1975 by the AAP.

Figure 9.3: Figure 6.5 from Categorical perception of speech sounds by infants. Siegler, DeLoache and Eisenberg: *How Children Develop*, Second Edition Copyright © 2006 by Worth Publishers

Figure 10.2: Adapted from Malcolm Owen Slavin, Ph.D. and Daniel Kriegman, Ph.D., Toward a New Paradigm for Psychoanalysis: An Evolutionary Biological Perspective on the Classical—Relational Dialectic (1990). *Psychoanalytic Psychology*, 7S: 5–31.

Figure 10.4: Adapted from Daly, M. & Wilson, M. (1985). Child abuse and other risks of not living with both parents. *Ethology and Sociobiology*, 6, 197-210. Copyright © 2010 Elsevier B.V. All rights reserved. ScienceDirect® is a registered trademark of Elsevier B.V.

Figure 10.5: Adapted from Sulloway, Frank (1997). *Born to Rebel: Birth Order, Family Dynamics, and Creative Lives.* Vintage.

Figure 11.3: Adapted from Shepard, R and Metzler. J. Mental rotation of three dimensional objects. Science 1971. 171(972):701-703

Figure 11.4: Adapted from *The adapted mind: Evolutionary psychology and the generation of culture* (pp. 533-549). New York: Oxford University Press.

Figure 12.2: Adapted from A Colby, L Kohlberg, JC Gibbs, M Lieberman. A longitudinal study of moral judgement. 1983. *Monographs of the society for research in child development*, 48, 1-2. John Wiley & Sons Ltd.

Subject Index

Name Index